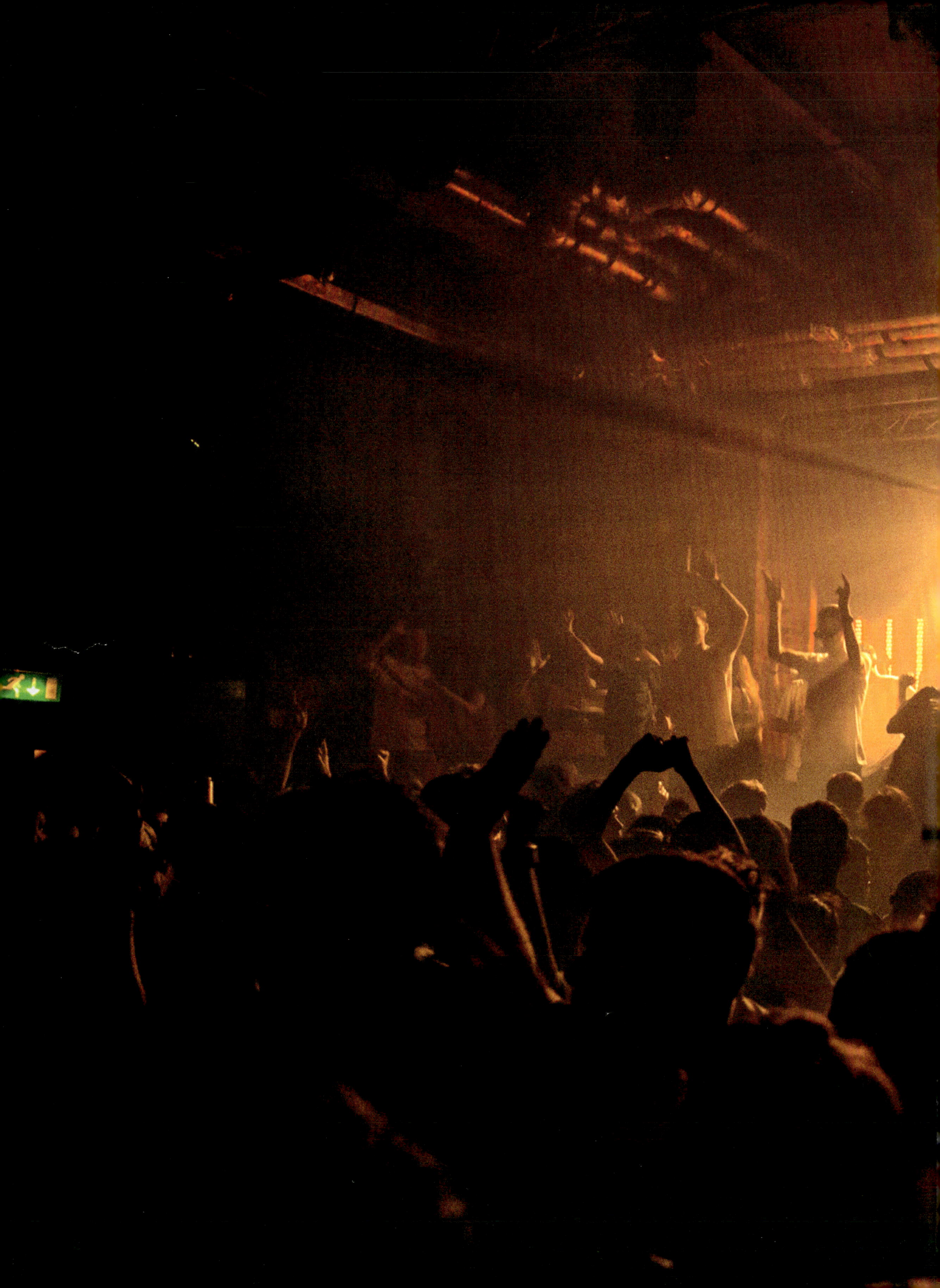

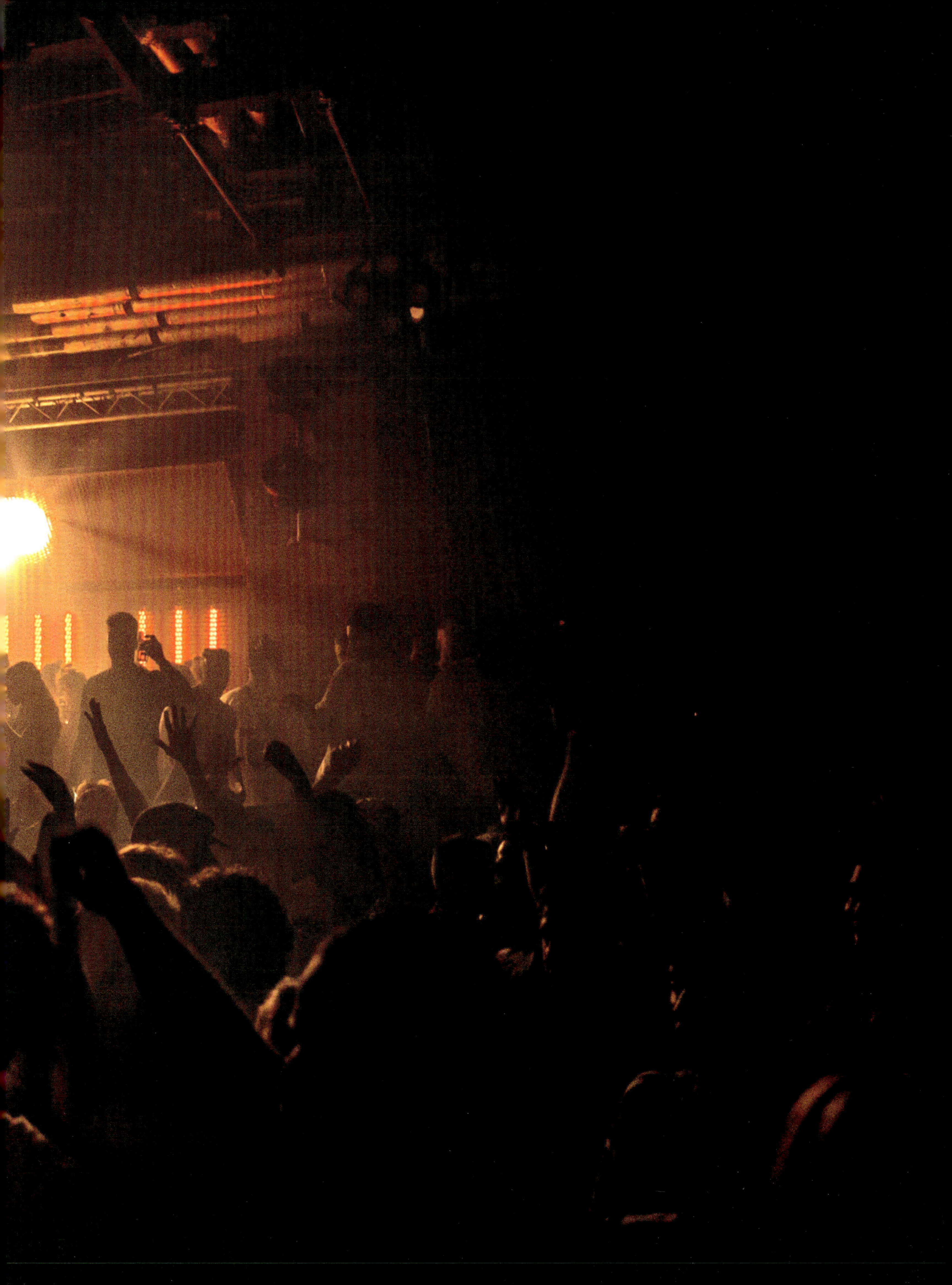

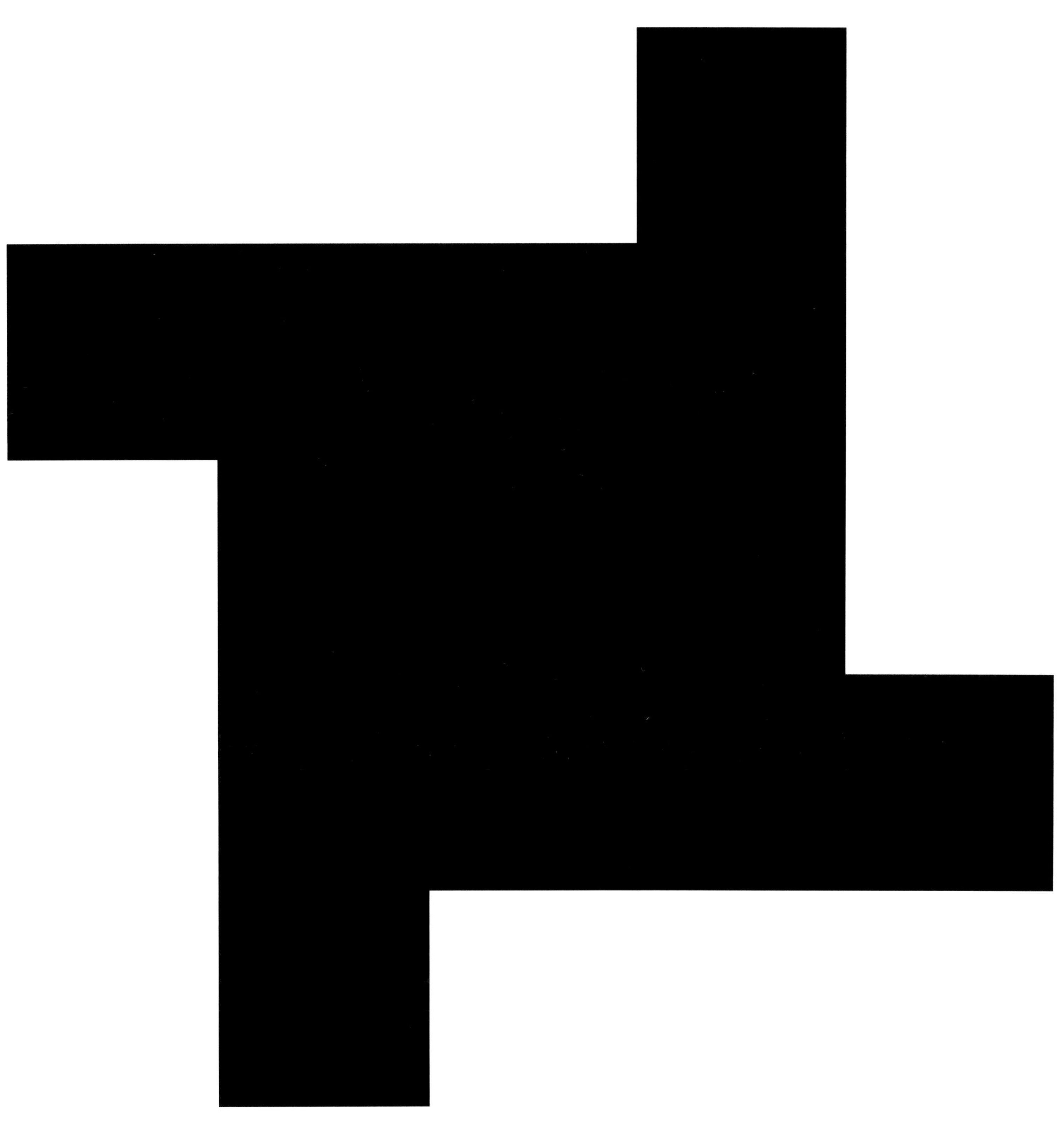

contents

foreword by annie mac 11

introduction by bill brewster 15

the history of fabric 27

the matter of matter 55

the music of fabric 69

birthdays 95

the art of fabric 115

the people of fabric 179

#savefabric 265

the meaning of fabric 275

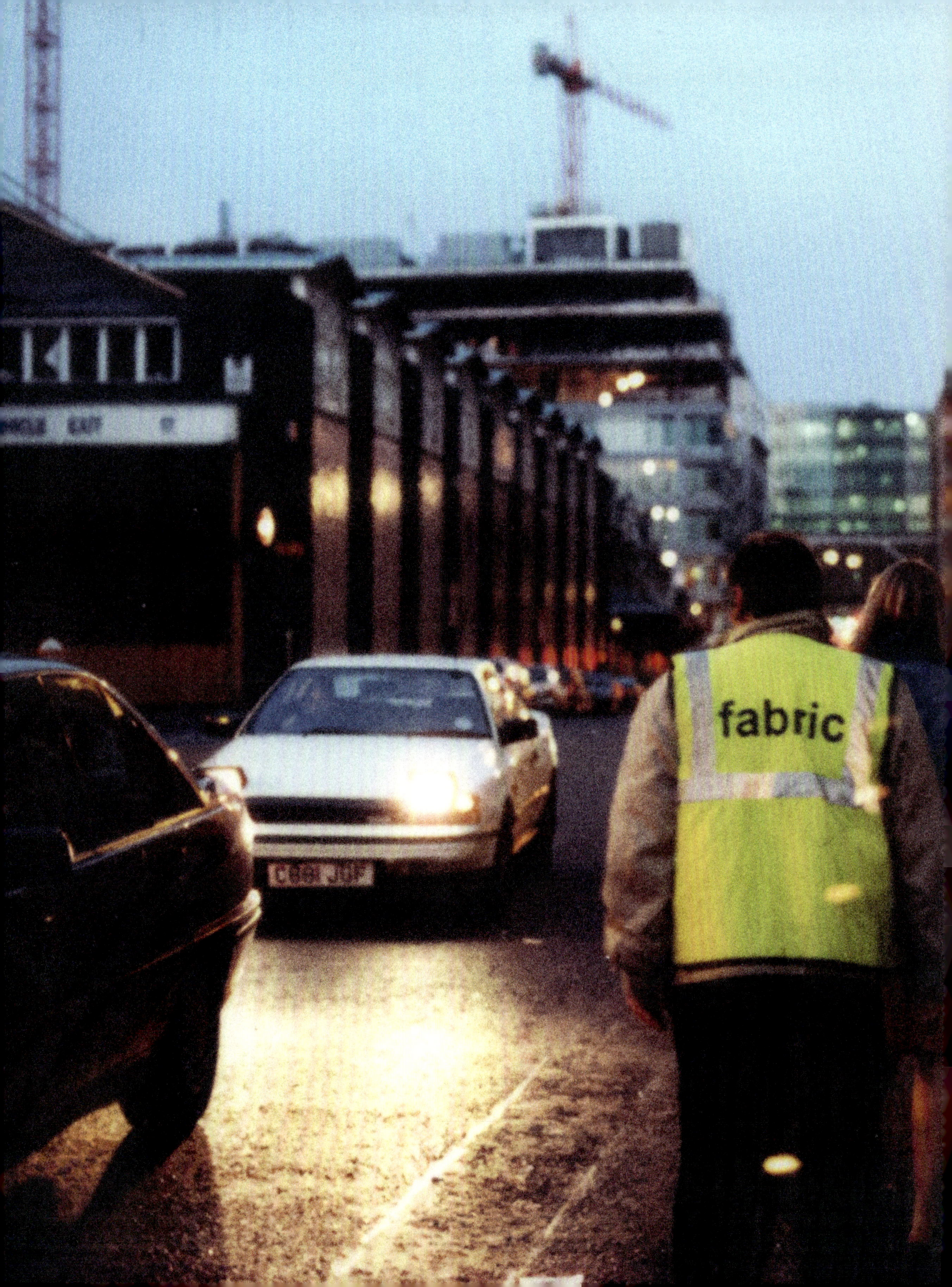
fabric

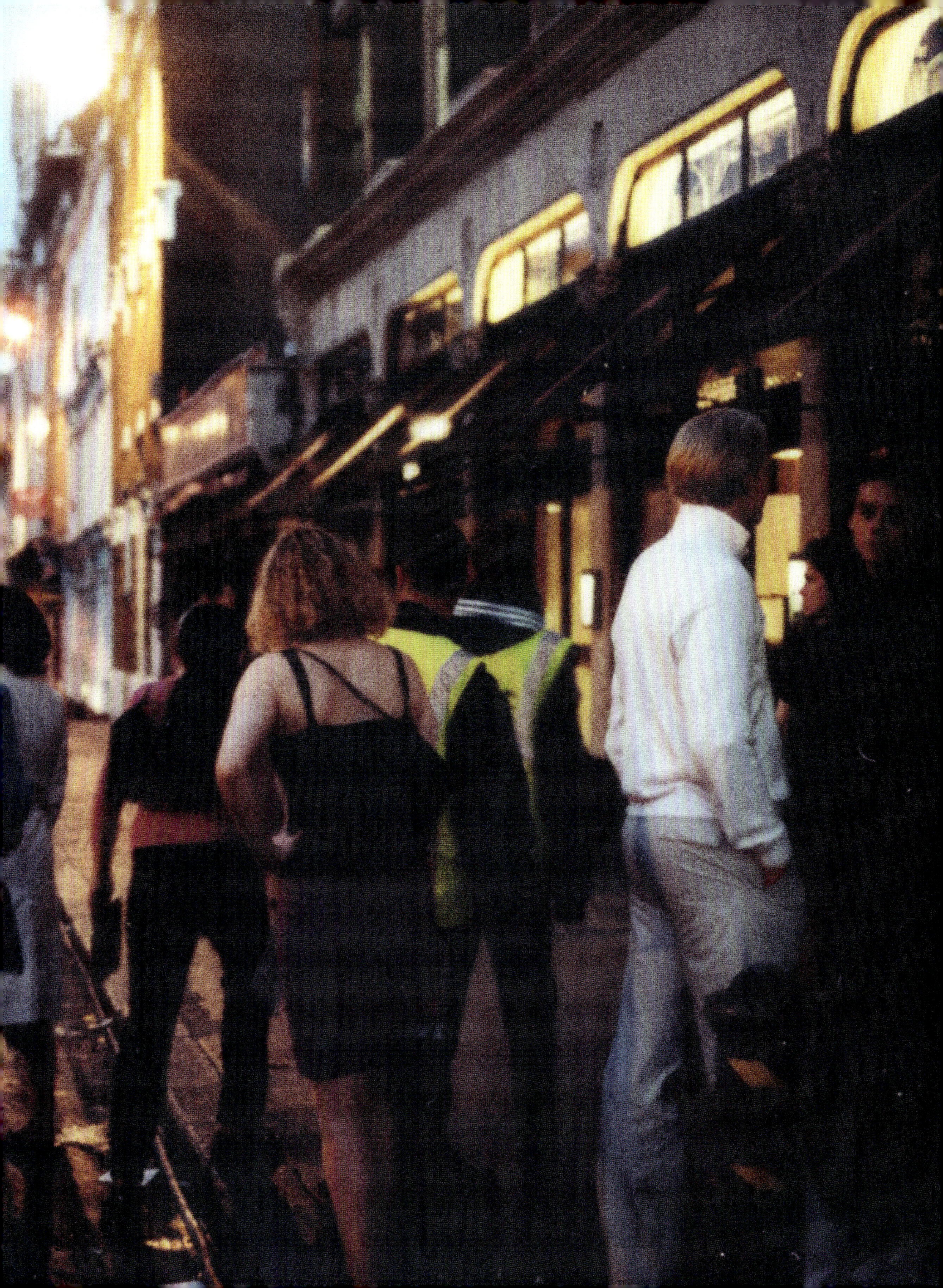

foreword by annie mac

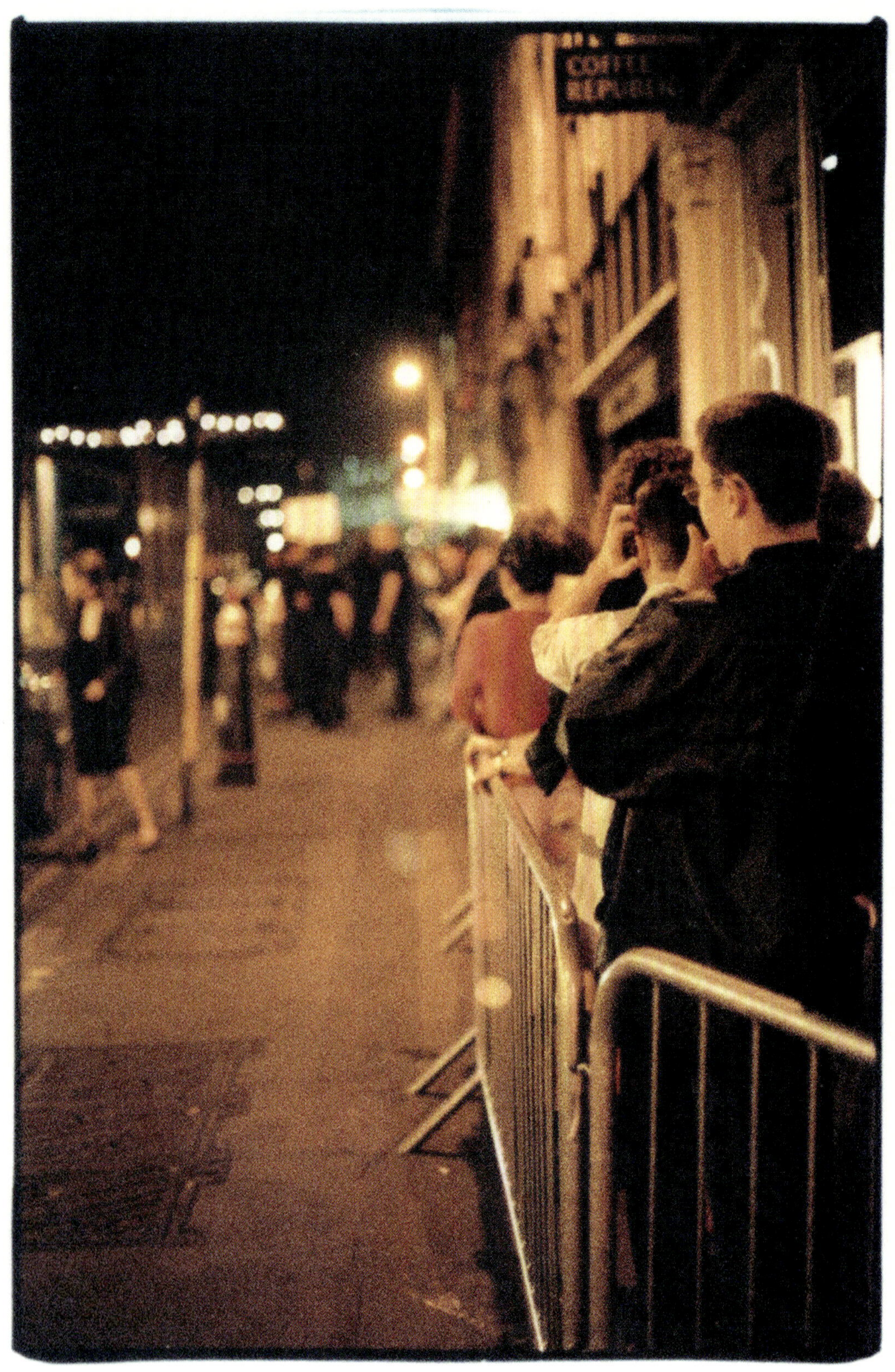

12—1

fabric is so important in the twenty-first century landscape. For me when it started it symbolised a kind of cross-pollination of genres, whereas before it felt like everything was quite categorised, so you were into garage, or jungle, or house music. What fabric did really well was to represent genres but put them in the same club on the same night, across the three different rooms. That felt new, and very exciting for it, and I think it pre-empted shuffle culture and the idea of genres blurring more generally as streaming came in.

Culturally it was just the North Star for electronic music. It was, and still is, a rite of passage for any DJ to play and to curate stuff there. The crowd at fabric were always open minded and up for new things: for hearing progressive music, music that pushed the boundaries of genre and pushed things forward. As a DJ it's a dream place to play for those reasons, and of course for the very practical reasons of it having an incredible soundsystem and incredible booths. It's a club designed for all the right reasons that clubbing exists.

The thing that really sticks in the memory from my early days going to fabric is it feeling really exciting getting in and walking down those stairs, every time. I met my now husband for the first time in the booth of Room 1 too, so that's obviously my most significant personal memory! Professionally, of course I had great times bringing my Annie Mac Presents brand in and watching it grow. The privilege of being able to bring together mad, brilliant people in music and have them DJ together was glorious.

For my own personal musical journey, it has been so huge. fabric put their faith in me as a curator before anyone else outside of Radio 1. The AMP brand really began in Room 3; I think the first people we had play for us were Paul Epworth and David Holmes. We had Xavier and Justice in there, we had Erol Alkan, we had Mylo, and those early days really felt like the beginning of a movement, the whole French takeover and developments in electro-house. Then moving from that start to being able to curate the whole club was really something: I'll never forget walking down those stairs, with the same excitement as when I'd first been to the club, and seeing the AMP logo projected on the walls. It really felt so special for fabric to put their faith in me, my manager, my agent and my team: we felt like they had our back.

Having my thirtieth birthday there was one of my favourite memories – not just fabric memories but all-time raving memories. Shaun Roberts allowed us to have the club to ourselves, us being myself and my friend Naomi, who was turning twenty-one. We invited lots of friends and family and took over Room 3, we had some brilliant people – Rob Da Bank, Yussef, Shy FX – and we had inflatable palm trees and flamingos all around the top balcony. My parents and my entire family came over from Ireland, and my dad even made a speech from behind the booth to a crowd of ravers congratulating me on my birthday. It was quite an incongruous situation, my Irish parents being in the middle of fabric, but it was such a fun night. However it was never about just one night. I have so many memories of Shaun – always there waiting with a bottle of Laurent Perrier Rosé at the bar for us – and of so, so many good nights.

Annie Mac

introduction by bill brewster

Back in my very early days as a fabric resident DJ, it wasn't unusual to turn up at 9.45 p.m., ready to start the Room 1 warm-up and find the booth already occupied, the space vibrating with deep resonant bass. The owner and founder, Keith Reilly, would frequently greet me, his bag of records neatly positioned next to the three Technics 1200s, pulling out a few tunes to play before the club opened.

I've met quite a few club owners in my time in the industry and, trust me, this is not a regular occurrence. I've encountered misbehaviour, rudeness, crookedness and arrogance, but Keith is one of the few driven by one thing: music. It has been well documented previously, and in this book you are currently reading, that Reilly lost a couple of homes, countless amounts of money in legal fees and, sadly, also his marriage. But his admirable – arguably foolhardy – stubbornness to support the things he believes in is probably the principal reason that the club he started in 1999 is still open today. October 2024 marks a quarter of a century of keeping London's feet moving.

Clubs rarely last more than a few years. Often the victims of gentrification, they help revitalise an area and are rewarded for their efforts by noise complaints that help shut down the very thing that brought them to the area in the first place. You can count the long-term British survivors on one hand: the granddaddy of them all, Heaven, Ministry of Sound, The Warehouse in Leeds and The Sub Club in Glasgow. So many others have arrived in a blitz of publicity only to disappear sometime later, residing only in the misty-eyed memories of grey-haired clubbers: Turnmills, Dance Tunnel, Cable, Madame Jojo's, Vibe Bar, Plastic People, The Coronet, The Cross, Baileys Studios, Herbal, The Astoria, The End or Home (we'll come on to Home, later). This is just in London.

My involvement with the club started back when I was living in New York in the mid-1990s. My buddy Frank Broughton and I were disciples at the Church of Junior Vasquez, the Sound Factory, where we'd stand underneath the DJ booth, which towered 3 metres above us, and dance all night. When the club closed in early 1995, we tried to fill the gaping maw in our lives by throwing a party in Frank's impressively large brownstone, looking onto one of Harlem's beautiful squares. Entry was free. We set up our $125 hired sound system in the living room, created a 'DJ booth' and myself and Tribal America's Rob Di Stefano played all night. *We'd got the bug.* We did another four or five parties in New York before moving back to the UK at the end of 1996. We didn't even have a name for the first handful of gatherings. The first one in London was in March 1997. Frank's mate Skelly had a loft on 54 Kingsland Road, which we cleared out, then installed a rather underwhelming set of speakers and filled it with a hundred of our friends. I played for eight hours, from start to finish, the greatest grounding I'd ever had in how to really control a hungry dancefloor.

24 May 1998 was an amazing day for two reasons. Firstly, Grimsby Town were promoted back to the Championship via the play-offs. We celebrated this incredible achievement by throwing a Low Life party in a warehouse in Bethnal Green. Attending that night was a delegation from Boy's Own, led by X-Press 2's Rocky and including Clive Henry, Stripey and Miami Mick. At the end of the night Rocky said simply, 'You should be playing every week.' At the next party, back in Skelly's loft, Rocky brought Nikki Smith with him – as well as a strong Boy's Own contingent. Nikki loved what I played: 'Are you interested in being a resident at this new club, fabric?' DJs get these offers all the time. Few of them get past bar talk. Fewer still an actual gig in an actual physical space.

'Would you like to come and see the space?' asked Nikki. So off we went to a then half-derelict Smithfield to check out this club. As soon as we stepped through the door, I knew this was not just real but mind-blowing. The space, empty as it was and littered with rubble, was immense, like a secret, newly excavated underground cathedral. Elevated ceilings, elegant arches and, back then, there were even plans to have a rooftop space (which never happened as far as I know). She told me who the residents for Saturdays would be: Craig Richards and Terry Francis (weekly) and then myself, Jon Marsh and Amalgamation Of Soundz (monthly).

In the late 1990s, British clubbing, especially house music, was largely in thrall to the superclubs and the superstar DJs who dominated their line-ups. They'd enjoyed endless coverage in magazines and the club nights reciprocated with generous advertising budgets. It was the golden era of dance music magazines, when *Mixmag* was overtaking stalwart rock weeklies like *NME* and *Melody Maker*, while *Muzik*, *DJmag* and MoS offshoot, *Ministry Magazine*, competed for shelf space.

Into this culture stepped Home, a new venue just off Leicester Square, led by James Barton's former partner in Cream, Darren Hughes, and financially backed by Ron McCulloch's Big Beat organisation, with residents like Paul Oakenfold, Steve Lawler, Tim Sheridan and Dave Haslam in place and regulars including Brooklyn's Danny Tenaglia. It seemed like a surefire winner. Big Beat owned a chain of clubs and bars that included Home in Sydney and The Tunnel in Glasgow, and were intent on building an empire.

Although fabric looked like a superclub in size, grandeur and ambition, it was anything but. Firstly, its list of residents, led by Craig Richards and Terry Francis on Saturdays, with me and others playing monthly. It was essentially a list of, as Terry Francis quipped to me, 'Who are *they* again?'

Both Home and fabric were quietly competing furiously to become the first to open – and fabric lost. Initially, it was scheduled to open its doors in September 1999, but had to delay the opening by about six weeks, leaving the match: advantage Home.

Home opened with the usual razzamatazz one expects with a big London launch, with pop stars like Rod Stewart, Ronnie Wood and Jay Kay from Jamiroquai in attendance. When fabric opened on 21 October 1999, by stark contrast, it was full of DJs and industry people with a generous smattering of clubbers on the blag. It was unapologetically where the underground lived (quite literally if you looked at how they'd burrowed into London's primeval earth below). 'I think opening in Leicester Square is a very bold move,' warned Ministry's Mark Rodol, presciently, before Home's opening night. 'These people are from Liverpool and Scotland and I wonder if there is an appreciation of what Leicester Square is all about.'

Slightly panicked by the delay, fabric ploughed on doughtily with a brilliant opening weekend that included a free Thursday night, the Steve Blonde-led Friday and, finally, a Saturday that featured Tony Humphries and Sasha, Craig and Terry, myself, Jon Marsh and Amalgamation Of Soundz, led by the irrepressible Jean-Claude 'JC' Thompson.

Personally speaking, it was not only a memorable night, but the following week was generally nuts. An hour or so after I'd finished DJing in Room 2, I was up in the VIP room chatting to Jon Marsh's wife Henny, when a woman sat next to me. Her name was Liz. We started chatting and got on famously. Took her number. Went on a date on the Monday. On the Thursday, myself and my writing partner Frank Broughton had a party to launch our new book, *Last Night A DJ Saved My Life*. Liz, naturally, came. On New Year's Eve, at midnight in fabric, just before my set and less than ten weeks after we first met, I proposed to her. We were married eighteen months later. Along the way, we had two little fabric babies, Lola and Ferdy. For Christmas last year, I bought Lola a Pioneer DJ controller.

The club 'rivalry' – which was never less than friendly – dissipated fairly swiftly. I would regularly bump into Darren Hughes in the VIP room after finishing my sets. Thanks to the endlessly shifting issues surrounding Westminster Council's capricious licensing rules, Darren would often be down long before fabric closed, thanks to the 3am closing at Home. One night, about a year into fabric's existence, I was chatting to Darren and he said to me, without any rancour, 'fabric got everything right.' In the lingering spaces during this conversation, I got the sense he was also admitting that Home did not. In March 2001, Westminster, alarmed at what they believed was wanton drug-dealing, revoked Home's Public Entertainment Licence. 'The city council will continue to work closely with the police and the entertainment industry to try and stamp out such illegal, dangerous and anti-social activity,' commented a Westminster Council spokesperson.

The victory for fabric wasn't that it outlasted Home, but that it changed the way a large club operated. Keith Reilly's vision was essentially in thrall to the party rather than the star DJ. fabric chose the DJs for what they did in the DJ booth and not how marketable they were. If anything, fabric was a basement, a red light and a feeling writ large. It might have had the body of a superclub, but it had the soul of a sweaty illegal rave. And it showed.

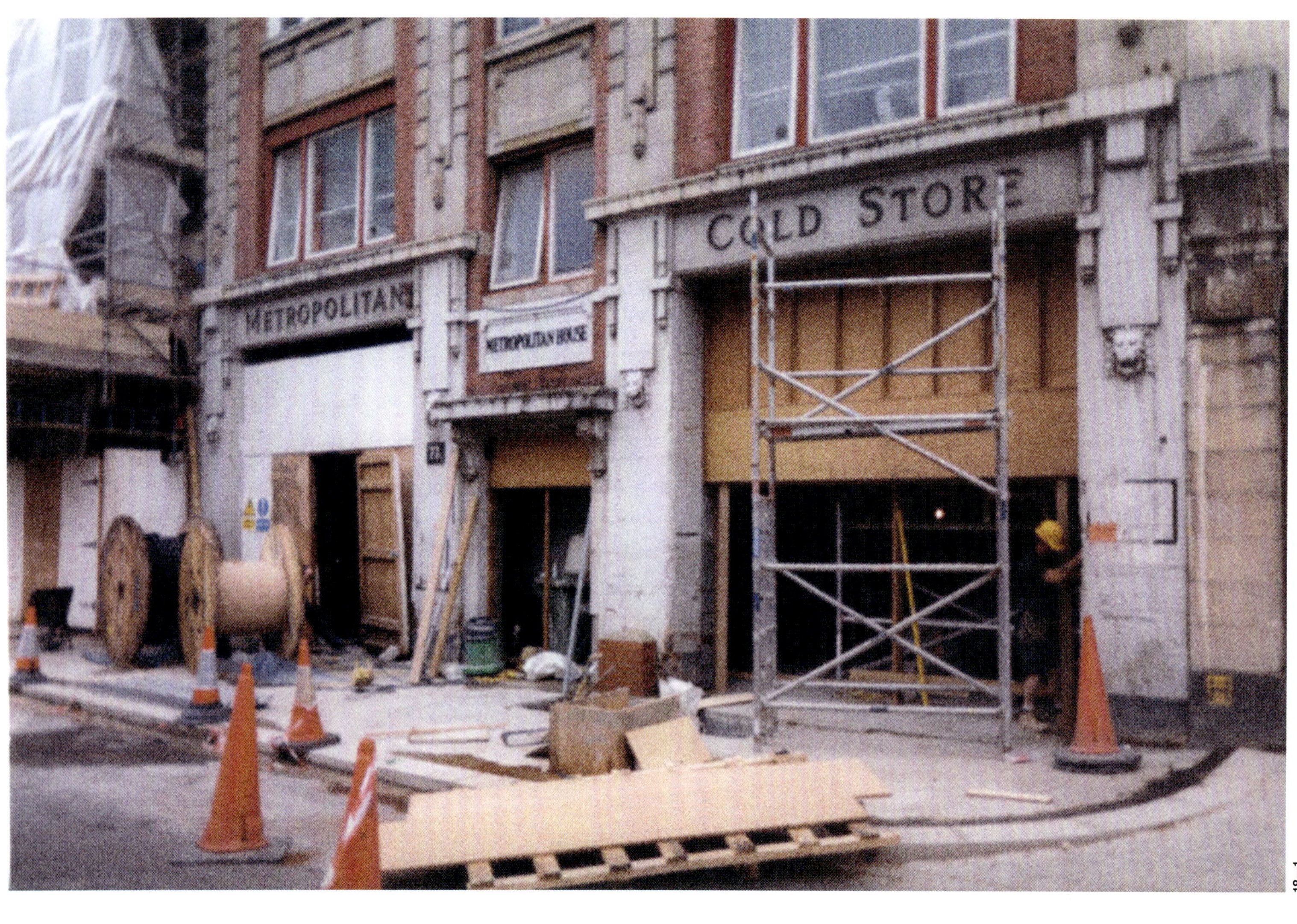

18—1

Although it wasn't without precedent, it certainly did not exist in the grand form that fabric had taken. One of his favoured DJs, Terry Francis, along with partner Nathan Coles, helmed one of London's best kept secrets, Wiggle, a party you had to know about to have any chance of even finding (memories of searching for a seemingly abandoned pub in the wastelands of pre-developed Docklands or the backstreets of Woolwich, hopelessly lost).

'Wiggle was one of the reasons why Keith was really interested in me doing it,' explains Terry of his residency, 'because he really liked our attitude: the upfront-ness of it, and our vibe was friends of friends and no tickets on the door. We had a nice atmosphere and a nice crowd. He always said that Wiggle was a major influence on the place.'

From the residents that were chosen, the boldness (or recklessness, depending on your point of view) is evident. I know it was something they worried about. Would people get it? Would they buy into it?

They did. In droves.

fabric was a success more or less from its first weekend, apart from a panicked hiccup leading up to the Millennium party when they arguably overcharged (a secret Chemical Brothers appearance helped to fill it to acceptable levels). fabric's attention to detail was unique at the time, from the quality and maintenance of the sound system to its bodysonic dancefloor. It was entirely staffed by people who not only knew their shit, but lived for it, from Nikki Smith and Judy Griffith, through to the lighting engineers (one per room) and Sanj the sound guy, who would always make sure that the right tech-spec would be waiting for you by the time you pulled your headphones out to play. If anything didn't feel right, he'd be back down in minutes with a new cartridge, needle, deck or Pioneer CDJ 1000 (the first actually useful machine on the market). It was like stepping out of a Morris Minor and into a Rolls Royce. There wasn't a club in the UK back then that matched the professionalism of the staff. At that stage, the UK hadn't long left the era of club nights being thrown in upstairs rooms in pubs with a tatty carpet for a dancefloor and antediluvian sound systems. fabric, like the Ministry of Sound, brought a new industry standard.

By the end of 2000, fabric had established itself as one of the best clubs in the world. Maybe even the *actual* best. And they'd done it with brilliant DJs, committed to music firstly, rather than the superstar circus that many elements of the nightlife world had succumbed to.

I played at the first six or seven birthday parties, as well as New Year's Eve, before my time was up. I'd still come back for the occasional party in October. By year three, fabric had become a world club rather than a London haunt, but continued its innovative booking policy. It was now in the position of being able to nurture and create new stars, such as Ricardo Villalobos, whose fame came through his many regular appearances at the club, or Skream, whose first encounter was at the tender age of fifteen (naughty boy), hearing one of his tunes getting a rewind. Daniel Avery admits that playing there and producing FABRICLIVE 66 changed his life; Erol Alkan, so early in his career he hadn't even decided what his DJ name actually was, established himself as a serious contender. I'm not sure any other club could have got away with booking John Peel – memorably so in Room 3 – who also did an early FABRICLIVE mix, too. Some got so famous – hello, Diplo – that fabric could no longer afford to book them.

This ability to lure in the cream of the underground made it impossible to define which genre of music it best represented. In fact, it somehow managed to keep the whole dance community happy: house, techno, drum and bass, breaks, big beat, hip hop, grime, UK garage. Whoever played there, whatever it was they played, it all seemed to fit. As Sasha commented, the club had a 'soul'.

Not only that, but it seemed to offer a way of playing that was often unrepeatable anywhere else. There are records I used to play twenty years ago that still don't work anywhere else *but* fabric. It could make you play in a different way. In fact, it seemed to *invite* you to do so, as though bricks and mortar were somehow communicating this desire to you. 'In fabric there's always a feeling of moving things much more forward than you'd play anywhere else,' claims Carl Cox, inside this book. 'And it's not just me; just about any DJ there will end up playing something extraordinary.'

I remember one night in Room 1, warming up for Sasha. He typically played harder and faster than me, so I decided to modify what I was doing so it seamlessly matched his style. Then he came on. He instantly slowed the groove down, and then spent the next hour playing fathoms-deep house that bore little resemblance to anything I'd ever heard him play: slower, funkier, anthem-free. fabric could do that to you. The Sasha that played Tyrant nights with Craig Richards and Lee Burridge was not the same guy who played Twilo with John Digweed. It's embedded in fabric's bricks and mortar, see?

Later into the first part of the twenty-first century, fabric threw their lot in with O2 and entertainment behemoth AEG, and began designing a club that would form part of the redevelopment of New Labour's turn of the century folly, the Millennium Dome. It was a chance to construct an ideal club space from the ground up, rather than sourcing an older building à la fabric. They brought in designers and architects Pentagram and came up with Matter, a multimedia space that would deliver more than just sweaty bodies on a Saturday night.

The timing was, unfortunately, awful. The opening night coincided with the crash of Lehman Brothers investment bank. Despite Matter's impressive monthly residencies (including a fast-rising Rinse FM), it was dogged by issues beyond its control, including the Jubilee Line's flaky service out to the boondocks in Greenwich. If it ran, the club would be full. If it didn't, well ... catastrophe. The club would probably have survived the recession if Transport for London had managed to deliver a reliable service, but sadly in May 2010, fabric decided to pull the plug on the club (which, in turn, plunged fabric into moments of difficulty, too).

For a whole range of reasons, 2016 was a monumentally shit year. In January, we lost David Bowie. In April, it was Prince's turn to leave us. In June, on the eve of Glastonbury, the country lost its mind and voted for Brexit (the whole festival existed in a shocked state of mourning that year). In December, George Michael, aged only fifty-three, passed away too. And in the middle of our annus horribilis, fabric was closed down. Islington Council had revoked fabric's licence, citing its 'culture of drug use'. The reason given was the allegation that two individuals' deaths, which had occurred on 25 June and 6 August, allied to an undercover operation undertaken by the police in July that year. Of course, no one wants to see any deaths at all in their spaces, whether it's a nightclub, football stadium or pub, but ignoring the wider issue of drug use in the UK is irrational. The police report was full of slightly comical vagueness, such as 'manifesting symptoms showing that they were (on drugs). This included sweating, glazed red eyes and staring into space.' I've had a worse reaction queuing in the Post Office.

Petitions were launched, campaigns started to save the club. The whole dance music community, worldwide, joined in the chant to save Clerkenwell's finest. Shaun Roberts, who'd recently left the club, came back to help coordinate the crusade. Letters were written, think-pieces in the nationals; there were news interviews, online agitation. I wrote in the *Guardian*, 'If we want our cities to be modern, vital, vibrant, inclusive spaces that are available to everyone and not just a gaggle of oligarchs with shit taste in Versace and football clubs, we need to save fabric.' We all did our bit. Islington Council was forced to take note.

British governments, often fearful of youth gathering together, have never been comfortable with this culture. Former Tory MP Oliver Letwin's memo in the aftermath of the inner-city riots in 1985 perfectly sums up the attitude towards street culture: '[Lord] Young's new entrepreneurs will set up in the disco and drugs trade; Kenneth Baker's refurbished council blocks will decay through vandalism combined with neglect; and people will graduate from temporary training or employment programmes into unemployment or crime.' As Frank Broughton and I wrote in our book, *Last Night A DJ Saved My Life*, 'dancing is political, stupid'.

In December 2021, there were widespread reports of drug-taking in the Houses of Parliament. Drug swipes found traces of cocaine in eleven out of the twelve bathrooms. It was alleged that cannabis use was common, while another source claimed, 'I have seen an MP openly snorting cocaine at a party.' Speaker Lindsay Hoyle said, 'The accounts of drug misuse in Parliament given to the *Sunday Times* are deeply concerning – and I will be raising them as a priority with the Metropolitan Police this week.' In 2022, there were 3,127 deaths attributed to drug abuse or addiction, while 7,423 deaths were alcohol-related. Were there calls for the House of Parliament to be shut down? Has anyone ever suggested that pubs should cease operations? They have not. Who has caused the most damage to British society over the past fifteen years, a disco in Clerkenwell or the Houses of Parliament?

As we now know, fabric did indeed reopen, buoyed by establishment comments such as those from District Judge Allison, who said the club was 'a beacon of best practice'. At last, it could get on with what it did best – promoting the best global electronic music, booking the most interesting DJs and acts, and throwing killer parties.

Entertainment spaces have never been needed as much as they are now. The pandemic, gentrification and urban redevelopments have had a deleterious effect on the UK's nightlife, which is now facing an existential threat. No club, however large, is immune from the threat of closure. Between 2005 and 2015, it was reported that more than 1,400 closed in the UK, with an estimated £200 million in value lost from British nightclubs in the five years after 2013. Early in 2024, Rekom UK, the biggest nightclub operator in the country, with nearly fifty sites, went into administration.

This country, riddled with class bias as it is, does not value or understand the cultural importance or value of our industry. The UK now exports far more talent abroad than it does cars or steel, yet receives little or no support from arts organisations who fall over themselves to keep opera houses and theatres afloat for the benefit of the few, while these crucial cultural (re)generators are left to flounder and close. Like far too many locations in London, they frequently end up as luxury flats owned by foreign entities looking for an investment opportunity rather than a home. According to the Night Time Industries Association there were 873 UK nightclubs in June 2023, a drop from 994 the previous year and 1,266 in 2020.

We have never needed nightclubs more than we do now. The need to dance is not a desire; it's innate. In repressive Iran, where the fear of dancing is currently so great they have outlawed it, people are gathering in cafes, bars and the street to dance as an act of social disobedience.

We've had more than four decades of club culture providing a pathway from the inner cities out to the world. fabric has been a key driver of that, from bringing in labels like Butterz, led by the inspiring Elijah, to promoting grime, dubstep and any number of the murky sounds that have risen out of the cracks of the UK's tattered pathways. So let's salute those pioneers who conceived the club, who founded it and carved it out of the ancient bricks of London's underworld. I'll forever be grateful for the kickstart they gave me all those years ago, particularly Nikki Smith, Shaun Roberts (RIP), Scott Paterson, Tubbs, Sanj the sound man, Steve Blonde, Cameron Leslie, Portia and, of course, Keith Reilly. As John Digweed says inside, 'To keep a club relevant for a few years is hard enough, but to stay at the top for twenty-five years is an incredible achievement.'

Just as I was completing this introduction, my daughter came up to me to ask a favour. 'Dad,' she said. 'Can you get me into fabric for my nineteenth birthday?' The circle of life keeps turning. Viva dancing. All hail fabric.

Bill Brewster

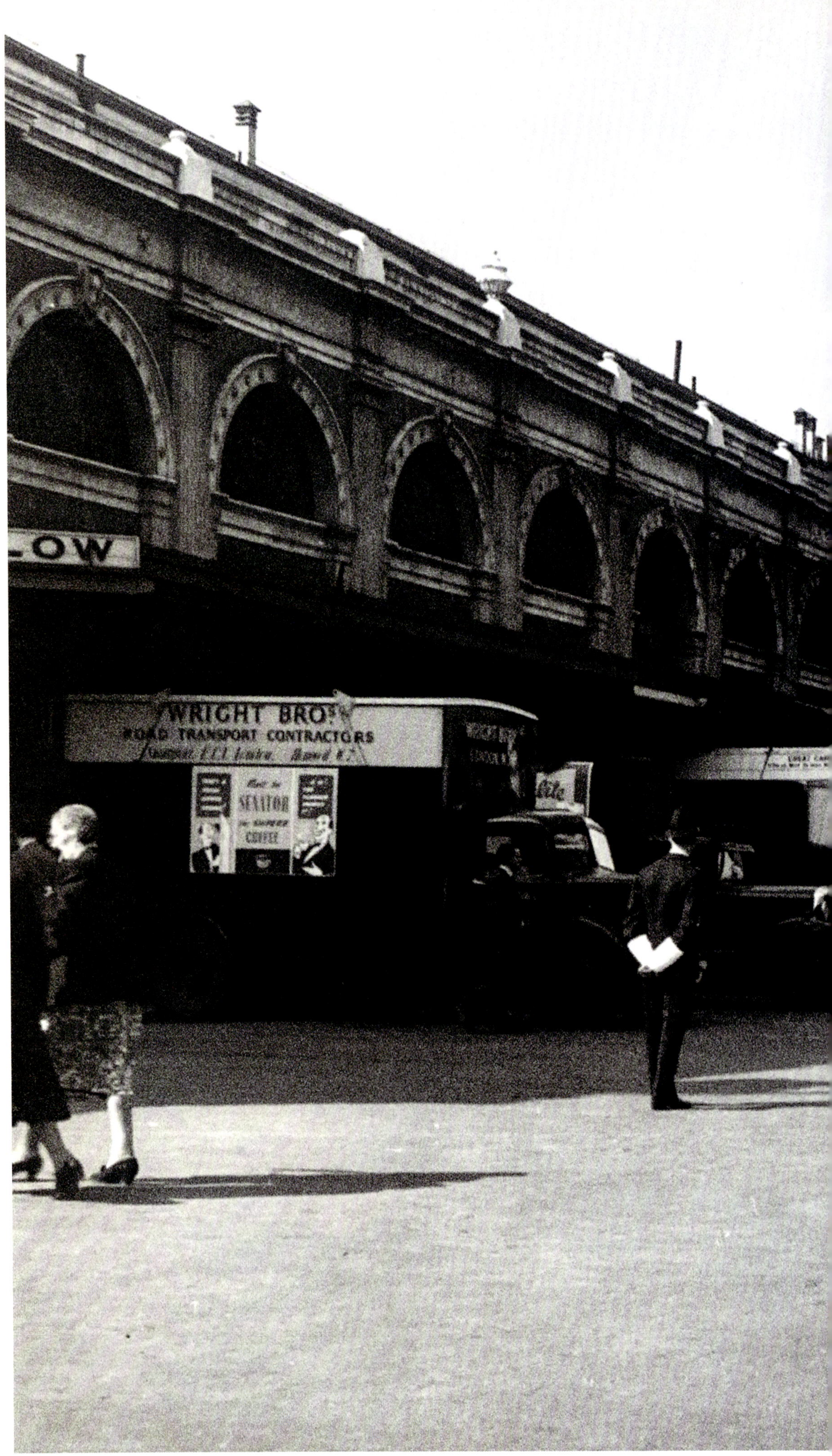
LOW
WRIGHT BROS
ROAD TRANSPORT CONTRACTORS
SENATOR
COFFEE

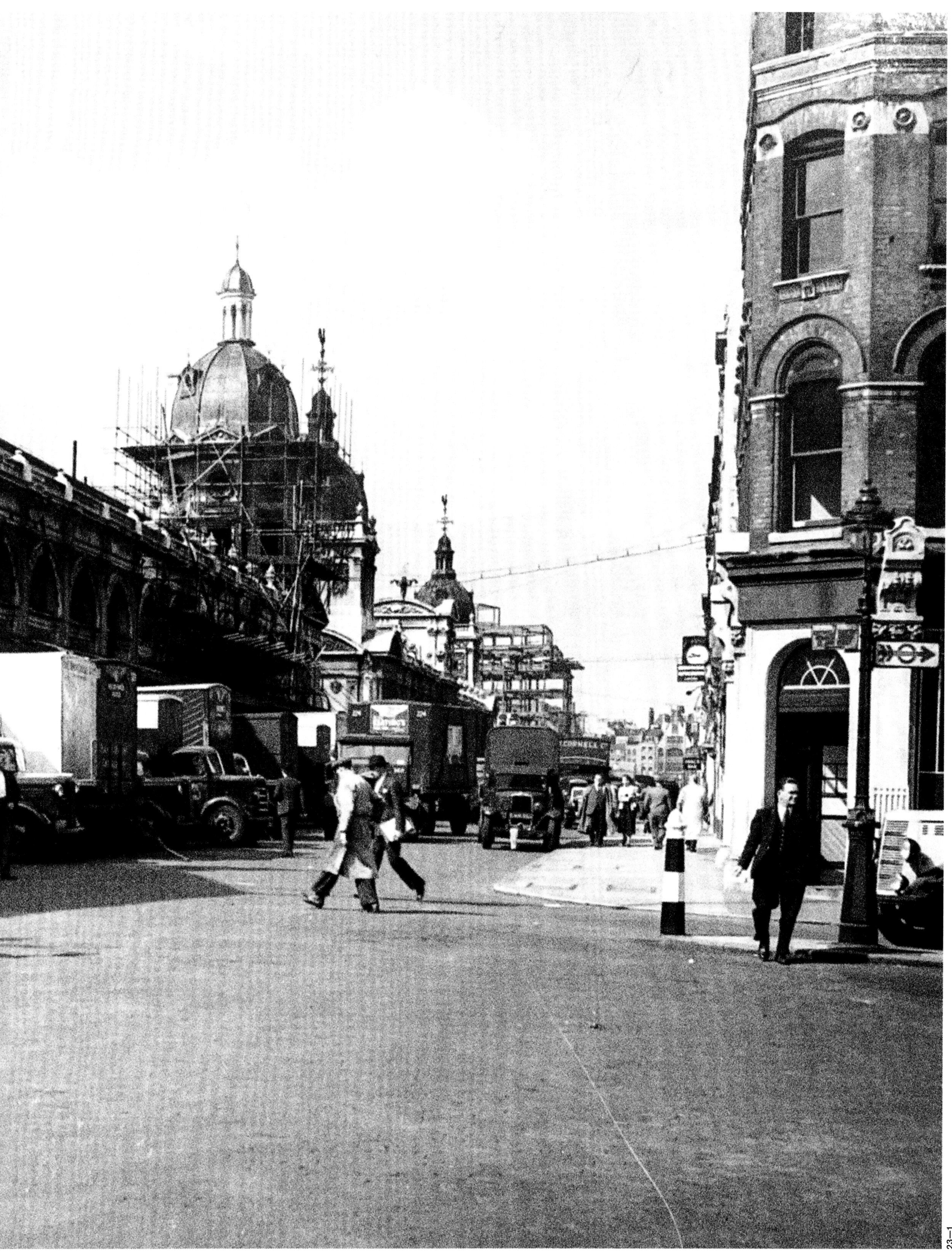

23—1

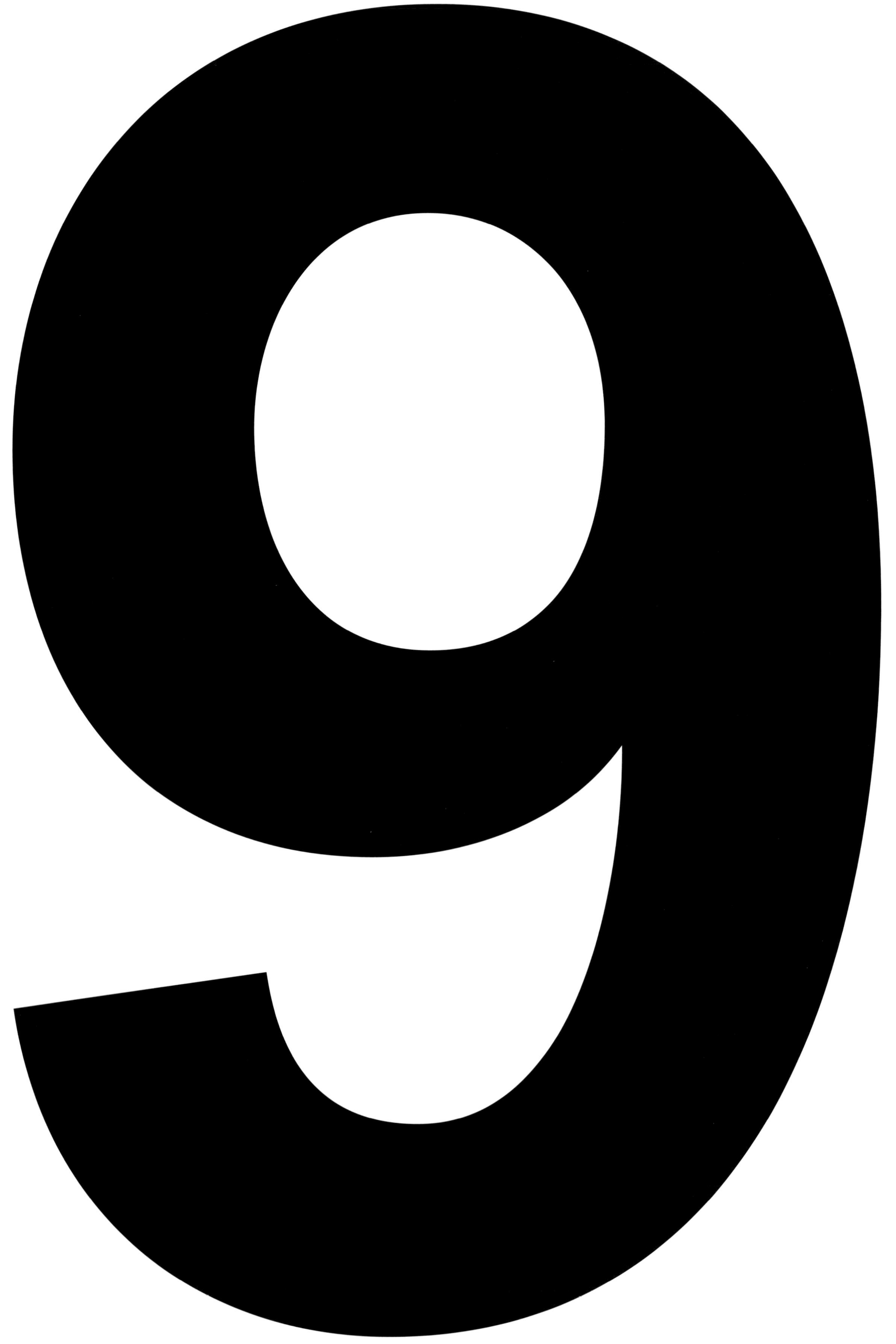

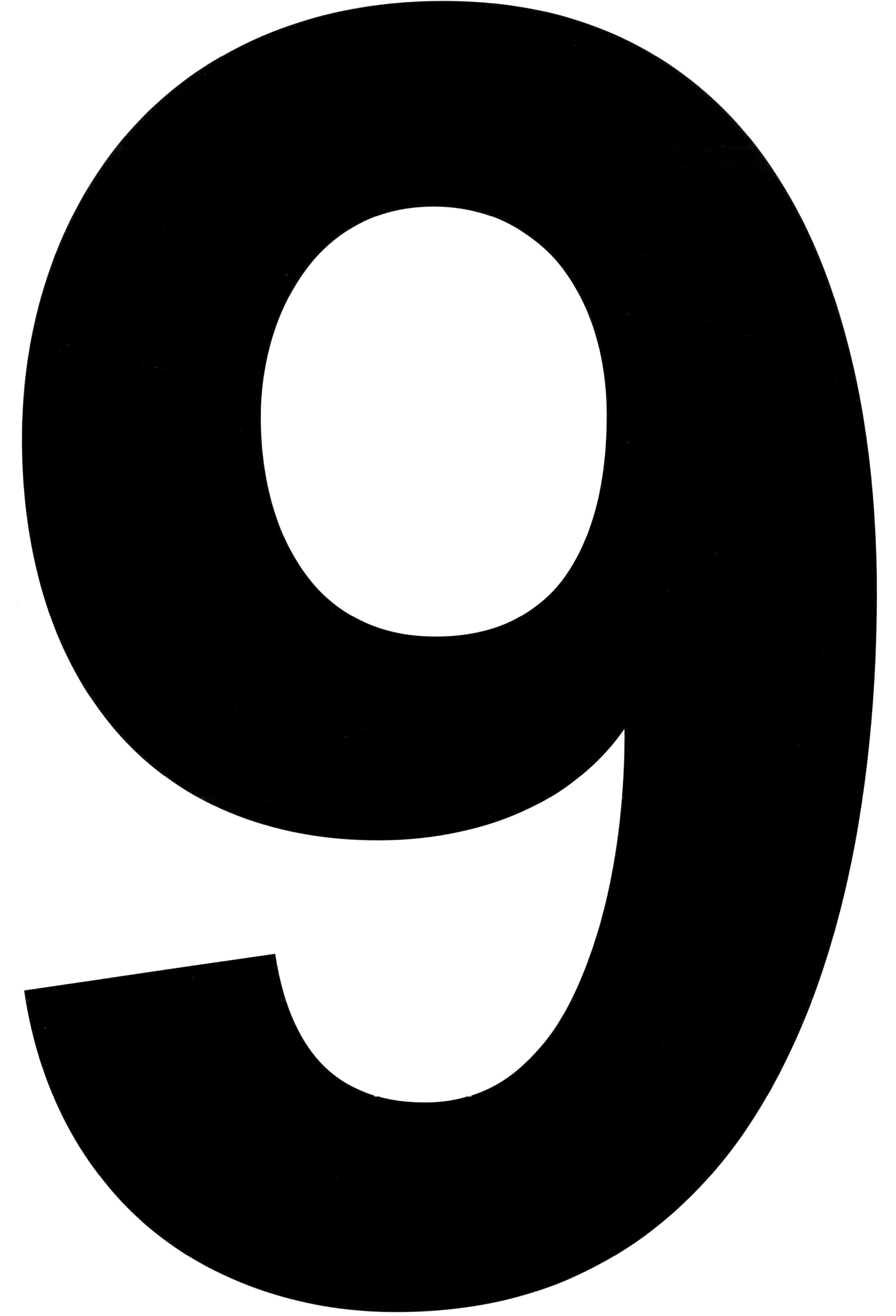

the history of fabric

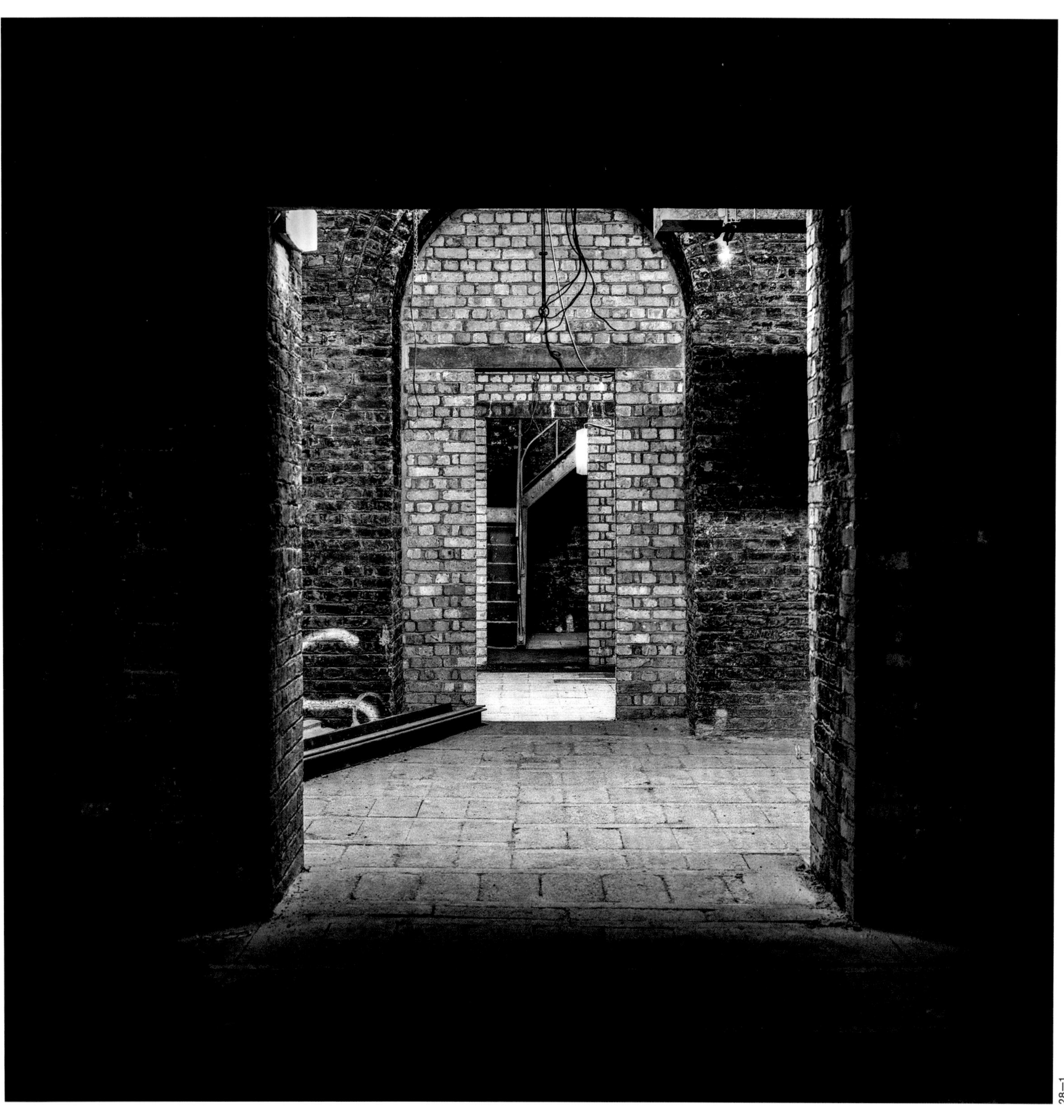

28—1

Late one Friday night, a little way into the 2000s, Keith Reilly was leaning on a railing watching DJ Hype smash the living daylights out of fabric's Room 1, when a teenager next to him turned to him and said, 'Fucking amazing, isn't it?' This kid clearly didn't know who he was talking to – he was just caught in the moment and wanting to share it. Keith beamed and replied – from the heart – 'Yeah!' But the kid continued, the fire of enthusiasm stoked, 'I cycled here from Colchester!' … then went back to dancing.

More than two decades later, Keith is almost speechless with joy as he recounts this: 'Honestly, I wanted to pick him up and hug him!' In that brief exchange, barely more than a couple of seconds, there was so much. A moment of intergenerational connection, an acknowledgement of shared passion, a sense that dance music still really mattered going into the new millennium. There was a fleeting feeling of 'mission accomplished' for Keith, too. He'd put blood, sweat and tears into the club, and its future was still far from assured – but this was everything he'd wanted from it, a piece of dancefloor alchemy that really brought home the fact that his dreams had been made real, and that other people shared his deranged drive to chase the beat. This youngster was who he'd done it all for.

And right there, in Keith Reilly and the unknown raver, are the alpha and omega of fabric, the two things without which it wouldn't exist, let alone have survived a quarter of a century as a cultural mainstay. Of course, fabric is much, much more, too. It's a family: from Cameron Leslie, who came on as the yin to Keith's yang at the beginning and steers the ship to this day, through the DJ keystones Craig Richards and Terry Francis and beloved characters like programmer Judy Griffith and the late and sadly missed promoter Shaun Roberts, all the way through to the toilet and cloakroom attendants, fabric as an entity is the sum total of all the people who've made it work. But without those individual punters coming in week in, week out, it would be nothing – and, likewise, it would never have existed and built the tight-knit family it has without Keith's unhinged vision.

In that quarter-century of existence, fabric has been from boom to bust and back again, multiple times. It was founded at a time when British dance music culture was characterised by flash and ego, but rejected that in favour of underground party values. It's been a pariah and a national treasure, faced existential threats from both sides of the law and nurtured multiple musical revolutions. It's seen the greatest tragedies and the greatest celebrations imaginable play out inside its walls, and weathered social and cultural storms gathering outside. It's come agonisingly close to closing for good more times than is comfortable.

Yet it's somehow come through all that stronger and sturdier, rising from underdog status even within dance culture to being nationally and globally recognised as a hub of creativity and connection. It has woven itself into the, well, fabric of London, the UK and the world's culture, and it continues to bubble with new ideas. There are, of course, untold eye-opening stories – even, as Keith puts it, 'achingly salacious and sordid' ones – from throughout its history. But before we get to those, to understand how they came about, we need to know more about the man whose vision spawned them.

Keith Reilly's childhood in Essex was comfortable, a little staid, even. Despite coming from a family of some notoreity, his dad was a scrupulously straight dealer, running a successful haulage company, and Keith, his brother and his sister grew up wanting for nothing. 'We had nice clothes, even a horse,' he remembers – although it was devoid of pop culture, with not even a record player in the house. The kids were expected to study and do normal jobs; Keith's mum was desperate for him to be a lawyer or accountant, though for a while his ambition was architecture, even taking extra technical-drawing classes after school.

The moment he discovered David Bowie, though, any hope of respectability was gone. Music became everything to him. He's long told an 'origin story' of how he scrawled 'DAVID BOWIE' and 'LOU REED' on his jeans at the age of thirteen, but just recently one journalist called him out on this, suggesting perhaps this was a bit precocious for a child of the early seventies whose friends cared only for Mud and Showaddywaddy. Keith fumed at this impugning of his tastes, but then just a couple of weeks later his mum messaged saying she'd been clearing out the loft and had found some photos – which, sure enough, included a picture of him in those exact Levi's, which he gloatingly texted to the journalist who'd slighted him.

It's quite a picture. His hair long and tangled and a glint of mischief in his eye, he looks borderline feral, like he's escaped from a hippie commune – a far cry from the commuter-belt gentility of his upbringing and a million miles from the wideboys of his extended family. This is without question a kid who, as he puts it, 'If you told me not to go over there, I'm there trying to find out what's so good over there that you didn't want me to see it.' His mother was distraught, of course, but Keith was entirely and irreversibly committed to 'hearing, archiving, sharing music' and the culture that came with it.

He worked two paper rounds for two years to buy his first hi-fi. He taped every John Peel show then spent hours with his friends poring over the tracklists and hunting down records. He hoovered up every genre that came along, especially Essex's very special soulboy/jazz-funk culture; he bought his first Technics turntables after an epiphany when seeing legendary DJ Froggy cut up the Brothers Johnson's 'Stomp!' at a Caister Soul Weekender. By seventeen he was DJing by default – a bar in the village calling him up on hearing he had a very cool record collection … though they'd neglected to tell the resident 'local cool guy DJ', who rocked up with his record box to find a whippersnapper in his place, a mortifying experience for poor young Keith. It was experiences like this which made him very quickly realise he did not enjoy the limelight. 'I loved DJing, but I didn't want to be a DJ,' as he succinctly puts it.

Keith did like a good get-together, though. He was still only nineteen, right at the end of the seventies, when he started throwing parties in warehouses. It was purely a matter of 'because it's there', really; he knew people with access to warehouses, so if he got a nod that a company had gone bust or a space was otherwise out of use, with his friends like Spencer Carroll he'd bring in a PA, a makeshift bar and get it going on. They played everything from raw funk to Talking Heads, rockabilly to Donna Summer, not just thrown together willy-nilly, but mixed with skill.

Keith is fiercely proud that the dancefloors of London and its surrounds in the late seventies and early eighties – Blitz, Le Beat Route and so on – had all the variety and DJ skill that any legendary New York or European club did. 'People go on about the Paradise Garage,' he says, 'but we had it all here!' For Keith, the culture mixing was crucial. With a smile he points out that 'people thought because the Blitz had Steve Strange on the door dressed as a clown it was all about the New Romantics, but it wasn't'. They were as likely to play James Brown as Spandau Ballet at the Blitz, and it's the first place he heard the Sierra Leonean Afro-synth disco of Bunny Mack's 'Love You Forever', a personal favourite to this day and as futurist in its way as any arch electropop. Again, he wasn't putting on parties to be in the limelight. The warehouse dos were just one-offs, a bit of opportunistic fun; he'd much rather have been out and about in London's clubs and after-hours spots with his fellow music fanatics. It should give some hint of where he was going that his clubbing buddies by this point included the likes of Linden C, Femi B and Rob Acteson, budding DJs who would go on to define the sounds of underground London in years to come.

As the eighties wore on, the offspring of disco and postpunk merged with incoming hip hop and electro, the rare-groove movement and sound-system culture, and other

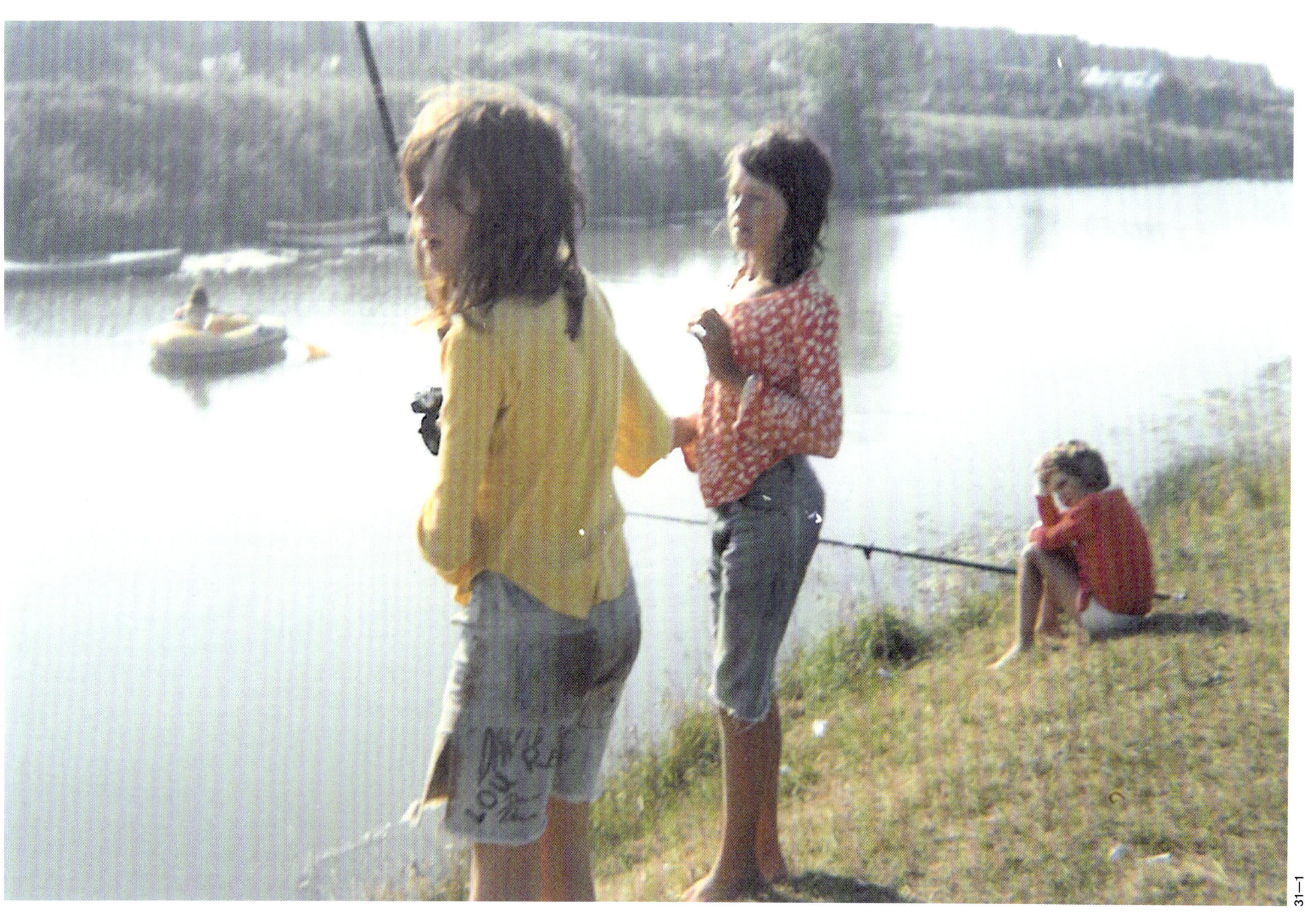

31—1

warehouse parties proliferated, providing a training ground for names like Norman Jay, Coldcut, Colin Dale, Mark Moore and many more now-household names. Keith ducked, dived and danced through it all, only ever wanting to be near the music. Eventually he founded and nurtured a successful cassette and CD manufacturing business, allowing him to earn a good living and build his musical contacts ever further.

And then there was house. It was already in the mix in the circles he was moving in from the minute it started filtering through from New York, Chicago and Detroit, so Keith didn't have the kind of grand awakening to it that some did with the acid house explosion of 1987 and '88. Rather it was a gradually blossoming love affair, and the more the London house scene grew, the deeper he got. He marvelled at the skills and soul of Derrick Carter and Kid Batchelor, made new friends like Sasha and Craig Richards; he felt at home among people who believed as he did that 'this was something pure and beautiful and very special that was ours'.

Of course, as the nineties began, the dance explosion kept on … exploding. Everything got bigger, bolder, rougher, tougher – and with that came, as Keith puts it, 'hard house, happy house, handbag house, all these silly variations to distract from the real thing – it was horrible!' From very early on in the nineties, Keith started to nurture dreams of having his own place, and he had a front-row seat, so to speak, to witness all these changes in clubland, too. At the start of this decade, his brother Billy – then working in a garage the family ran – had also got in on the raving game. Discovering that a building next to the notorious rave sweatpit Bagley's in the then exceedingly down-at-heel King's Cross area was available, he decided to open a pre-club bar and asked Keith to get involved.

However, when it was granted a late licence, it became another club: the Cross, a haven for more glamorous clubbers, in stark contrast to its down-and-dirty neighbour Bagley's. From 1994 Keith put on some midweek nights called Fluid and Big Picture, representing the real house he loved, bringing over US singers like Michael Watson, Byron Stingily and Robert Owens, and lesser-known DJs like Marques Wyatt, and generally having a fine time. But the main business of the club was glam nights – fluffy bras, cowboy hats and glitter predominated, and proponents of the growing superstar DJ culture like Judge Jules, Seb Fontaine and Danny Rampling delivered ever-cheesier anthems to the dressed-up party people.

Keith *really* didn't like it. 'If I was in on a Friday or Saturday, I'd just be going, "This is so awful!"' he winces. 'It wasn't about the music anymore, this was something else.' He could see people were having fun, he could respect his brother's successful running of the place, but it wasn't where he wanted to be. With unusual diplomacy, he won't mention particular names that turned him off, rather, 'It wasn't any one person or DJ set, but bit by bit I just started to think this isn't right, fuck this, something's got to be done.' The drive to find a space of his own built gradually – not out of any desire to be an impresario, or really as any kind of business decision, but out of a deeply felt need. He was *willing* something truer to his clubbing ideals to exist. And his reaction to the radically different culture of weekends at the Cross tipped him over into making that a reality.

It helped a great deal that as he was out flyering for the Cross he would see another face – Steve Blonde – doing the same job outside clubs. The two hit it off and ended up pooling their resources, starting a new business for flyer distribution. Keith talked of his dreams of opening a club space, and eventually said he wanted to sell off his share of the business to do it; Steve didn't need any encouragement – he decided he'd do likewise and came on board as a key part of the founding fabric team.

Some way into the mid-nineties, they started looking in earnest for a venue. As Keith checked out places with potential, the would-be architect in him came out; his imagination ran wild as he walked around spaces imagining how he'd transform them. Although, as Craig Richards points out, 'places like Smithfields and King's Cross felt east because they were away from the West End, where people still went clubbing', this was all pretty much in what we now see as central London. It's hard for anyone not alive at that time to envisage, but there were still more or less empty buildings across the heart of the capital that weren't packed with chain cafés, Sports Directs or office spaces. The area between the West End and the City absolutely reeked of insalubrious history: just around Smithfield, Scots rebel William Wallace had been hung, drawn and quartered, and the Peasants' Revolt leader Wat Tyler stabbed by the king's men; for centuries the debauchery of Bartholomew Fair was notorious, and in Victorian times the 'rookeries', or slums of houses built willy-nilly with barely even alleys between them, were famously lawless.

The disused Aldgate tube station was in the running for some while; indeed, it had been used for one-off rave events, and Keith went as far as to pay for safety assessments, but, still nervous after the 1987 King's Cross fire, London Transport ultimately weren't having it. Another possibility was even closer to where fabric ended up: a suite of buildings in the old Smithfield Market known as the Annexe, which is now becoming the new home of the Museum of London. Keith put on a charm offensive, including lavishing the 75-year-old market superintendent with attention, taking him to the Cross suited and booted 'and looking like Louie Austen', literally getting young women to feed him grapes. He was suitably charmed, but that one didn't work, partly because although Keith was ready to try and raise the five million pounds needed to renovate the building and make it viable, the Corporation of London – 'a strange bunch', he calls them – wanted to only offer him a five-year lease. There was further light relief when a rival bidder for the lease on another Corporation of London building, a well-known TV personality, snaffled a Corporation coat of arms during a viewing, but was later spotted with it in his house on a TV broadcast and banned from the process. This was tough going, though; Keith was burning through money just on assessing venues – to the point that he had sold not one, but two houses.

But then an unlikely saviour appeared, in the form of a 'six feet four inches Norwegian lumberjack-looking guy', Rolf Munding. Keith's new friend, the dapper market superintendent, alerted him to the fact that Rolf had a couple of former meat storage arches opposite the market. Craig Richards remembers Keith showing the space to him. 'It was a dripping Victorian cellar,' he says, 'nothing like a nightclub, but Keith could see exactly how it was going to work and his enthusiasm was infectious.' Keith wasn't just enamoured with the space – he immediately took to Rolf, who was, and is, a genial wheeler-dealer with financial interests in pubs, Czech breweries, mopeds and skateboard paraphernalia, among various other things. He'd owned the arches since the eighties and was trying to make a go of them as a club/bar and restaurant project, which would become Smiths of Smithfield. Until this point he'd been nurturing Philip Sallon as a possible partner, which worked in Keith's favour, as Keith was able to look sober and sensible in contrast to the notorious nightlife eccentric.

Having charmed Rolf, Keith had 'a difficult conversation' on the phone with Sallon, who was in the bath at the time; Keith winces at remembering 'the sound of the water slapping about'. With this unlikely business call and Sallon out of the picture, the venue that would become fabric was underway ... kind of. In 1996, Keith, Rolf and a team of investors Rolf and Sallon had previously assembled – a mixed bunch but all from an accountancy background – began the transformation of the venue. Musical talent was already being gathered together, with Keith's first hires including Craig Richards, Steve Blonde and the well-established club promoter Nikki Smith. Into this mix came one other element: a consultant from Deloitte, brought in by Rolf originally to do due diligence on his putative restaurant project, by the name of Cameron Leslie.

When Keith and Cameron met, alchemy happened. As personalities they were opposites in almost every way; Cameron jokes that the fact that he'd also fancied the idea of being an architect as a kid was 'just about the only thing we had in common'. Where Keith is mercurial and completely led by his vision, with practical matters just something to overcome during the pursuit of that vision, Cameron is a practical person, a problem-solver by nature – 'the reality maker', as Keith liked to put it. He, too, loved club music, having had his student days in Brighton and fallen in love with the vibe and culture of 'the Zap, the Escape and all those places along the seafront' – but he'd never envisaged being in the music world. Having studied hospitality and worked his way up to management level in international hotels, then into hospitality and leisure consultancy, he already had a neat career path mapped out.

But the first time he sat down to lunch with Keith to hear his plans, Cameron was enthralled – and Keith in turn instantly realised what Cameron was capable of: here was someone who could bring method to his madness. As their lunch stretched to hours, they scrawled notes onto the tablecloth, eventually rather sheepishly requesting to take it away with them, as it had become a working document of how the club would work. Cameron would have joined up with the new enterprise like a shot, but his role as a consultant meant there was an irreconcilable conflict of interest: legally, he couldn't work with Keith. It seems like the luck plane was tilted in fabric's direction, though, because within 24 hours of being told his contract was watertight and there was no way he could join fabric, a restructuring in Deloitte turned everything on its head and he left there and then. He came on as general manager and that was it – he'd joined the club.

But though the pieces seemed to be in place, this was far from a glorious beginning. The investors hired a building contractor despite Keith sounding alarm bells about his 'say yes to everything' attitude – rightly, it turned out, as the contractor went into liquidation halfway in, which led to a major falling out among the partners. The falling out was so bad, in fact, that a meeting in the mews office behind the club degenerated into a screaming stand-up row, and Keith (who's 'never had a fight in my life') and an investor squared up to one another – it got so heated that a large glass ashtray was raised in anger, before everyone stormed out, the rift irreparable. The investors tried to put the club into administration. Keith feared they then planned to buy it back for a song, but managed to do financial judo on them: with lightning speed, he found a new backer and made an offer to the insolvency practitioner to clear the debts and provide contingency funds on top – which, given his opponents didn't have anything similar in place, the court ratified, and the club was his again.

Thus concluded fabric's first brush with obliteration. But it was far from the last, and indeed more trouble was already on the horizon – though this didn't become apparent for a little bit. To make that offer, Keith and Rolf had needed to call in help from a friend of Billy's, a regular at the Cross and another flamboyant clubland personality. They'd much rather have had a more sober and boring partner, but this was not the time to look a gift horse in the mouth. With eight million pounds of ready cash sitting in the bank, he was able to bail them out in short order, becoming the majority shareholder, and work was able to begin in earnest on realising Keith's vision.

As well as disliking the music, Keith never wanted all the hoopla and folderol that went with the ever-expanding superstar DJ culture of the nineties, epitomised by the fancy-pants capering at the Cross. His heart was still with the warehouse-party vibe, where music was paramount, and his closest musical allies were people like Terry Francis, whose notorious Wiggle tech-house parties were in illegal venues as often as legal ones. However, he'd long since got fed up with the faff of 'opening somewhere up, securing it, cleaning it, working out how to have toilets, finding somewhere for the bar, setting up the sound system each time, all of that'. He wanted something no-frills, but with everything just so. As Craig Richards says: 'It was a case of raising the standards of the things that you believe in – security and sonics and toilets and drinks – and not worrying about the other stuff.'

So they went hell for leather to make the space – that 'Victorian cellar' with 'METROPOLITAN COLD STORE' on the front and sticky, tarry caulk on its internal brickwork into … well … almost exactly what you can see today. The clean, spacious unisex toilets, the easily accessible bars and stairs that wouldn't create bottlenecks, and, of course, the three rooms of dancefloor space with impeccable sound were the be-all-and-end-all of the plans. Given both Keith and Cameron's architectural leanings, it was always going to be made to look nice, but never with whistles and bells; any extra spending and effort would be put towards going the extra mile with those fundamentals – as with the 'bodysonic' dancefloor of Room 1, which effectively turned the whole floor into a giant bass speaker.

There were all the hassles of any big build. As Cameron says, 'We were supposed to open on 1 October 1999, but the electrics still weren't right, and even on the day we did finally open three weeks later, we were still painting – like, there was still wet paint when the doors actually opened!' The logistics were fraught, enough to lead their operations manager to collapse with exhaustion on the day of launch, meaning Cameron would end up having to run all the operations – bars, toilets, security and more – for the first forty nights it was open; literally, forty nights non-stop with mid-week outside hires as well as the weekend public club nights.

They had bigger worries still, though. During all this preparation, gangs were demanding access to fabric to sell drugs inside. They found Keith's home address, and numerous threats were made, but he was adamant that he had to face them down, with the police involved: 'I wasn't going to walk away. I know the ropes, I know how things operate, and I know if you don't draw a line, you'll end up with someone else running your business before you know it.'

He and Cameron both wore bulletproof vests for an uncomfortably long time, right through the opening of fabric. 'I was telling them,' Keith says, 'I'm not having it, this club's going to be clean, this is nothing to do with the rest of my family and if you want me you know where to find me. I'll be outside the club!' It took months of facing down the threats, but Keith says, 'Once it died down, I knew that we'd sent a message that this wasn't how we worked.' It was a bittersweet victory, though; Keith's bull-headed focus on getting his dream realised without it getting corrupted cost him his marriage, his wife Sarah understandably exhausted by being woken in the night when new threats came, and for a while having to ship out to Spain to stay out of the line of fire.

fabric eventually arrived – to some bemusement from the dance-music establishment. 'Even when it was still just a hole in the ground,' says Keith, 'agents were coming to see us and then walking away shaking their heads.' Inevitable comparisons were being made with Home, which was being fitted out down the road in Leicester Square as a seven-story behemoth, with Darren Hughes, formerly of Liverpool's Cream – which by this time was one of the biggest promotions organisations in Ibiza to boot – as its figurehead. Home had everything that suggested commercial success in 1999: association with a known 'superclub' brand, megastars Paul Oakenfold and Danny Rampling as residents, and a West End location.

Keith remembers one industry figure pointing all this out to him and asking who he had as residents. 'Craig Richards and Terry Francis,' he replied, which was met with: 'WHO are THEY?' He actually looks slightly smaller and wide-eyed, like a defensive scolded schoolboy, as he recalls his response: 'They're my friends!' Likewise, he was determined to rep drum'n'bass in the club, though at this point it was anything but fashionable and the swanky superclubs weren't having any of it. There was, on the surface of things, no reason to think that what they were doing was anything but micro-niche stuff: the economy of superclubs and the superstar DJ culture of helicopters, egos and conspicuous excess was still on the rise, and fabric seemed a ramshackle organisation in comparison; after all, they'd even had to recruit Cameron's dad to run the cloakroom.

Nonetheless, fabric opened on 21 October 1999 with queues round the block despite Home having beaten them to the punch by a month, and the punters and DJs loved it. A team was building of dancefloor lifers, people with the values of underground club music coming through their veins – people like Steve Blonde and Nikki Smith, like Shaun Roberts, who came on before opening as a flyer-boy and quickly graduated to assisting with programming Friday nights, and like Judy Griffith, who was cannily poached from Home by Nikki and brought on board as her assistant. The dancefloors themselves thronged with party people who appreciated the focus on exquisite sound, and DJs who focused on the groove rather than the Jesus poses and obvious tunes of the superclub 'personality' DJs. This was part design and part luck – as Steve puts it: 'With Home leading with the biggest, most obvious names, I think we became known as the destination for people looking for leftfield music almost by default.'

That didn't stop the team's flamboyant funder, however, who didn't seem to have got the memo that this keep-it-underground approach was working. He'd invite big name commercial DJs he'd met at private members' bars – including hard-house luminaries like Fergie and Judge Jules, perfectly fine DJs in their own milieu but anathema to fabric's rapidly coalescing musical ethos – to come and play. 'You'd get a call from some guy,' says Cameron, 'saying, "I just met the owner, and I'm going to be coming down on Friday night to play ..."'

'And of course you'd have to say, "No, you're bloody not!"' laughs Keith. He would bring oddball Soho drinking characters he'd met the night before into meetings too, or even give them jobs, and steadily more and more red lights started to flash for Keith and his team.

'He was a very different animal to us,' says Keith. 'We were just music people wanting to make the thing happen; he was the sort of idiot who'd turn up to the office in a red-lined black cape like bloody Dracula!'

Cameron laughs ruefully as he remembers his first meeting with him in a Pizza Express: 'He's the sort of guy who'd introduce himself going, "I'm really, really rich!"'

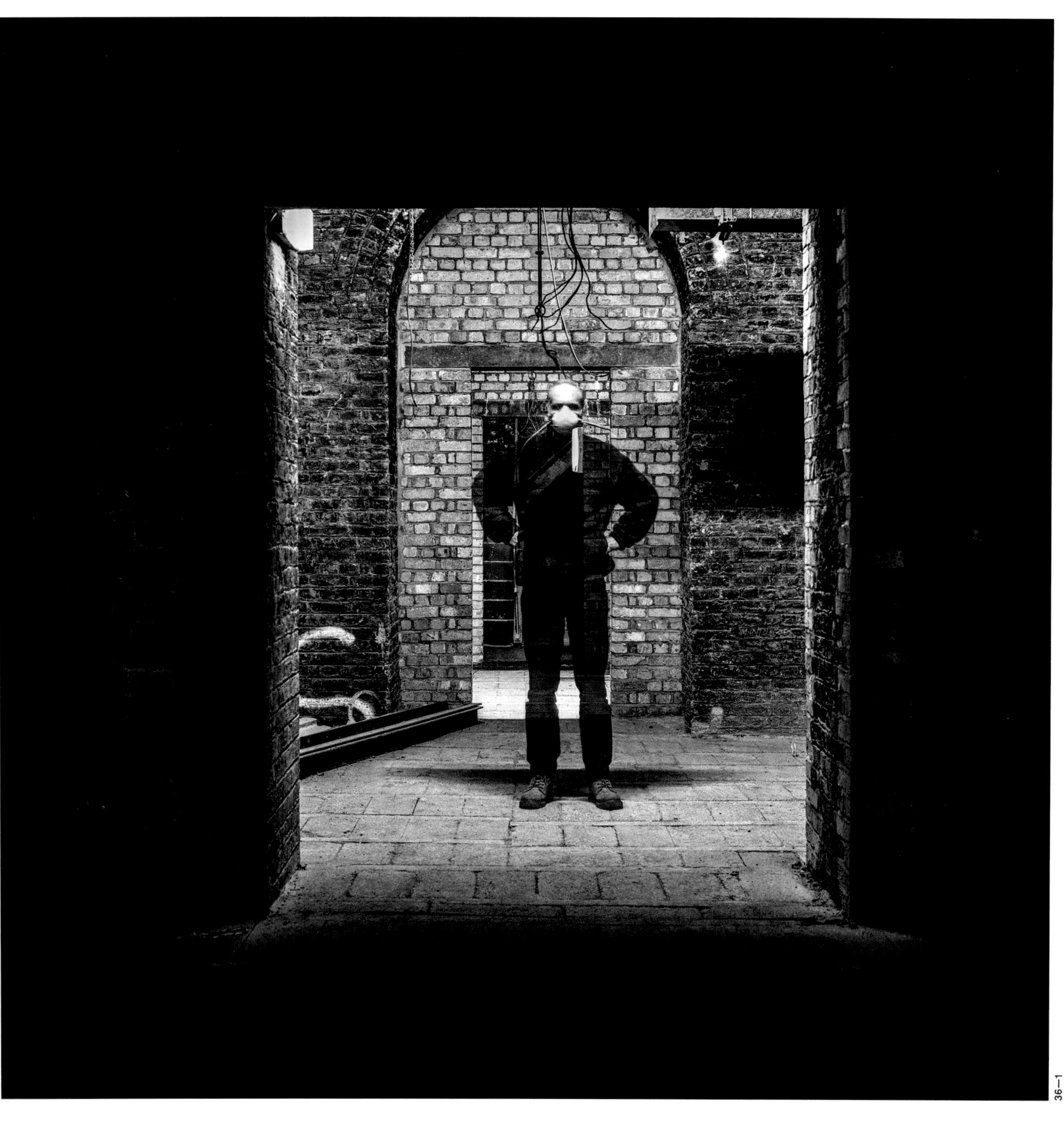

36—1

In fact, he dragged Cameron away from his pizza just to show him his bank balance on a cashpoint outside. 'Not Coutts or some investment bank, just his current plus account, but he wanted to show this off.'

'This was someone who couldn't see people,' says Keith, 'only money.'

And all too soon, it became apparent that he was not just a flash Harry, but someone with a dubious past. The fortune that made him seem like such a safe bet for fabric came from a business deal which ended with a bitter fallout with his partners. And what's more, he was now in the process of doing the same to Keith and Rolf, bleeding them dry by funnelling money out of the company into offshore entities.

As soon as Rolf stumbled on this elaborate scheme, their wayward investor went on the counter-attack and accused Keith and Cameron of stealing, suspending them summarily and barring them from the building. This was his first major tactical mistake, and the first galvanising of the familial solidarity that would be a feature of fabric's reaction to crises over the years. The club had only been up and running three years, but such was the staff's relationship to the place and its management that they spontaneously called a meeting and told the interim manager he had appointed that if Keith and Cameron weren't brought back, they would walk out en masse. This was still a new company, yet the staff were willing to risk their livelihoods to stand by its founders. The interim manager, who had been brought in from Ministry of Sound, turned round and told him that he didn't have a company without Keith and Cameron.

From here, the legal wranglings were long and intense. Keith, despite never being one for admin, can still quote the obscure statutes they had to invoke. As former business partners came out of the woodwork, the investor's fate was all but sealed, but he made things difficult to the last. Even after fabric as a business was wrested away from him, he still maintained one contract relating to the lease, which needed to be signed back over to Keith. Keith offered to clear £130,000 of debt and give him £1,000,000 in cash to go and start a new life, only to be met with a 'fuck you'. 'That,' says Keith, 'is the level of animosity we'd reached.' Soon after, there were rumoured sightings in some scary and unlikely parts of the world, but to all intents and purposes he then vanished off the face of the earth.

They were finally shot of their toxic partner, but it was not plain sailing – far from it. Another investor came in, this time a billionaire with cash to spare, who sadly proved prone to unnecessary antics too – again trying to stitch the founders up on contracts with ultimatums to beef up his share. This time, they responded dramatically, Keith going as far as faking a suicide attempt (complete with mocked-up clinic admissions) to signal the seriousness of the situation and scare their new partner into playing ball. At this point, as when the gangs were trying to hold fabric to ransom, people were asking him why he didn't call his uncles in to put on a bit more serious pressure, but he holds it up as a prime example of how 'there's always another way – I'd much rather be more creative about these things!' They laugh about this overdramatic dodging and diving now, but both Keith and Cameron shudder, too, at the knowledge of how close they were to the edge in the early years. 'You've got to stand up to the challenges,' says Cameron, 'because what's on the other side of that edge is just destruction. There were existential threats to the club all the time.'

'And all we wanted,' says Keith, almost wailing at the injustice of it all, 'was to run a disco!'

Somehow, though, a little way into 2004, as fabric's fifth birthday hoved into view, things settled down. Or rather, the balance of chaos and control became just about manageable, and what chaos there was involved marshalling mercurial DJ talents in and out of hotels and parties, rather than boardroom battles and agonising court cases. Outside its walls the culture had shifted, too, with the late-nineties superstar DJ scene looking downright quaint, and sounds like electroclash, grime, rowdy French electro and more arising to shake up the scene. Inside, the focus on connoisseurs' choices and friends-of-friends over hype and flash continued to pay off. From 2001 its twin mix-CD series had been rolling along in its iconic packaging, a calling card for the variety and quality of the club, and all in all, it started to feel like maybe, just maybe, there might be a future in this …

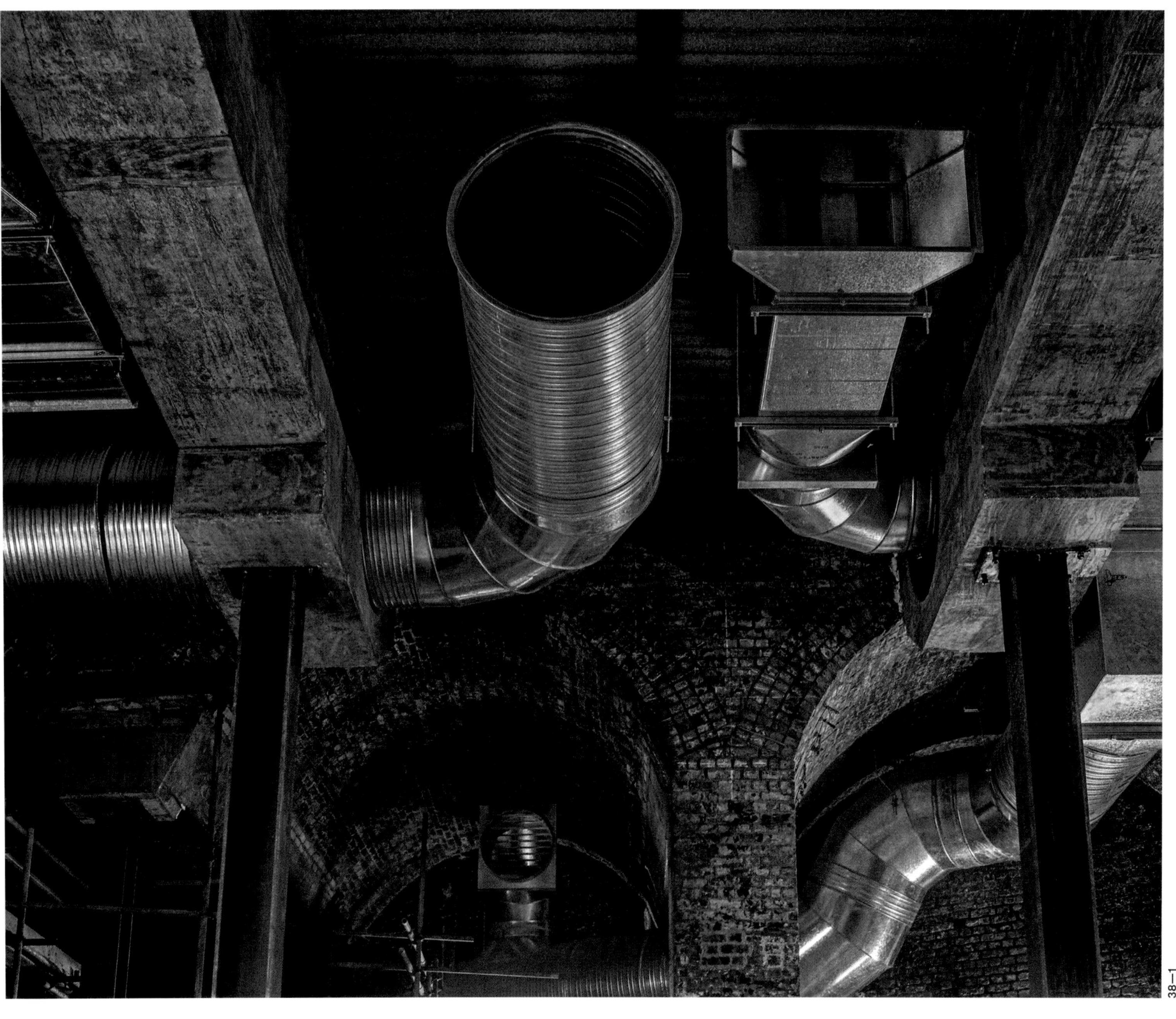

38—1

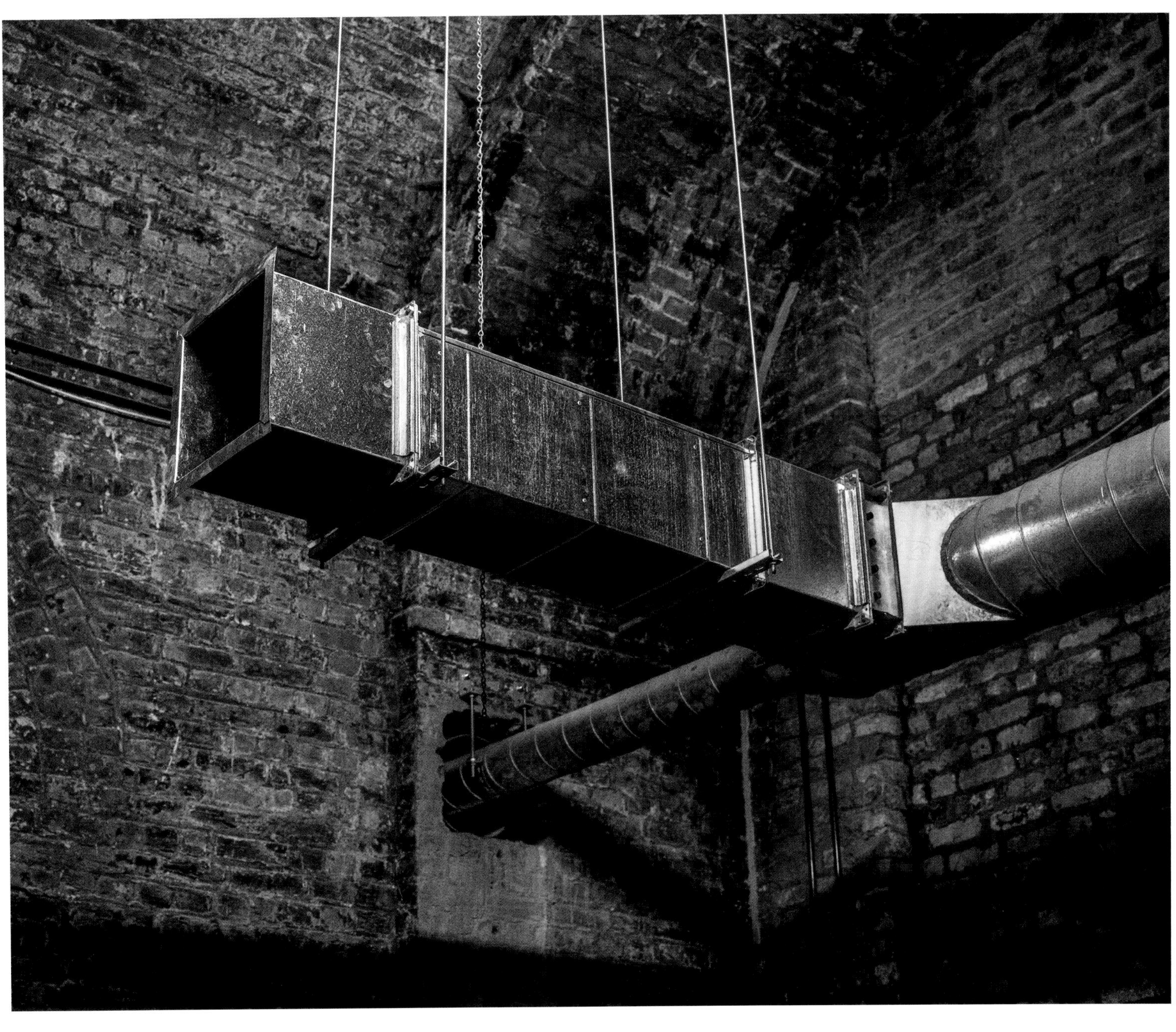

39—1

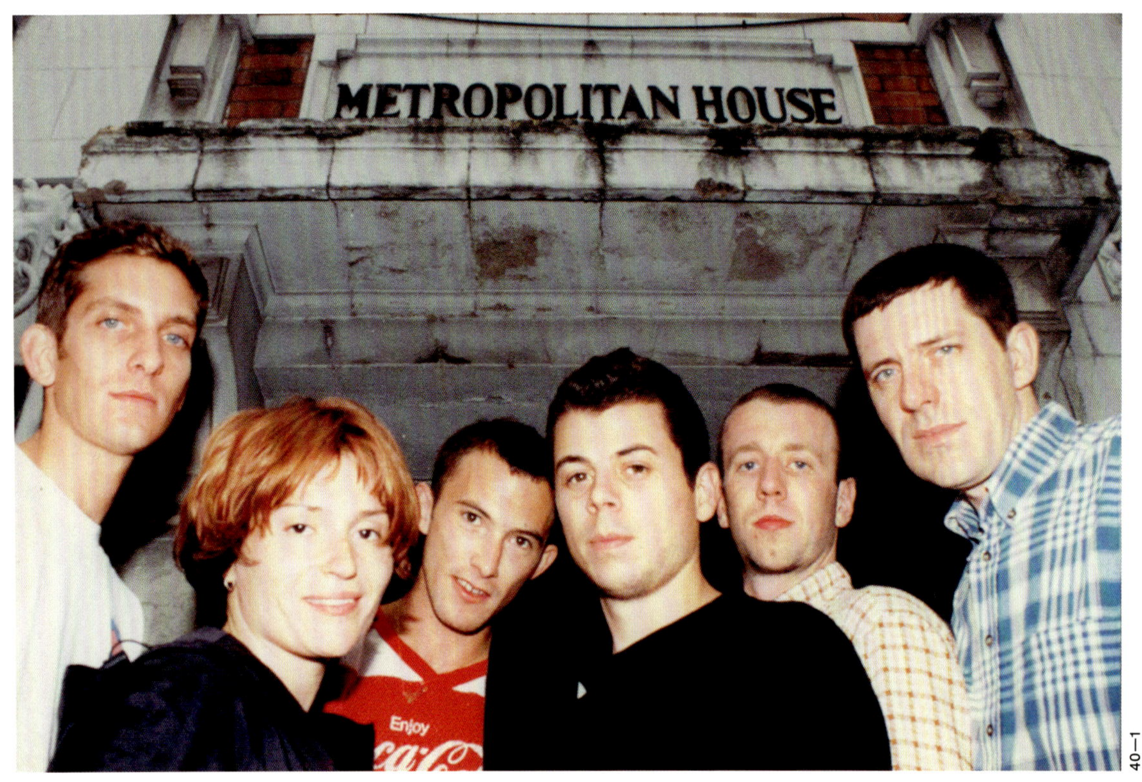

40—1

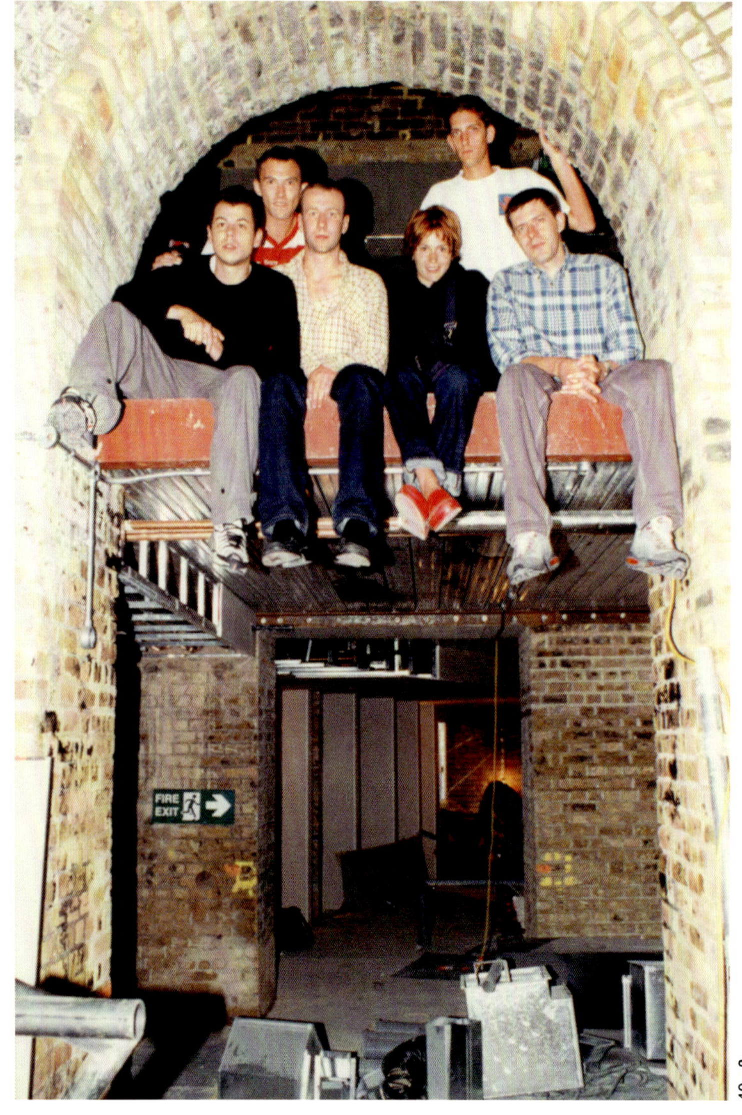

40—2

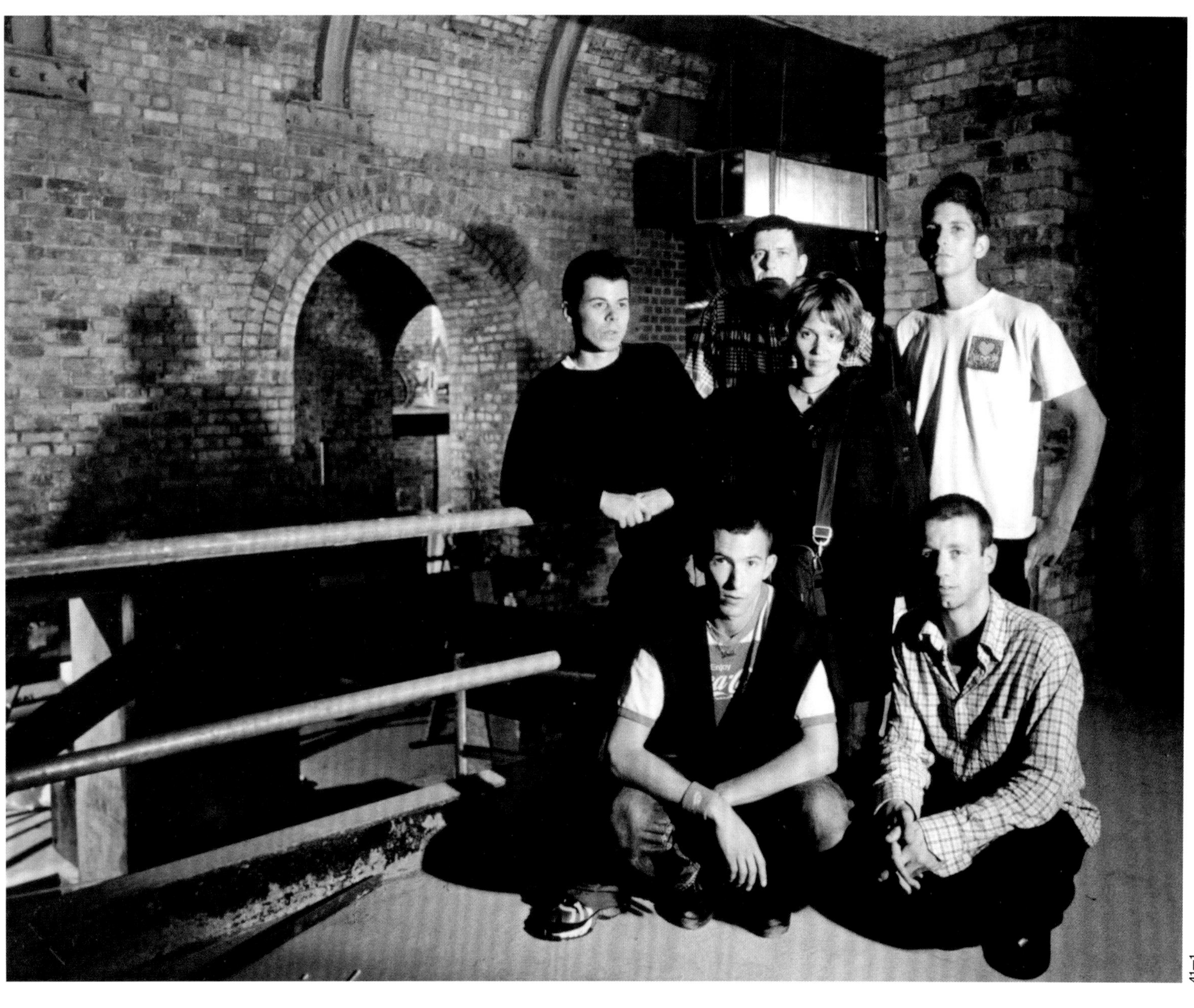

41—1

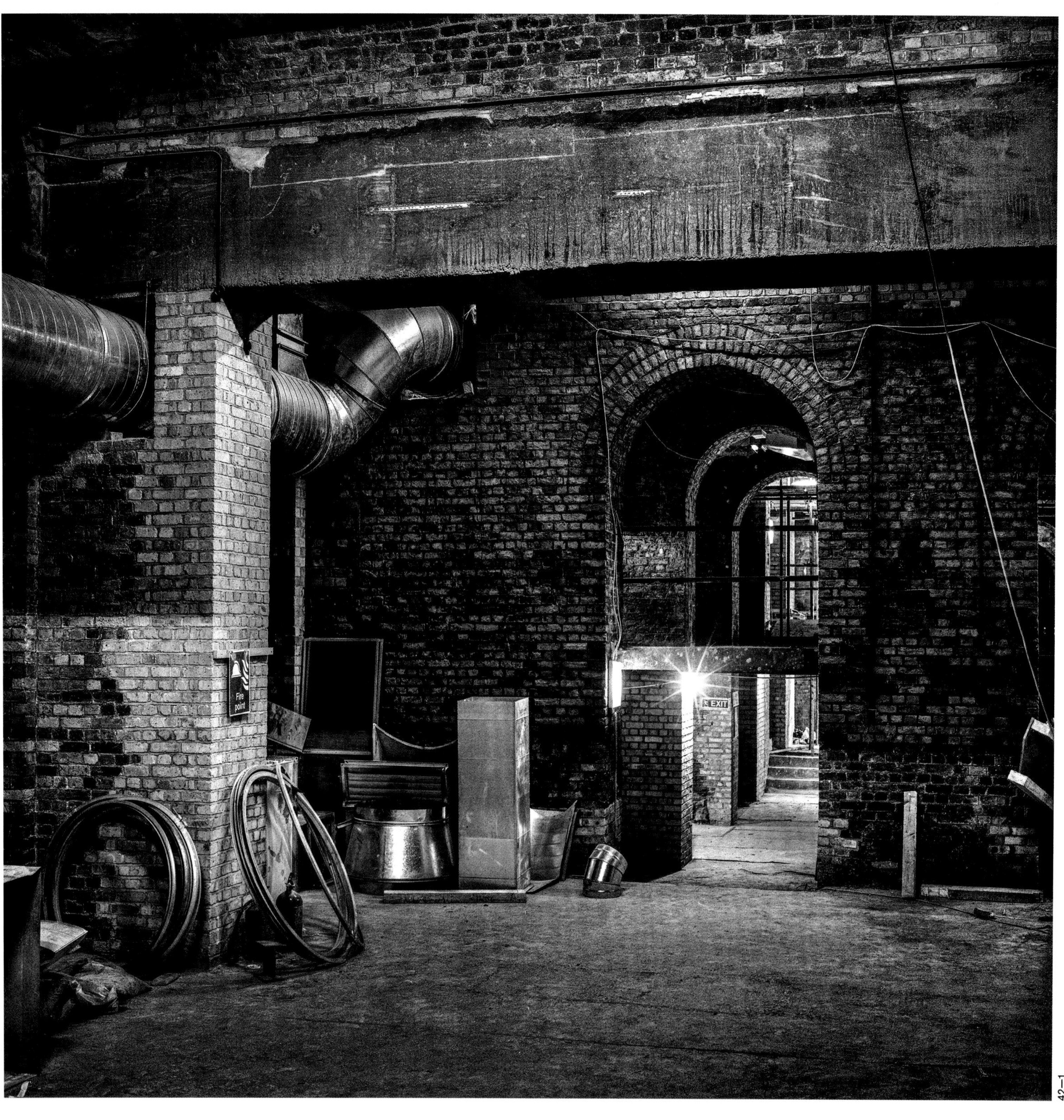

42—1

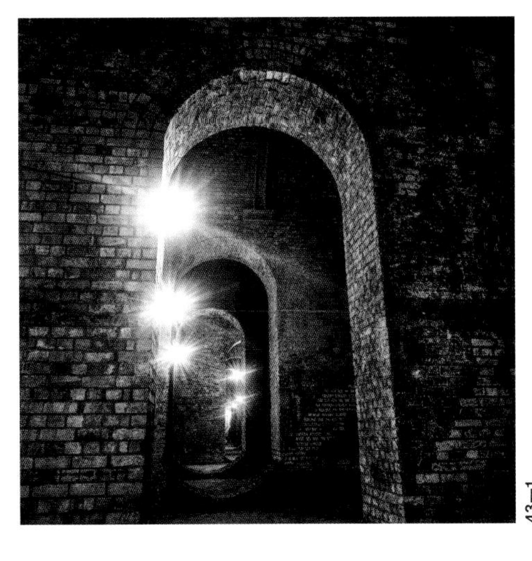
43—1

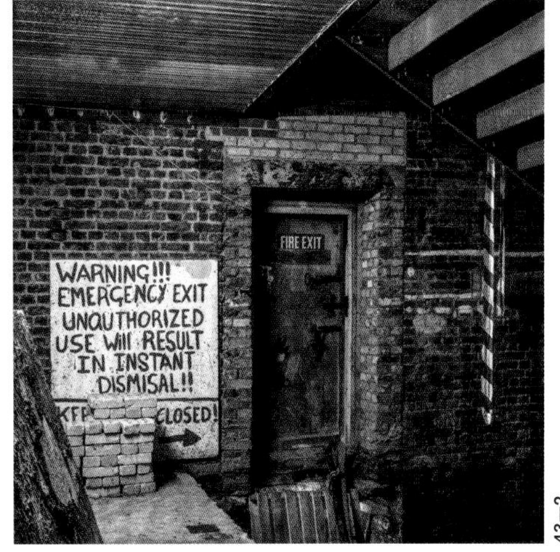

43—2

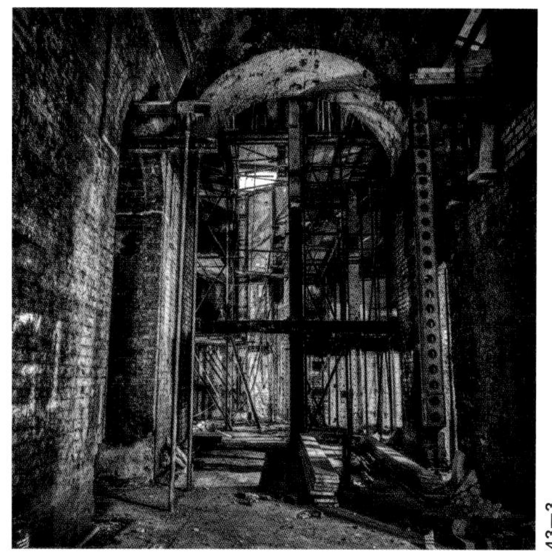
43—3

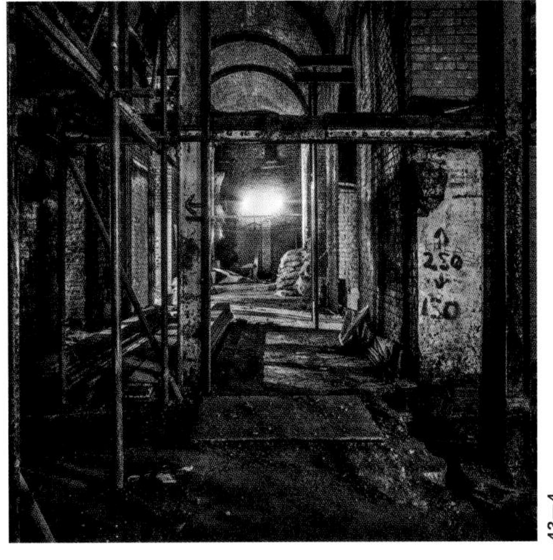
43—4

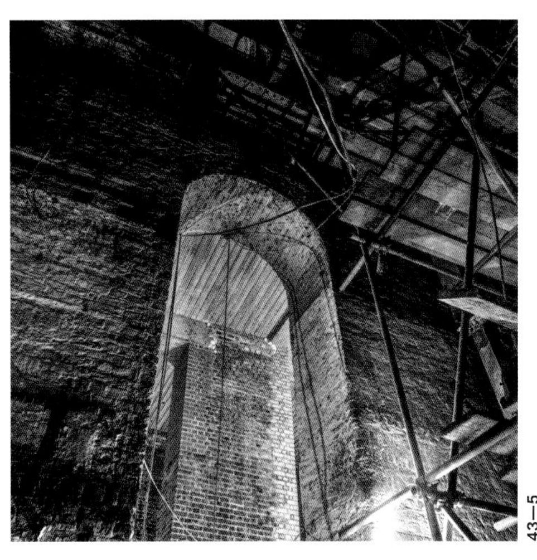
43—5

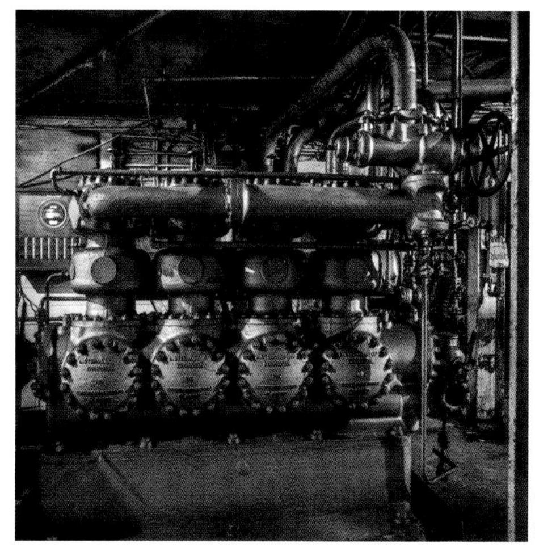
43—6

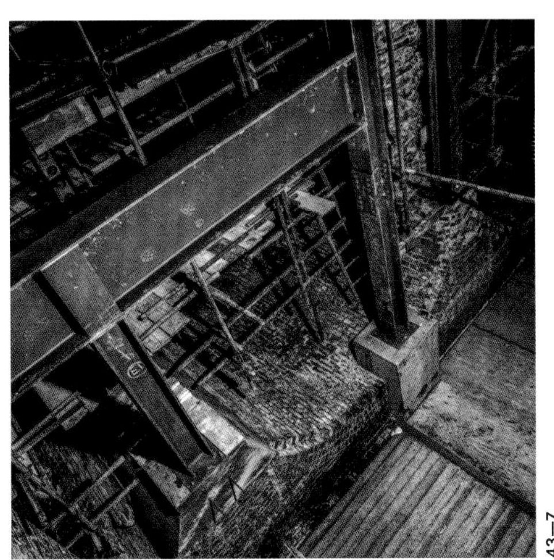
43—7

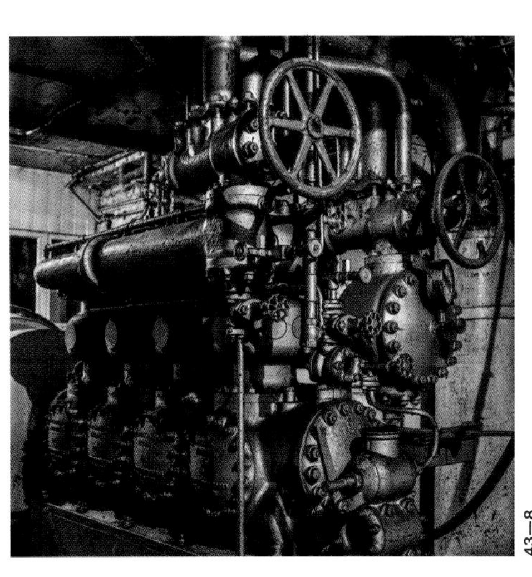
43—8

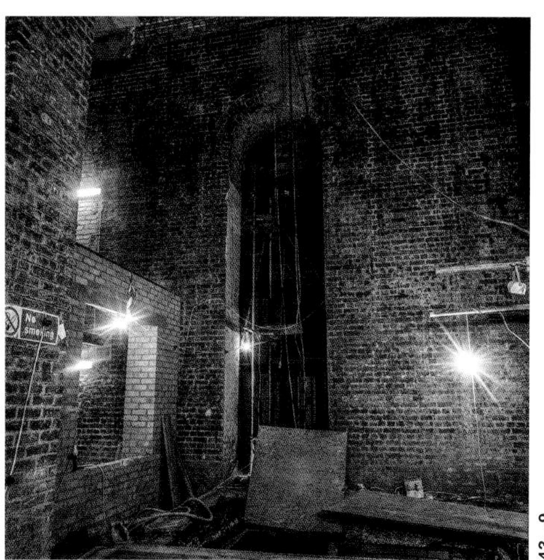
43—9

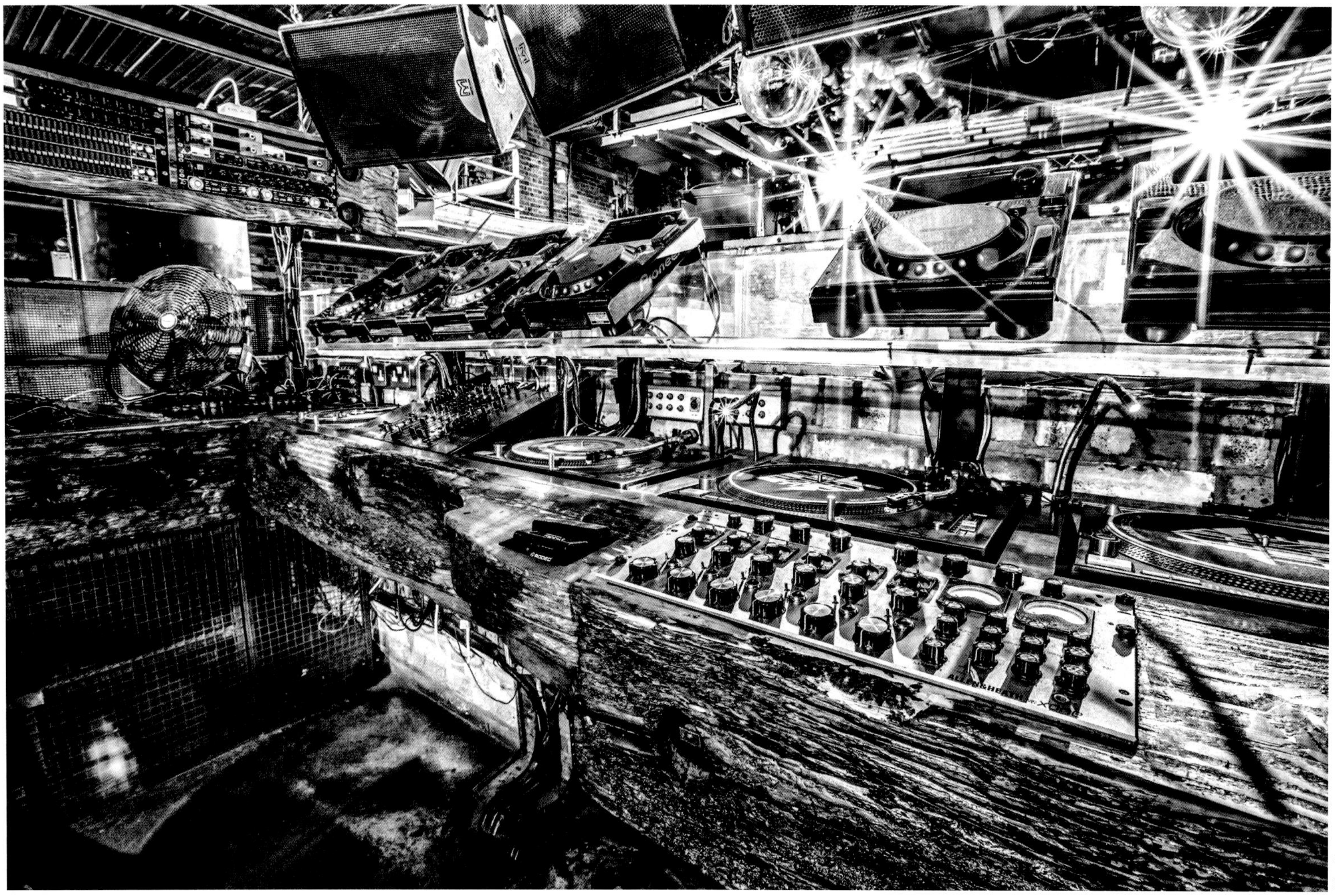

44—1

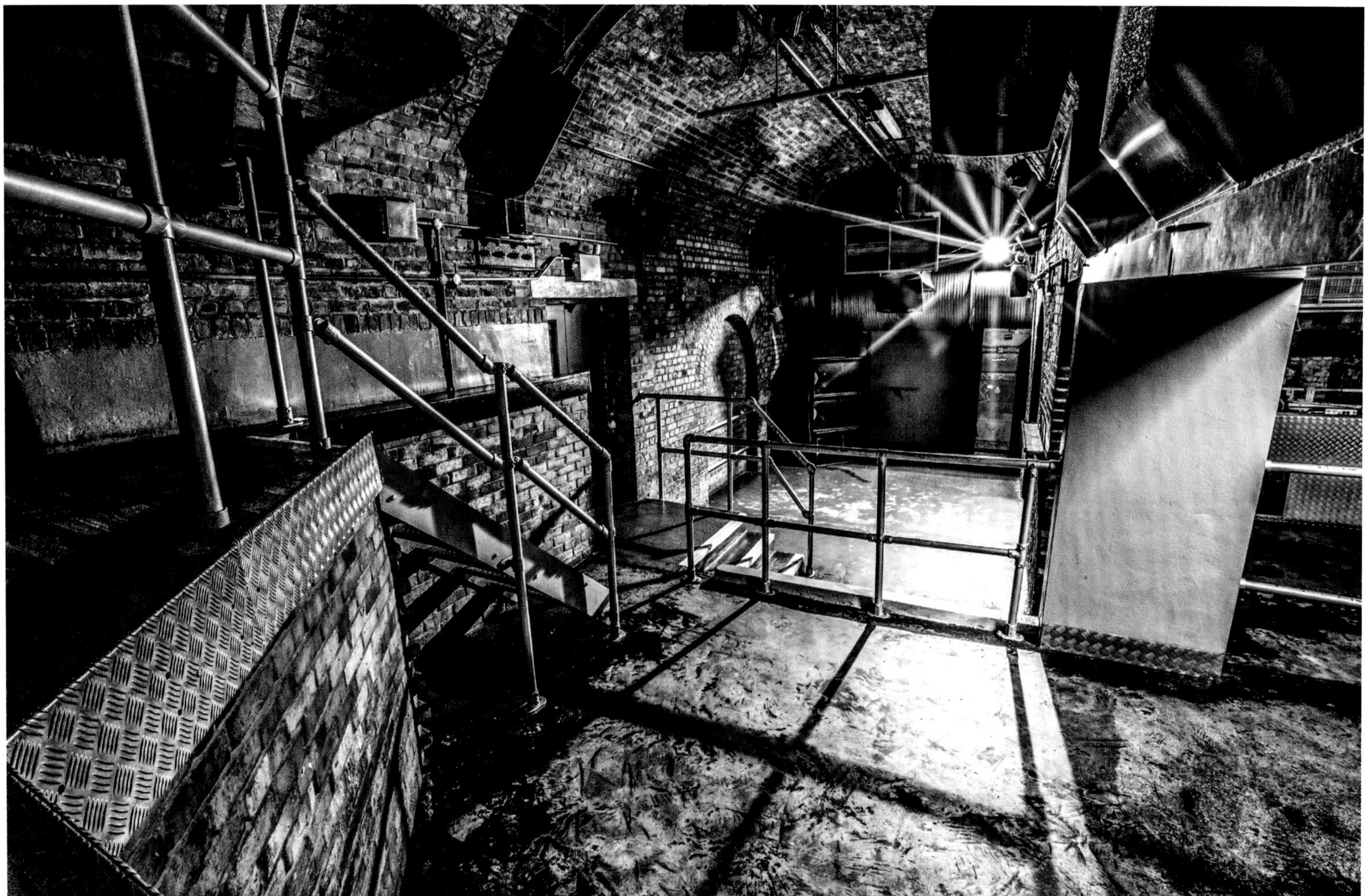

44—2

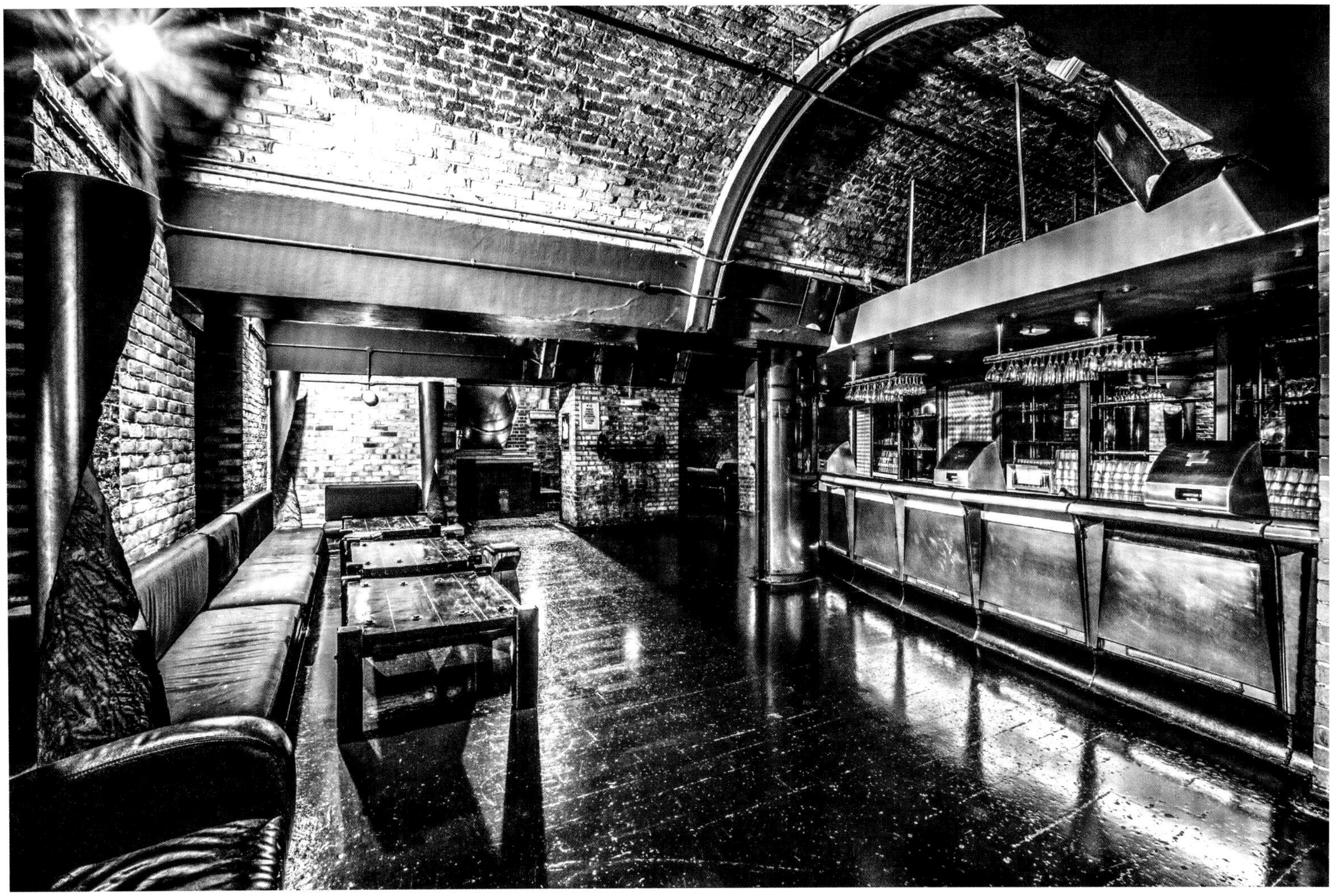

45—1

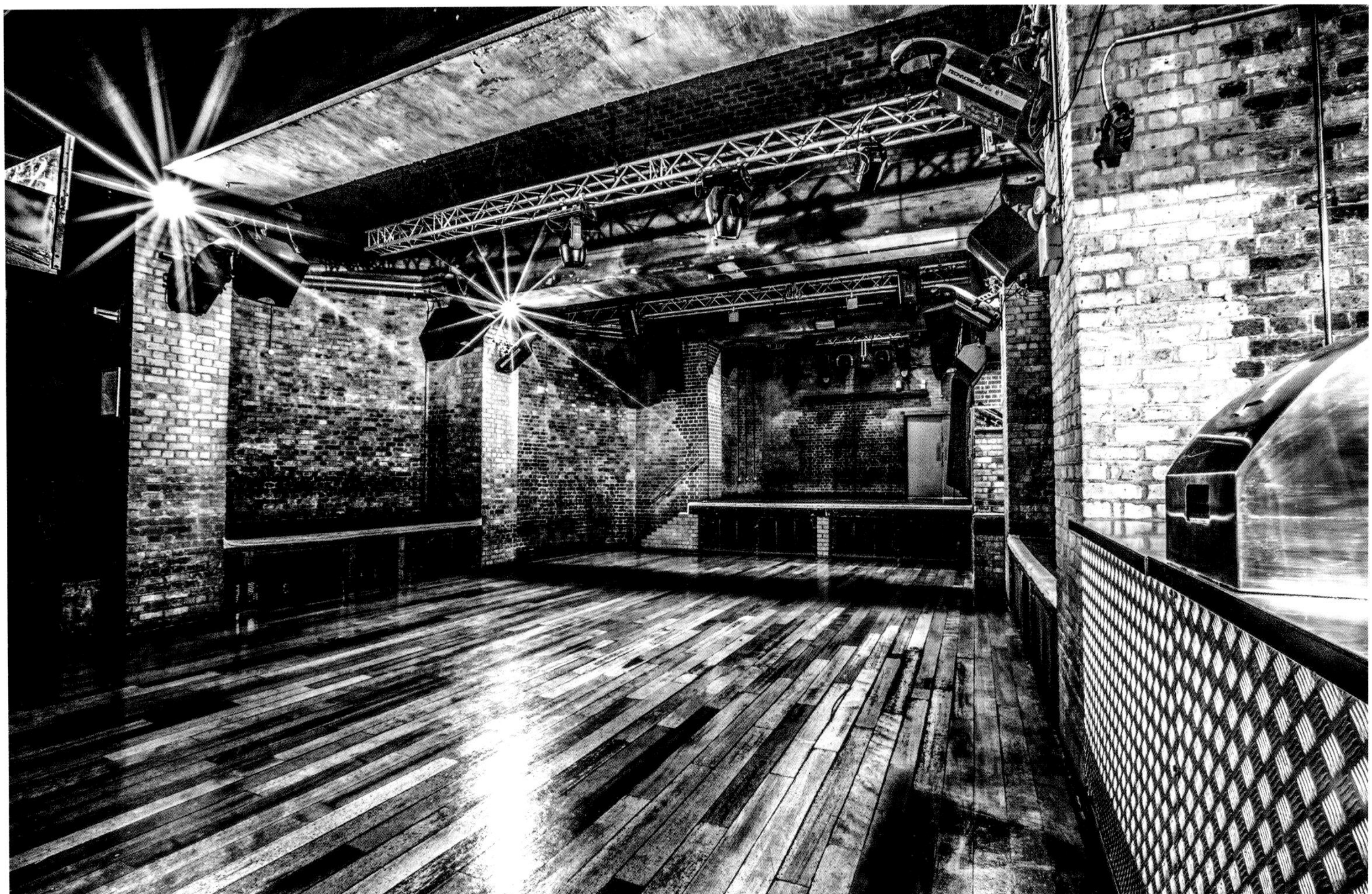

45—2

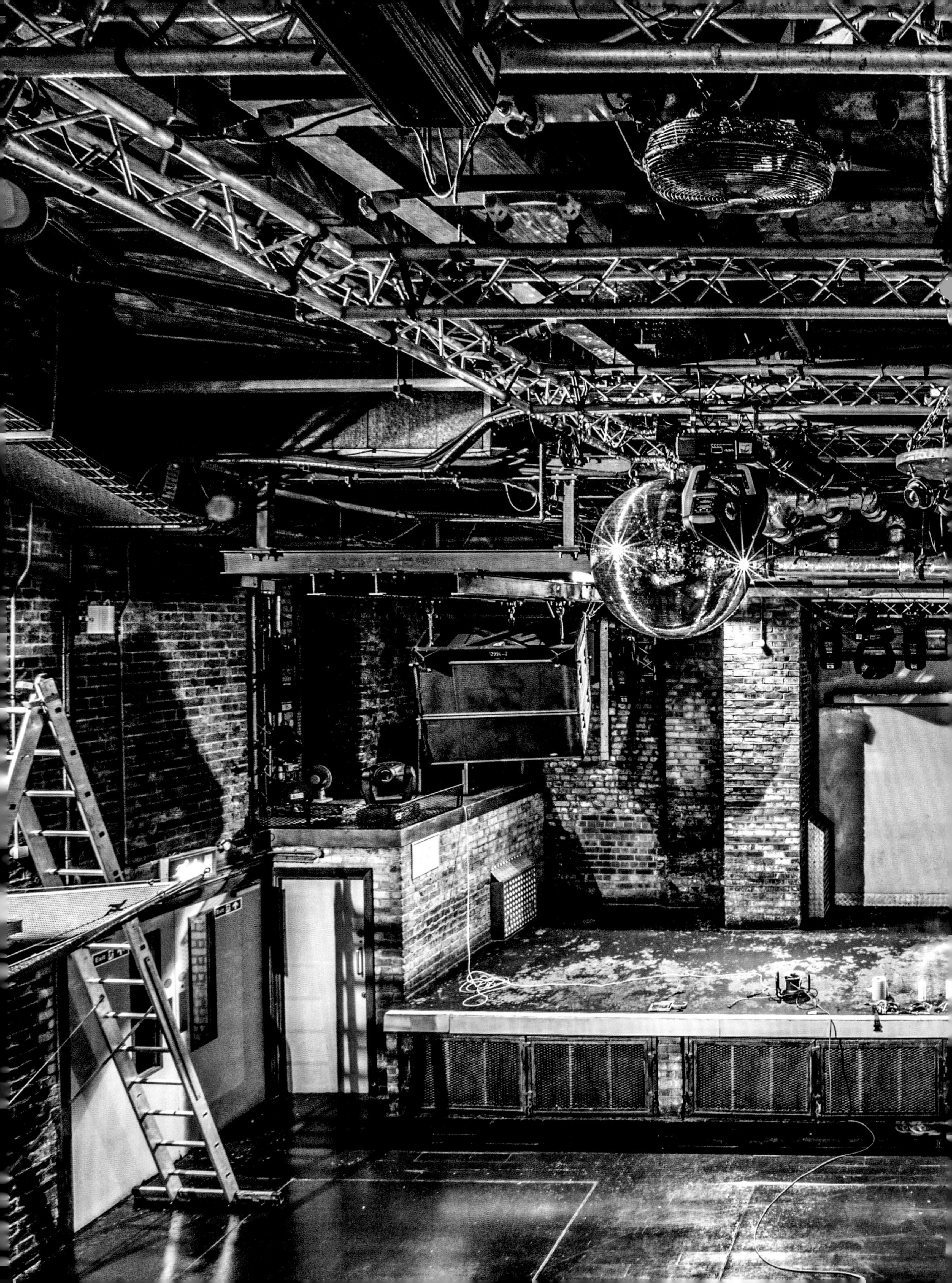

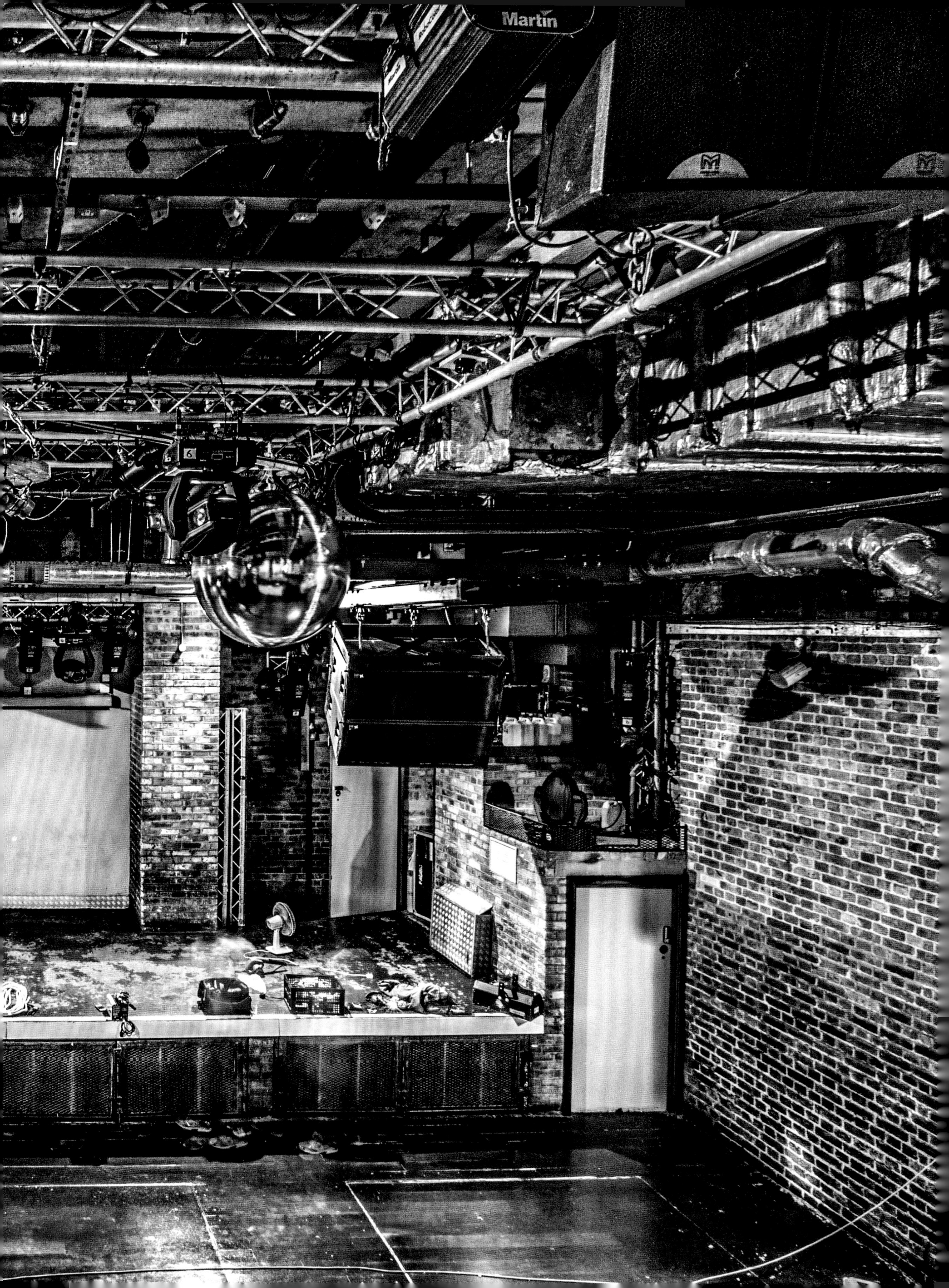
Martin

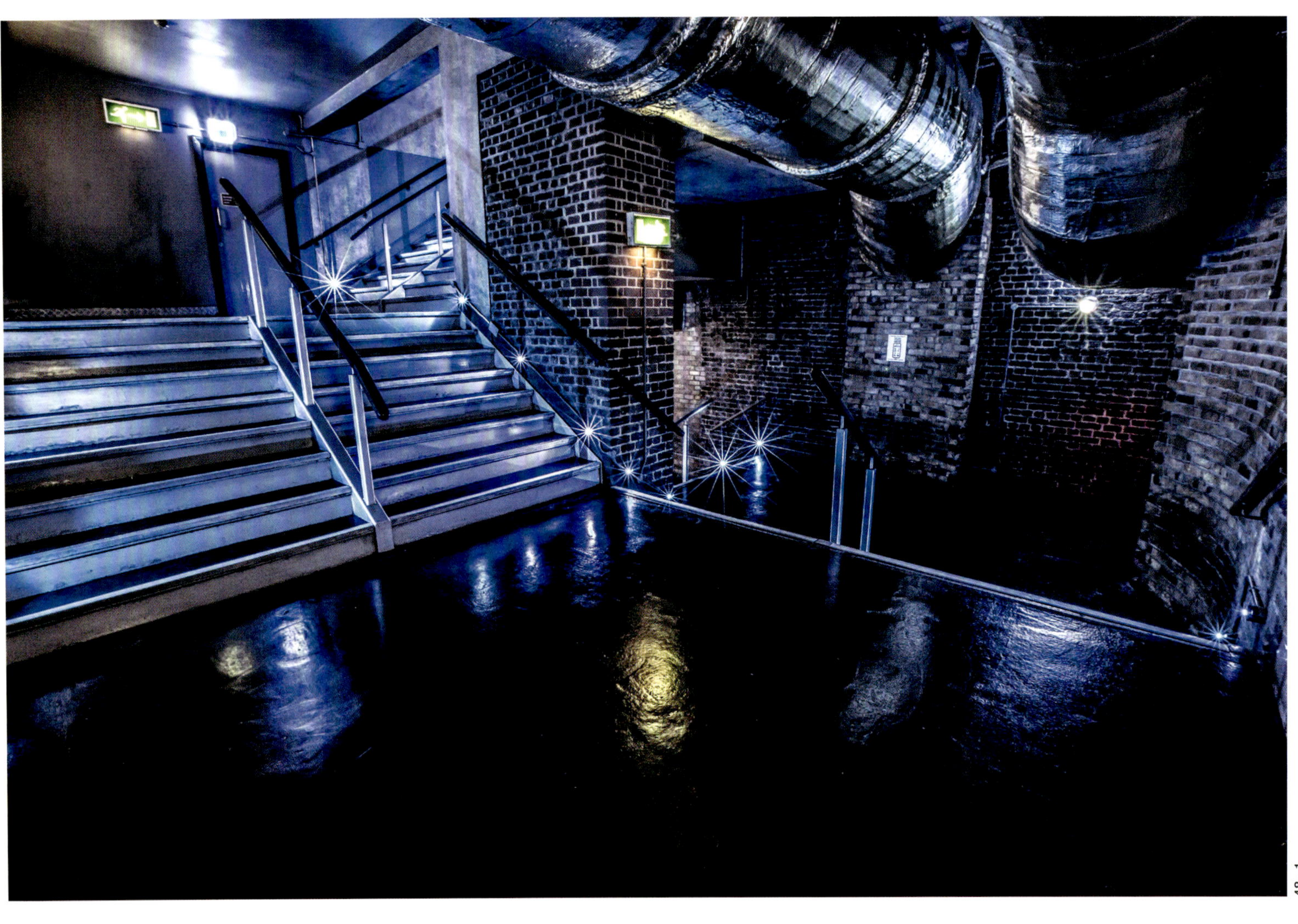

48—1

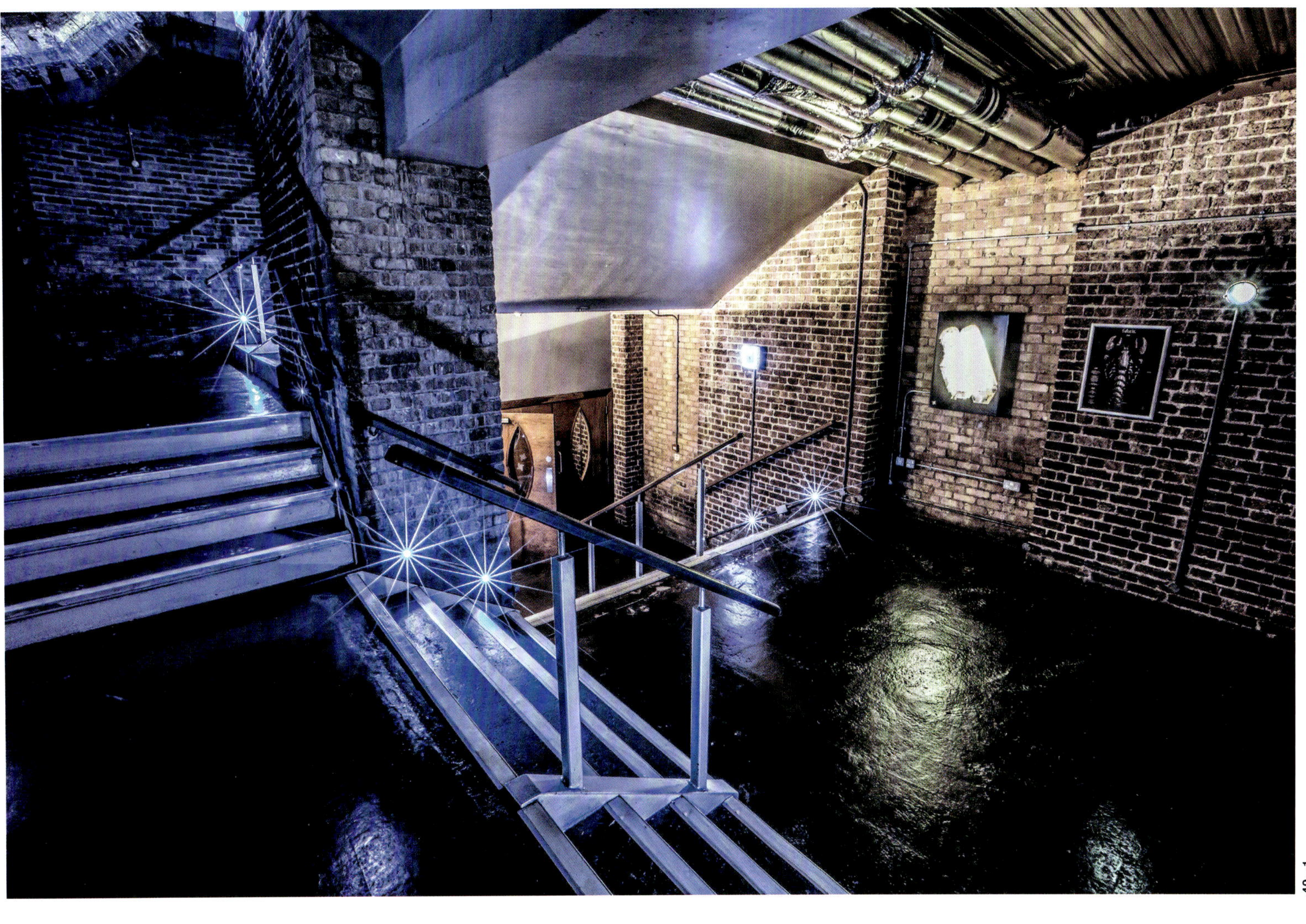

49—1

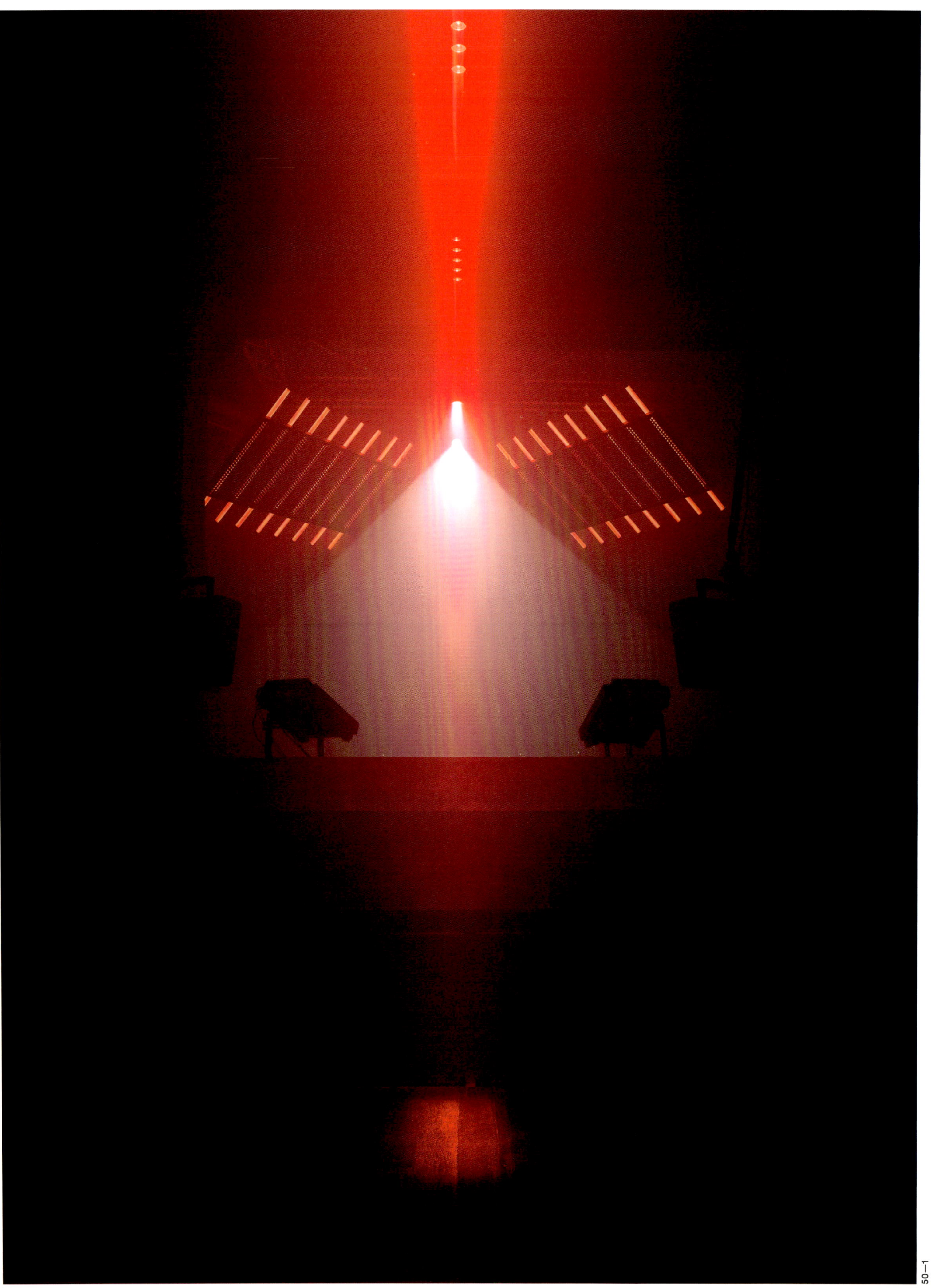

50—1

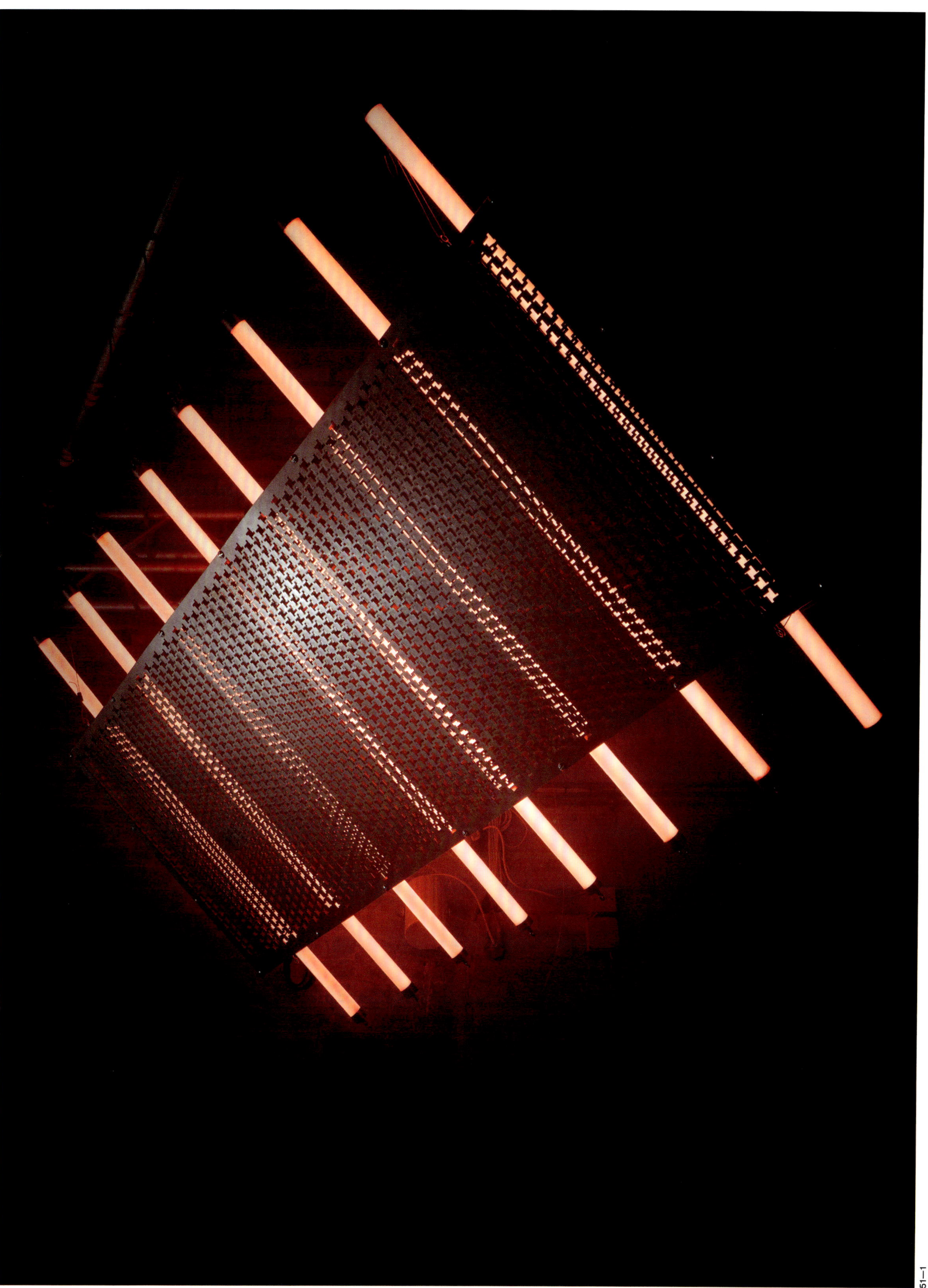

51—1

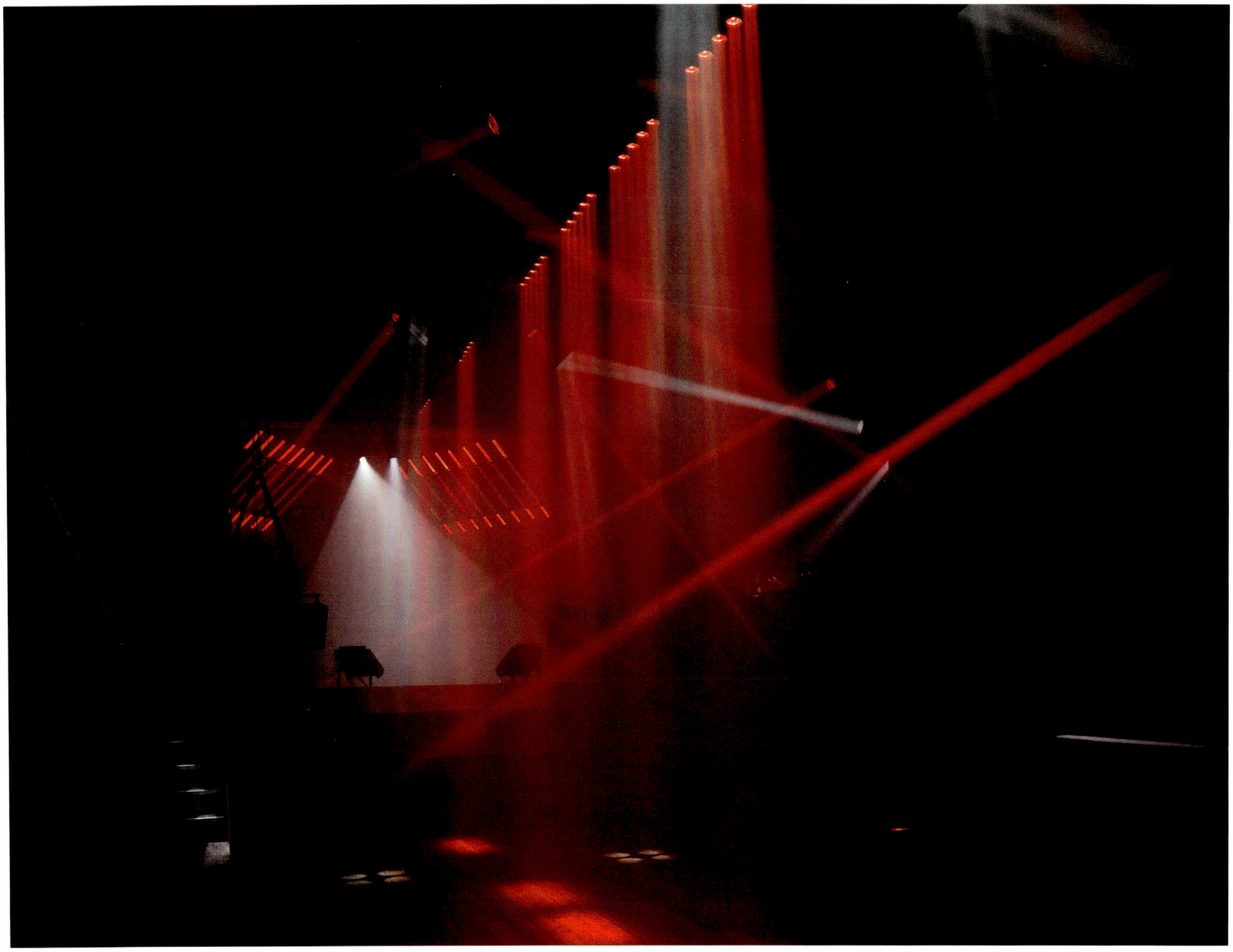

52—1

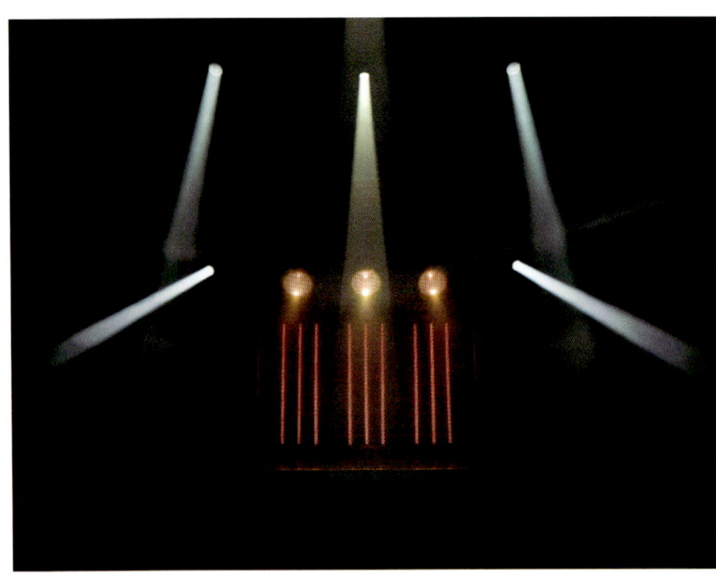

52—2

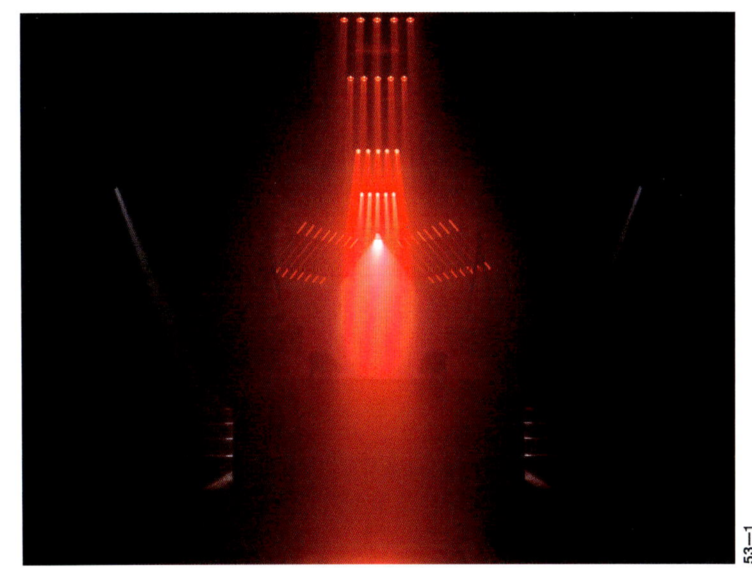
53—1

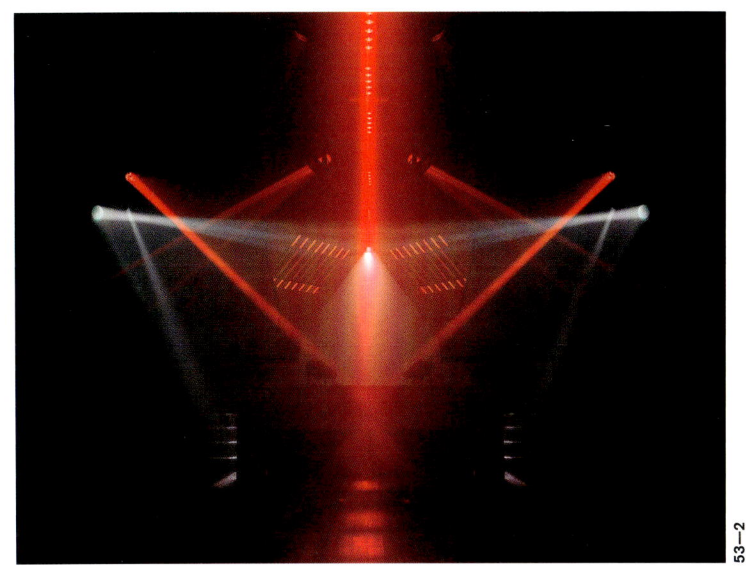
53—2

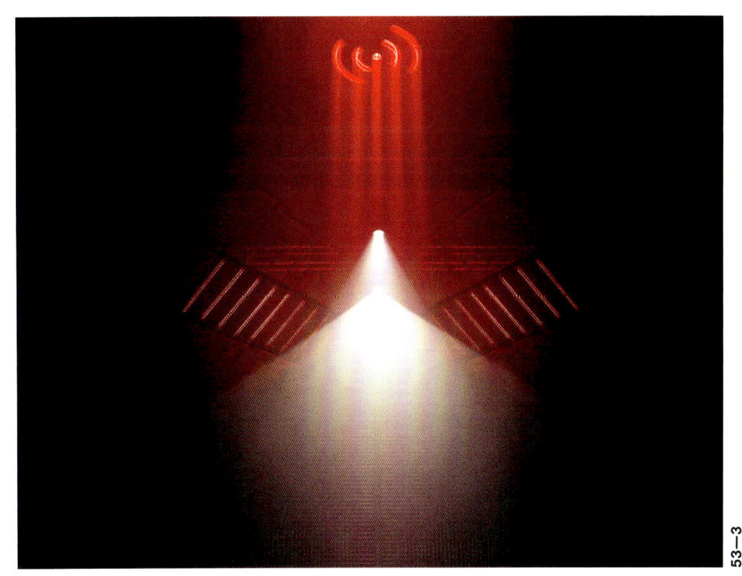
53—3

the matter of matter

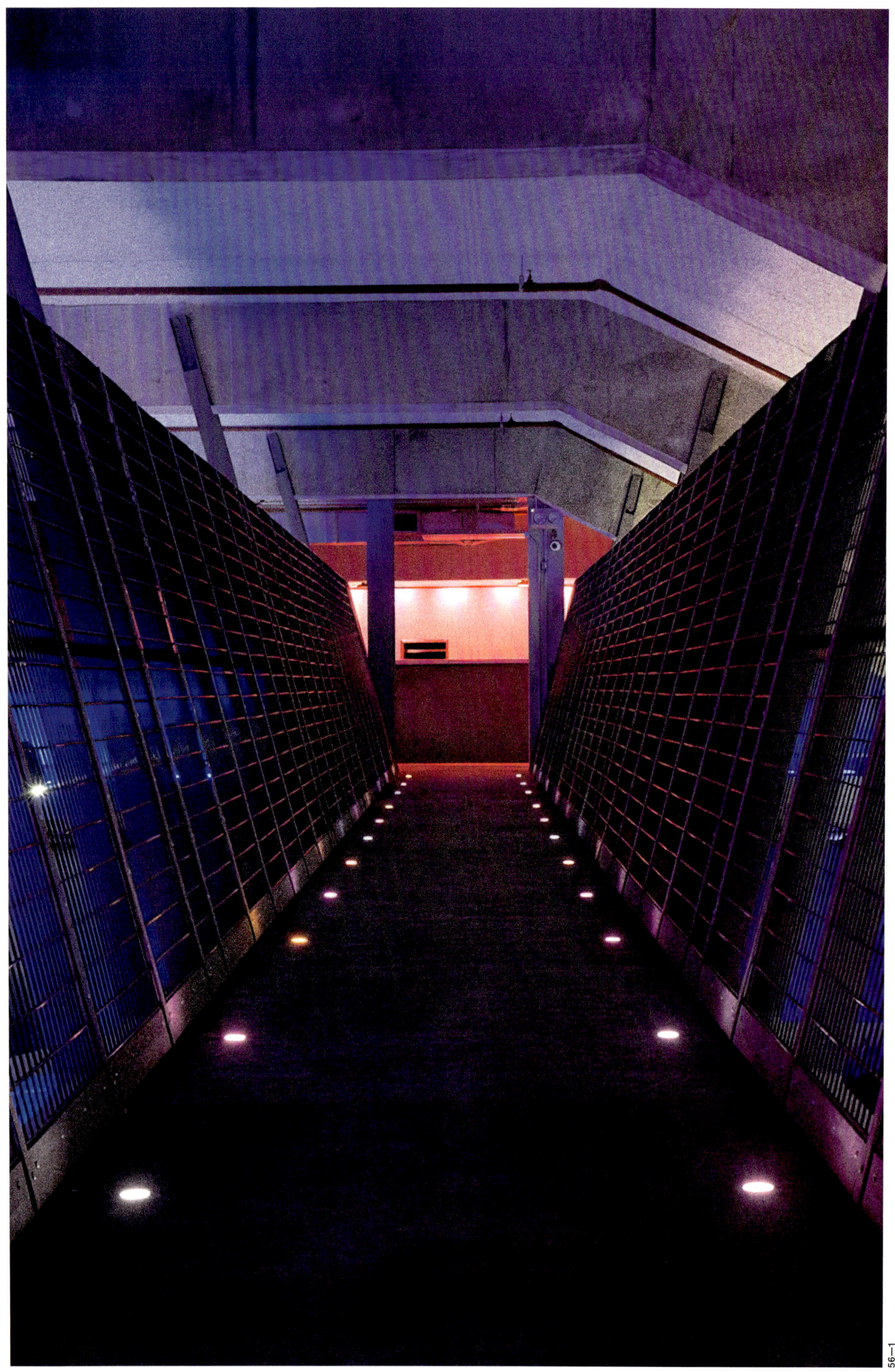

56—1

Against all the odds, fabric was doing well in the mid-2000s. Really well. It had weathered the dramatic shifts in clubland, very quickly built a faithful regular crowd, and was able to be diverse and exploratory without losing touch with the fundamentals it had been founded on – and from 2004 the internal business wranglings that had plagued it from the beginning finally died down to negligible levels. It was as close to plain sailing as clubland gets – so, of course, Keith and Cameron went haring off after a whole new, preposterously ambitious and quite possibly deranged project.

The building known as the Millennium Dome was originally meant to be temporary. A symbol of the Blair-era boom economy, it was built on post-industrial wasteland where the Thames flows out through the east of London. It's huge – the ninth most capacious building in the world, in fact – and was made as a millennium exhibition and celebration venue, with little thought to what would come next. Through the early 2000s there were various plans to turn it into a business park or giant shopping centre, or move it to Swindon to become a research centre, but generally it hung around like a gigantic white elephant, until finally, in 2005, an agreement was cut with O2 telecoms and the entertainment giant AEG to build an events venue inside its shell.

This became, of course, the O2 Arena, and the fabric team were offered the chance to have a space of their own within it. And they went for it. Like, really went for it. The O2 opened in 2007, and matter in 2008; even given all that has transpired since, Keith and Cameron visibly glow with affection for that time. 'Actually, the process of it was really enjoyable,' Keith says. 'Working with the architects and designers Pentagram on it – I loved the name "matter", I loved the logo, I really loved the place, it was a great, great process.'

'We stuck our necks out,' says Cameron, 'but it seemed like a good bet. You looked at AEG and they'd rejuvenated the whole of East Los Angeles with the Staples Center arena, they had countless others across the US – they knew what they were doing!'

Even though fabric's foundation had been against the megaclub ethos, doing something on this scale was too great an opportunity to pass up. 'We weren't going to do another club,' says Cameron, 'but this was of interest to us because it wasn't going to be a nightclub. It was going to be something else.'

'It was going,' jumps in Keith, 'to be a laboratory!' It appealed to each of their ambitions: Cameron with his hospitality-business head on saw the potential of 'secondary and tertiary businesses to the main arena benefiting' – something they could build on and build relationships through; and Keith's mercurial imagination was given a huge canvas to paint on. As soon as he's onto the topic, he waxes lyrical about his fandom of architects like Tadao Ando, and how Pentagram's William Russell is the British master of this style of minimalism – which in turn inspired his own ideas.

'In almost everything in the world we operate in,' Keith says, 'creativity amounts to: book a venue, put the act on stage, throw some lights on it. I always had this idea about getting different artists from different fields collaborating, using lots of different artistic resources, and I had this dream of getting sculptors and photographers and painters involved. If people do big-scale multimedia shows it's usually fucking awful, just big geometric shapes, bloody terrible colours. So I've always had this idea I wanted to get more existing talent involved, make everything have more art in it, very collaborative, properly open up the possibilities. In the warehouse party days, in our naive way, we'd have showreels of weird films, there'd be banners and graffiti. In fabric, obviously we had art on all our promotional material. But I wanted more, I wanted art everywhere.'

It was a serious undertaking, as ever – Cameron tempted his even more business-minded brother Nathan, who'd left the UK in 2004 for a 'proper job' in New York, back with the promise of being general manager. The dream was to make a venue that could stage club nights, pre- and after-show parties for the big events at the O2, but also be 'a creative arts laboratory'. They were imagining all kinds of possibilities with immersive projection, LED lighting and anything else that technology had to offer. Keith and his old friend Howie B even started thinking about possibilities for reinventing the musical on a truly grandiose scale, with credible music and cutting-edge presentation, and started bringing in quite an array of talent – PJ Harvey, Brian Eno, Pascal Comelade, Nick Cave – to start conceptualising shows.

It didn't quite get that far, but it did become something magical for a brief while. 'This wasn't an old meat warehouse,' says Cameron, 'where we had to work round the quirks of the building. This was a blank sheet of paper to work on. There was freedom to make it how we wanted.'

William Russell's design and layout created a space where even the shapes of the walkways, balconies and corridors felt like part of the creative experience, and the main arena with a ramped-up take on fabric's bodysonic dancefloor was a human-centred space wherever you were standing in it. 'I've never before or since seen a system that powerful but crisp and clear,' says Nathan. 'We'd demo it to people with a Skream track and watch their eyeballs start rattling!' And audiences responded in kind. 'I'm an old raver,' he continues. 'I went to the big, big raves of the early nineties – and this was as close to getting a proper rave inside a club as I've ever seen.'

'If you went to Hospitality or Ram,' says Cameron, again glowing with pride, 'it was a big room show, totally different to fabric where things revolve round the three rooms. It was about the one big arena – BOOM. The energy of that big crowd was off the charts.'

Just like fabric, though, the fact that it had the vision of Keith – a music lover and clubber above all else – underpinning it meant that it was never only about the big spectacle. Perhaps the perfect expression of its possibility in its brief existence was the couple of raves that Rinse FM put on there. At the time – 2009–10 – Rinse was in a limbo space, its pirate broadcasts on hold as it waited to see if it would get legal community radio status. But the music it played was reaching a peak: dubstep was on the exponential rise, UK funky was everywhere, grime was still vital and weirder sounds were coming in to the Rinse world via Scottish crews like Numbers and LuckyMe. Those raves became a high-water mark for British bass music, and are immortalised in the video for Katy B's 'Katy on a Mission' – turning the song's love letter to raving into a love letter to the venue itself.

It started with a bang. 'On the opening night,' says Nathan, 'I was watching the door numbers like a hawk, and we hit targets so early in the evening I knew we had a monster on our hands. I started to wonder just how big it could get.' It was glorious. But it couldn't last. It was swimming against the tide from the start; that very opening night was the day of the Lehman Brothers collapse, bringing the global financial crisis to boiling point and ushering in an era of belt-tightening. 'Our audience,' says Cameron, 'had never had to worry about anything like that, kids had money on Friday nights, they weren't worried about mortgages. But now suddenly we're into mass youth unemployment kicking in, people getting laid off everywhere, so it was a perfect storm of forces against it – and the crisis meant we couldn't raise any more finance, or even restructure the huge debt we already had, to weather that storm either.'

The fabric team's relationship with AEG was rocky from the start, too, with promised infrastructure and contracts for O2 Arena aftershow parties not materialising. Even so, all of that might have been survivable if it hadn't been for the Jubilee Line – the branch of the tube that provided the only easy public-transport access to the venue from the rest of London – consistently being out of service as a promised digital upgrade dragged on by months and months. This transport issue wasn't just the straw that broke the camel's back, says Keith, but a sledgehammer. 'You can chart it week by week,' he says. 'Tube running, four and a half thousand people in; no tube, five hundred in there.' They didn't stand a chance. 'We were haemorrhaging cash,' winces Cameron. 'You'd come in after the weekend, look at the books and just … ugh. These were big boy numbers – really scary, scary numbers.'

When, in May 2010, they finally made the decision to pull the plug, there was just time for one last escapade. They felt they'd invested so much in the light and sound kit for the venue, maybe they could rescue some of it for fabric, so Cameron and Nathan hired a truck, derigged the club and loaded it up. He thought they'd got away with it, but in fact a security guard recognised them, dobbed them in, and a booming voice belonging to one of the O2 management came over the tannoy, bellowing, 'Cameron! What do you think you're doing?' The game was up, and he had to unload and call Keith. With their tails between their legs, they had to speak to their partners and admit that was it. 'It was beyond frustrating,' says Nathan. 'We'd put heart and soul into that place, we'd done everything right, but it wasn't enough.' Matter was done for.

And so, it transpired, was fabric. They tried to battle on, but though matter was a separate company, fabric had been guarantor for a £3.2 million loan to help build it. When it became clear that matter couldn't keep going, fabric became liable and eventually went into administration. And when it did, it was public. 'It was mad,' says Cameron. 'All the stuff with our initial investor we'd managed to keep under wraps, nobody really knew what trouble was going on behind the scenes, but this time our dirty laundry was being aired in public, and the rumours were flying around everywhere.' The air of gossip and suspicion was majorly lightened by a rallying of support from clubbers and the fabric family, though – a first inkling of the wave of solidarity that would rise the next time fabric faced serious threats to its existence.

Once again, Keith and Cameron found themselves having to buy back their own club. This time they enlisted the help of Gary Kilbey. An old schoolfriend of Keith's who he'd known since he was twelve, Gary had been a partner in his CD and cassette business, and an early backer of his attempts to open the club before drifting away. 'He's not a music person,' says Keith, 'and he thought we'd never make anything of it, not surprisingly given all the madness – he's a lot more prudent and sensible than me.' This time round, though, he could see that his old friend had built something of lasting value, and he came on as director of the new company Fabric Life Limited. And despite several bids being in the ring for the premises, the receiver saw value in the original owners running it too, and they won out in the final round.

Once again, fabric was back on track. Nathan was still on board, now as assistant managing director, overseeing a shake-up – effectively a relaunch, in fact – that blew away the cobwebs and made sure it was running smoothly. Gary's presence gave it the stability that it needed, not just financially but by cementing the family feeling of the business even more. As Keith puts it: 'To have someone I've known almost all my life, and who's always had my back, next to me, that's beyond valuable. That's something not many people can say they have in business, and it's helped make us what we are.'

Nonetheless, of all the parts of the fabric saga, talking about matter is the one where you can really hear regret in Keith, Cameron and Nathan's voices – purely because of what could have been. It clearly breaks its founders' hearts that its real glory lasted less than two years, but matter showed what could be done with a huge space without compromising dance culture – its legacy has certainly lived on in subsequent London megavenues like Printworks – and for that brief period, it created magic on a huge scale.

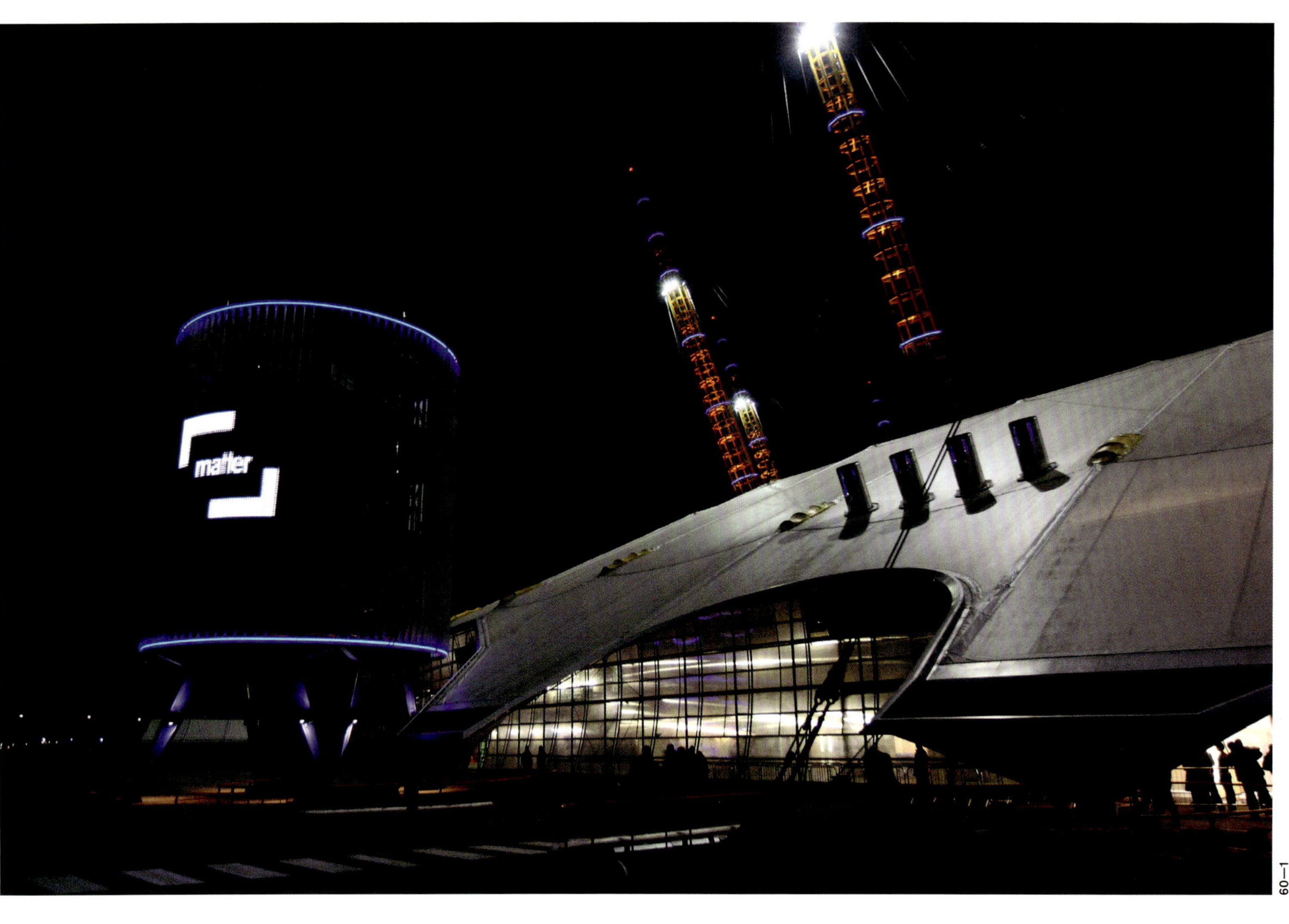

60—1

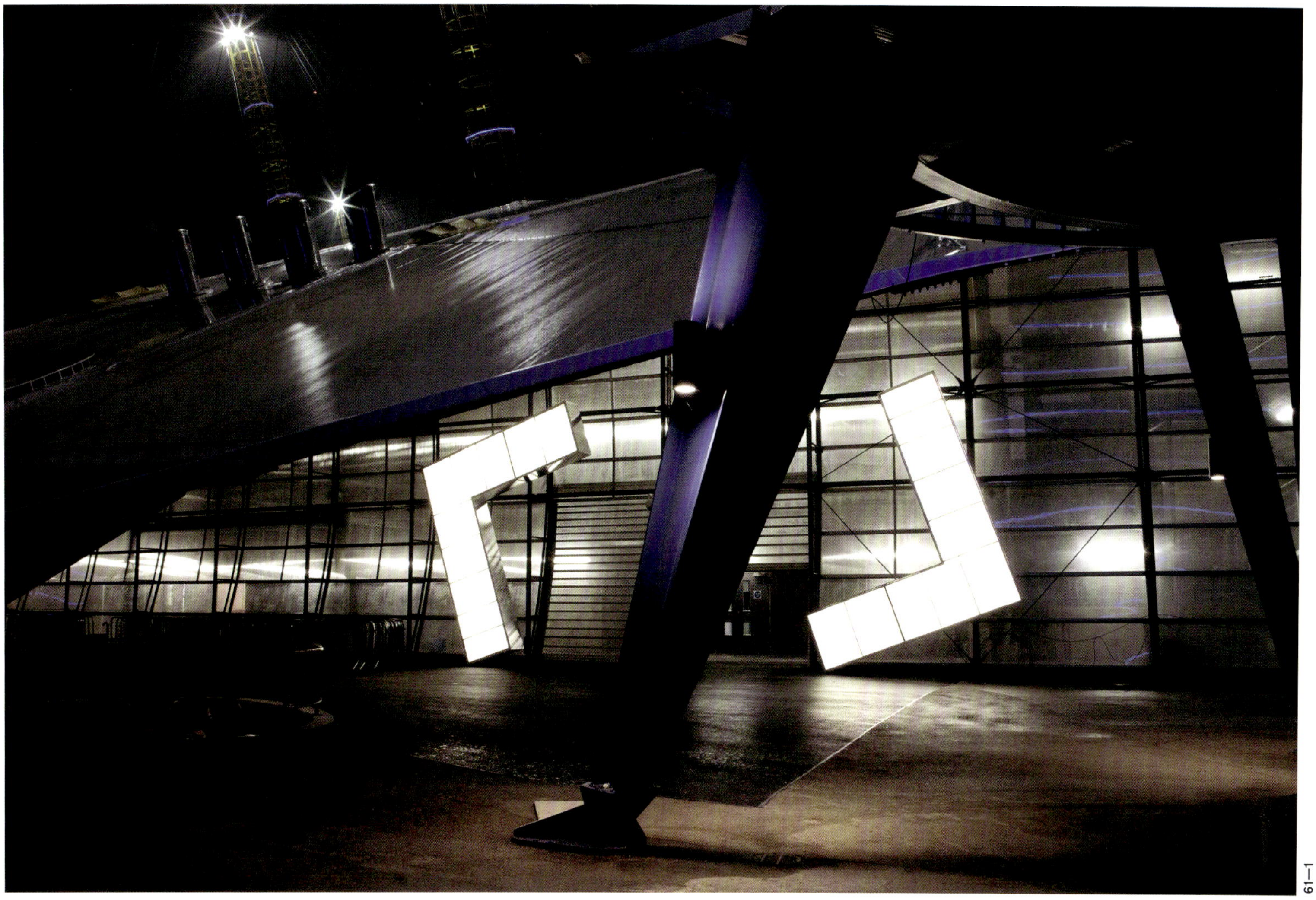

61—1

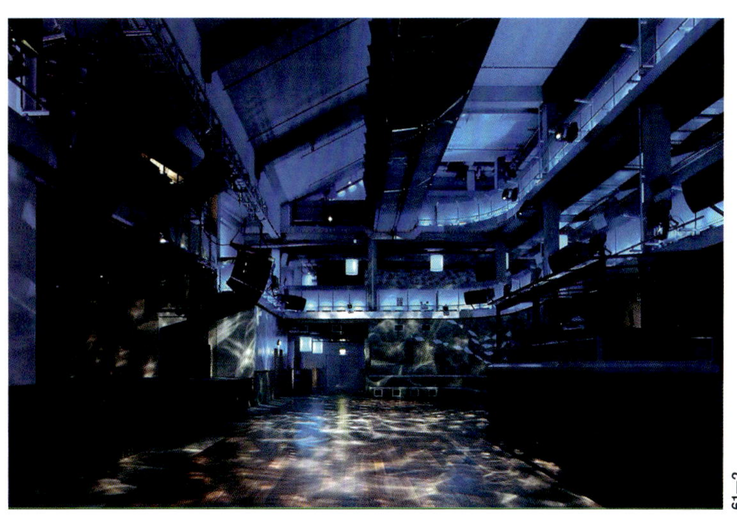

61—2

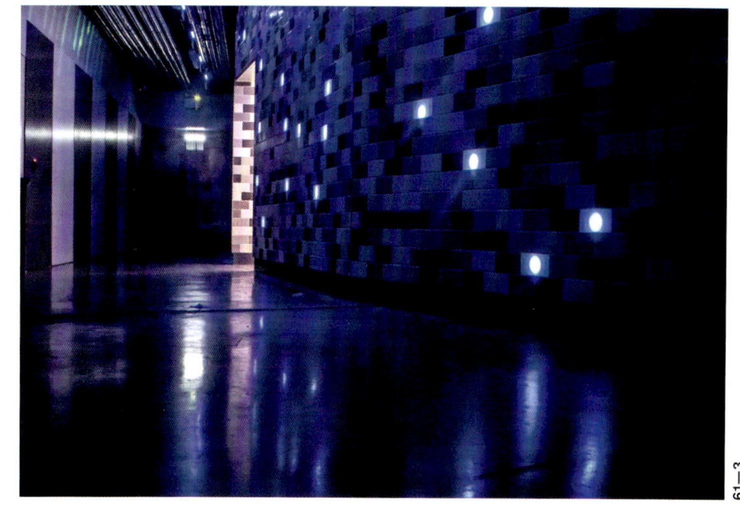

61—3

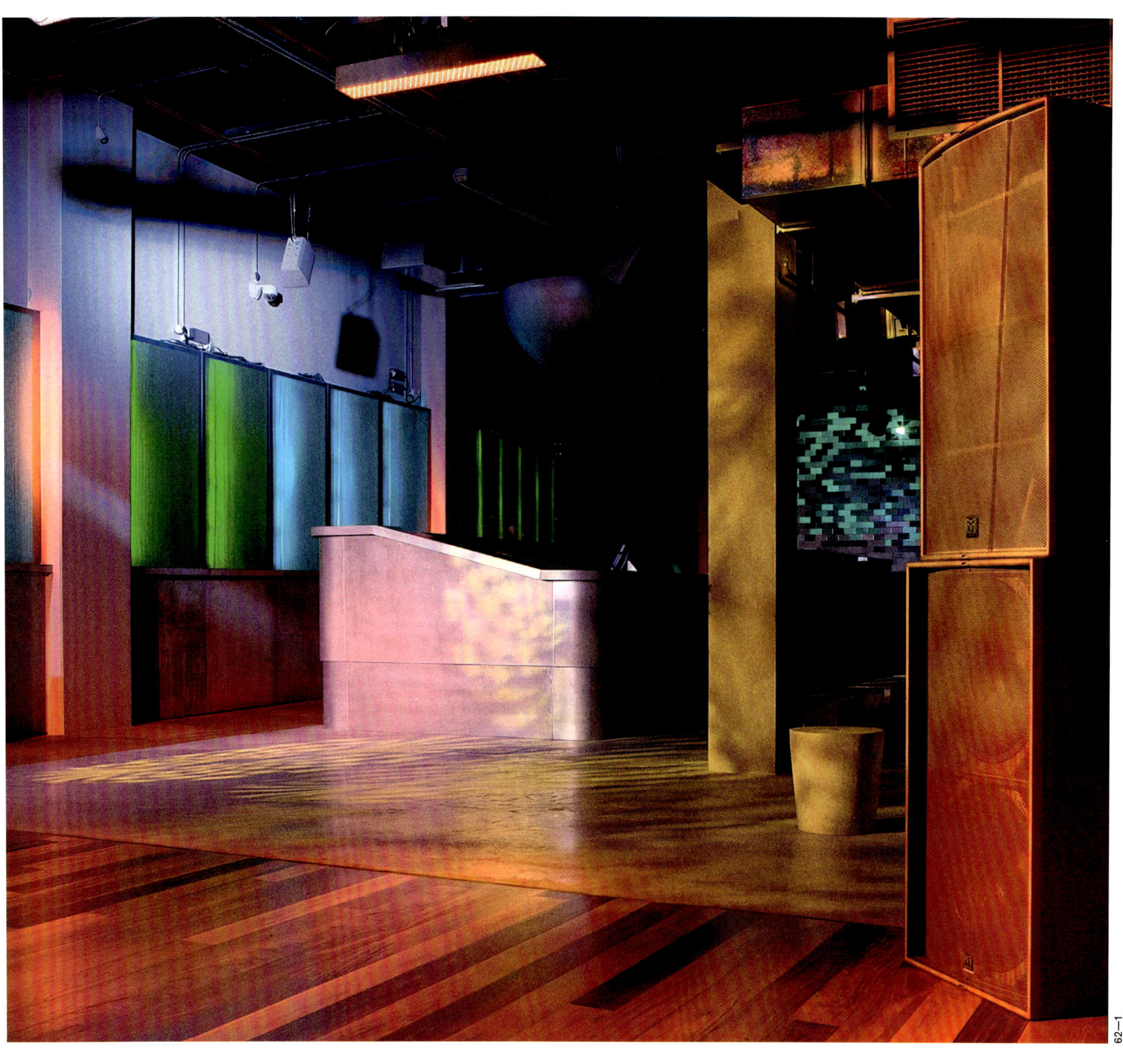

62—1

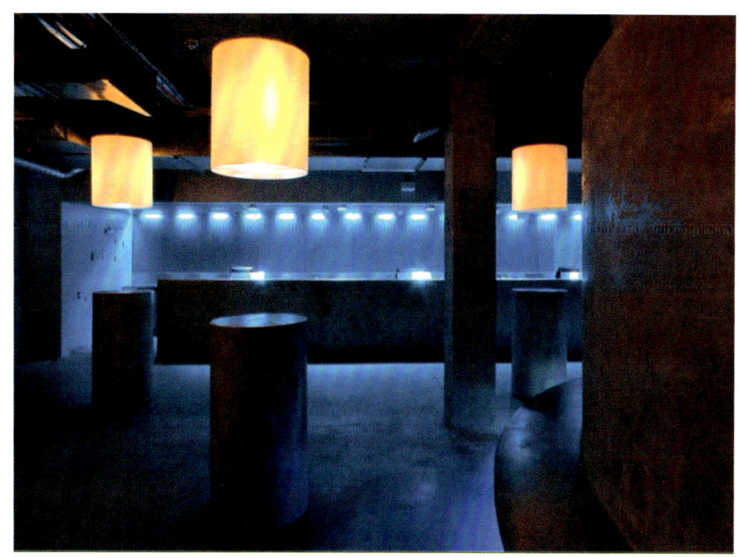
63—1

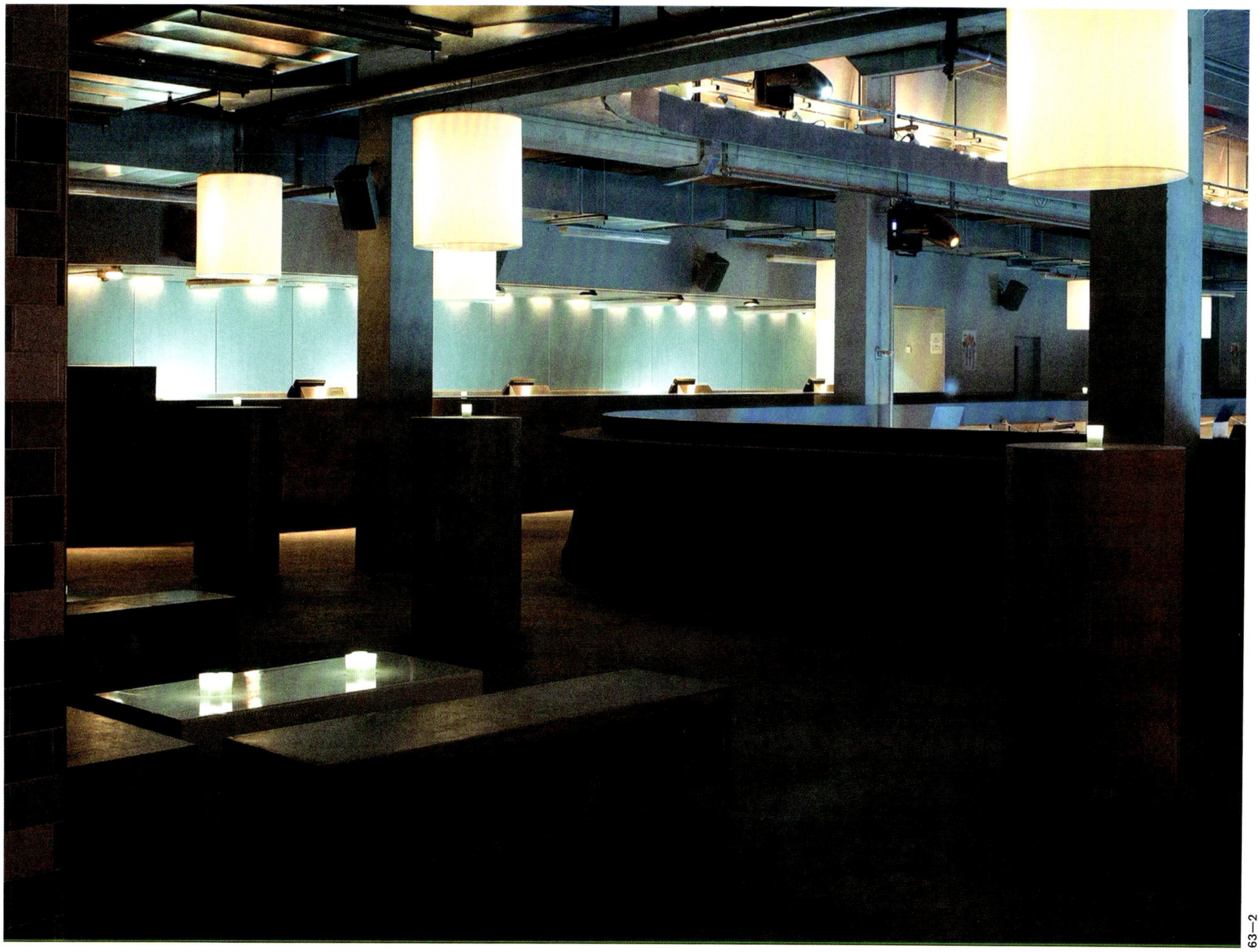

63—2

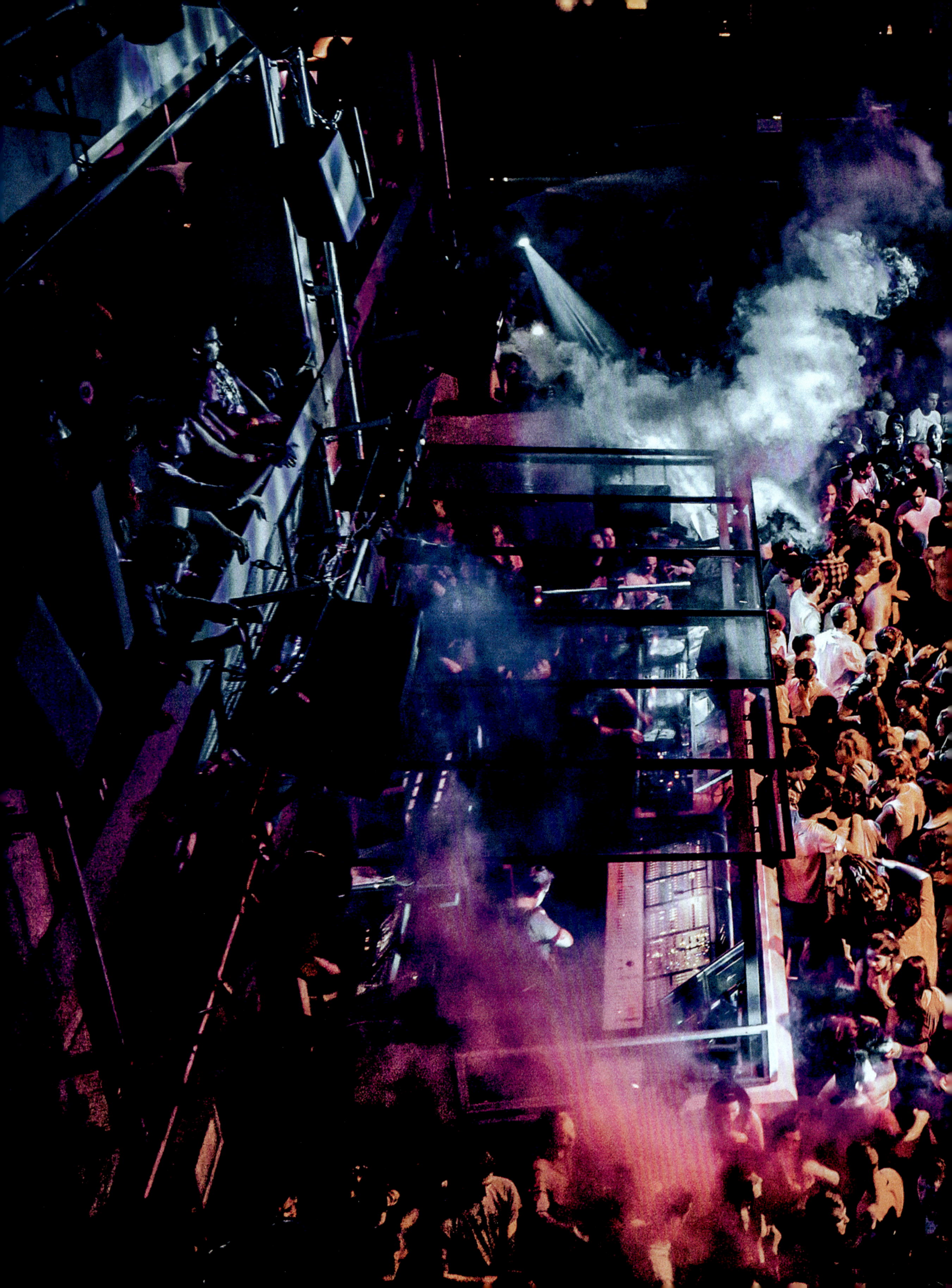

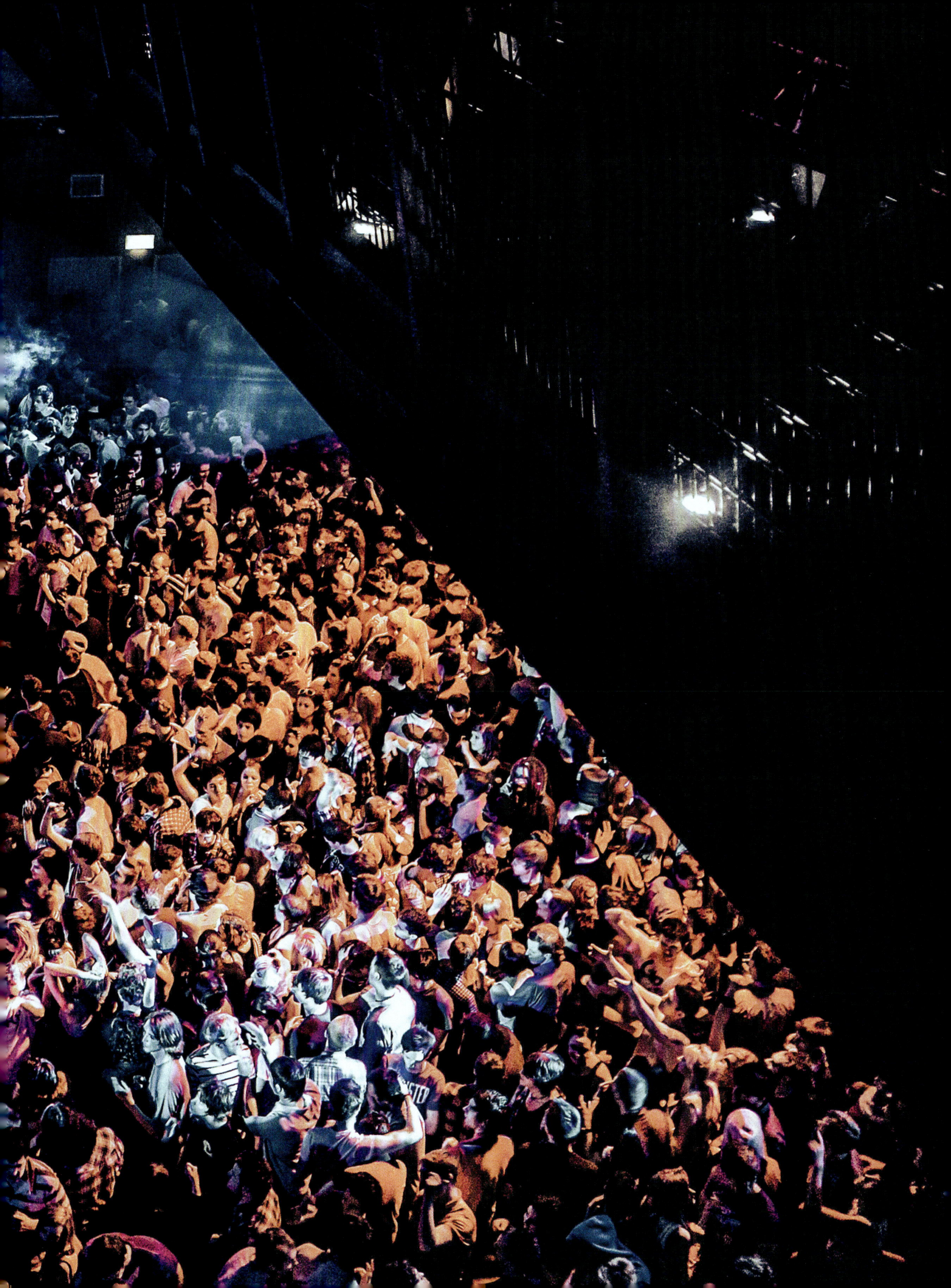

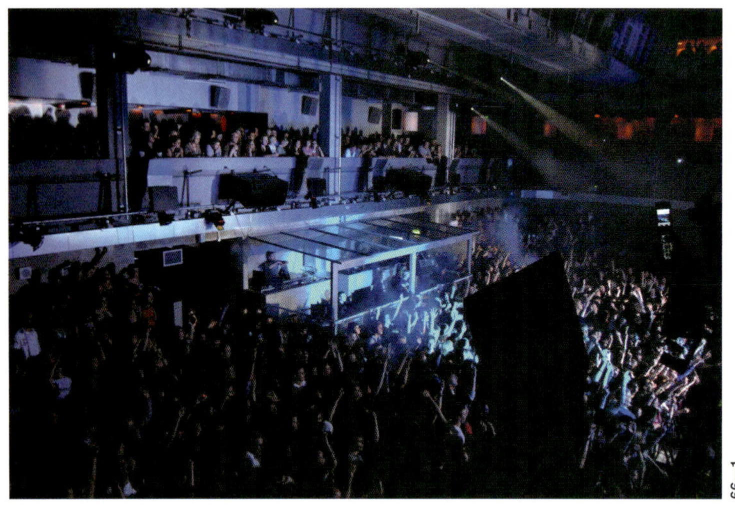
66—1

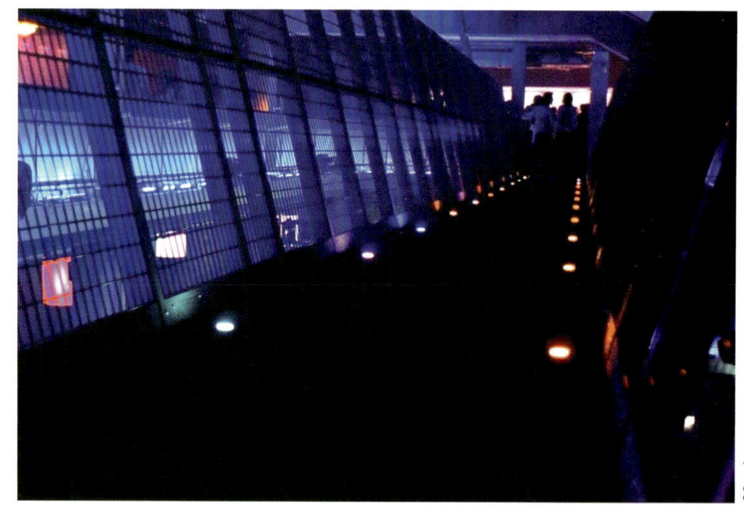
66—4

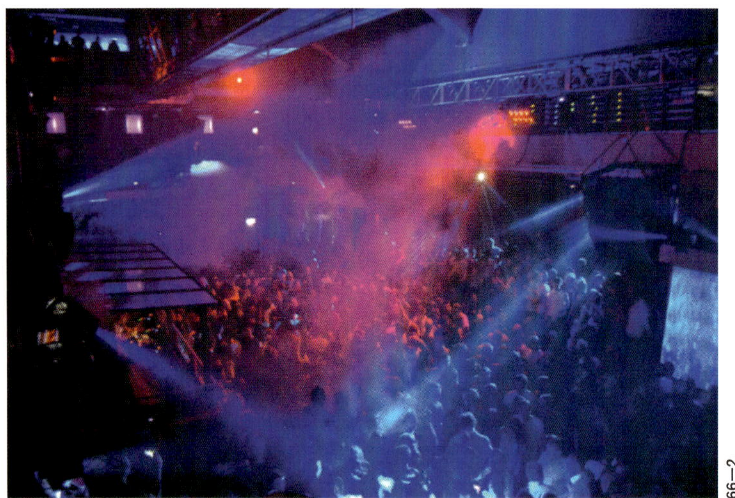
66—2

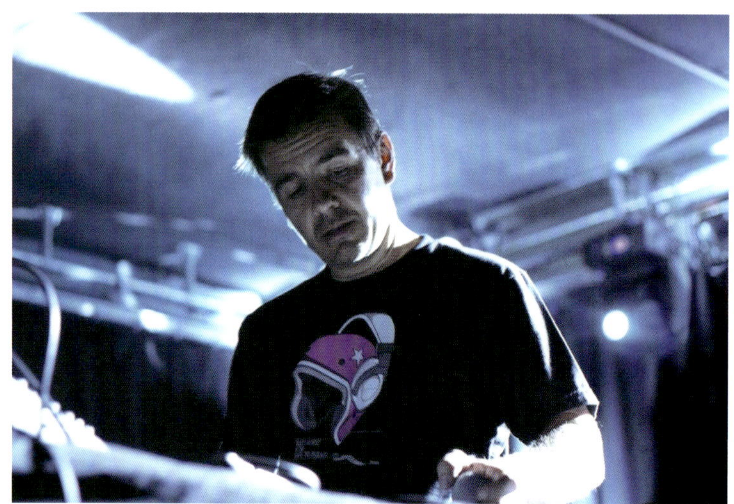
66—5

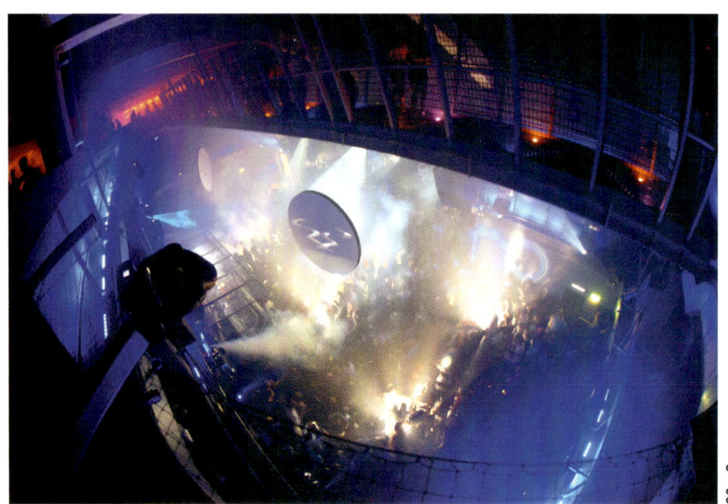
66—3

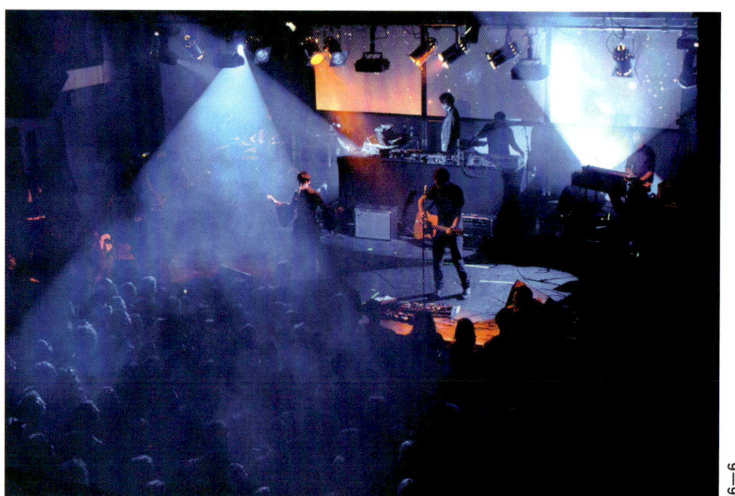
66—6

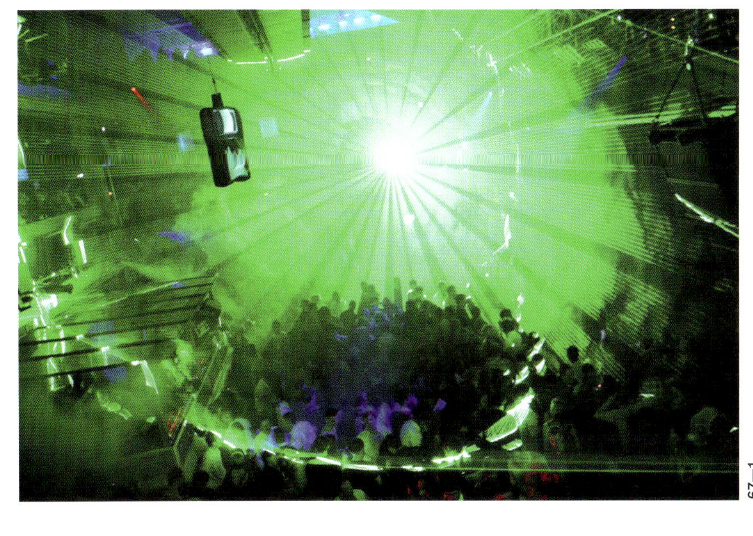
67—1

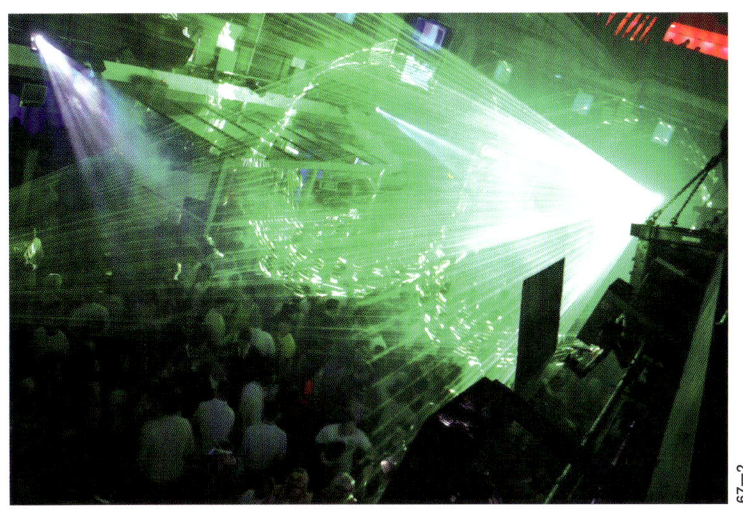
67—2

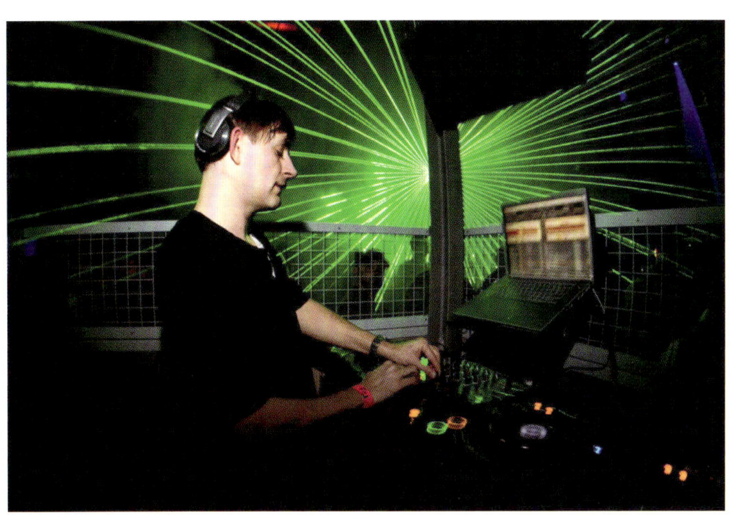
67—3

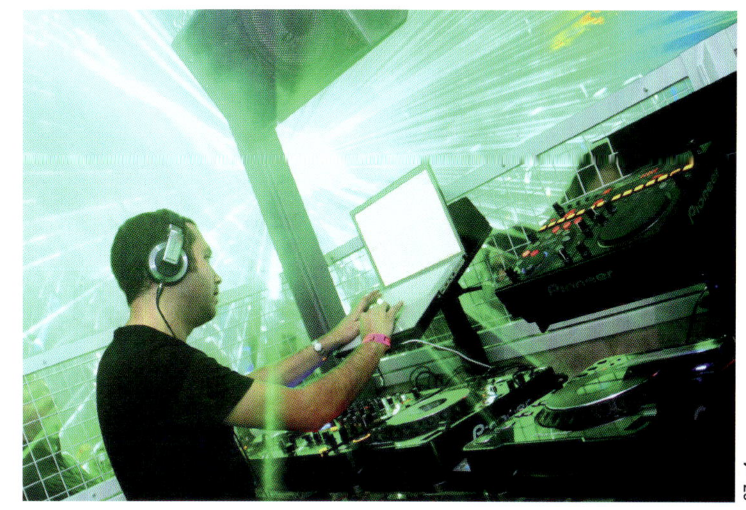
67—4

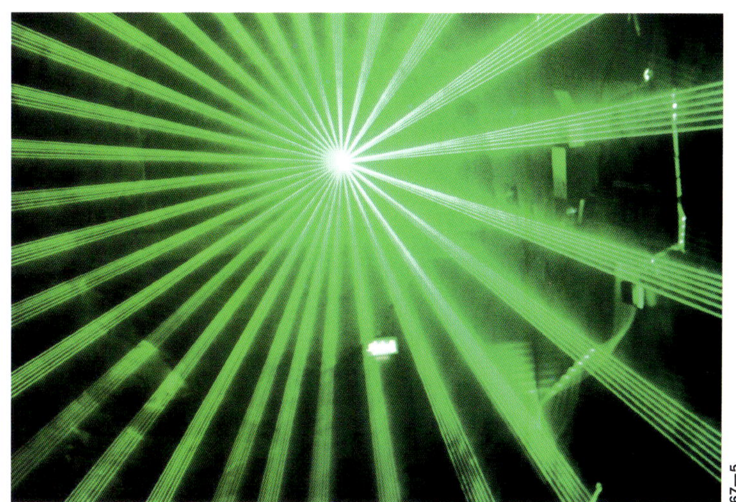
67—5

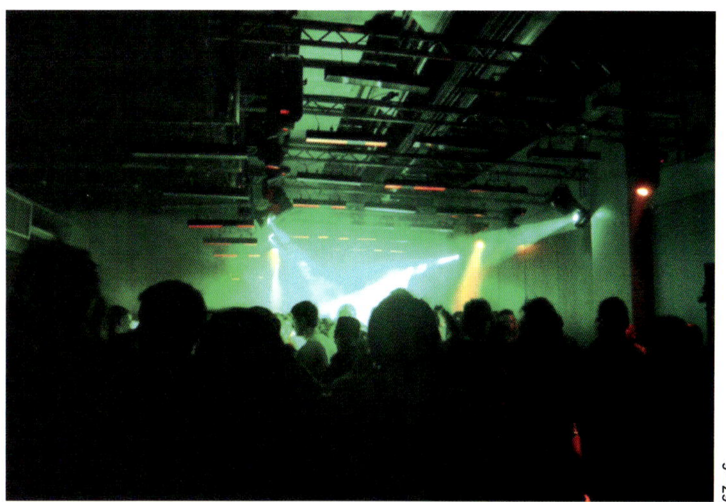
67—6

the music of fabric

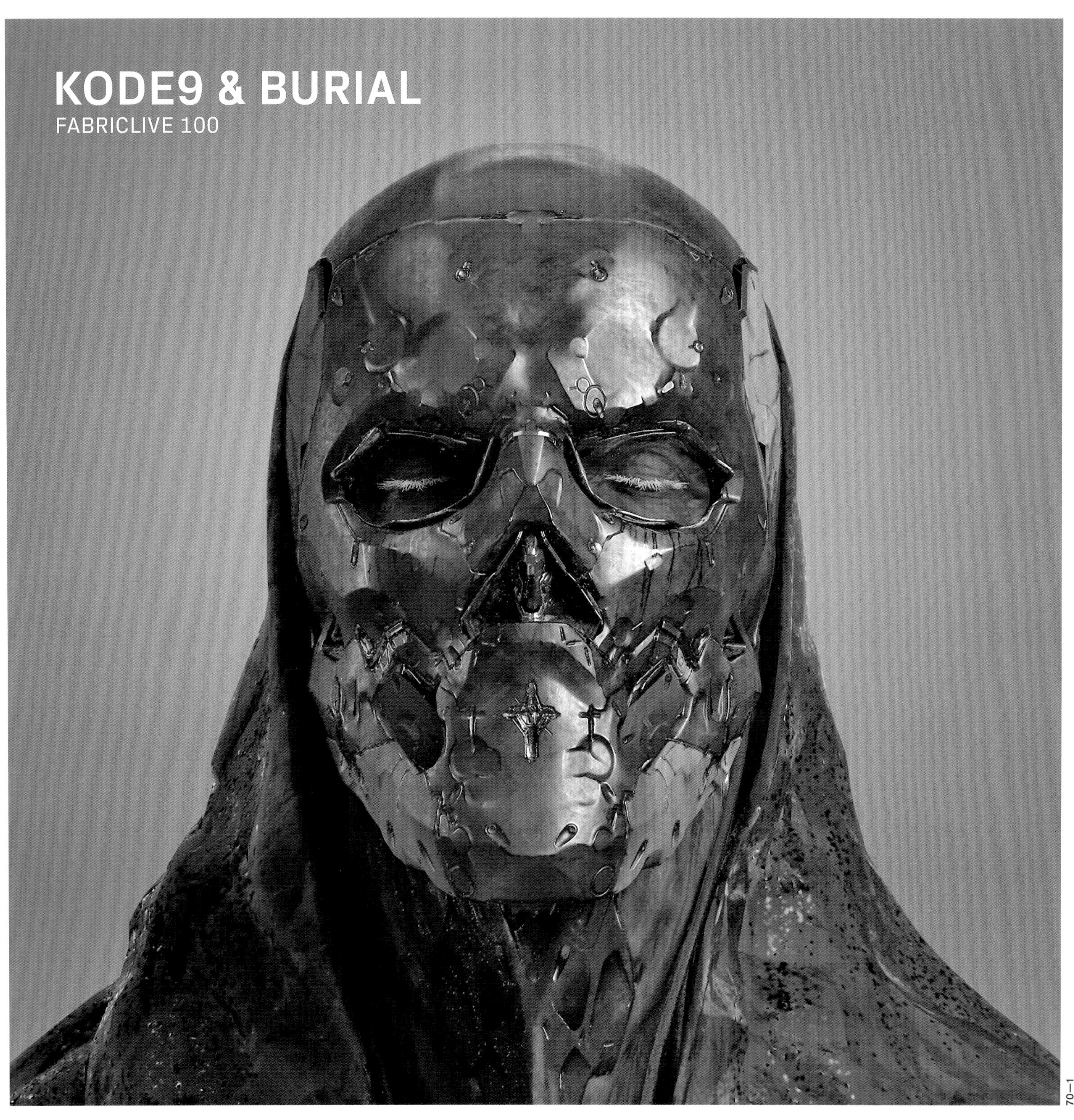

70—1

fabric didn't arrive in a vacuum. Though it was founded to be different – with Keith Reilly's distaste for the fancypants flash of mid-nineties superstar DJ culture as its prime mover – it had clear predecessors and peers, and it was always part of a London music ecosystem. Keith himself cites Ministry of Sound as the club that 'cut the turf' when it opened in 1991, though he thought it had some flaws in layout and feel, and by the time fabric was conceived it was all too frequently succumbing to the lowest common denominator in its programming, it absolutely nailed the fundamentals in terms of sound, functionality and providing a home for his beloved US house originators, and there's no question it had set the pace for 'destination' venues in London clubland.

Other clubs represented more leftfield sounds and decent audio too, of course. In 1995 Mr C, Layo and Bushwacka! had opened The End a little way to the west from where fabric would be. It, too, prided itself on its high-end sound systems and became an important home for drum'n'bass, but most famously of all it was a hub for the London tech-house movement – a prime player in which was one Terry Francis. And since 1993, Eddie Piller's the Blue Note had been running in the then distinctly ungentrified Hoxton Square off to the east, the absolute epitome of a down and dirty, late-opening basement rave-up with the most exquisite line-ups. 'The Blue Note had everything,' says Steve Blonde, whose tastes would do so much to lay the foundations for fabric's musical identity. 'Ninja Tune did their nights there, Talvin Singh … James Lavelle … DJ Harvey … Metalheadz on a Sunday, of course. It was everything I wanted from a club!'

There were more: Bar Rumba, Velvet Rooms, Leisure Lounge, Turnmills, Plastic People, the venerable Heaven – all part of the weekly merry-go-round for clubbers with well-developed tastes beyond the obvious. But it was those first three that really formed the coordinates for fabric's vision: the bold ambition of Ministry, the sense of a truly purpose-made space by and for clubbers in The End, and those line-ups in the Blue Note. Not that this was consciously decided at any point, mind. It was simply a matter of the constellation of people who came together around Keith's vision, their tastes and connections, and the places and spaces that inspired them. Beyond that, there was no grand plan for music policy; as Steve Blonde puts it: 'We weren't gunning to be the most underground club, it was still a commercial venture, and we were ready to let outside promoters in, whoever they might be.'

There may not have been a plotted-out music policy as such, but there was something vital from the beginning, something which would prove to be the beating heart of fabric's identity right through to today: the residencies of Keith's friends Craig Richards and Terry Francis on Saturdays. First up, this plugged the club into a great British tradition. Clubs like Back to Basics in Leeds and the Sub Club in Scotland were proving that having residents who were as beloved to punters as any star guest was a key to longevity. It's this probably more than anything else that helped fabric put clear water between itself and the more obviously superclub-ish Home down the road with its parachuted-in big-name residents.

The rest of the line-up for Saturdays tended to be booked on equally organic principles – it was all about DJs who the team themselves loved. 'I was out every night in those days,' says Judy Griffith, who was integral to the way Saturday nights fell together, working hand in hand particularly with Craig to find the cream of current talent. 'Most of us were! And we were always looking out for people who could really do it – we weren't interested in famous names or big egos, it was all the people who'd be more likely to be playing in the downstairs or the backroom of the clubs we went to.'

'I think initial successes came from just getting on with it,' says Craig. 'We might not have known what we were doing, but we were always booking from the heart, and I think that showed. People saw that this was honest, and would give us leeway and go with it.'

One crucial aspect where good taste and good luck intersected was in the internationalism of the line-ups they were booking. It feels bizarre to say this now, but in 1999, outside of the hard techno scene, very few British DJs ever went to Berlin, let alone Frankfurt. Craig, however, was an exception, as were his close friends like Parisian Ivan Smagghe and the ever ahead-of-the-curve Andrew Weatherall. This in turn led the whole programming team to look to the international scene centred on the city, and fabric provided early platforms for then-obscure artists like the Germans Steve Bug and Michael Mayer, North American names like Levon Vincent, Matthew Dear and Mathew Jonson, and, of course, the Chileans-in-Germany Luciano and Ricardo Villalobos. The then fabric publicist

Scott Paterson remembers Ricardo arriving for the first time 'just playing a warm-up, but I had to help him in with like forty boxes of records, and of course it turned into a three-day afterparty, and I really had a moment of, "Oh, OK, this is where this is going ..."!'

These wide horizons in booking policy helped sow the seeds for a cosmopolitan crowd even early on; this wasn't just the London scene any more, it was attracting Italians, South Americans, Germans and plenty more besides – something that would only increase with time. And this seeking out of relatively obscure acts destined for big things became a recurring feature of the club. Even Justice got their UK break playing Room 3 of fabric as part of an Ed Banger showcase, devoid of hype, there not because they were a Next Big Thing but because the team simply liked what they were about. 'We've always championed the underdog right from the start,' says Judy, 'but the flipside of that is we will stick with them, too. So someone like Jamie Jones or Nina Kraviz has come through Room 3, Room 2, until they're headliners, then eventually they're too busy or we can't even afford them!'

While Saturday nights fell into their identity almost immediately – thanks partly to the presence of Craig and Terry, and partly to the natural stability of the underground house and techno, which provided the night's backbone – Fridays, with Steve Blonde at the helm, took a while longer to find their identity, which wasn't surprising. From the beginning they represented the flux of genres available at the time, so would never have the stability of the eternal late-night groove that Saturdays plugged into. They generally attracted a younger and/or more alternative crowd; Terry Francis, with a wry eyebrow raised, says: 'A bit more college students, not so much the serious clubbers we had on Saturday.' This represented a new wave of music fans coming into the mix as the acid house generation grew up, bringing all kinds of extra influences into the mix as they did.

To start with, all bar one week of the month, the Friday would be run by outside promoters – Bugged Out! vs Big Beat Boutique set the tone early, as did people like Talvin Singh, Ali B and James Lavelle who'd been cut adrift when the Blue Note closed in 1998. The most commonly used overarching term was 'breakbeat', but this covered the entire tempo range from trip hop through nu-skool breaks to raging drum'n'bass, and stylistically from the most refined jazziness to fuzzy, scuzzy indie trash. 'Basically,' says Howie B, 'I could buy anything I liked in the record shops and make it fit, even if I had to speed it up or slow it down!'

Jungle and drum'n'bass would, of course, be a core part of the club. In fact, the first ever Friday was a V Recordings night with Bryan Gee and Jumpin Jack Frost; you could hardly have a more foundational, back to basics, junglist rave-up than that – and news of the subsonic force of the bodysonic dancefloor spread quickly through the faithful. It's emblematic of fabric's dedication to quality that one of the very earliest nights was Reinforced Records' tenth birthday – where 4hero and friends programmed the cream of London drum'n'bass talent next to a room with Underground Resistance, Carl Craig, Rolando and other heroes of Detroit techno. But in those early days, Fridays were extremely diverse – you were as likely to find someone like Gilles Peterson, or heads from the original UK Balearic generation like Boy's Own's Cymon Eckel, programming nights.

When it came to the one Friday a month put together inhouse, as Steve self-effacingly puts it: 'You throw a lot of shit at the wall and see what sticks, don't you?' Of course, that doesn't mean just putting on any old thing – fabric from the beginning was run from the top down by obsessive music lovers, so they knew what was good – but the leftfield of clubland around the turn of the millennium was defined by flux and generational shifts, and it wasn't always obvious which sounds and scenes were going to last and which remain just curios. But quickly Steve – assisted by the young Shaun Roberts, who thanks to his networking skills and golden ear for talent had quickly made the leap from flyer boy to programming team – started to realise that bringing everything inhouse might help to provide some cohesion in the chaos. 'We could see the bigger picture,' says Steve. 'We knew the club inside out, and we would maybe invest more and be able to think long term more than an outside promoter.' With Ali B and James Lavelle as residents, FABRICLIVE quickly settled to be another pillar of the club's identity in the public eye.

Then there were Sundays. If Saturdays were for 'serious clubbers', that went tenfold for the Sabbath, which truly was for the die-hards, with the club running through the day and into the night. For this, the team decided to bring in just one outside promoter: DTPM, which had previously run for almost four years at The End and established itself as one of

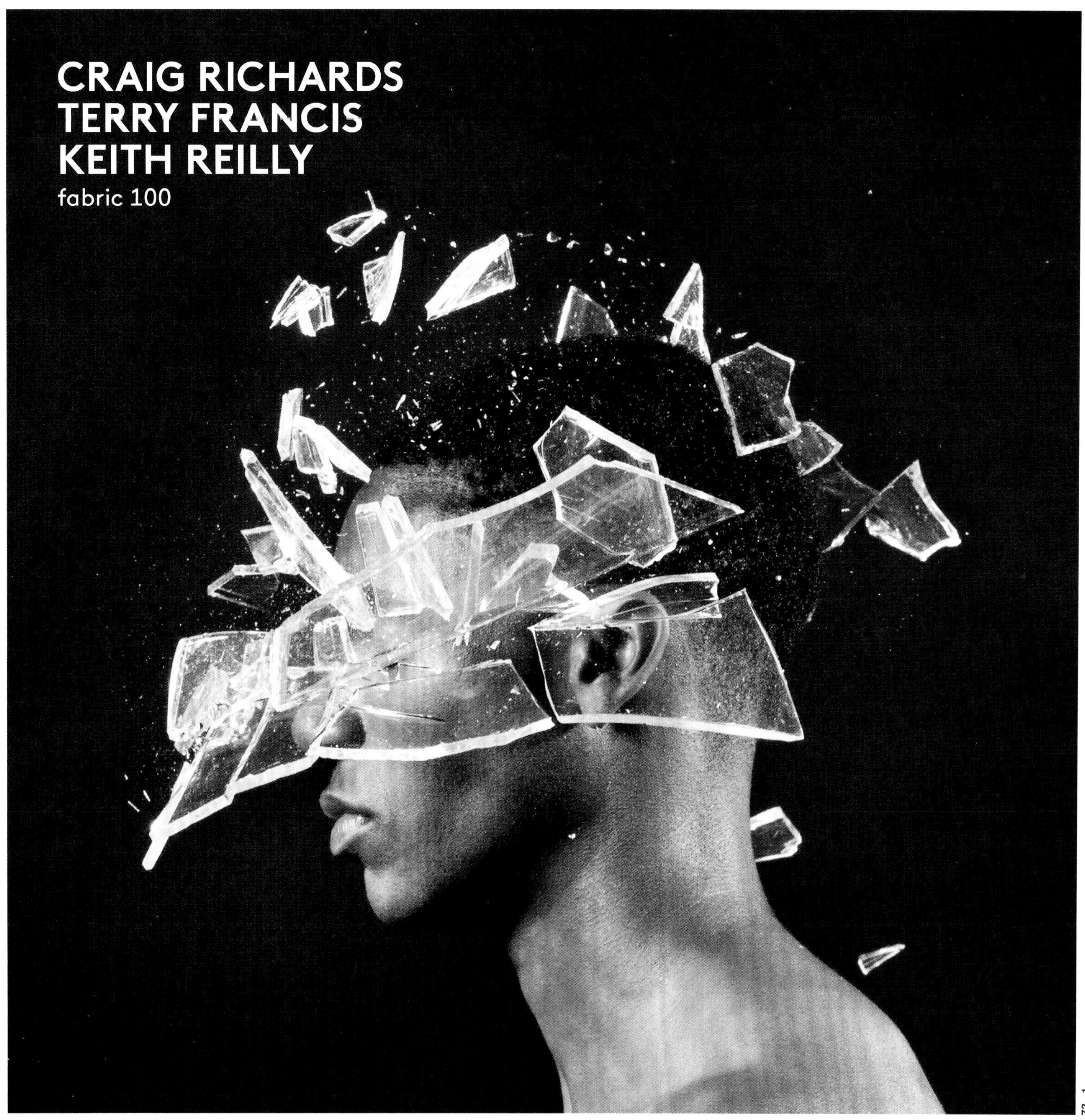

73–1

the capital's most reliable 'gay and polysexual' parties for people who wanted the weekend to never end but still cared about the quality of music and dancing. It was an astute choice. 'We already had a "family",' says DTPM founder Lee Freeman, 'and we were just moving house, really. We'd been closed for a couple of months leading up to the relaunch at fabric, so it just gave it momentum. The opening night was a resounding success, and after a bit of fine tuning we slotted in quite nicely. I think the following New Year's Day, 2000, was probably the moment we knew we had settled into our new home and everything was working out nicely.'

DTPM had its music policy locked down already and, with that 'bit of fine tuning', it slotted perfectly into fabric's particular spaces. Room 1 was party central with house, house and more house, at the higher energy end of the spectrum. 'Always cutting edge, but never up its own arse,' as Lee puts it, with beloved names like Miguel Pellitero, Smokin Jo, Alan Thompson, Steve Thomas and Justin Ballard coming through, as well as bigshots like Shapeshifters, Freemasons and a pre-EDM David Guetta. Room 2 was tech and tribal house for the more intense dancers, led by residents Ariel, Malcolm Duffy and Lisa German. Room 3, meanwhile, had an anything-goes approach, where DJs like Fat Tony and Jodie Harsh, electro, pop and anything else could fit. All of this provided a failsafe vibe that continued week in, week out for eight solid years from fabric's first weekend.

By 2001 fabric had pretty well found its groove, and was pretty unique for a club of its size in having such regularity to its programming. This was given an extra boost when Keith decided that he wanted to have a record label too, and with no knowledge of how to start one, reached out to Geoff Muncey. Geoff had worked with Craig Richards's partner Amanda at BMG/ Deconstruction, so had a ringside seat as fabric was dreamed up and realised, and partied at its early wild weekends. When the call came from Keith, Geoff was non-committal – he was away travelling and didn't want to cut short his trip. But when he returned and met up with Keith, he found out – after an extremely long and rambling music conversation – that the job was still going, and took it on the spot.

Like so much about fabric, the success of the label rested on its simplicity: a furious drive to do one thing and do it well. Its core from the start was simply one mix album a month, alternating between fabric (representing Saturdays) and FABRICLIVE, starting with the residents for the first two editions of each, then branching into the guests that gave the nights their character. Of course, as with the club itself, this simplicity was anything but simple to accomplish. As Geoff says, 'Twelve CDs a year, rain or shine, with inflexible deadlines and all the licensing of tracks, was pretty stressful at times! We came close to the wire on a number of occasions, but we never missed one.' In fact, this really captured the spirit of fabric through and through: a crack team tearing their hair out, losing sleep and working frantically behind the scenes to get something seemingly effortless happening on a never-ending regular schedule.

With their distinctive metal tins and artwork based on the themes that Jonathon Cooke was creating for the monthly flyers, the CD mixes went out to fabricfirst members and on general sale. Very quickly, it became clear they were succeeding in their stated purpose to, in Geoff's words, 'showcase what was being played in the club, and to distinguish between the two nights musically'. Now, even someone who hadn't set foot in the club – including, crucially, international music lovers – could get a real handle on what Fridays and Saturdays were about as they grew and evolved – how they had their own identity … but also how they overlapped.

The fabric mixes started, of course, with Craig, then Terry, laying the foundation of trippy electronic house, but in just the first couple of years, branched out through soulful US house (Tony Humphries), heavy electro (Radioactive Man) and pure techno energy (Slam). And it wasn't long before they could incorporate the kind of funky eclecticism of people like Rob da Bank, Amalgamation of Soundz and Rub'n'Tug that could easily sit in a Friday line-up. FABRICLIVE started off with the diverse but definitely breakbeat-centric sounds of James Lavelle, then Ali B, with DJ Hype staking out the drum'n'bass territory next – but by its seventh edition had blown the doors completely off the hinges by throwing in John Peel. Though Keith's long-time idol turned friend loathed the idea of playing in a nightclub, Keith had badgered him until he accepted, and Peel was blown away by the reception, the crowd staying with him through every curveball then carried him through the club on their shoulders after he finished – of course – with the Undertones' 'Teenage Kicks'. His FABRICLIVE mix condenses this into seventy minutes and stands as a bold statement of endless possibility within the limits of the club-and-label format.

From there, FABRICLIVE was comfortably able to encompass, alongside hip hop, breaks and jungle big names, the slick collision of indie and electro of Stuart Price as Jacques Lu Cont and the psychedelic disco-boogie of Bent, both not implausible on Saturday nights. Then there was the party-starting broken beat of Bugz in the Attic and the cross-tempo global fusions of Nitin Sawhney. It's notable that the latter two's instalments in the mix series each included tracks from the nascent dubstep scene in 2003 and '04, when it was barely even named as such. In fact, dubstep had been in fabric since before it was even dubstep; the foundational FWD>> night was doing Room 3 during True Playaz jungle nights from 2001. Skream remembers the first time he ever heard one of his own tunes out, at the first of these – as he says, 'For me it literally all started there!' Grime, too, found its way in early, with the Run the Road showcases from 2005 providing a platform when mainstream clubs were shunning the genre. Shaun Roberts in particular was an aficionado of the new mutations of UK bass, which would become an ever greater strand of Friday programming after Steve Blonde moved on and Shaun took the reins in 2006.

Of course, in the middle of all this were Craig's friends and close associates Andrew Weatherall and Ivan Smagghe, who frankly played whatever they wanted, whichever side of the Friday/Saturday divide they happened to be on. And just off to the side of them was the noisy, anything-goes indie-electro-disco genre flux that ran turbulently right through the 2000s, epitomised by the likes of Annie Mac and pre-megastardom Diplo and Erol Alkan. The latter is the absolute 'Friday version' of the kind of artist development Judy described happening with DJs on Saturdays; a last-minute fill-in for an absent David Holmes in a Bugged Out!-curated Room 3 was his great career breakthrough (he signed with the agent who still represents him to this day immediately afterwards), and he too made that step-by-step progress through the rooms to headliner, eventually curating his own nights.

But among all this genre turbulence, the real shift was longer, slower, more seismic: the one that Shaun presided over – from 'breaks' to 'bass' as the overarching theme of Fridays. Dubstep really broke out of its micro-niche status at the start of 2006, and just over a year after that, fabric was instrumental in its global expansion. French electro overlords Justice had been signed up to deliver FABRICLIVE.37, but because of copyright issues it couldn't be licensed in time, so two rising stars of dubstep were called to see if they could make a replacement in short order. Caspa and Rusko were just twenty-five and twenty-two respectively, but had their publishing signed to fabric so could license their own tunes easily, and they were skilled DJs trusted to put together a mix quickly. In the event, they came into the club on a Monday following a weekend gigging, banged out the mix from vinyl and dubplates in a single take, and it was mastered and being sent out on promo by the end of the week. It's no exaggeration to say it was world-changing; for better or worse, its rapid-fire barrage of the more rambunctious end of the sound was the spark that caused the genre's explosion – and rendered it unrecognisable from its deep and brooding origins. It remains probably the most talked-about, and certainly the most controversial, fabric mix to this day.

The club wouldn't shy away from the most rowdy, ravey sides of dubstep; indeed, Caspa's Dub Police would become one of the biggest names on Friday nights, rivalling the big drum'n'bass brands like True Playaz and Ram for energetic crowds. But it also supported all the many-splendoured facets of the bass-music galaxy that followed dubstep and grime into clubland, providing a home for the deeper grooves of the likes of Hyperdub, Hessle Audio, Night Slugs and Numbers. This both reasserted the experimental edge, which had always been part of Keith and Craig's musical dream, and also further blurred the boundaries between the house/techno world; indeed, as Judy says, 'About 2010, some of the guys who'd come through dubstep, especially the Hessle boys, started pushing for slots on Saturday.' People like Four Tet, Daphni and Optimo started coming through with the eclectic Weatherall-like ability to fit comfortably on a Friday or Saturday, and as the 2010s moved on they began to feel less like exceptions and more representative of an increasingly fluid scene.

Shifts in sound came in parallel with – and were sometimes amplified by or even caused by – gradual changes in personnel. When DTPM wound down in 2007, Shaun and Judy together headhunted the WetYourSelf! team of Cormac, Peter Pixzel and Jacob Husley, who'd built a unique mixture of serious minimal house/techno heads and an East London fashion/queer crowd for their nights at the Aquarium club. After some persuading – they were nervous about upscaling – they took over Sundays, bringing them closer to Saturdays musically, with Jacob particularly becoming a crucial part of the fabric team. Andy Blackett came from six years working at Ministry of Sound – but being not-so-secretly in love with fabric's line-ups – to do bookings at matter in 2010. Thankfully he survived that trial by fire and was invited into fabric to work on Saturdays, bringing with him a love of the more intense and weighty techno sound. He naturally fell into championing the direction of Room 2 in his early years and formed long-term partnerships with the likes of Ben Klock and Marcel Dettmann, helping with that sound's increase in global influence and cementing its place at fabric.

Rob Butterworth was another case in point: having come on board in 2005 working in finance, he'd got a world-class training in the music industry and publishing from Geoff Muncey and colleagues, and gradually worked more on the label. He championed the deep bass of the likes of Shackleton and Kode9, among other sounds, and when Geoff left in 2012, Rob took over as head of the label. Negotiations had already been in place to start a new imprint for all-original music when he started, and one of his earliest tasks was to recruit a new A&R. This was already well underway, with final interviews locked in, when Kirsti Weir – then fabric's press officer, as well as being a mainstay in the underground electro world – thought to suggest Rob Booth.

Booth at the time was in the third year of running his own café in the Lake District, but he was better known in the music world for his Electronic Explorations blog and podcast. Set up five years previously, it had been almost unique in the burgeoning blogosphere in providing downloadable mixes in high-quality audio, and traversed the gnarlier, darker, weirder fringes of dubstep and techno. He'd picked the best of the best, and the 61-track compilation he pulled together to pay his spiralling site-hosting costs showed he had a fantastic ear, goodwill from artists and the ability to get support from tastemakers like Mary Anne Hobbs and Dave Clarke. He was the perfect person for the job, and the team persuaded management to let them upset the interview process, while Booth made the hard decision to completely upend his life and move to London.

Together, the two Robs would launch Houndstooth – taking its name from the checked cloth pattern that gave fabric its original logo, and its sonic cues from Electronic Explorations – to expand the sonic and visual palette outwards from the club. Through 2013, it pushed out a relentless stream of music from ultra-distinctive artists – Call Super, House of Black Lanterns, Throwing Snow – at first tethered to dark and strange club music, but quickly branching out with Throwing Snow's bleak mutant project Snow Ghosts, signalling how far Houndstooth was willing to go from the dancefloor. A new pillar for fabric's music was in place, once again perfectly timed to channel the changing times. The 2010s were far less about tumultuous change in trends, and much more about individual musicians and DJs who stood out and joined cultural dots in unique ways. And from the very start, Houndstooth showed that it was a place for committed artist development, allowing its stable to flex their creative talents and spread out in all directions over time, protected from cycles of hype.

Houndstooth developed apace through the decade. It was able to dive into straight-up dance music, as with Marquis Hawkes's classic house sound or the supercharged rave of Paul Woolford's Special Request guise, as well as being an important nexus for the dark and complex 'deconstructed club' sound, which was evolving worldwide and providing space for mysticism, queer identities and radical expansion of imagination. Houndstooth's position within the fabric family, internally and in the global public eye, was cemented in 2016 following the club's forced closure, when Butterworth – one of the few remaining skeleton staff – suggested an endeavour similar to Booth's previous compilation to keep his podcast running. Booth was 'glad to have a reason to be back in the office and working', and the resulting, deranged 111-track box set served not just as a symbol of support from musicians, but a musical joining of the dots between eras, styles, sounds, nights of the weekend and between Houndstooth and fabric as a whole. WetYourSelf!, too, became further integrated into fabric at this point, as Jacob became crucial to the wider #savefabric campaign, as we'll see later.

As with everything in the club, though the work on the labels was tightly focused, the ambition was off the hook with the release schedules and aesthetic, and Houndstooth almost tripped itself up in 2019 when it accepted Paul Woolford's challenge to release four lavishly packaged double Special Request albums in a year. The two Robs can laugh wearily about it now and are back on good terms with 'Woolly' now, but they definitely discovered the limits of their patience – and almost their sanity too – there. Meanwhile, they were also stewarding the fabric and FABRICLIVE series to their final, hundredth editions – ending on a bang with a triple mix of eternal Saturday night grooves from Craig, Terry and Keith for fabric.100, and a strange and wonderful one from Kode9 and Burial for FABRICLIVE.100 – only to almost immediately launch a whole new mix series. fabric Presents untethered itself from the Friday and Saturday club restraints, allowing the label itself to bring DJs into the fold, creating a new feedback loop with the club programming.

Finally – for now, at least – in 2022 came fabric Originals, a chance for the original artist commissions to come back to club music. 'Houndstooth has come around to singer-songwriters with great sound design,' says Booth, 'which is great, and allows a lot of it to be licensed for film and games, but now with fabric Originals we can still do what we started out doing!' By its tenth anniversary in 2023, Houndstooth had become a fully fledged industry presence, able to do showcase gigs in churches and art venues – perfectly placed to dovetail with fabric's increasing ambitions in the cultural world outside clubland. But with fabric Originals the pure dance party spirit was still being represented, showing what the building in Farringdon was still about every weekend of the year.

All this time, all the way through the 2010s and into the 2020s, the three rooms of fabric had continued to represent the swirls and cyclical shifts of the never-ending flow of club culture. Bass music and other elements may have made incursions into Saturdays, but house and techno remained the eternal four-to-the-floor pulse of the party, with Judy and Andy consistently plugged into the global network that linked Berlin, Ibiza, LA, New York, Chicago, Detroit, Cape Town and beyond.

Sundays, too, kept the groove – often very deep, sometimes very strange, but always joyful – and then in 2018 diversified, with WetYourSelf! going monthly, interspersed with new nights on rotation, most notably Love Child, in which WYS!'s Jacob Husley and Paranoid London collaborator Josh Caffé re-emphasised the queer roots of fabric Sundays and then some, with vogueing balls and a showcase of young international LGBTQ+ talent. Fridays kept drum'n'bass as their staple, but with every flavour and variant of bass and experimental electronics ebbing and flowing in and out of the mix, representing sound-system culture as something intergenerational and expressive of London's evolving character.

The intergenerational aspect couldn't be better represented than by the fact that Rob Cracknell, who took over booking from Shaun in 2015, 'grew up going to FABRICLIVE as a teenager, and now I was working at the club to create line-ups that needed to stack up against some of the best nights of my life!' Newer resident DJs, too – Anna Wall, Harry McCanna, Tapefeed, Jossy Mitsu among others – all have fabric's culture in their blood-stream, often having had their very first clubbing experiences in there. Josh Caffé attended DTPM 'religiously' in the 2000s, and is explicit about how the building itself has 'so much that's important in its DNA', which feeds into Love Child's new generation programming.

As with the whole of fabric's history, you could get vertigo if you think too hard about everything that's happened musically. Thousands of nights, tens of thousands of hours of music played (including one thirty-hour set by Keith Reilly himself), tens of millions of profound moments of people experiencing that music just within the walls of the club – and beyond that, the presence of the mix albums and original record releases out in the world, producing new experiences and inspirations in people's lives globally through the decades. Huge careers have been born, genres have risen and fallen, and new ones inspired by fabric moments. It's more than could ever be documented.

And yet, for all the multiplicity of it, it remains rooted in a very simple, profound belief in the music itself. Keith may have gradually, year by year, handed over the club he dreamed up to new talents to keep it vital, looking on now like a proud father whose kid has grown up, but his vision remains at the heart of every booking, every record release, every artistic collaboration. Everything has changed, but at the same time, nothing has: the fundamental, primal groove of house, the power of subsonic bass, the necessity of diversity and artistic curveballs – all are present and correct as they were in 1999. The amount of work that has gone into fabric in all its manifestations in a quarter of a century is eye-popping to consider, and yet musically, the same sense of possibility infuses everything as much now as then.

fabric 1–100

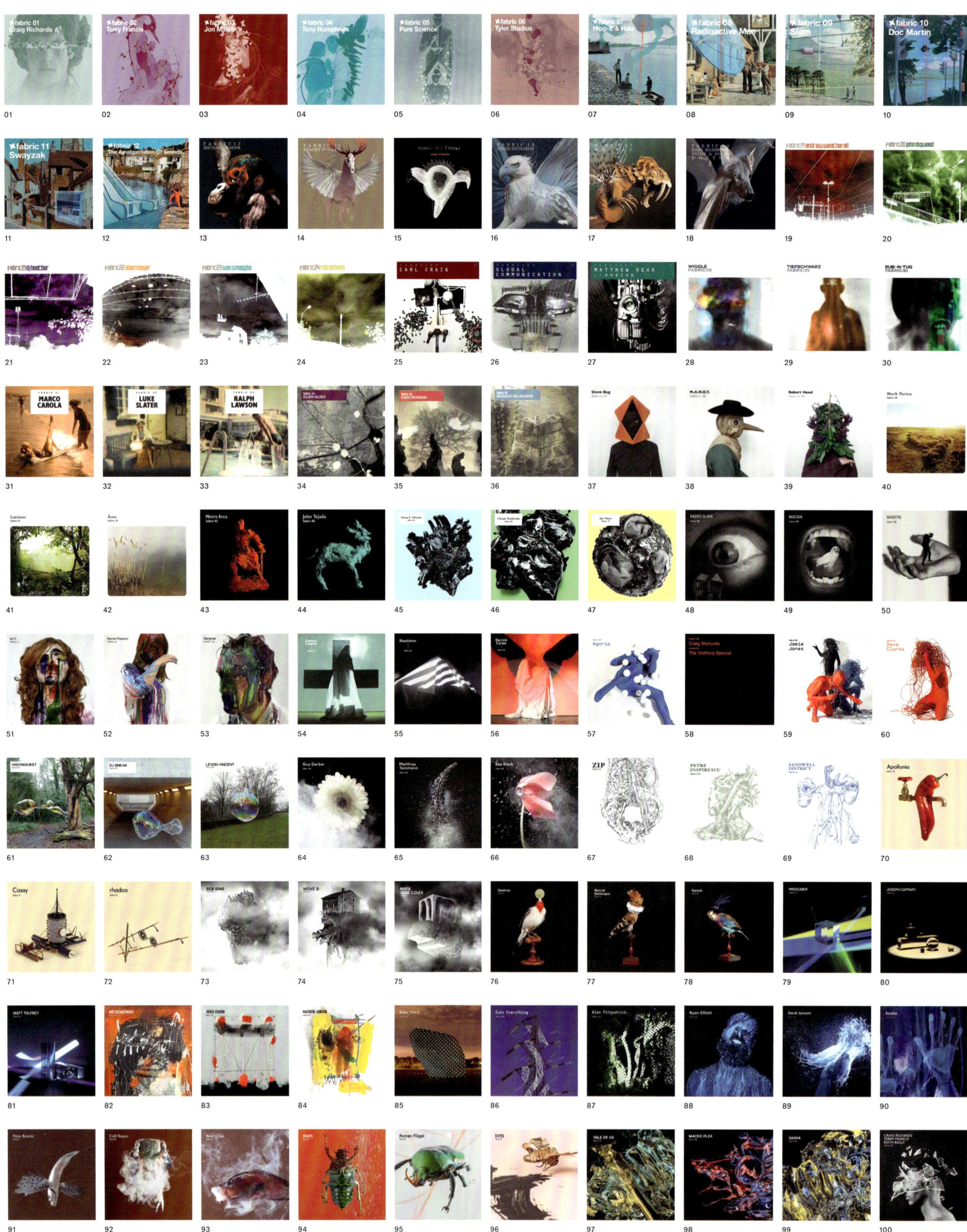

FABRICLIVE 1–100

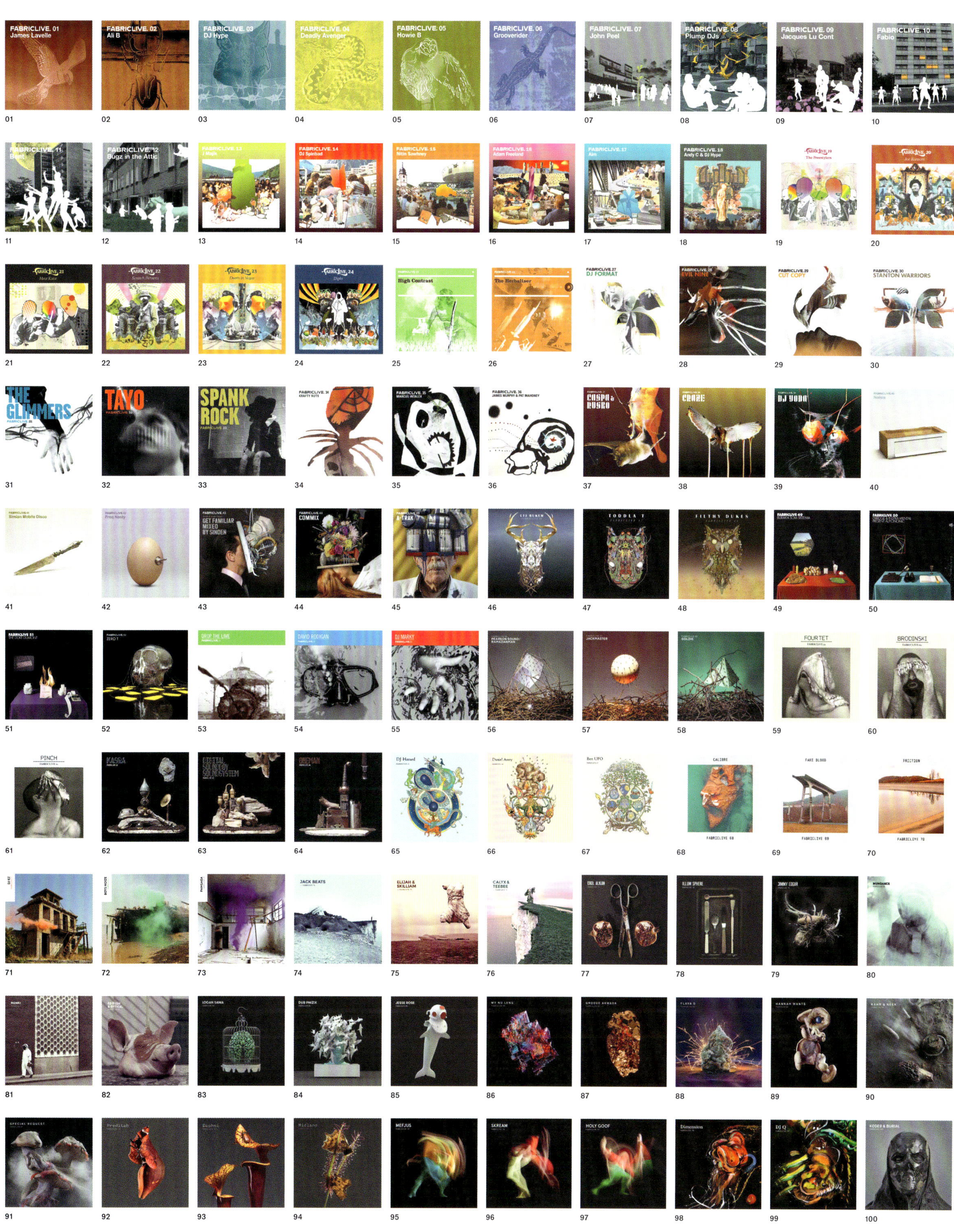

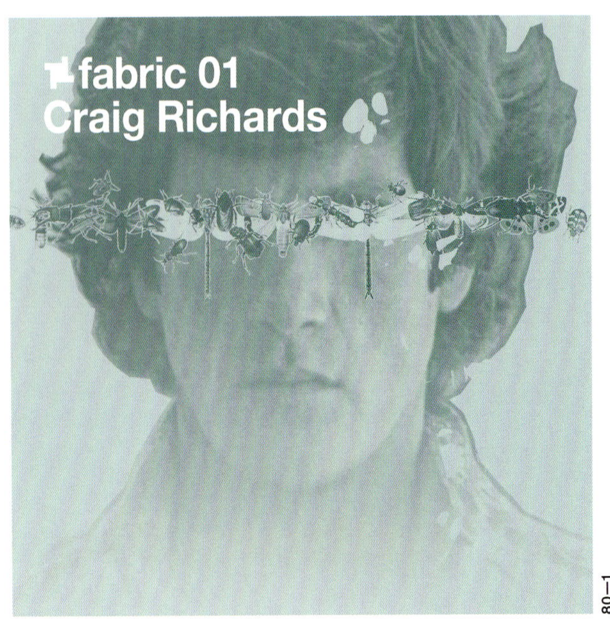

80—1

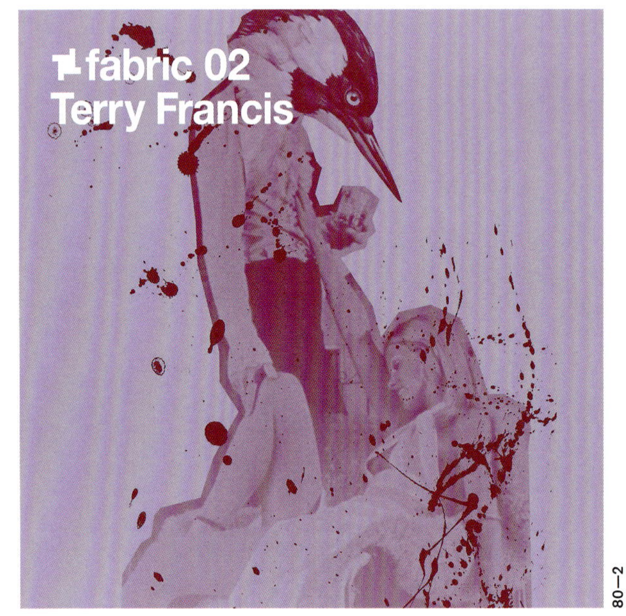

80—2

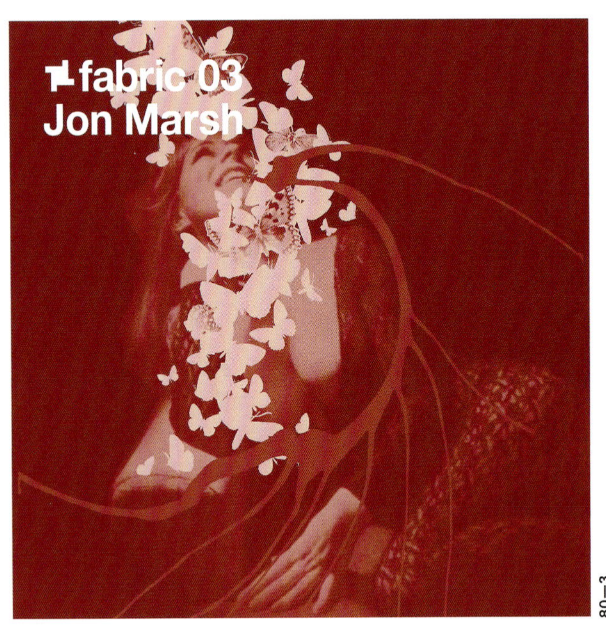

80—3

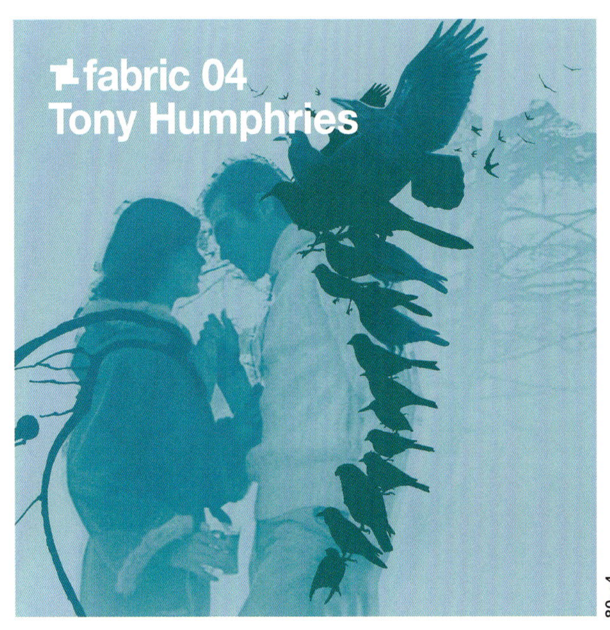

80—4

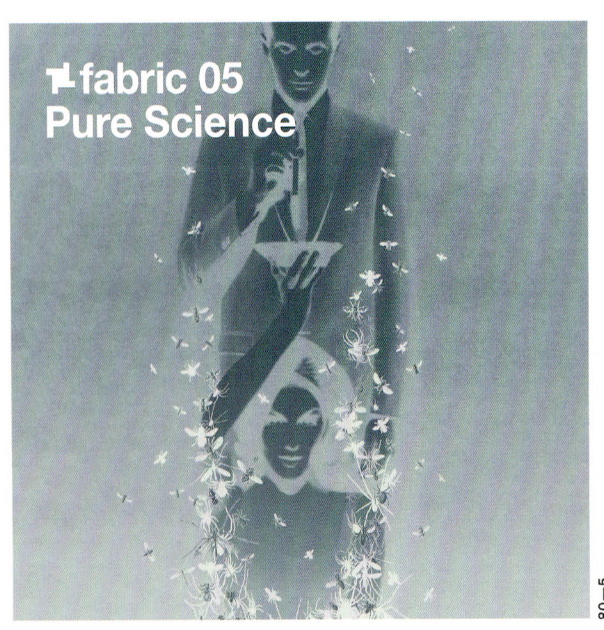

80—5

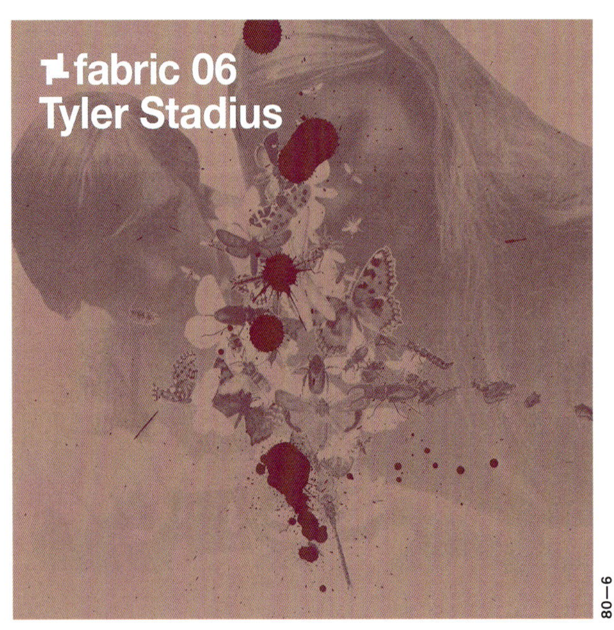

80—6

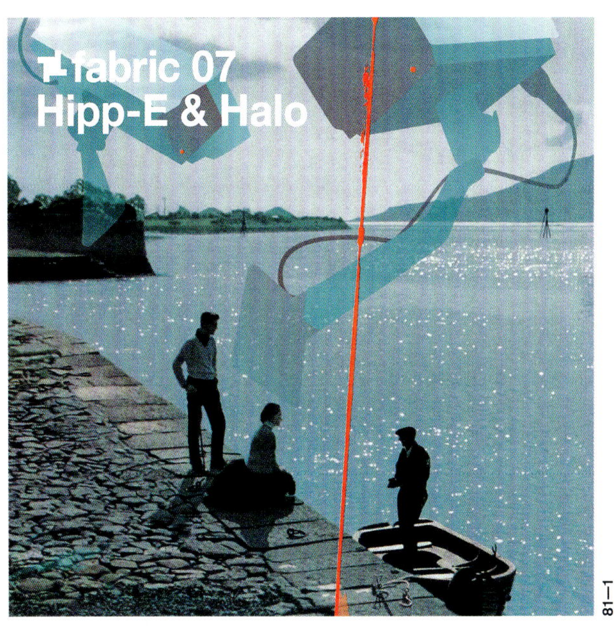

81—1

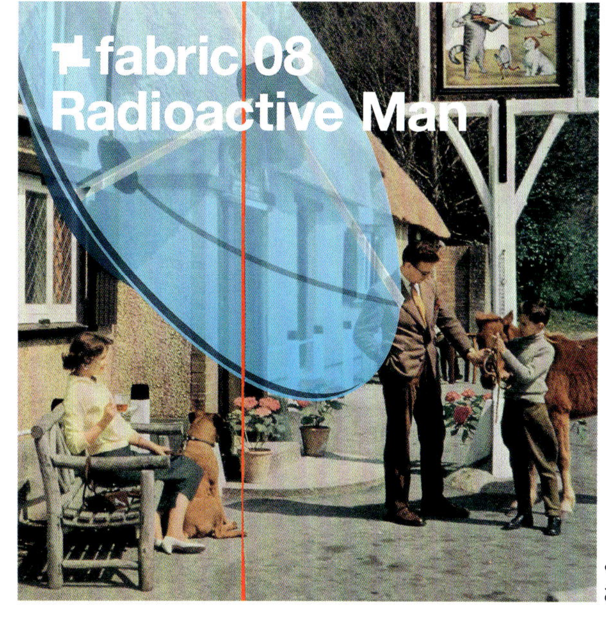

81—2

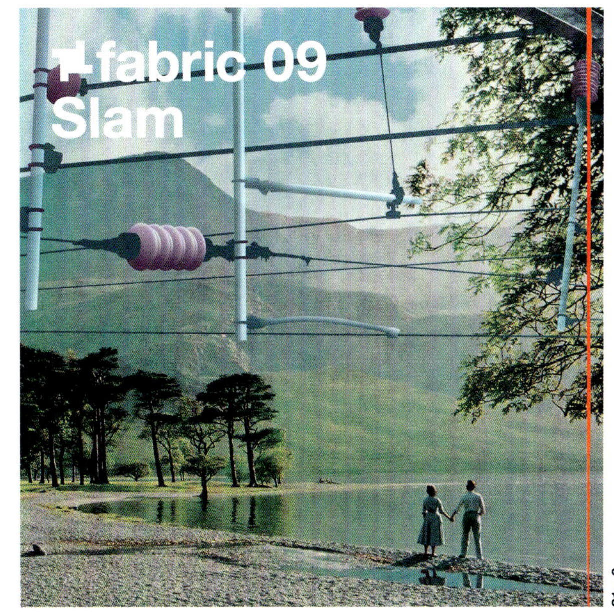

81—3

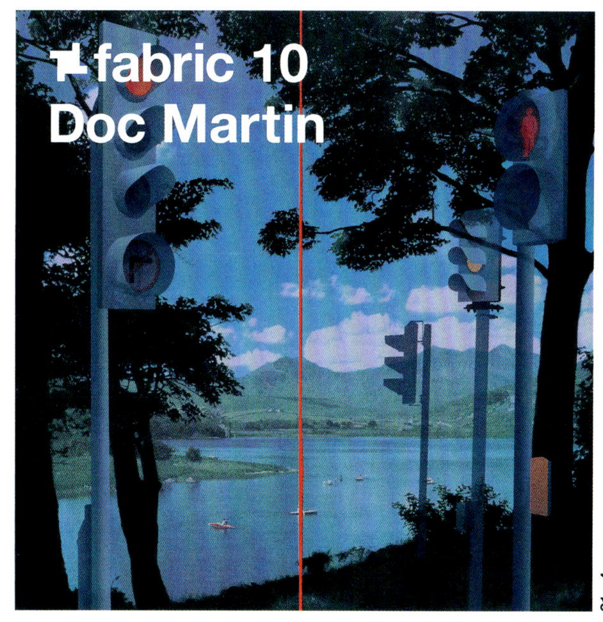

81—4

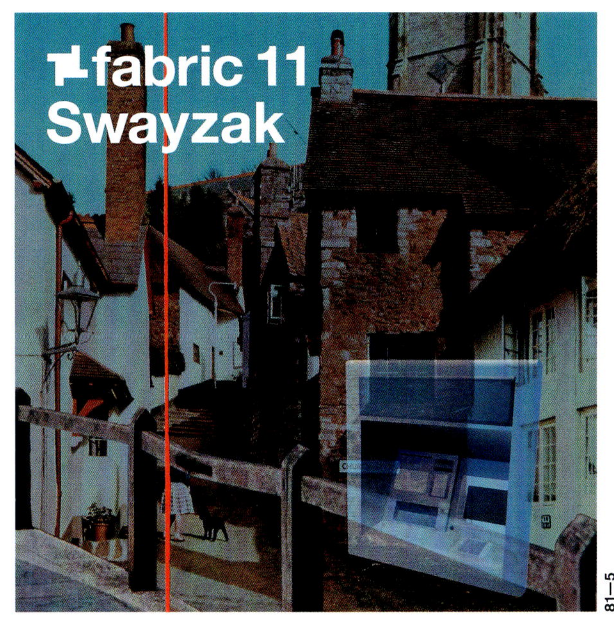

81—5

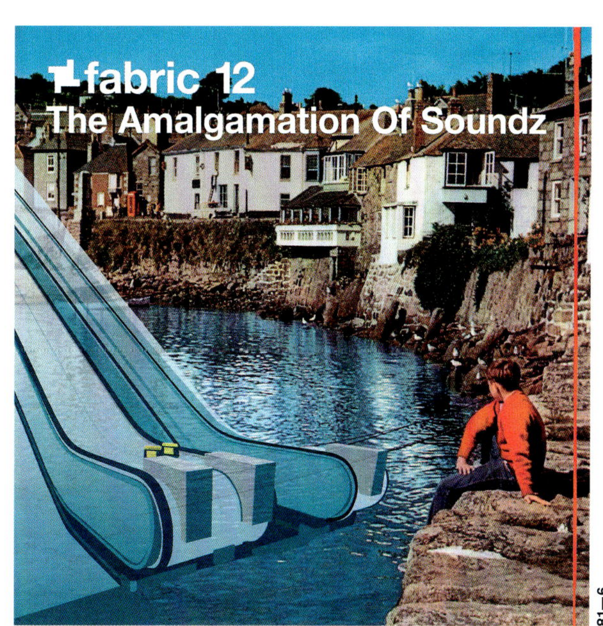

81—6

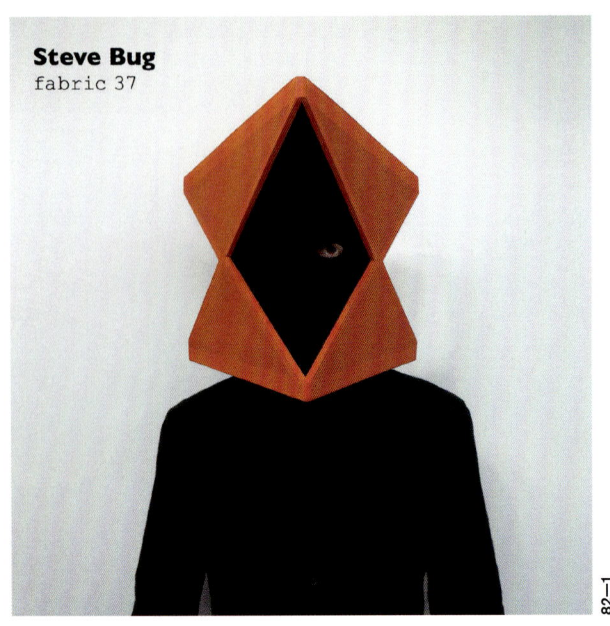

82—1

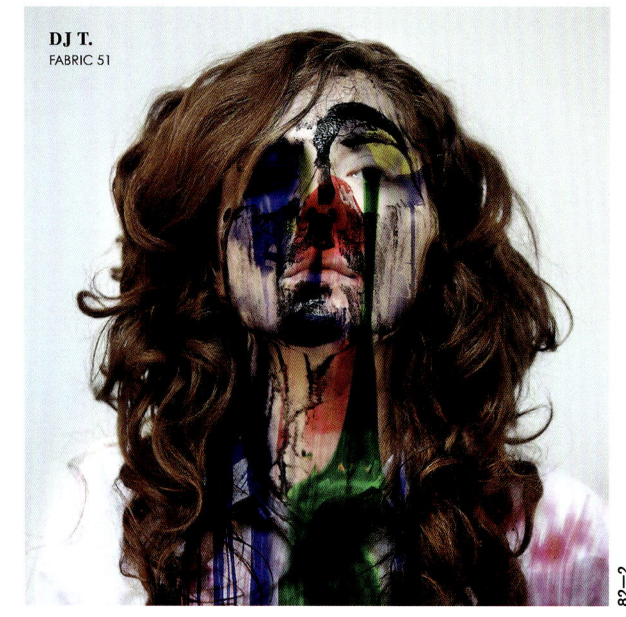

82—2

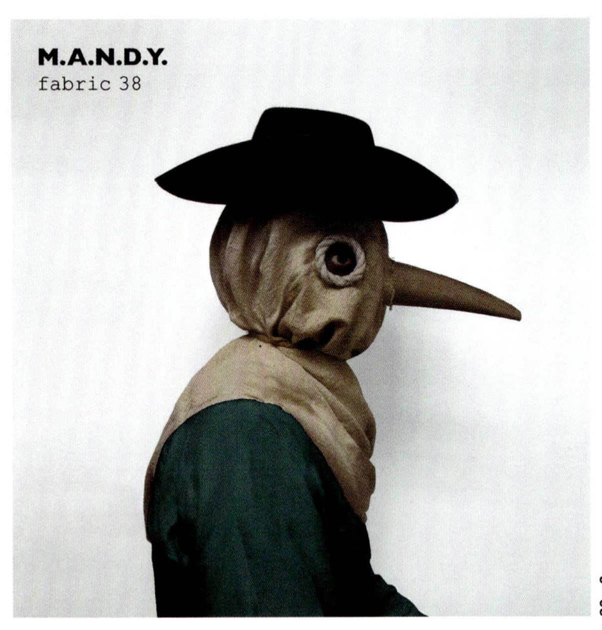

82—3

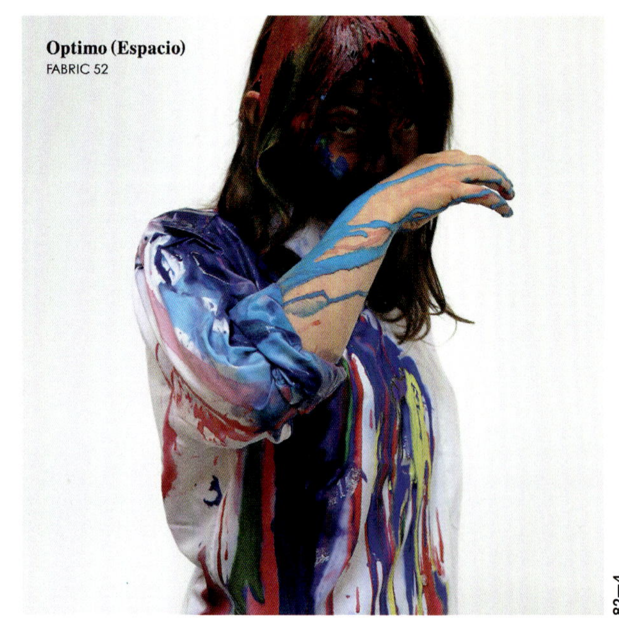

82—4

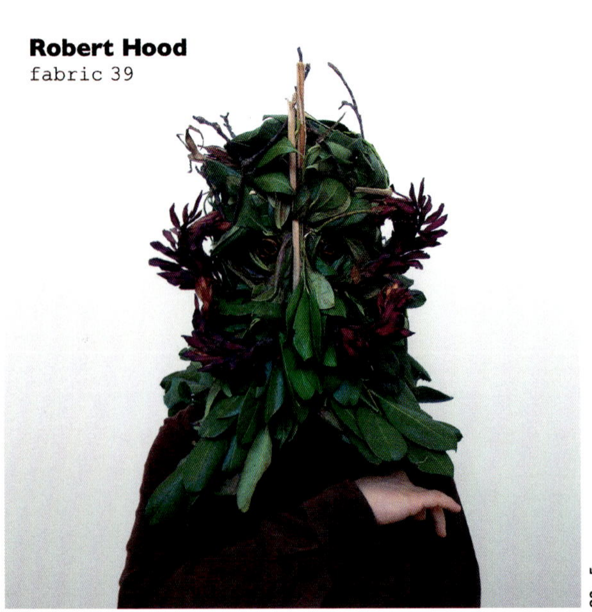

82—5

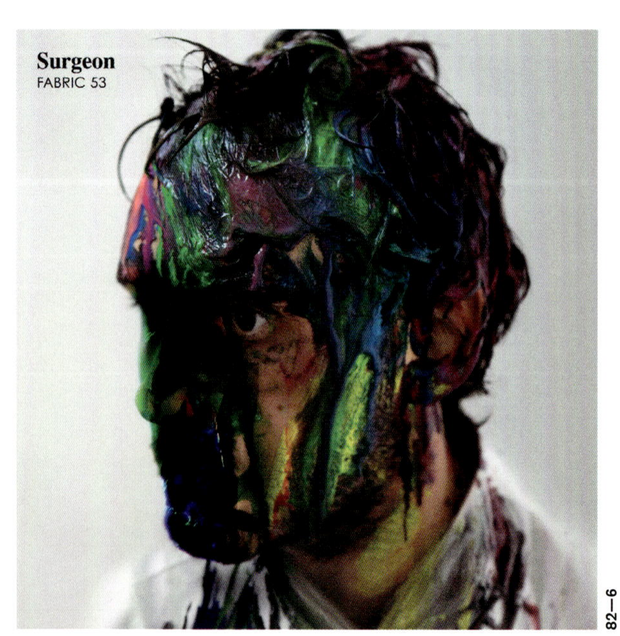

82—6

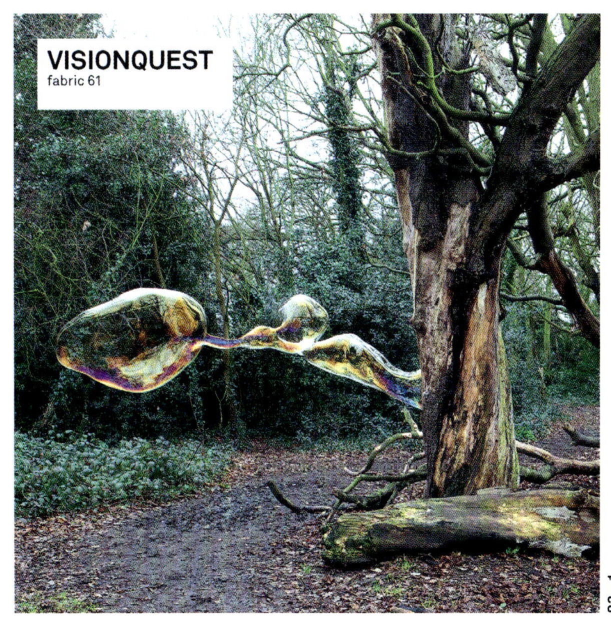

83—1

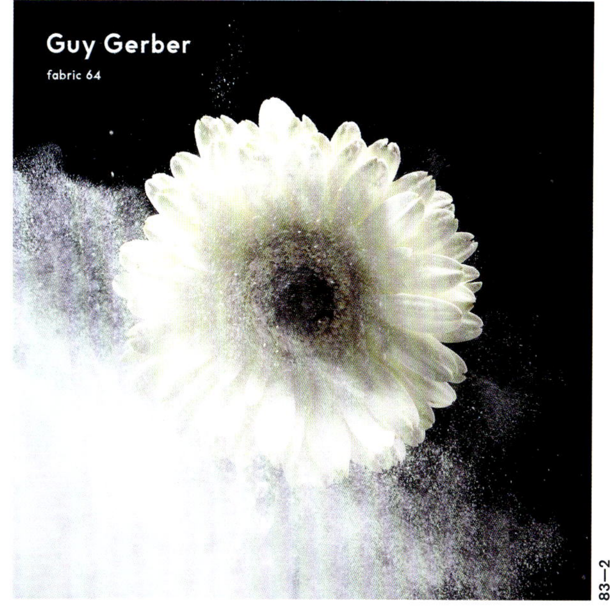

83—2

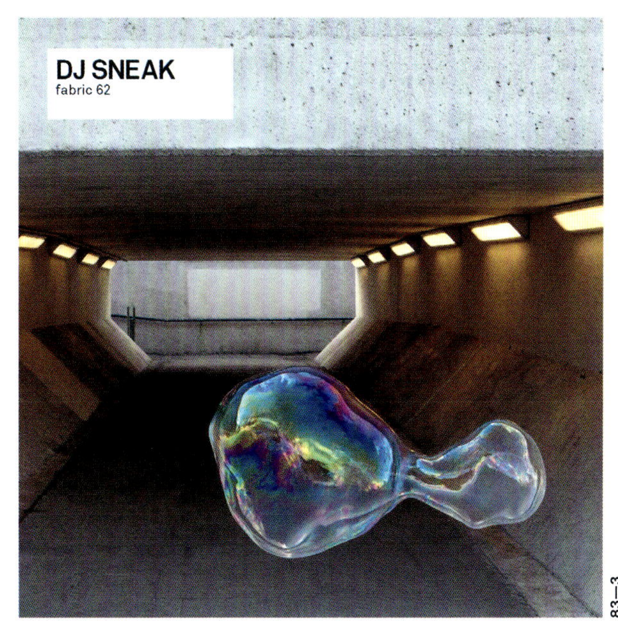

83—3

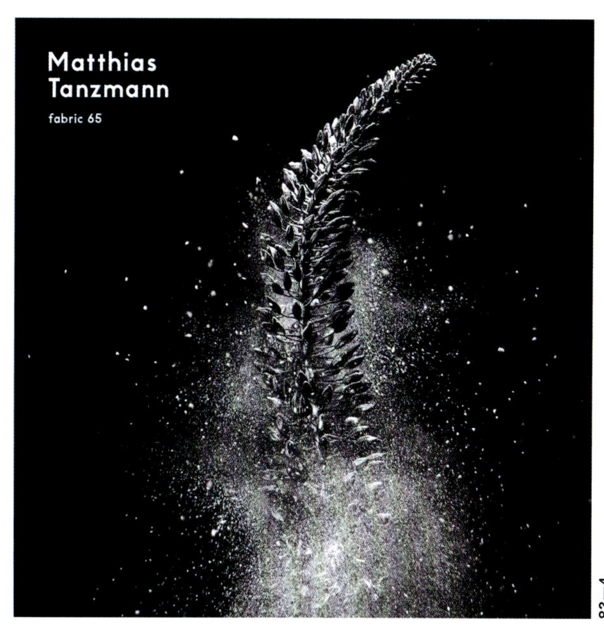

83—4

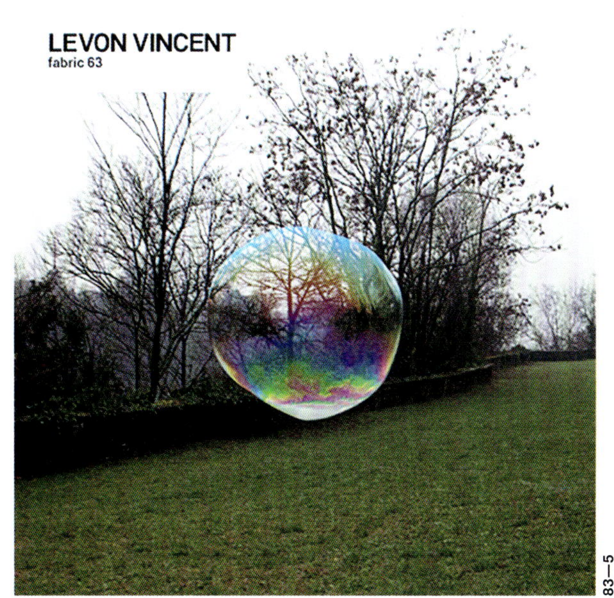

83—5

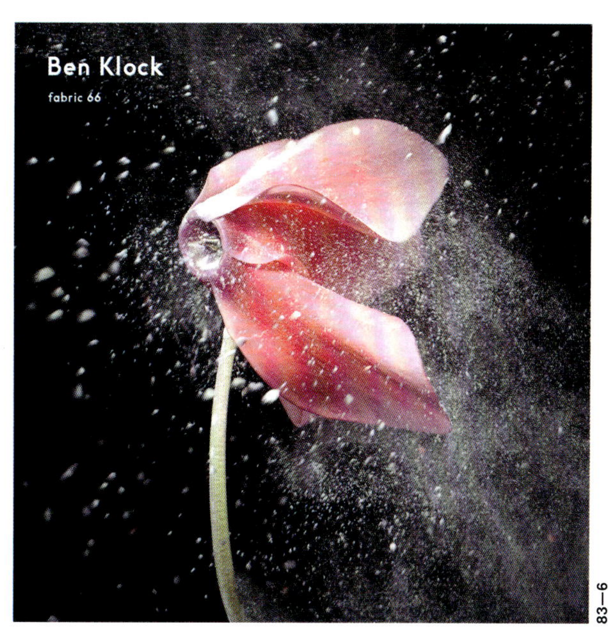

83—6

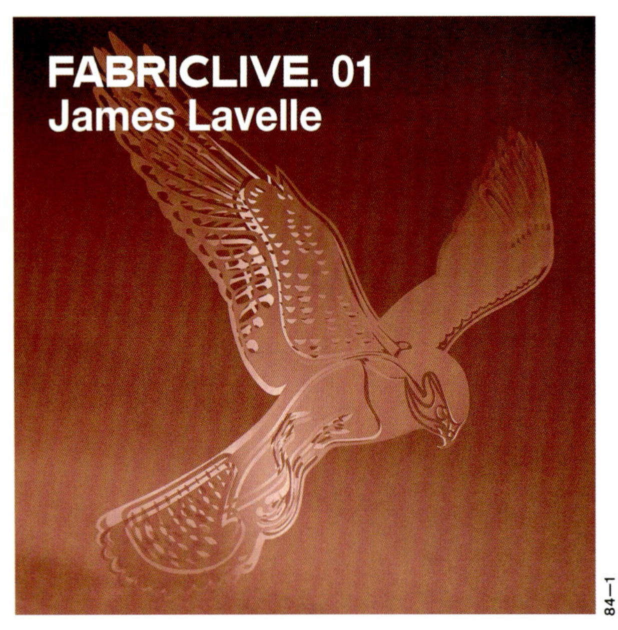

84—1

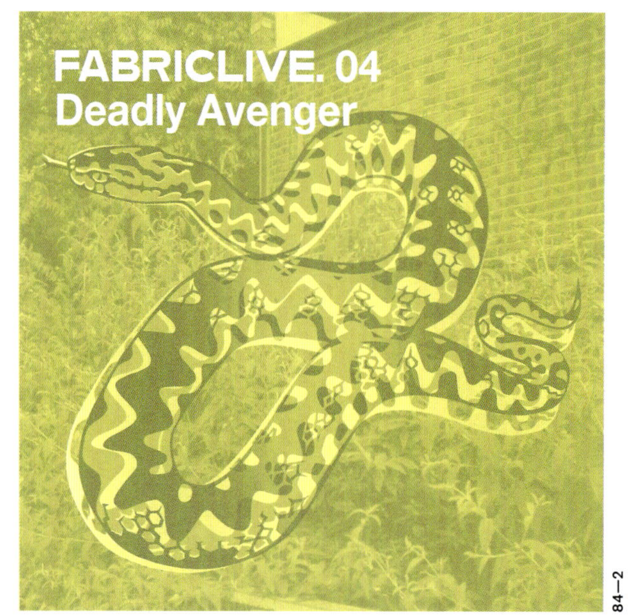

84—2

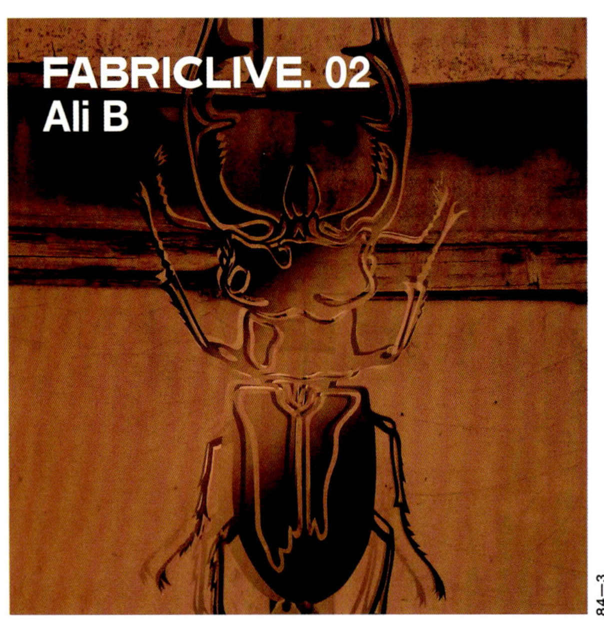

84—3

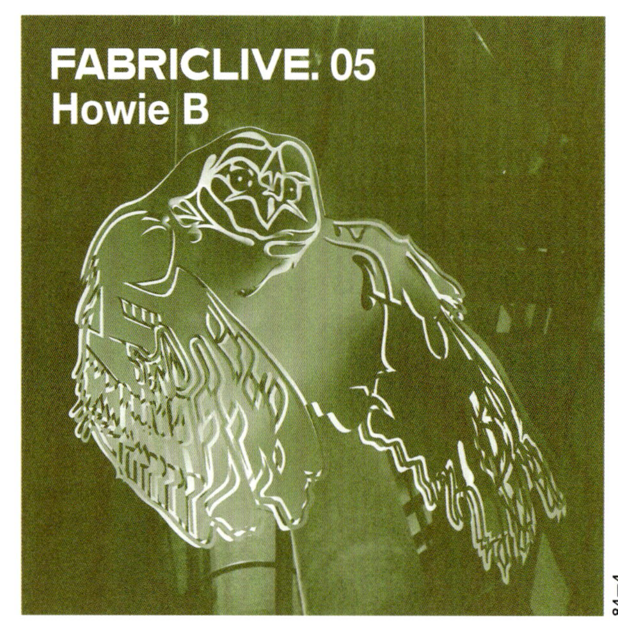

84—4

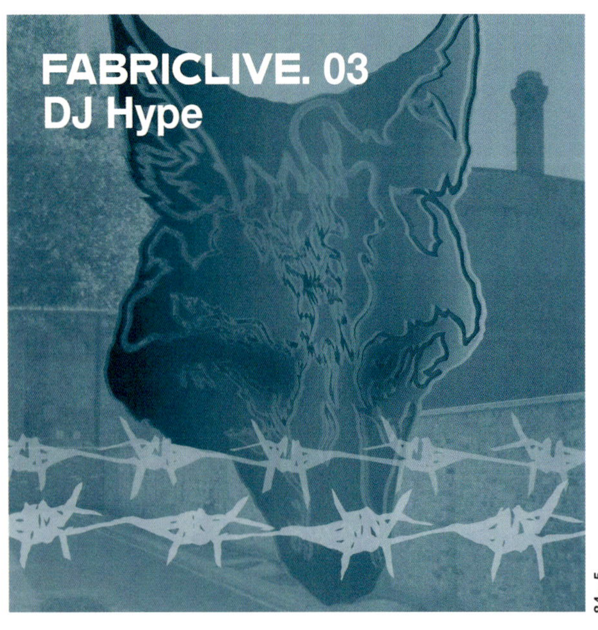

84—5

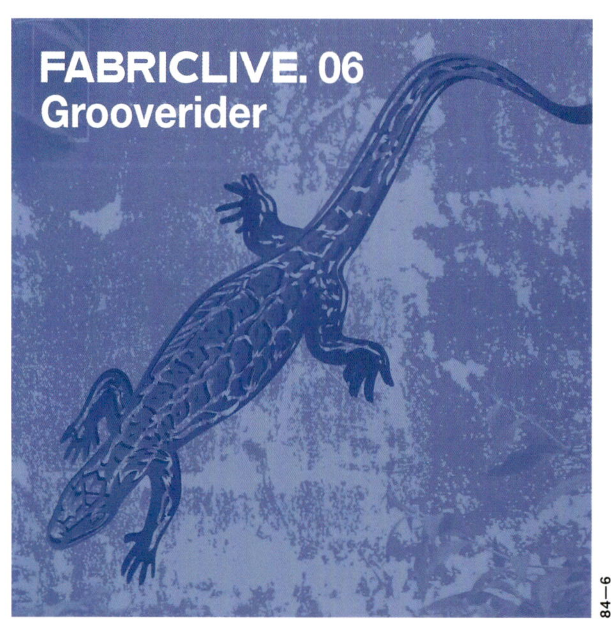

84—6

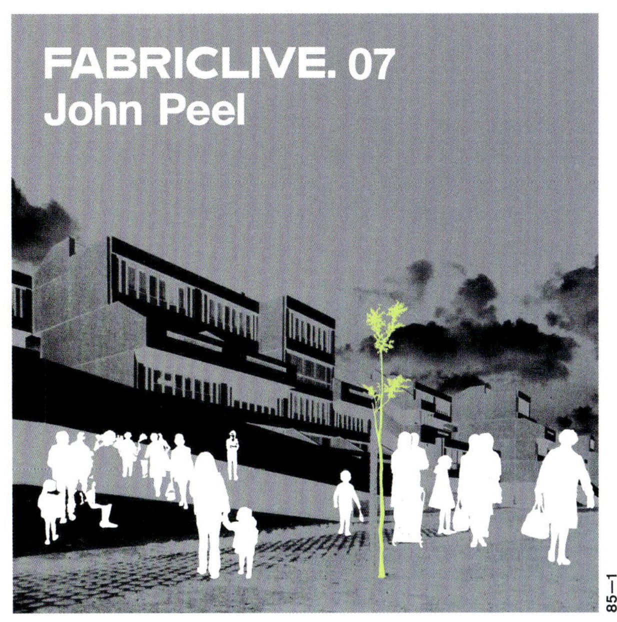

85—1

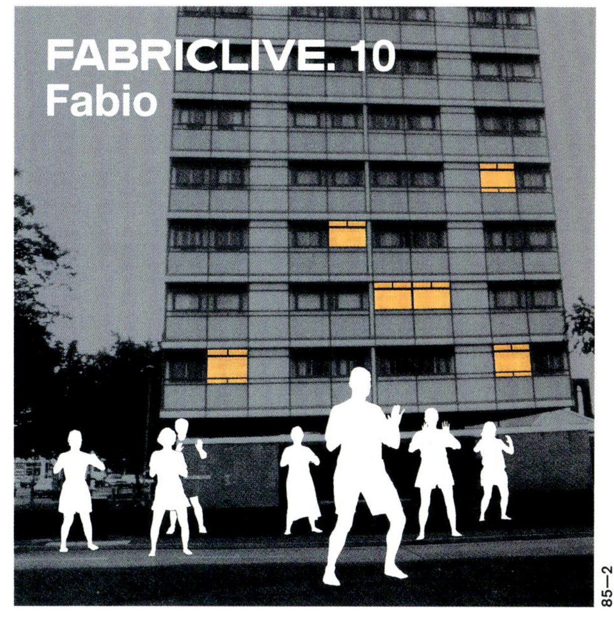

85—2

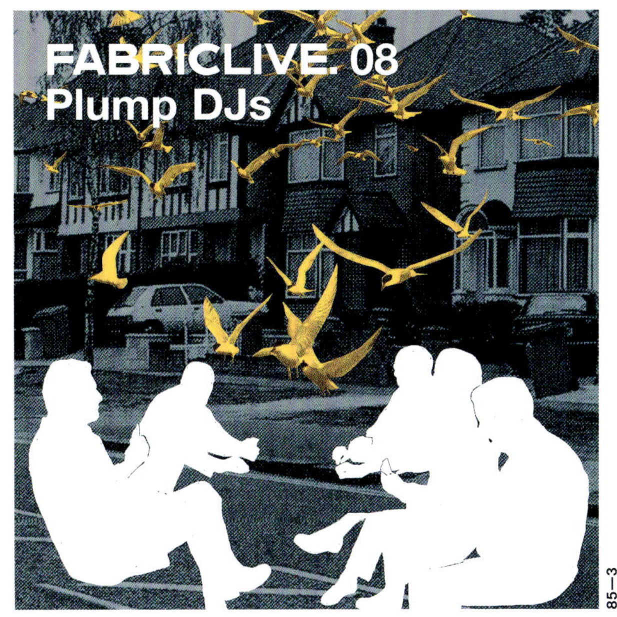

85—3

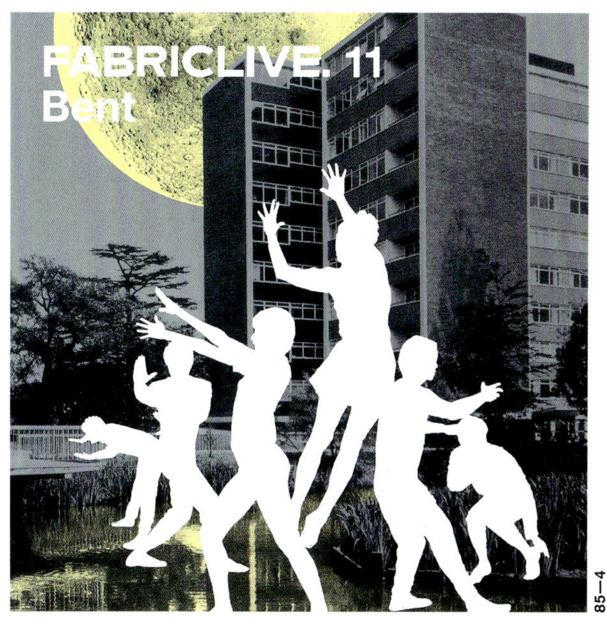

85—4

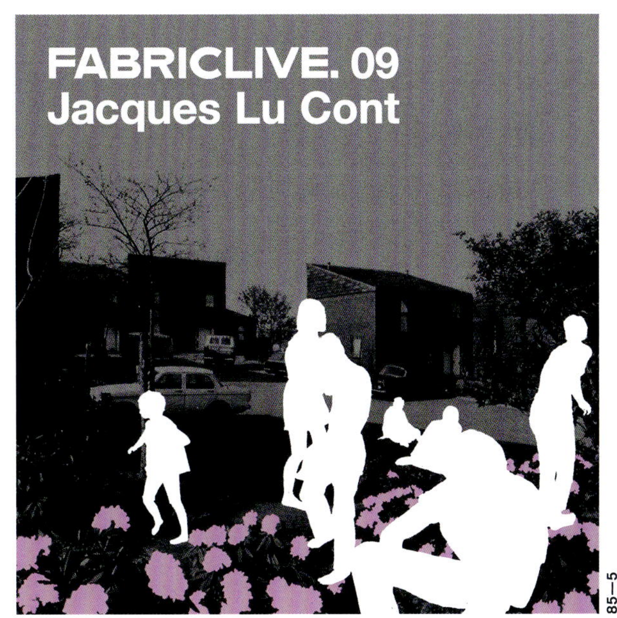

85—5

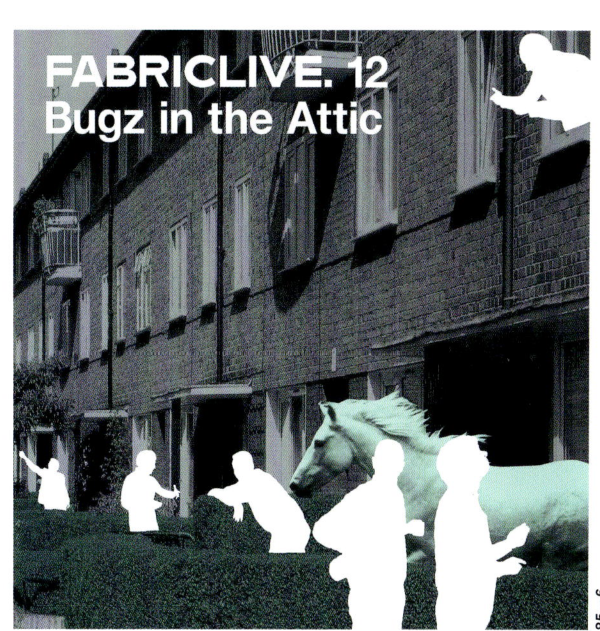

85—6

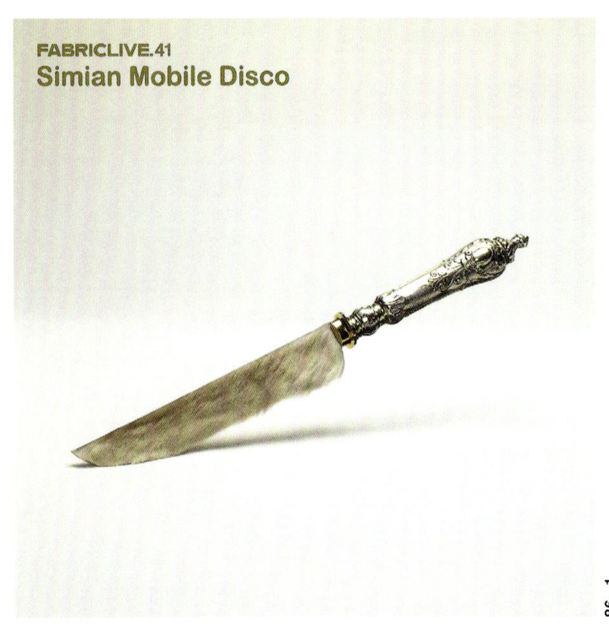

86—1

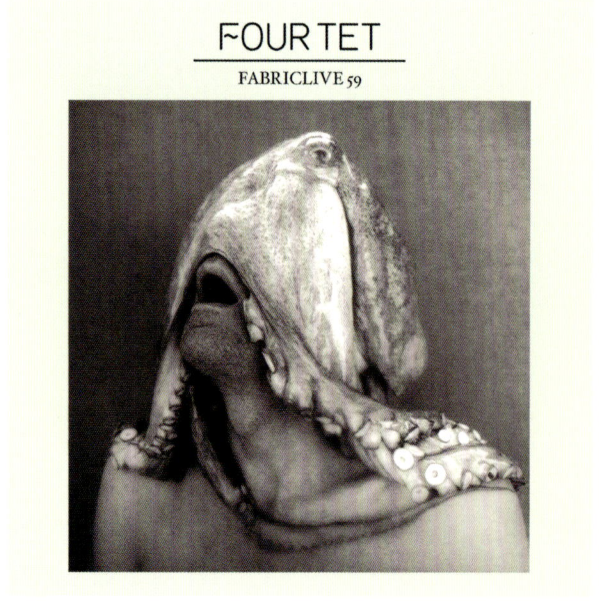

86—2

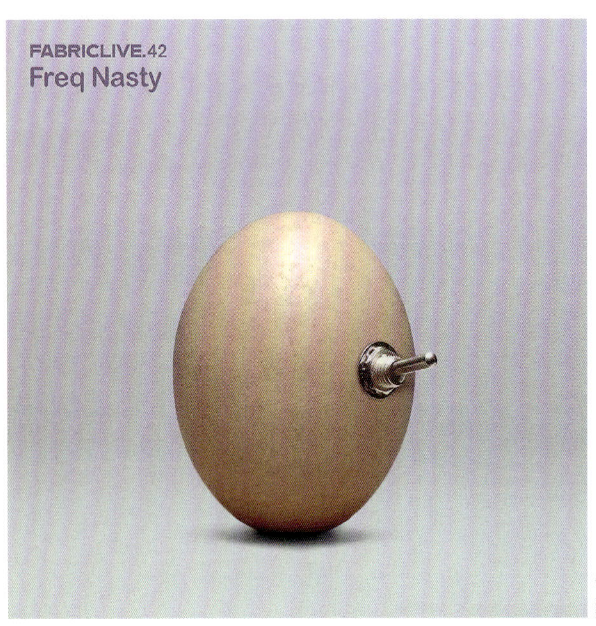

86—3

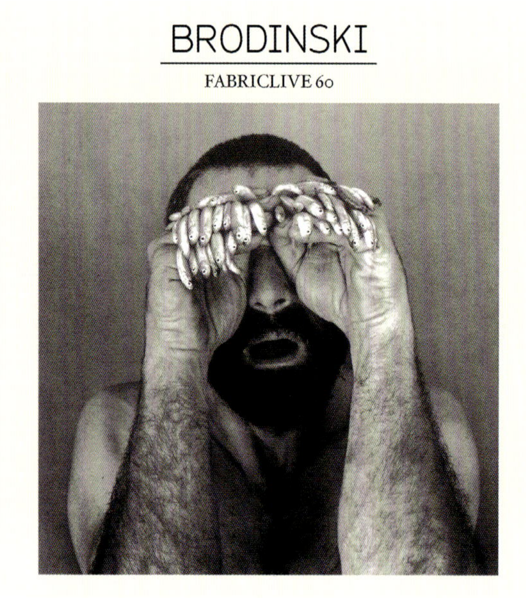

86—4

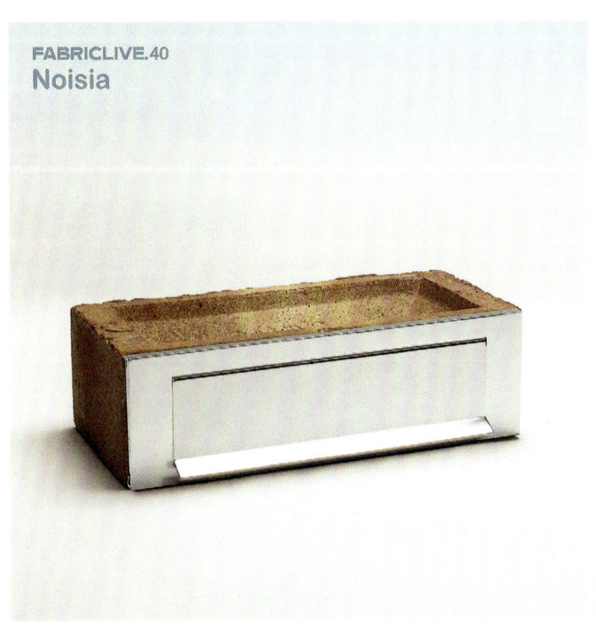

86—5

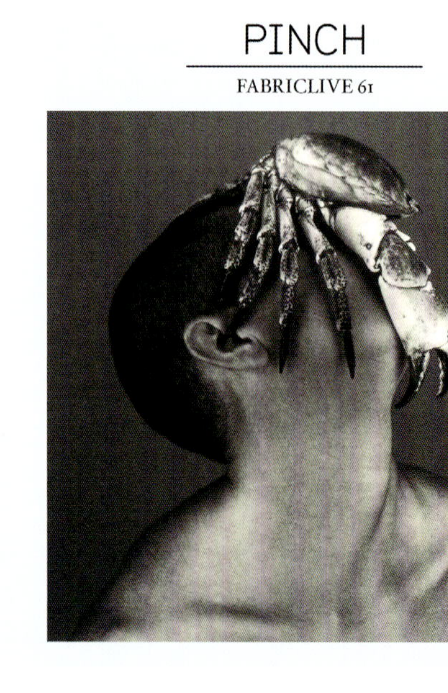

86—6

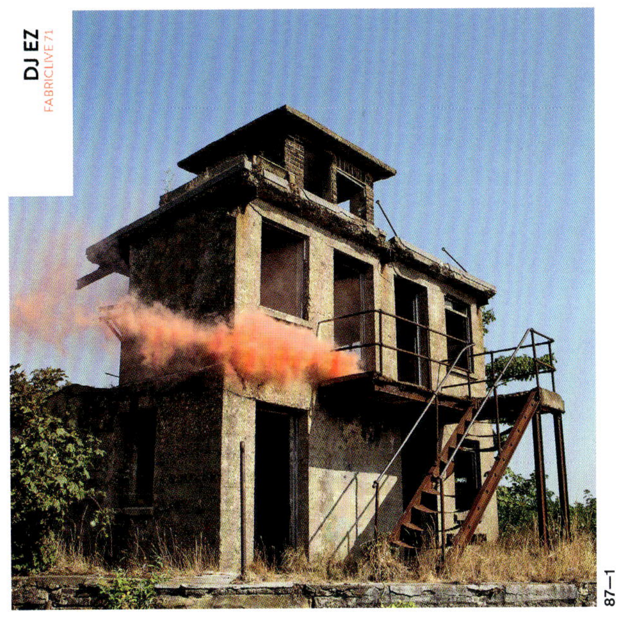

87—1

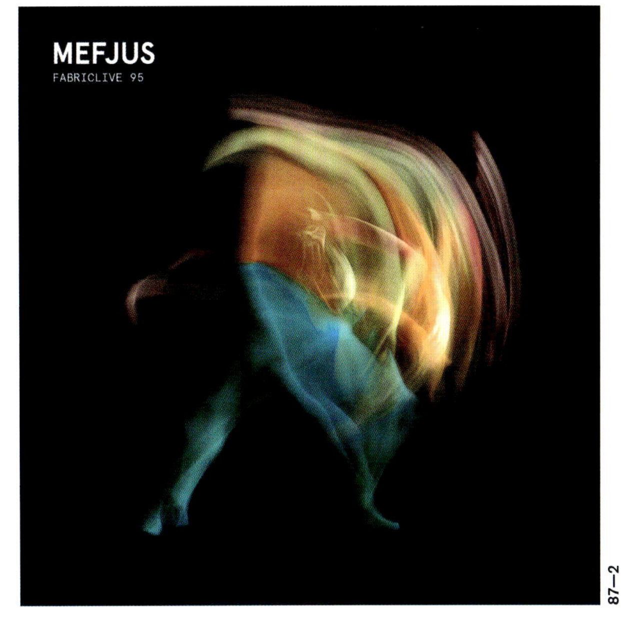

87—2

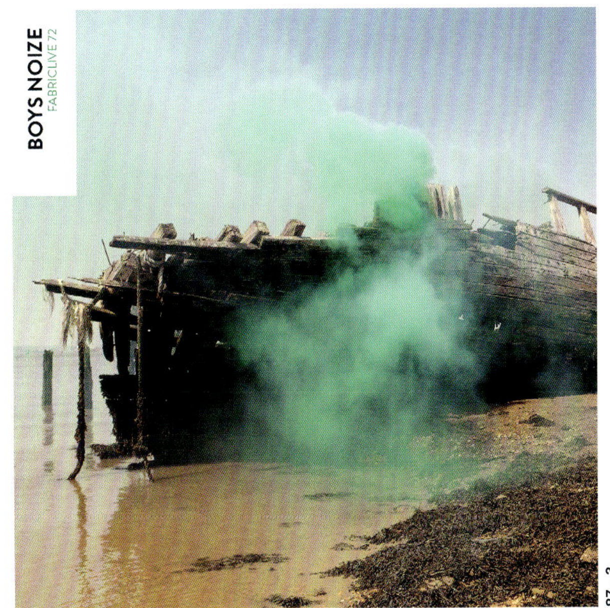

87—3

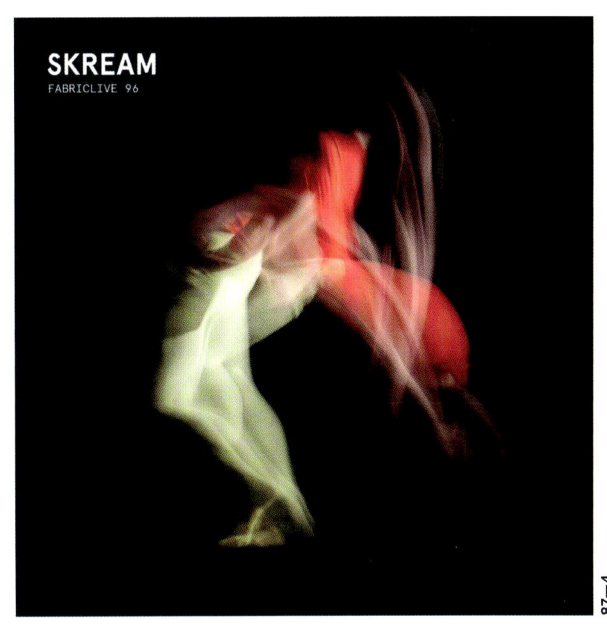

87—4

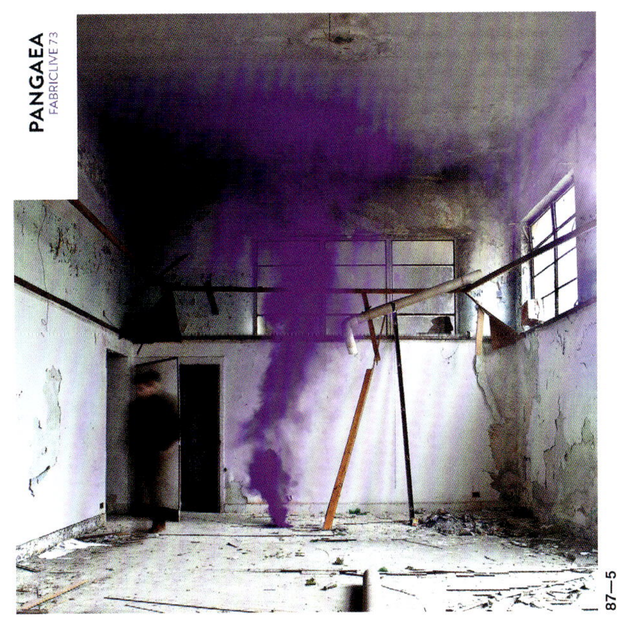

87—5

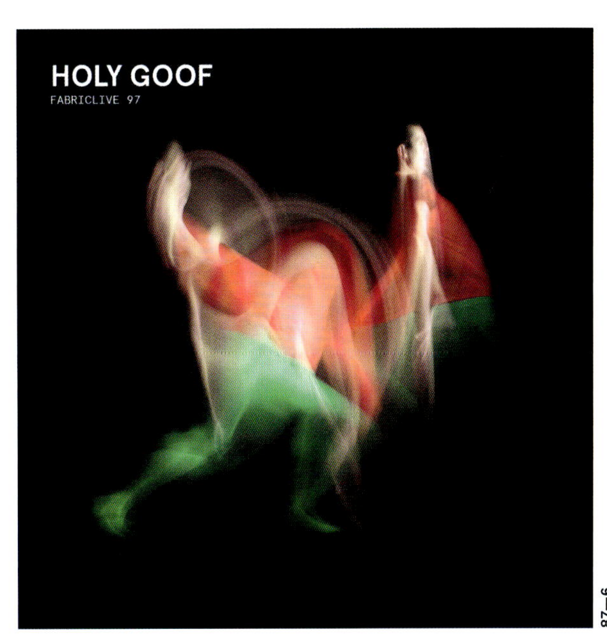

87—6

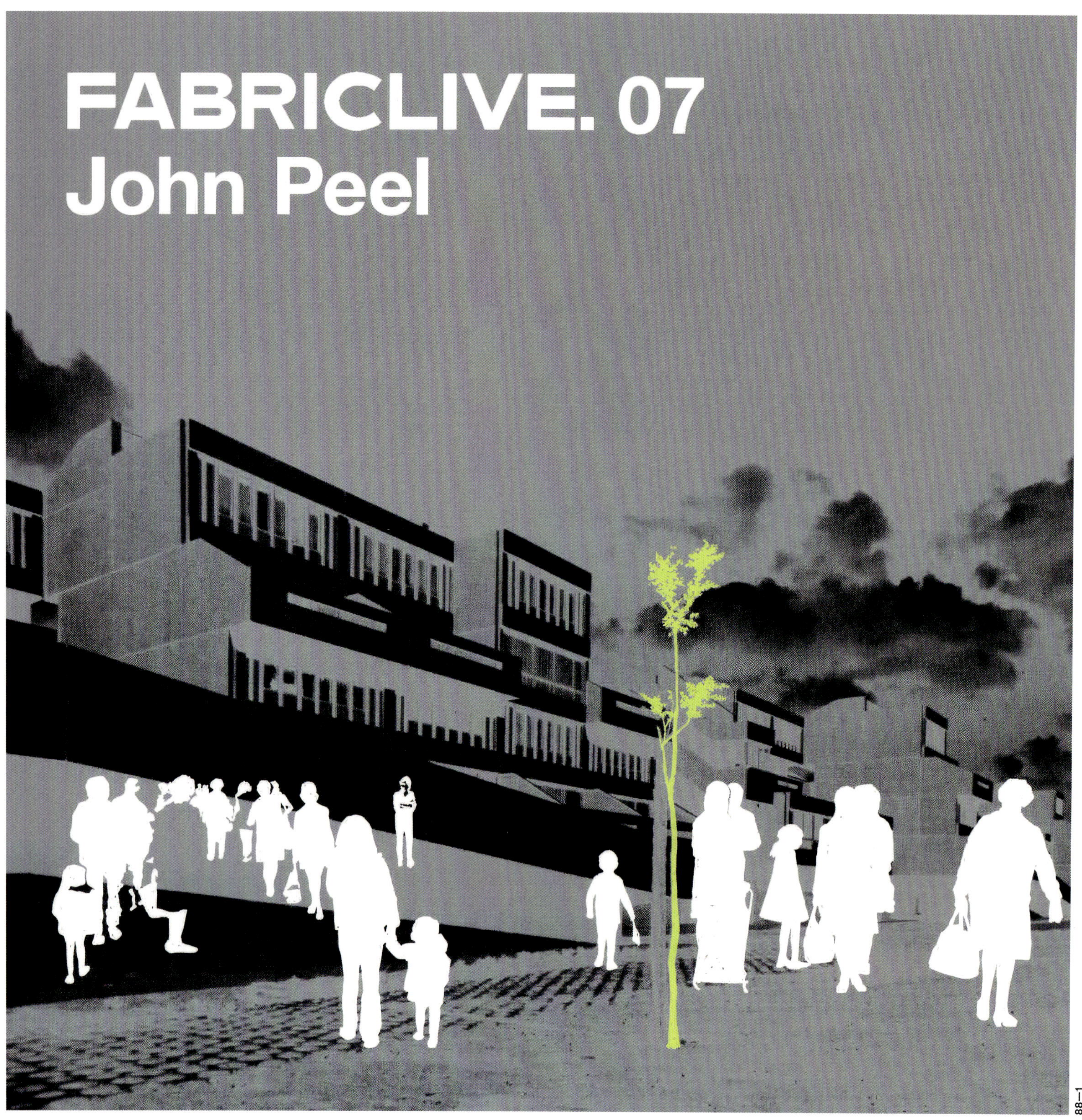

Intro	(01a / 01b)		
01a	Asa-Chang & Junray	Hana (Excerpt)	
01b	Peter Jones	BBC Commentary, 1981 European Cup Final – Liverpool v Real Madrid (Excerpt)	
02	The Soledad Brothers	Break 'Em Down	[Estrus]
03	Don Carlos	Late Night Blues	[Ras]
04	MC Det	Hipsteppin'	[Times Two]
05	The Velvelettes	Needle In A Haystack	[Universal]
06	The Bad Livers	Lust For Life	[Mark Rubin]
07	Trouble Funk	Let's Get Small	[Universal]
08	The Capris	There's A Moon Out Tonight	[Sony]
09	The Fall	Mr. Pharmacist	[Beggars Banquet]
10	Christian Smith & John Selway	15.5 Remake	[Tronic]
11	Jimmy Reed	Too Much	[Charly]
12	Maloko	In The Midnight Hour	[London]
13	Derrick Morgan	Moon Hop	[Rounder]
14	The Datsuns	In Love	[V2]
15	The Kingswoods	Purty Vacant	[Kingswoods]
16	Sinthetix	Liar	[TOV]
17	Culture	Lion Rock (Peel Session)	[Cultural Foundation]
18	Act 1	Tom The Peeper	[Polydor]
19a	Joy Division	Love Will Tear Us Apart	[Factory]
19b	Alan Parry	BBC Commentary, 1978 European Cup Final – Liverpool v FC Bruges (Excerpt)	
20	Elementz Of Noize	Clock	[Emotif]
21	The Cheviot Ranters	Corn Rigs Tunes	[Topic]
22	Marc Smith vs. Safe n' Sound	Identify The Beat	[Bonkers]
23	The Kop Choir	You'll Never Walk Alone	[Cherry Red]
24	The Undertones	Teenage Kicks	[Sanctuary]

fabric 36
RICARDO VILLALOBOS

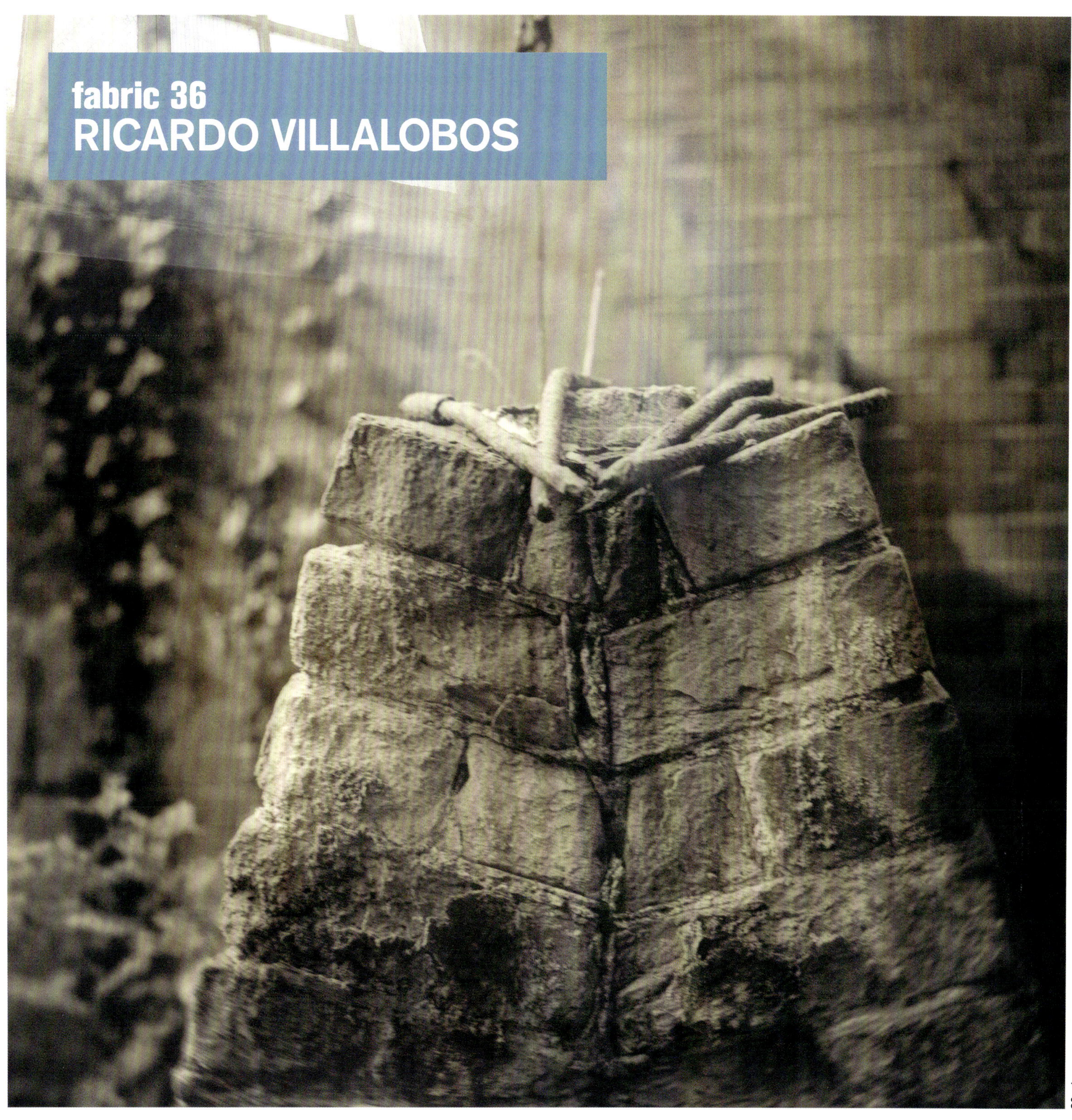

89—1

01	Ricardo Villalobos	Groove 1880	[Unreleased]
02	Ricardo Villalobos	Perc and Drums	[Unreleased]
03	Ricardo Villalobos	Moongomery	[Unreleased]
04	Ricardo Villalobos	Farenzer House	[Unreleased]
05	Ricardo Villalobos & Patrick Ense	M.Bassy	[Unreleased]
06	Ricardo Villalobos	Mecker	[Unreleased]
07	Ricardo Villalobos & Jorge Gonzales	4 Wheel Drive	[Unreleased]
08	Ricardo Villalobos & Patrick Ense	Fizpatrick	[Unreleased]
09	Ricardo Villalobos & Andrew Gillings	Andruic & Japan	[Unreleased]
10	Ricardo Villalobos	Organic Tranceplant	[Unreleased]
11	Ricardo Villalobos	Prevorent	[Unreleased]
12	Ricardo Villalobos & Fumiya Tanaka	Fumiyandric 2	[Unreleased]
13	Ricardo Villalobos	Won't You Tell Me	[Unreleased]
14	Ricardo Villalobos	Primer Encuentro Latino-Americano	[Unreleased]
15	Ricardo Villalobos	Chropuspel zündung	[Unreleased]

fabric19 andrew weatherall

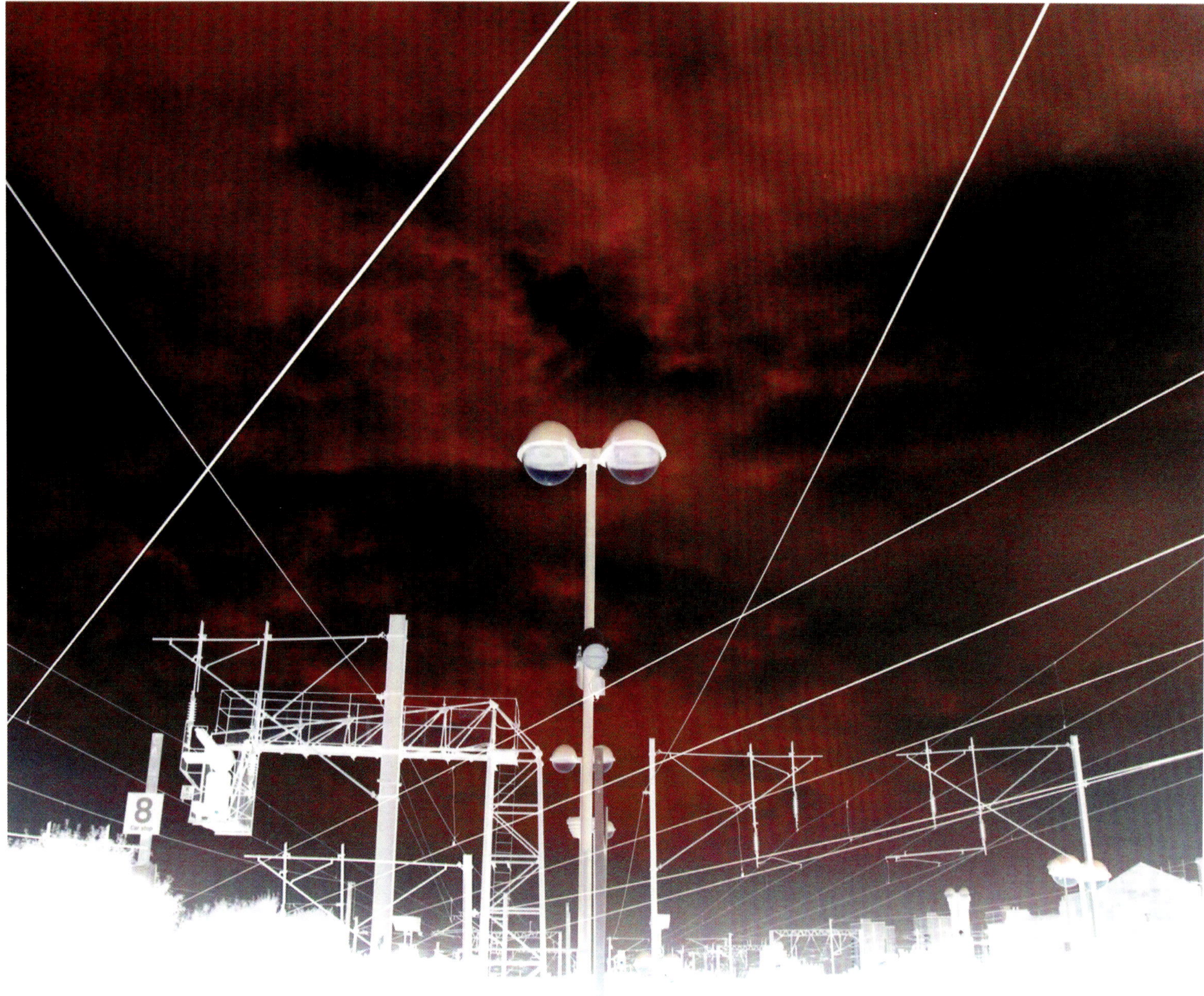

90—1

01	Sexual Harassment	I Need a Freak	[Montage Records]
02	Egyptian Lover	Freak-A-Holic	[Egyptian Empire]
03	Kango's Stein Massive	M/S Langåra (Syntax Erik Mix)	[Trailerpark Recordings]
04	DJ T.	Time Out (Acid Dub)	[Get Physical Music]
05	Alexkid	Don't Hide It (Alexkid's Vocal)	[F Communications]
06	Tomboy	She Hit My Head	[Gomma]
07	Delon And Dalcan	Dunufus	[Boxer Recordings]
08	Marc Romboy Vs. Booka Shade	Everyday Of My Life (Martin Landsky Remix)	[Systematic]
09	Jesper Dahlbäck	Robot Dance	[DK Recordings]
10	Steve Bug	That Kid (Hate Mix)	[Poker Flat Recordings]
11	Metope	Second Skin	[Sender Records]
12	Miwon	Brother Mole (John Tejada Remix)	[City Centre Offices]
13	Black Devil	Timing, Forget The Timing (Kerrier District Mix)	[Rephlex]
14	The Emperor Machine	Bloody Hell	[DC Recordings]
15	Ricardo Villalobos	Dexter (2 Lone Swordsmen Remix)	[Playhouse]
16	Technova	Atmosphere	[Hydrogen Dukebox]

FOUR TET

FABRICLIVE 59

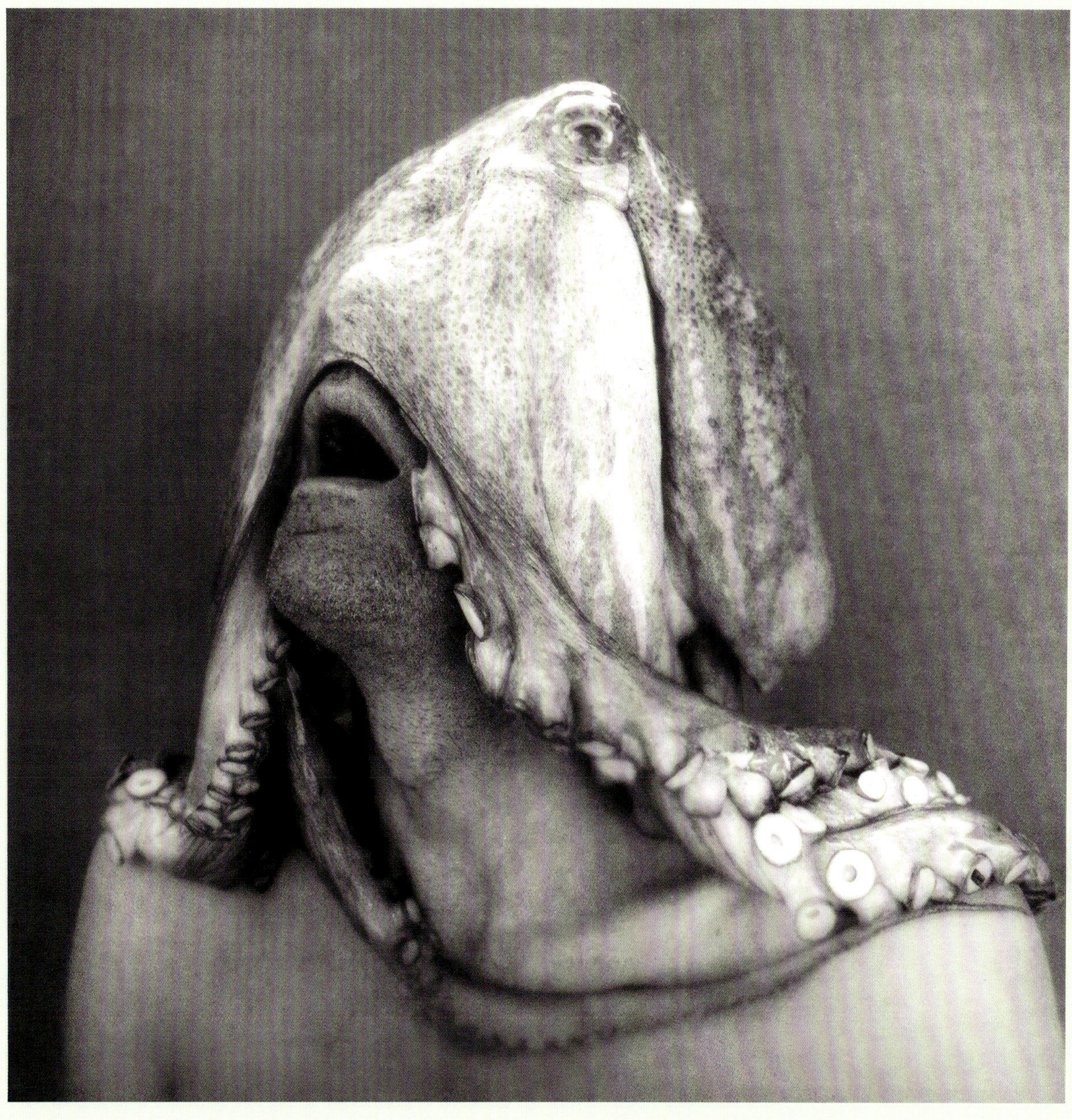

91—1

01	Intro		
02	Michel Redolfi	Immersion Partielle	[GRM]
03	Crazy Bald Heads	First Born	[On-Tick]
04	Persian	Feel Da Vibe	[Same People]
05	KH	101112	[unreleased]
06	Youngstar (Musical Mob)	Pulse X	[Inspired Sounds]
07	Crazy Bald Heads	First Born (Four Tet Remix)	[unreleased]
08	Floating Points	Sais (Dub)	[Eglo]
09	Apple	Mr Bean	[Appsolute]
10	Caribou	Webers	[The Leaf Label]
11	Big Bird	Flav (Urban Myths Remix)	[Nice n Ripe]
12	Genius	Waiting	[Kronik]
13	Four Tet	fabric	[unreleased]
14	David Borden	The Continuing Story Of Counterpoint, Part Nine	[David Borden]
15	STL	Dark Energy	[Something]
16	Percussions	Percussions One	[unreleased]
17	C++	Angie's Fucked	[Music For Freaks]
18	Burial	Street Halo	[Hyperdub]
19	KMA	Cape Fear	[KMA]
20	WK7	Higher Power	[Power House]
21	Ricardo Villalobos	Sieso	[Cadenza]
22	Four Tet	Pyramid	[Text]
23	Red Rack'em	How I Program	[Bergerac]
24	Active Minds	Hobson's Choice (Tune For Da Man Dem)	[white]
25	Armando Gallop & Steve Poindexter	Blackholes	[Muzique]
26	Outro		
27	Four Tet	Locked	[Text]

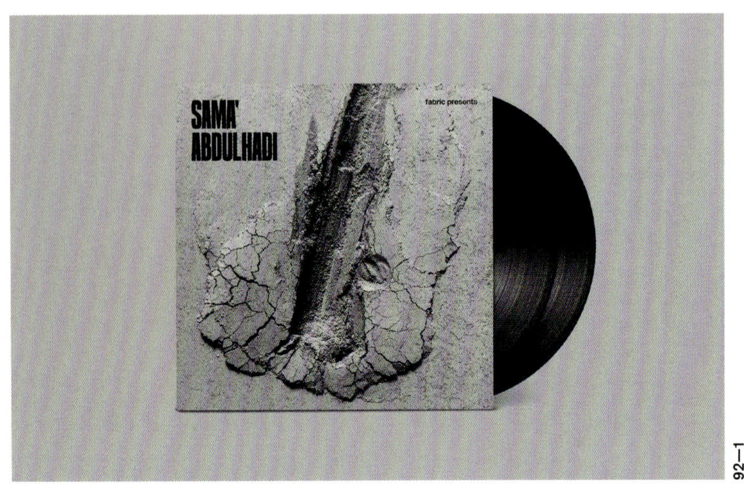

92—1

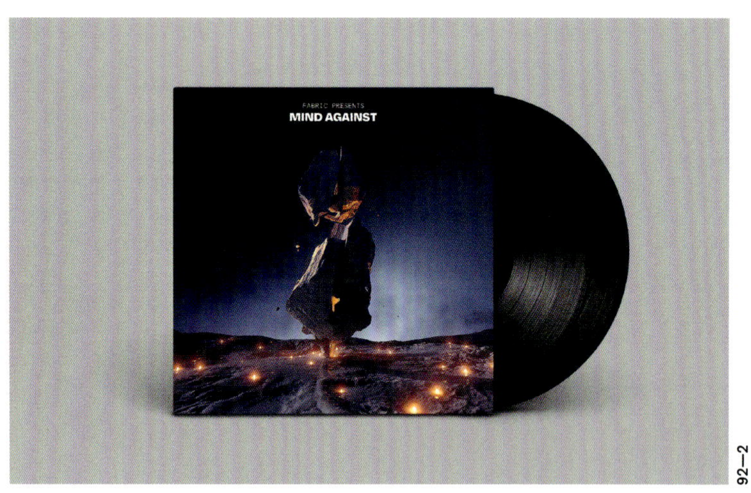

92—2

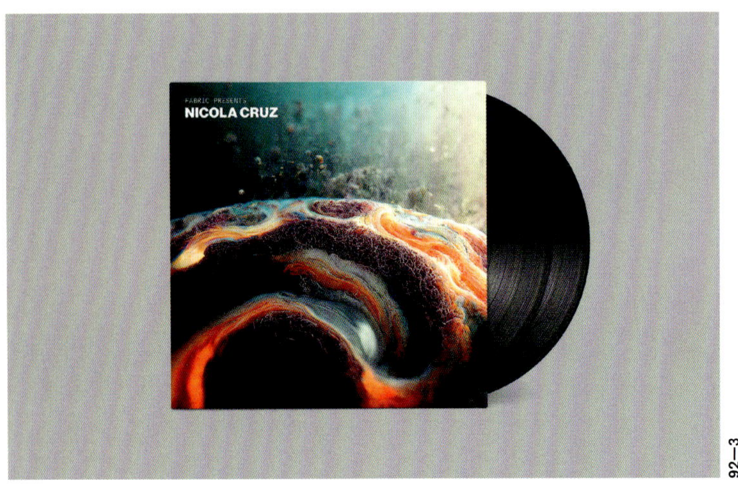

92—3

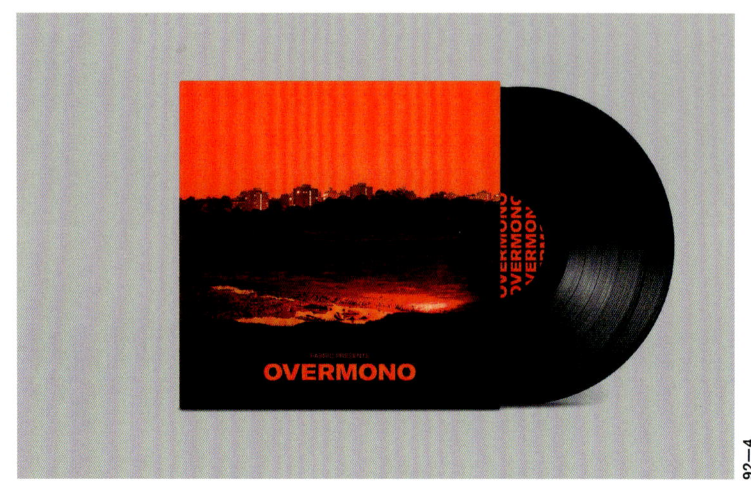

92—4

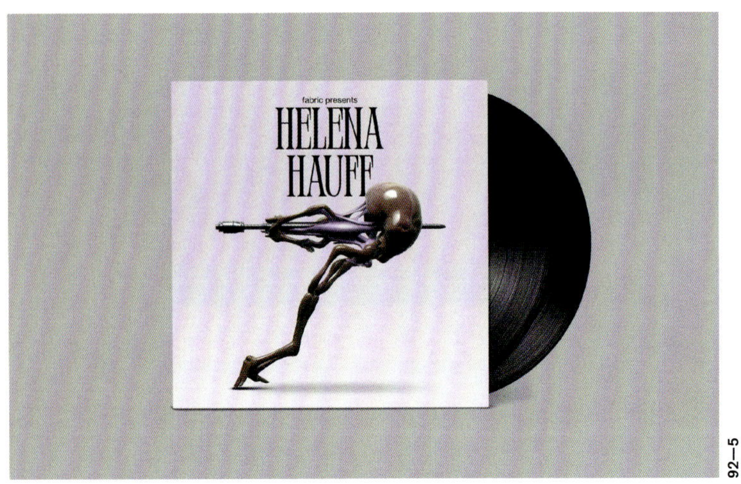

92—5

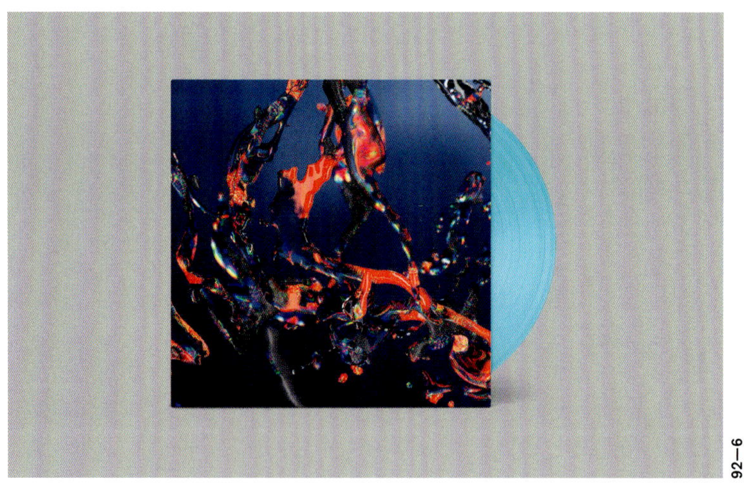
92—6

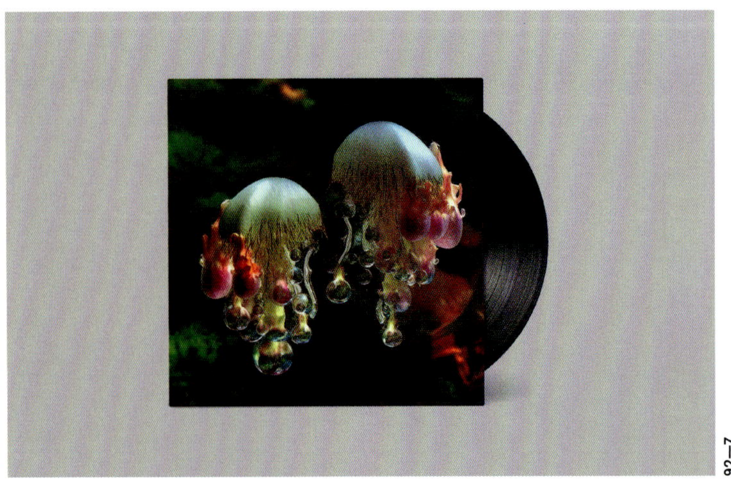
92—7

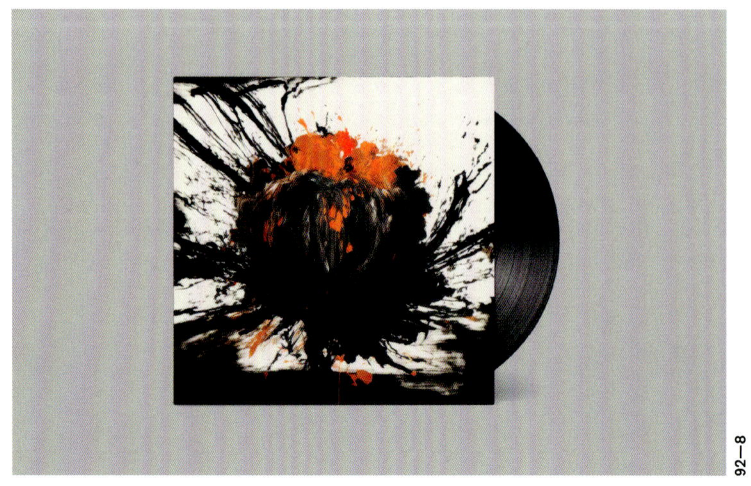
92—8

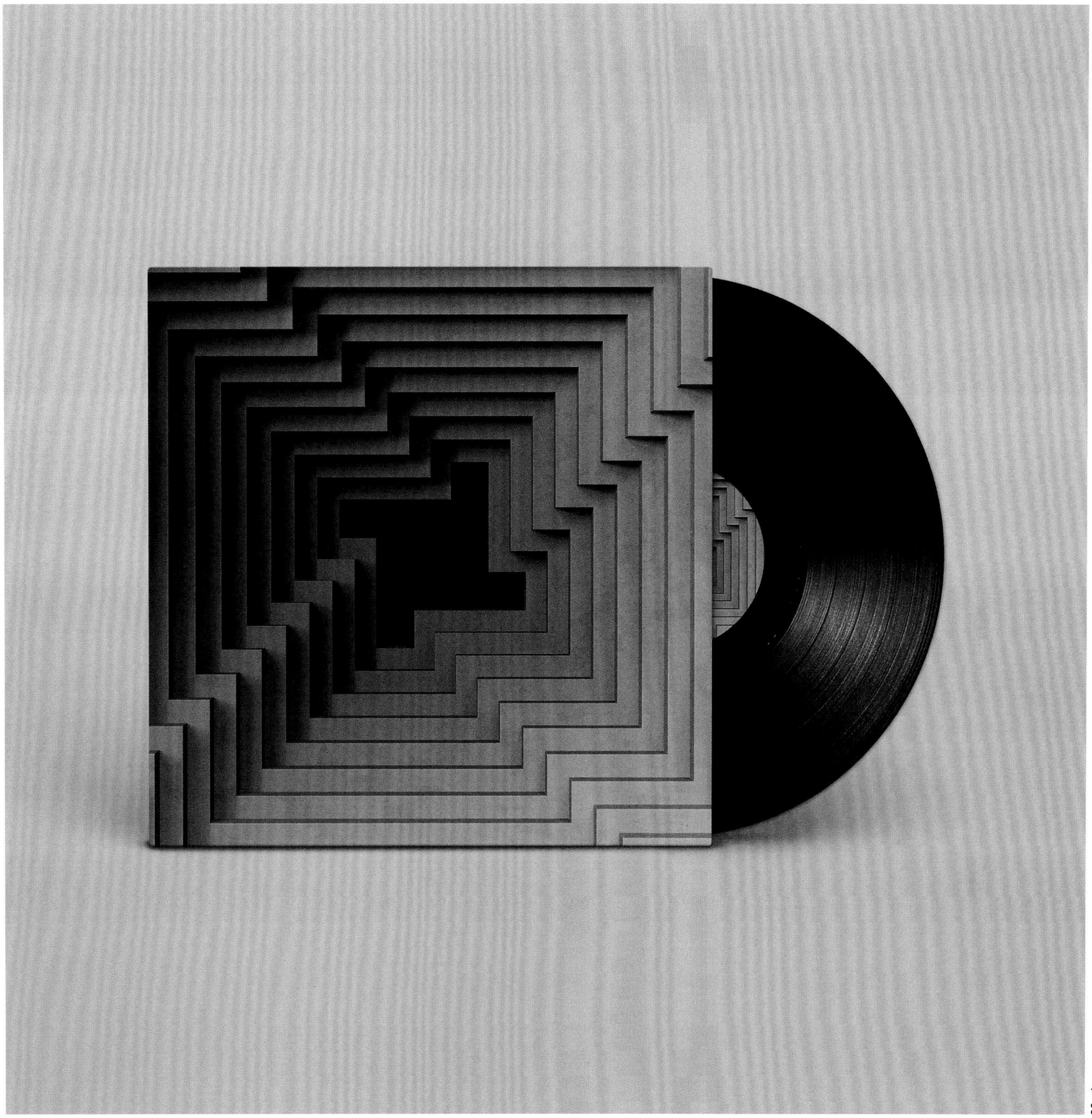

93—1

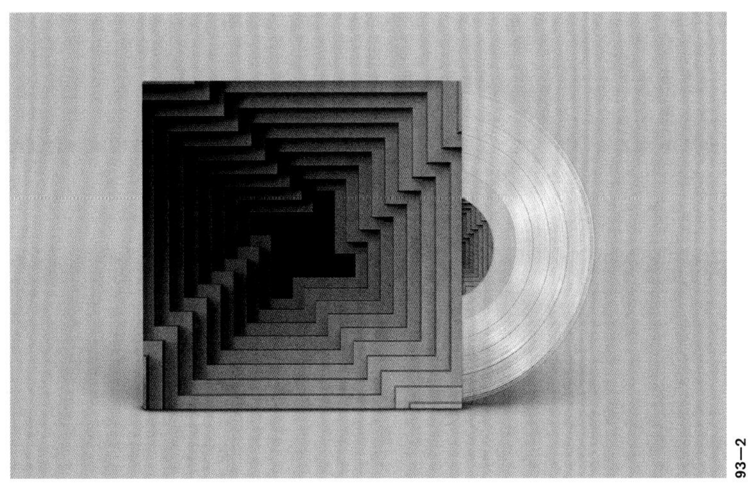

93—2

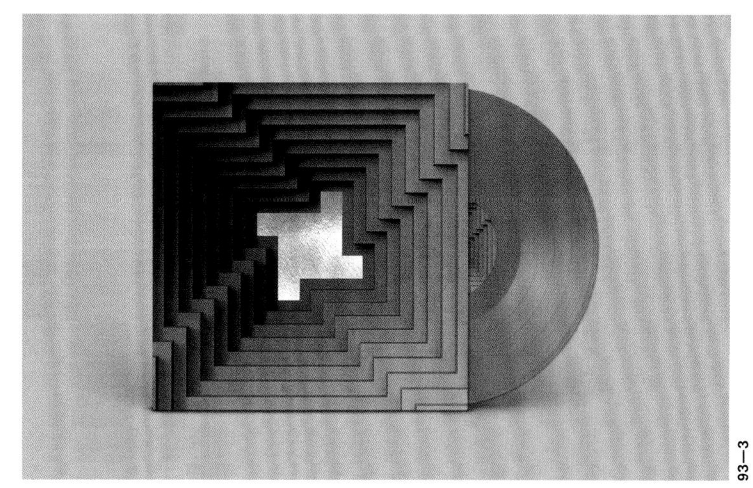

93—3

birthdays

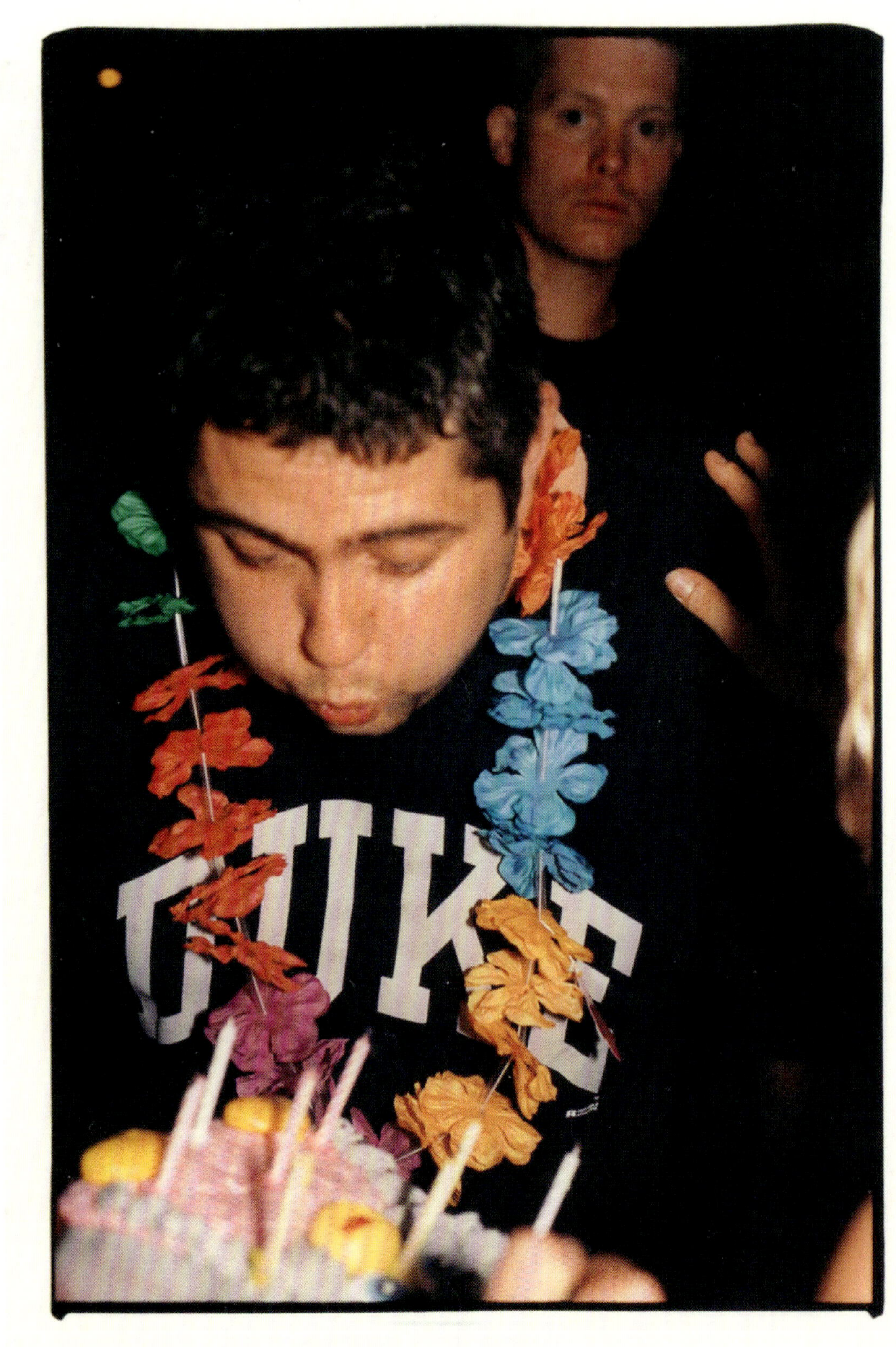

96—1

fabric has always been a party above all else. That's precisely what's kept it alive all these years; where other institutions have focused on spectacle, commerce or fashionability, fabric remained at heart about people socialising, having fun and cutting loose, whether that be the customers or the members of the wonky family that keep the place running. So celebrating that – throwing a party for the party, so to speak – presents a special challenge: when you're in the business of revelry every week of the year, what can you do on your birthday?

The answer is pretty simple: MORE. From the very beginning, fabric's birthdays were the stuff of legend, and they have snowballed over the years to become important not just for the venue, not just for London, but as much a part of the global club music calendar for those who know as huge events like Glastonbury, Burning Man or Miami Winter Music Conference.

As with all things fabric, it started with a simple brainwave. When the club opened, there was a policy of no fancy dress. This was partly down to Keith Reilly's dislike of the then-dominant 'glam house' superclub culture, where sequinned cowboy hats and fluffy bras were the name of the game, and partly to deter hen parties and other unserious clubbers. fabric was about dressing down to get down, and that was part of what gave it its identity as the home of the underground. But, as Cameron Leslie puts it, 'We decided the birthday was time to allow a bit of silliness,' so the team put together the mother of all dress-up boxes.

The first birthday party in 2000 carried on until 2 p.m., and was instantly the stuff of legend. The following year's went right through twenty-four hours, only stopping so the club could reopen for DTPM on Sunday night. From 2009 – the tenth birthday, with a dream line-up including Ricardo Villalobos, Andrew Weatherall, Ivan Smagghe, Craig and Terry among others, all playing in endless solo and back-to-back iterations – Saturday 'nights' on the celebration weekend started to stretch to thirty hours, absorbing the Sunday session and going through into Monday morning, and then eventually to a full thirty-six hours.

This became a playground for the music to spread out and sprawl, for fabric's residents and their friends to really paint on a broad canvas and explore the full range of moods. It was where the likes of Villalobos and Weatherall – and later Ben UFO, Seth Troxler, Nina Kraviz or Joy O – plus, of course, Craig and Terry could play sets that sprawled through day and night. Looking back over line-ups now, you can see the concentrated essence of fabric as breaks, electro, dubstep and minimal all make their way into the line-ups, and techno and drum'n'bass keep pulsing through the years.

This, too, was where fabric's ability to have people come and go at any time of day or night was pioneered – the 'pilgrimage' that Bradley Zero describes to see Villalobos play on a Sunday morning (and then for the rest of the day) is not unusual – and set the pace for fabric to increasingly stagger entry, more in the Berlin style of clubbing. But most of all, it was still the party to end all parties – still as deadly serious about good music as ever, perhaps even more so, but completely cut loose, a time to drink, dress up and act the fool.

The closures in October 2016 and during the Covid lockdown have only made this yearly bacchanal more important and fabric's loyal dancers more eager for the next – and its place in the global calendar has only helped to cement the sense that fabric is in it for the long haul. Living for the moment can, paradoxically, build foundations for the future, it turns out.

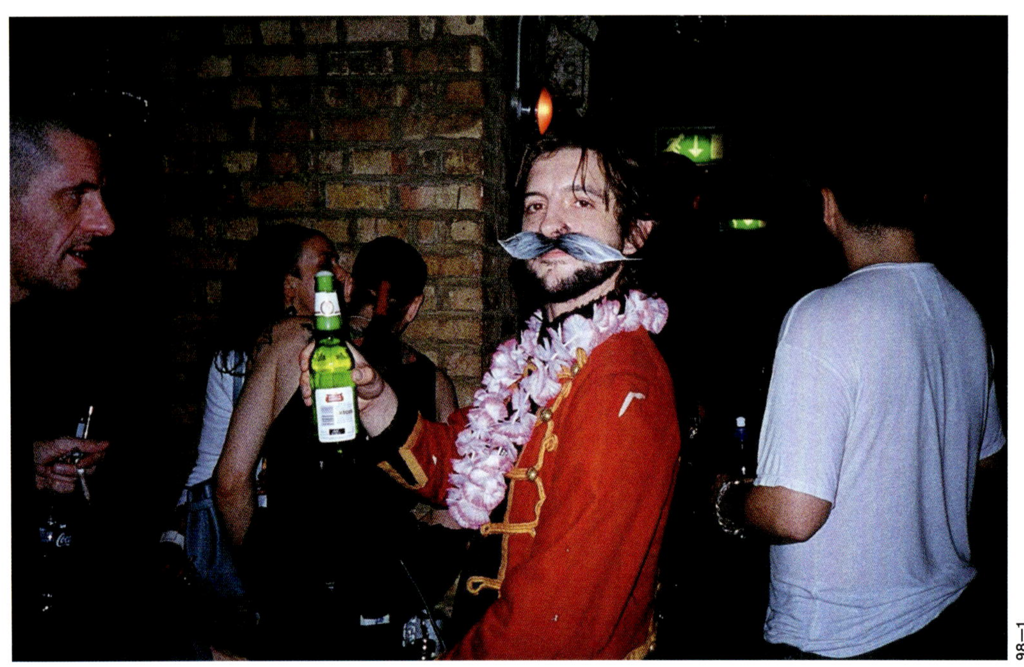

98—1

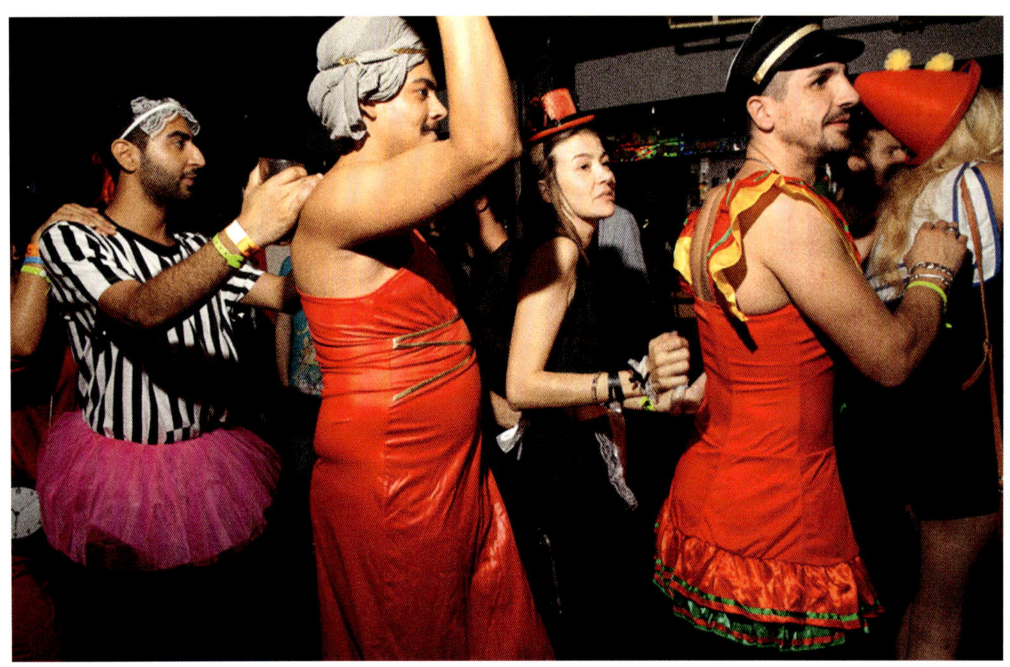

98—2

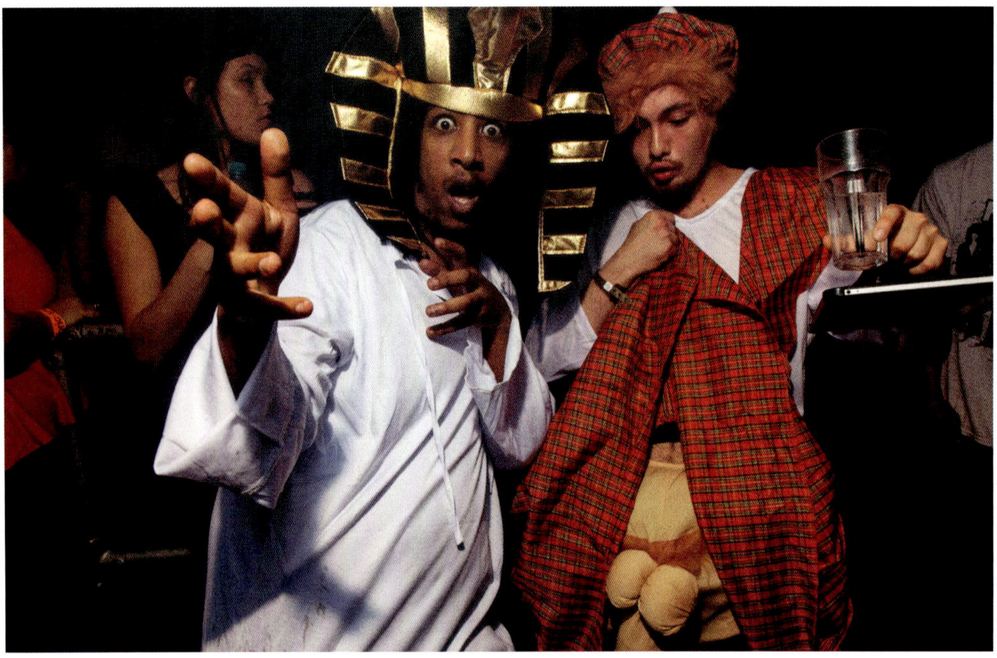

98—3

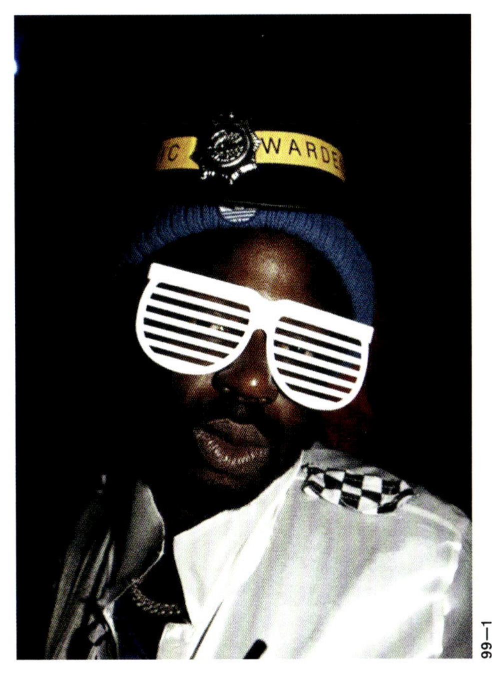

99—1

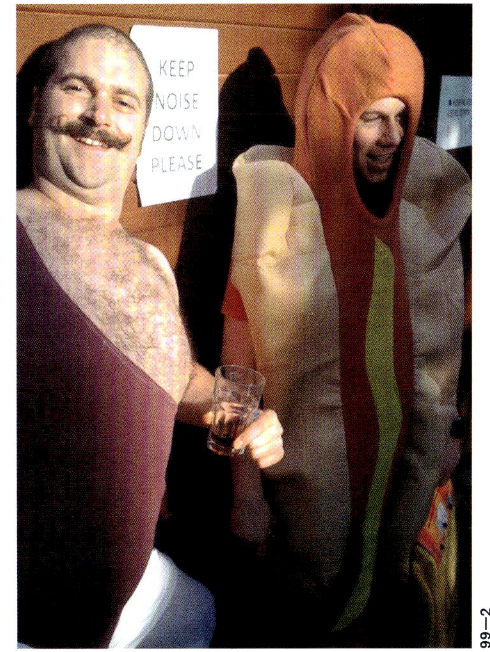

99—2

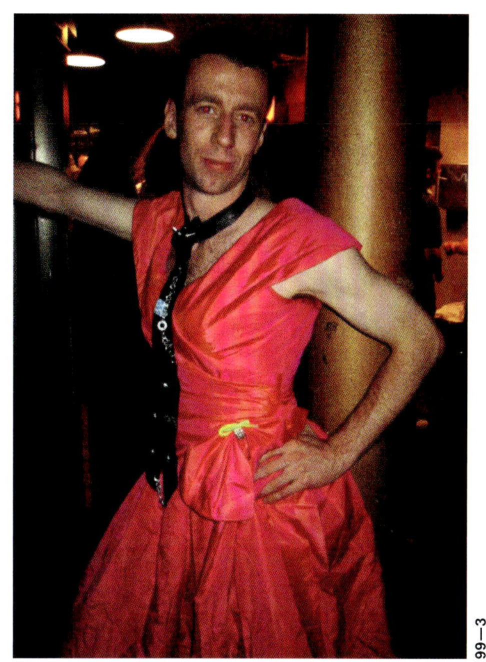
99—3

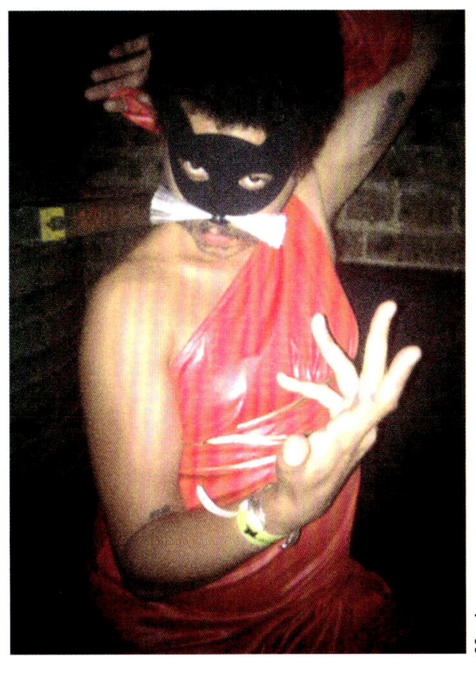
99—4

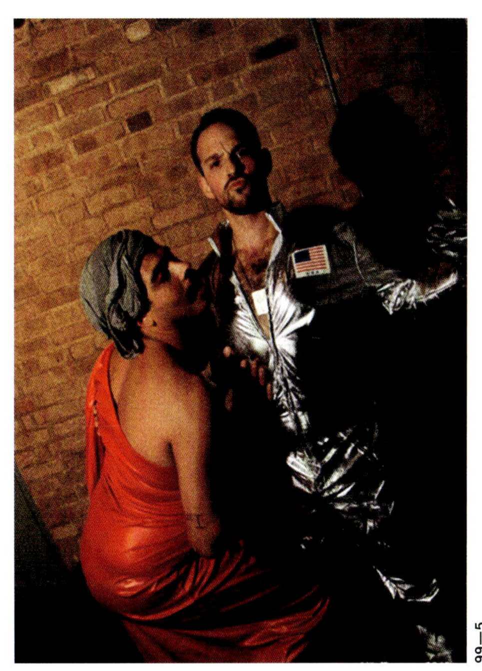
99—5

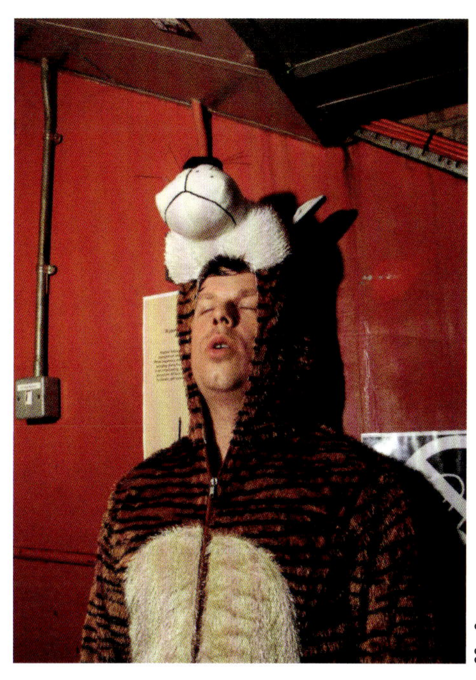
99—6

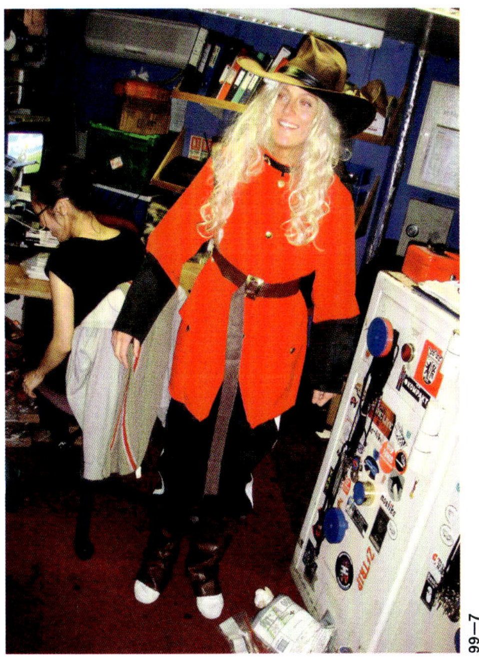
99—7

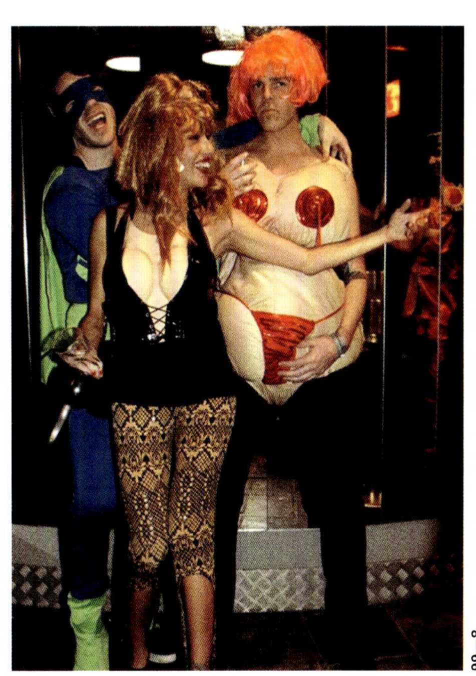
99—8

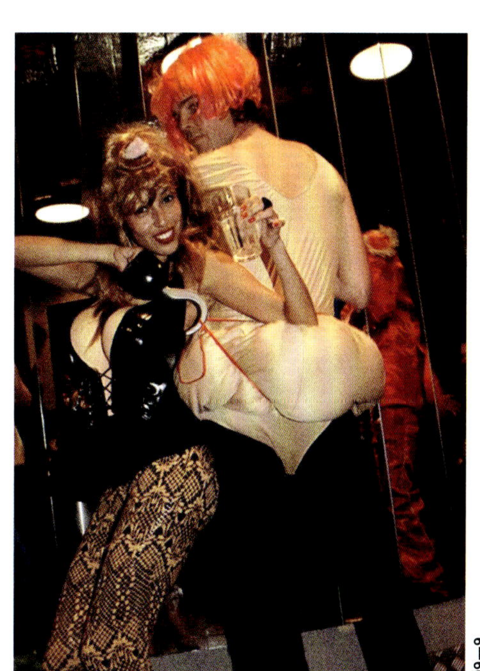
99—9

TEN YEARS OF FABRIC
1
10.30-1 HIPP-E & HALO
1-3.30 MICHAEL MAYER
3.30-6 ANDREW WEATHERALL
6-7 MATHEW JONSON (live)
7-10 CRAIG RICHARDS
10-1 RICARDO VILLALOBOS
1-3 DOC MARTIN
3-5 TERRY FRANCIS
5-6.45 IVAN SMAGGHE
6.45-7.45 IVAN SMAGGHE b2b CRAIG RICHARDS
7.45-10.15 STEVE BUG
10.15-11.15 DANIEL BELL (live)
11.15-1.15 RICARDO VILLALOBOS
1.15-3 CRAIG RICHARDS b2b RICARDO VILLALOBOS
3-4 TERRY FRANCIS
4-5 CRAIG RICHARDS
2

100—1

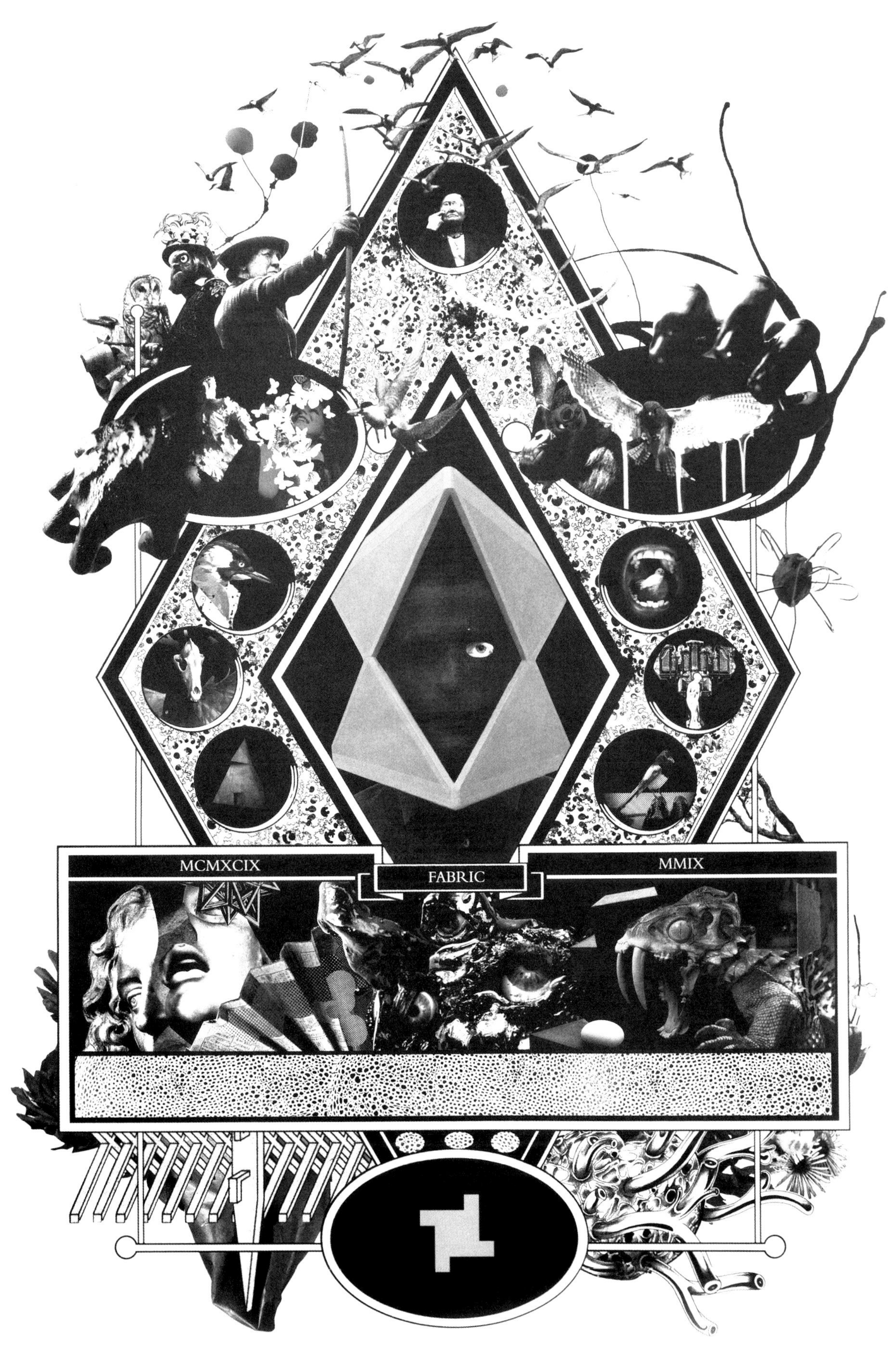

101—1

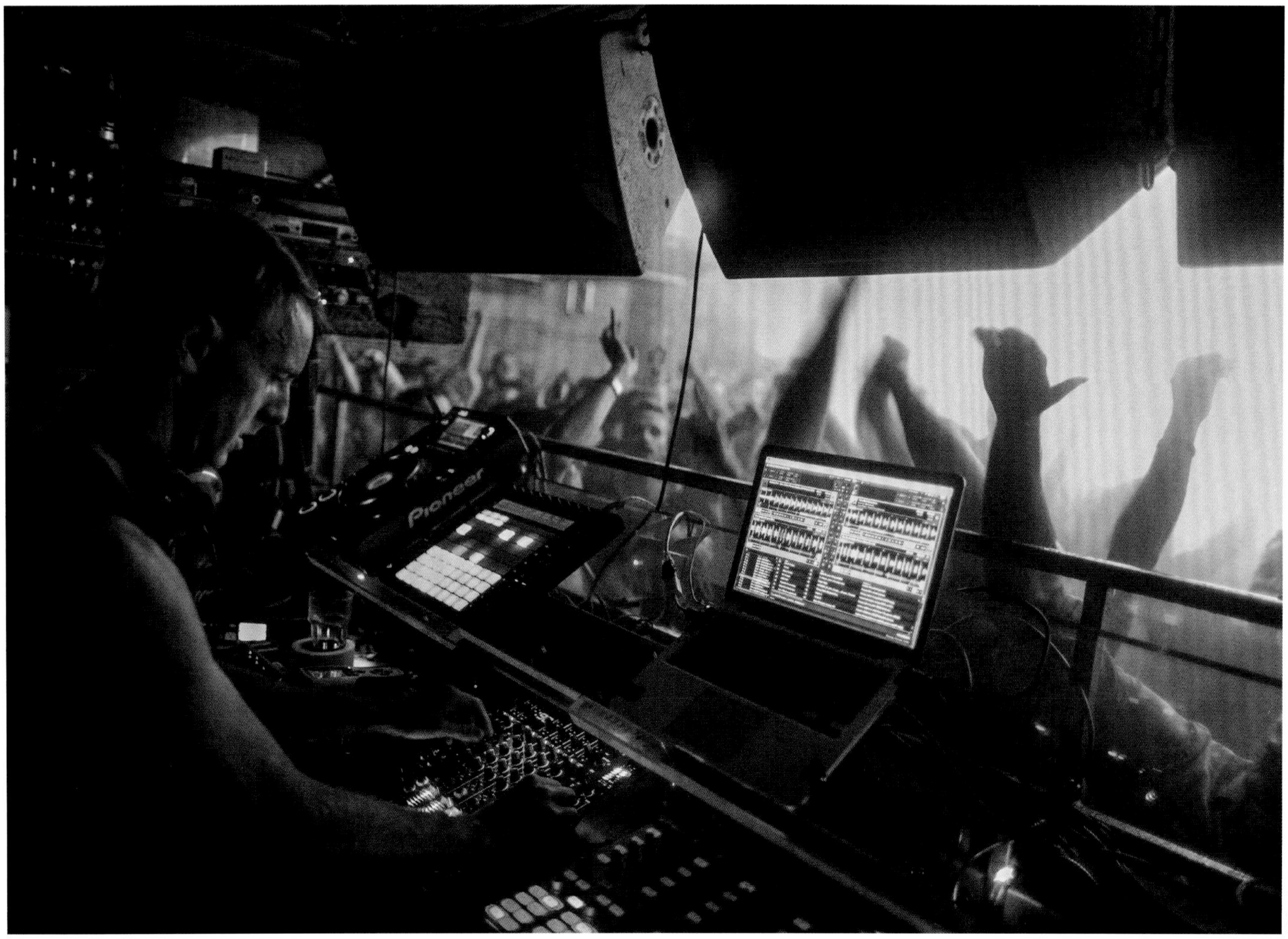

102—1

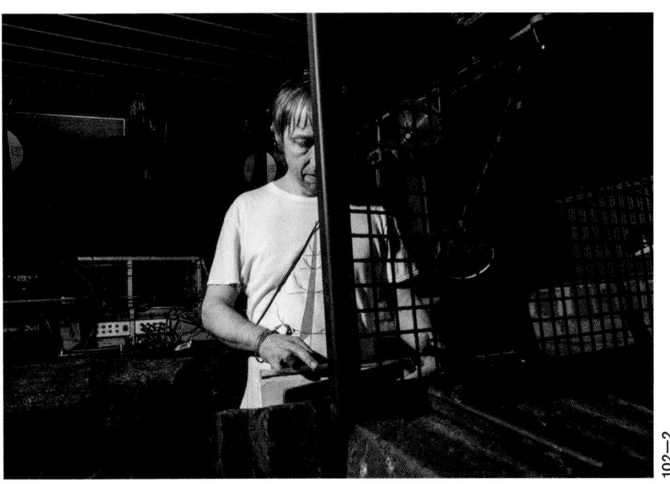

102—2

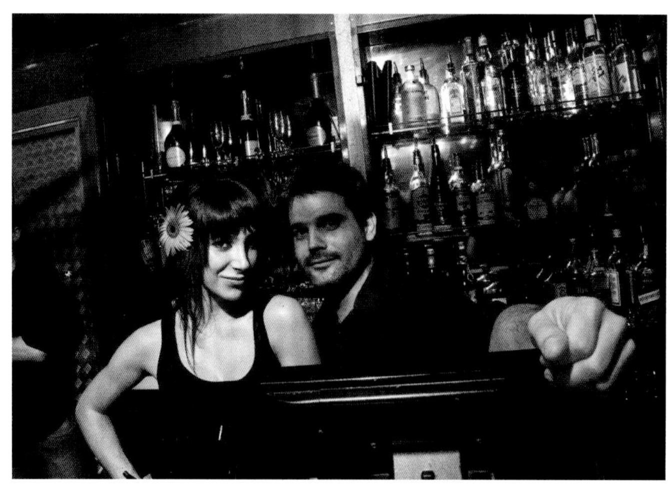

102—3

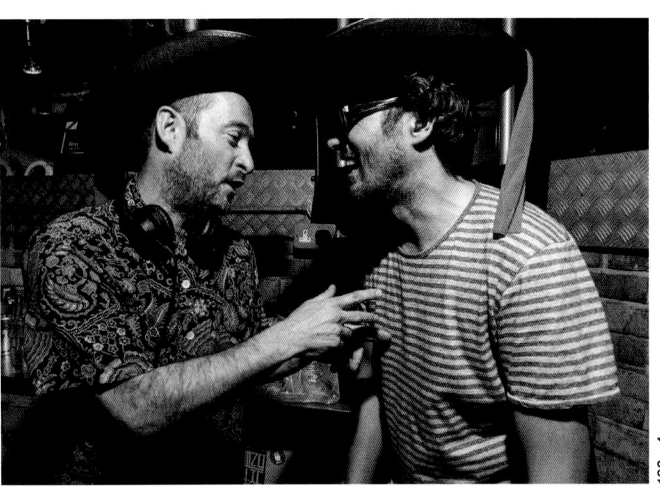

102—4

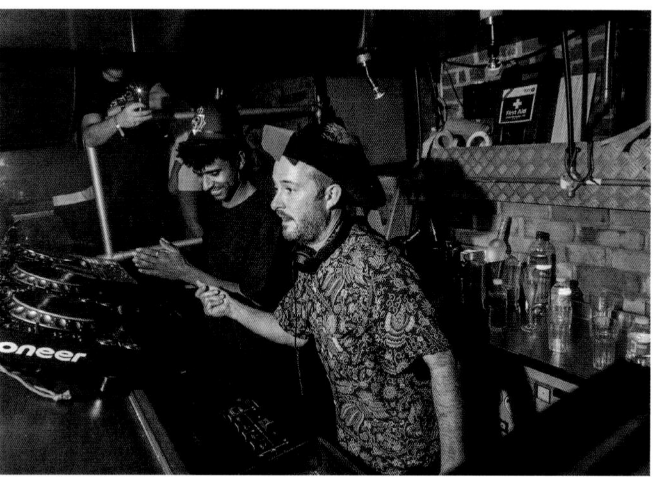

102—5

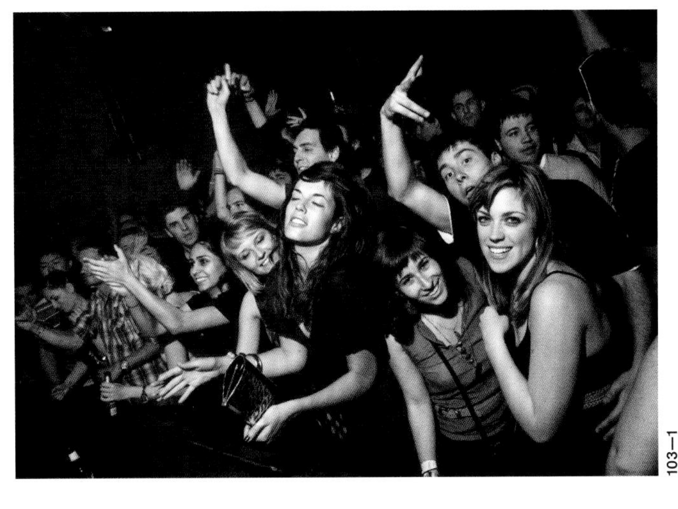
103—1

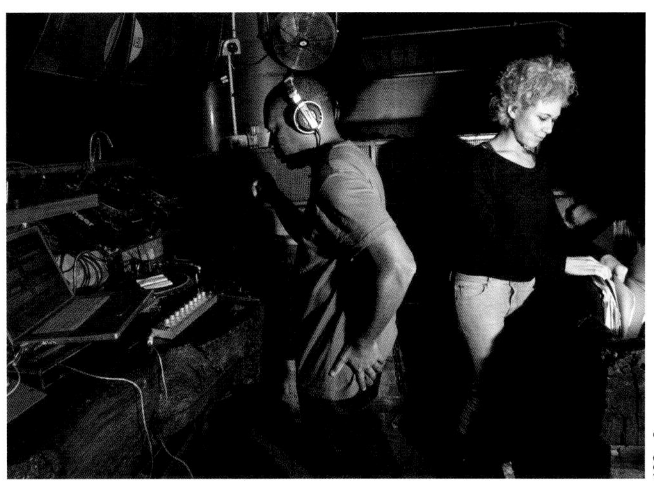
103—2

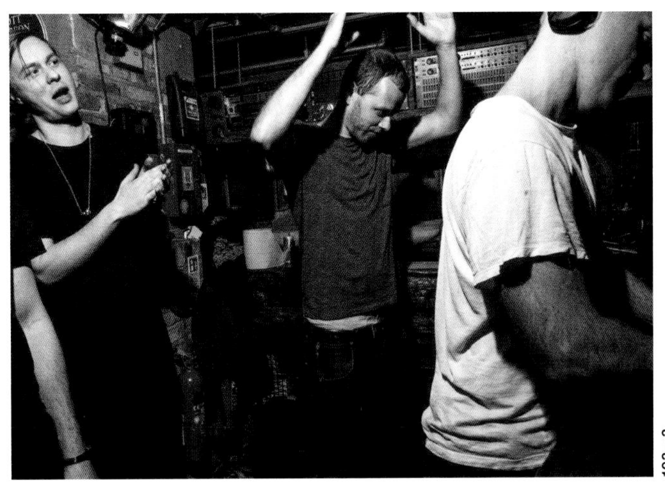
103—3

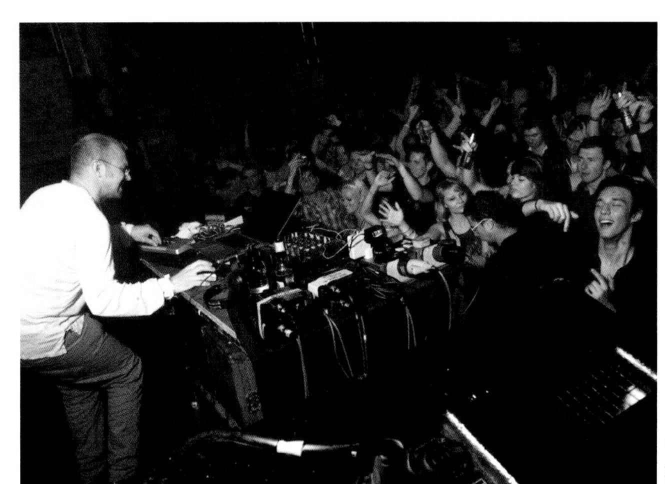
103—4

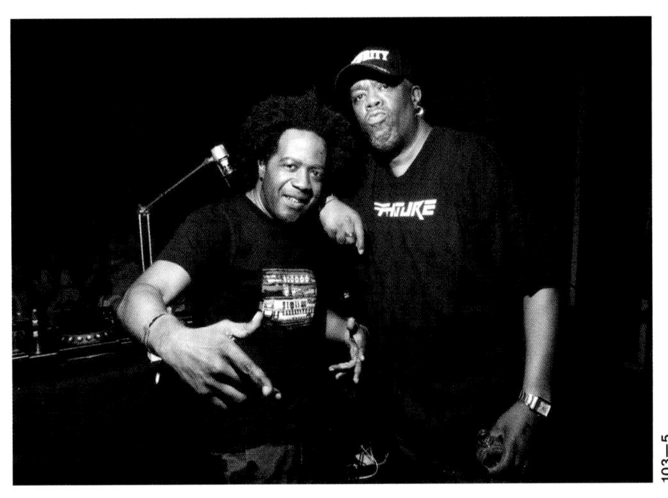
103—5

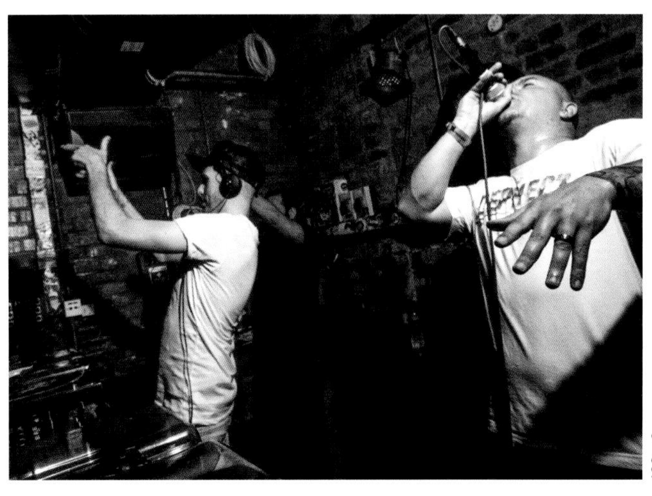
103—6

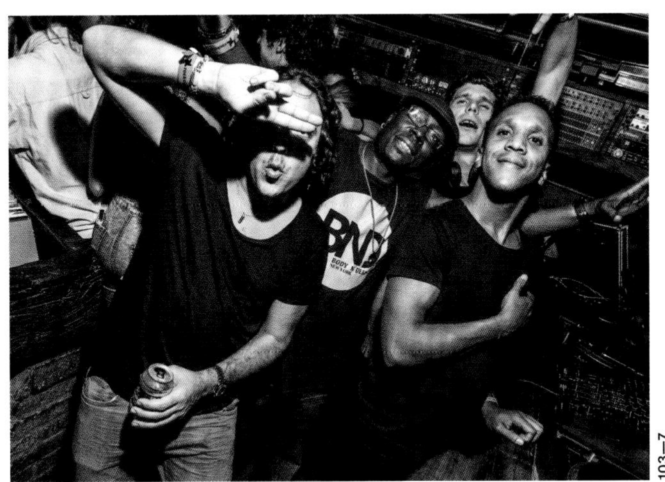
103—7

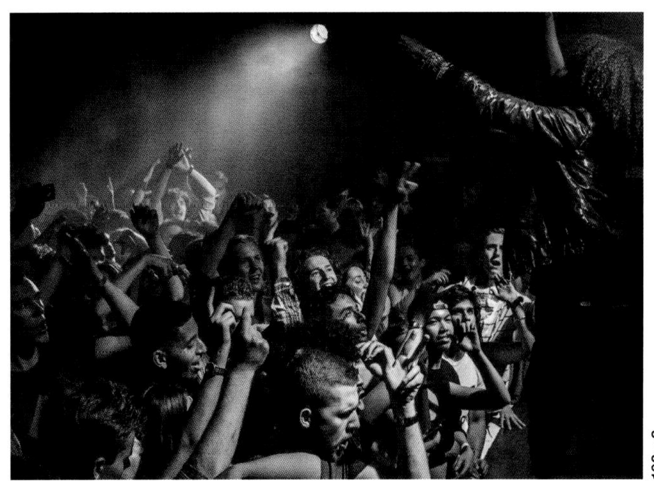
103—8

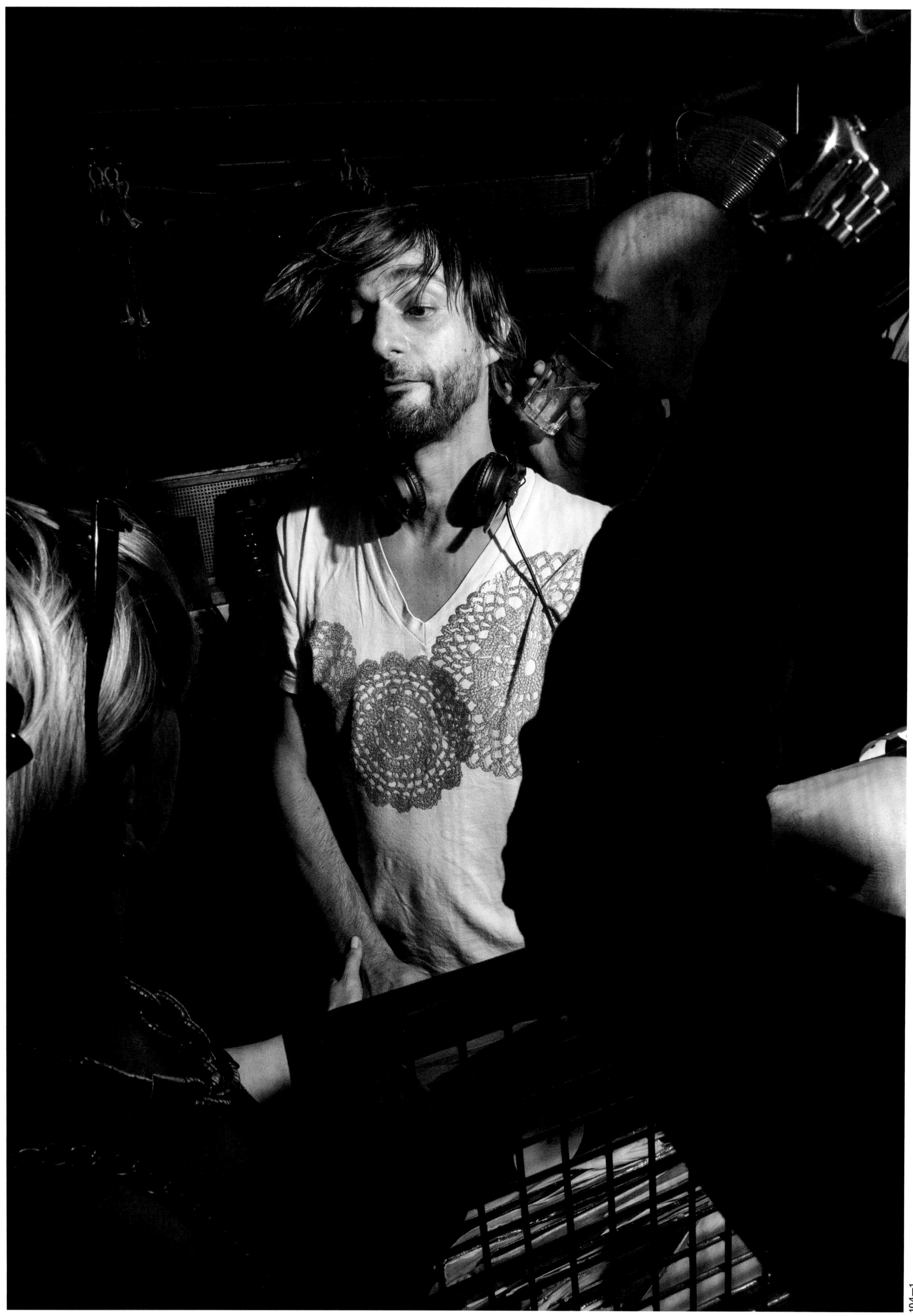

104—1

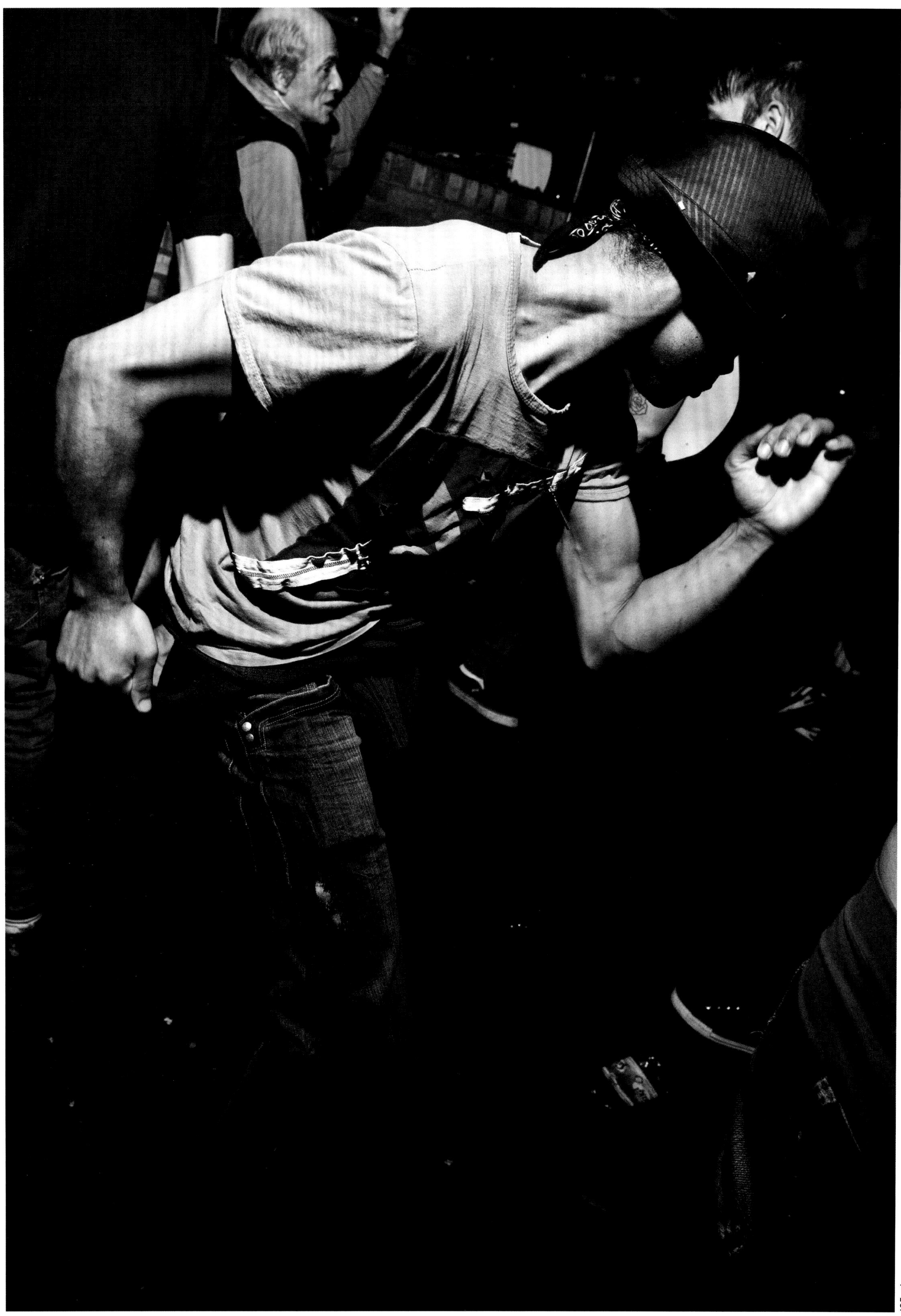

105—1

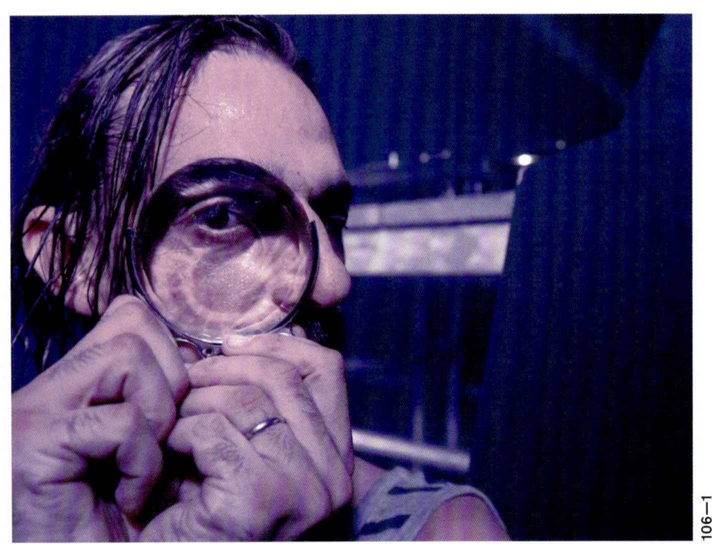
106—1

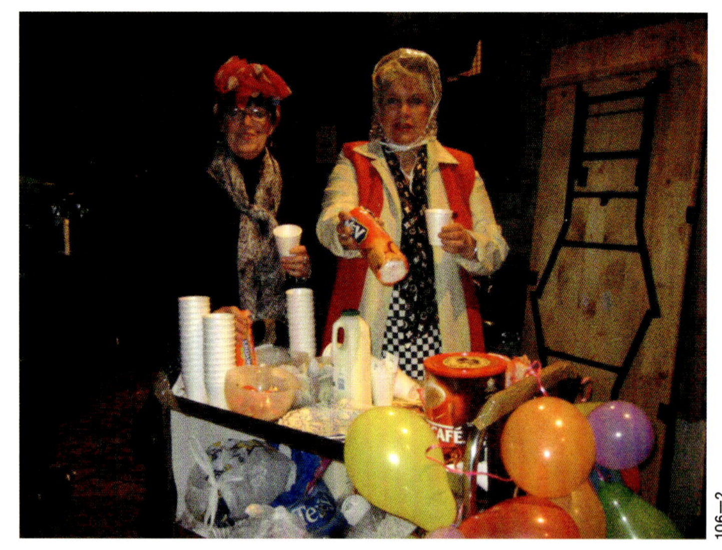
106—2

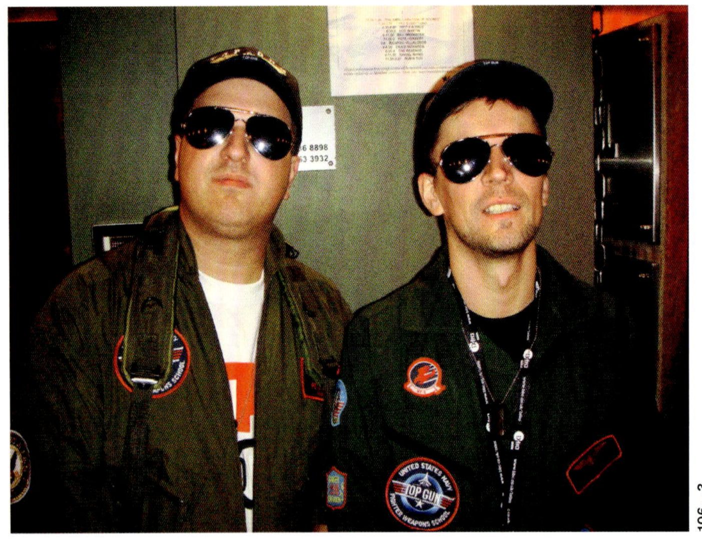
106—3

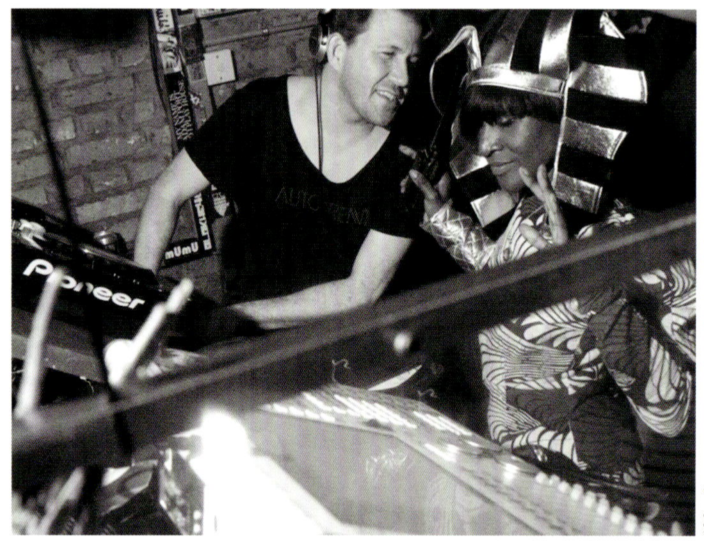

106—4

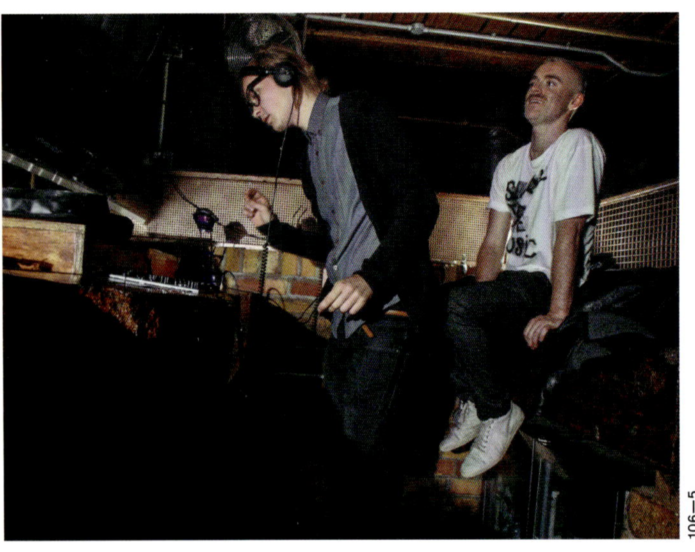
106—5

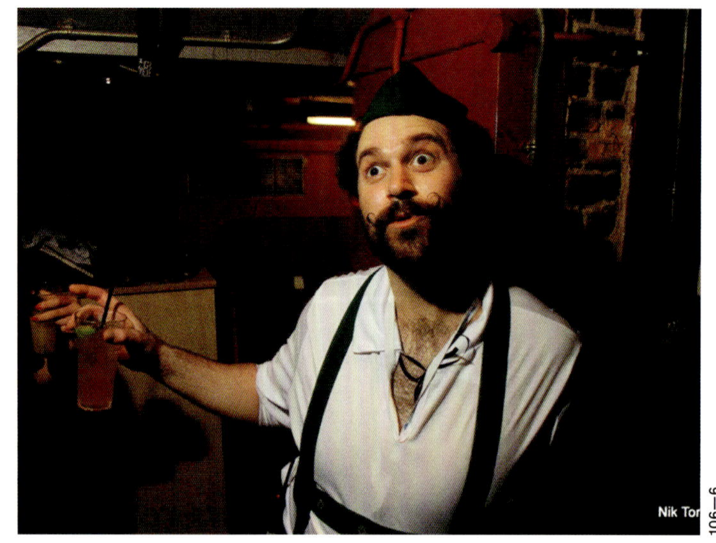
106—6

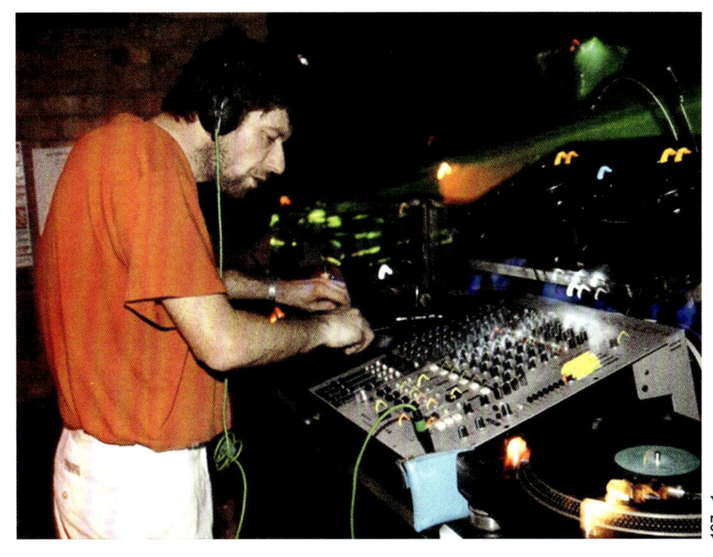
107—1

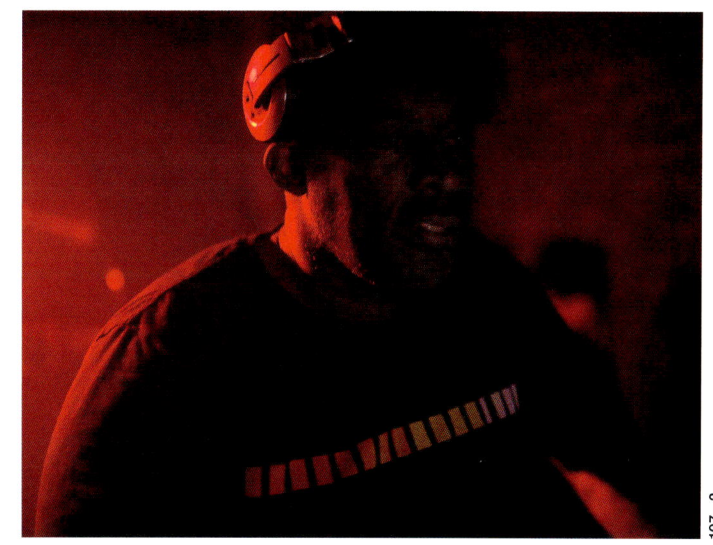
107—2

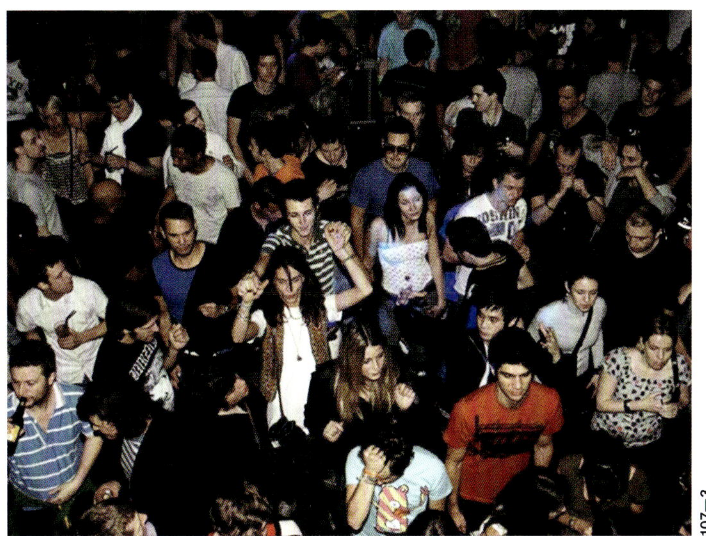
107—3

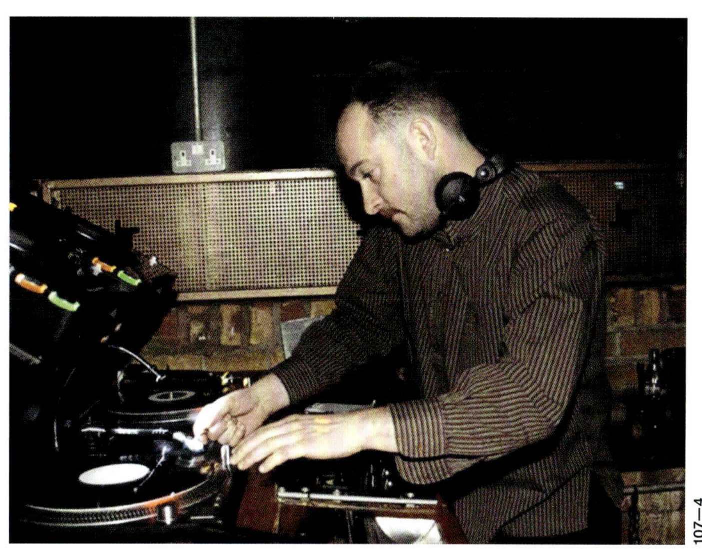
107—4

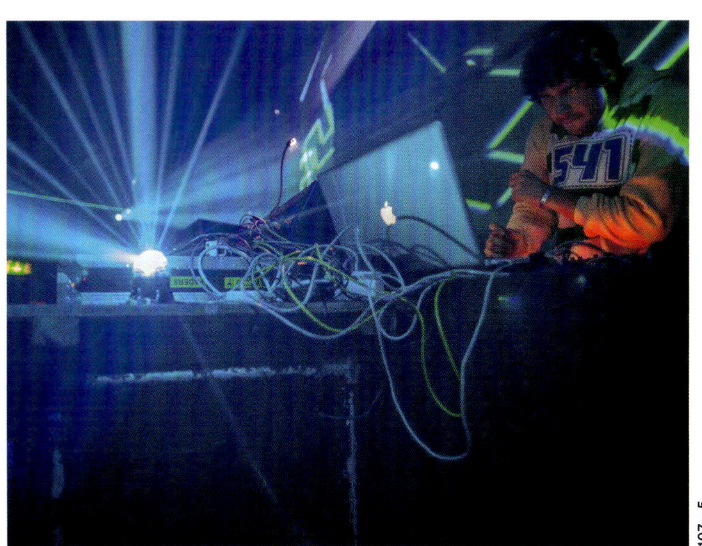

107—5

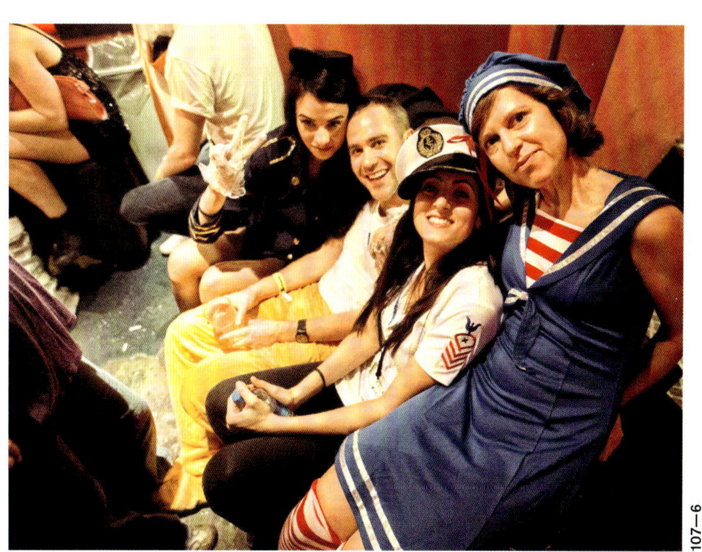
107—6

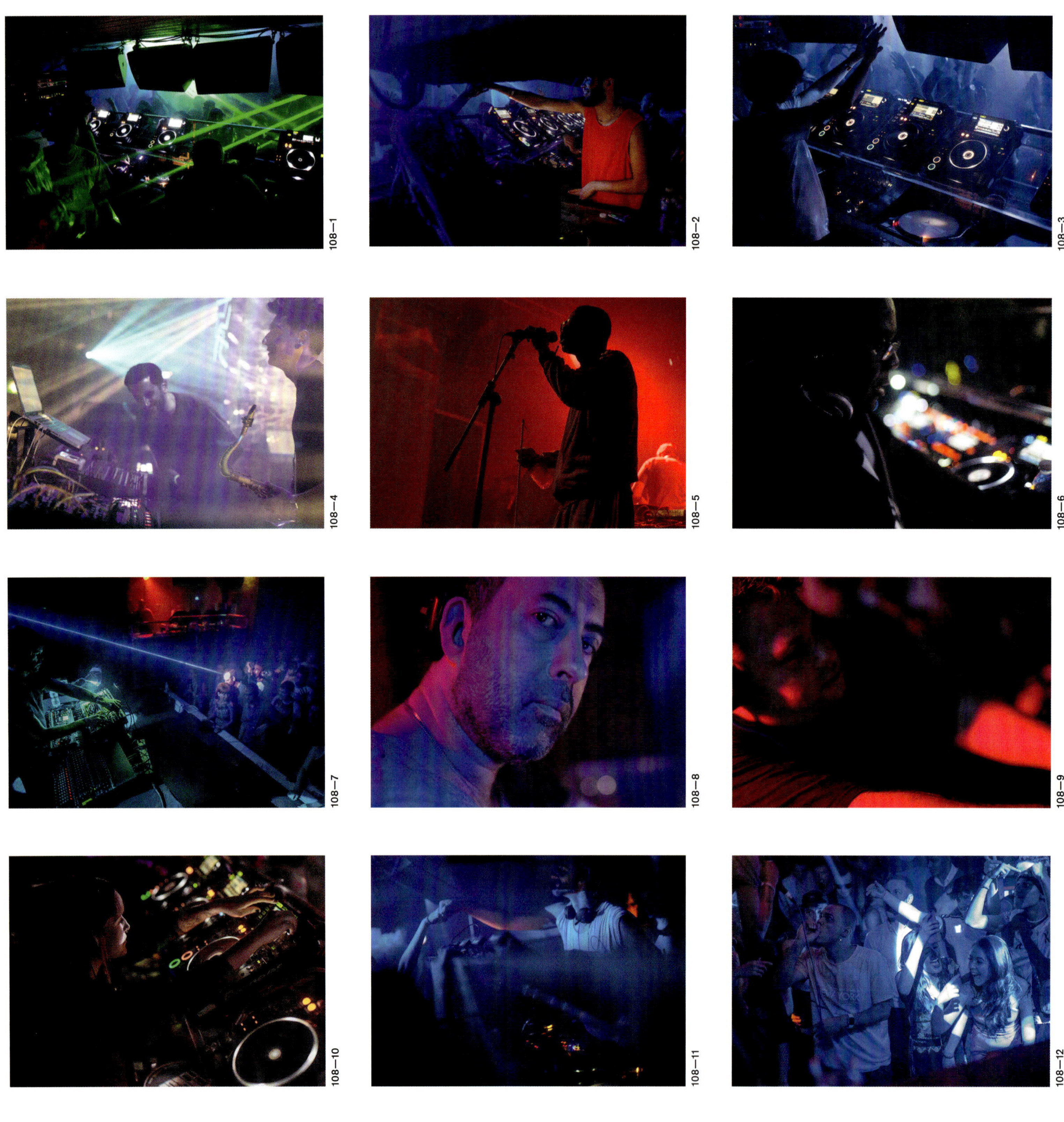
108—1
108—2
108—3
108—4
108—5
108—6
108—7
108—8
108—9
108—10
108—11
108—12

1999
2000
2001
2002
2003
2004
2005
2006
2007
2008
2009
2010
2011
2012
2013
2014
2015
2016
2017
WE
ARE
18
fabric

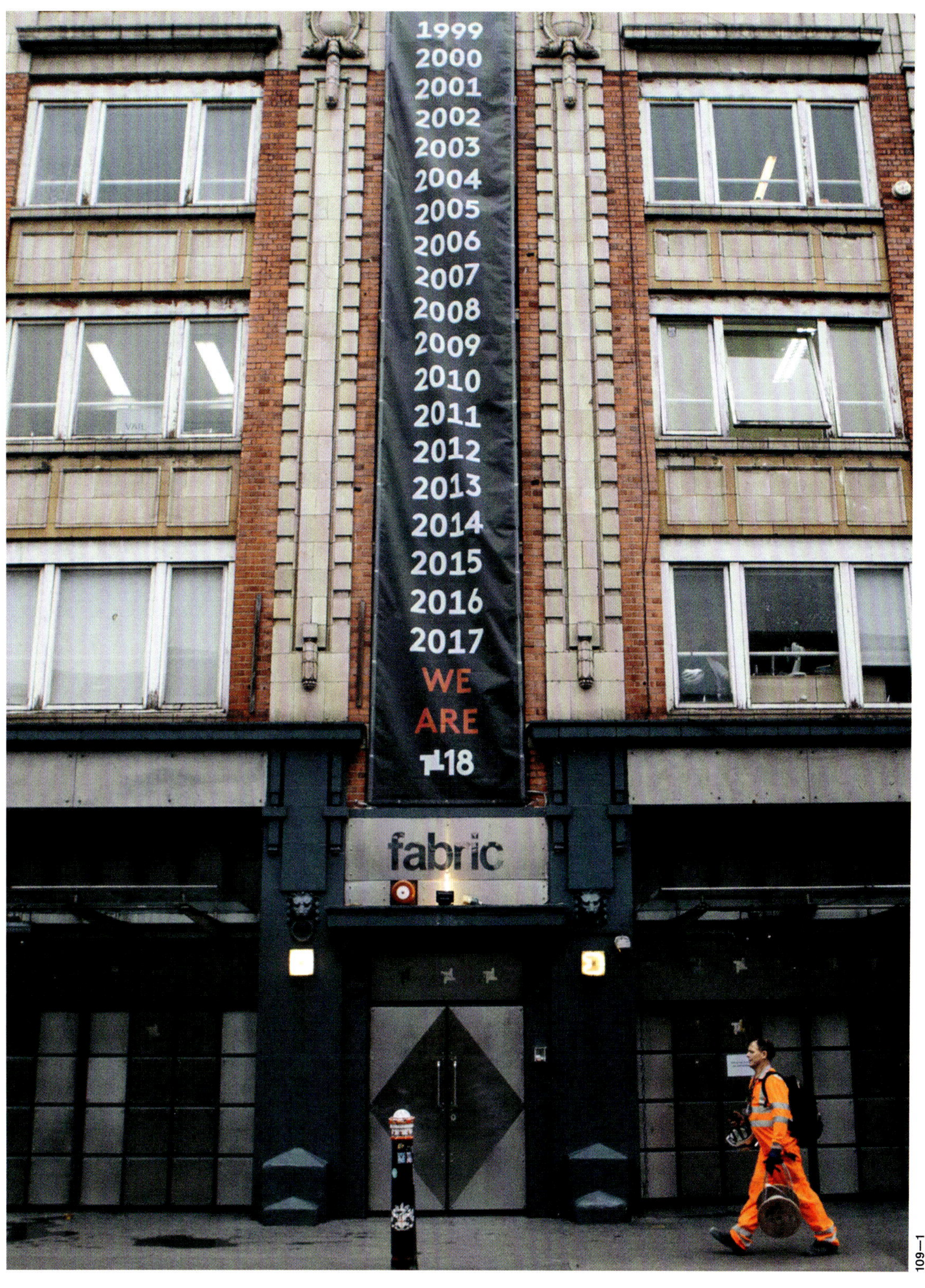

109—1

fabric
15th Birthday
Sat 18th 11pm
to Mon 20th 5am
October 2014
-
30 hours of
non-stop music
Craig Richards
Terry Francis
Ricardo Villalobos
Âme
Arnaud Le Texier
Ben Klock
Ben UFO
Dixon
Doc Martin
Marcel Dettmann
Jay Tripwire
Mathew Jonson (Live)
Matt Tolfrey
Seth Troxler
Three
www.fabriclondon.com

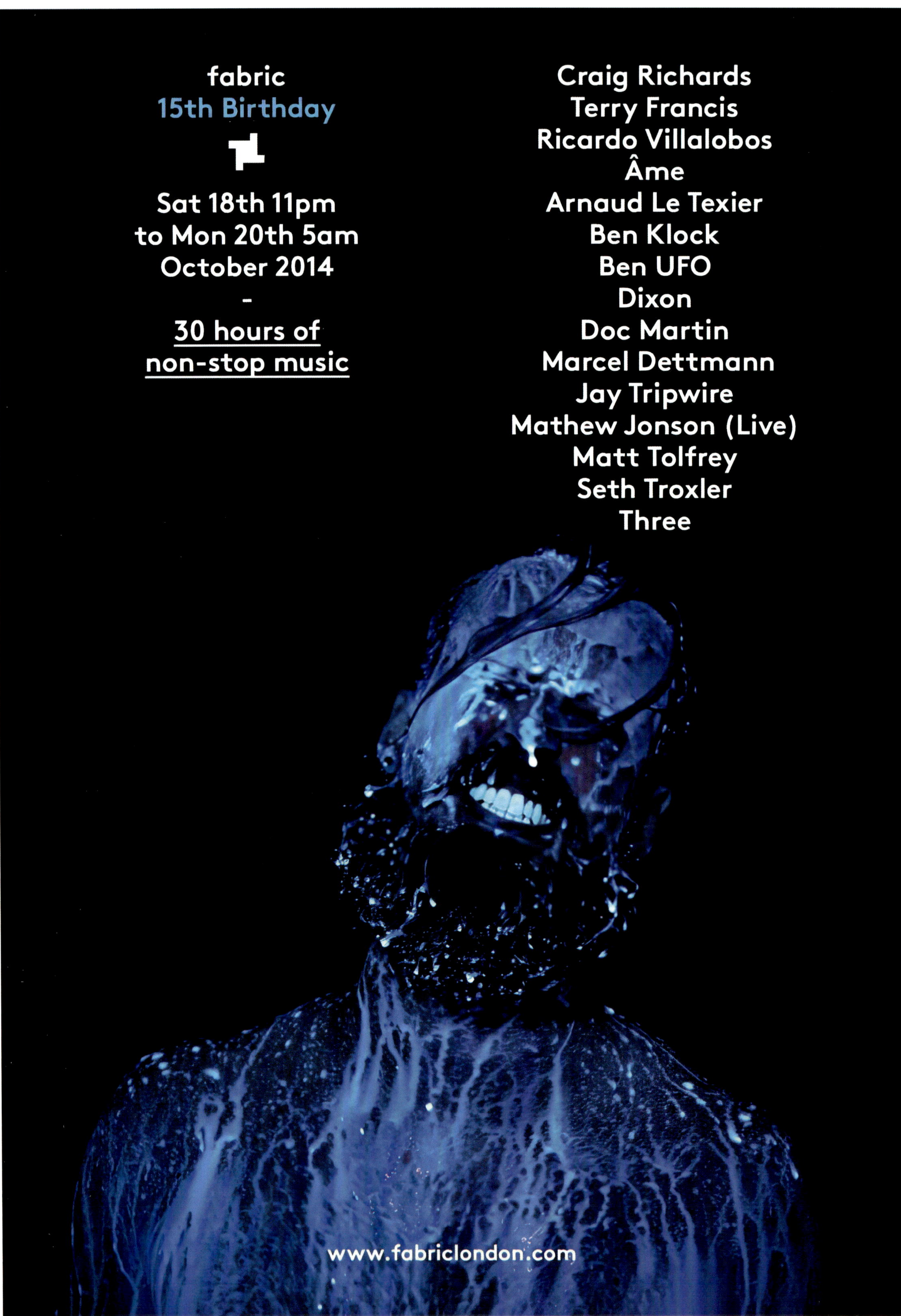

110—1

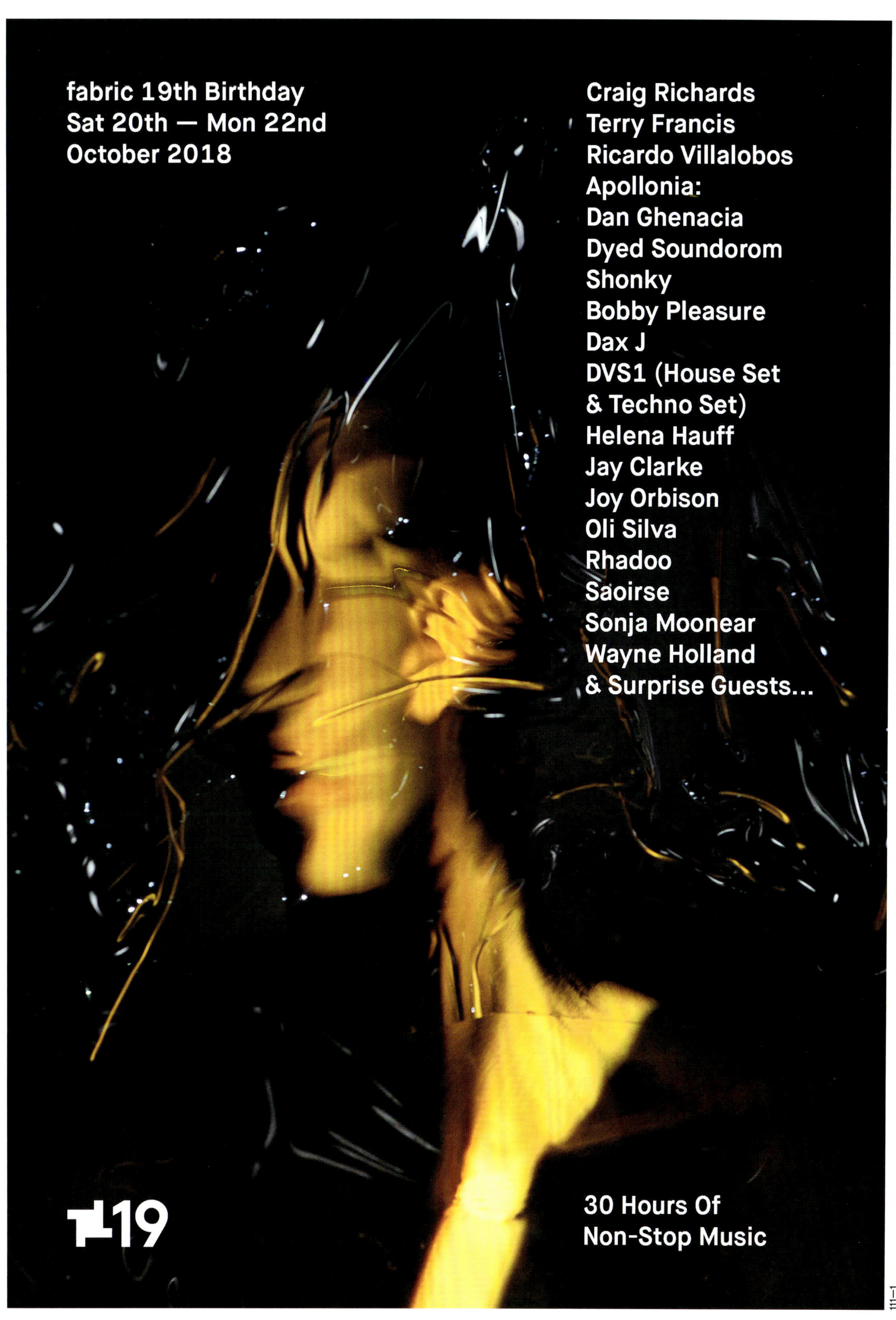
fabric 19th Birthday
Sat 20th — Mon 22nd
October 2018
Craig Richards
Terry Francis
Ricardo Villalobos
Apollonia:
Dan Ghenacia
Dyed Soundorom
Shonky
Bobby Pleasure
Dax J
DVS1 (House Set
& Techno Set)
Helena Hauff
Jay Clarke
Joy Orbison
Oli Silva
Rhadoo
Saoirse
Sonja Moonear
Wayne Holland
& Surprise Guests...
19
30 Hours Of
Non-Stop Music
111—1

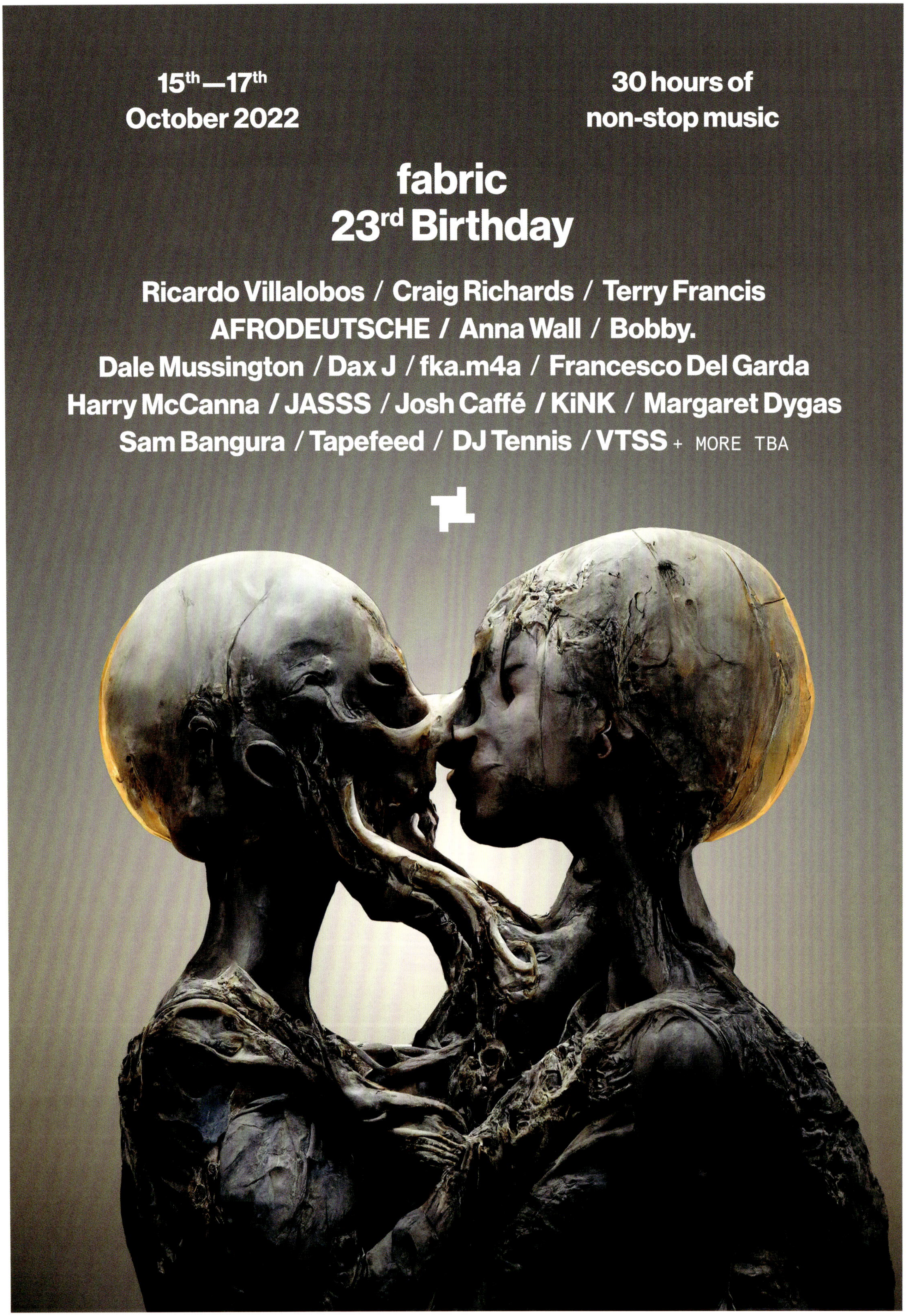

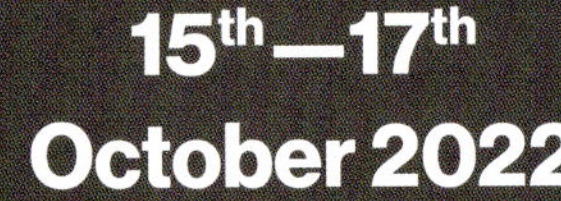
15th—17th
October 2022

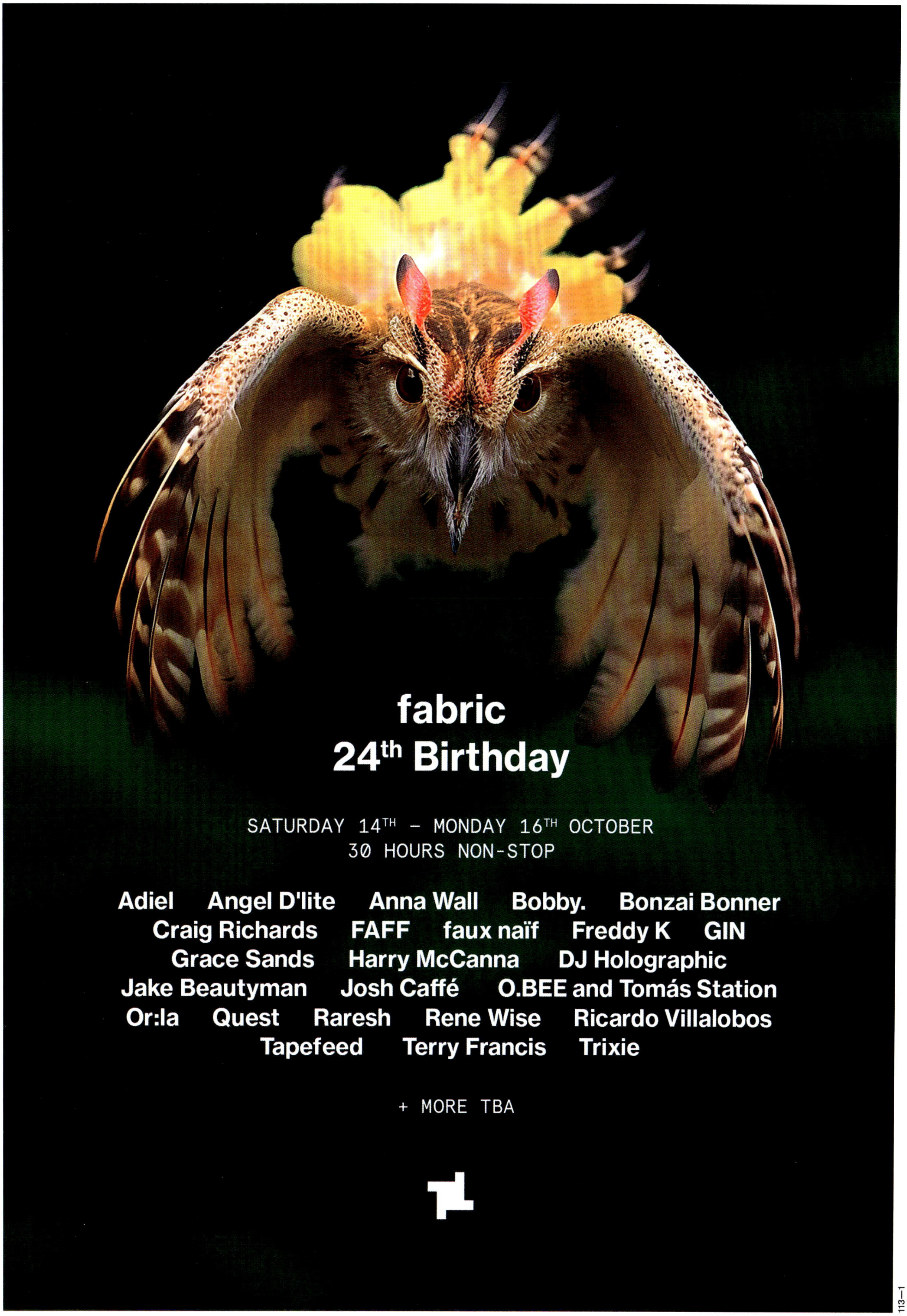

the art of fabric

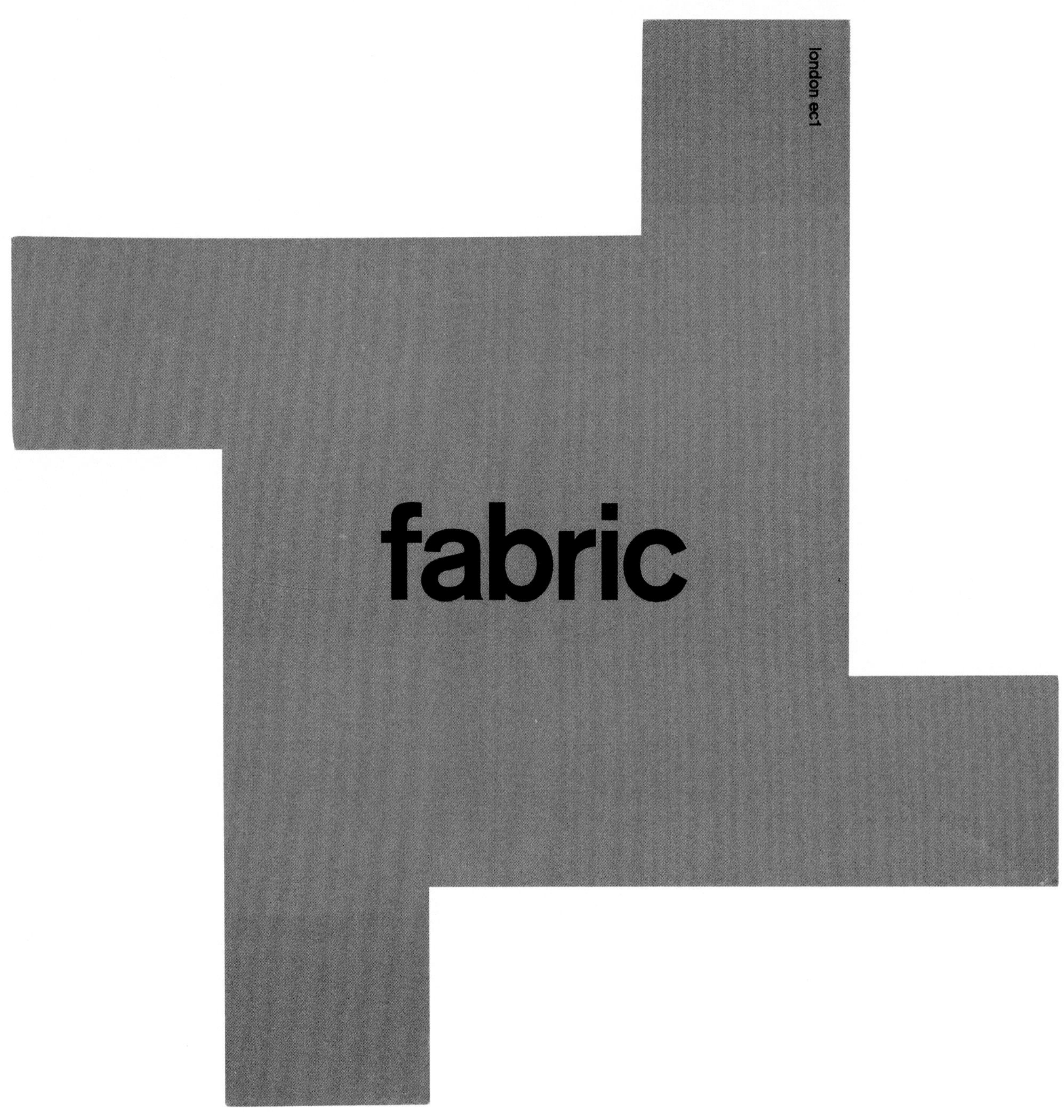

116—1

fabric on the whole is a collaborative endeavour. Necessarily so, given the volume of culture and customers that have flowed through it week in, week out over the years. But there's one place that this isn't the case: the artistic style which helped make it stand out at the start and which has kept its weirder, more bohemian edge intact over all these years. This style has taken inspiration from a number of places, not least the original vision for the club from Keith Reilly – which was first cemented by design company Intro, who did the pre-launch graphics and, crucially, the club's endlessly iterated logo – but ultimately the art itself is the work of just two people: Jonathon Cooke and Roberto Rosolin.

In proper fabric style, the initial meeting took place at a party. Craig Richards met Jon at a do in Barcelona around 1997 and liked the cut of his jib. Jon wasn't a formally schooled artist or designer, but had come up through the music industry since his teens. Straight out of school, as a young mod, he worked briefly in an independent studio in Holborn, but soon talked his way into Stiff Records, where he became a junior in the art department under Simon Ryan, working on releases by the likes of the Pogues, Madness and Furniture. From there he went to the even more mod Stiff-offshoot Countdown, run by a pre-Acid Jazz Eddie Pillar, where he became tour manager for raw Kent garage rockers, the Prisoners. By this stage he was 'embedded in the music industry', as he puts it, and went through design jobs at major labels and promoters until he ended up at Blue Source, who were working with the likes of Placebo and The Chemical Brothers. Most notably during his time there, he designed Leftfield's Leftism and Rhythm & Stealth covers.

By the end of the nineties, he was branching out on his own, so the meeting was fortuitous. At Craig's invitation, Jon came to see the cavernous space that was going to be fabric with him and Keith, and tentatively accepted the invitation to create flyers for them. But it was after bumping into Keith at an event at the Scala up the road that he really grasped what he was getting into. 'We had a long talk about what he had planned,' said Jon, 'and I realised that what he was doing was something very different; there was a punk feel about it that I really liked, and I was inspired by Keith himself.' This inspiration led him in turn to assert his own punk ideals and say to Keith that he'd only embark on the project if he was given creative freedom to develop the aesthetic exactly as he wanted, which was instantly agreed – and so it began.

'They got me, and I got them,' says Jon. 'And it was honestly a match made in heaven. It was such an exciting thing to be part of. I could tell from the off that it was driven by a passion for music above all else; they put real work into all the detail that mattered, and it was a thorn in the side for the boring, predictable fluffy-bra brigade that were dominating clubs of that size at that time. People noticed straight away that it was something different, and I wanted the flyers to be part of that and to reflect that. I just enjoyed the fact that the flyers had nothing to do with club culture at all!'

As the founding FABRICLIVE promoter Steve Blonde, who met Keith Reilly while both were out flyering, says: 'In those days, flyers were the way to know what was going on. You had the national dance music mags, but really to know what was going on – in London at least – the flyer pack was everything.' Come out of any club in the capital and you would likely be handed literally dozens of flyers, many of them bundled together in packs with rubber bands or zip-seal bags. So something radical was needed to stand out.

The vibe Jon brought – in radical contrast to both the swishy glitz of the 'fluffy-bra brigade' and the macho sci-fi imagery rampant in techno and drum'n'bass of the time – was influenced by 'a growing interest in paganism, nature and the dark side of the country!' Gnarled wood, antlers, human–animal hybrids all came together in his deeply psychedelic collages. For inspiration he would trawl second-hand shops around Farringdon, finding dusty old Playboy magazines and Ladybird books, blending glamour shots with wood-peckers and magpies, all scanned and cut up in Photoshop. All of this was showcased on big fold-out flyers that would highlight a month of fabric nights at a time, so Jon's work had a broad canvas.

It all stood out a mile compared to anything else in clubland, and while in retrospect Jon may find some of the pieces better than others, he remains happy that it built an atmosphere, a body of work, an ongoing statement – and left its mark on the collective psyche. 'I loved the idea,' he says, 'of some kid coming out of a club, maybe a bit the worse for wear, getting in a taxi to go home or go to an afterparty, getting a bunch of those flyer packs, coming to the fabric one, unfolding it and getting all these beautiful images that had connections to nature and the countryside – and just for one moment making them think about that. Just a flash of beauty in people's lives, a reconnection.'

As years went on, with assistance from other designers like Juan Cortes and Ryan Belmont, the work went through all kinds of iterations, repeating themes of nature, architecture, abstraction, absurdity – all with a psychedelic edge. Jon never lost his sense of the preposterous; for one series he bought a lampshade from a junk shop, put it on his head with a toilet-roll holder in his mouth, photographed it, photocopied the photograph 'and came out with something that looked like it was from the Bauhaus in the 1920s!' The fabric and FABRICLIVE CDs would take the themes of the month's flyers out into the wider world, and helped increase the sense of the club's work as a living gallery – although Jon never stopped to think about the sense that it was building into a grander work. 'We just had to keep doing it each month,' he remembers, 'so it was about whatever would work at the time. There wasn't a moment to stop and take stock. But there was just naturally a running thread through it all.'

After a decade, Jon was starting to tire of the relentlessness of the fabric work – and just as pertinently had plenty of other work to be getting on with via his Village Green design studio – 'because having the fabric art out there constantly, with a full-page advert on the back of Jockey Slut magazine every month, was the best advert for my studio I could have asked for!' So a replacement was recruited in the form of Roberto Rosolin. After art college in Italy, he'd moved to London and done bits of agency work here and there; in classic fabric torch-passing style, he'd had his clubbing epiphanies at fabric, a Friday night faithful from very early on, gradually graduating to Saturdays as his music tastes evolved. He was completely schooled in what fabric was about and ready to pick up where Jon left off.

It was a dramatic start, though. He was originally recruited in 2010 to work on the gigantic matter project, but the month he was due to start – also the month his daughter was born – it closed. The fabric management didn't want to waste his potential, though, so they invited him over to the club – and against all the odds he managed to ride out the fabric administration. In fact, with the new-broom approach that Nathan Leslie brought as fabric's assistant managing director, it perhaps made sense to have fresh talent brought to the club's publicity material. All of which was pretty daunting for Roberto; his challenge was to keep continuity with the 'flyers that were a proper piece of art' that he'd admired as a young clubber, while keeping the sense of fabric moving forward.

His way forward was to 'try and keep doing things that felt like fabric art, that kept this weird and surprising feeling every month', but to focus on process, and let the work evolve with changing technology. 'Photography was becoming less expensive,' he says, 'so I could take pictures myself, work with more photographers, use these pictures in the collages. And because it wasn't about the big paper flyer anymore, but online, we began to work a lot with video, too.' Following Jon's model, he let himself be led by the images that came to hand, in a kind of extended process of free association. 'I never really conceptualised,' he says. 'Each thing would suggest something new – so maybe one month I'm working with leaves, so it suggests, OK, why not trees? Or why not leaves made from another material?

'It's a mixture of instinct and plan,' he continues, 'but really more instinct than plan. Having randomness helps keep things fresh. We have so many things to do, fifty-two weekends a year, and after twenty-five years everything has been covered – people, buildings, plants, animals, minerals, landscapes ... But I'd say that now it's really exciting times because we're moving into AI, and that helps keep me moving – because I can control it, but also ... can't control it! So this is where the magic sometimes comes out.' In the social-media era, too, he says it gets easier to take inspiration from the artists who are playing. 'Everyone has a brand now,' he says, 'so when someone is playing or headlining, there's always an idea I could take from them and incorporate, whether that's messy or tidy, funny or serious. Though sometimes you might go all the way for the opposite – that's why, with Ricardo Villalobos, who's one of the most random DJs in the world, I went for something very slick and polished.'

Roberto has certainly brought his own signature to the artwork. Though he says fabric's style is 'subtle and minimal, with darkness always present', he's allowed himself occasional daring uses of light, colour and dynamism; his pictures with his regular photographic collaborator Mads Perch for fabric's sixteenth birthday in 2015, of human bodies leaping through explosions of powder paint, stand as emblematic of his style.

Likewise, his 'marble bust' portrait of Ricardo for the twentieth anniversary of the DJ's arrival at fabric in 2023 remains – in the truest sense of a much overused word – iconic. But he has always kept that continuity, too, paying tribute not just to Jon's work before, but above all else to fabric itself, to the abstract collective personality of the club. 'That's why I don't have to think too consciously,' he says, 'because whatever I do, I can see whether it's "fabric" or not straight away!'

And that remains as true now as it was from the very first few weeks Jon forged the aesthetic. The two designers' work for fabric has found its way into multiple exhibitions and books, but for all that each piece might charm and fascinate as a thing in itself, it remains above all a part of a much greater artwork: fabric as an entity. The art fuses in the mind with the architecture of the building itself, as created by the Forward architects studio and etched into millions of clubbers' memories, and now rejuvenated by Giorgio Badalacchi with his subtly witty abattoir aesthetic and re-emphasis of the building's original materials in tribute to its tarry-bricked origins as a meat store – as well as the brief fever dream of matter and its amazing layout.

And this in turn is filtered to the outside world via the club pictures of a sequence of in-house photographers: Nick Ensing, Sarah Ginn, Danny Seaton, Anna Wallington and Enrico Policardo (the latter also contributing photography to Roberto's artwork, alongside Mads). All of these snappers are clubbers in their own right – Nick, for example, is an original 1988 acid-house raver, and for periods of his life 'was in fabric every week, sometimes multiple times a week!', while Sarah has been deeply immersed in UK bass music of the twenty-first century. Given that there are few cameras in fabric, these few lucky snappers' work comes together to create a seething, surging visual identity that merges into the musical and personal experiences of the club. There were photographers, too – Chris Davison and Jimmy Mould – who worked specifically for the fabric label: again, adding cumulatively to the ever-evolving visual identity. While the technology of promotion and artistic production might change, as long as the club, the labels and the projects that go with them keep doing what they do, the drive and inspiration to keep that flow of images coming will remain – always different, always the same.

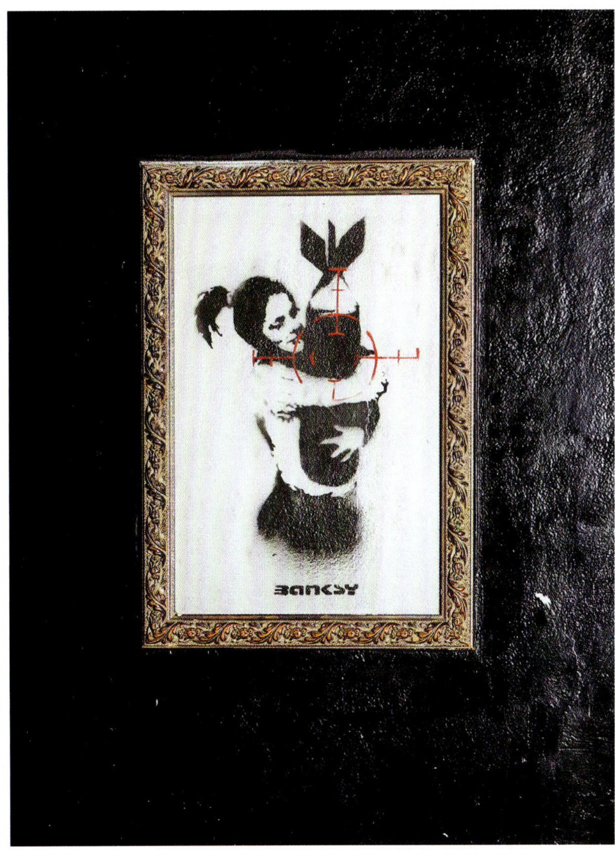

119—1

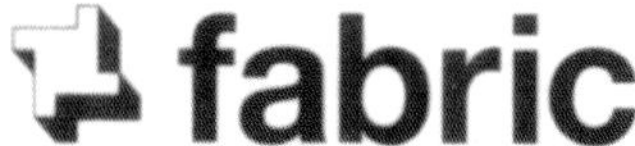

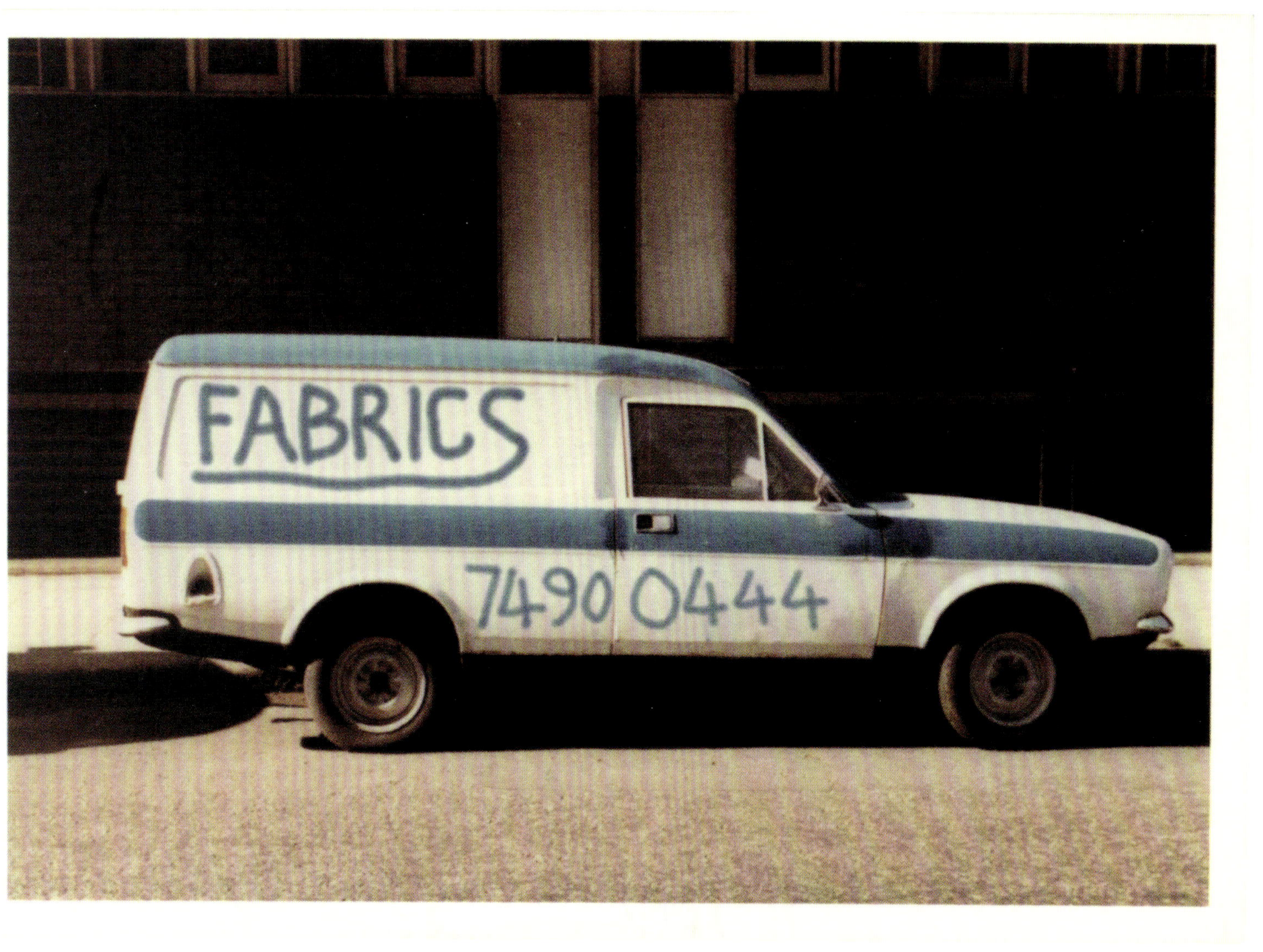

121—1

fabric

Fabric
Saturdays
Room 1
Room 2
Room 3
02 October
Sasha
Pure Science - live
Terry Francis
Craig Richards
Tony Humphries
DJ Pierre
Kid Batchelor
Friction
Adam Freeland
Tayo
Danny McMillan
£12
10pm–7am
09 October
Danny Tenaglia
Craig Richards
Kojak - live
Tom Middleton
Terry Francis
Kenny Hawkes
Amalgamation of Sounds
77a Charterhouse Street
London EC1M 3HN
16 October
Derrick Carter
Gene Farris
Craig Richards
Presence - live
Richard Sen - Bronx Dogs
Clive Henry - Peace Division
Eddie Richards
Air
Ben Wilcox
Ali B
DJ Orange
fabric info 0207 490 0444
www.fabric-london.com
23 October
John Digweed
Brother Brown - live
Jon Marsh
Craig Richards
Bill Brewster
Groove Armada
30 October
Felix Da Housekatt
Craig Richards
Pete Herbert
Derrick May
Terry Francis
Kid Batchelor
Phil Mison
Nancy Noise
fabric

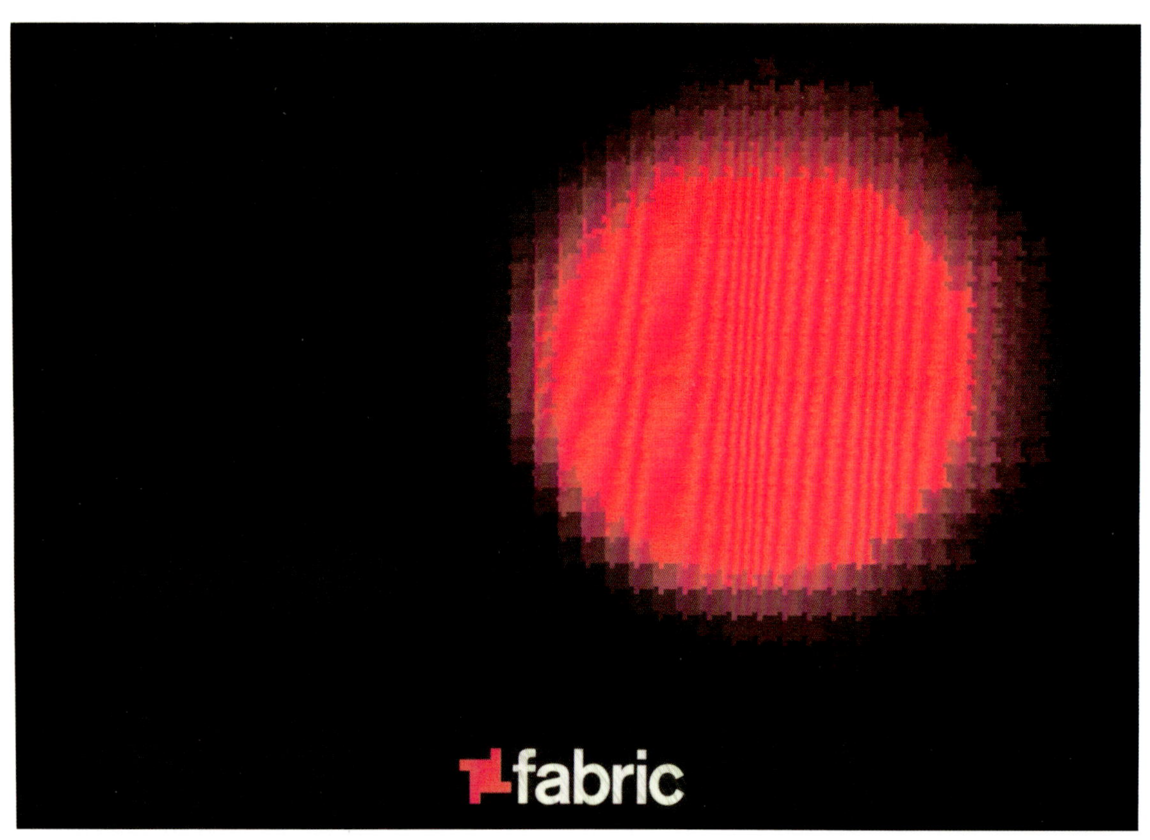

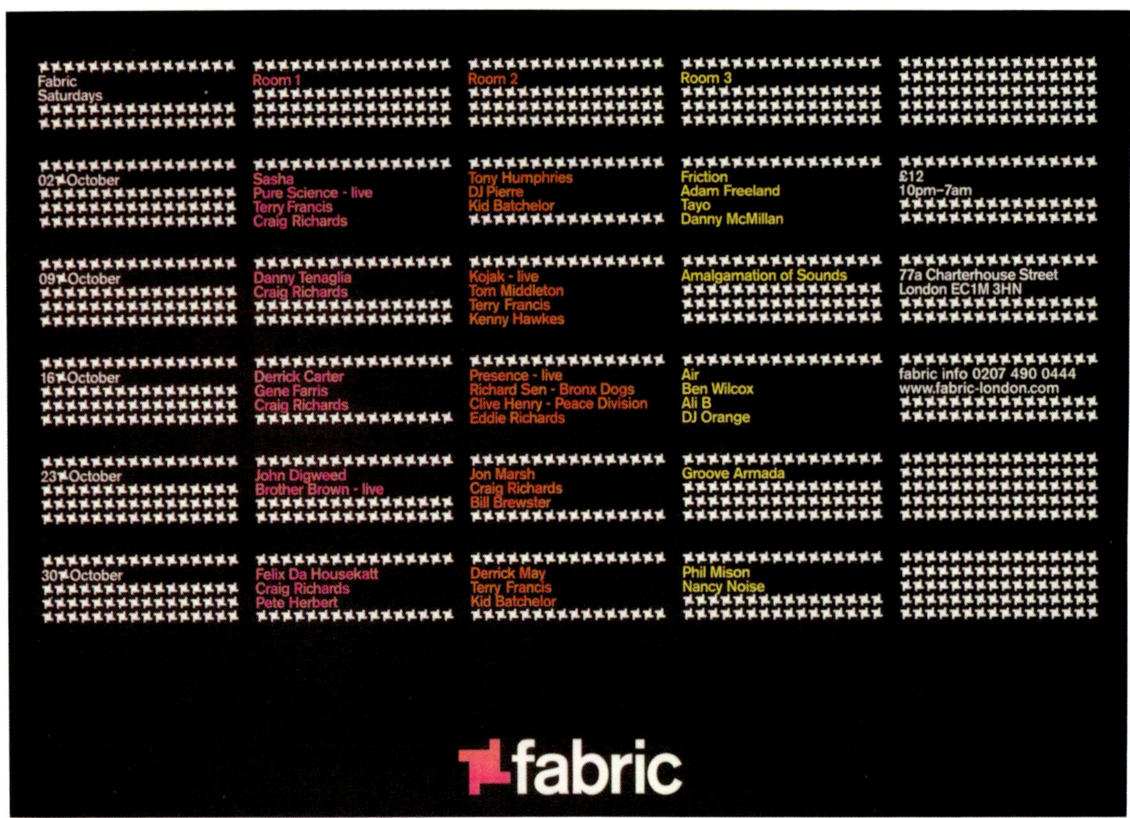

122—1

fabric

Fabric
Saturday
Room 1
Room 2
Room 3
30 October
Felix Da Housekatt
Craig Richards
Pete Herbert
Derrick May
Terry Francis
Kid Batchelor
Phil Mison
Nancy Noise
£12
10pm–7am
77a Charterhouse St
London EC1M 3HN
fabric info
020 7490 0444
www.
fabric-london.com
fabric

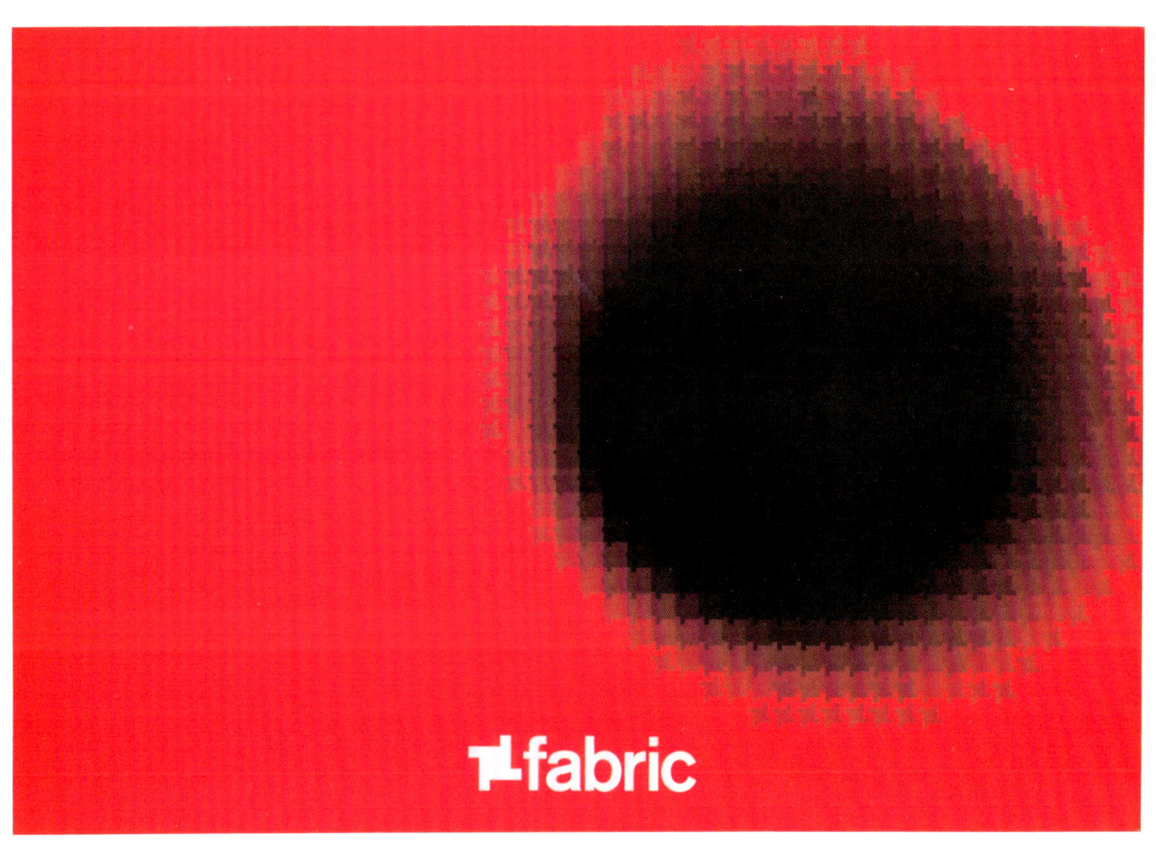

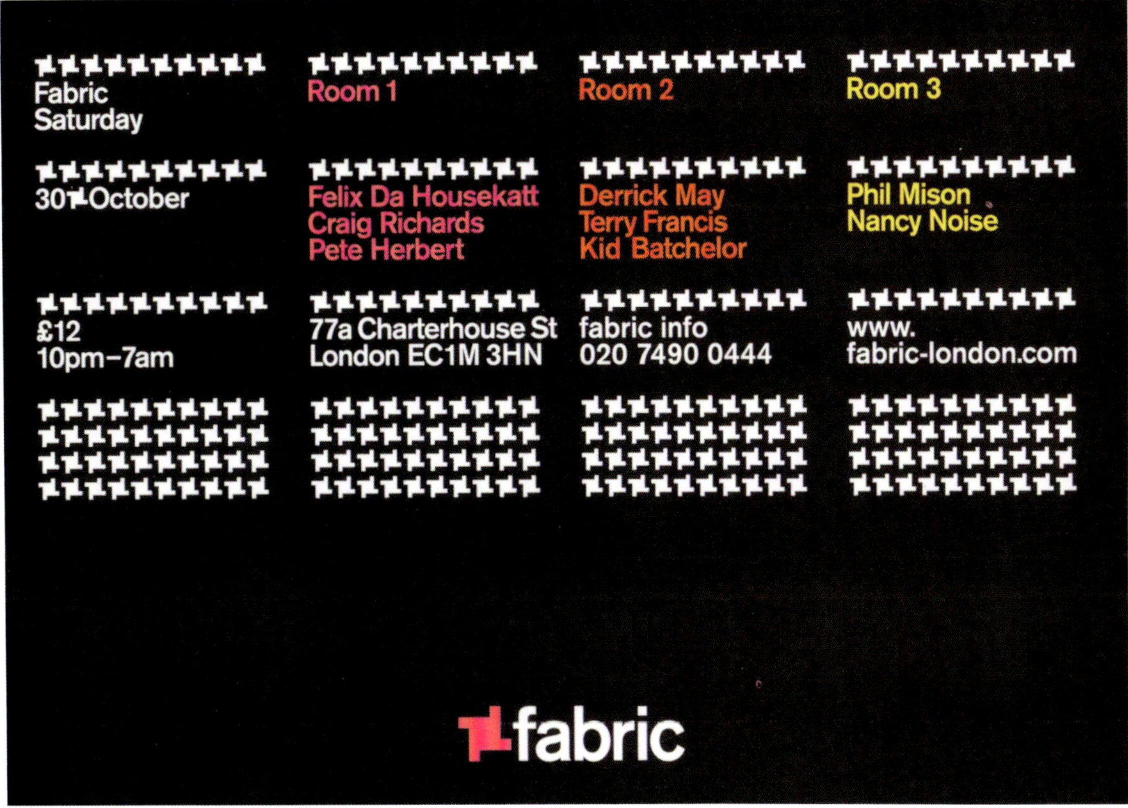

123—1

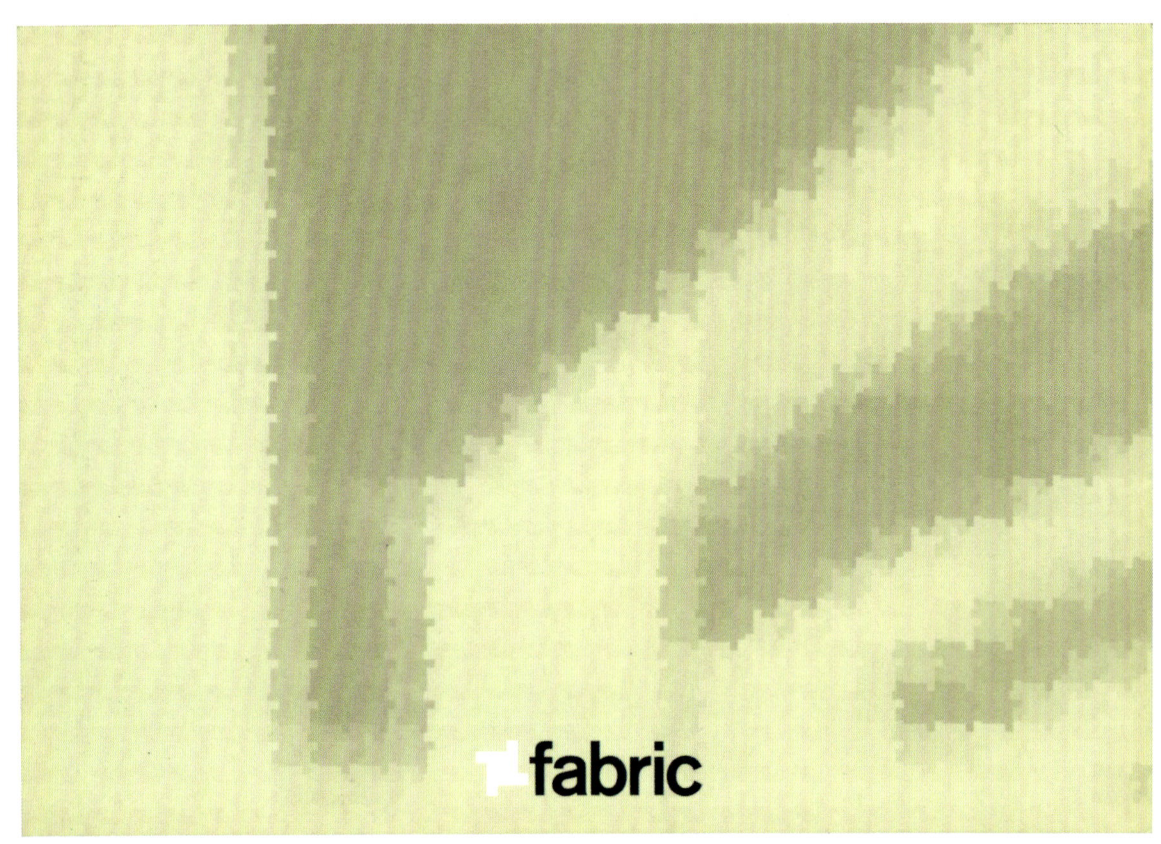

Fabric Saturdays

	Room 1	Room 2	Room 3	
06 November	Tyrant Sasha Craig Richards Lee Burridge	FRICTION Adam Freeland Rennie Pilgrim Tayo	Passenger Shut Up And Dance Ali B Steve Blonde	£12 10pm–7am
13 November	François K Ben+Pete	Kevin Saunderson Swayzak (live) Craig Richards	It's a Finger Lickin' Tour Krafty Kuts Soul of Man Plump DJs	77a Charterhouse St London EC1
20 November	Pete Heller Jon Marsh David Alvarado	Jeep Girlz (live) DJ Dan Craig Richards Bill Brewster	Grass Roots Launch Ashley Beedle Q & Rossano Strut Bert Bevans	Info 020 7490 0444
27 November	Luke Slater (live) Terry Francis Pure Science (live)	Cosmos (live) Tom Middleton Craig Richards	Fraser Cooke Michael K	www.fabric-london.com

fabric

124—1

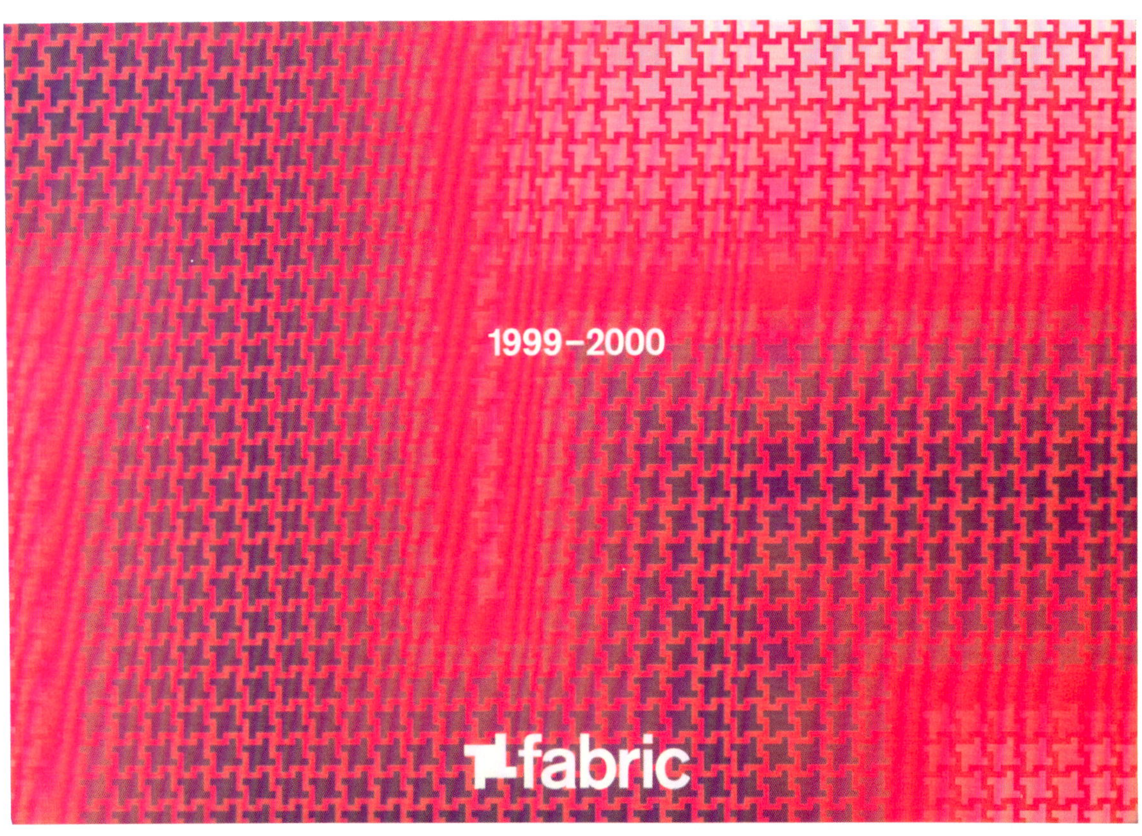

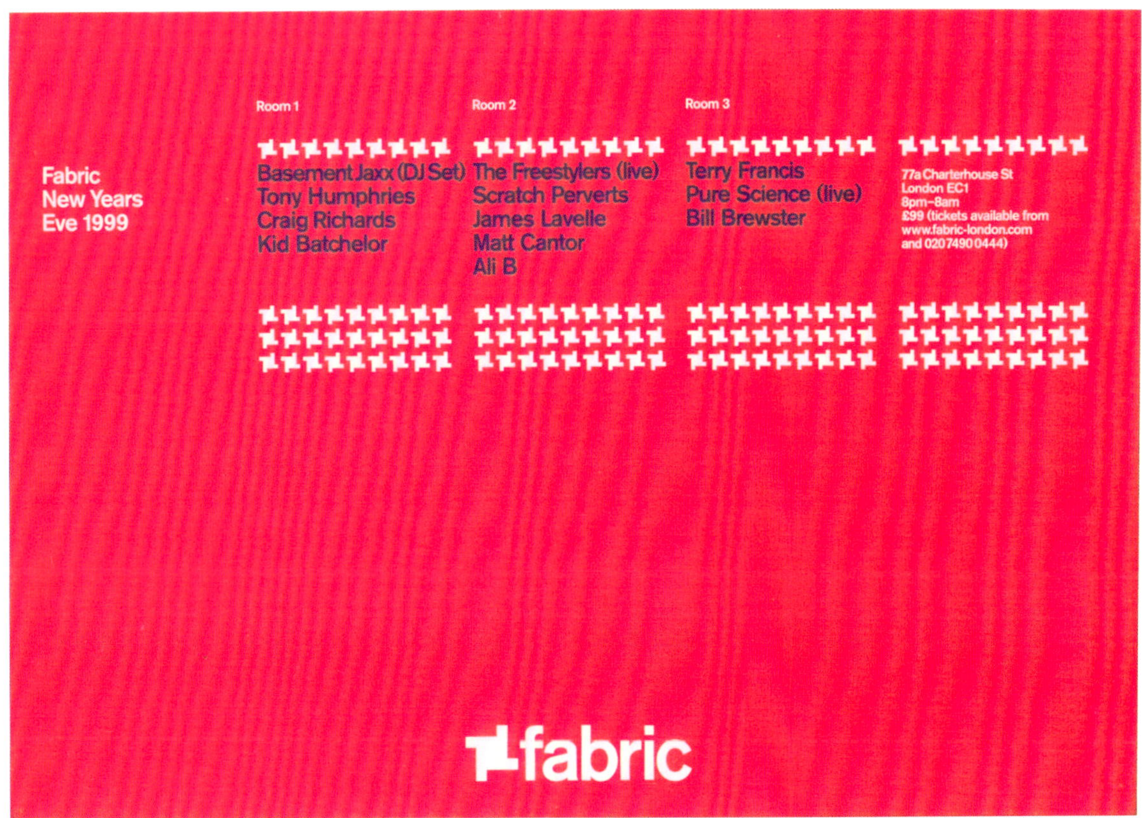

125—1

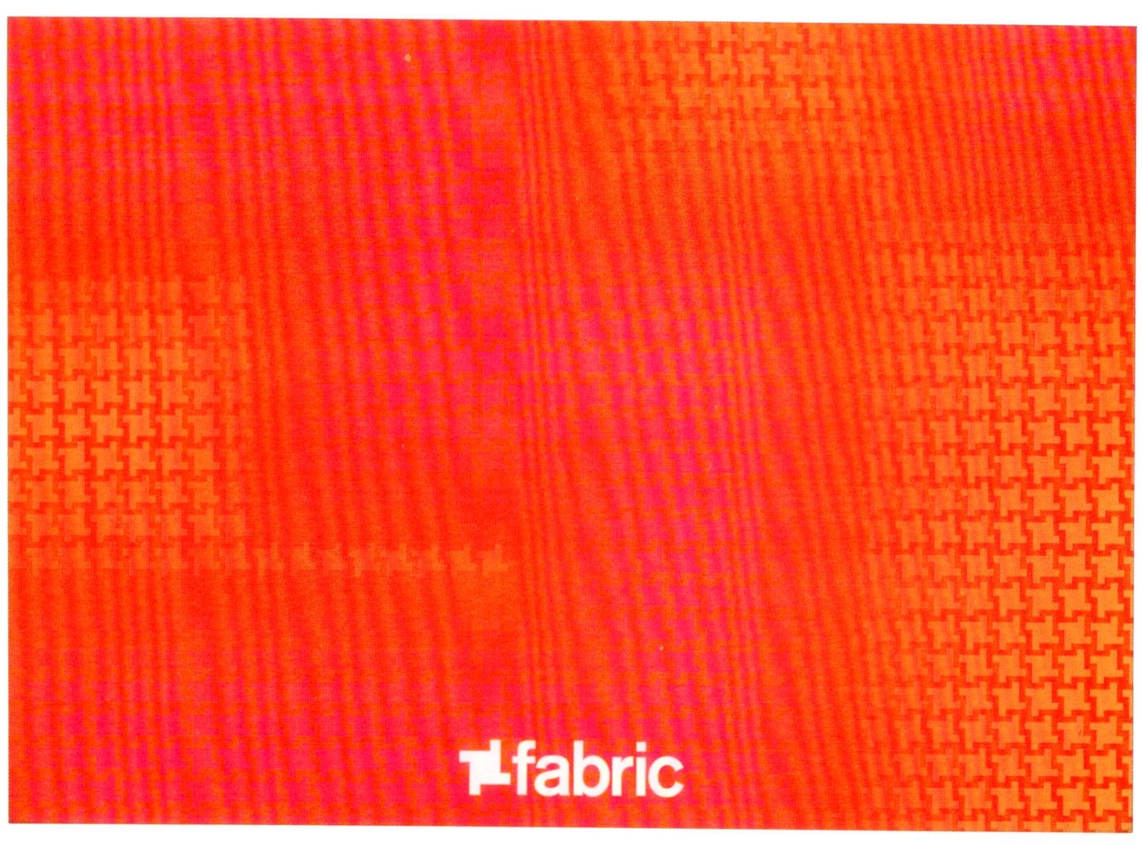

Fabric
Saturdays

	Room 1	Room 2	Room 3	
04 December	Tyrant Sasha Craig Richards Lee Burridge	FRICTION Hybrid (live) Rennie Pilgrim Tayo	Amalgamation of Soundz	£12 9pm–7am 77a Charterhouse St London EC1 Info 020 7490 0444 www.fabric-london.com
11 December	Wamdue Kids Kid Batchelor Tim Webster	Terry Francis Craig Richards Bill Brewster	air Luke Vibert Ali B DJ Orange	
18 December	Felix Da Housekatt Kojak (live) Jon Marsh JP	Dave Angel Terry Francis Craig Richards Get Fucked (live)	Groove Armada	
Fabric New Years Eve 1999	Basement Jaxx Tony Humphries Craig Richards Kid Batchelor	The Freestylers (live) Scratch Perverts James Lavelle Matt Cantor Ali B	Terry Francis Pure Science (live) Bill Brewster	8pm–8am £99 (tickets available from www.fabric-london.com and 020 7490 0444)

fabric

126—1

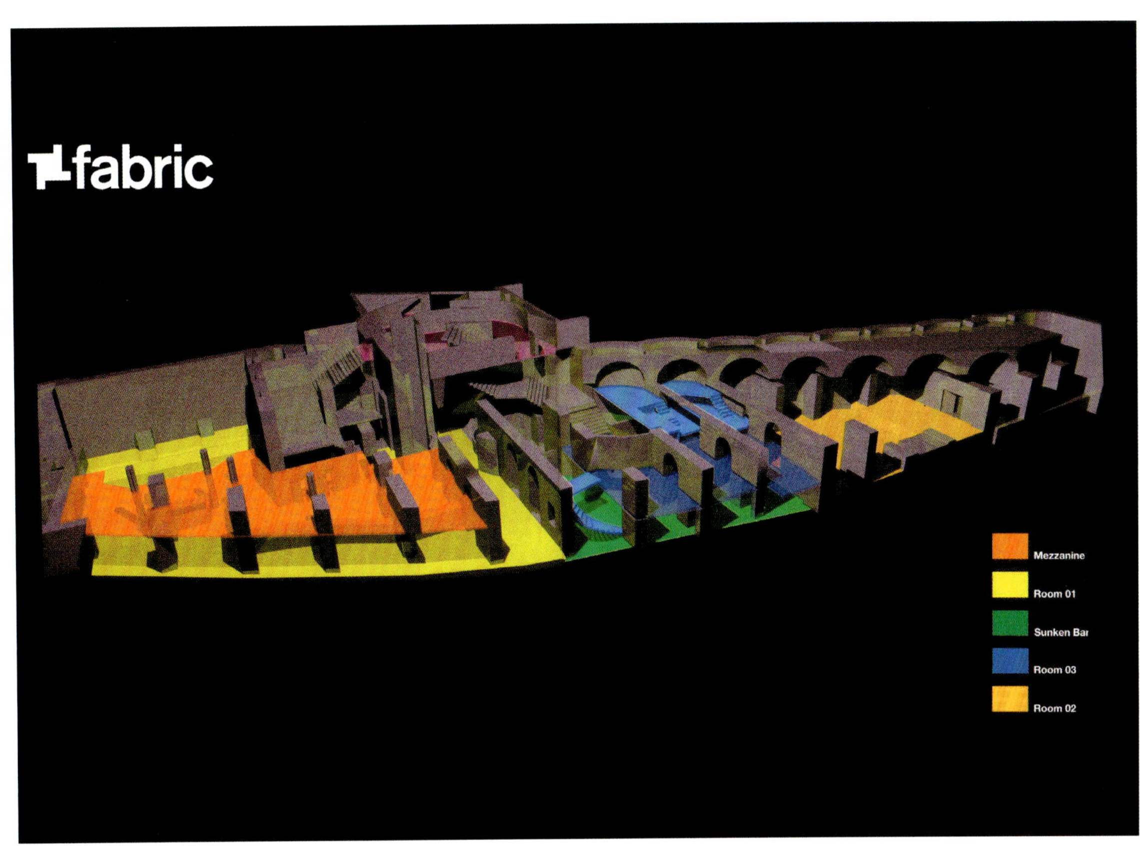

Venue Capacity

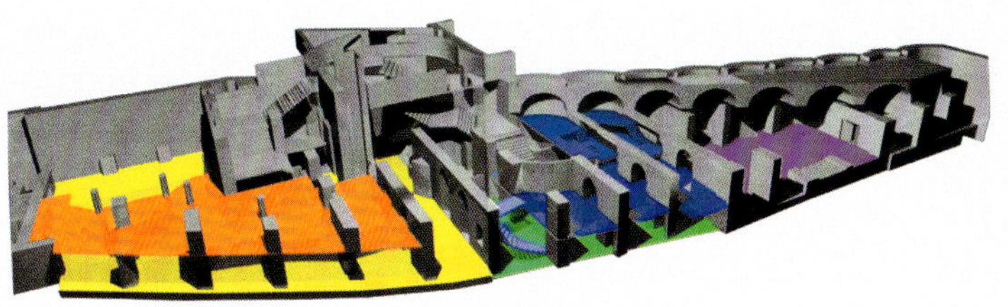

Room One

CAPACITIES:
RECEPTION 300 TO 800
BANQUET 160
THEATRE 220

Considered a template space within the industry, the first room encapsulates **fabric**'s core values: state-of-the-art technology in an unforgettable environment. It features a mezzanine 'VIP' Lounge, a large DJ booth, an extendable stage and changing facilities. Buried underneath the dancefloor is Europe's first bass-loaded "Bodysonic" system.

Room Two

CAPACITIES:
RECEPTION 100 TO 500
BANQUET 80
THEATRE 90

The second stage area reinforces the venue's flexibility: weekend crowds aren't likely to know they're listening to a TiMax ImageMaker sound system comparable with that of The Bolshoi Ballet. The space has a raised level DJ booth, light and sound gallery, a fully equipped recording studio, laser systems, changing rooms and multi access points to the stage. The deep stage area can also be converted into a catwalk and is ideal for live acts and presentations.

Room Three

CAPACITIES:
RECEPTION 50 TO 200
BANQUET 30

The "club within a club" micro space reflects **fabric**'s attention to detail: intimacy, excitement and a house party atmosphere are guaranteed, right in the heart of the venue. This third room has an equally-highly equipped sound system, dedicated entrance points, a separate bar, mini balcony lounge, stage area and DJ booth across its four split levels.

Sunken Bar

CAPACITIES:
RECEPTION 50 TO 150

The lower level's centre space is dedicated to relaxation, whatever the event. Here you will find banquette seating, couches, easy access to the unisex toilets and its own bar area.

Mezzanine

CAPACITIES:
RECEPTION 50 TO 250
BANQUET 60
THEATRE 40

The eye-catching balcony bar overlooks Room One can be auxiliary or self-containing as the event dictates. It has its own unisex toilets, a large bar, signature tables, seating and occasional furniture.

One Venue. Infinite Possibilities.

127—1

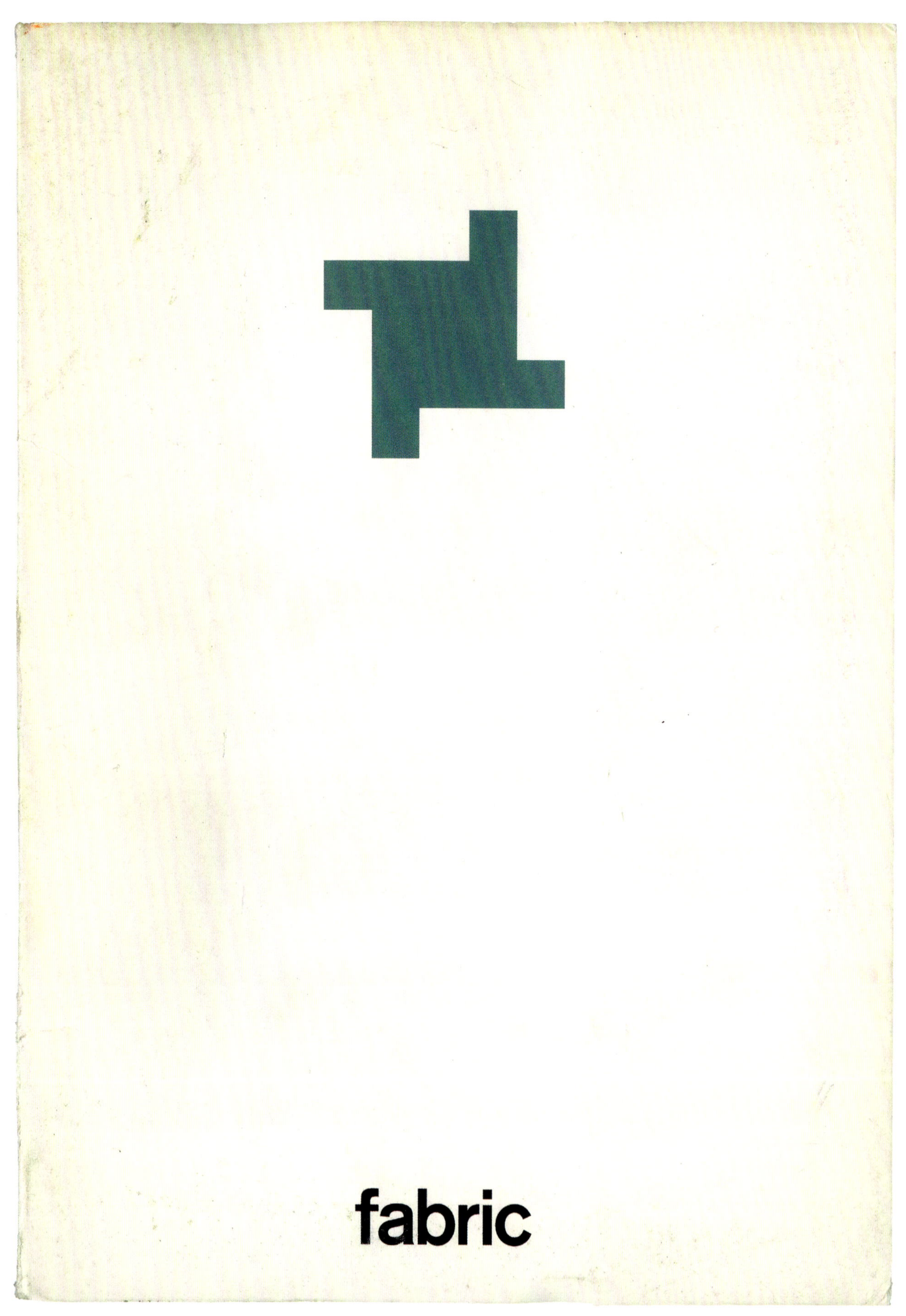

128—1

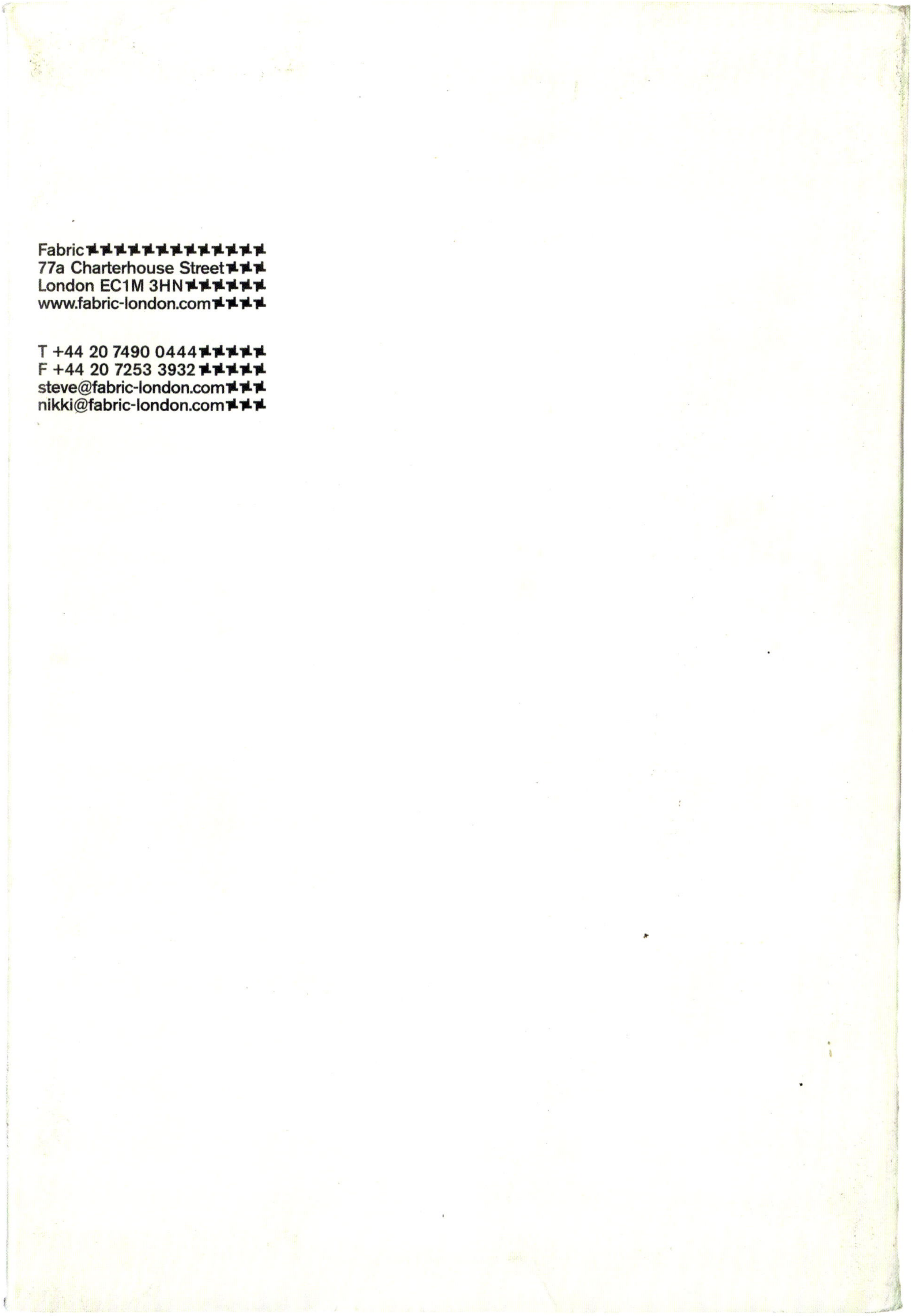

Fabric
77a Charterhouse Street
London EC1M 3HN
www.fabric-london.com

T +44 20 7490 0444
F +44 20 7253 3932
steve@fabric-london.com
nikki@fabric-london.com

129—1

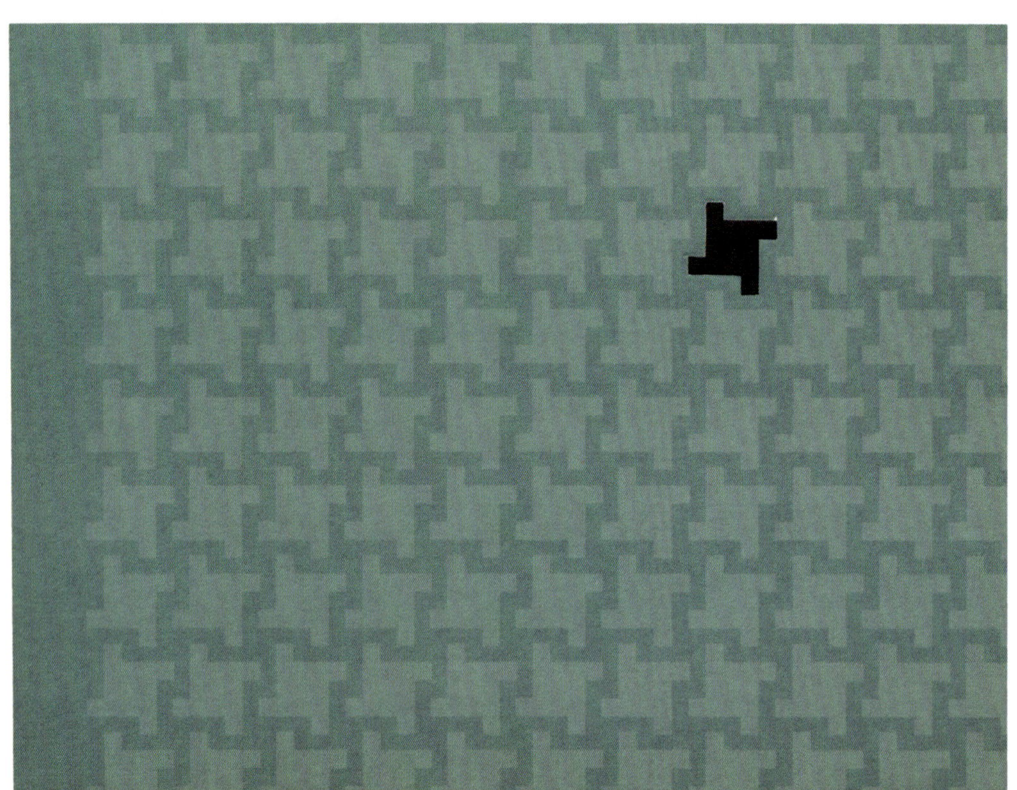

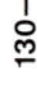

130—1

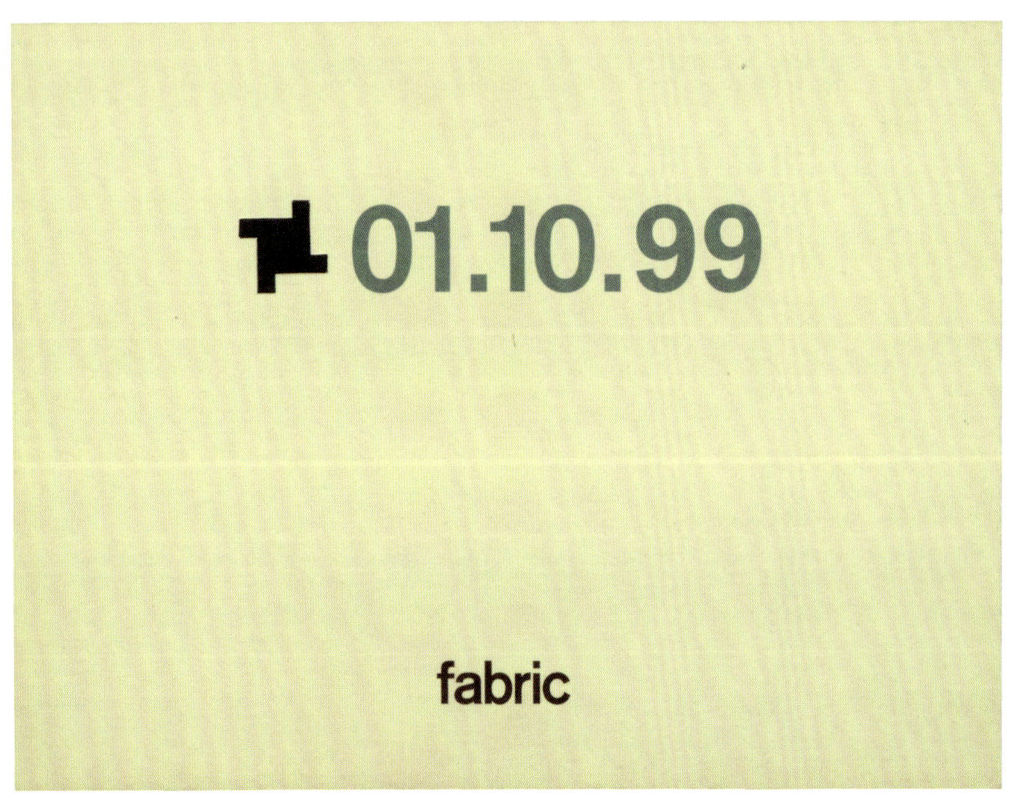

130—2

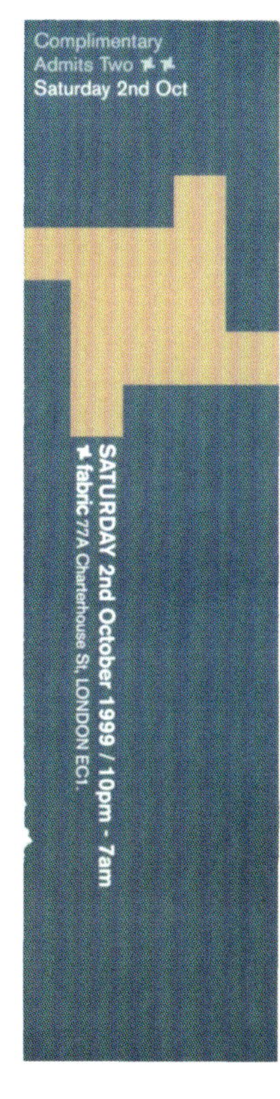

131—1

131—2

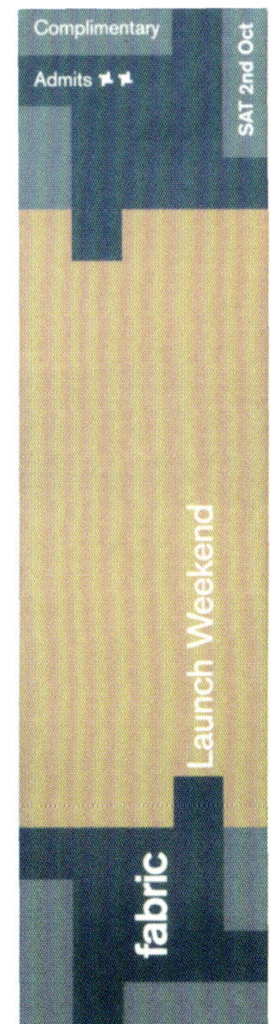

131—3

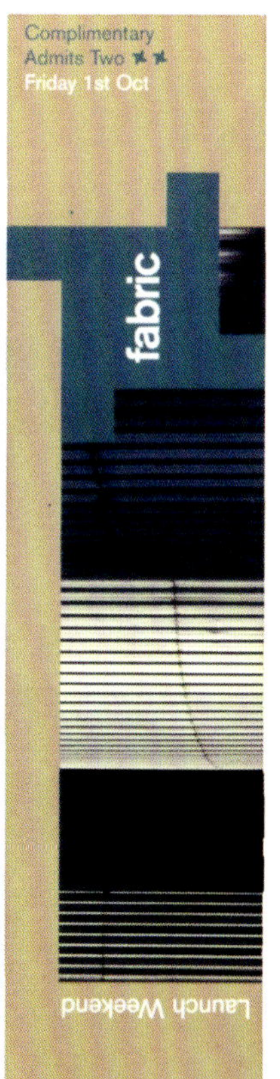

131—4

77A CHARTERHOUSE ST. LONDON EC1 www.fabric-london.com
fabric info: 0207 490 0444
fabric
the
launch
weekend

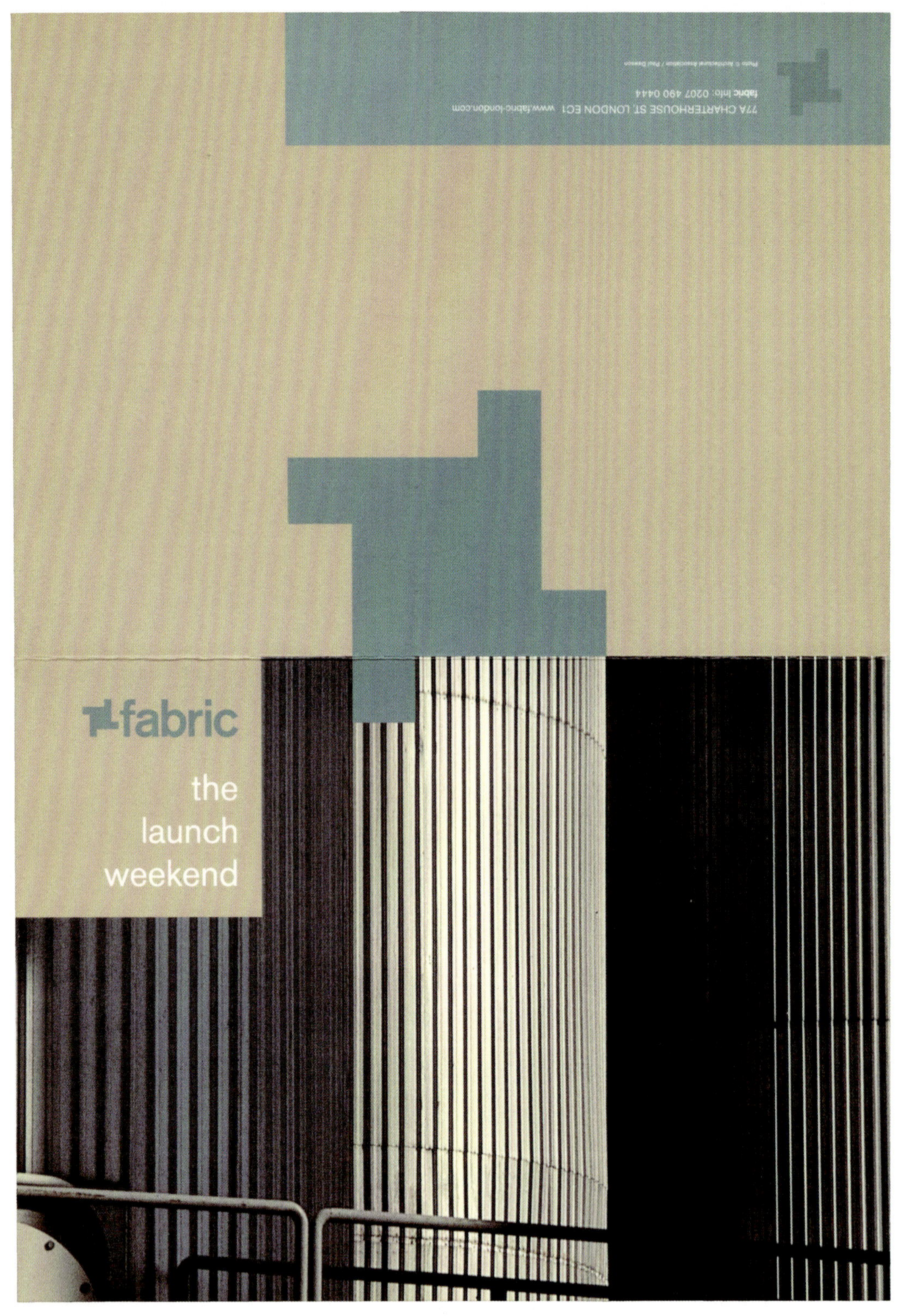

132—1

FRIDAY 1ST OCTOBER
10pm - 5am (£10)
ROOM 1
Monkey Mafia (live)
Schoolly D (live)
Kid Swift
Scratch Perverts
ROOM 2
E-Z Rollers (live)
Ed Rush & Optical
DJ Die
Jumping Jack Frost
J Majik
ROOM 3
Groove Armada
Harvey
SATURDAY 2ND OCTOBER
10pm - 7am (£12)
ROOM 1
Sasha
Terry Francis
Craig Richards
Pure Science (live)
ROOM 2
Tony Humphries
DJ Pierre
Kid Batchelor
ROOM 3
FRICTION
Adam Freeland
Tayo
Danny McMillan

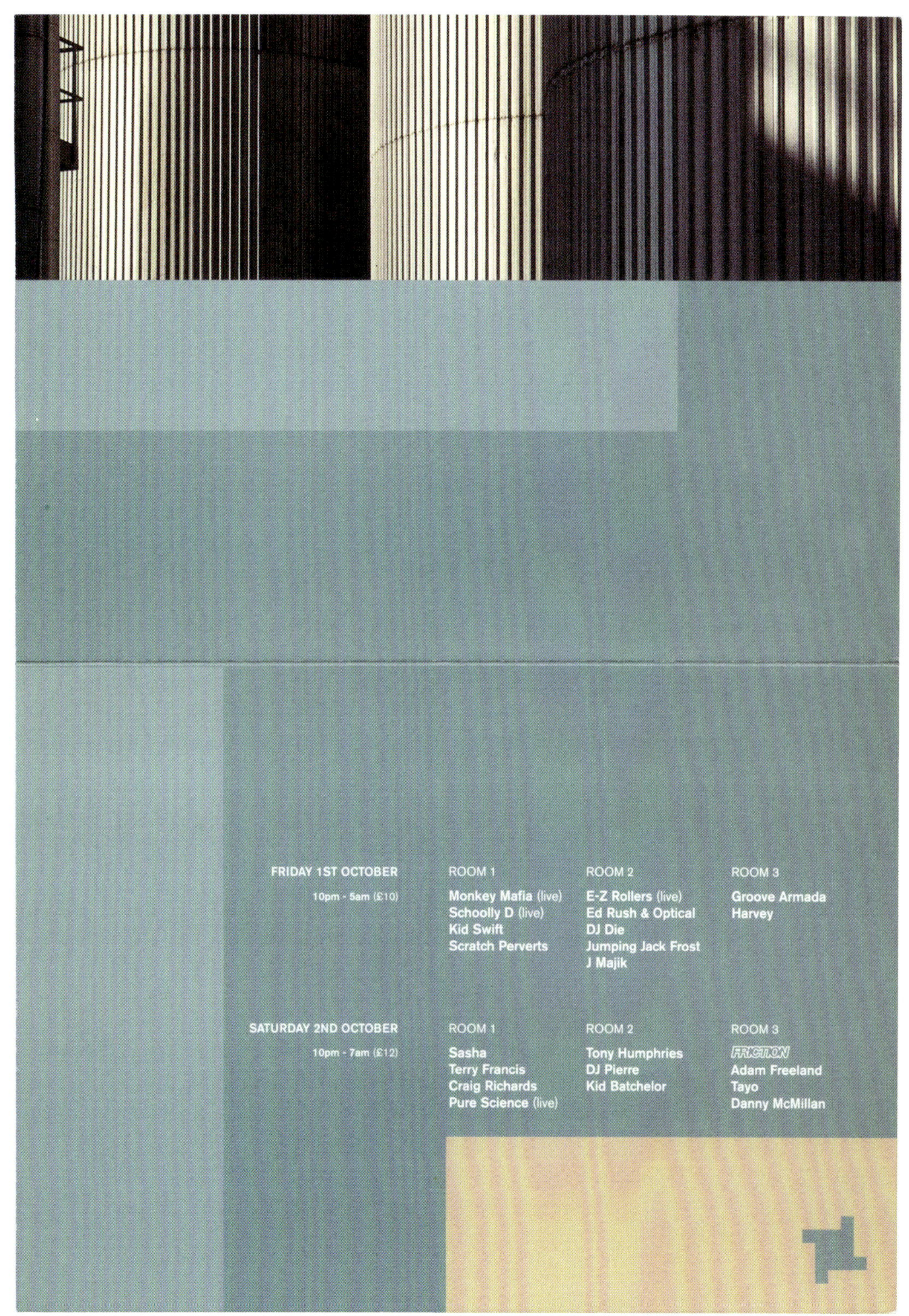

133—1

the freestylers@fabric
monkey mafia@fabric
danny tenaglia@fabric
derrick carter@fabric
scratch perverts@fabric
terry francis@fabric
sasha@fabric

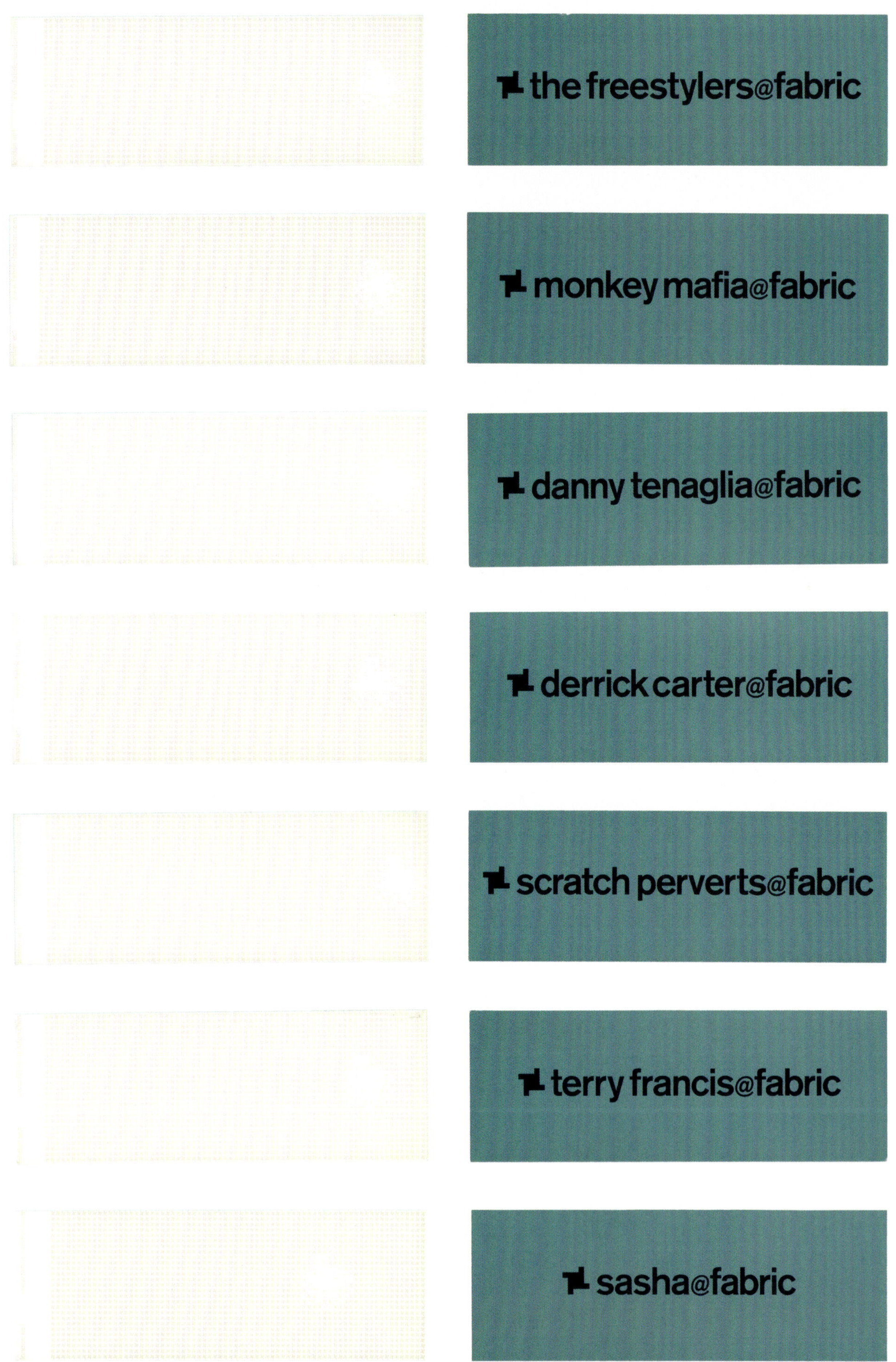

134—1

tony humphries@fabric

craig richards@fabric

grooverider@fabric

françois k@fabric

john digweed@fabric

fabio@fabric

135—1

Saturdays
April
fabric April

136—1

Saturdays
November
fabric November

04 11 00
Room 01
20:20 Vision 5th Anniversary
Ralph Lawson.
Random Factor
Fred Everything. Huggy.
Room 02
Dave Angel. Terry Francis.
Dave Mothersole.
Room 03
Strut Records.
18 11 00 Tyrant
Room 01
Sasha. Craig Richards.
Lee Burridge.
Room 02
Nick Rapaccioli.
Terry Francis.
Clive Henry
Room 03
Bob Jones & St. John Da Zilva.
fabric
www.fabriclondon.com
11 11 00
Room 01
Gemini Planet-E. Jon Marsh.
Bill Brewster.
Room 02
Kevin Saunderson.
Terry Francis. Colin Dale.
Room 03
Finger Lickin' Records.
25 11 00
Room 01
Idjut Boys. Craig Richards.
Akwaaba DJ Set.
Room 02
Richard Thair – Red Snapper.
Amalgamation Of Soundz.
Richard Grey.
Room 03
Groove Armada.
Ed Dimmock

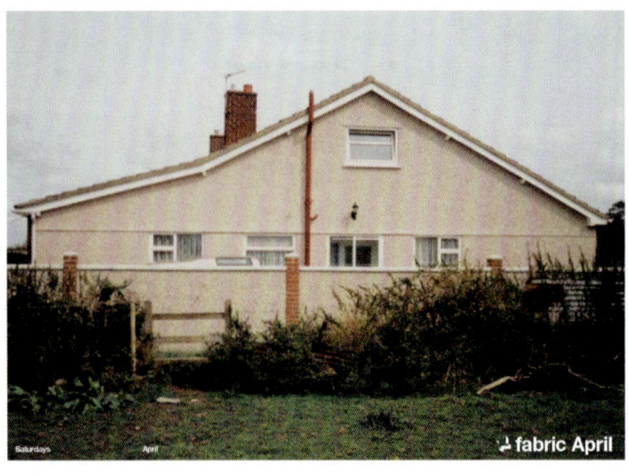

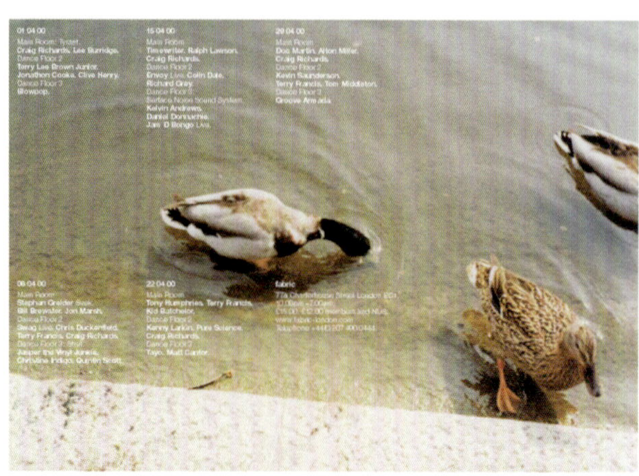

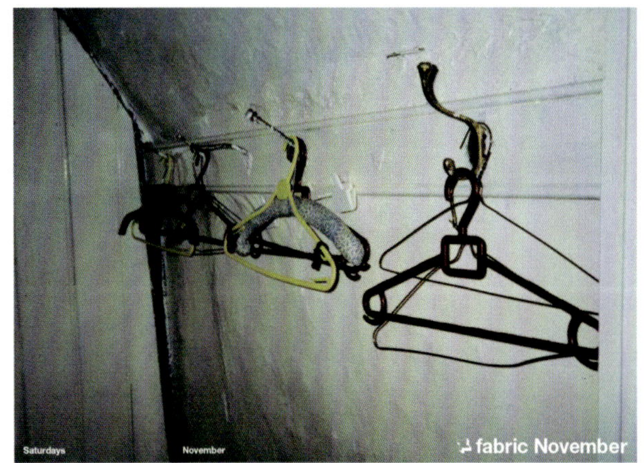

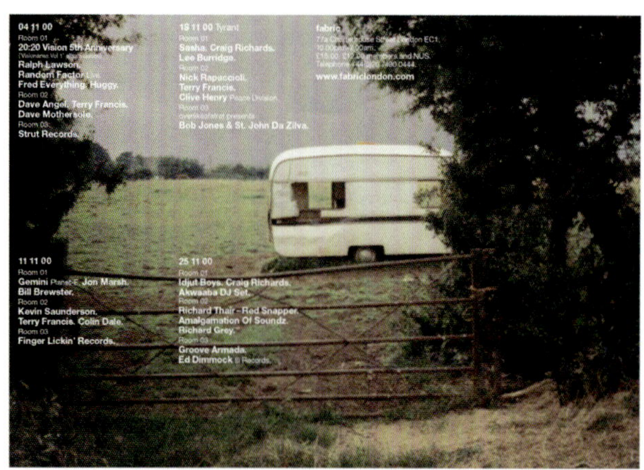

136—2

Saturdays
October
fabric October

07 10 00
Room 01
Tyler T-Bone Stadius Sonar, Vancouver.
Swag Live. Craig Richards.
Room 02
Luke Slater Live
(Wireless out now on Novamute).
Terry Francis.
Eddie Richards.
Room 03:
Amalgamation Of Soundz.
21 10 00 fabric is one.
10.00pm – midday 22nd.
£15.00. £12.00 members and NUS.
£10.00 after 5.00am.
Room 01
Craig Richards.
Terry Francis.
Sasha.
Bill Brewster.
Jon Marsh.
Deep C & Udoh.
Room 02
Adam Freeland.
Nathan Coles.
Lee Burridge.
Circulation Live.
Room 03
Amalgamation Of Soundz.
Tom Middleton.
fabric
77a Charterhouse Street London EC1.
10.00pm–7.00am.
£15.00. £12.00 members and NUS.
Telephone +44(0)20 7490 0444.
www.fabriclondon.com
14 10 00
Room 01
Doc Martin.
Herbert Live.
Craig Richards.
Room 02
Fabric presents
The Fuse Club Belgium:
Trish & Kash.
Deg & Terry Francis.
Room 03
Surface Noise Sound System.
Soul Mekanik Live.
Kelvin Andrews.
Danny Donnachie.
Jam D Bongo.
28 10 00
Room 01
Terry Lee Brown.
Swayzak Live.
DJ Heather.
Craig Richards.
Room 02
Terry Francis.
Nathan Coles.
Jonathon Cooke.
Room 03
Groove Armada.

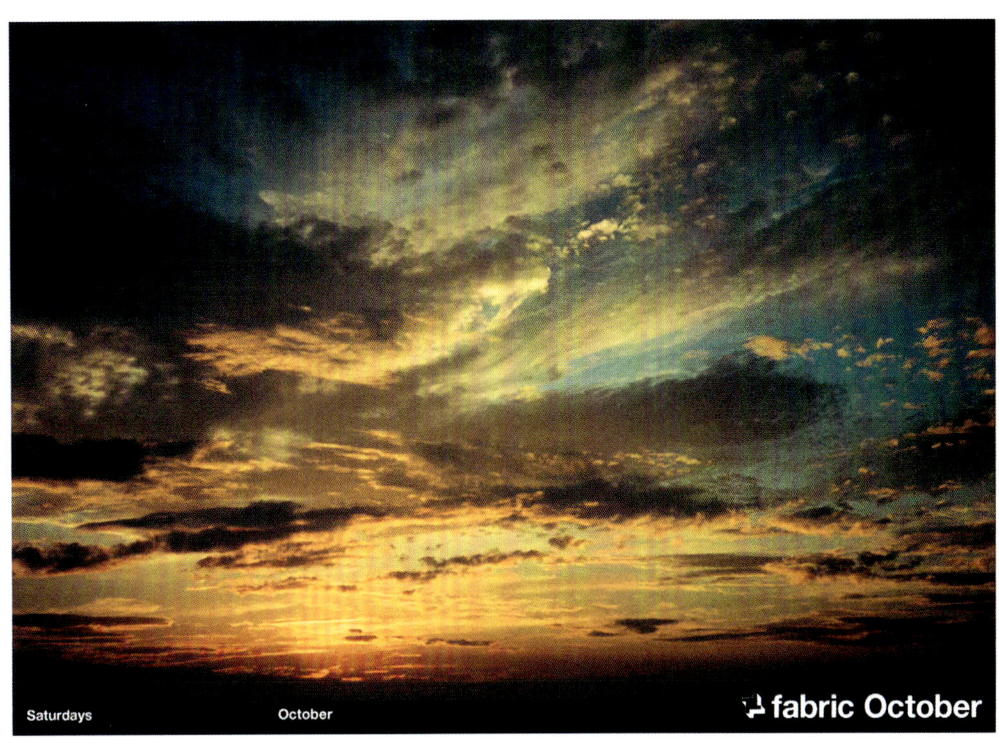

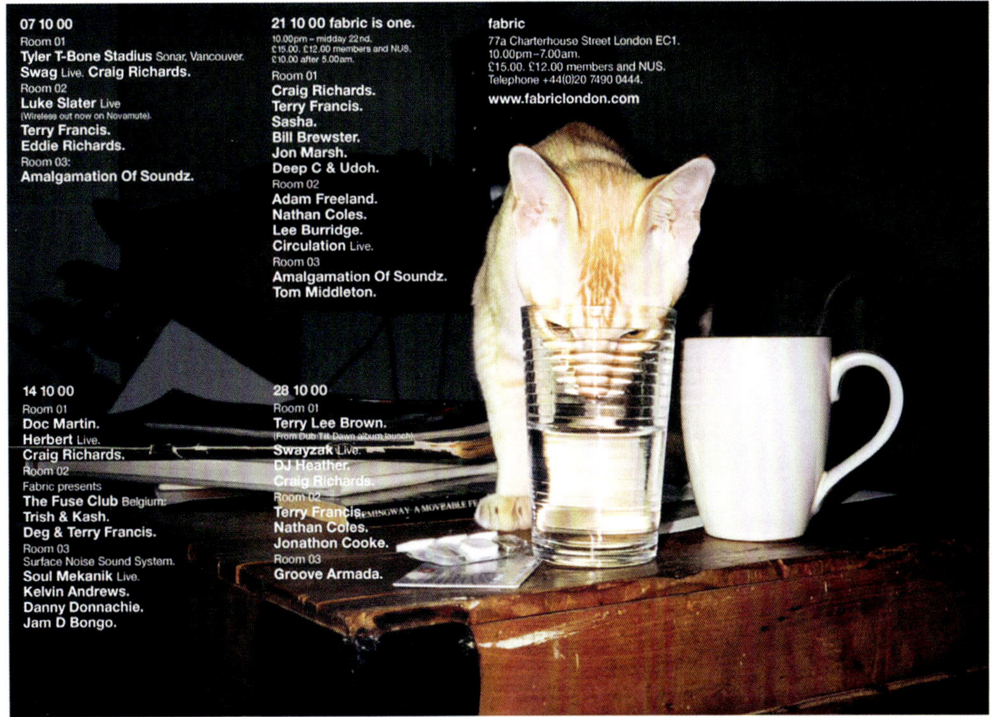

137—1

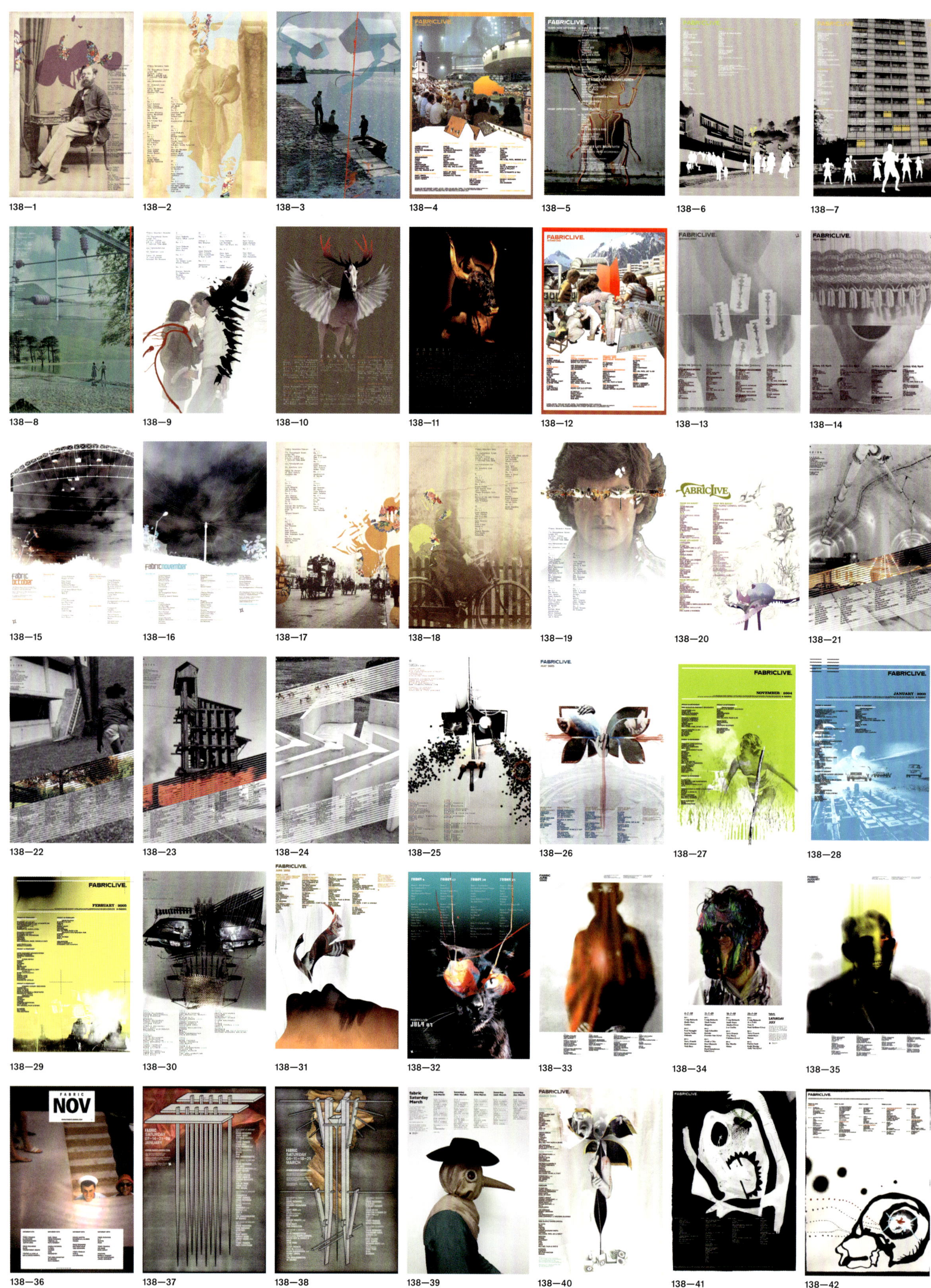

138—1 138—2 138—3 138—4 138—5 138—6 138—7

138—8 138—9 138—10 138—11 138—12 138—13 138—14

138—15 138—16 138—17 138—18 138—19 138—20 138—21

138—22 138—23 138—24 138—25 138—26 138—27 138—28

138—29 138—30 138—31 138—32 138—33 138—34 138—35

138—36 138—37 138—38 138—39 138—40 138—41 138—42

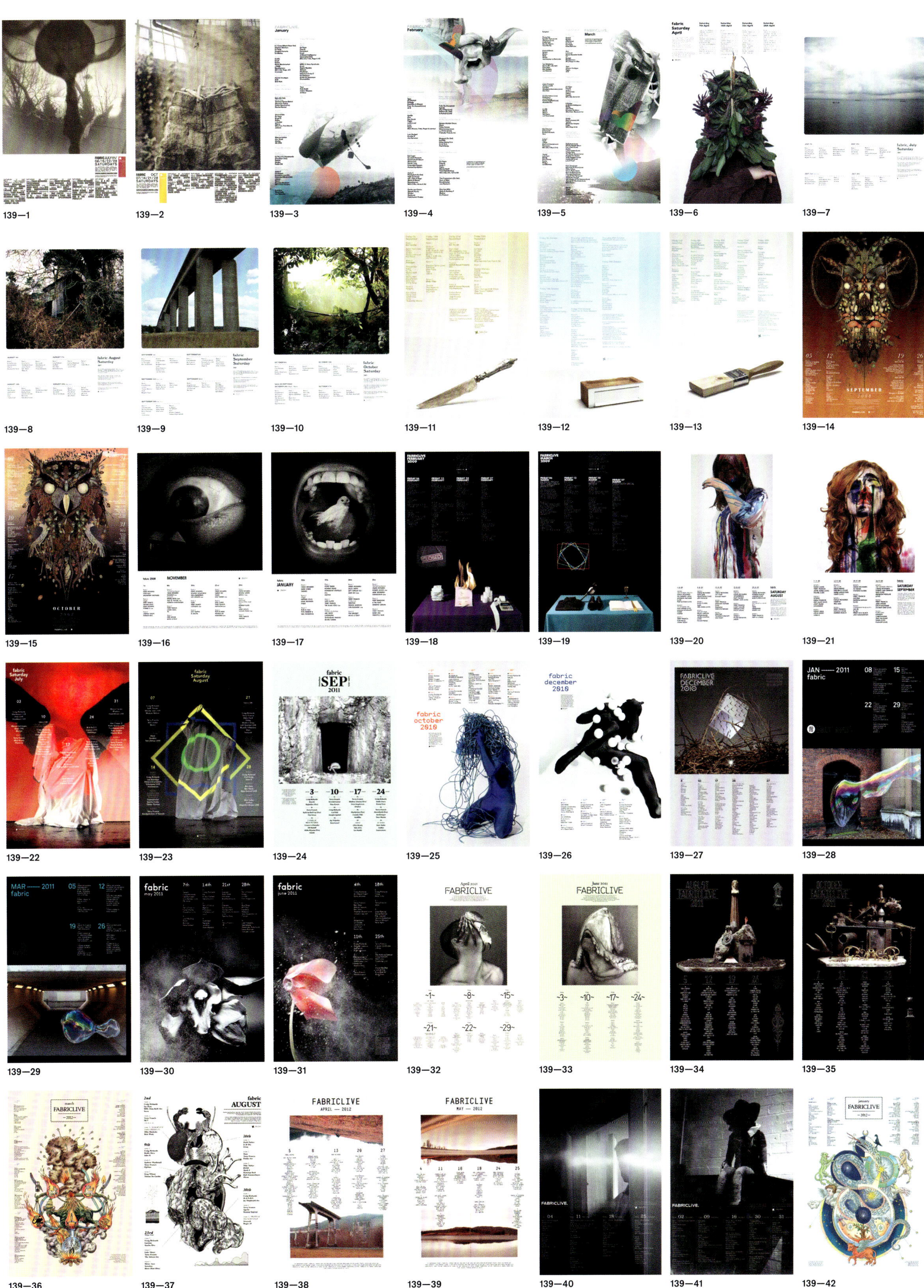

139—1 139—2 139—3 139—4 139—5 139—6 139—7

139—8 139—9 139—10 139—11 139—12 139—13 139—14

139—15 139—16 139—17 139—18 139—19 139—20 139—21

139—22 139—23 139—24 139—25 139—26 139—27 139—28

139—29 139—30 139—31 139—32 139—33 139—34 139—35

139—36 139—37 139—38 139—39 139—40 139—41 139—42

Friday 2nd May
Friday 9th May
room 1
UNKLE
SCRATCH PERVERTS
J WALK live
ALI B
room 2
PROTOTYPE
GROOVERIDER
FABIO
ANDY C
ED RUSH
TWISTED INDIVIDUAL
L DOUBLE
MCs RAGE, FLUX & FOXY
room 3
SCRATCH vs
BADMEANiNGOOD
SCRATCH PERVERTS
SKITZ
DJ BIZNIZZ
RICHY PITCH
MATT SMOOTH
ROB MAC
Friday 16th May
room 2
THE CHEMICAL BROTHERS dj set
JAMES LAVELLE
ALI B
room 1
ZINC PRESENTS FASTER
ZINC
GROOVERIDER
TOM MIDDLETON
ZED BIAS
JOE RANSOM
MCs DYNAMITE, SLARTA JOHN
& ANGELA HUNTE
room 3
DAVID HOLMES
DISASTRONAUT
Friday 23rd May
room 1
PLUMP DJs
JAMES LAVELLE
FALLACY live
STANTON WARRIORS
DEKKER
room 2
METALHEADZ
GOLDIE
LEMON D
DOC SCOTT
STORM
DANNY C
CLARKEE
MCs GQ, RAGE & 2SHY
room 3
ROOTS MANUVA dj set
JOE RANSOM
DJ SS
room 2
HYBRID
MEAT KATIE
DJ HYPER
room 3
SKITZ & RODNEY P
JOE RANSOM
BEAT MONKEYS
9.30PM – 5.00AM / PRICE £12 (£10 NUS). FABRIC. 77A CHARTERHOUSE STREET LONDON EC1.
INFORMATION: 020 7336 8898. TICKETS AVAILABLE FROM TICKETMASTER 0870 902 0001 AND FROM OUR WEBSITE.
FABRICLIVE CD SERIES: 09 JACQUES LU CONT AVAILABLE NOW. ART DIRECTION & ILLUSTRATION: LOVE.
www.fabriclondon.com

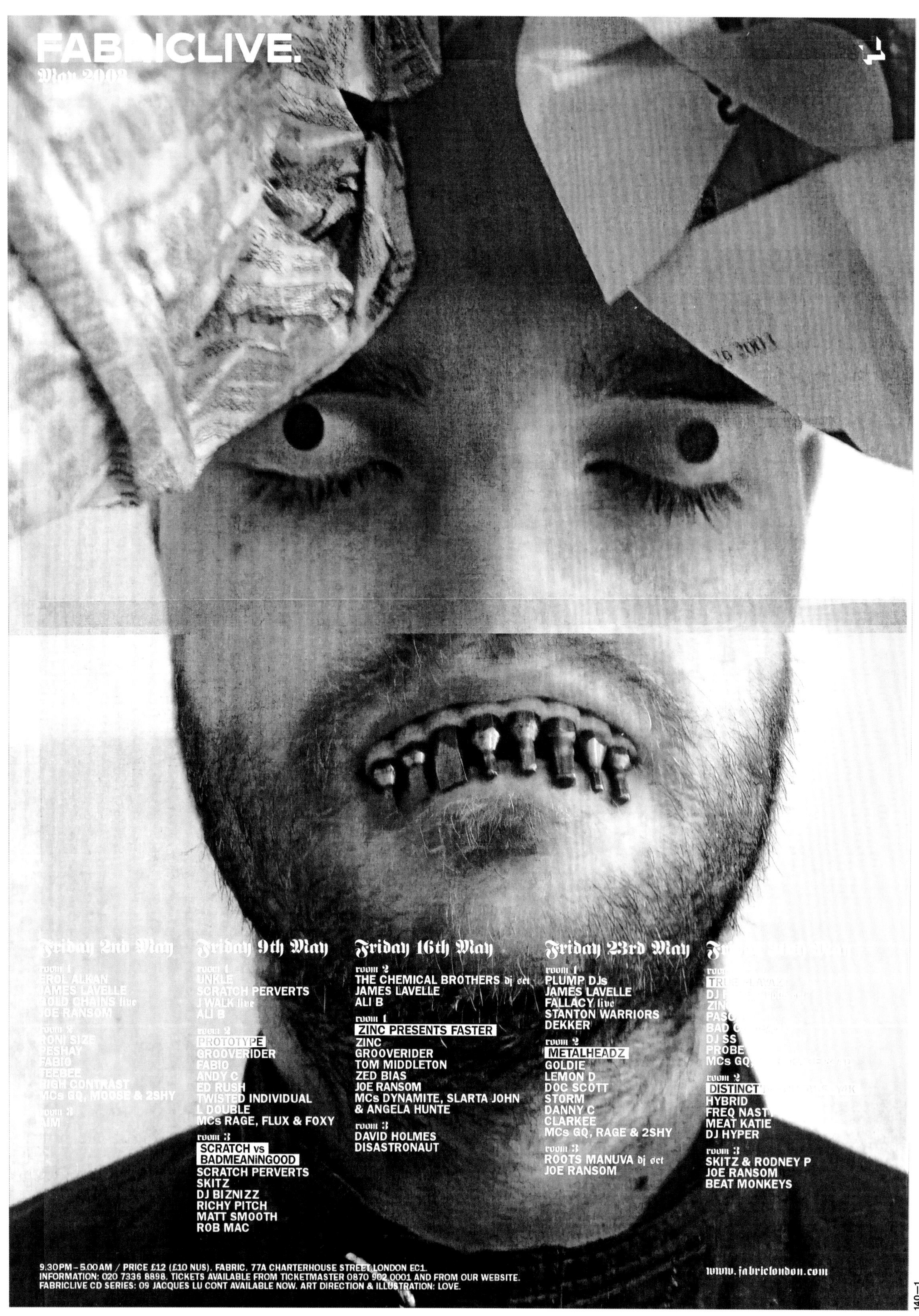

140—1

FABRICLIVE.

NOVEMBER | 2004

77A CHARTERHOUSE STREET LONDON EC1. 9.30PM–5.00AM. £12 (£10 NUS) INFORMATION: 020 7336 8898 TICKETS AVAILABLE FROM TICKETMASTER 0870 902 0001 AND FROM OUR WEBSITE: WWW.FABRICLONDON.COM FABRICLIVE. 19 THE FREESTYLERS. RELEASED 13 DECEMBER. ART DIRECTION: LOVE WWW.LOVELIMITED.CO.UK

FABRIC

FRIDAY 05 NOVEMBER

THE SCRATCH PERVERT BEATDOWN

RM01
IAN BROWN (LIVE)
JAZZY JEFF
SCRATCH PERVERTS
THE MIXOLOGISTS

RM02
DILLINJA & LEMON D
SCRATCH PERVERTS
ED RUSH & OPTICAL
J MAJIK
MAMPI SWIFT
MAXIMUS
MCs RYME TYME, SP:MC & 2 SHY

RM03
ROOTS MANUVA (DJ SET)
JOE RANSOM
DJ VADIM
DJ BLAKEY
MC TRIP

FRIDAY 12 NOVEMBER

RM01
THIEVERY CORPORATION
JAMES LAVELLE
STANTON WARRIORS
WILL SAUL

RM02 BREAKBEAT KAOS
ADAM F
DJ FRESH
DJ HYPE
PENDULUM
BARON
COMMIX
LE LUTIN
TKO & BOOM TAC
MCs GQ, DET & DARRISON

RM03 SCRATCH
THE NEXTMEN
DJ BIZNIZZ
RICHY PITCH
MATT SMOOTH
ROB MAC

FRIDAY 19 NOVEMBER

RM01
PLUMP DJs
KID KENOBI & MC SURESHOCK
JOE RANSOM
THE FREESTYLERS (DJ SET)
ALI B

RM02
GROOVERIDER & FABIO (LIVE ON RADIO 1)
ANDY C
DJ ZINC & JENNA G
DJ DIE
HIGH CONTRAST
M.J. MACPHERSON
MCs GQ & EKSMAN

RM03
NITIN SAWHNEY
NIHAL
BOBBY FRICTION

FRIDAY 26 NOVEMBER

RM01 TRUE PLAYAZ
DJ HYPE & DJ MARKY (BACK2BACK)
ZINC
PASCAL
GROOVERIDER
BROCKIE
HAZARD
MCs GQ, FATS, RAGE & AD

RM02
MEAT KATIE
LEE COOMBS
ALI B
WESTERN ALLSTARS

RM03
JOE RANSOM
SHORTEE BLITZ
MR THING
MC TRIP

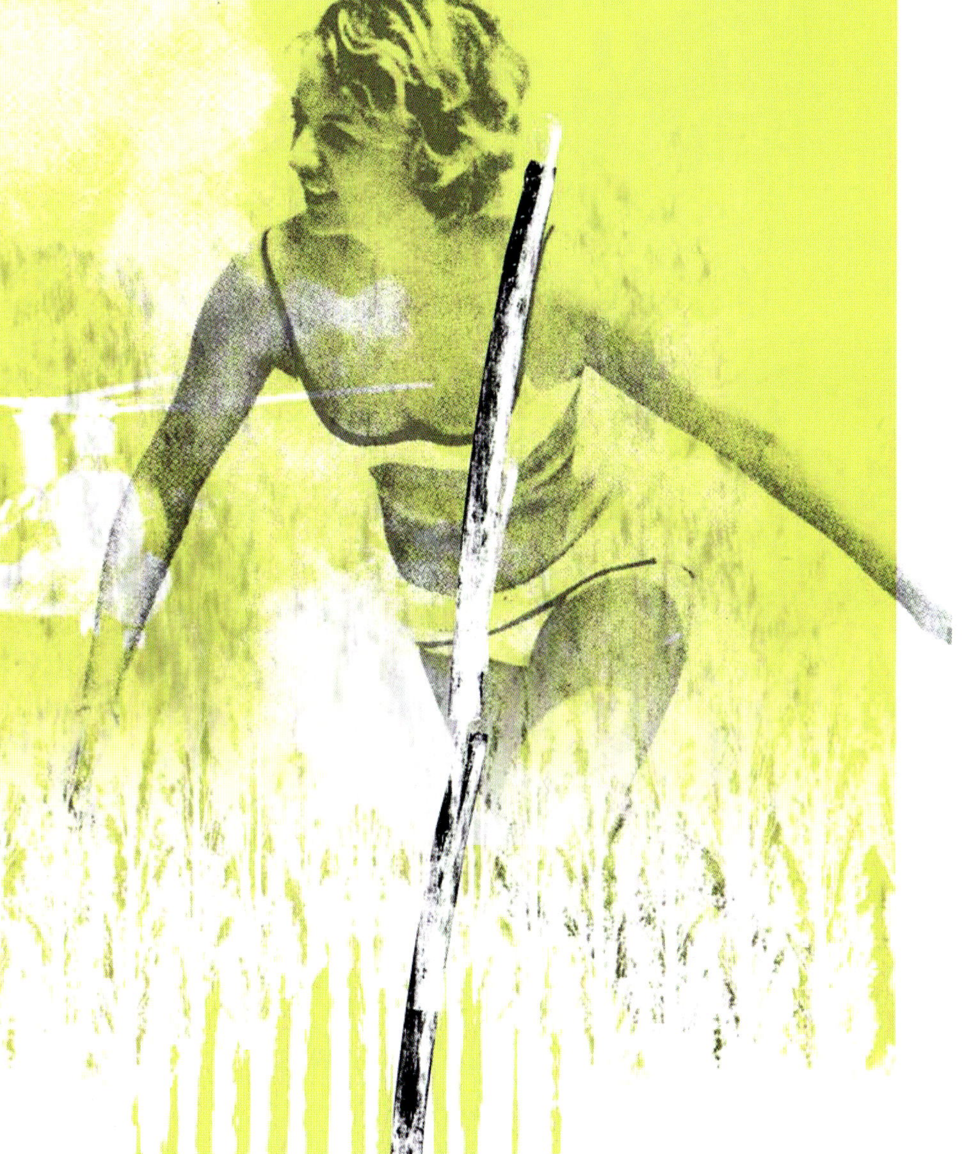

141—1

FABRIC JULY 2005

77A CHARTERHOUSE STREET
LONDON EC1
10PM—7AM. £15/£12 NUS
TELEPHONE: +44(0)20 7336 8898

ADVANCE TICKETS AVAILABLE FROM
TICKETMASTER 0870 902 0001
& FROM OUR WEBSITE:
WWW.FABRICLONDON.COM

FABRIC CD SERIES:
23 IVAN SMAGGHE
RELEASED 18TH JULY

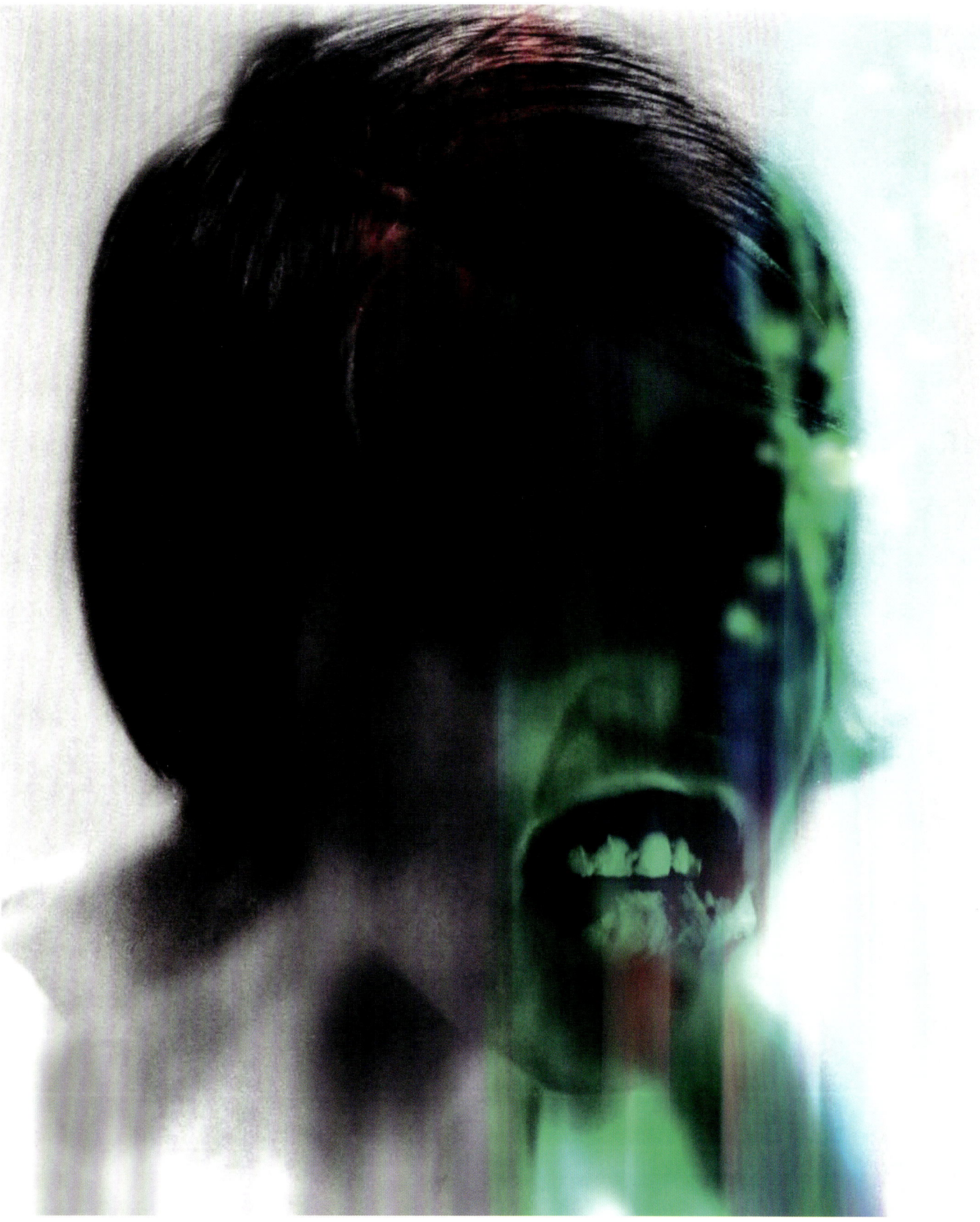

2ND
ROOM 1
CRAIG RICHARDS
MICHAEL MAYER
JENNIFER CARDINI
ADA LIVE
ROOM 2
TERRY FRANCIS
AGORIA
ASAD
ROOM 3
SUNKISSED:
G-HA
KANGO'S STEIN MASSIV LIVE
OLANSKII

9TH
ROOM 1
DOC MARTIN
IZ & DIZ
ROOM 2
CRAIG RICHARDS
ALTER EGO LIVE
SPECTRAL SOUND:
MATTHEW DEAR AUDION
& RYAN ELLIOTT
ROOM 3
TERRY FRANCIS
CHARLES WEBSTER

16TH
ROOM 1
CRAIG RICHARDS
STEVE BUG
WIGHNOMY BROS.
ROOM 2
SENDER RECORDS:
BENNO BLOME
METOPE LIVE
FRANK MARTINIQ
ROOM 3
OPTIMO
JAMES HILLARD

23RD
ROOM 1
CRAIG RICHARDS
IVAN SMAGGHE
ISOLEE LIVE/PLAYHOUSE
ROOM 2
TERRY FRANCIS
ROLANDO
COLIN DALE
ROOM 3
CHATEAU FLIGHT
ROB SUMMERHAYES

30TH
ROOM 1
TIEFSCHWARZ
EWAN PEARSON
GILES SMITH
ROOM 2
TERRY FRANCIS
BEN SIMS
RENATO COHEN
ROOM 3
TIRK RECORDS:
MAURICE FULTON
GREG WILSON CREDIT TO THE EDIT
MATTY J

142—1

FABRIC
SATURDAY
01–08–15–22–29
APRIL
WWW.FABRICLONDON.COM
77A CHARTERHOUSE STREET, LONDON EC1.
10PM–7AM. £15 / £12 NUS & FABRIC FIRST
MEMBERS. PHONE: +44(0)20 7336 8898.
ADVANCE TICKETS AVAILABLE FROM TICKETMASTER
0870 902 0001 & FROM OUR WEBSITE.
FABRIC CD SERIES: 27 MATTHEW DEAR AS AUDION.
AVAILABLE NOW.
PRINTED ON PAPER SOURCED
FROM SUSTAINABLE FORESTS.
ART DIRECTION & DESIGN: LOVE.
WWW.LOVELIMITED.CO.UK
fabricfirst
JOIN THE CLUB
SATURDAY 01 APRIL
RM. 01
FRANÇOIS K
TERRY FRANCIS
RM. 02
CRAIG RICHARDS
JAMES HOLDEN
MISC. LIVE
RM. 03
CHILLIFUNK 10TH ANNIVERSARY:
LOFTY
DR. BOB JONES
MARATHON MEN
GAVIN FRASER
DONNA WILLIAMS LIVE P.A./
FUNK ADDICTION
MC BUNZI D
SATURDAY 08 APRIL
RM. 01
CRAIG RICHARDS
ANDREW WEATHERALL
ATA PLAYHOUSE
RM. 02
TERRY FRANCIS
AGORIA
SHINEDOE INTACTO REC.
RM. 03
GREG WILSON
IDJUT BOYS
SATURDAY 15 APRIL
RM. 01
CRAIG RICHARDS
AKUFEN
MATTHEW DEAR
RM. 02
KILL THE DJ:
IVAN SMAGGHE
JENNIFER CARDINI
ASWEFALL
[T]EKEL LIVE
RM. 03
TERRY FRANCIS
TRISTAN DA CUNHA
SATURDAY 22ND APRIL
RM. 01
CRAIG RICHARDS
KOMPAKT:
SUPERPITCHER
DJ KOZE
FERENC LIVE
RM. 02
SLAM
TERRY FRANCIS
RM. 03
CHATEAU FLIGHT
IN FLAGRANTI
SATURDAY 29TH APRIL
RM. 01
CRAIG RICHARDS
LUCIANO
SWEETN' CANDY LIVE
JAMIE JONES
RM. 02
TERRY FRANCIS
MARCO CAROLA
TECHNASIA LIVE
RM. 03
RUB 'N' TUG
TIM SWEENEY DFA

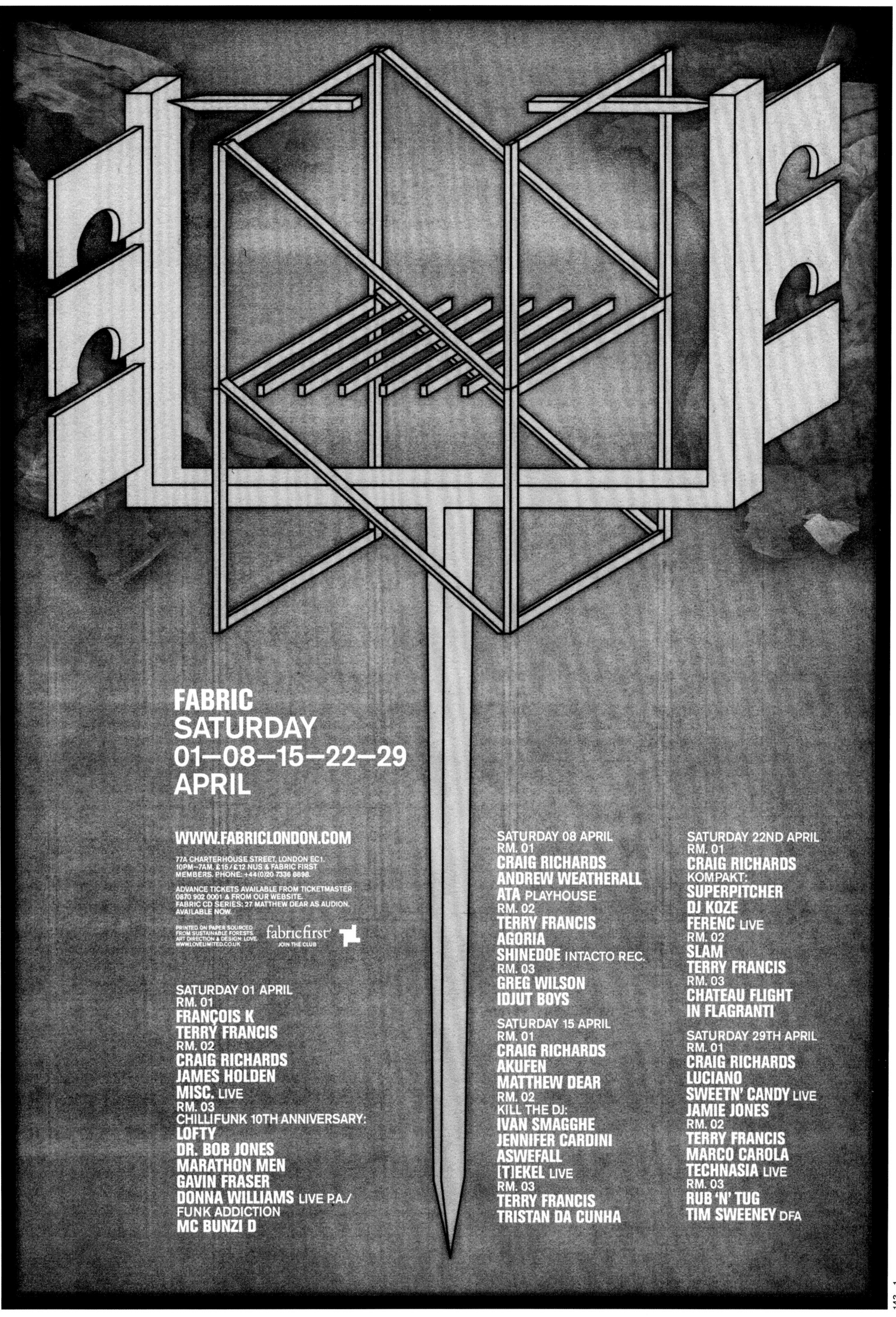

143—1

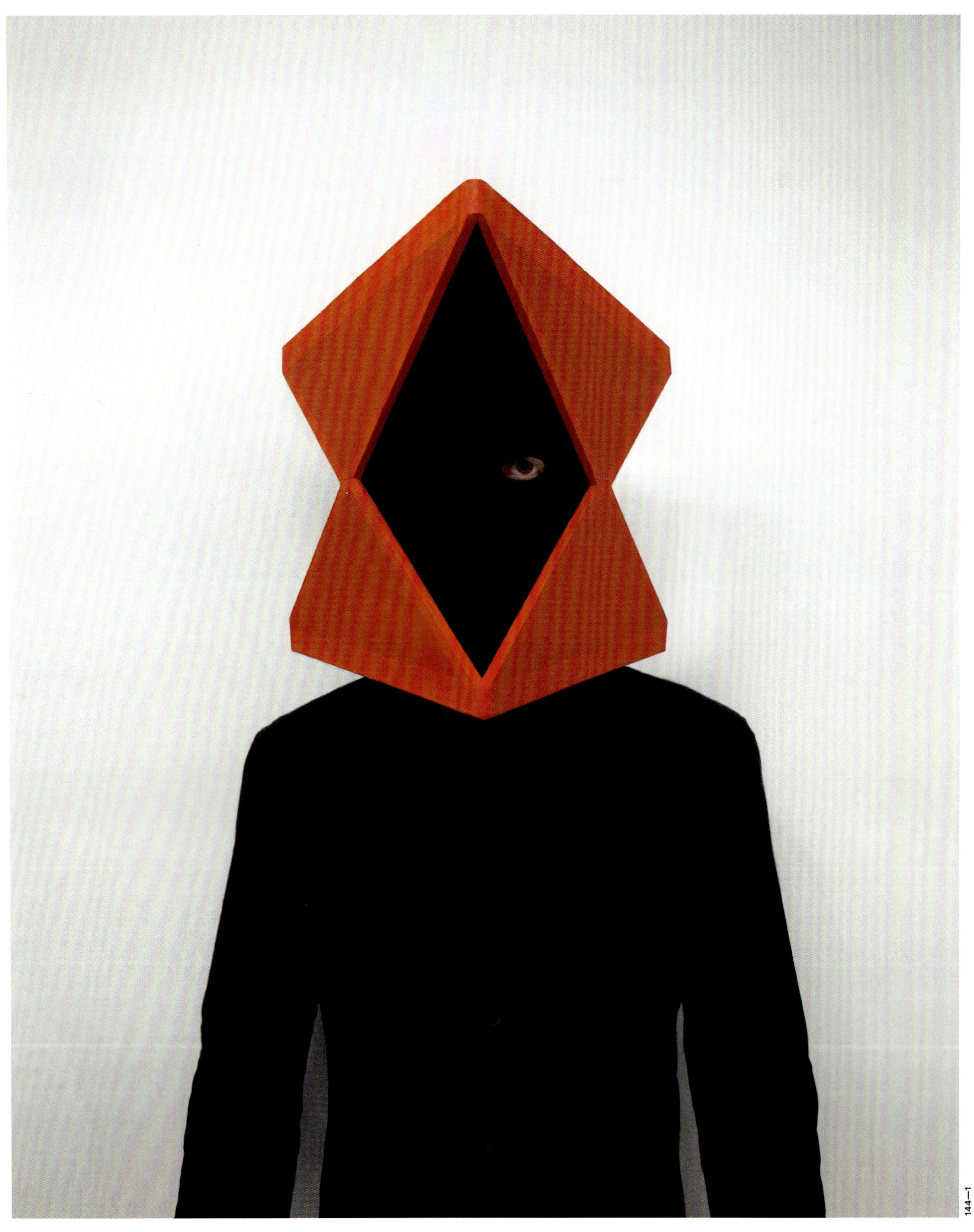
144—1

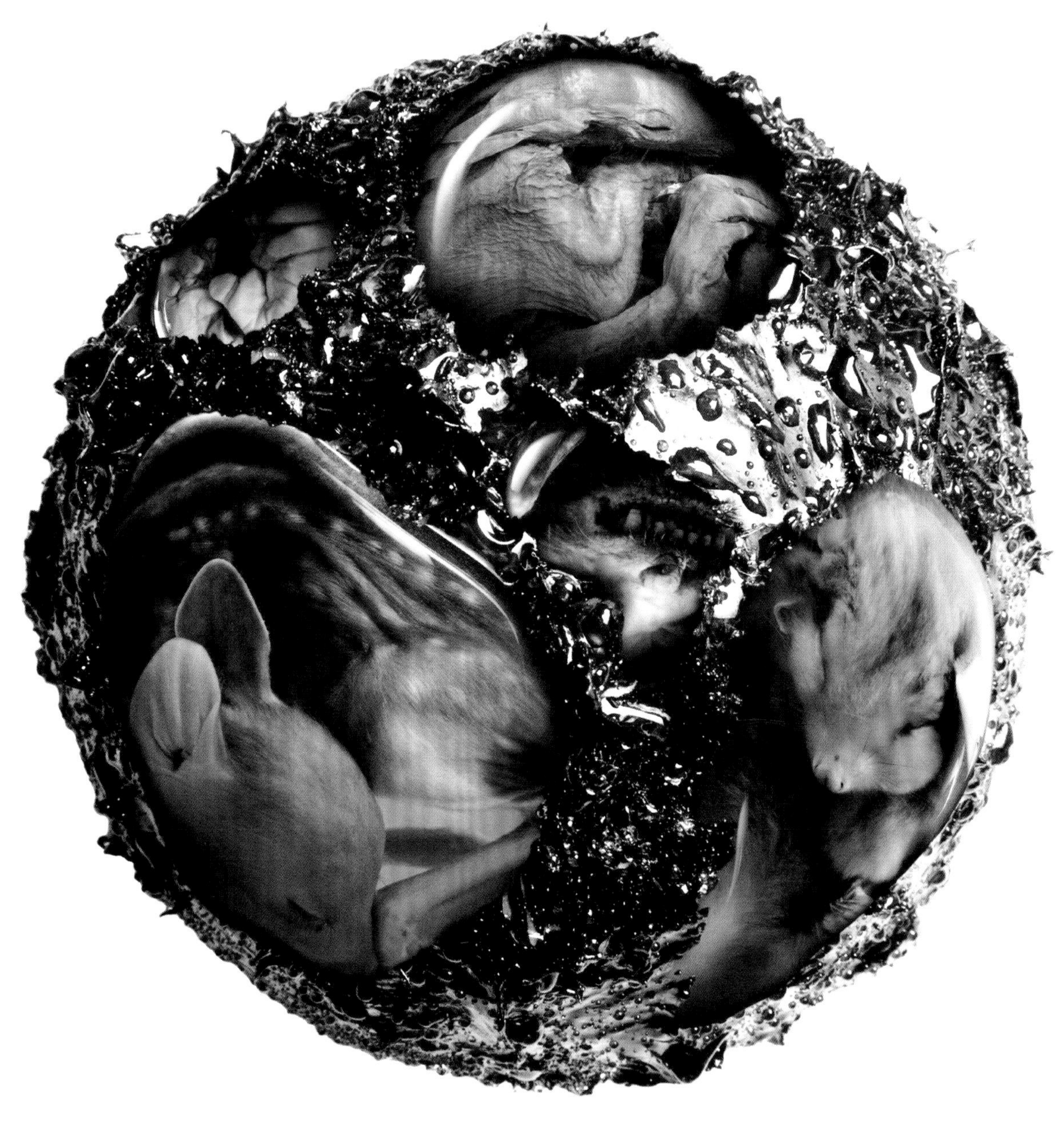

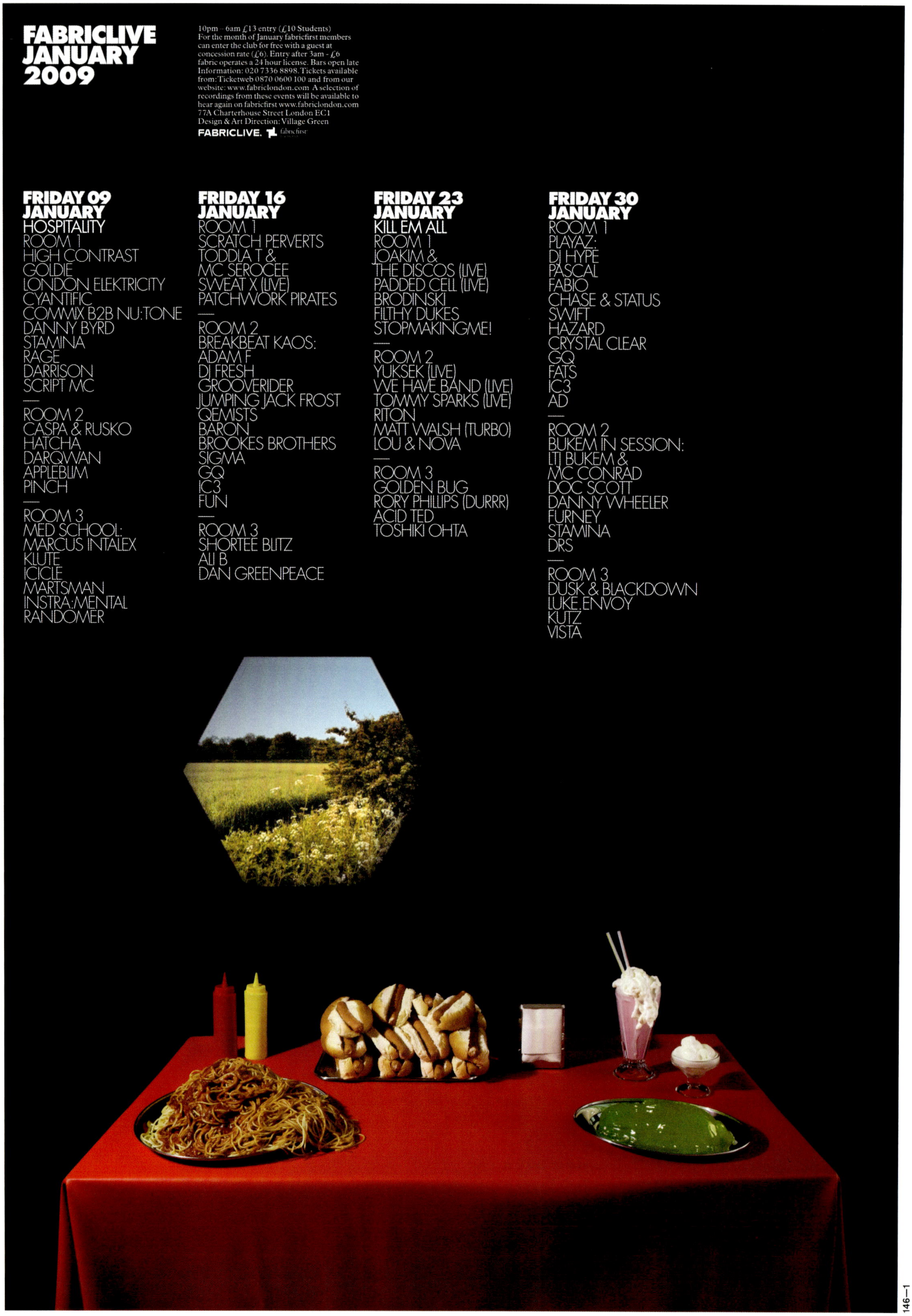

FABRICLIVE
JANUARY
2009

10pm – 6am £13 entry (£10 Students)
For the month of January fabricfirst members can enter the club for free with a guest at concession rate (£6). Entry after 3am - £6
fabric operates a 24 hour license. Bars open late
Information: 020 7336 8898. Tickets available from: Ticketweb 0870 0600 100 and from our website: www.fabriclondon.com A selection of recordings from these events will be available to hear again on fabricfirst www.fabriclondon.com
77A Charterhouse Street London EC1
Design & Art Direction: Village Green
FABRICLIVE. fabricfirst

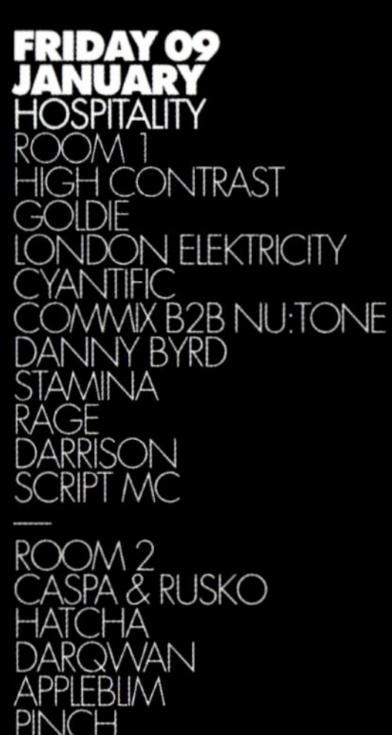

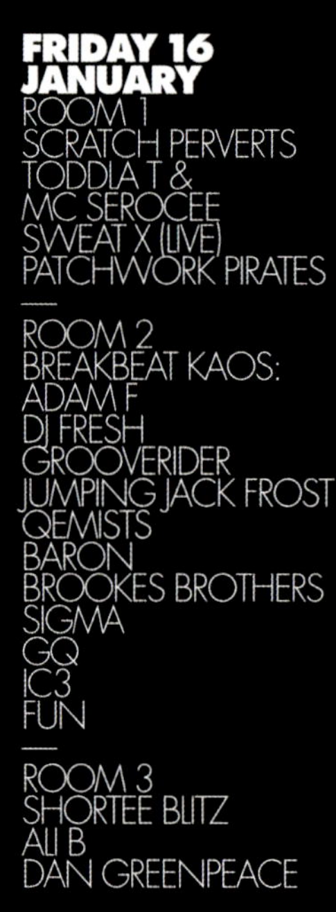

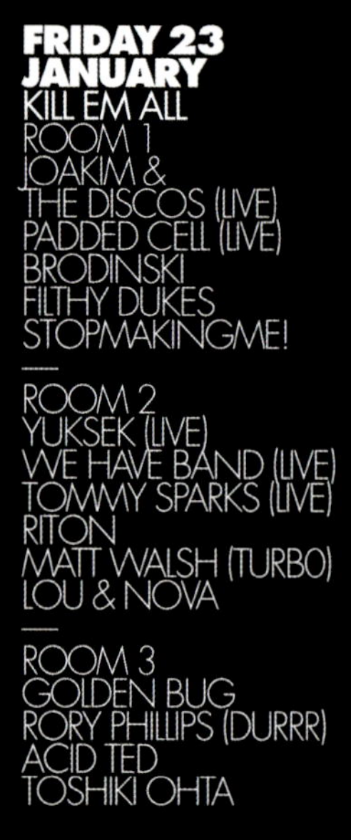

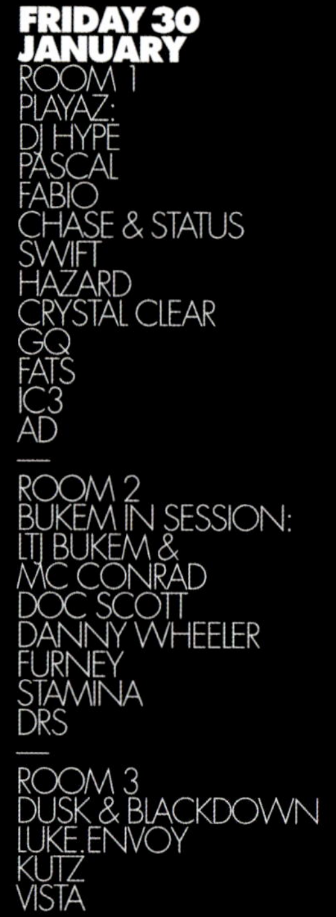

146—1

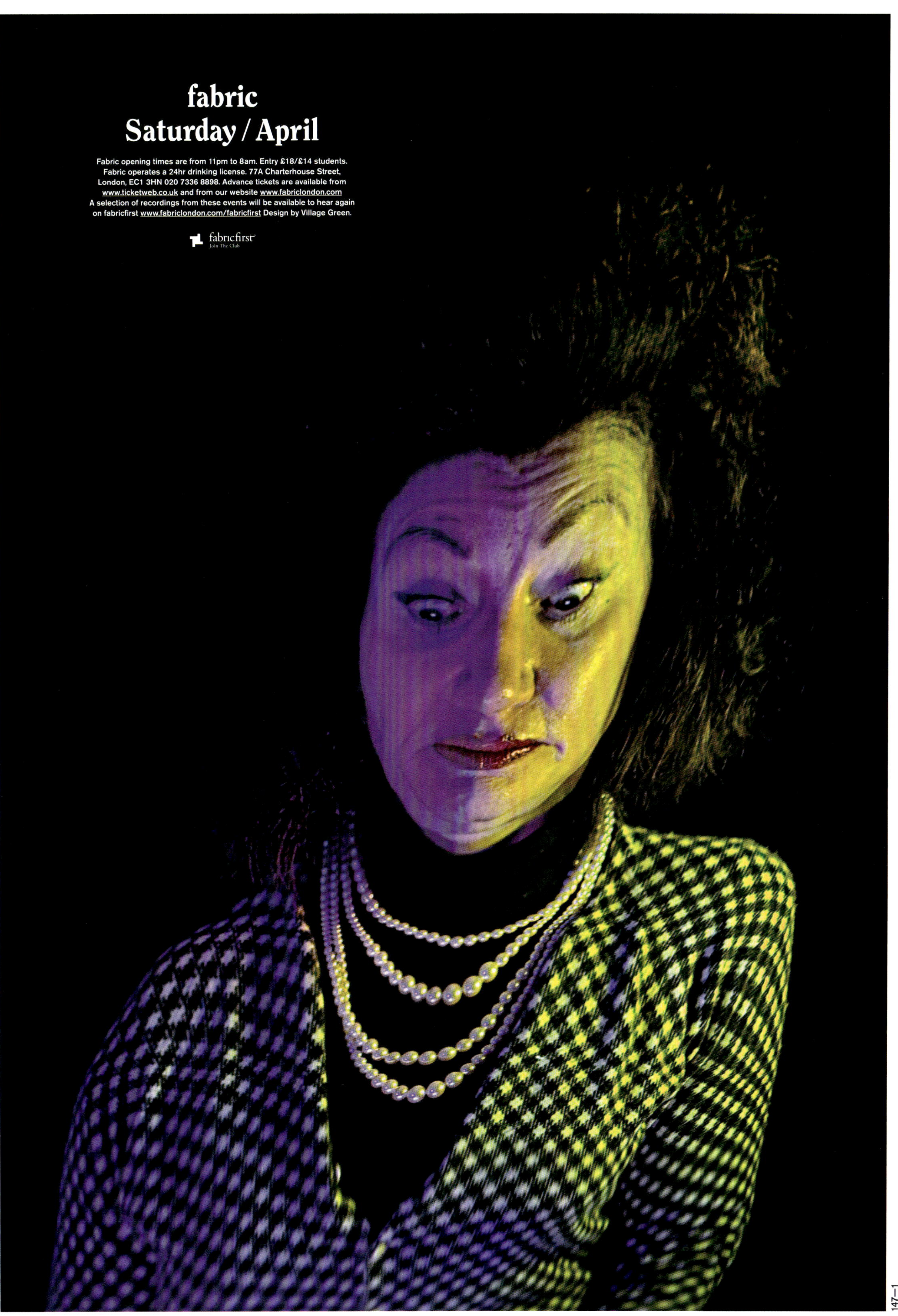
fabric
Saturday / April
Fabric opening times are from 11pm to 8am. Entry £18/£14 students.
Fabric operates a 24hr drinking license. 77A Charterhouse Street,
London, EC1 3HN 020 7336 8898. Advance tickets are available from
www.ticketweb.co.uk and from our website www.fabriclondon.com
A selection of recordings from these events will be available to hear again
on fabricfirst www.fabriclondon.com/fabricfirst Design by Village Green.
fabricfirst
Join The Club
147—1

fabric

JUNE

2012

77A Charterhouse Street, London EC1. Opening times: 11pm to 8am. Check www.fabriclondon.com for advance tickets, prices and further info. fabric operates a 24hr drinking license. A selection of recordings from these events will be available to hear again on www.fabriclondon.com/fabricfirst.

fabric 63: Levon Vincent — Out Now.
fabric 64: Guy Gerber — 25th June.
fabric 65: Matthias Tanzmann — 20th August.
fabric 66: Ben Klock — 15th October.
Design and Art Direction by plusyes,
Illustration by Luca Zamoc.

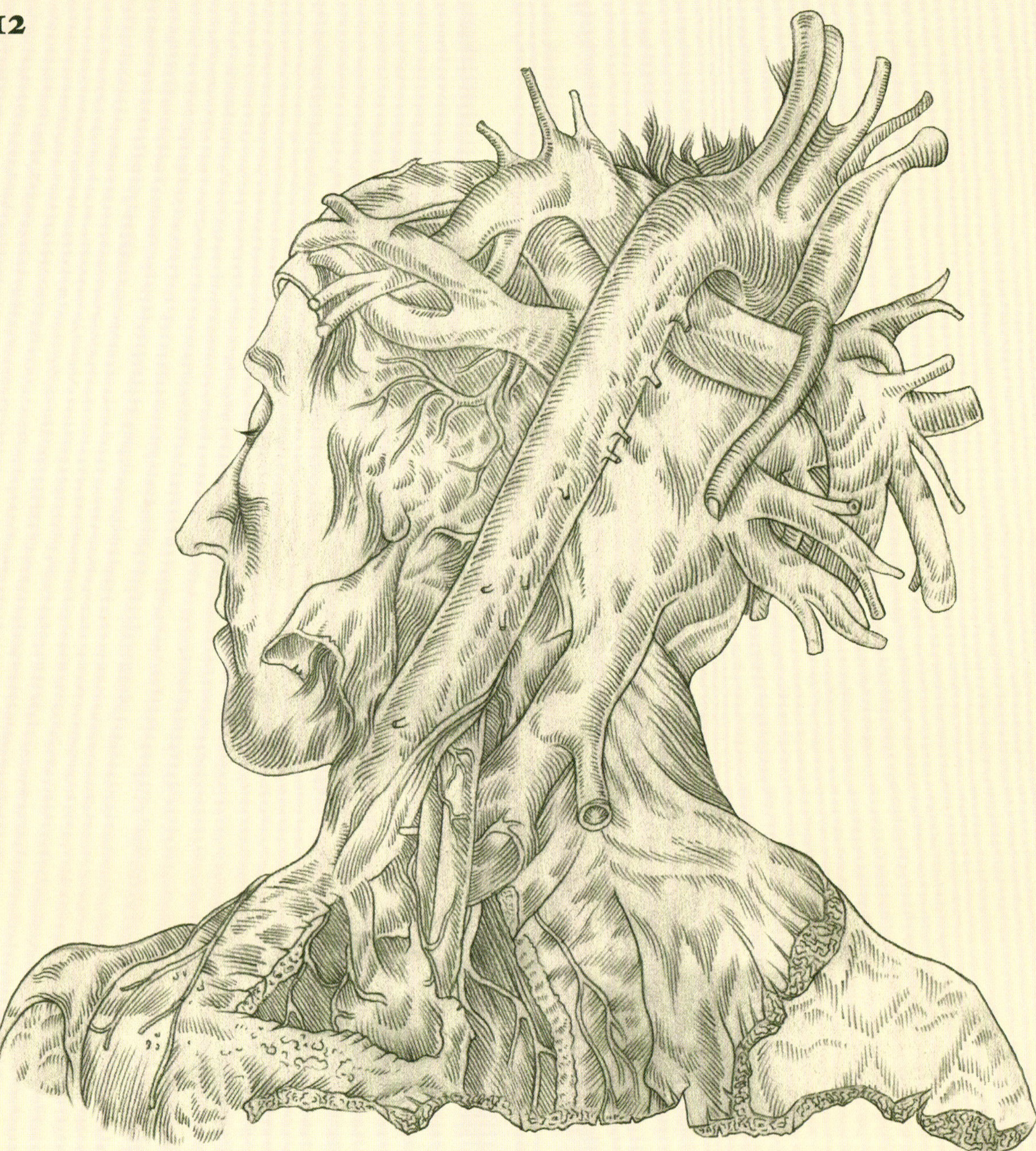

2nd

—

ROOM 1
CRAIG RICHARDS
APOLLONIA:
DAN GHENACIA
DYED SOUNDOROM
SHONKY

—

ROOM 2
TERRY FRANCIS
BEN KLOCK
DVS1

—

ROOM 3
TALE OF US
FB JULIAN

9th

—

ROOM 1
DIRTYBIRD
CLAUDE VONSTROKE
JUSTIN MARTIN
SASCHA BRAEMER

—

ROOM 2
THE NOTHING SPECIAL
CRAIG RICHARDS
MARTYN *(live)*
JUJU & JORDASH *(live)*
PEVERELIST

—

ROOM 3
TERRY FRANCIS
THUGFUCKER

16th

—

ROOM 1
DERRICK CARTER
NICK CURLY
MAKAM *(live)*

—

ROOM 2
LUKE SLATER
TERRY FRANCIS
THE ADVENT *(live)*

—

ROOM 3
BIGGER DEER RECORDS
SAMU.L
LEWIS RYDER
ROSS CAIDEN

23th

—

ROOM 1
CRAIG RICHARDS
CASSY
H FOUNDATION:
HIPP-E & HALO

—

ROOM 2
MARCEL DETTMANN
SHED *(live)*
BLAWAN

—

ROOM 3
TERRY FRANCIS
ROB MELLO
NICK DARE

30th

—

ROOM 1
CRAIG RICHARDS
RADIO SLAVE
TERRY FRANCIS
MR G *(live)*

—

ROOM 2
LOST
OMAR S
MIKE PARKER
STEVE BICKNELL

—

LOUCHE
DJ QU
TEVO HOWARD *(live)*
BRINSLEY KAZAK
BRUNO SCHMIDT

148—1

03
1
Pure Intec
Carl Cox
Jon Rundell
05
1
10 Years of Phonica
Levon Vincent
A Guy Called Gerald (Live)
Heidi
Hector
2
Terry Francis
Anthony Rother (Live)
Hrdvsion
3
10 Years of Phonica
Lord Of The Isles (Live)
Anthea & Soho
Simon Rigg
Jonny Rock
Nick Williams
Brian Not Brian
07
1
Darkside (Live)
Nicolas Jaar &
Dave Harrington
12
1
Craig Richards
Jamie Jones
Tone of Arc (Live)
2
Matt Tolfrey &
Ryan Crosson B2B
Ryan Elliott
Avatism (Live)
3
Terry Francis
Kate Simko
19
fabric
14th Birthday
—
30 Hours Of
Non Stop Music
Craig Richards
Terry Francis
Ricardo Villalobos
Clockwork
Cosmin TRG
Derren Smart
DJ Qu
Juergen Junker
Marcel Dettmann
No Regular Play (Live)
PBR Streetgang
Shed (Live)
Skream (Disco Set)
Sonja Moonear
Soul Clap
Tama Sumo
Wolf & Lamb
Zip
26
1
Craig Richards
Maceo Plex
DJ Tennis
2
One Records
Adam Shelton B2B
Subb-An
Shaun Reeves
John Dimas (Live)
Jack Wickham
3
Terry Francis
H: Foundation:
Hipp-E & Halo
77A Charterhouse Street, London EC1. Opening times: 11pm— 8am. Check www.fabriclondon.com
for advance tickets, prices and further info. fabric operates a 24HR drinking license.
A selection of recordings from these events will be available to hear again on www.fabriclondon.com/fabricfirst
fabric 71: Cassy — Out Now. fabric 72: rhadoo — 21st October. fabric 73: Ben Sims — 2nd December
Art Direction and Design by plusyes. Photography by Mads Perch.
fabric
October
2013

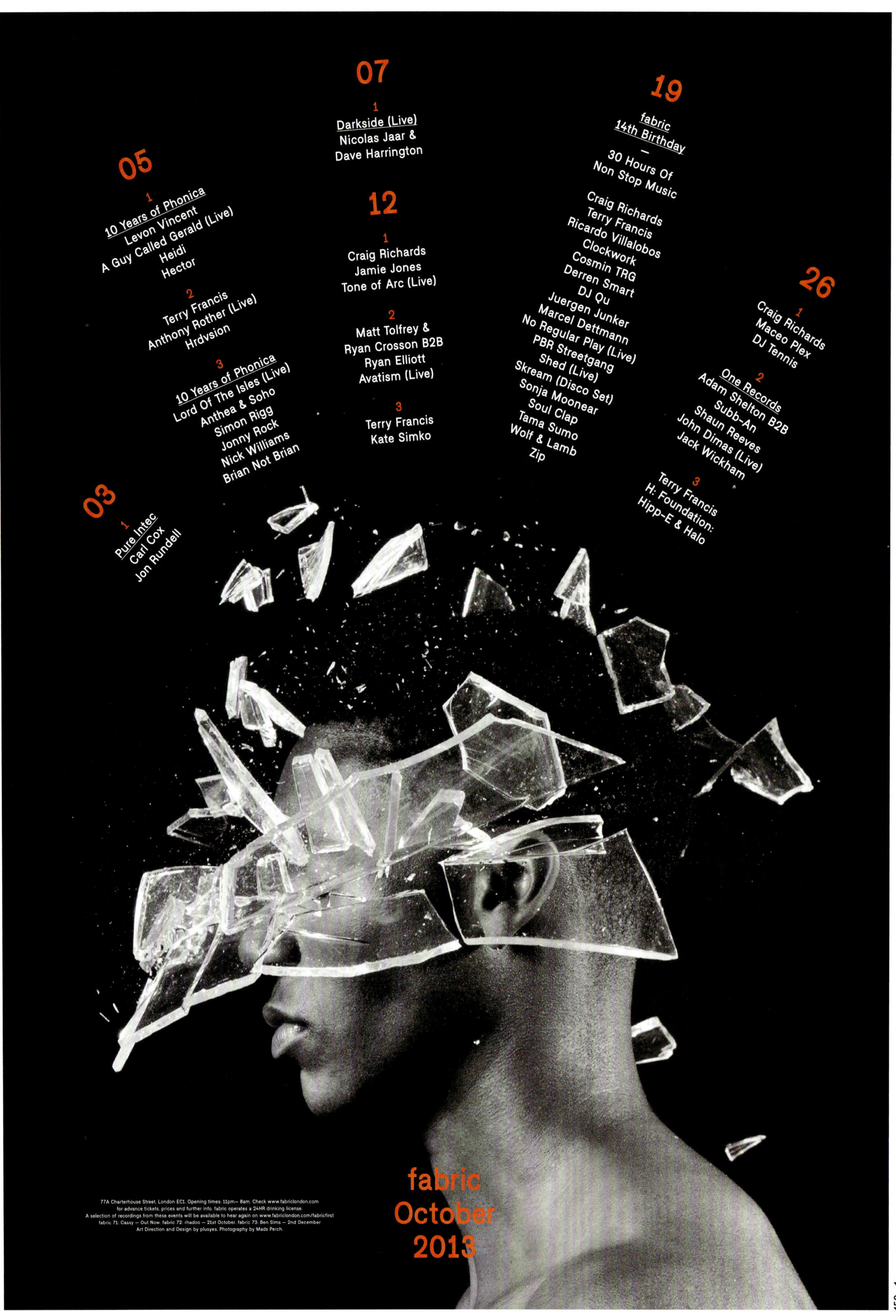

150—1

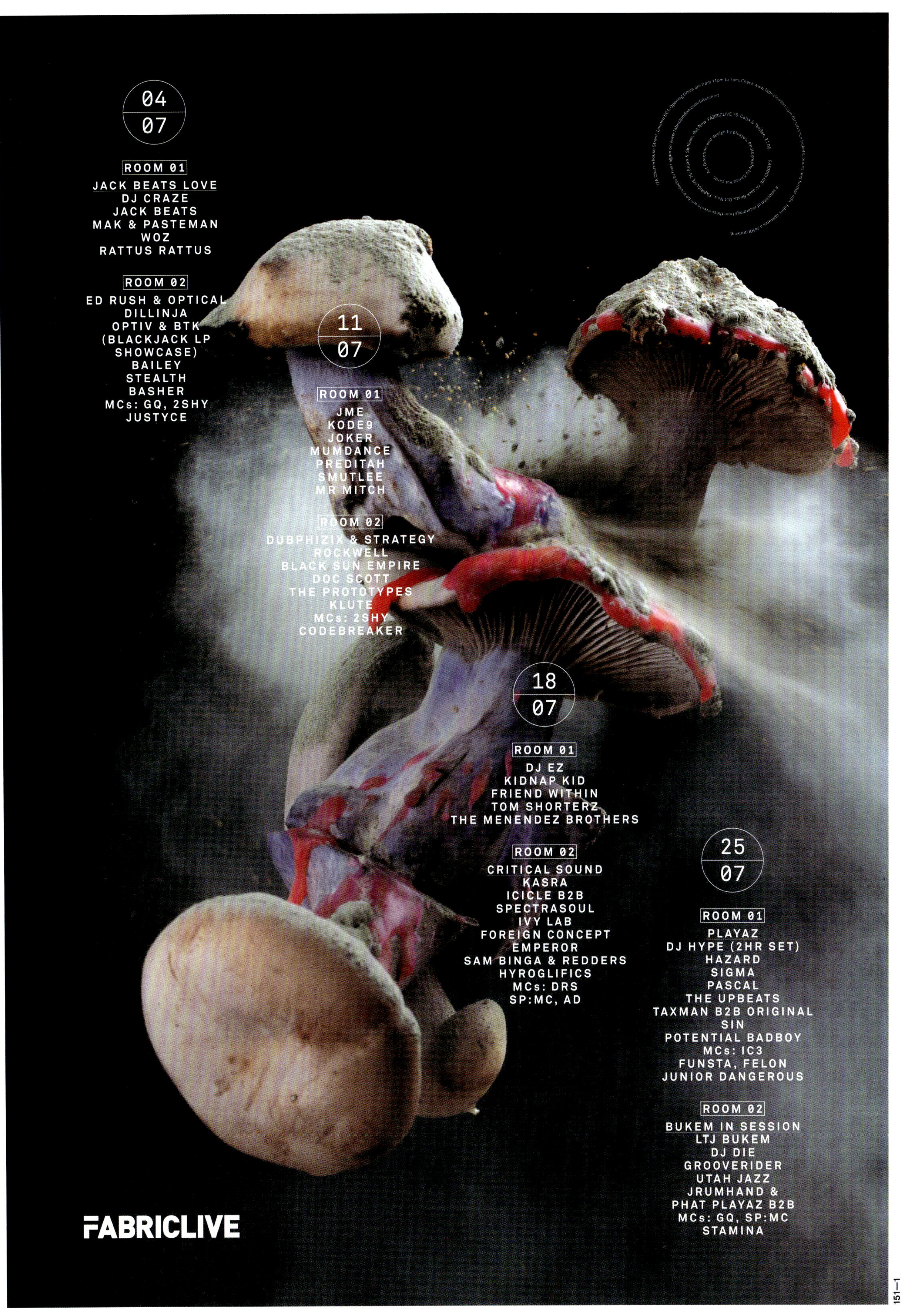

04
07
ROOM 01
JACK BEATS LOVE
DJ CRAZE
JACK BEATS
MAK & PASTEMAN
WOZ
RATTUS RATTUS
ROOM 02
ED RUSH & OPTICAL
DILLINJA
OPTIV & BTK
(BLACKJACK LP
SHOWCASE)
BAILEY
STEALTH
BASHER
MCs: GQ, 2SHY
JUSTYCE
11
07
ROOM 01
JME
KODE9
JOKER
MUMDANCE
PREDITAH
SMUTLEE
MR MITCH
ROOM 02
DUBPHIZIX & STRATEGY
ROCKWELL
BLACK SUN EMPIRE
DOC SCOTT
THE PROTOTYPES
KLUTE
MCs: 2SHY
CODEBREAKER
18
07
ROOM 01
DJ EZ
KIDNAP KID
FRIEND WITHIN
TOM SHORTERZ
THE MENENDEZ BROTHERS
ROOM 02
CRITICAL SOUND
KASRA
ICICLE B2B
SPECTRASOUL
IVY LAB
FOREIGN CONCEPT
EMPEROR
SAM BINGA & REDDERS
HYROGLIFICS
MCs: DRS
SP:MC, AD
25
07
ROOM 01
PLAYAZ
DJ HYPE (2HR SET)
HAZARD
SIGMA
PASCAL
THE UPBEATS
TAXMAN B2B ORIGINAL
SIN
POTENTIAL BADBOY
MCs: IC3
FUNSTA, FELON
JUNIOR DANGEROUS
ROOM 02
BUKEM IN SESSION
LTJ BUKEM
DJ DIE
GROOVERIDER
UTAH JAZZ
JRUMHAND &
PHAT PLAYAZ B2B
MCs: GQ, SP:MC
STAMINA
FABRICLIVE
151—1

03
ROOM 01
Hessle Audio
Pearson Sound
Ben UFO
Pangaea
Special Guest:
Surgeon
Bruce
ROOM 02
Hoya:Hoya
Legowelt (DJ Set)
Krystal Klear
Illum Sphere
Jon K
Jonny Dub
Hosted by Chunky
10
ROOM 01
Critical Sound
Mefjus B2B Ed Rush
Kasra B2B Foreign Concept
Emperor B2B The Upbeats
Alix Perez B2B Ivy Lab
Sam Binga B2B Chimpo
Hyroglifics
MCs: GQ / Mantmast
Redders
ROOM 02
Renegade Hardware
Loxy B2B Ink
Maztek
Audio
Optiv & Btk
Cold Fusion
MCs: Stapleton
K Eye / Remedy
17
ROOM 01
DJ EZ
DJ Haus
Benton
Moxie
Dorsia
ROOM 02
Fred V & Grafix
Culture Shock
Mat Zo (DnB set)
Hamilton
Frankee
Macpherson
MCs: Texas
Tonn Piper / Felon
24
ROOM 01
Butterz
Ruff Sqwad
Bonkaz
Elijah & Skilliam
Mumdance
Swindle
Flava D
Parris
ROOM 02
Blackout
Black Sun Empire
State Of Mind
Phace
Misanthrop
Neonlight
Prolix
MCs: SP:MC
2 Shy / Carasel
31
ROOM 01
Playaz
DJ Hype (2 hour Set)
Hazard
DJ Marky
TC
Pascal
Original Sin B2B Taxman
Potential Badboy
MCs: IC3 / Biggie
Stamina / Funsta MC
Junior Dangerous
ROOM 02
LTJ Bukem
Lenzman
Bailey
The Jazzassins
Blade
MCs: GQ
Ribbz / Moose
77A Charterhouse Street, London EC1. Opening times are from 11pm to 7am. Check www.fabriclondon.com for advance tickets, prices and further info. fabric operates a 24HR drinking license. A selection of recordings from these events will be available to hear again on www.fabriclondon.com/fabricfirst
FABRICLIVE 80: Mumdance, Out Now. FABRICLIVE 81: Monki, Out Now. FABRICLIVE 82: Ed Rush & Optical, available 20th July.
Art direction and design by plusyes, photography by Enrico Policardo
Jul
FABRICLIVE
2015

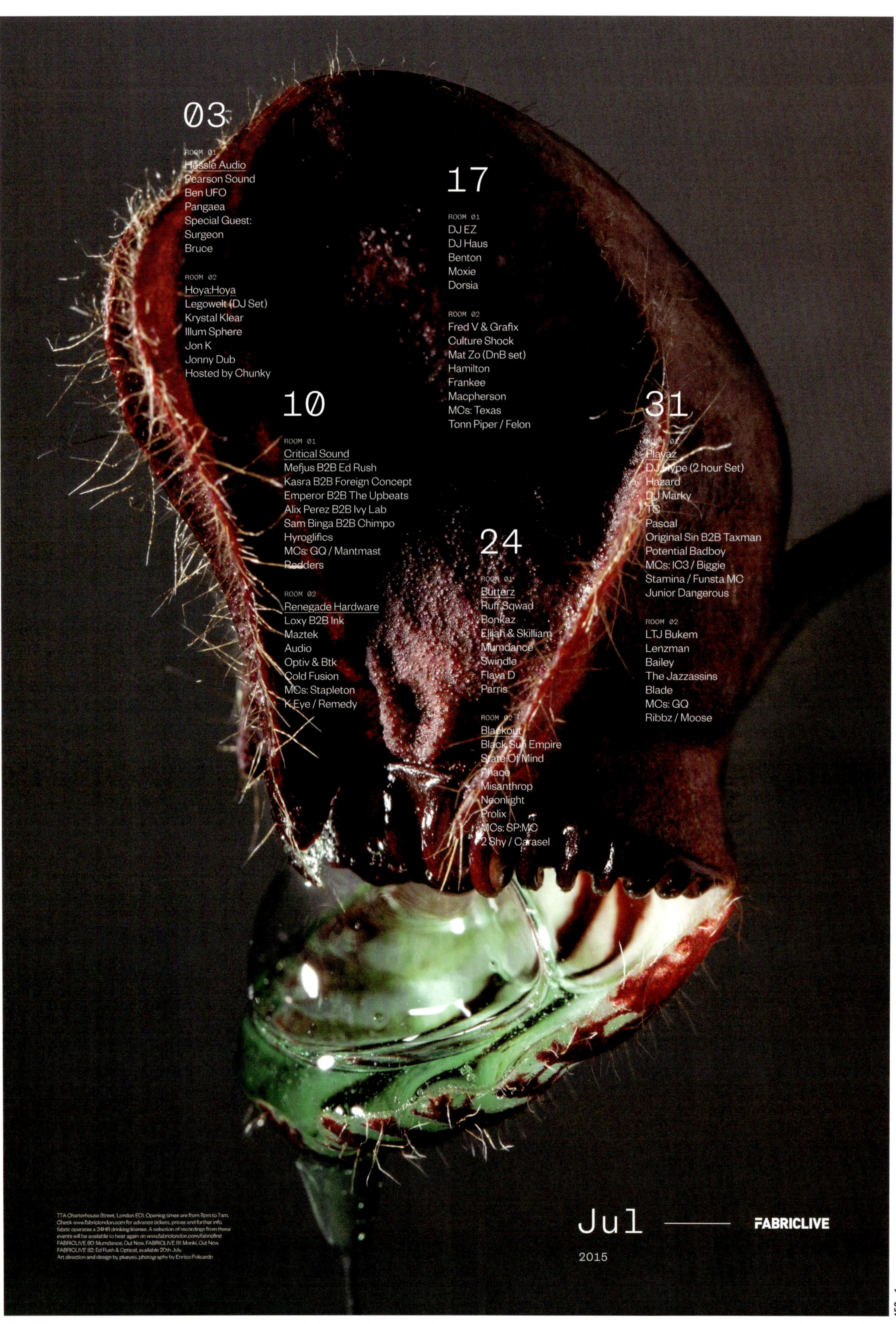

152—1

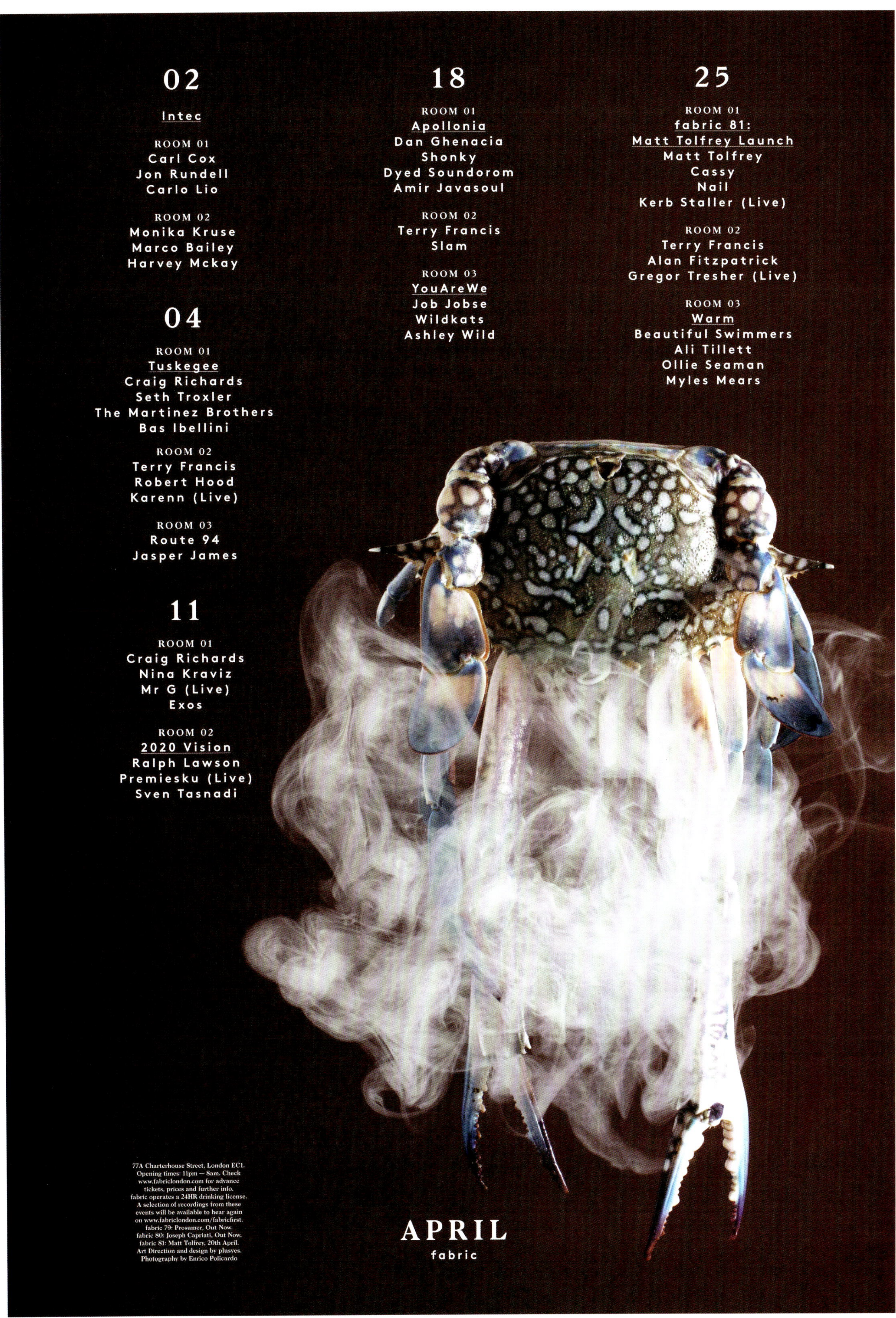

02
Intec
ROOM 01
Carl Cox
Jon Rundell
Carlo Lio
ROOM 02
Monika Kruse
Marco Bailey
Harvey Mckay
04
ROOM 01
Tuskegee
Craig Richards
Seth Troxler
The Martinez Brothers
Bas Ibellini
ROOM 02
Terry Francis
Robert Hood
Karenn (Live)
ROOM 03
Route 94
Jasper James
11
ROOM 01
Craig Richards
Nina Kraviz
Mr G (Live)
Exos
ROOM 02
2020 Vision
Ralph Lawson
Premiesku (Live)
Sven Tasnadi
18
ROOM 01
Apollonia
Dan Ghenacia
Shonky
Dyed Soundorom
Amir Javasoul
ROOM 02
Terry Francis
Slam
ROOM 03
YouAreWe
Job Jobse
Wildkats
Ashley Wild
25
ROOM 01
fabric 81:
Matt Tolfrey Launch
Matt Tolfrey
Cassy
Nail
Kerb Staller (Live)
ROOM 02
Terry Francis
Alan Fitzpatrick
Gregor Tresher (Live)
ROOM 03
Warm
Beautiful Swimmers
Ali Tillett
Ollie Seaman
Myles Mears
77A Charterhouse Street, London EC1.
Opening times: 11pm — 8am. Check
www.fabriclondon.com for advance
tickets, prices and further info.
fabric operates a 24HR drinking license.
A selection of recordings from these
events will be available to hear again
on www.fabriclondon.com/fabricfirst.
fabric 79: Prosumer, Out Now.
fabric 80: Joseph Capriati, Out Now.
fabric 81: Matt Tolfrey, 20th April.
Art Direction and design by plusyes.
Photography by Enrico Policardo
APRIL
fabric

153—1

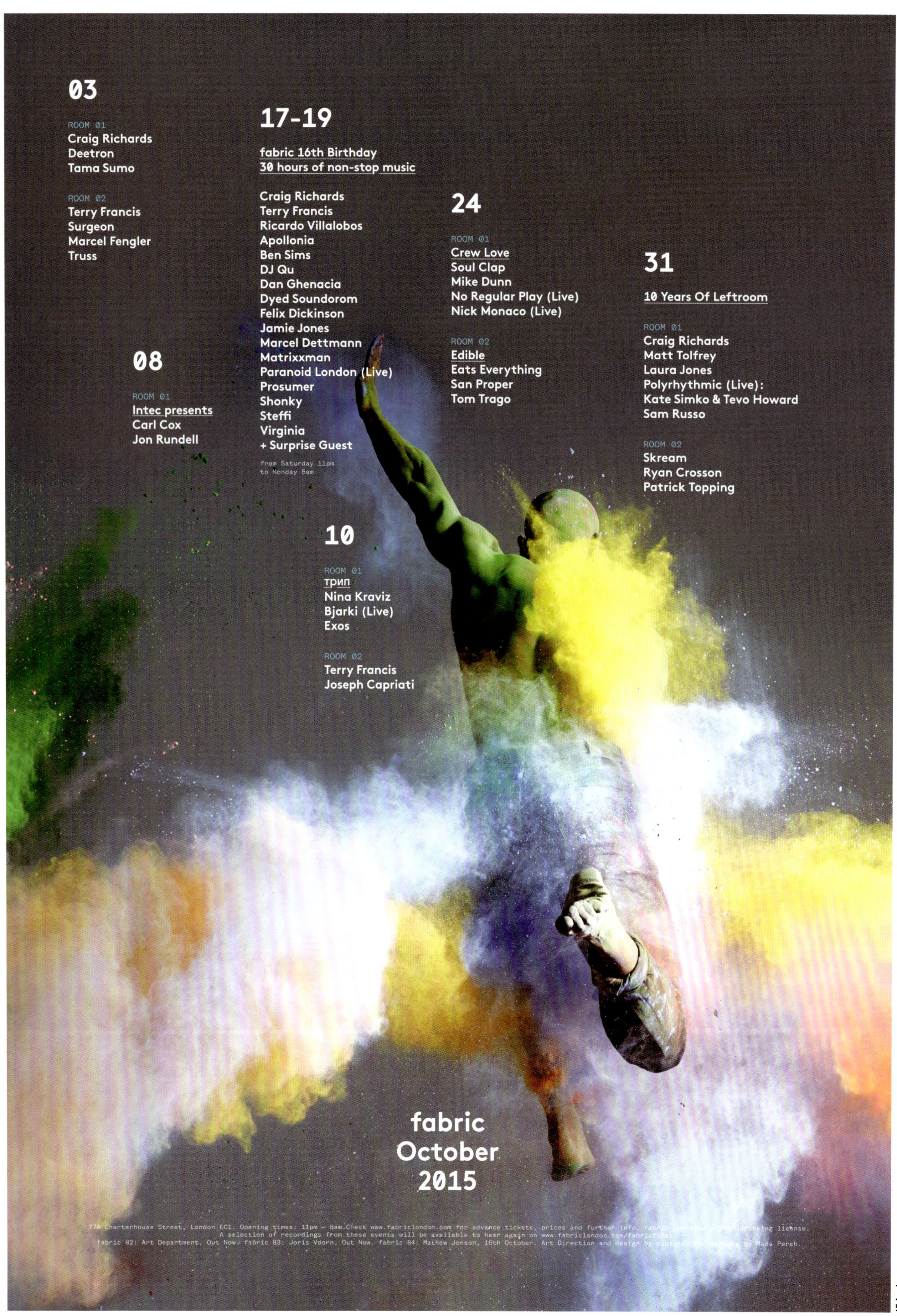
03
ROOM 01
Craig Richards
Deetron
Tama Sumo
ROOM 02
Terry Francis
Surgeon
Marcel Fengler
Truss
08
ROOM 01
Intec presents
Carl Cox
Jon Rundell
17-19
fabric 16th Birthday
30 hours of non-stop music
Craig Richards
Terry Francis
Ricardo Villalobos
Apollonia
Ben Sims
DJ Qu
Dan Ghenacia
Dyed Soundorom
Felix Dickinson
Jamie Jones
Marcel Dettmann
Matrixxman
Paranoid London (Live)
Prosumer
Shonky
Steffi
Virginia
+ Surprise Guest
from Saturday 11pm
to Monday 8am
10
ROOM 01
трип
Nina Kraviz
Bjarki (Live)
Exos
ROOM 02
Terry Francis
Joseph Capriati
24
ROOM 01
Crew Love
Soul Clap
Mike Dunn
No Regular Play (Live)
Nick Monaco (Live)
ROOM 02
Edible
Eats Everything
San Proper
Tom Trago
31
10 Years Of Leftroom
ROOM 01
Craig Richards
Matt Tolfrey
Laura Jones
Polyrhythmic (Live):
Kate Simko & Tevo Howard
Sam Russo
ROOM 02
Skream
Ryan Crosson
Patrick Topping
fabric
October
2015
77A Charterhouse Street, London EC1. Opening times: 11pm – 8am.Check www.fabriclondon.com for advance tickets, prices and further info.
A selection of recordings from these events will be available to hear again on www.fabriclondon.com/fabricfirst.
fabric 82: Art Department, Out Now. fabric 83: Joris Voorn, Out Now. fabric 84: Mathew Jonson, 16th October. Art Direction and design by plusyes. by Mads Perch.

154—1

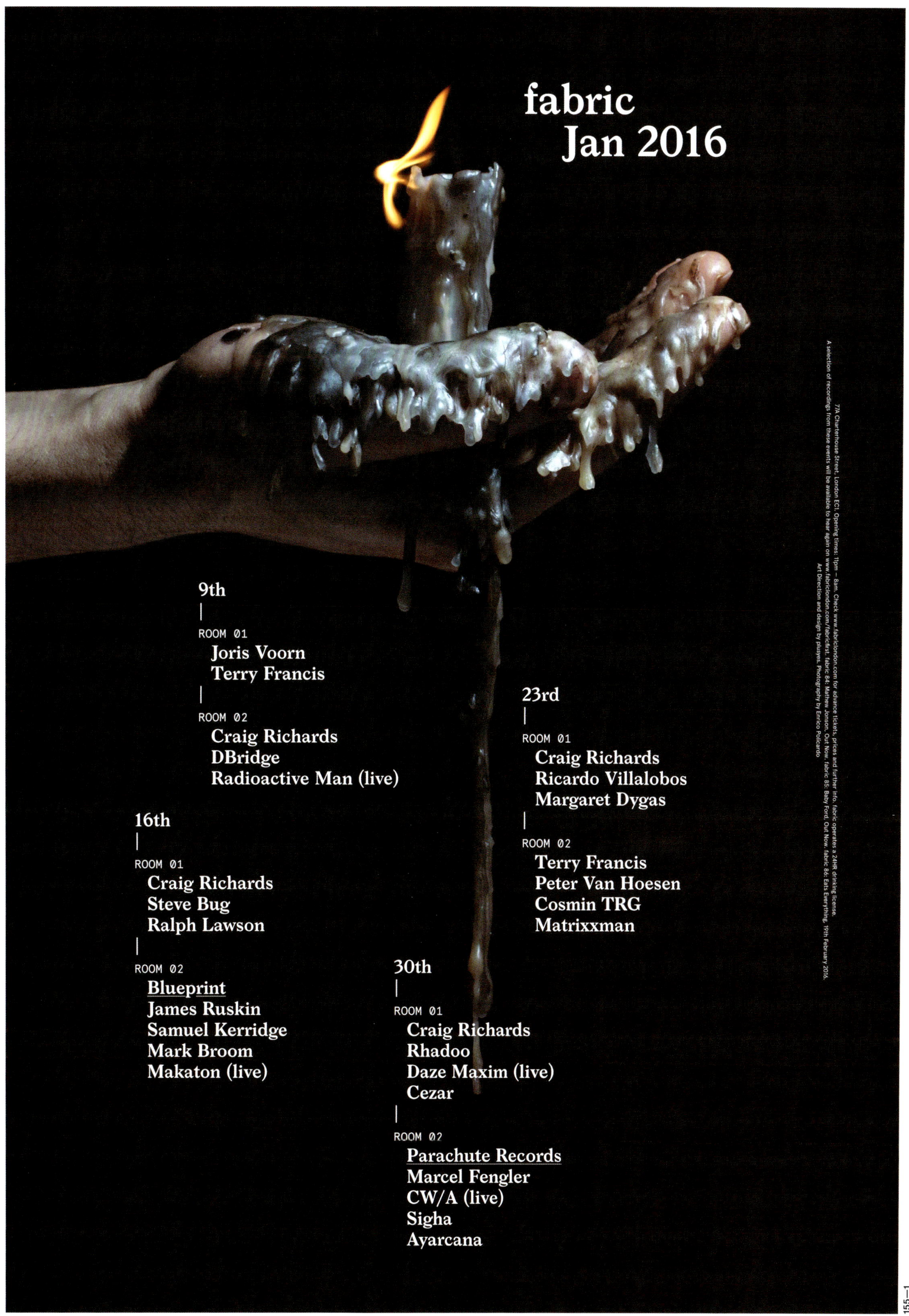

fabric
Jan 2016
9th
ROOM 01
Joris Voorn
Terry Francis
ROOM 02
Craig Richards
DBridge
Radioactive Man (live)
16th
ROOM 01
Craig Richards
Steve Bug
Ralph Lawson
ROOM 02
Blueprint
James Ruskin
Samuel Kerridge
Mark Broom
Makaton (live)
23rd
ROOM 01
Craig Richards
Ricardo Villalobos
Margaret Dygas
ROOM 02
Terry Francis
Peter Van Hoesen
Cosmin TRG
Matrixxman
30th
ROOM 01
Craig Richards
Rhadoo
Daze Maxim (live)
Cezar
ROOM 02
Parachute Records
Marcel Fengler
CW/A (live)
Sigha
Ayarcana
77A Charterhouse Street, London EC1. Opening times: 11pm – 8am. Check www.fabriclondon.com for advance tickets, prices and further info. fabric operates a 24HR drinking license.
A selection of recordings from these events will be available to hear again on www.fabriclondon.com/fabricfirst. fabric 84: Mathew Jonson. Out Now. fabric 85: Baby Ford. Out Now. fabric 86: Eats Everything. 19th February 2016.
Art Direction and design by plusyes. Photography by Enrico Policardo
155—1

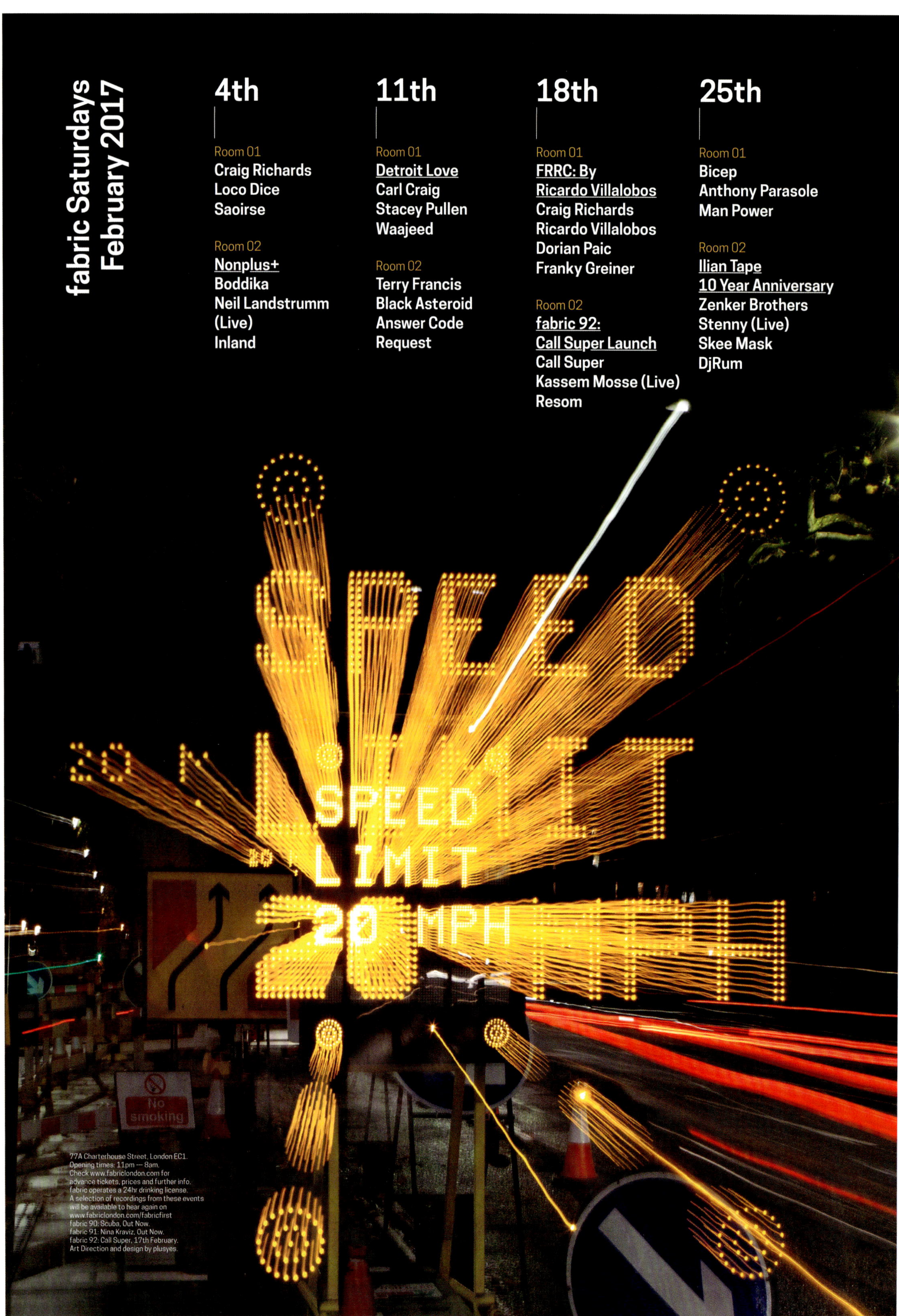
fabric Saturdays
February 2017
4th
Room 01
Craig Richards
Loco Dice
Saoirse
Room 02
Nonplus+
Boddika
Neil Landstrumm
(Live)
Inland
11th
Room 01
Detroit Love
Carl Craig
Stacey Pullen
Waajeed
Room 02
Terry Francis
Black Asteroid
Answer Code
Request
18th
Room 01
FRRC: By
Ricardo Villalobos
Craig Richards
Ricardo Villalobos
Dorian Paic
Franky Greiner
Room 02
fabric 92:
Call Super Launch
Call Super
Kassem Mosse (Live)
Resom
25th
Room 01
Bicep
Anthony Parasole
Man Power
Room 02
Ilian Tape
10 Year Anniversary
Zenker Brothers
Stenny (Live)
Skee Mask
DjRum
SPEED
LIMIT
20 MPH
No
smoking
77A Charterhouse Street, London EC1.
Opening times: 11pm — 8am.
Check www.fabriclondon.com for
advance tickets, prices and further info.
fabric operates a 24hr drinking license.
A selection of recordings from these events
will be available to hear again on
www.fabriclondon.com/fabricfirst
fabric 90: Scuba, Out Now.
fabric 91: Nina Kraviz, Out Now.
fabric 92: Call Super, 17th February.
Art Direction and design by plusyes.

156—1

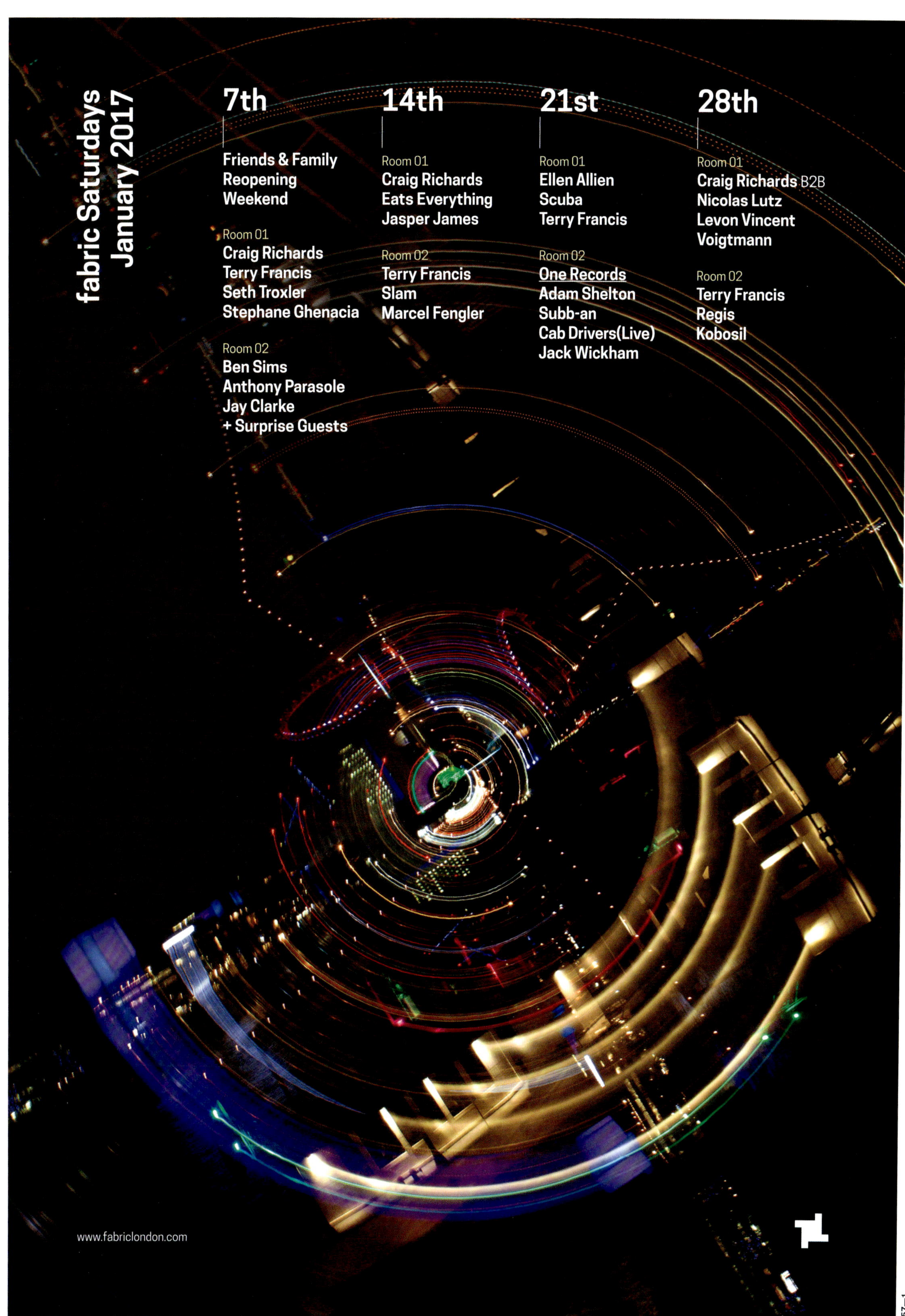
fabric Saturdays
January 2017
7th
Friends & Family
Reopening
Weekend
Room 01
Craig Richards
Terry Francis
Seth Troxler
Stephane Ghenacia
Room 02
Ben Sims
Anthony Parasole
Jay Clarke
+ Surprise Guests
14th
Room 01
Craig Richards
Eats Everything
Jasper James
Room 02
Terry Francis
Slam
Marcel Fengler
21st
Room 01
Ellen Allien
Scuba
Terry Francis
Room 02
One Records
Adam Shelton
Subb-an
Cab Drivers(Live)
Jack Wickham
28th
Room 01
Craig Richards B2B
Nicolas Lutz
Levon Vincent
Voigtmann
Room 02
Terry Francis
Regis
Kobosil
www.fabriclondon.com
157—1

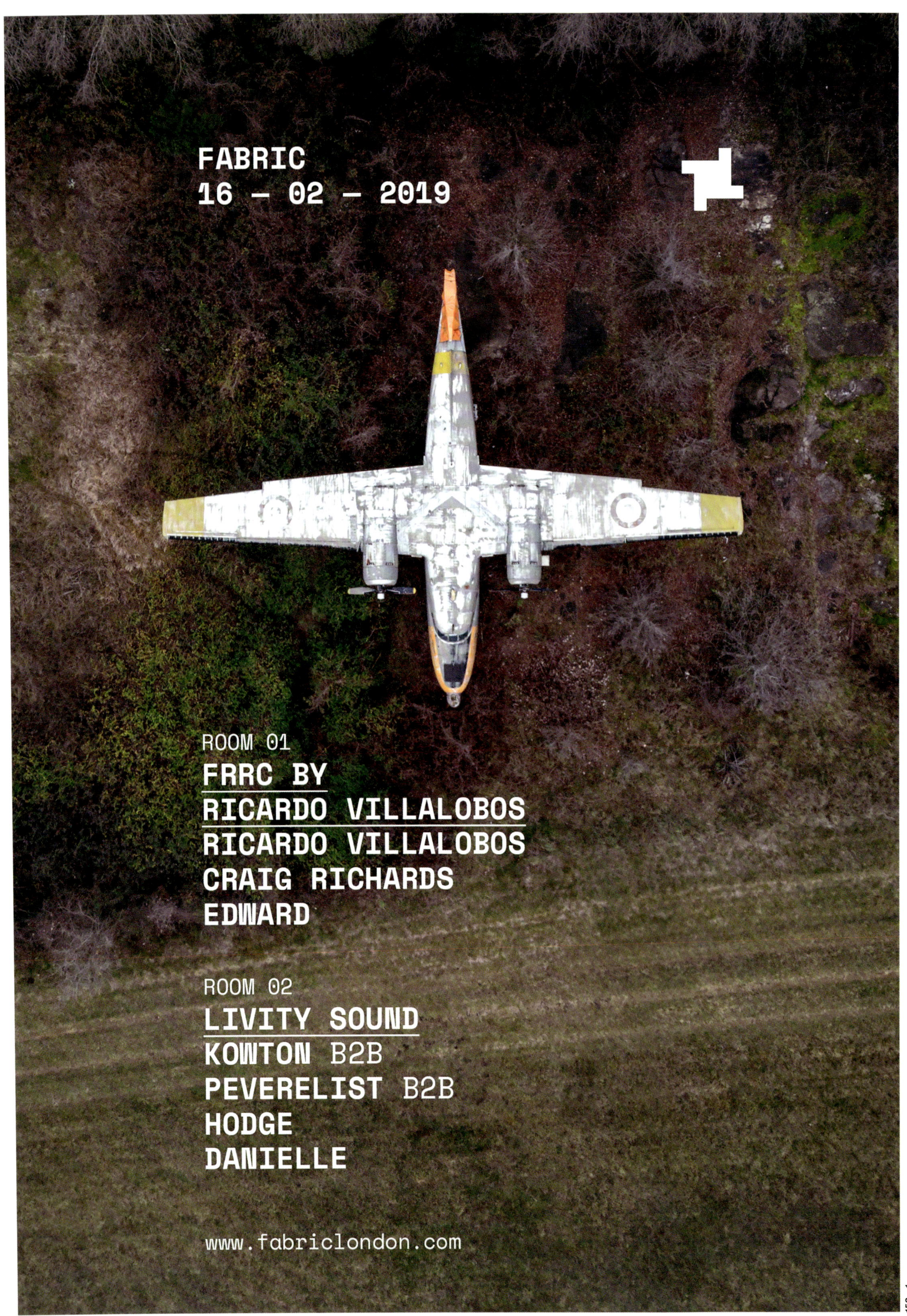
FABRIC
16 – 02 – 2019
ROOM 01
FRRC BY
RICARDO VILLALOBOS
RICARDO VILLALOBOS
CRAIG RICHARDS
EDWARD
ROOM 02
LIVITY SOUND
KOWTON B2B
PEVERELIST B2B
HODGE
DANIELLE
www.fabriclondon.com

158—1

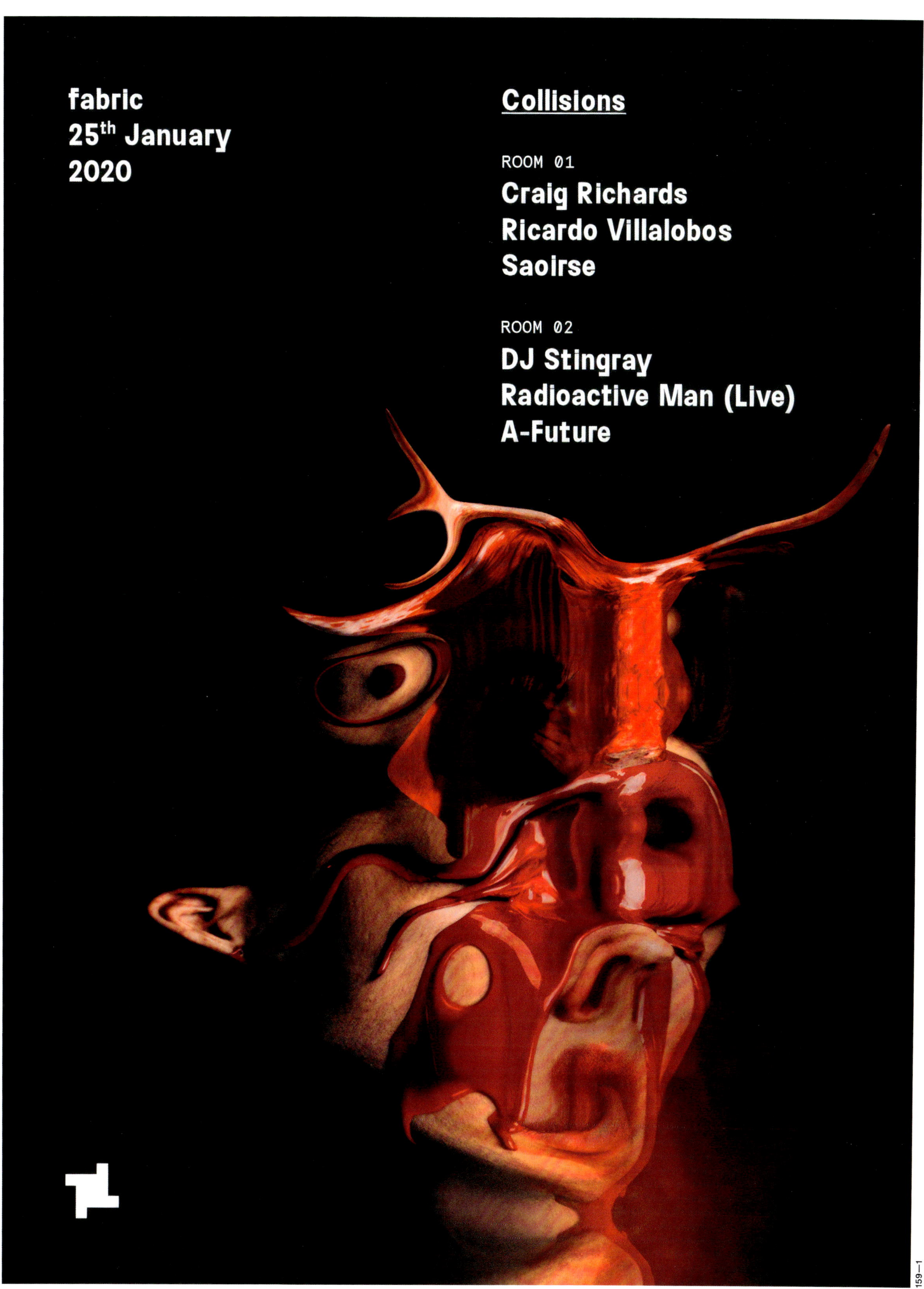
fabric
25th January
2020
Collisions
ROOM 01
Craig Richards
Ricardo Villalobos
Saoirse
ROOM 02
DJ Stingray
Radioactive Man (Live)
A-Future
159—1

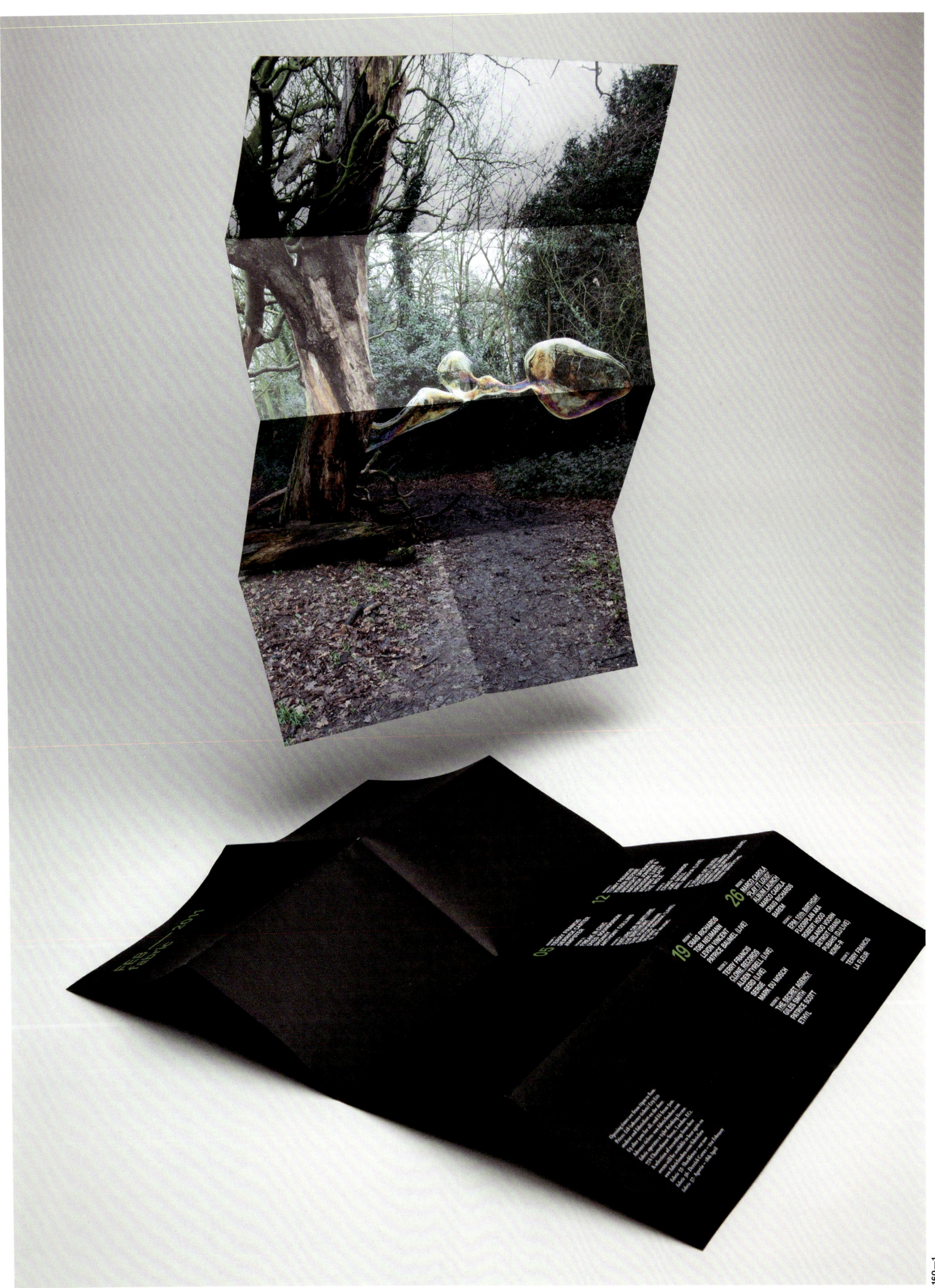

160—1

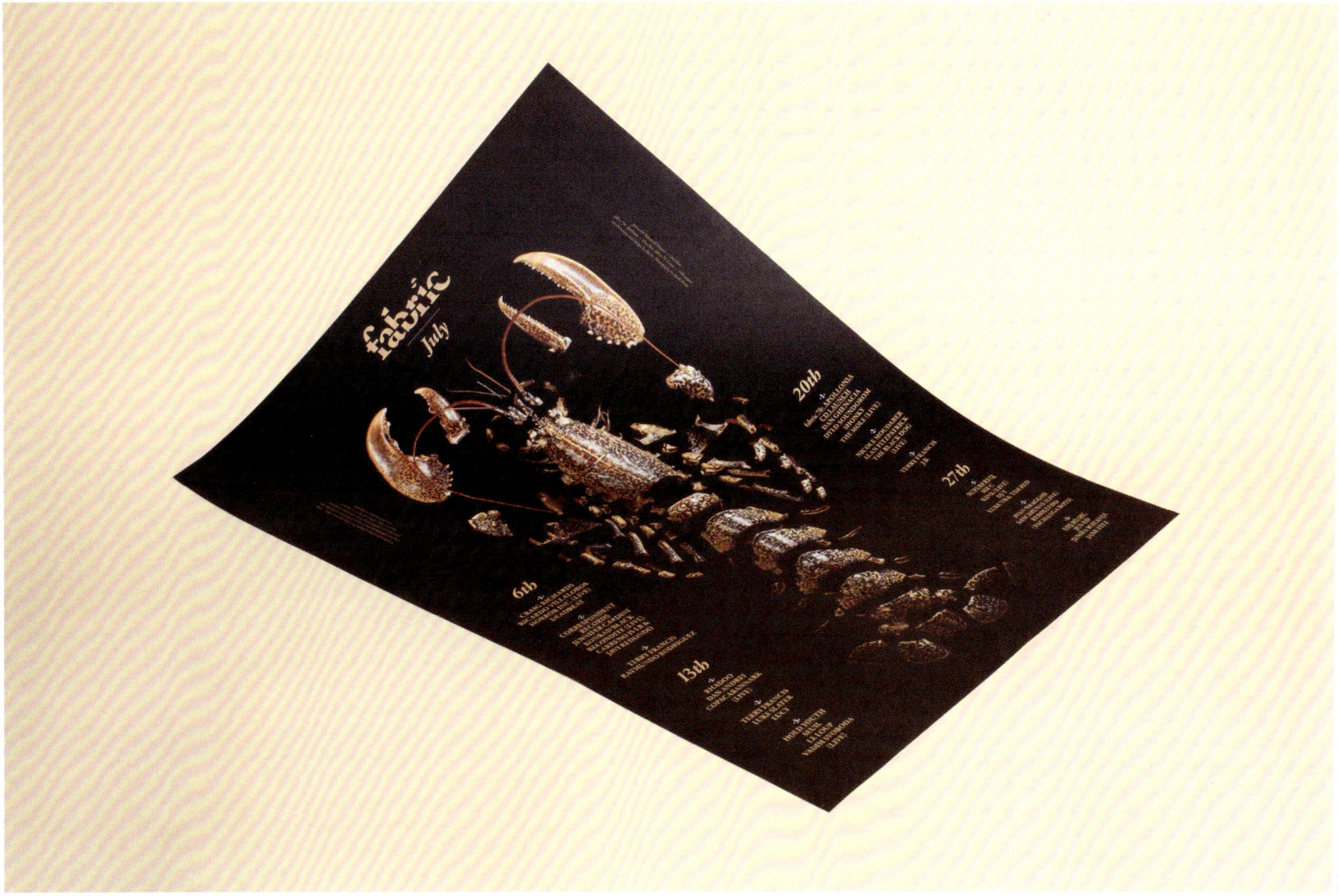

161—1

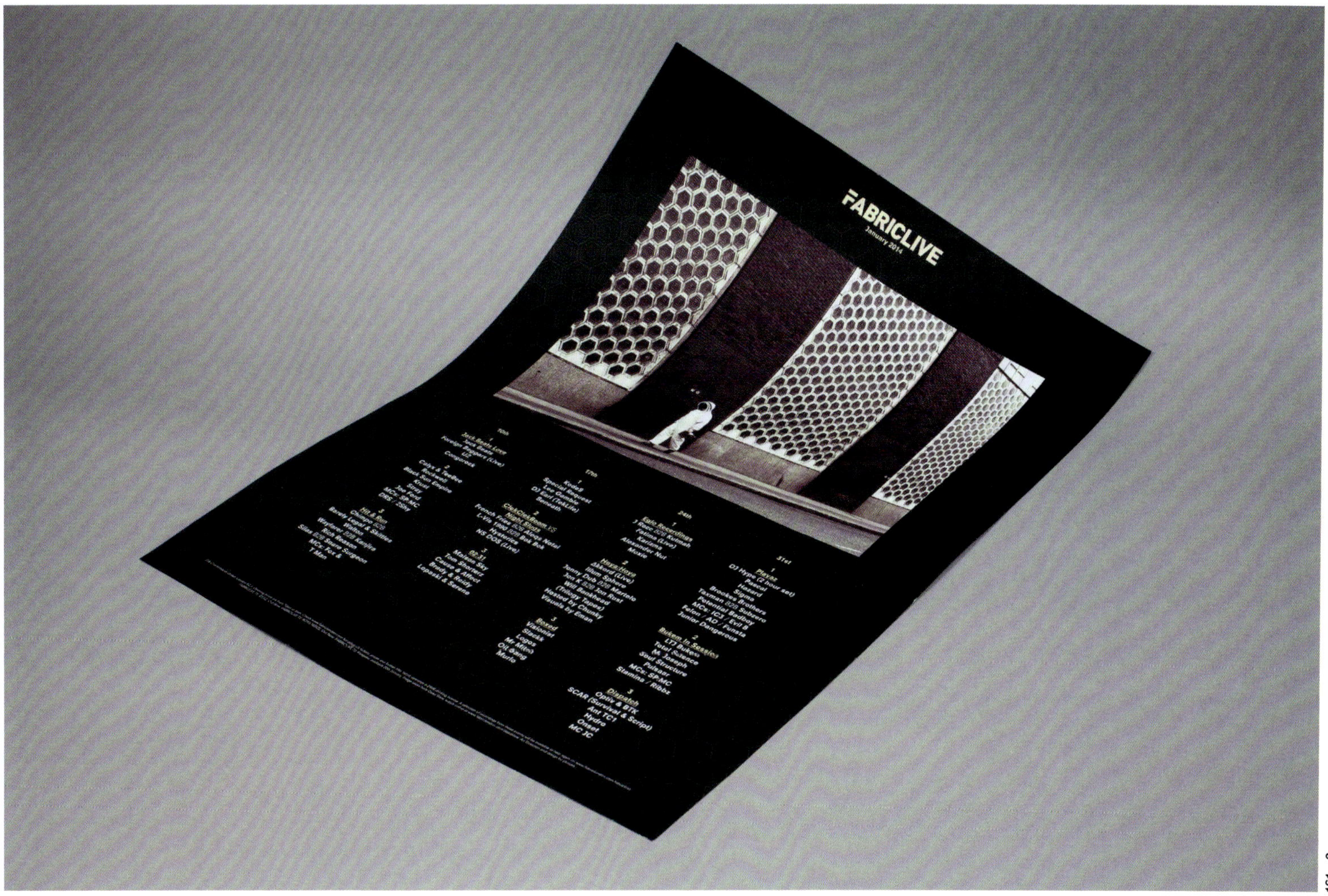

161—2

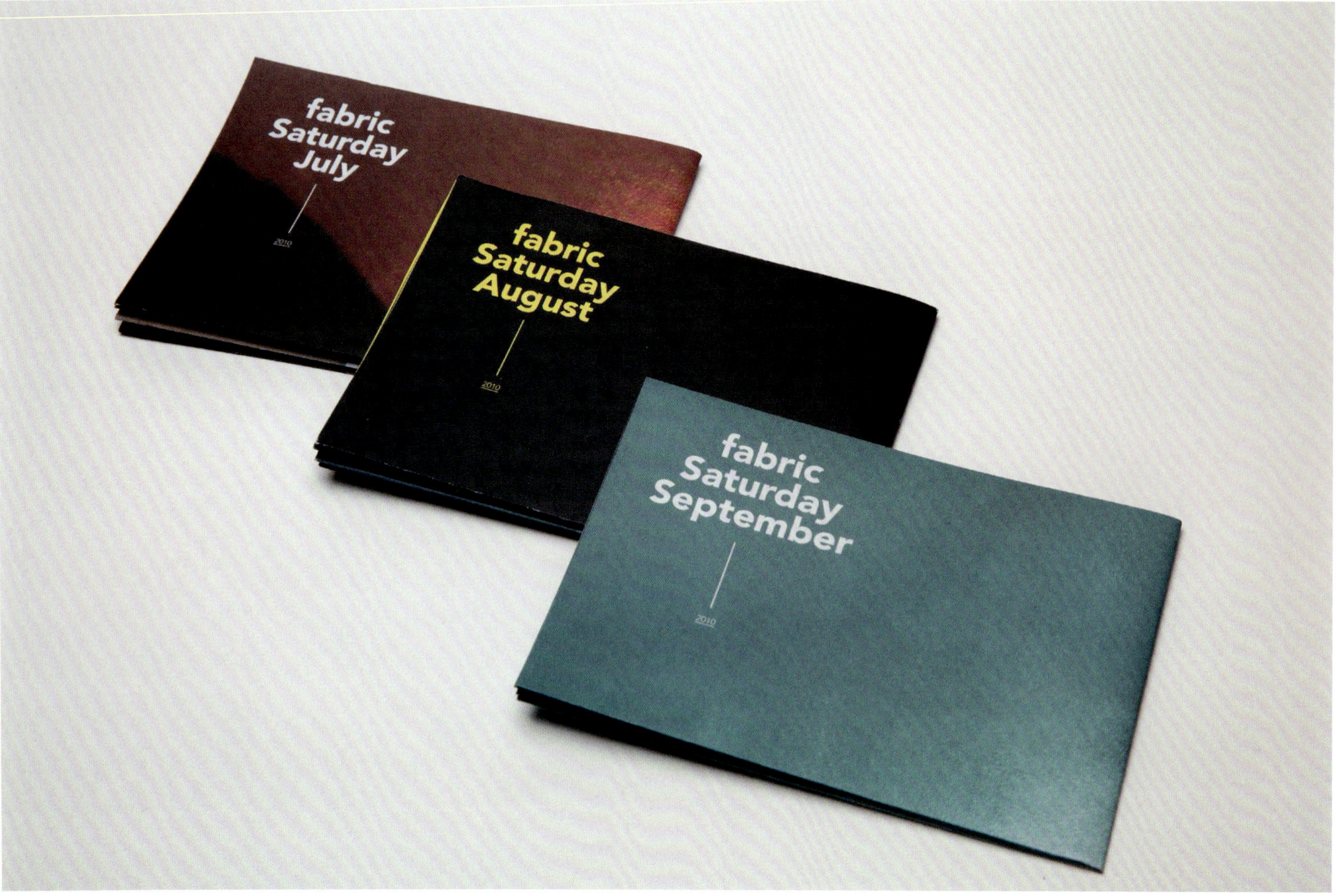

162—1

162—2

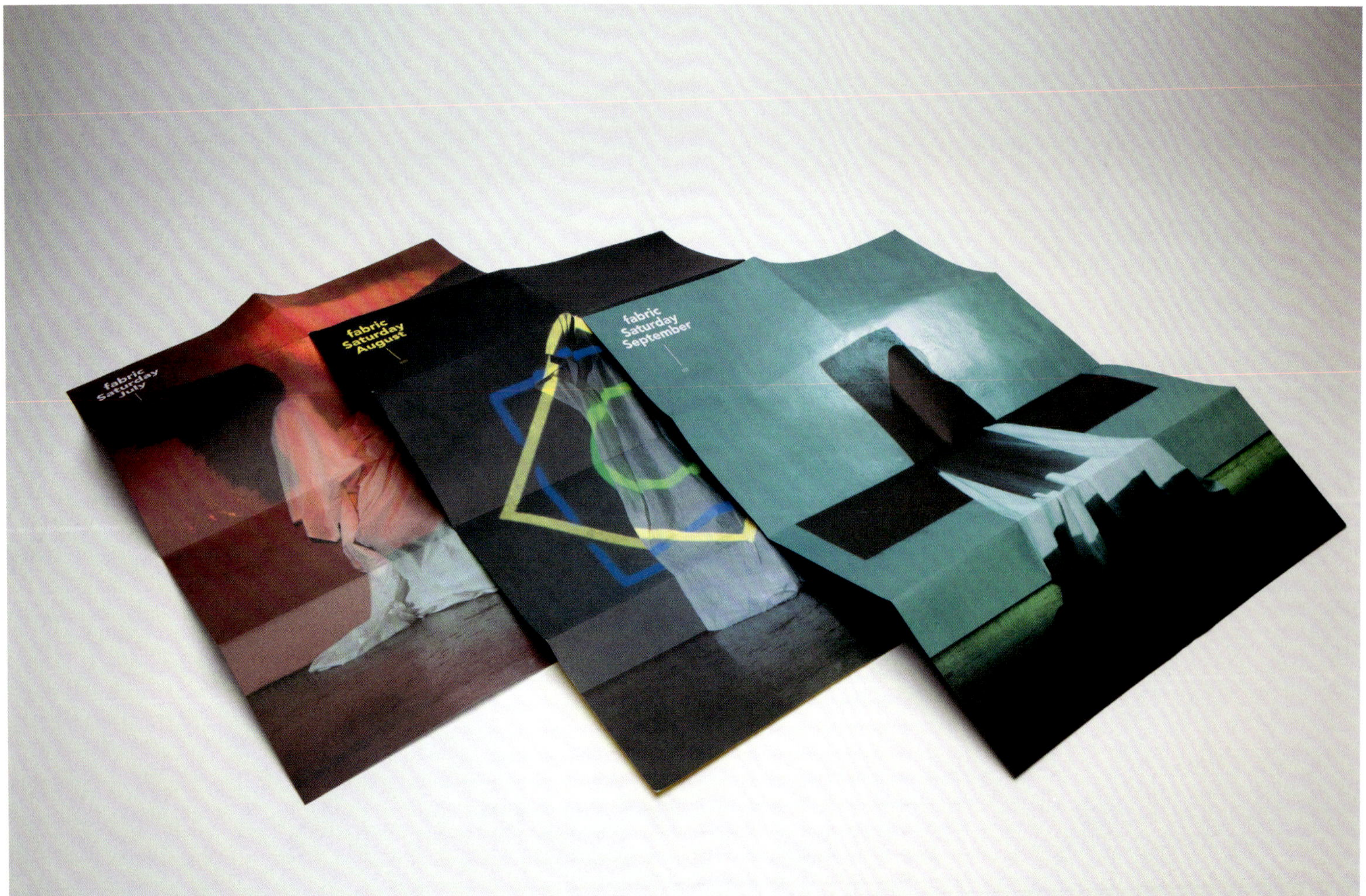

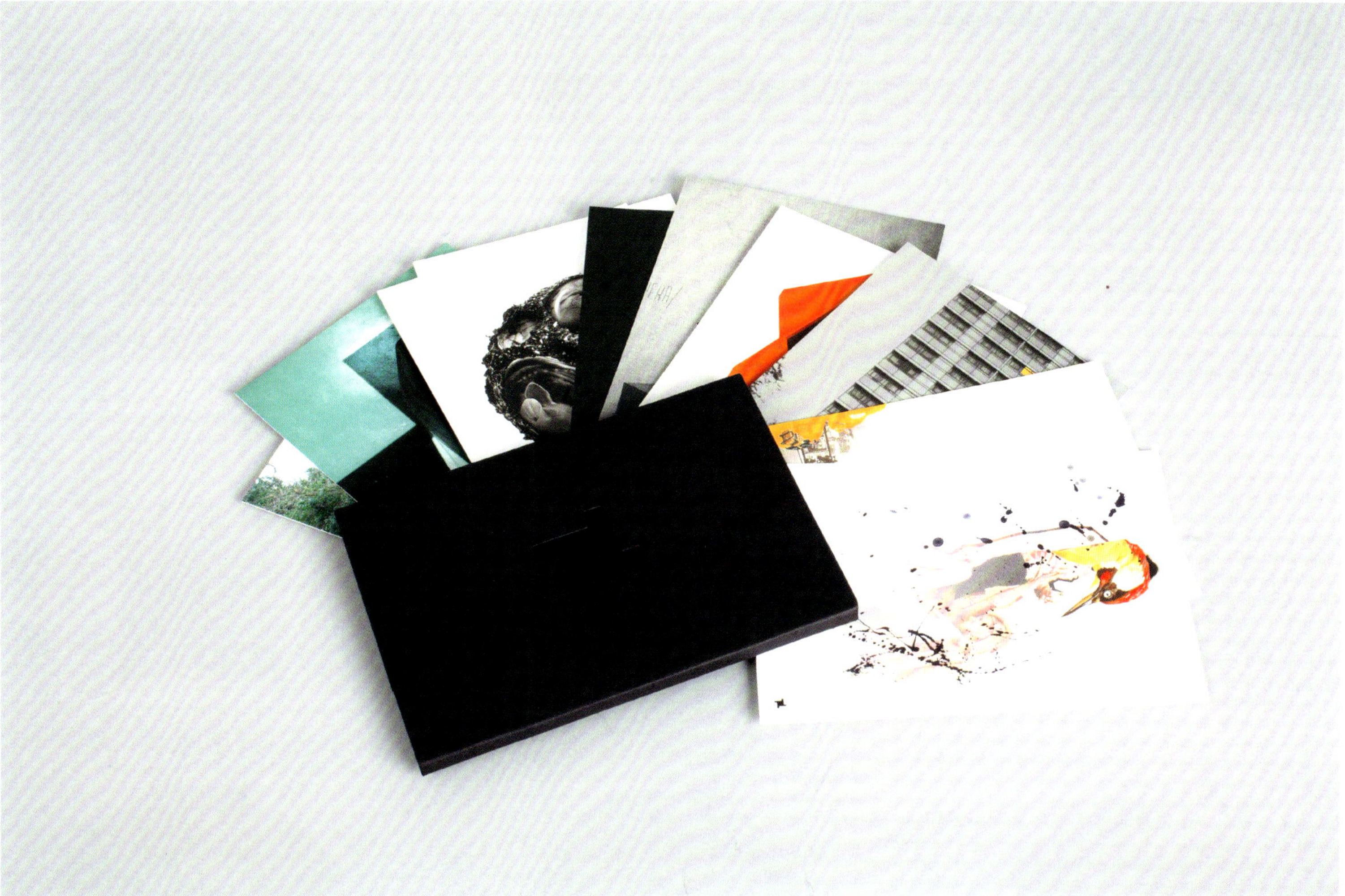

163—1

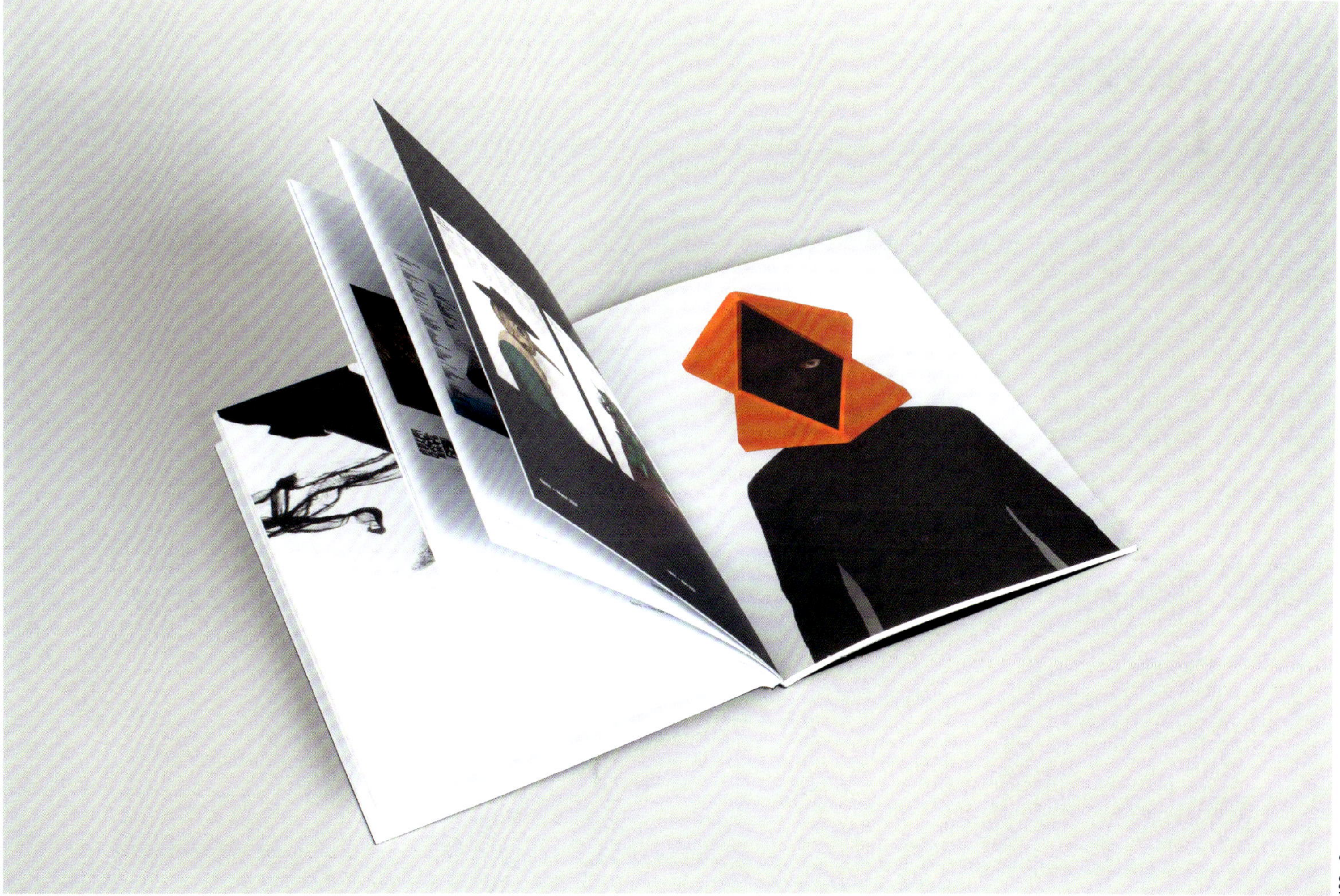

163—2

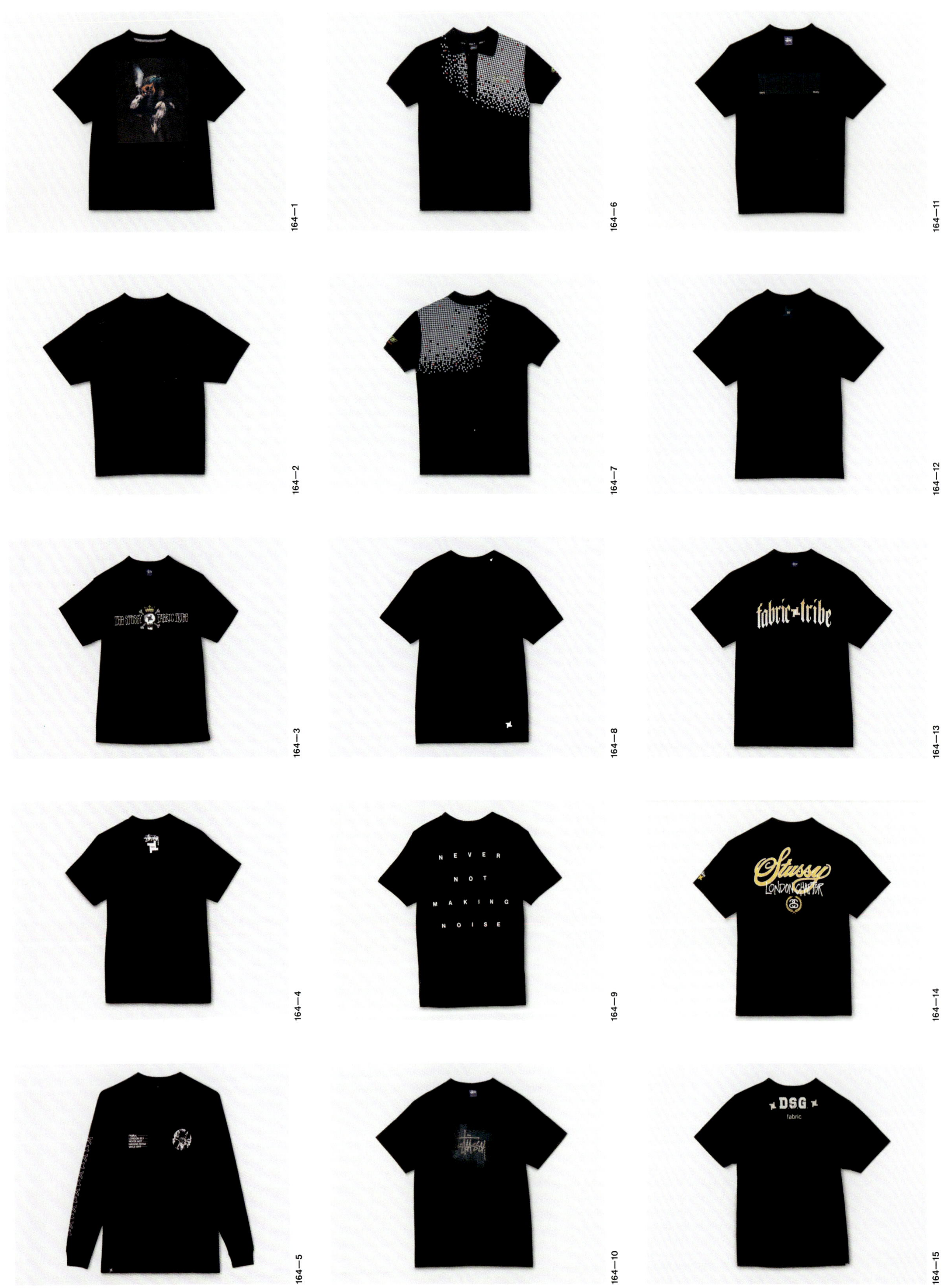

164—1 164—6 164—11
164—2 164—7 164—12
164—3 164—8 164—13
164—4 164—9 164—14
164—5 164—10 164—15

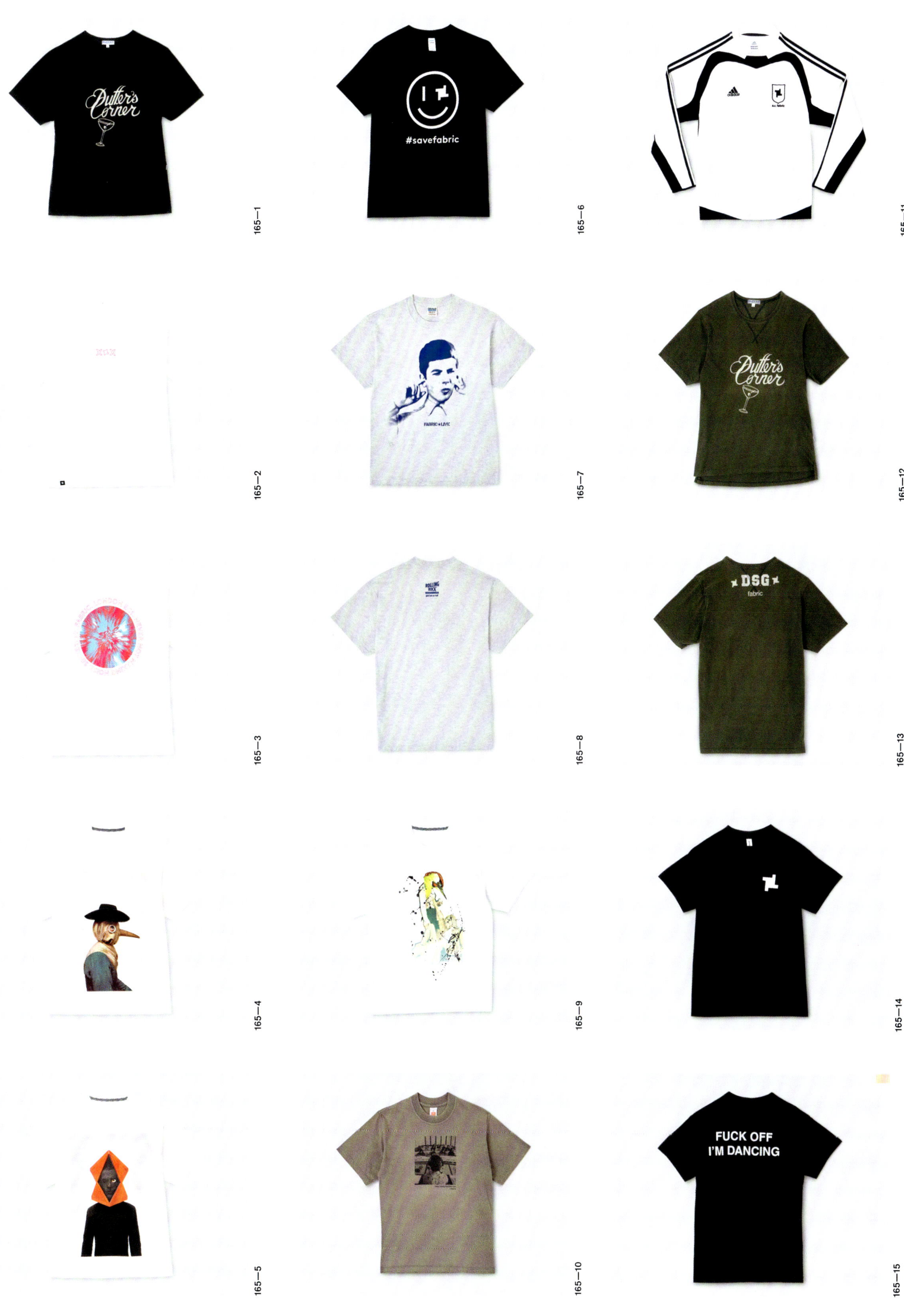

165—1
165—6
165—11
165—2
165—7
165—12
165—3
165—8
165—13
165—4
165—9
165—14
165—5
165—10
165—15

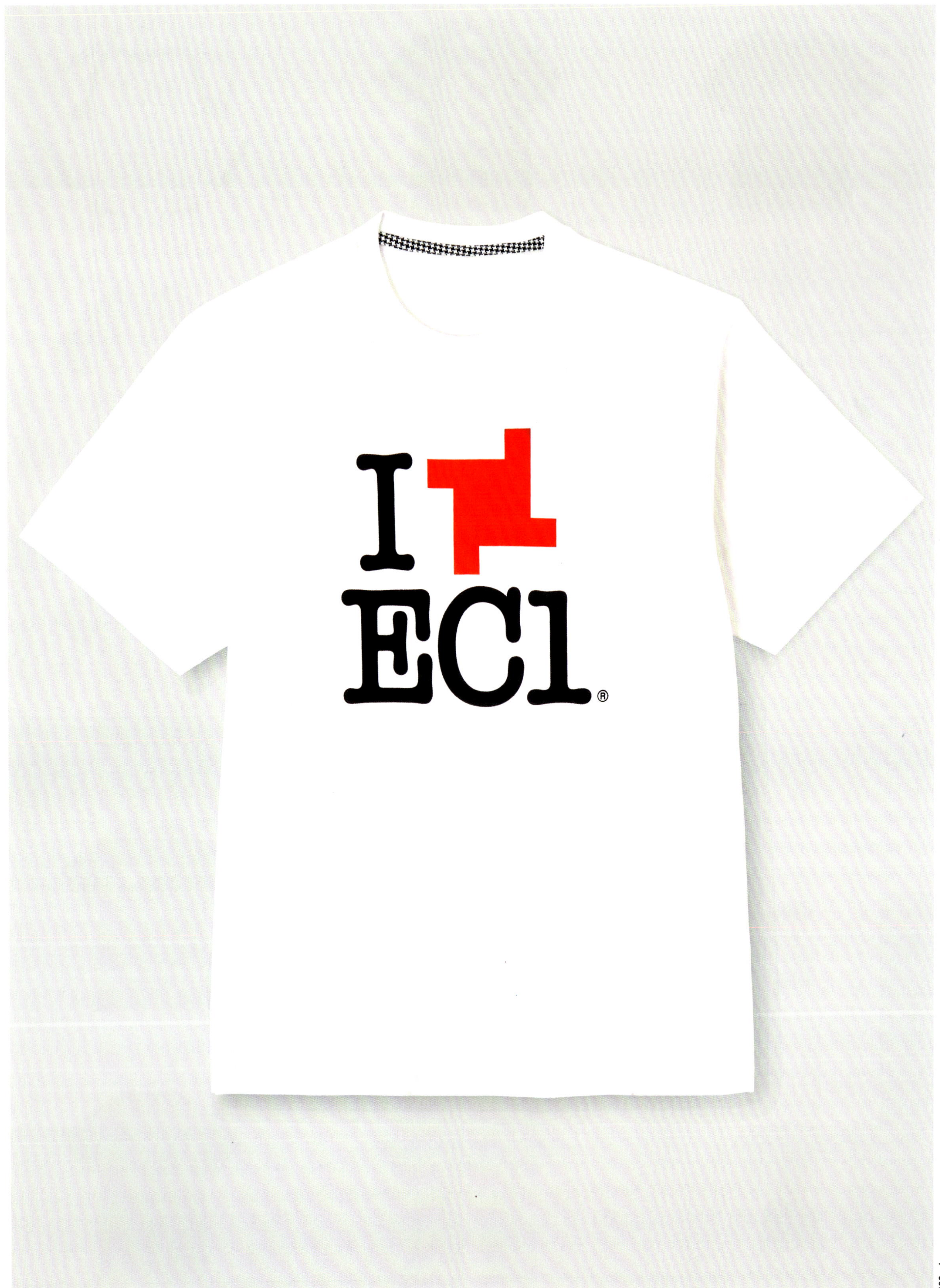

166—1

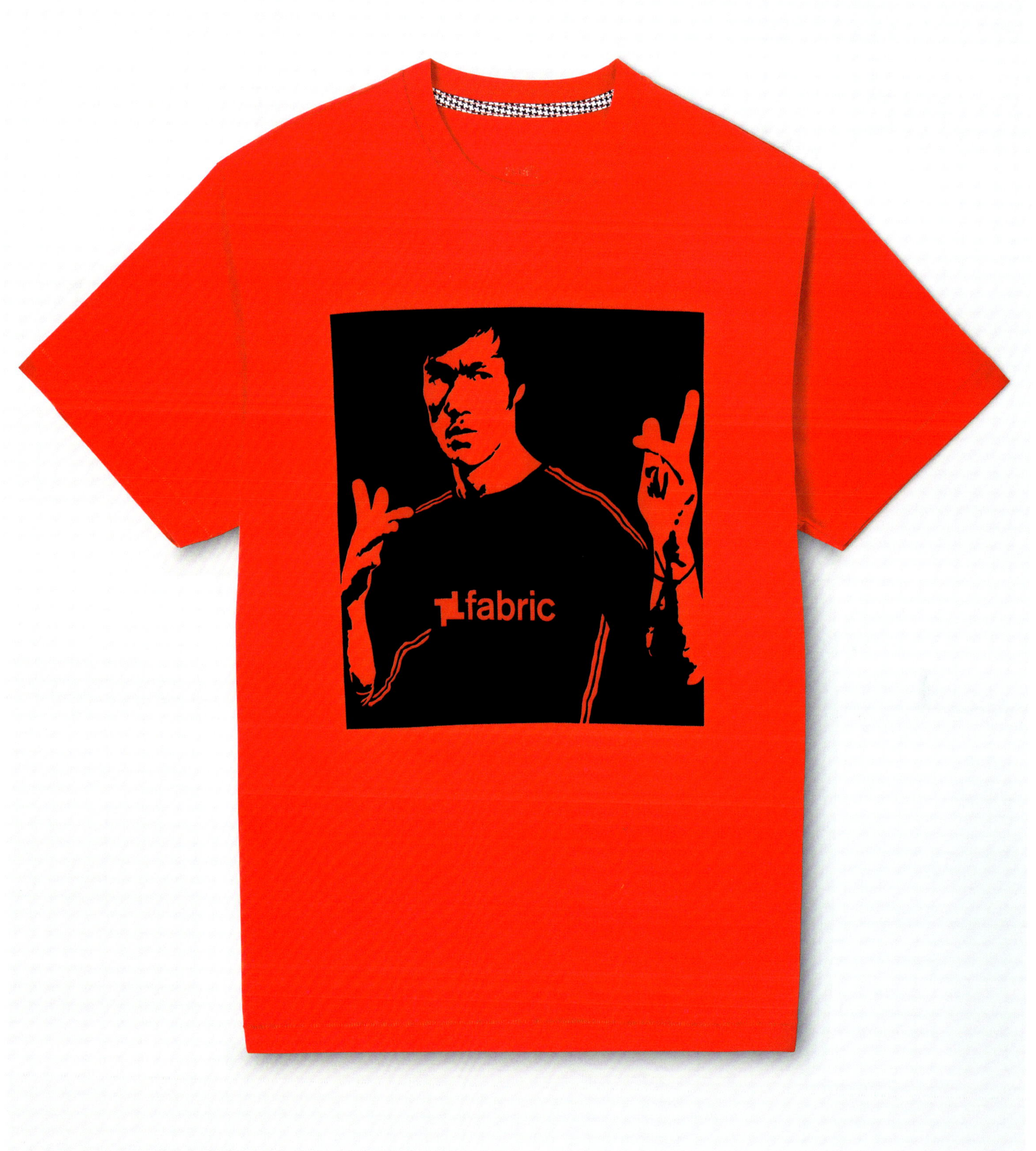

167—1

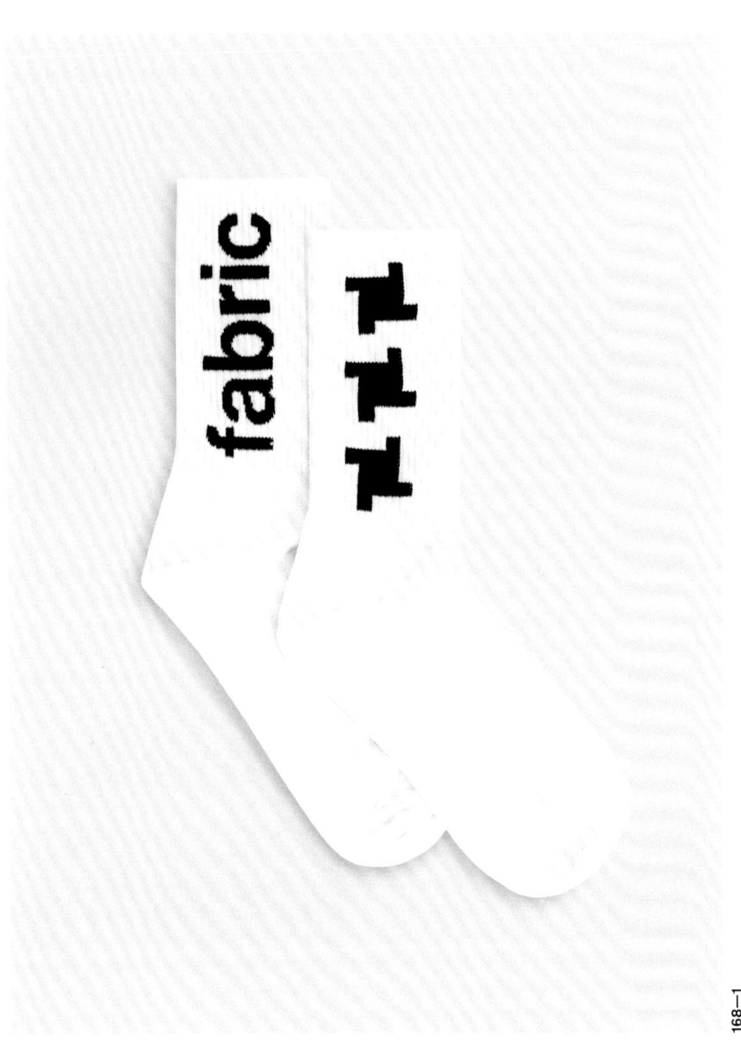

168—1

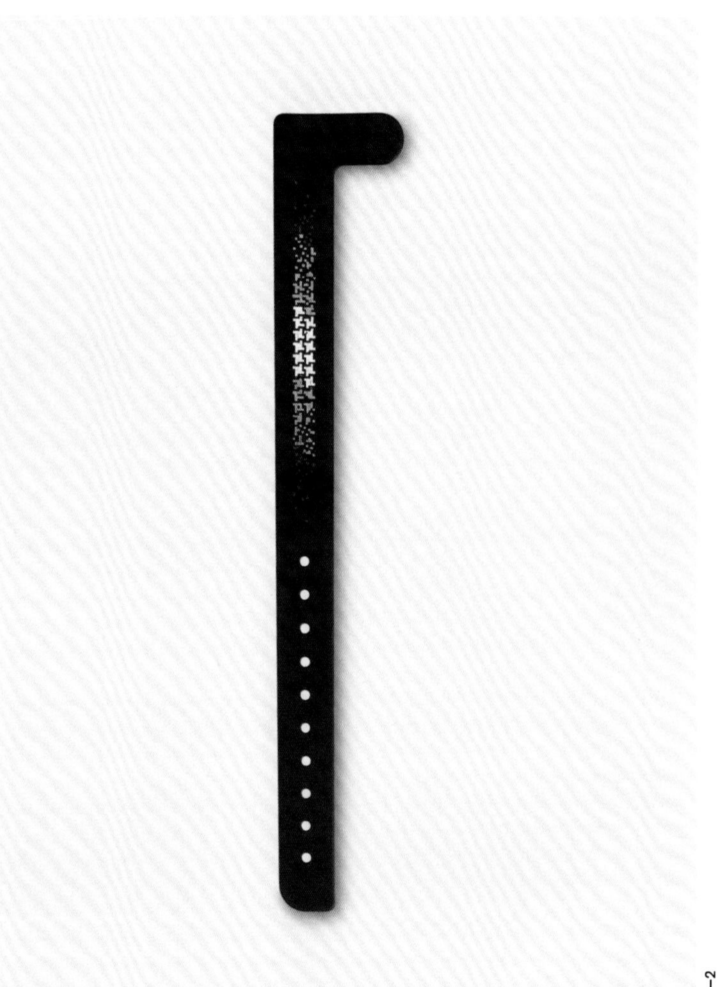
168—2

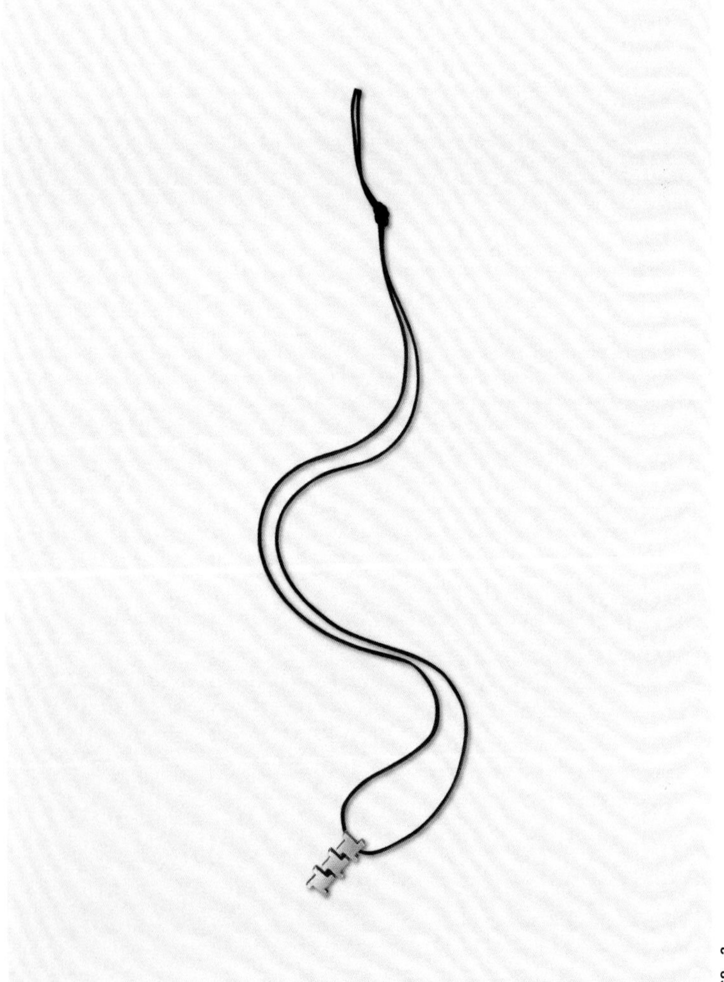
168—3

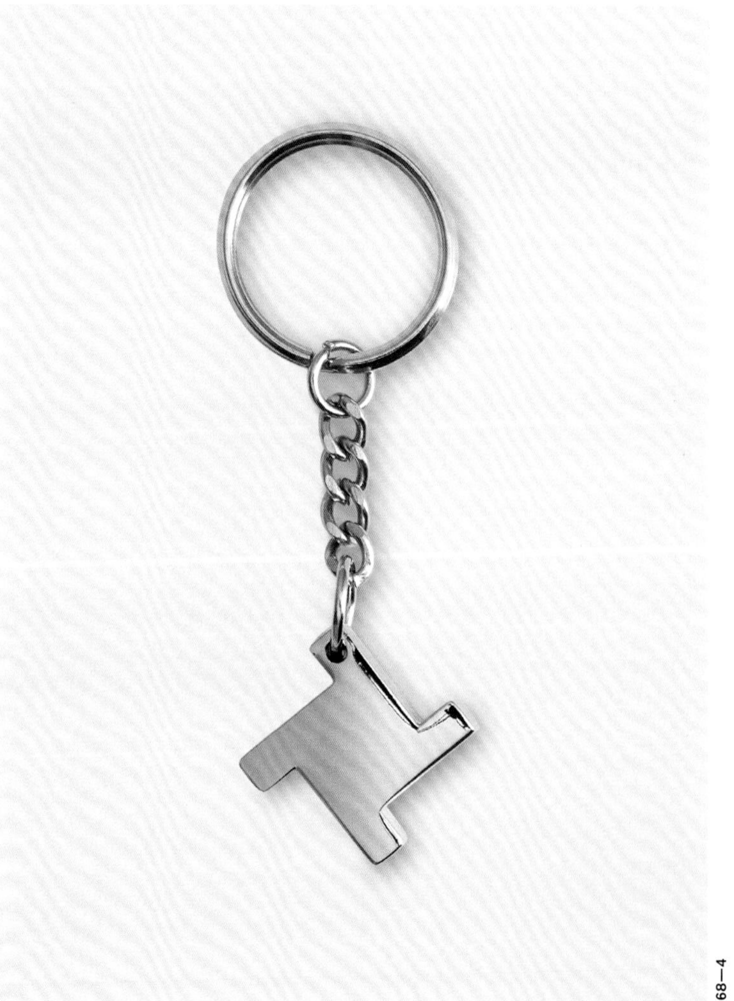
168—4

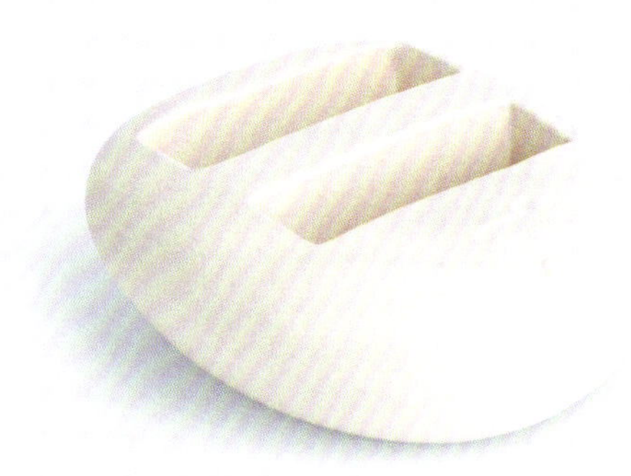

169—1

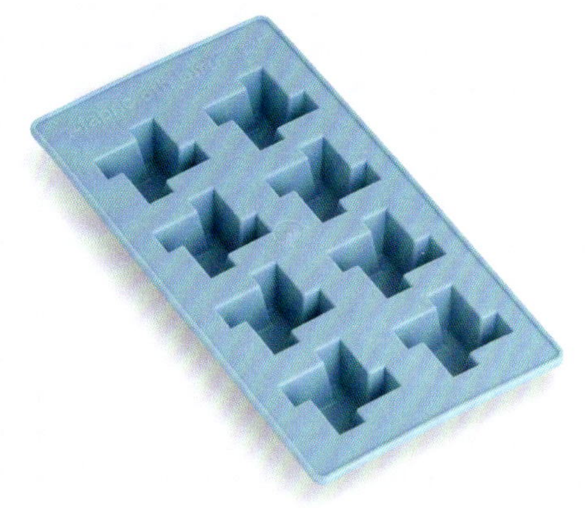

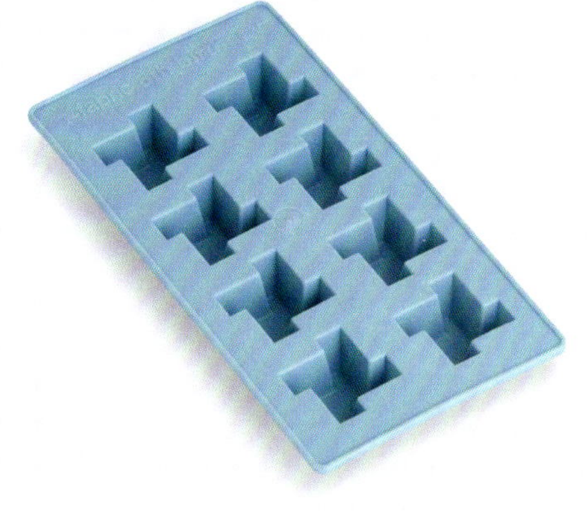

169—2

BAKE LOVE
169—3

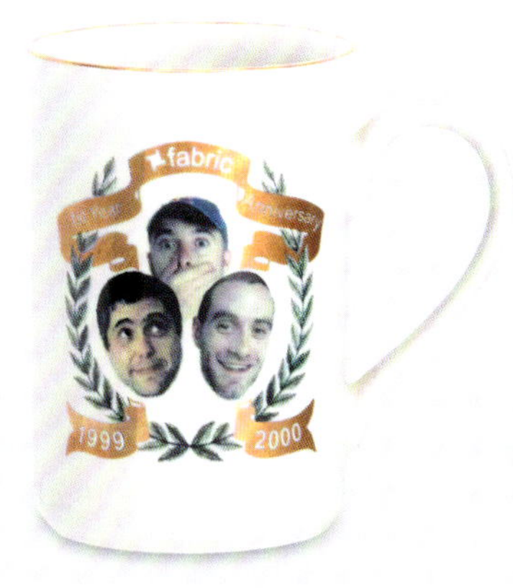

169—4

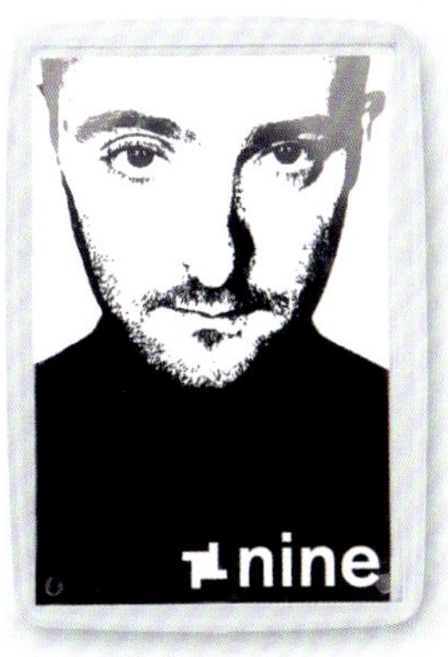

169—5

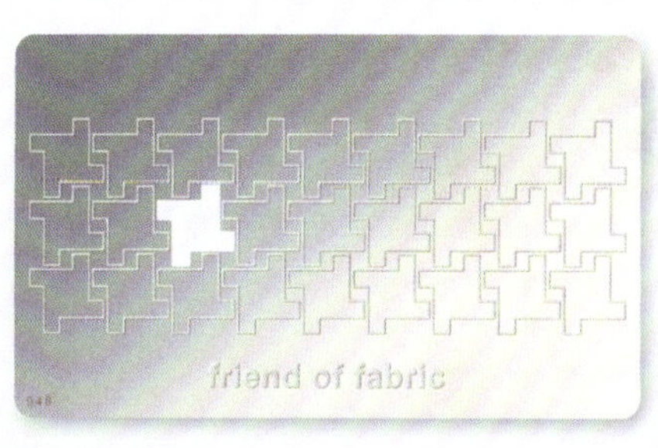

169—6

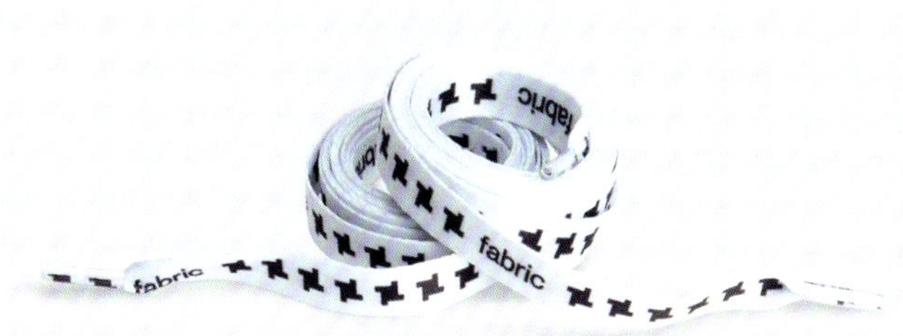

169—7

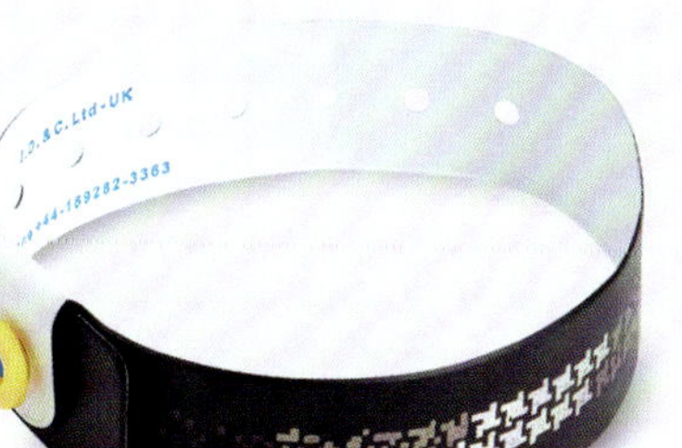

169—8

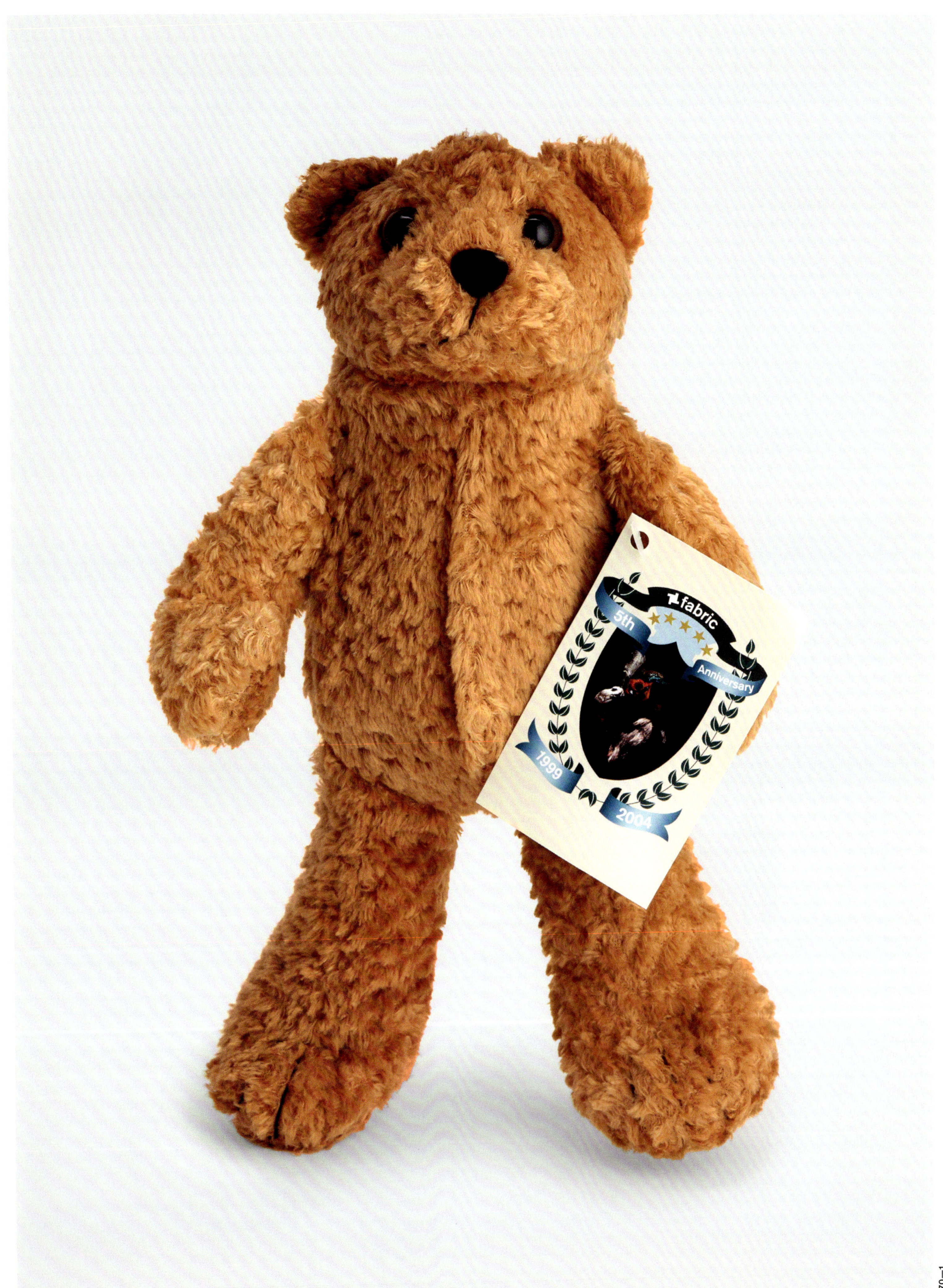

170—1

fabric
JAMES
CRAIG
Goodus et funkus
discotequm
TERRY
ALI
Years
3
Young
Est. MCMXCIX
100% Cotton

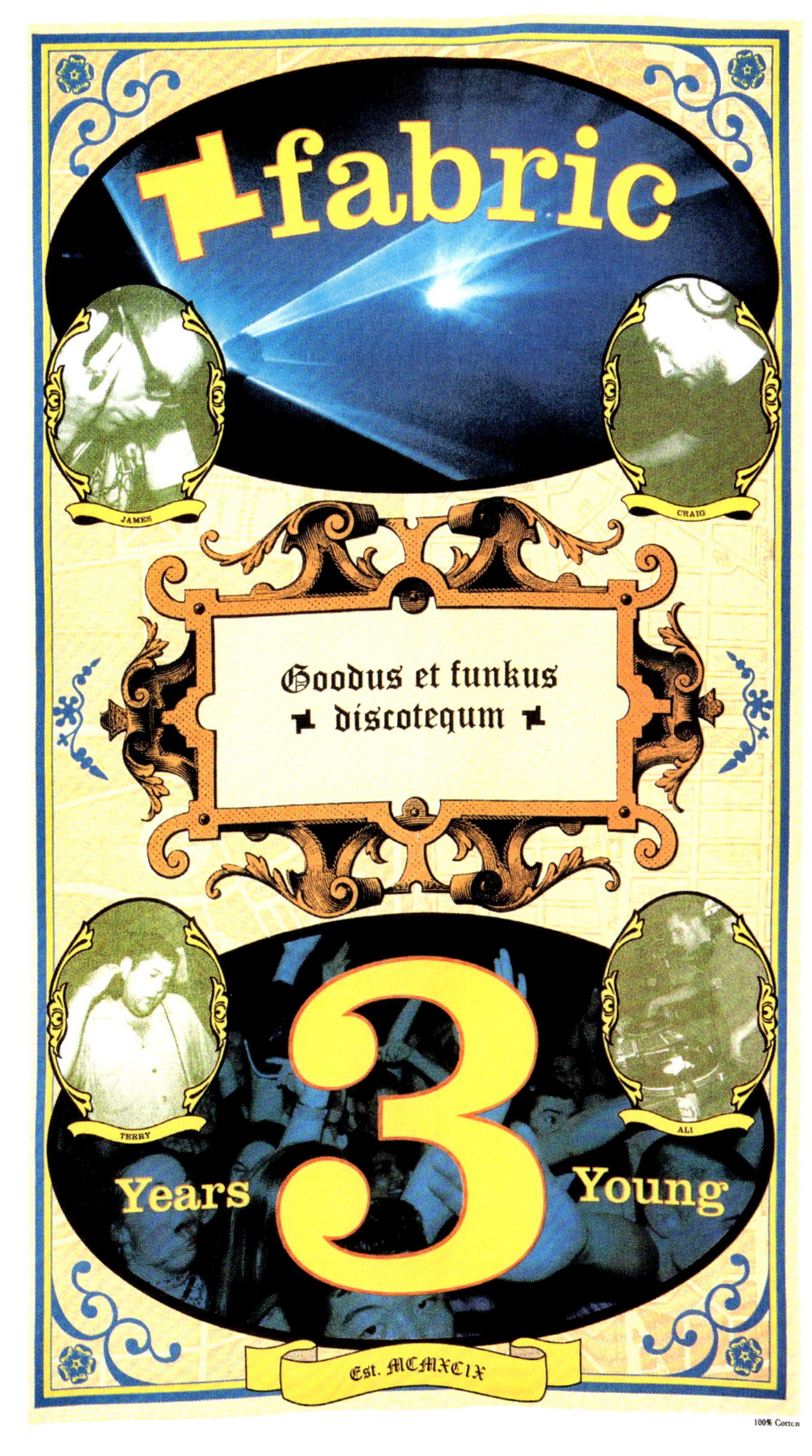

171—1

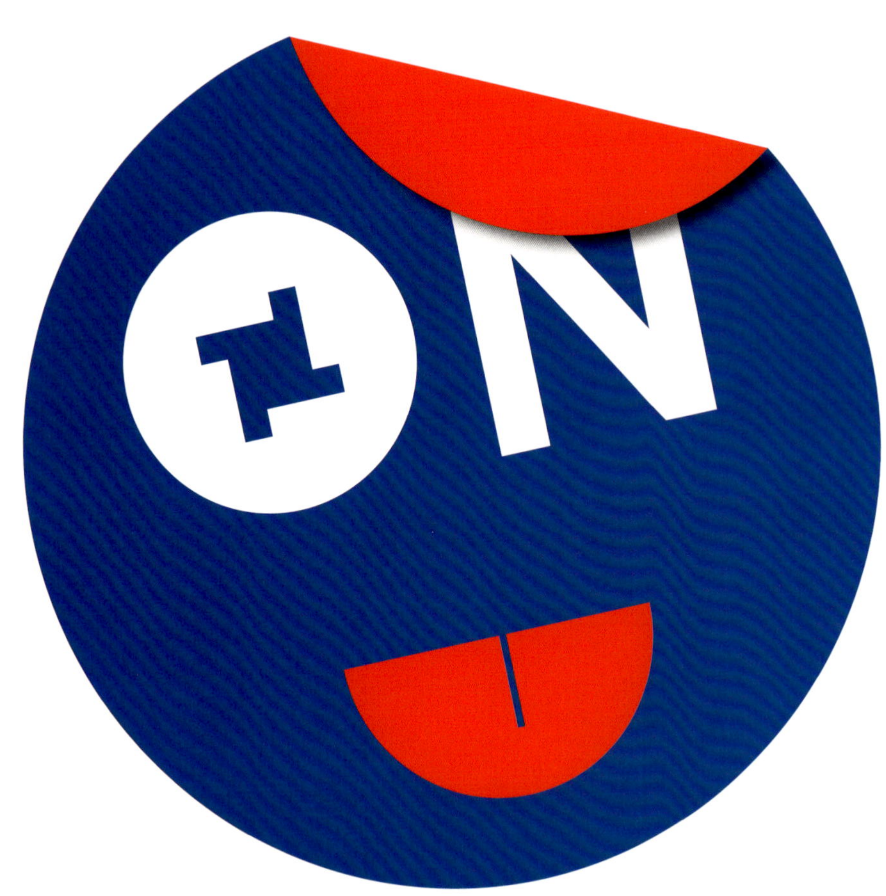

fabric

11pm
Saturday
21st August
TO ——
2pm
Sunday
22nd August

ON ——
15 hours of non-stop music

CRAIG RICHARDS
TERRY FRANCIS
BABY FORD
DINKY
MODERN DEEP LEFT QUARTET (LIVE)
RICARDO VILLALOBOS
SLAM
SWAYZAK

Prices: £15 Early bird /// £22/£10 students & fabricfirst Sat11pm – Sun 2pm /// £15/£10 students & fabricfirst Sun 5am – Sun 10am /// £10/£5 students & fabricfirst Sun 10am – close.
77A Charterhouse Street, London, EC1 3HN T 020 7336 8898. Fabric operates a 24hr drinking license.
Advance tickets are available from www.ticketweb.co.uk and from our website www.fabriclondon.com
A selection of recordings from these events will be available to hear again on www.fabriclondon.com/fabricfirst

172—1

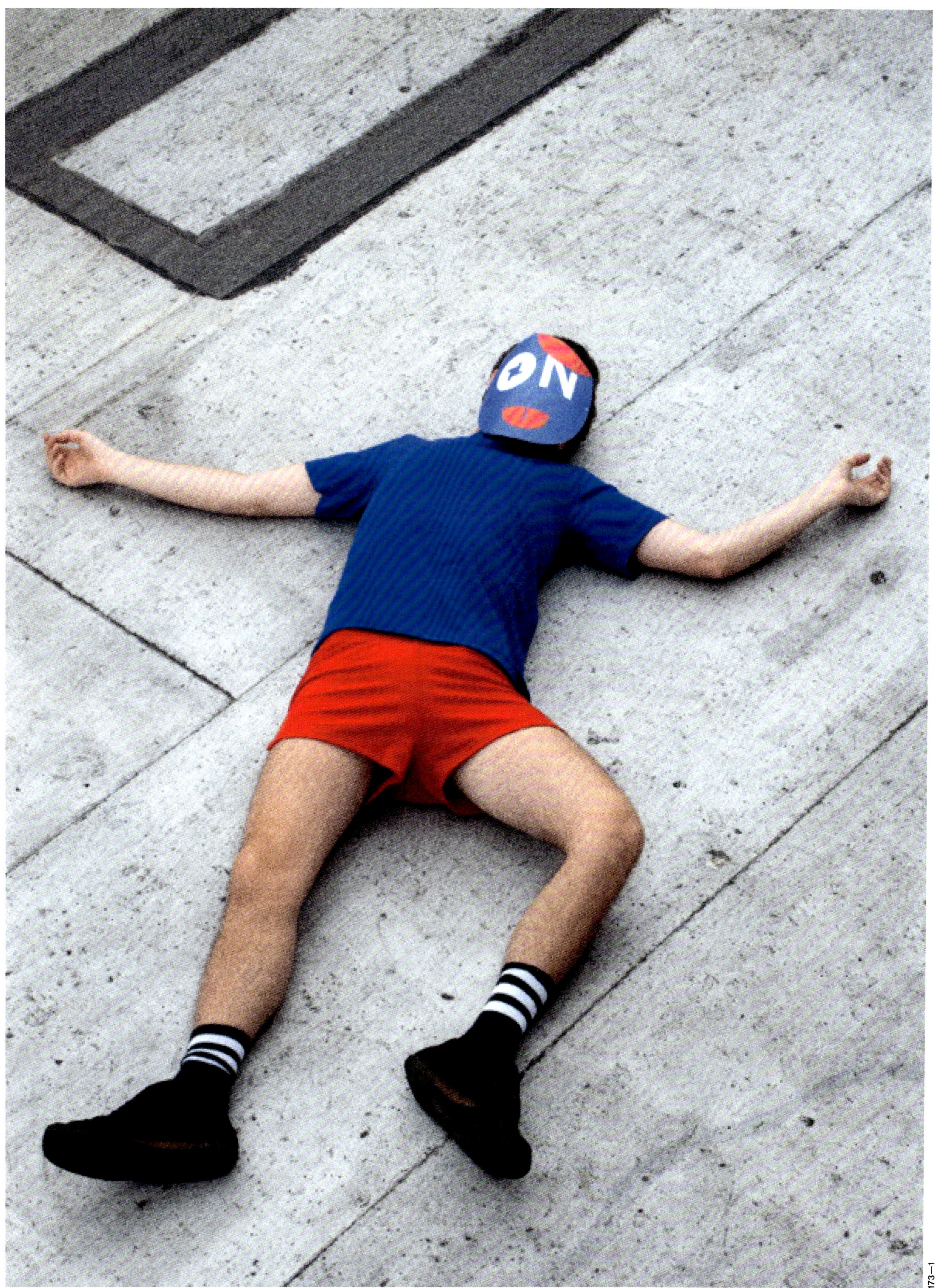

173—1

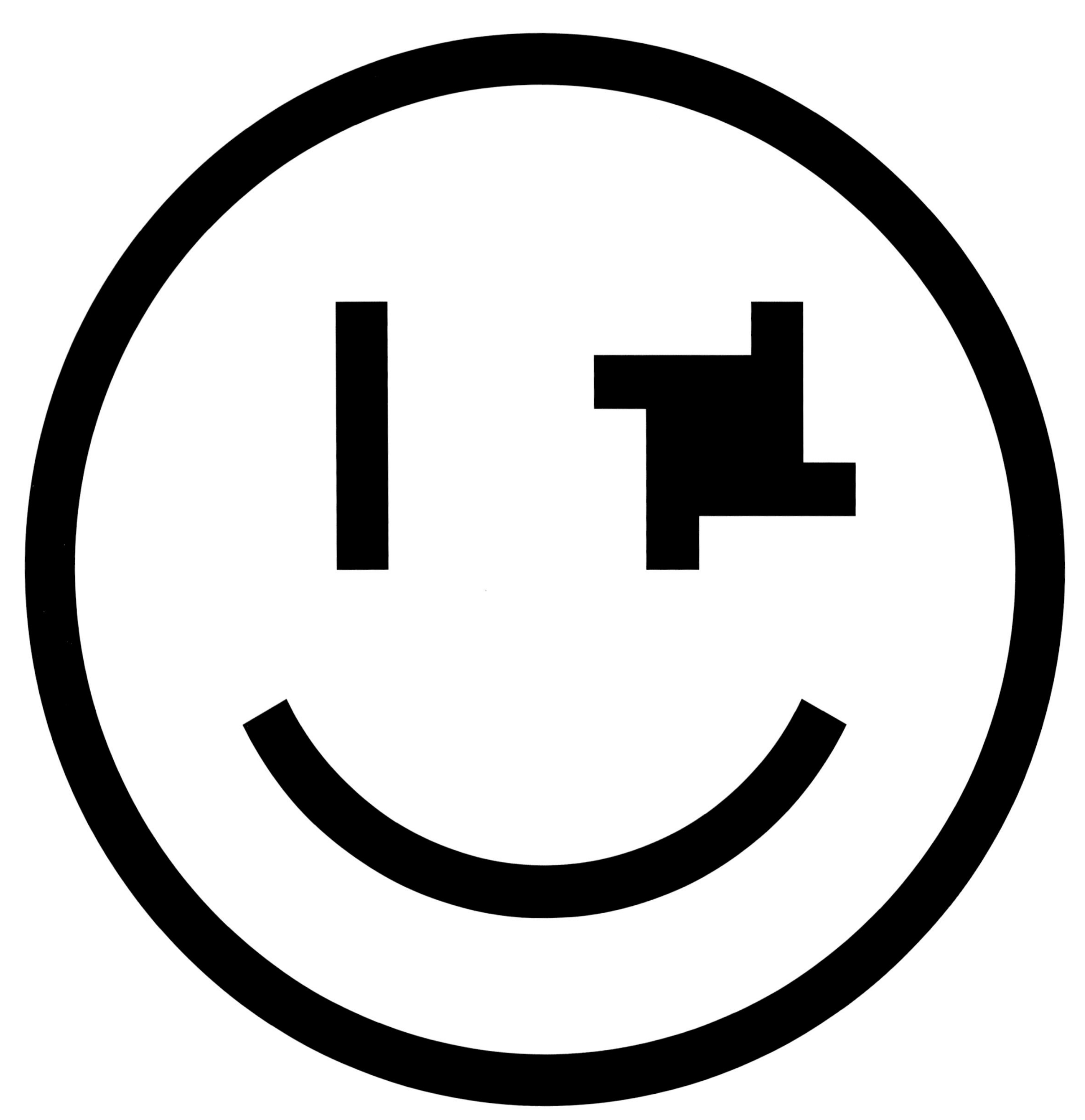

174—1

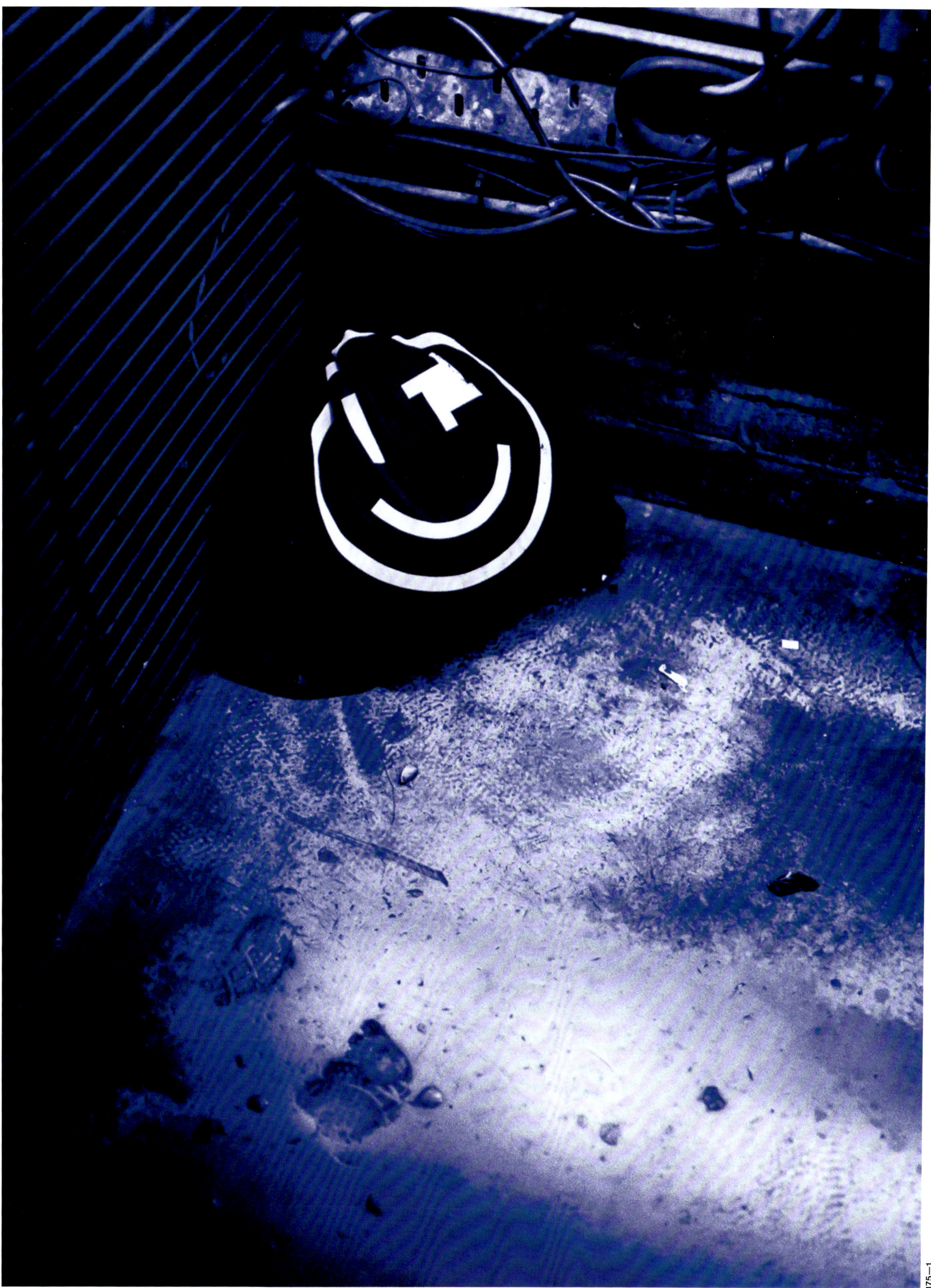

175–1

It was an enormous honour to have David Shrigley contribute his humorous and poignant scribbles to our afterparty concept. That concept being accommodating an enormous amount of people with nowhere to go and more to give after a long night on the fabric dancefloor. At this moment in time these post-club gatherings were not called afterparties; the term was yet to be coined. It was pre-internet and the multitude of options involving not going home had yet to be imagined. We simply wanted to continue the energy created within the club. With this in mind, we found various local premises to facilitate our needs... David's unique drawings provided flyers with strange and funny messaging which complimented our intentions. The aim being to attract a committed group of revellers desperate for a few more hours to a welcoming local venue. It was a time before mobile phones, and word of mouth was the currency. We distributed invitations adorned with David's work to a select few. They were very different days. Innocent and unchartered. No better, no worse, just different and now fondly remembered. We were privileged, excited and surprised to work with David, whose star was already in the ascendant. David has subsequently realised great success for his work, relentlessly challenging and celebrating human life in his inimitable way. We are deeply honoured to have collaborated with him.

Craig Richards

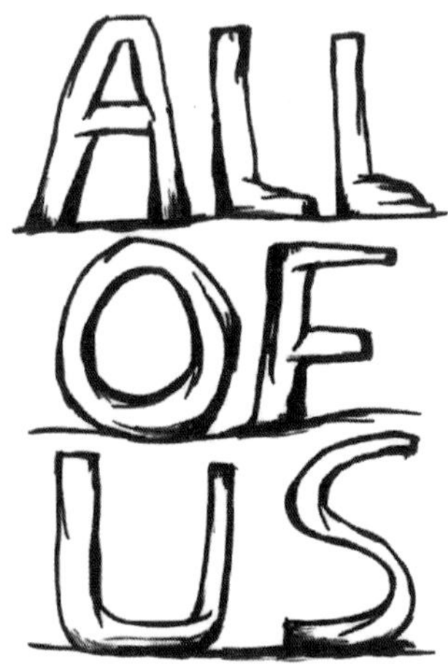

And **ON**... in celebration of Villalobos &
10years of treating our ears to
much inspiring music at fabric... and more.
Sunday 7th September from Midday till 8pm
on the roof terrace of : **South Place Hotel,
3 South Place, London EC2M 2AF**.
DJs: Amazing ones with vinyl.
Entry: £10 with flyer..

176—1

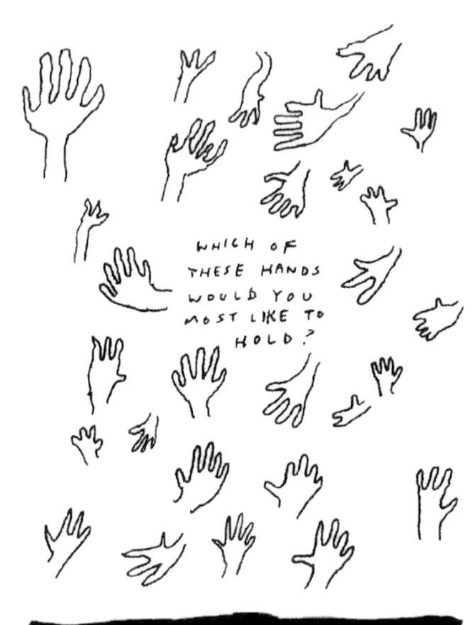

Fabric's Acid House Aftermath. Sun 28th. 6PM - 1AM
TBar: Corner of Shorditch High St & Bethnal Green Rd, E1
DJs: Craig Richards, Ricardo Villalobos, Tobi Neumann + more. Entry with invite obtained at Fabric Sat 27th.

176—2

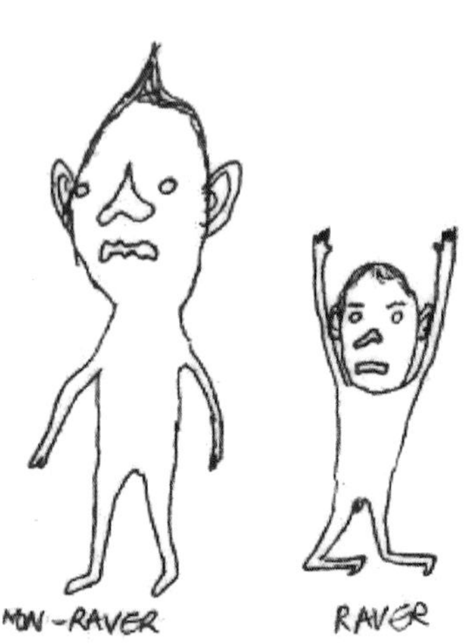

Celebrating 10 years of Villalobos at fabric
and Hamids birthday. Sun 28th April. Midday – 10pm
at 4th Floor Studios, 255-259 Commercial Rd, E1 2BT.
DJs: Amazing ones with vinyl. Entry: £10 with invite.
Bring Your Own drinks...

176—3

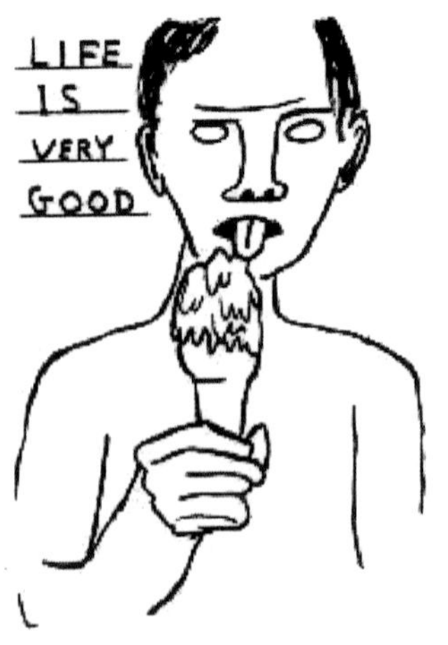

Afters Action, post Villalobos
for a special few on Sunday 10th August at:
THE SOULS, UNDER. Off Broadway Bar,
BROADWAY MARKET, E8 4PH
From 12 midday-8pm... DJs: Quality ones only...
Entry with Invite...

176—4

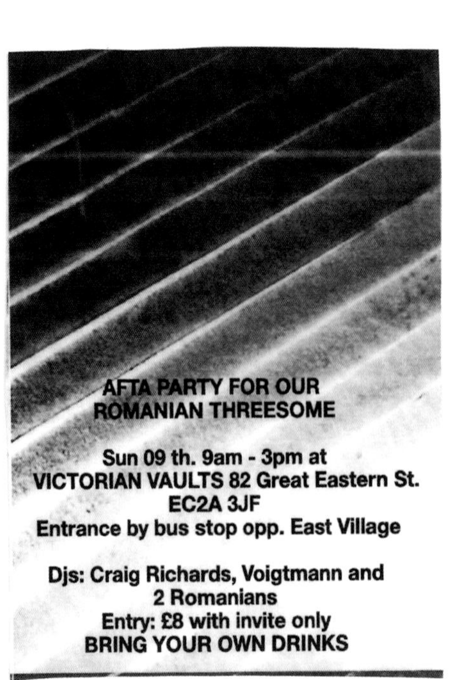

176—5

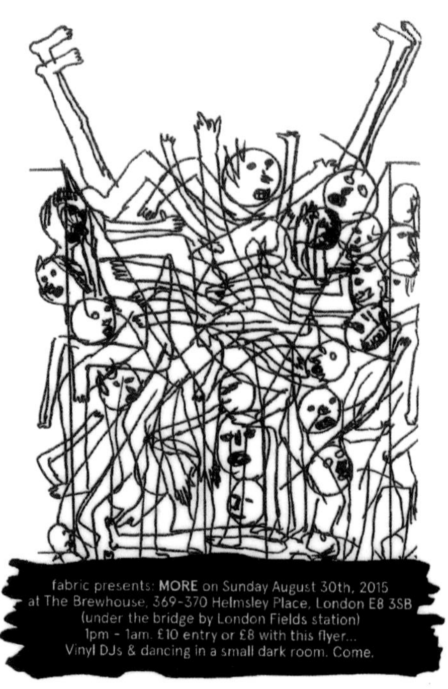

176—6

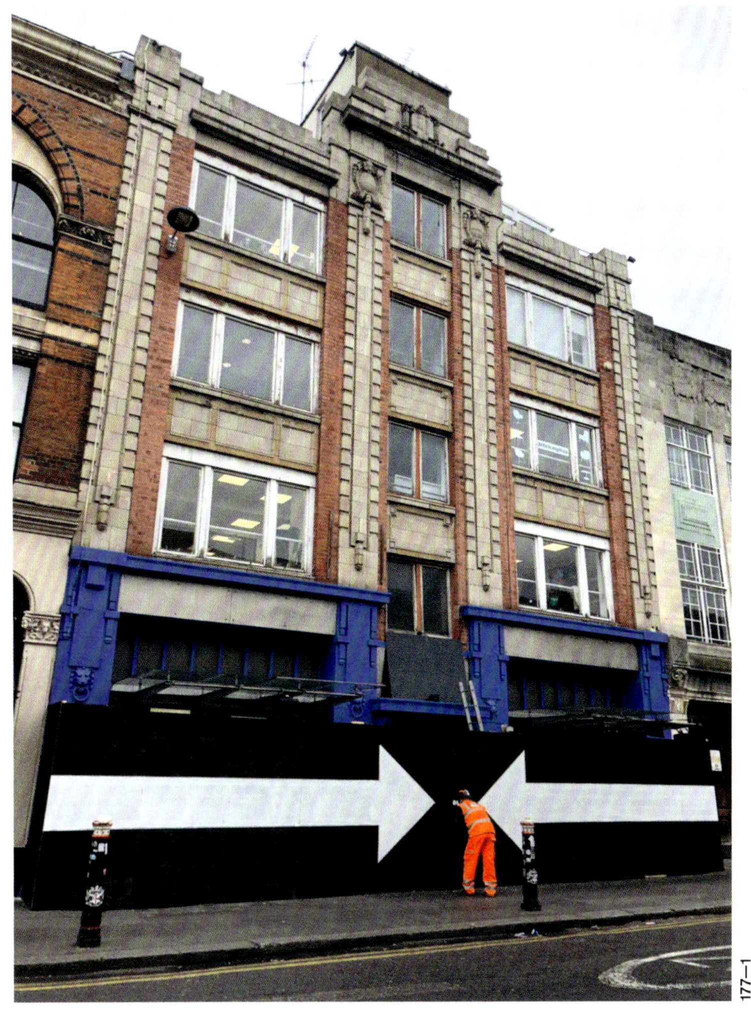

177—1

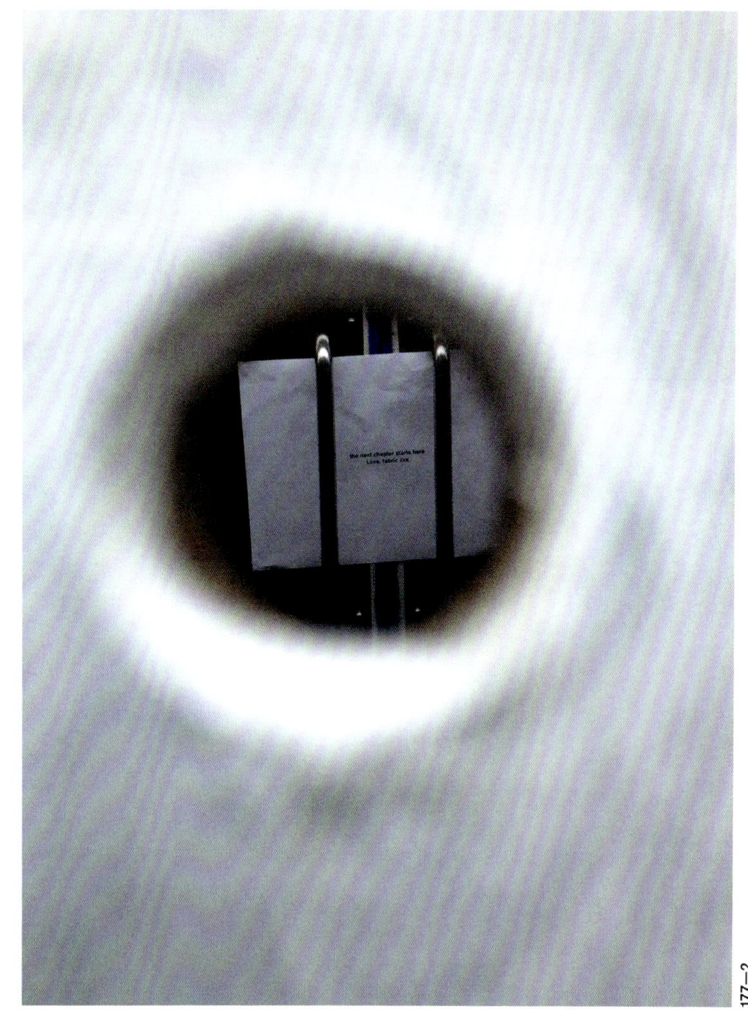

177—2

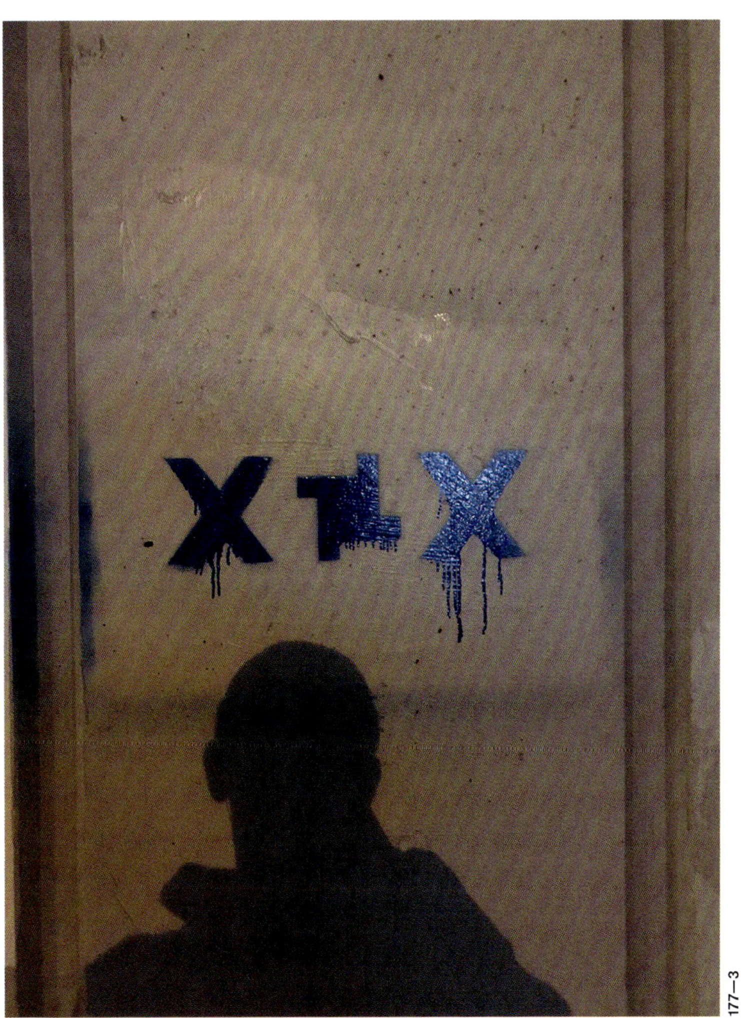

177—3

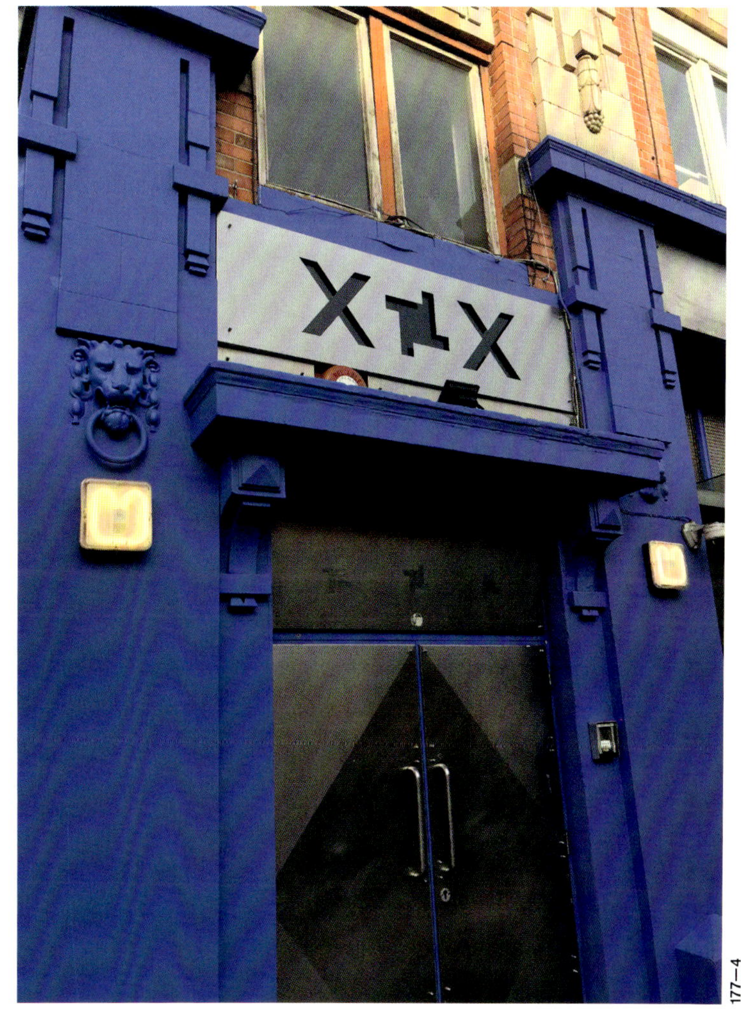

177—4

the people of fabric

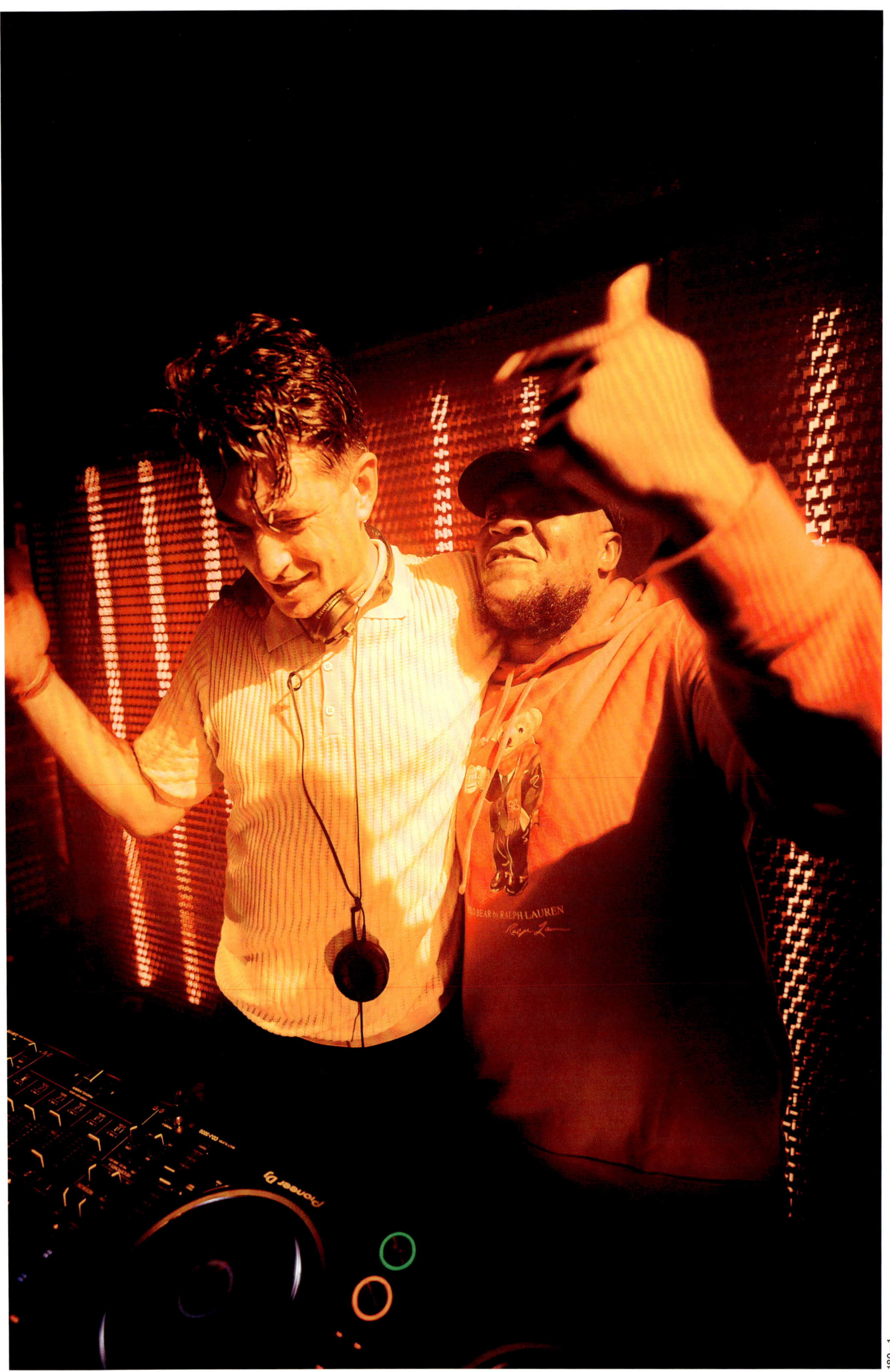

180—1

A club isn't just made for people – a club *is* people. For all that we like to talk about fabric's sound system, DJ booths, artwork, records and DJ sets, all of that is just stuff. The actual beating heart of fabric as an entity is the people who come through the doors, who interact with each other and the music, who play the CDs and records and keep the flyers, who accumulate memories and friendships. The intangible, ephemeral, endlessly moving flow of experiences and interactions is the substance, the artwork, the essence of the thing, above and beyond anything else. That's what generates the love and commitment from audiences, and ultimately the longevity of any nightlife organisation – and that goes tenfold for fabric.

That might sound like starry-eyed rave-boomer idealism, and sure, there is an aspect of that, but ... well ... why not? After all, fabric's origins lie in Keith Reilly's monomaniacal dedication not just to his love of music, but to his love of the networks that build up around people equally committed to the groove – that elusive assemblage people casually allude to as 'underground'. From his very first Soul Weekenders and parties in Essex bars, Keith was 'finding the others', plugging into those never-ending late-night conversations out of which culture is born. The focus on dancefloor experience above spectacle, and DJ line-ups made up of friends rather than superstars, is precisely why fabric was seen as an underdog at the start – but is also precisely why they're still here quarter of a century later.

The VIP area is really no more than a respite from the crowds rather than some lavish place to lord it over them, and DJs and staff alike are at least as likely to reminisce over memories from mingling on the main dancefloors as anything going on there or in the DJ booth. It's vital to note too that actual superstars have come through the doors, but only inasmuch as they were willing to be punters, not superstars. George Michael, Robbie Williams, Grace Jones, Liza Minnelli, Macy Gray, Ian Brown, Kiefer Sutherland, Macaulay Culkin and Vivienne Westwood have all graced fabric's dancefloors – and even at the peak of his fame, Dizzee Rascal was often sighted head down, hood up, raving like a champ to drum'n'bass. Keith fumes as he remembers Madonna deciding that she would grace them with her presence and sending ahead a list of demands for how she and her entourage should be accommodated. 'I thought she knew what clubs were about!' he says. 'That's not us at all!' She was not made welcome.

Which is not to say that fabric is a happy-clappy utopia. Of course it isn't. It's always been a commercial undertaking, and the night-time economy is a cut-throat realm. fabric has faced repeated existential threats over the years, and with each of those came conflict, condemnation and sometimes mass redundancies. Even on a day-to-day level, fabric's existence is based on gruelling work, from the practicalities of glasses and toilet roll to maintaining relationships – personal, financial and legal – with DJs and musicians, and managing public and institutional perceptions of the club. Every glittering, joyous peak moment in the club is built on hard graft. Putting on thousands of events for millions of people, releasing dozens of records a year, and perhaps most emblematically putting on those days-long birthday parties requires a lot of unglamorous, stressful hours invested with all the exhaustion, frustration and aggro that entails.

Nonetheless, fabric is something special. Speaking to staff, DJs and long-time regular punters alike, again and again, you'll hear the world 'family'. It's not just used casually as a shorthand for a close-knit workplace, but said with a real weight of meaning – generally affectionately, sometimes knowingly with a sigh, but almost always in that literal sense of the family as something that you belong to, that shapes you, that becomes part of you. In some cases it's even more literal: Cameron Leslie recruited both his dad Ian and his brother Nathan to work in varying capacities.

Nathan provided the extra level of business savvy to steer the matter project in 2008–10, and maybe even more crucially to get fabric back on track after matter's closure. Ian not only came in to run the cloakroom and cashiers in the early, wobbly days of the club – ending up there for three and a half months as 'a trusted pair of hands who could galvanise the team, watch the cash and look after the customers and not lose coats', in Cameron's words – but then ended up as membership secretary for fabricfirst for five years. In that time he probably had more face-to-face or ear-to-ear dealings with punters than anyone else in the team – to the point where he was invited to join holidays and even weddings by regulars.

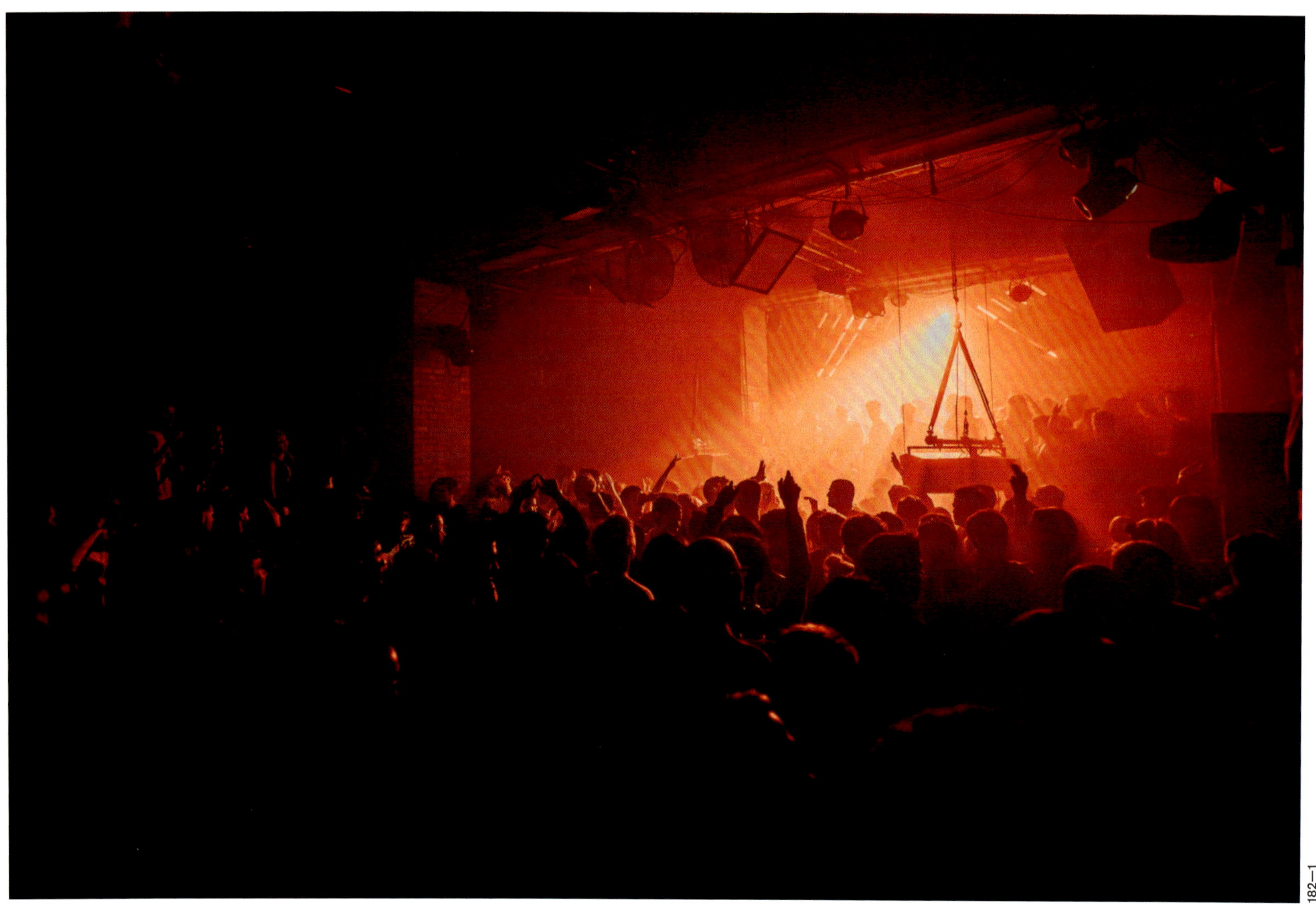

182—1

Yes, that's weddings, plural. Even on the very first night that fabric opened, Richard Welch, the club's first PR, met the man he would marry on the dancefloor. Annie Mac and Toddla T met in the DJ booth; techno legend Luke Slater met Heidy van den Broek, the former promotions assistant, on the dancefloor; BPitch Control mainstay Sascha Funke hit it off with another fabric promotions assistant, Julienne Dessange – and years on all the above are now married with children. There have been plenty more relationships sparked, kindled and kept alight by shared experiences on those dancefloors over the years. It's only natural; just in statistical terms, with millions of people through the door over twenty-five years, it's inevitable a few would find someone compatible – but there's more than just chance to it, too. Given the nature of fabric – its longevity and the commitment people have to it – its name once again feels strangely appropriate; it has become part of the fabric of people's lives and relationships, and those lives in turn become part of the wider fabric family. Add the bespoke household items like oven gloves, ice-cube trays, socks and tea towels that were given as presents to punters at fabric's birthdays or sent out to fabricfirst members, and fabric was even in people's pockets, their living rooms, their kitchen drawers. It's no wonder that clubbers feel a deep personal attachment and want someone like Ian to be part of their life outside the club, even in a small way.

And that growing-up-with-the-club experience constantly feeds back into the machine that keeps it running. fabric is made up of dance-music lifers, and – just as Keith, Craig and the rest of the initial team still had both feet firmly on the best dancefloors of London and further afield as they were willing the club into reality – younger staff members have very frequently come to their roles via a musical coming of age in fabric itself. For some of them, that musical schooling was consciously sought out. Danna Takako, who became the club's head of press later in the 00s, grew up in Chicago, but, on discovering drum'n'bass at an illegal rave there, made a pilgrimage to London in 2002. She vividly remembers walking into fabric for the first time and telling her friend: 'Mark my words, I'm gonna work here someday.' Andy Blackett, who has been a key part of booking Saturday nights since he joined in 2010, spent a decade before that looking enviously from Ministry of Sound where he worked and enjoying the last few hours of fabric most weekends 'because Ministry closed at five or six, and fabric carried on till eight, nine, ten, and it was only the other side of Blackfriars Bridge!'

There's a definite sense, too, that a lot of those people were made for the role they ended up in, or vice versa. Another recurring theme in talking to long-term staff is how many of them fell into their places – the team realised when they arrived in fabric's orbit that they were right, so made sure they stuck around. Andy Blackett, operations director Luke Laws and art director Roberto Rosolin joined not fabric but matter during its turbulent couple of years' existence. On matter's collapse, the talents of all three were noted and, in a moment of massive turmoil for fabric itself, they were all brought on board and have been key parts of the club for the decade-plus since. For Andy this was doubly daunting, as Saturday-night supremo Judy was off on a trip to Detroit at the time Cameron and Keith hired him to effectively be her partner in booking fabric Saturdays, so he had no clue if they could even work together. Of course, the founders' instincts for a music head were sound, and he settled into the role like it was his natural home.

Likewise, Geoff Muncey, who would mastermind the fabric and FABRICLIVE mix series, effectively had a job held open for him, as he was away traveling when the idea of starting a label was first floated – and Keith's intuition that he was the right person for the job proved right with bells on. The same went for the next phase of fabric's music releasing, with the launch of Houndstooth; as soon as Rob Booth's name was mentioned, the entire recruitment process was upended to make space for him, even though it meant coaxing him down from the other end of the country.

Then there were people who simply seemed to fall in by a natural process of clubland gravity. Scott Paterson, now a successful artist manager, started out as a flyer boy for fabric's arch-rivals Home when he first came down from Scotland as a fresh-faced young raver. His first contact with fabric was via fierce competition for poster space, but he struck up a friendship with his rival-in-flyering Shaun Roberts nonetheless, and got to know Judy in her brief time at Home too, plus he spent many Fridays at Bugged Out! nights in fabric. So by the time Home shut down he was almost part of the family already, and it just took a call from Steve Blonde and he was in – soon making himself indispensable as marketing manager. Sanj Bhardwaj had worked as a technician at Ministry and the Camden Palace previously. When he heard about the new venture he 'didn't want to hassle because I knew everyone would be on their case', but just a couple of days into fabric's opening he came in to fix a fuse box 'and never left!' From odd jobs and fixing up, he moved through operating the club's lasers to becoming 'Sanj the Man', tuning the fabric systems to the needs of each DJ that came through.

Of course, Judy and the much-missed Shaun sit right at the heart of all this. Speaking to artists and DJs who've come up through fabric over the years, again and again the first thing they'll mention will be the welcome they've been given, and not in the 'waheyyyy' tone that marks most generic anecdotes about clubland characters. Sure, both Judy and Shaun are/were party people and would always be ready to crack a bottle of champagne or several with their charges and continue the party after the club – but it was never just dumb hedonism. The reason they remain beloved among artists and the wider clubbing community is that they have always been smart, interesting, authentic people. Both of them were not just scholars of club music to a degree few people in the world could compete with, but broad in their interests, true conversationalists, always keen to make real connections. The fabric welcome that DJs love isn't just about hospitality in the material sense, it's about being seen as people and engaged with as such.

A club can't just run on vibes, though – it needs people to serve drinks, move boxes, replace toilet rolls, plug in cables and all the rest. Here you might see a little bit of an upstairs–downstairs divide; operations director Luke Laws chuckles a little ruefully when he talks about the 'fabric family', given that he and his team have to do the literal heavy lifting and are often close to invisible to the public ('people only notice us if something's gone wrong!'). But he absolutely sees a 'real, serious' family bond within the ops team itself, and speaks with great fondness of the club, even when he's wincing his way through the list of things that need to be kept tabs on through a fabric birthday weekend. And shot through everything is huge pride in the fact that that invisibility is actually a sign that the original vision of, in Craig Richards's words, 'raising the standards of security and sonics and toilets and drinks – and not worrying about the other stuff' is working.

On the sonics front, like all sound engineers who have to be on duty essentially problem-solving all night long, the head of tech Matt Smith also has a slightly world-weary tone when he talks about his workload. But at least he does get recognition; another common thread among DJs is the joy at having Matt, or previously his then boss Sanj, on the case with the sound and lights all night, not leaving anything to chance – and Matt recalls being recognised and accosted by sound nerds at Craig's Houghton Festival in 2023. And, of course, the joy of being able to work with one of the world's great sound and light set-ups is something that even hundreds of hours of graft can't dim – as Sanj puts it, 'It's worth it to know that there's people talking about you running the best sound in the best club!' That's evolving still, with the recent dramatic refit of Room 2. As Matt says, 'The chance to be there and have something do to through lockdown was a lifesaver, but also it's great to have it open and refreshed and giving people a new experience, while still being fabric.' Once again, after twenty-five years, it's still about the actual moments of interaction between people and sound above all else.

Through all of this has been a core of people who've held it together from the very start. Terry, Craig and Judy, all keeping the musical spirit constant even as the landscape shifts around them, still there and – while Terry and Craig may no longer do the marathon sets every week that made fabric's name – still plugged into the groove. And above all, there's Keith and Cameron. Keith hasn't involved himself in the day-to-day running of the club and label for some while now – his is more of a ceremonial role – but his presence is everywhere as a 'father figure'. It's clear that the same bloody-minded creative vision that turned the damp, tarry tunnels into fabric, that provided a home for weird music in the centre of London, that had people raving all night to John Peel, is still somewhere in people's minds when any decision is made.

Cameron, on the other hand, absolutely is in the thick of things every day, twenty-five years, three closures, and untold conflicts and heart-in-mouth moments later. And when they come back together to discuss something like the twenty-fifth birthday celebrations, the connection is immediately obvious – they absolutely, unquestionably seem like brothers. They're in almost all ways as different as it's possible to be, practically personifications of chaos and order, and you wouldn't need them to tell you that they've been at each other's throats many, many times over the years. But when Cameron pulls out a 'thank you and congratulations' note that Keith's mum sent him after an exhibition – yes, she did manage to come to terms with her son not becoming the strait-laced accountant she'd dreamed of – and they're reminiscing about that time, the closeness is impossible to miss. It's easy to be cynical about an organisation calling itself a 'family', but when you see the relationship that allowed fabric's twenty-five years to happen in the first place, it'd take a hard heart indeed not to understand that that's really what this is.

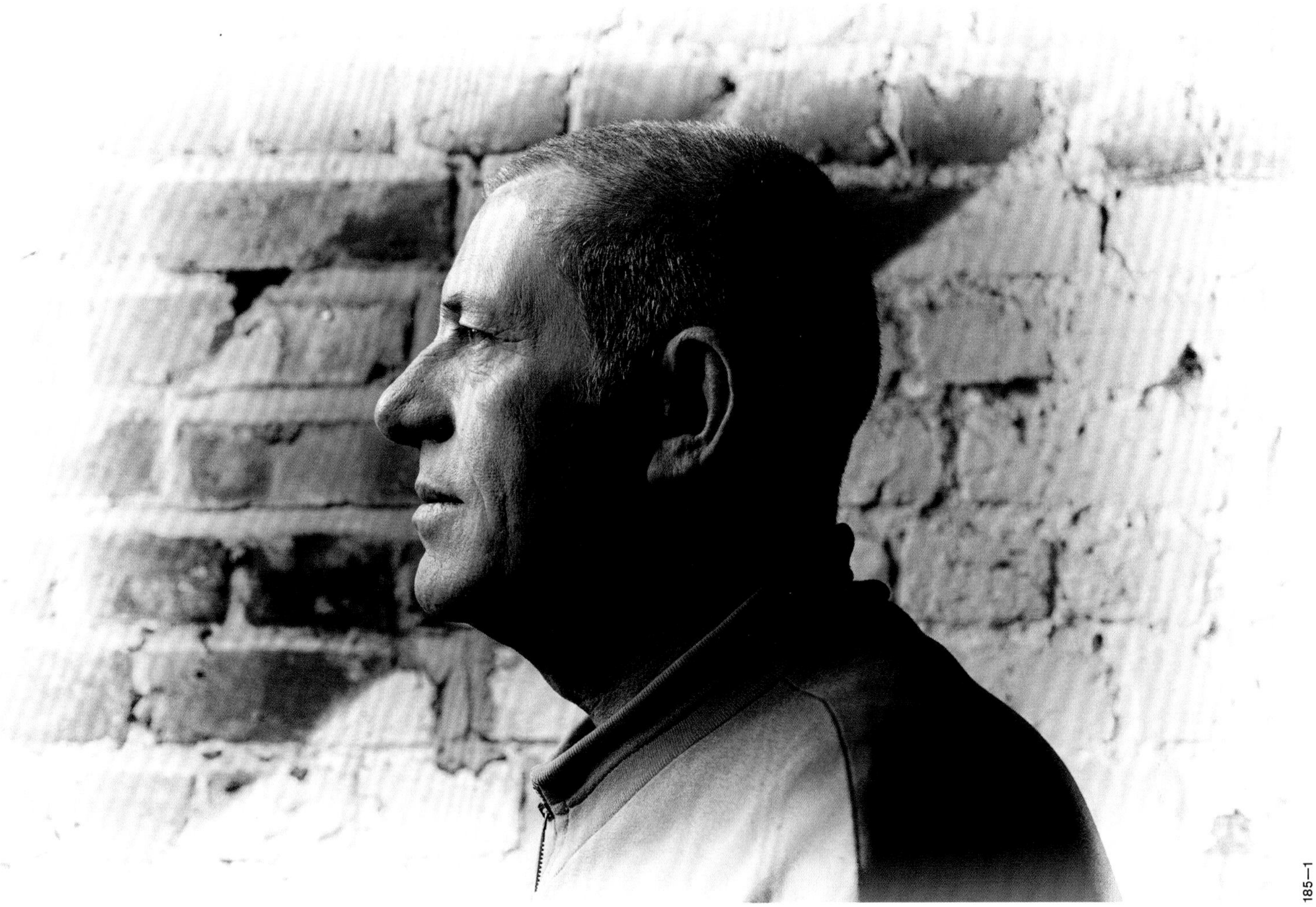

185—1

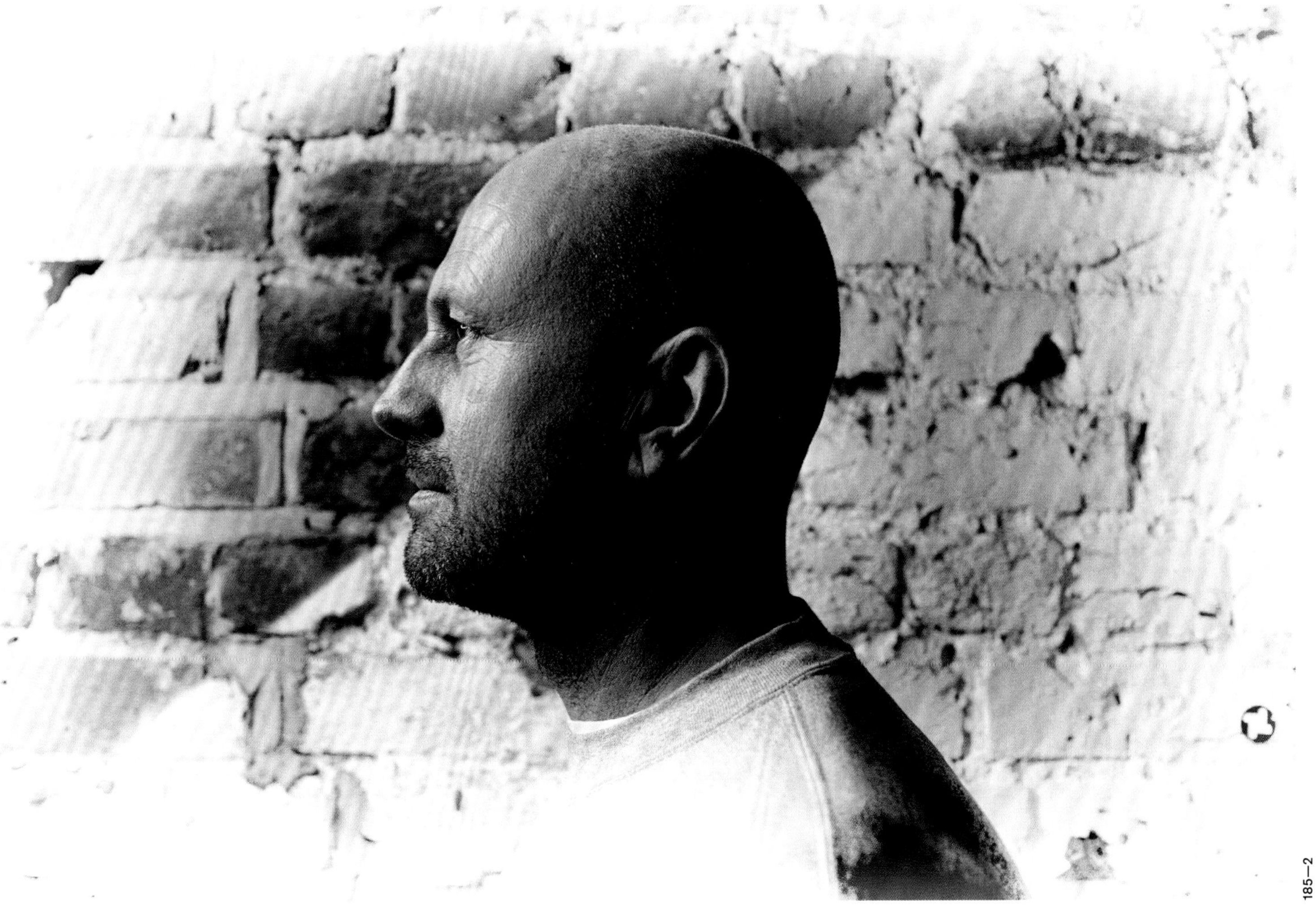

185—2

some of the key team – past and present

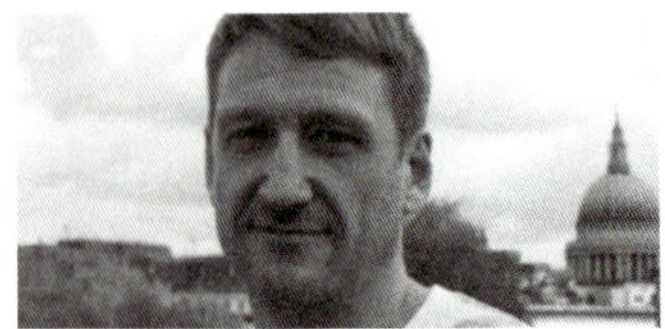

Andy Blackett (2010–present)
fabric:
A club I always wanted to programme,
A club that makes me proud,
A club that's part of my DNA,
A club that will go down in history.

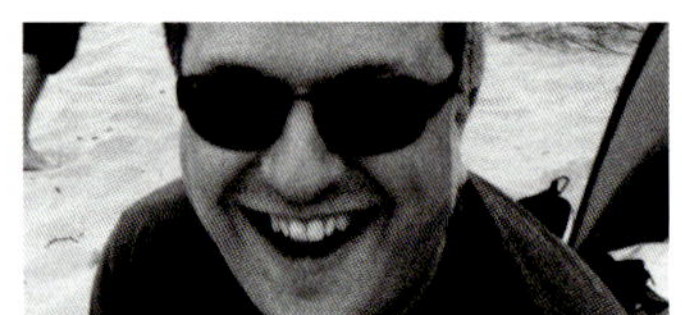

Dan Coshan (2000–2010)
It's hard to convey in words what fabric means to me; it's a community rather than a club or ex-employer. It simply embodies everything that you want to experience in a disco, with a collective of people you never want to be without.

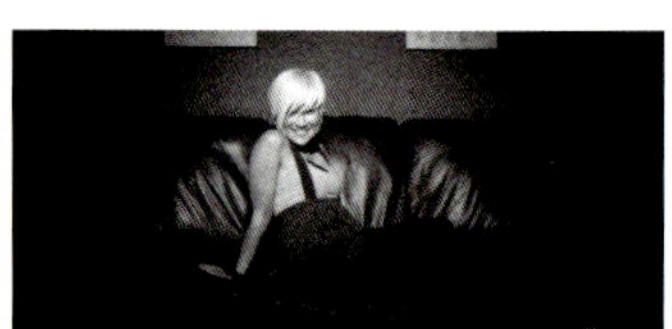

Danna Takako (2004–2010)
Anyone who's been lucky enough to be part of the fabric family understands that there's truly no words for it. ❤

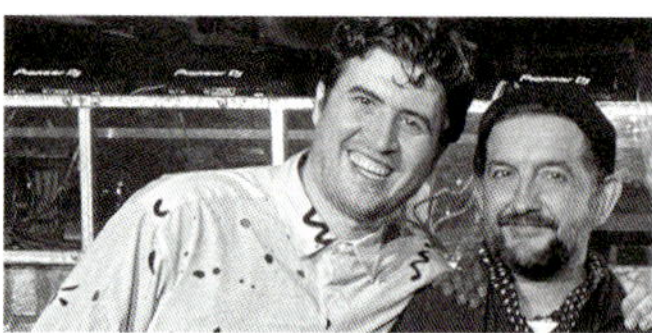

Dave Gamble (2010–2015)
fabric is the ultimate byword for a big night out and I feel so proud to have been a small part of that legacy, long may it reign.

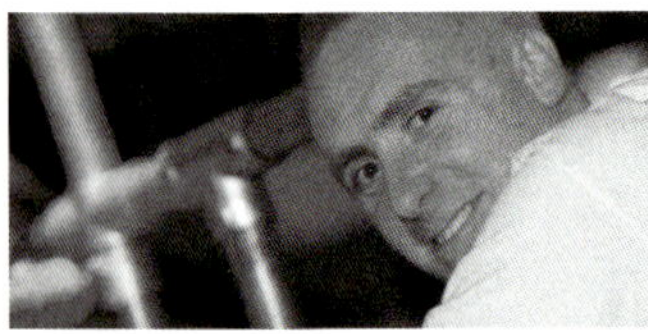

Dave Parry (1999–2004)
fabric meant the world to me. It allowed me free reign to experiment with audio and visual technology and push the boundaries of production. We did so many groundbreaking and wonderful things within the space and pretty much set the standards for club and DJ tech over the past twenty-five years.

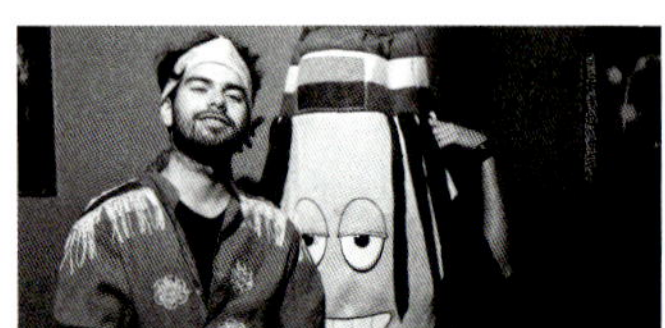

Ellis Coles (2018–present)
The space really does make up the fabric of what makes London clubbing so special. From the start it has always been about the finer details and getting the basics right. To play a small part in its history is an honour.

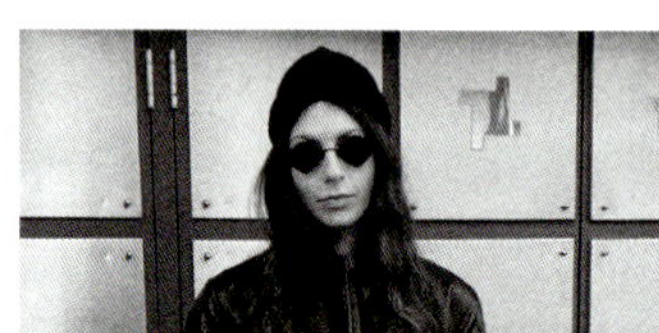

Flaminia Agrimi (2021–present)
Working at fabric means contributing to London's position as the heart of innovation and cultural resonance in the electronic music landscape.

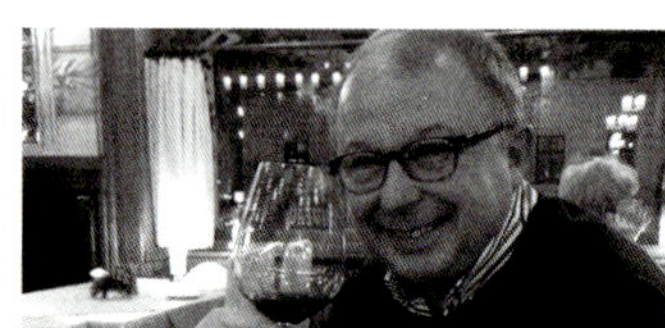

Gary Kilbey (2010–2020)
fabric to me was the dream team Keith and Cam put together that gave years of love and fun to all the fabric family. Helping them rebuild it was my honour x

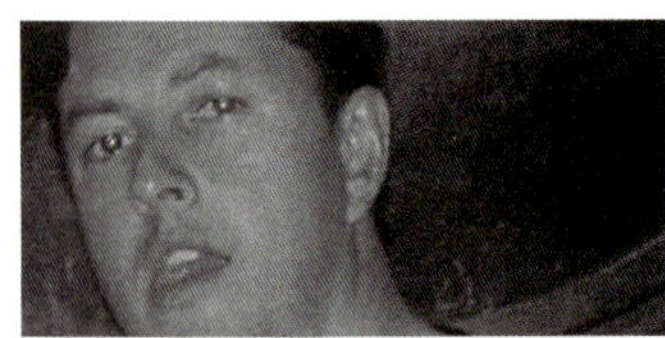

Geoff Muncey (2001–2012)
An education, an experience, friendships and memories that will stay with me forever.

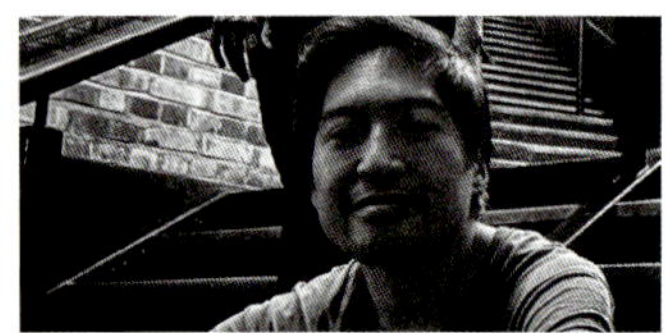

Hiroki Beck (2023–present)
fabric as a brand continues to represent an unwavering commitment to underground electronic music while continually pushing boundaries – most seen in our fabric mix series with its iconic CD tins, which remains a legacy to this date.

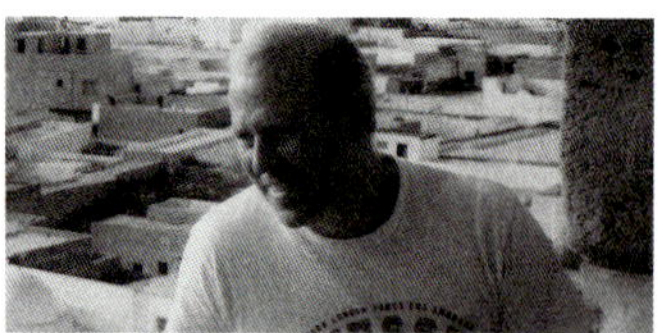

Ian Leslie (1999–2010)
Exciting to be part of a new enterprise, working with positive, happy people with such a great vibe in the club.

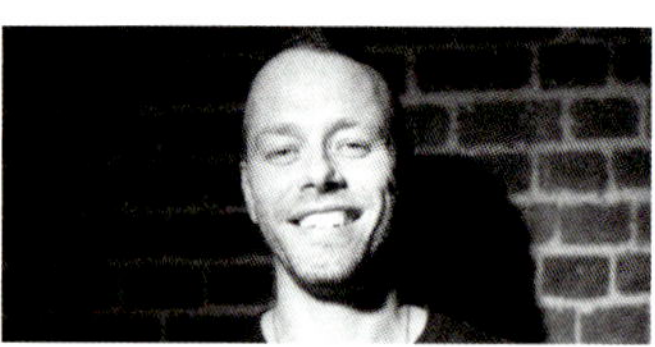

Jacob Trier Hansen aka Jacob Husley (2009–present)
It's hard to put into words how much fabric has meant to me, having practically lived there for the past fifteen years! The fabric community – from staff to ravers and artists – has become my extended family over the years. It makes fabric what it is, and I am so grateful and proud to be part of it.

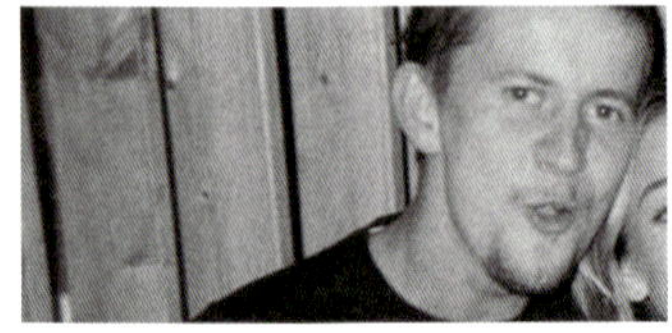

JJ Szilagyi (1999–2010 / 2012–2013)
I can honestly say I have never worked in a more welcoming place. I will always remember it as one big happy family running a disco on weekends. From the day I started, I felt part of this incredible team. I am so proud of the decade spent there. I have nothing but love to all at the club and here's to another twenty-five years at least ! ❤

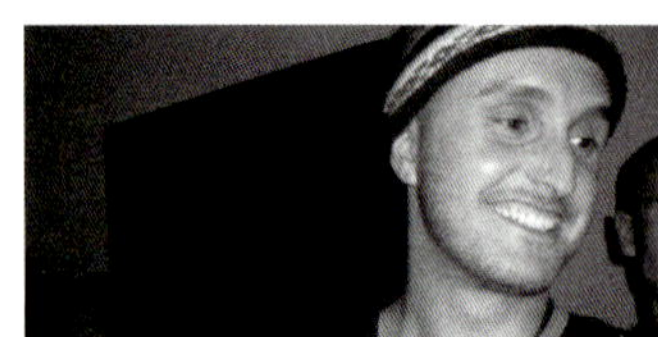

Josh Robinson (2006–2010)
fabric is fundamentally the seed that every part of my life has grown out of. It was the rave experience that made me commit to a career on the dancefloor and to never having a job where I wore a suit. It was the most enjoyable work and lifestyle any young man could ever receive in his early twenties, and it's a constant source of inspiration and peace every Friday and Saturday night to know that the venue is still there, and there are still people like me having that same experience.

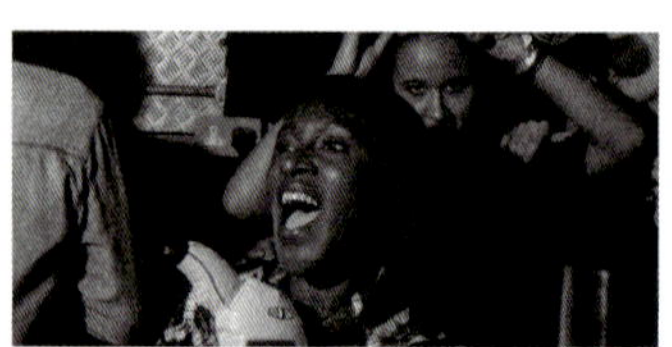

Judy Griffith (2000–present)
fabric is my life, my legacy, my London, my passion, my baby, my love – and the music programme is an extension of my soul.

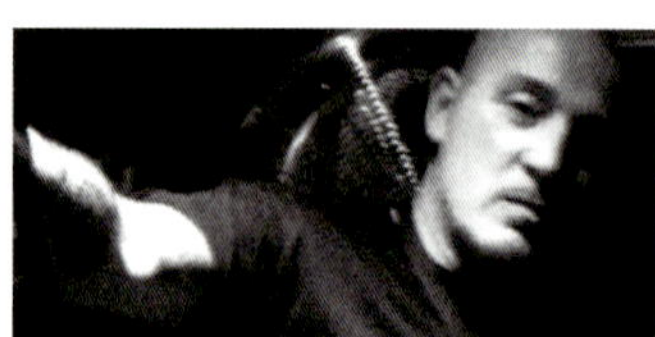

Keith Reynolds McGovern (2005–2016)
It was a pleasure and a privilege to be part of the fabric family for eleven amazing years. Every night you felt you were part of something special.

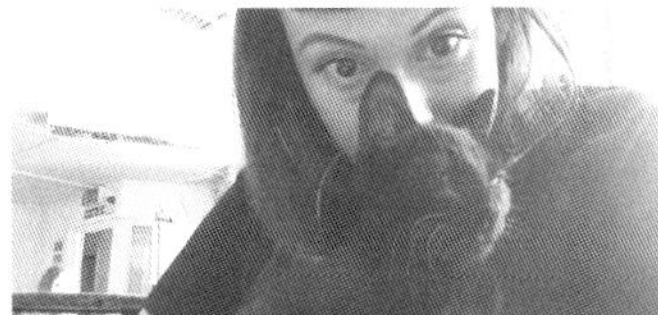

Kimi Otsuka (2012–present)
fabric is the glue that binds London's past and present clubbing scenes. It's a family, a place where I've met some of the best people in my life – it has given me and many others a feeling and circumstance in our discovery of music, love, escapism, knowledge, growth, friendship and family. I owe some of my best experiences to the club – goosebump moments and pride in being a part the team … tbh I can't imagine my life without fabric being here still.

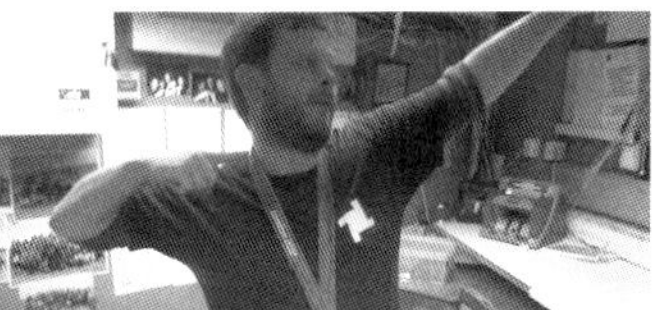

Luke Laws (2008–present)
fabric is like trying to solve a Rubik's cube that is fighting back – fun, challenging, infuriating, reassuring and never finished!

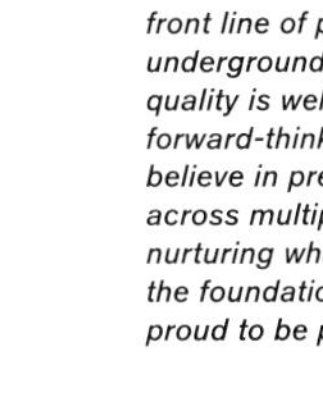

Matt Smith (2007–present)
For me fabric has always been at the front line of progressive electronic and underground music. Its dedication to sound quality is well known. There's a brave and forward-thinking team at its backbone who believe in presenting exciting new sounds across multiple genres, championing and nurturing what often goes on to become the foundations of global scenes. I feel very proud to be part of this legendary outfit.

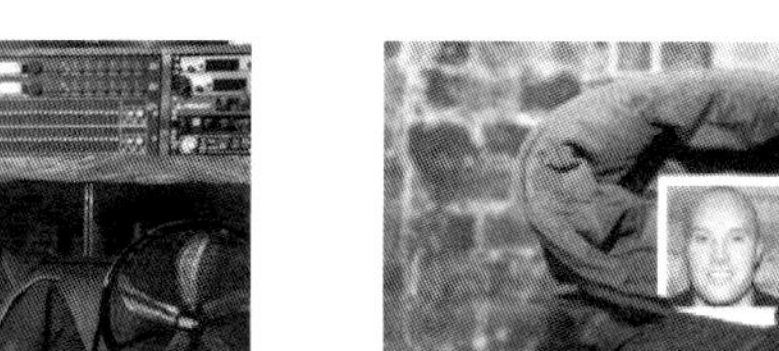

Nathan Leslie (2008–2013)
With ever-increasing amounts of terrible, commercial, low-quality 'dance music', we need clubs like fabric more than ever to ensure the pipeline for proper underground, quality dance music remains in place.

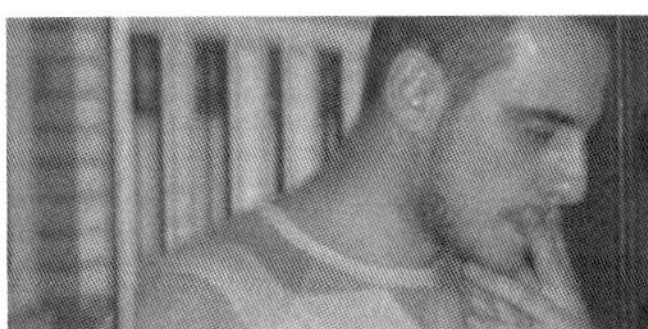

Nick Doherty (2000–2006)
Everyone involved cares deeply about making every night memorable, and it shows – there's nowhere better. Viva fabric.

Jorge Nieto (2020–present)
fabric meant a far away dream. It started from only accessing the flyers when I was growing up in Colombia, then inspiring me to move to London. It feels surreal and an honour to work here and be part of an incredible music institution.

Nikki Smith (1998–2001)
Nikki was very special to the fabric team and instrumental in shaping fabric at launch and in the early years.

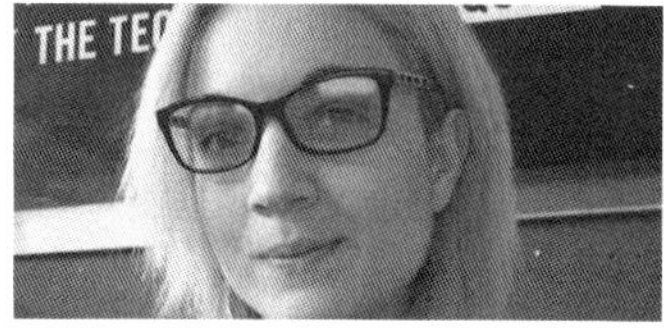

Nikolett Nemet (2012–present)
fabric to me is a piece of my heart that I always take with me no matter where I go. It's the place where I met the most important people in my life and made memories that I will cherish forever.

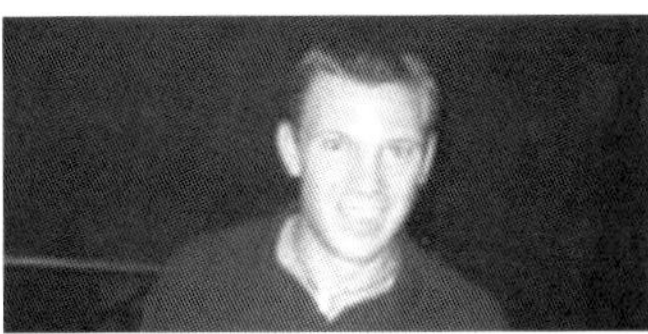

Paul Durand (2000–2016)
An experience where we worked hard, played hard and made lifelong memories and friends.

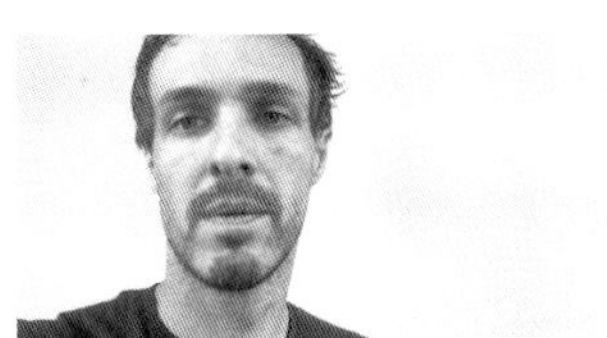

Piotr Brzezinski (2020–present)
fabric is a place of chaos inside and out — joyous energy. It is simultaneously an institution representing the 'old school' way of doing things and a venue at the forefront of what's latest and greatest today. And, above all, it represents an honest focus on the music, the artists that create the music and the crowd enjoying it.

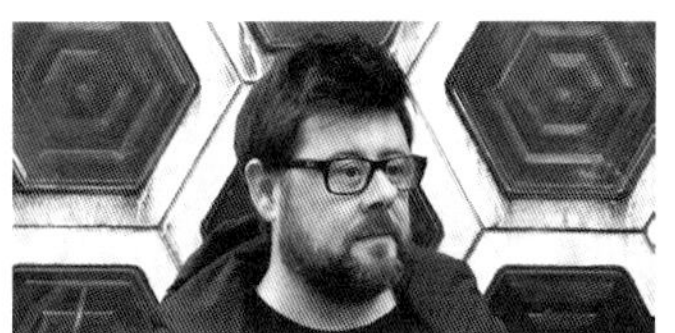

Rob Booth (2012–present)
fabric is my second family. Everyone who works for the club is on the same level; I've never experienced a workplace like it, and maybe never will. From assisting in setting up Houndstooth, fourteen years after the doors opened in EC1, and seeing it grow, to now working on the new exciting Originals label, using my experience to keep pushing new music to all electronic music fans, is the stuff of dreams. fabric has enabled this, and I owe a lot for their belief in me.

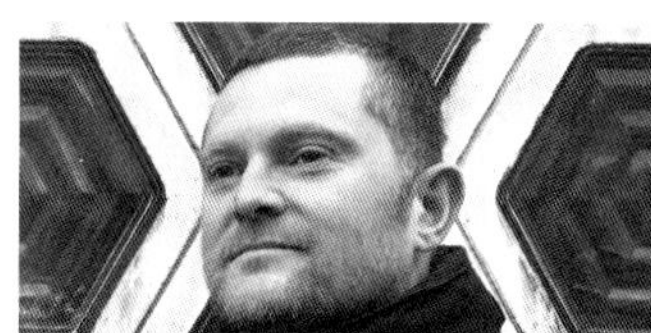

Rob Butterworth (2005–2023)
fabric for me is about pure escapism and joy; time spent in the club is losing yourself from everything else to just be in the moment. As someone who worked for the label, our mixes hopefully offered a vision of that to those who couldn't be there physically.

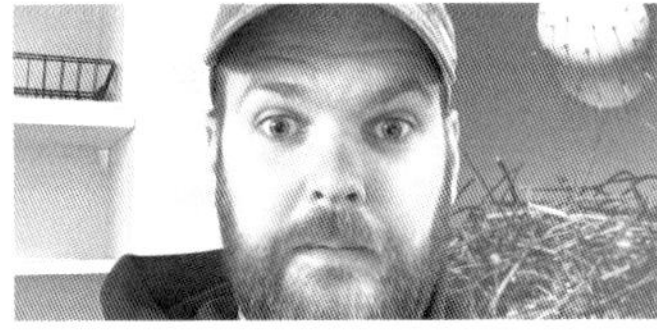

Rob Cracknell (2015–2018)
fabric was everything when I was growing up and going to Playaz in my teens, so to work there and work with Hype was a true dream come true … not many people get their dreams coming true, thank you team fabric.

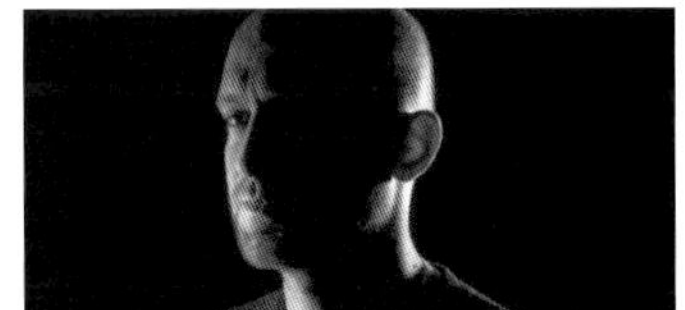

Roberto Rosolin (2010–present)
fabric has been the cornerstone of my creative journey as a designer, shaping me into the person I am today.

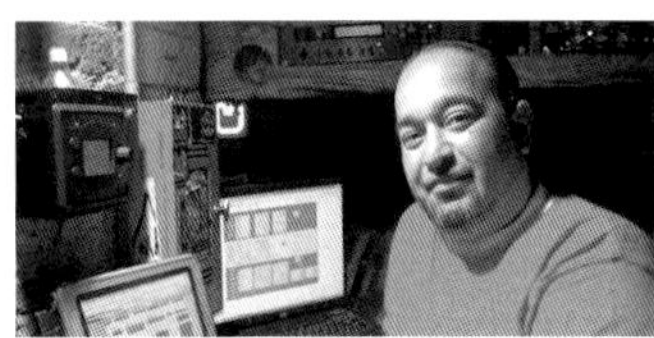

Sanj Bhardwaj (1999–2015)
fabric is all about sound, sound and sound. Getting the cleanest sound out of the system and working with the DJs.

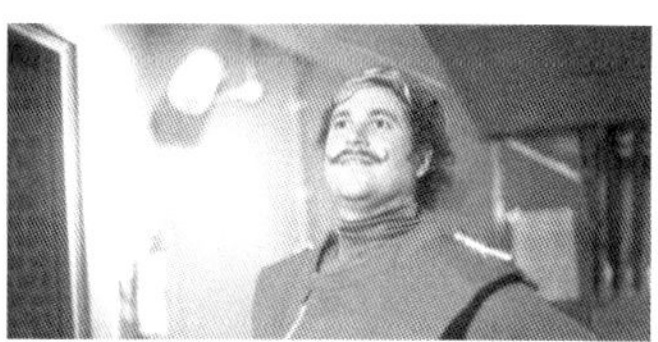

Saul Press (2008–2016)
To me fabric means family. We had our highs and lows, but we were always there for each other.

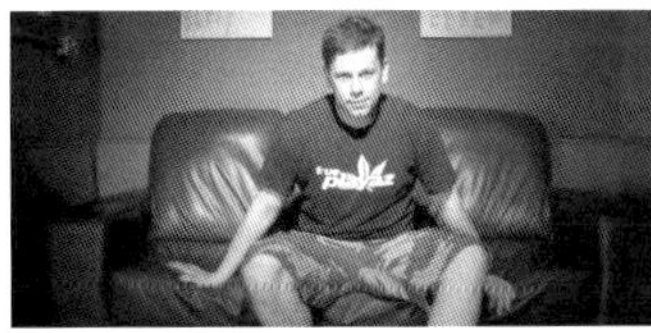

Scott Paterson (2001–2012)
My time at fabric meant the world to me. The club still does. We weren't actually trying to achieve anything apart from just making fabric the best personal experience we could in every way.

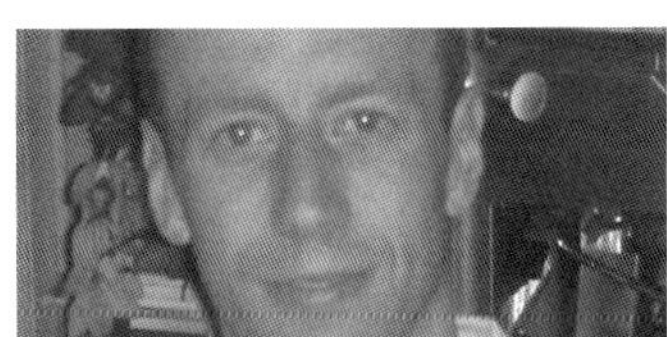

Steve Blonde (1998–2006)
fabric was always much more than just a club.

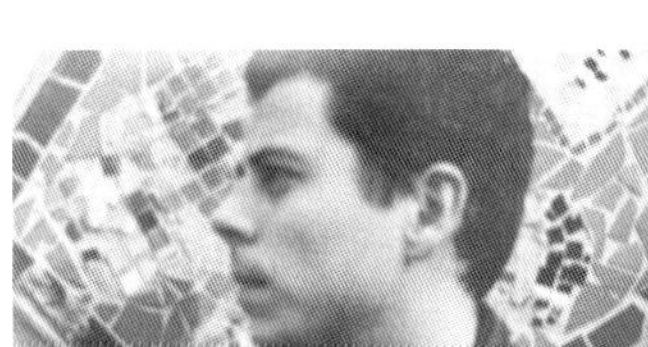

Toby 'Tubbs' West (1998–2001)
The achievement of fabric was through a collision of some special people, timing and pure belief it could happen.

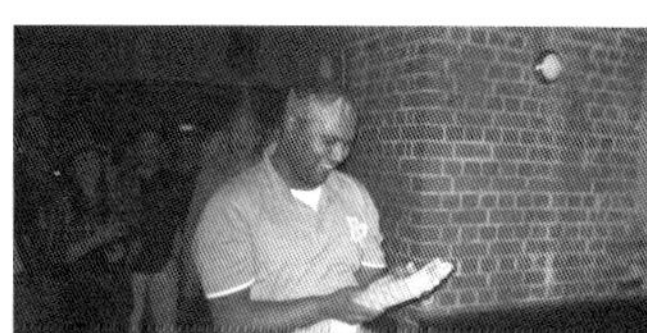

Uma Bala (1999–present)
I started as an intern when fabric opened – I'm still here through the highs and lows, accepted the challenges and enjoyed every moment!

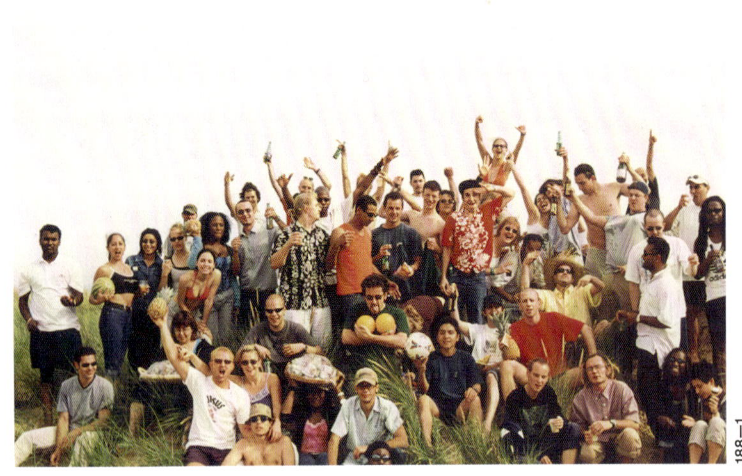

188—1

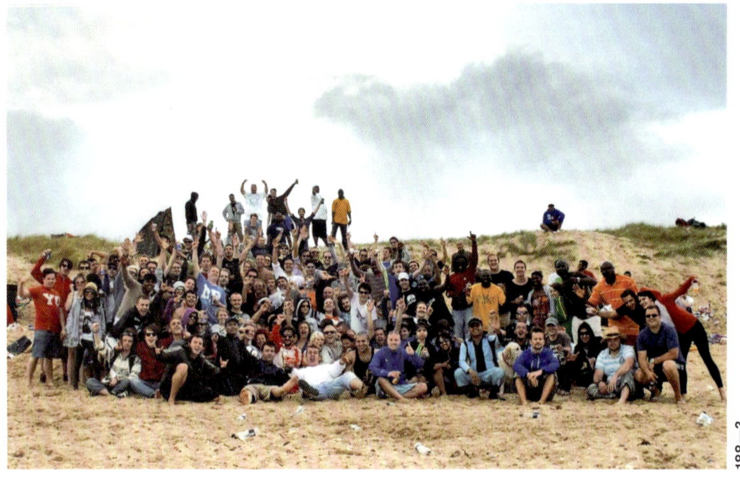

188—3

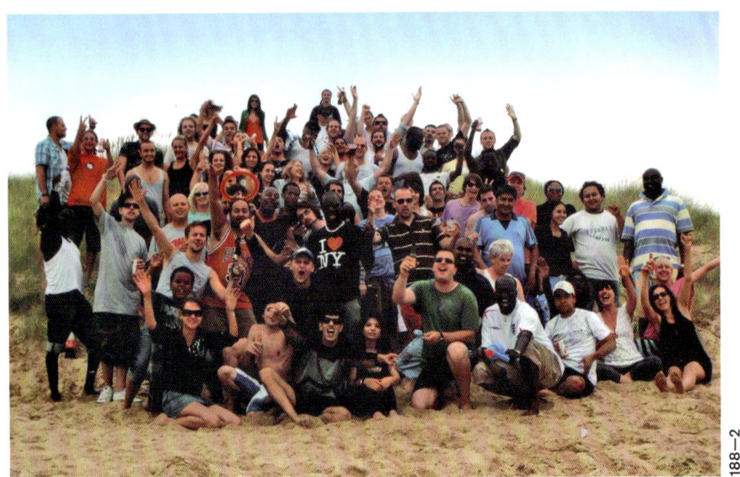

188—2

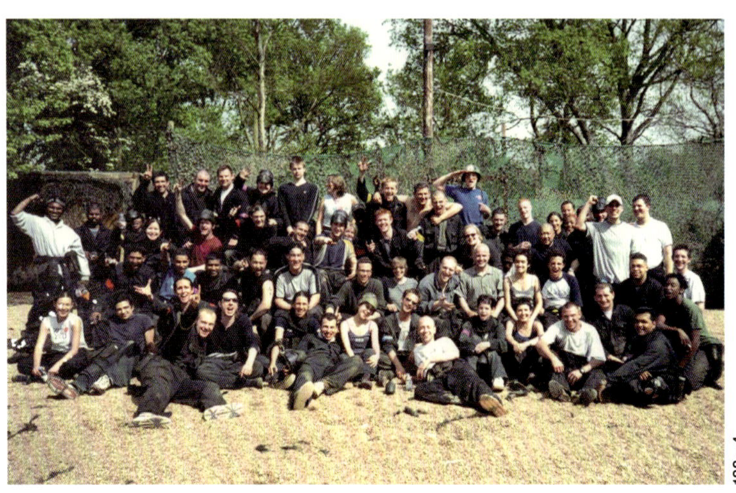

188—4

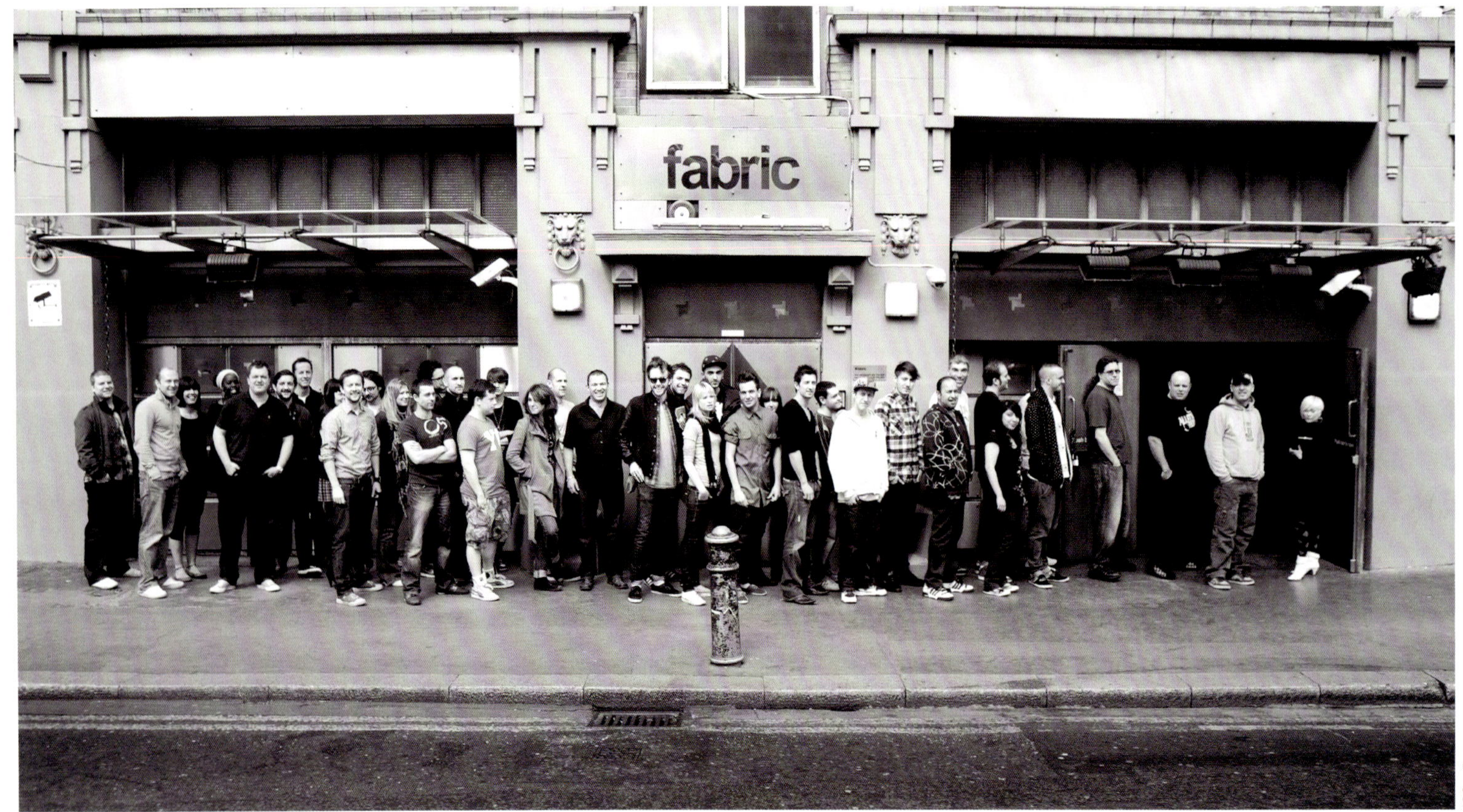

188—5

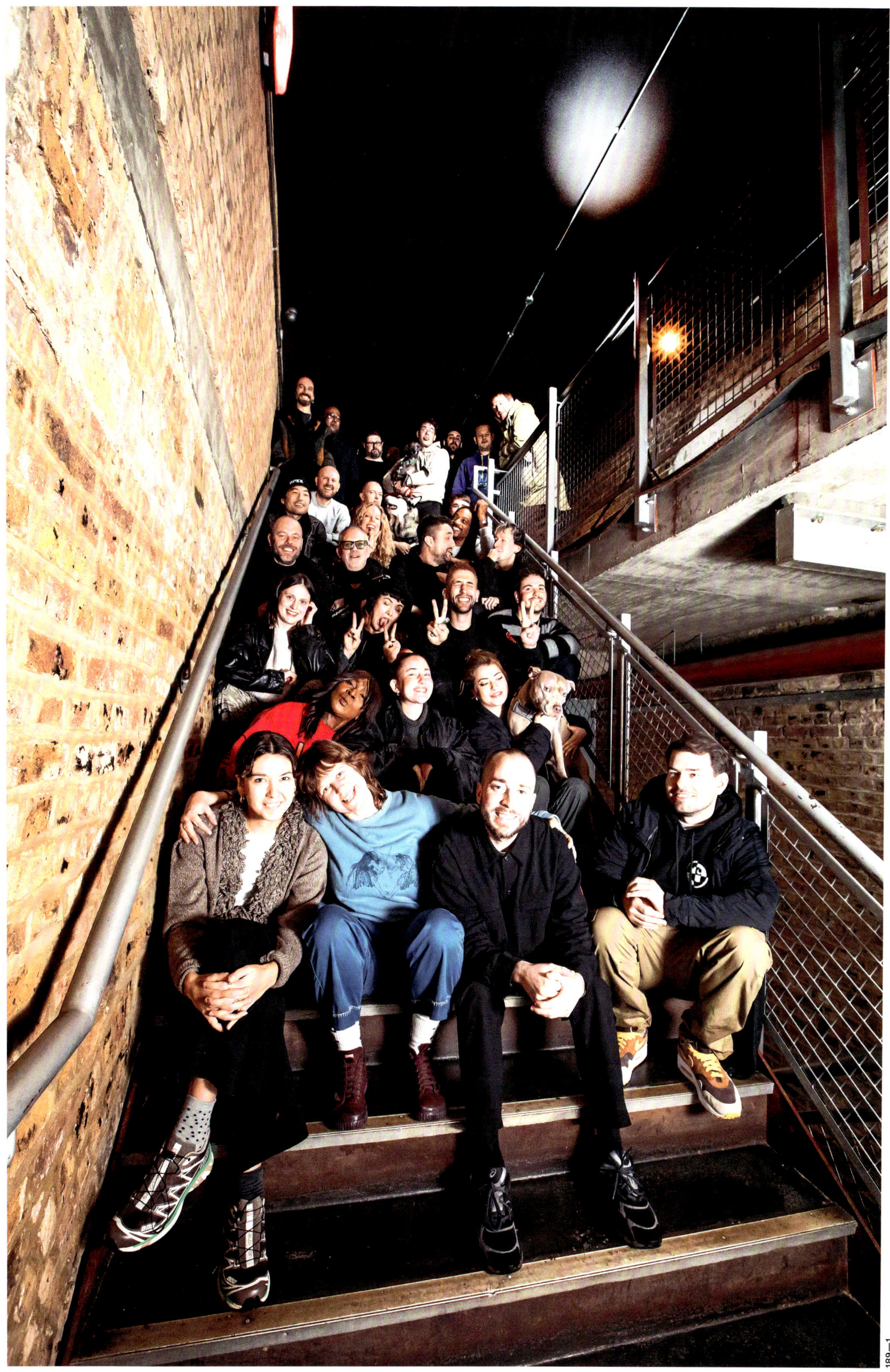

189—1

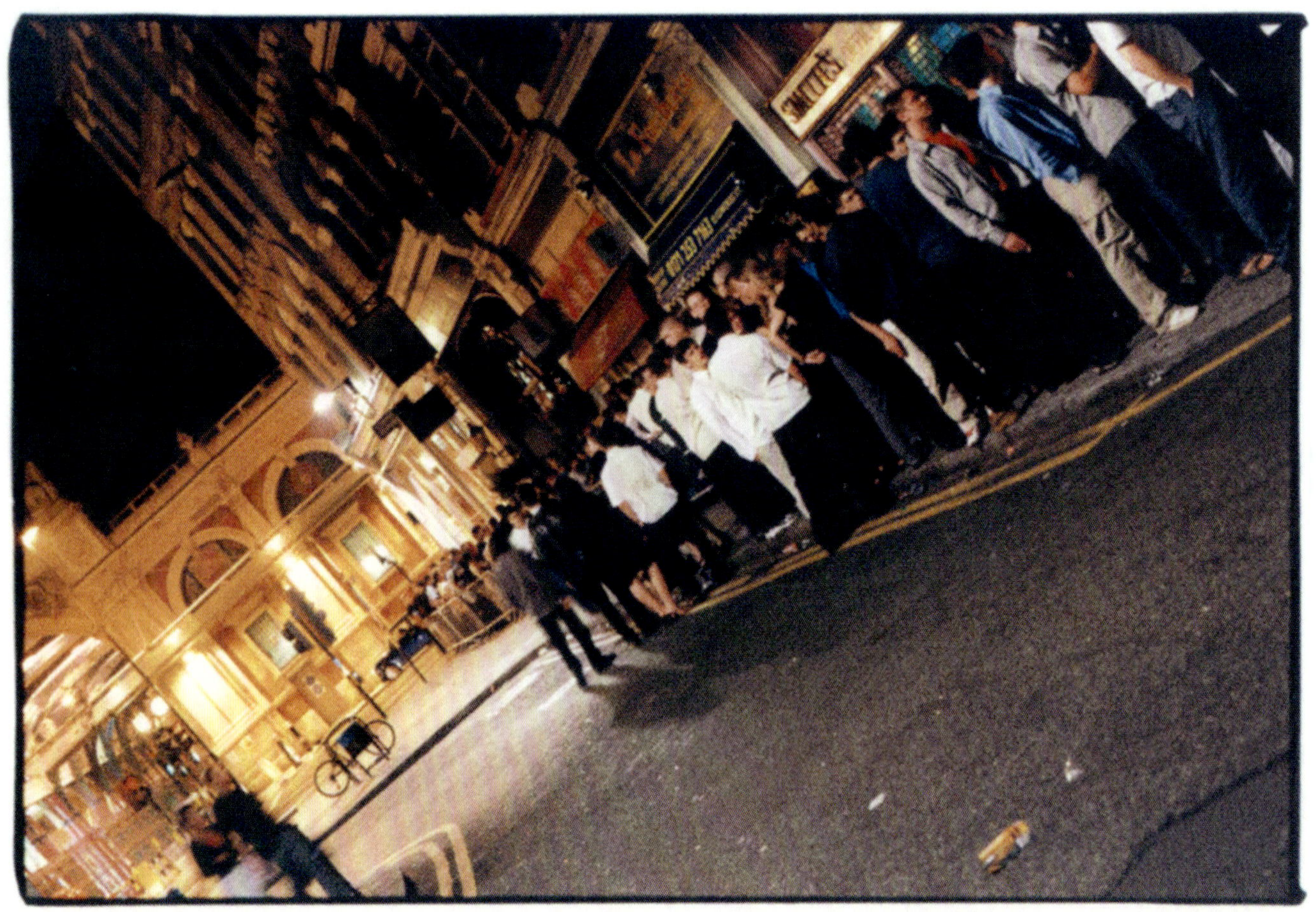

190—1

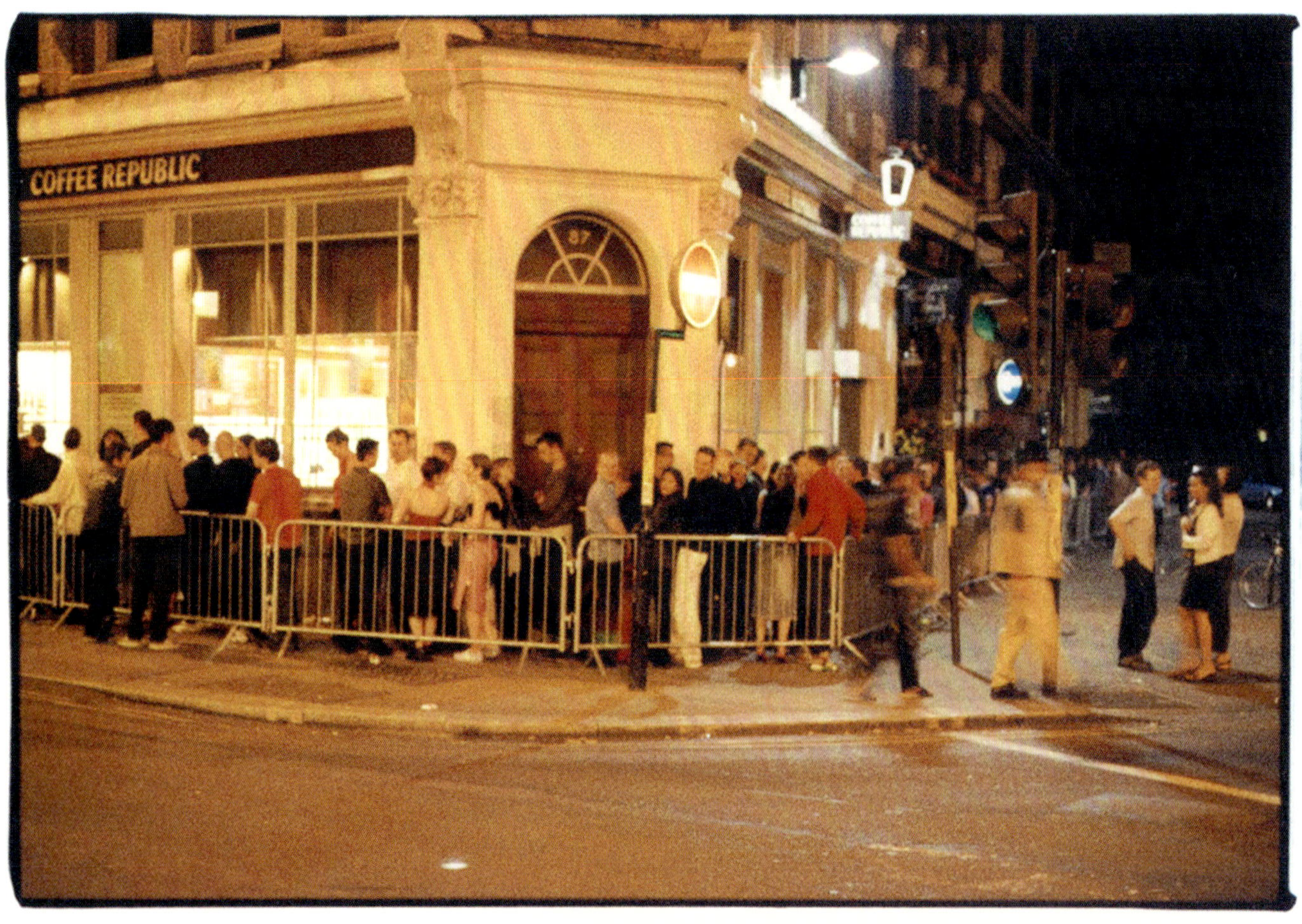

190—2

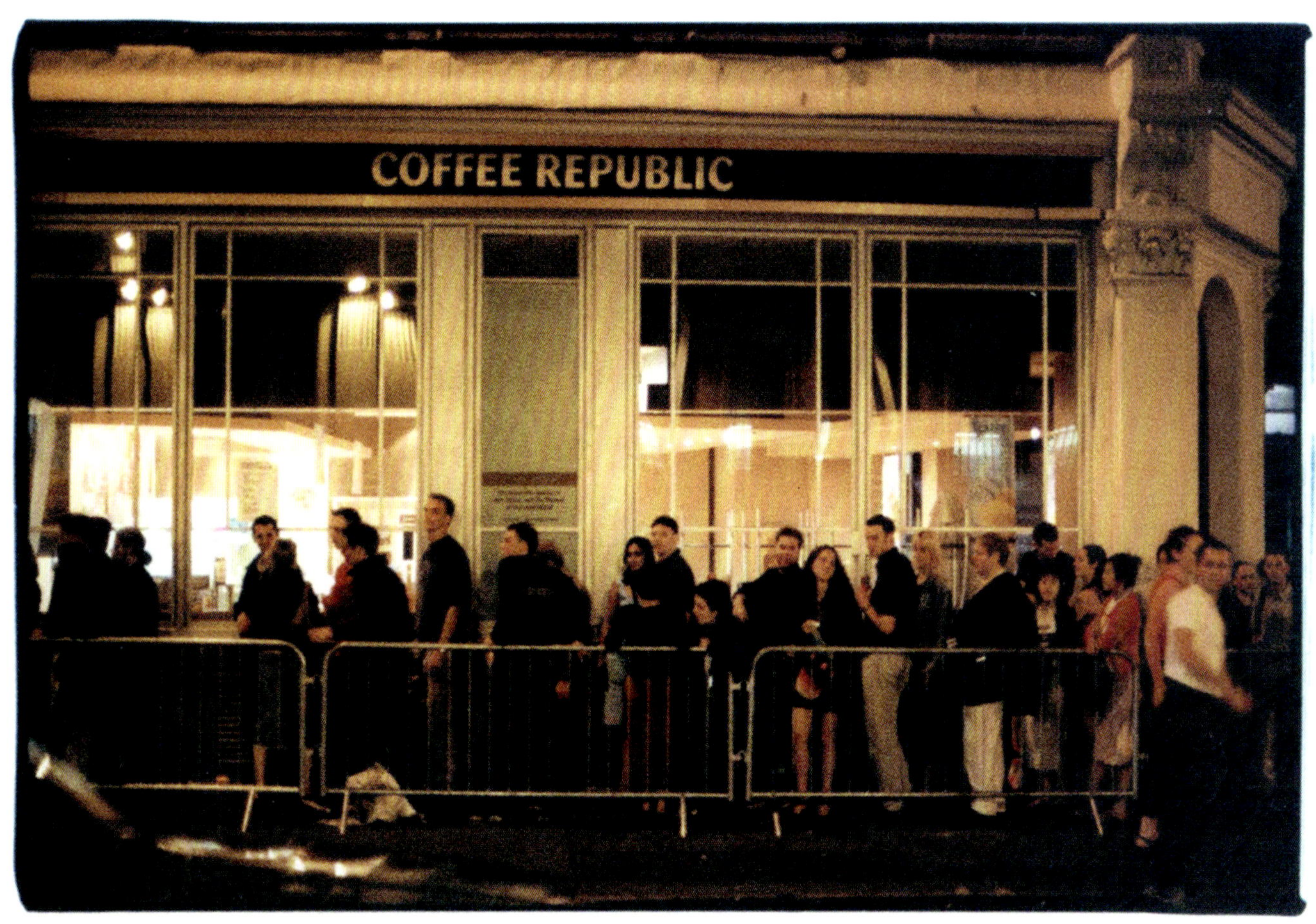

191—1

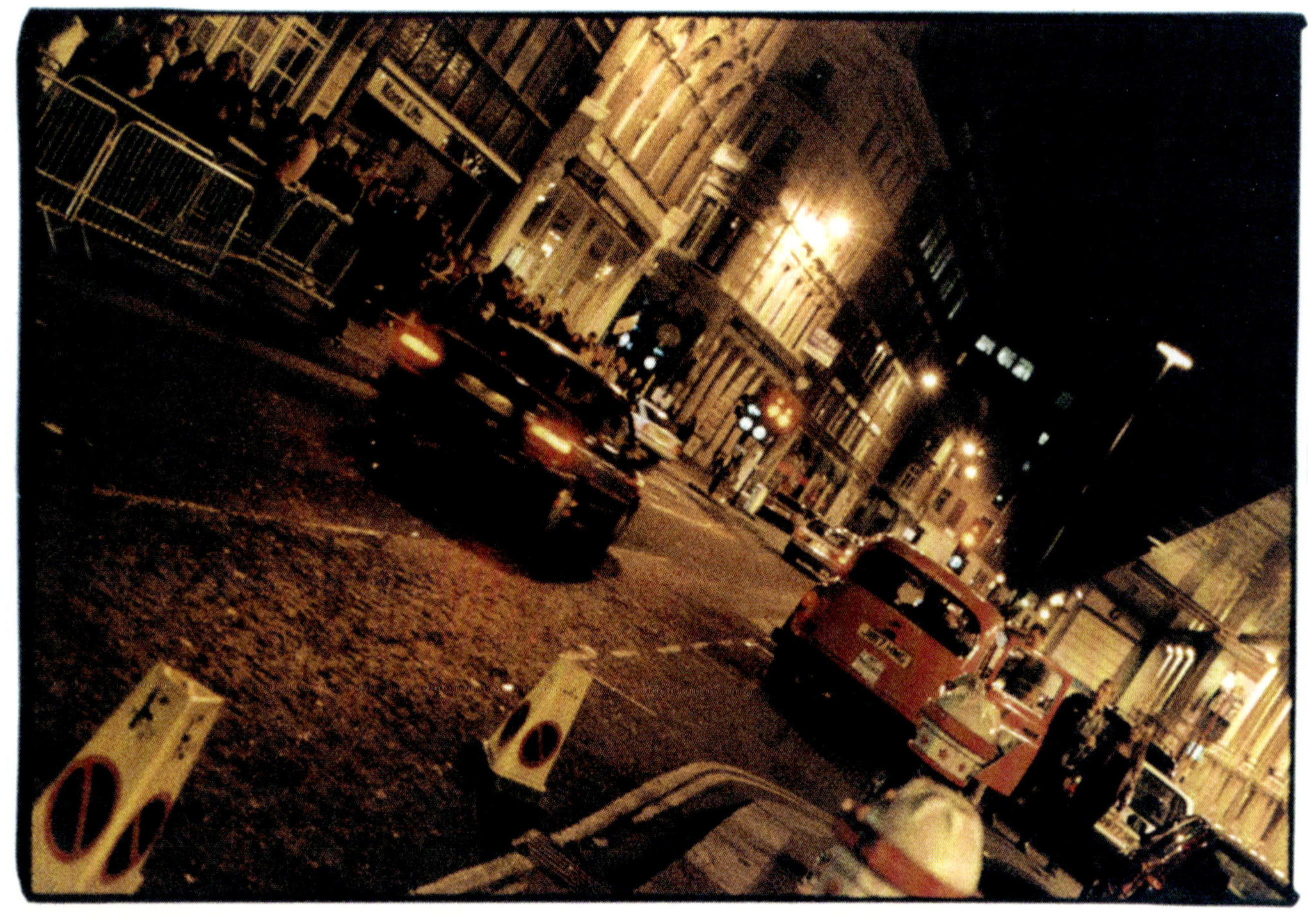

191—2

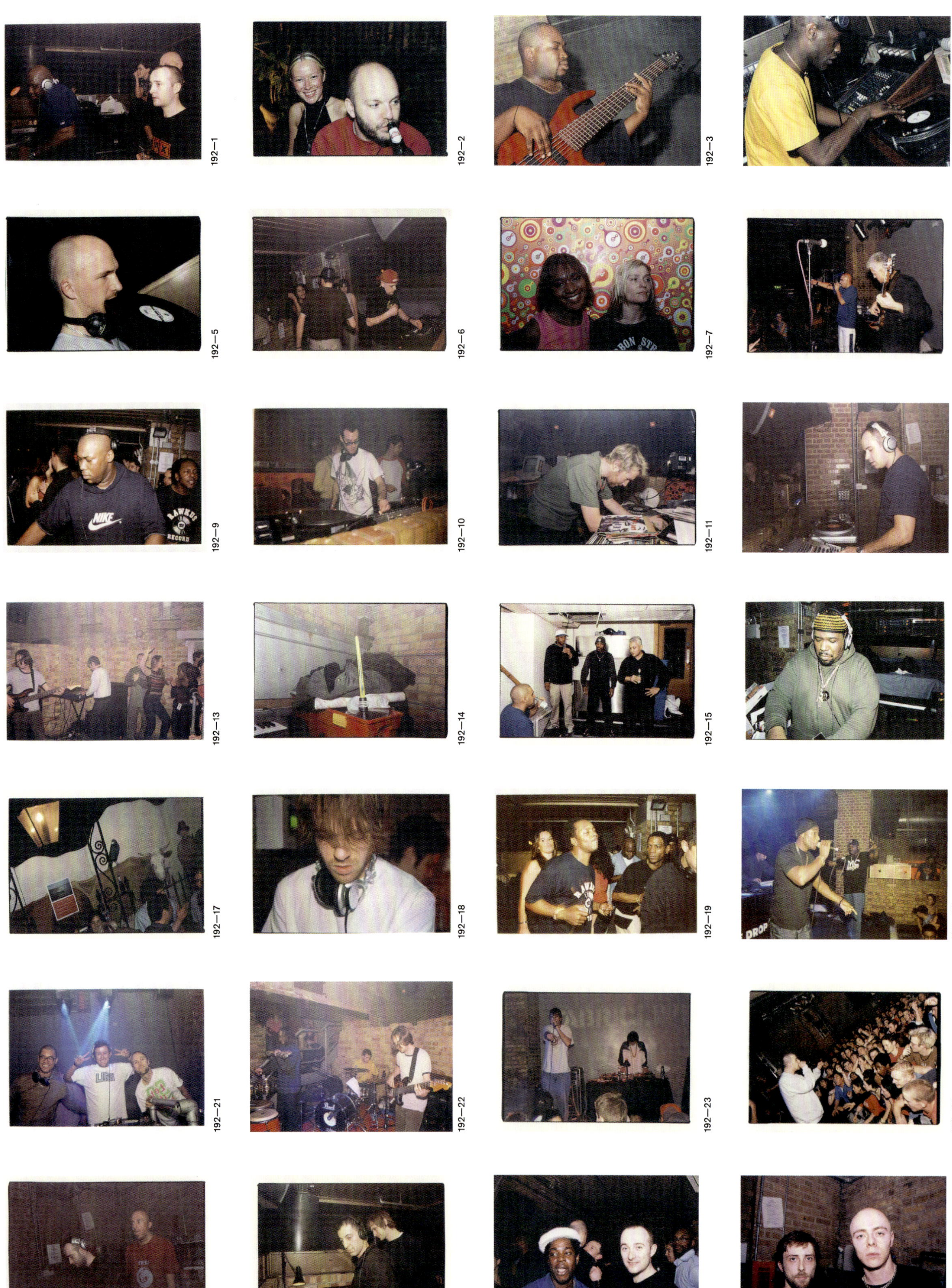

192—1 192—2 192—3 192—4

192—5 192—6 192—7 192—8

192—9 192—10 192—11 192—12

192—13 192—14 192—15 192—16

192—17 192—18 192—19 192—20

192—21 192—22 192—23 192—24

192—25 192—26 192—27 192—28

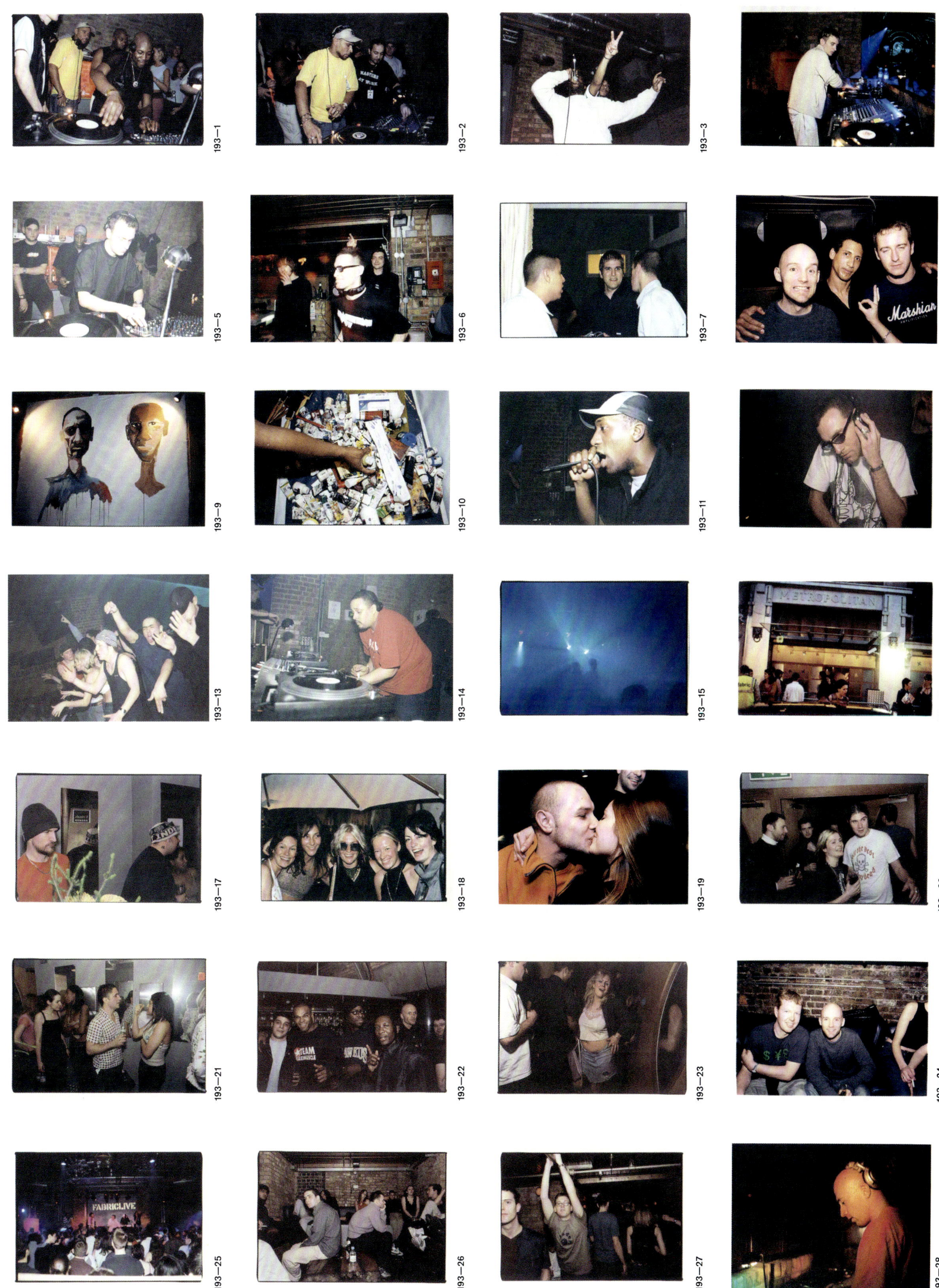

193—1 193—2 193—3 193—4

193—5 193—6 193—7 193—8

193—9 193—10 193—11 193—12

193—13 193—14 193—15 193—16

193—17 193—18 193—19 193—20

193—21 193—22 193—23 193—24

193—25 193—26 193—27 193—28

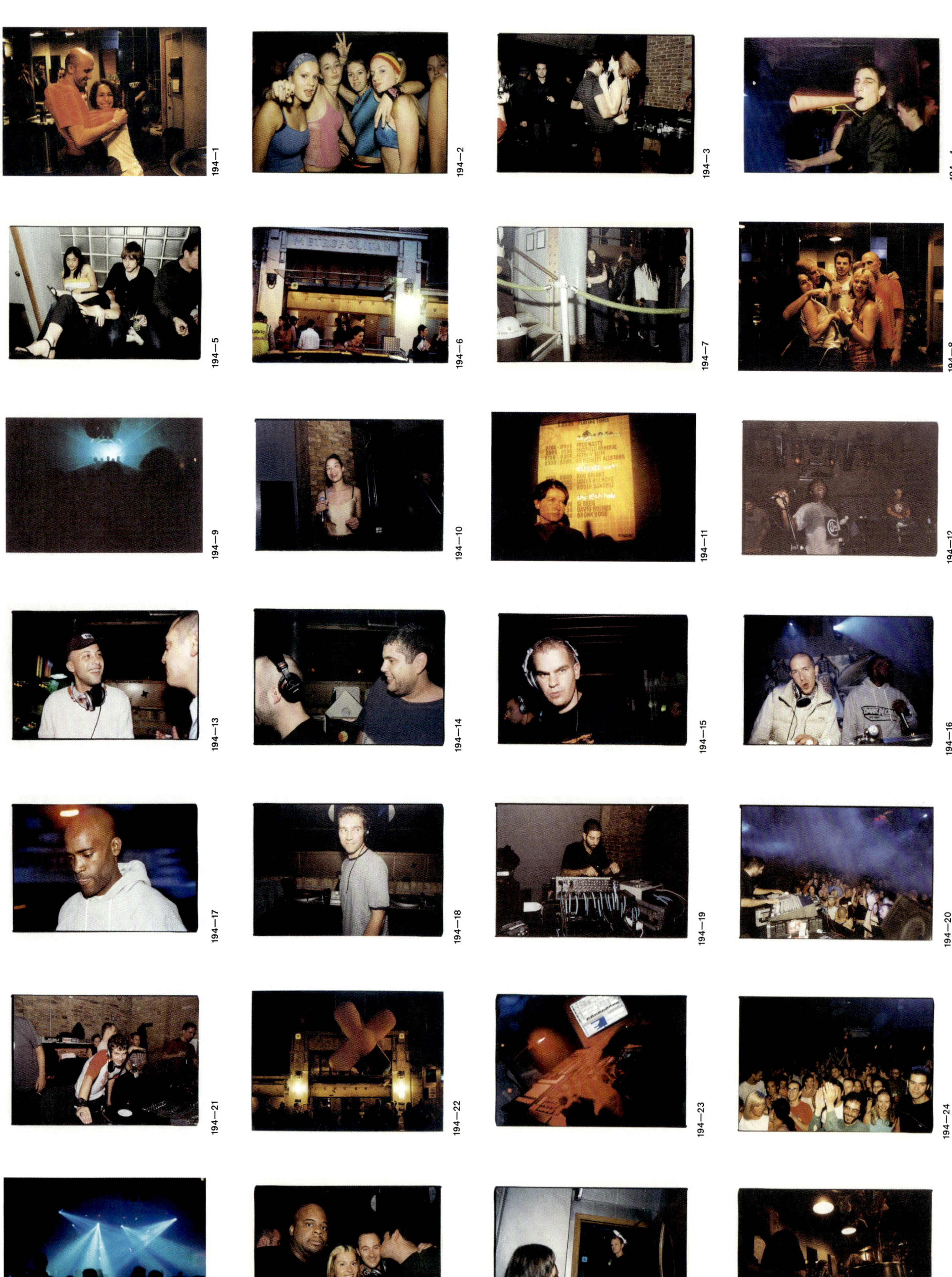

194–1 194–2 194–3 194–4
194–5 194–6 194–7 194–8
194–9 194–10 194–11 194–12
194–13 194–14 194–15 194–16
194–17 194–18 194–19 194–20
194–21 194–22 194–23 194–24
194–25 194–26 194–27 194–28

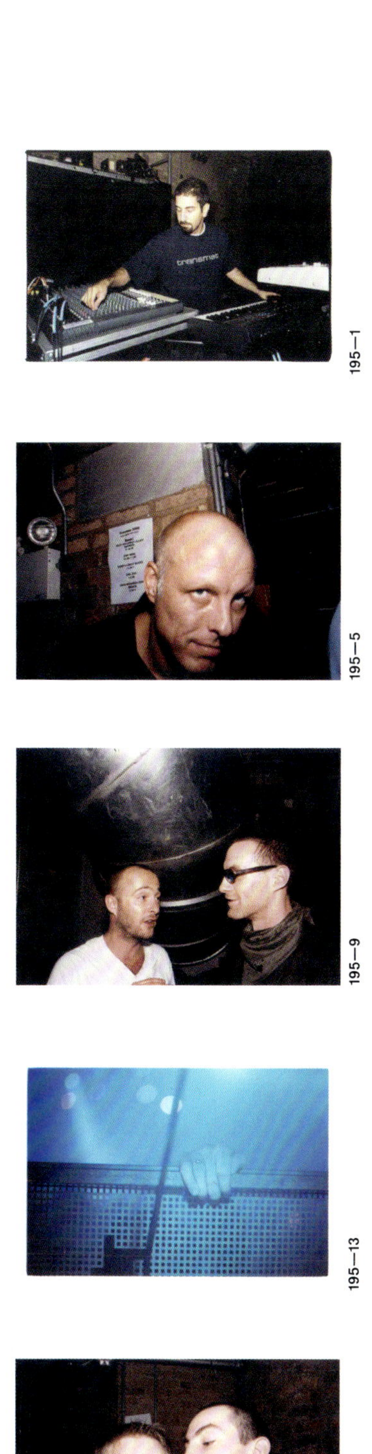

195—1

195—2

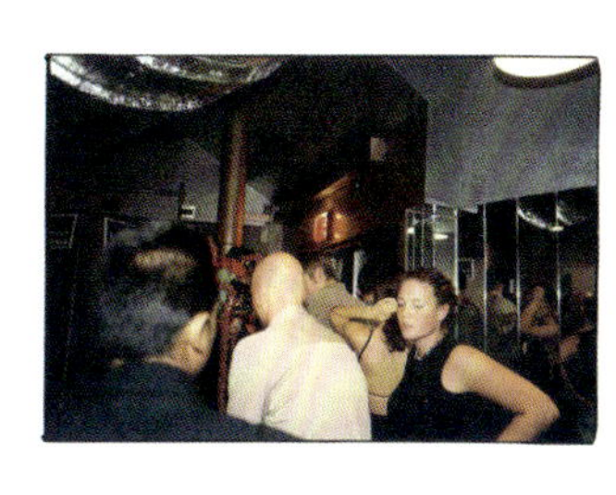

195—3

195—4

195—5

195—6

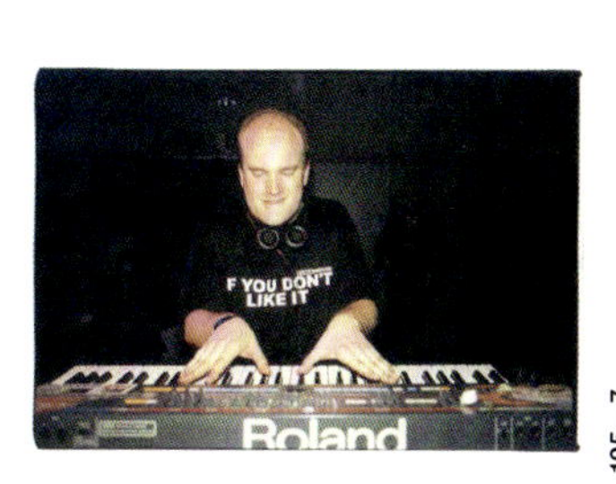

195—7

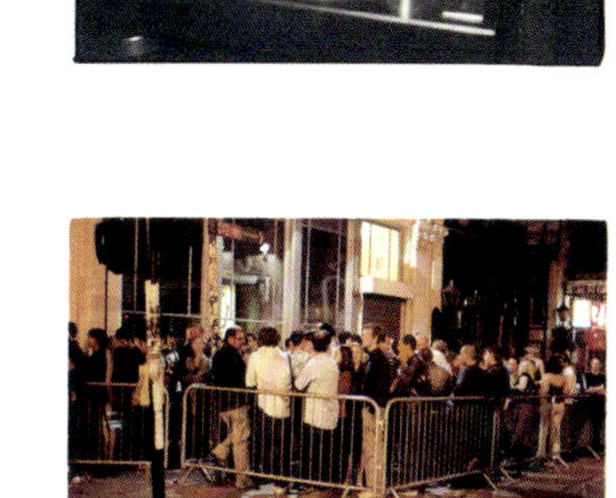

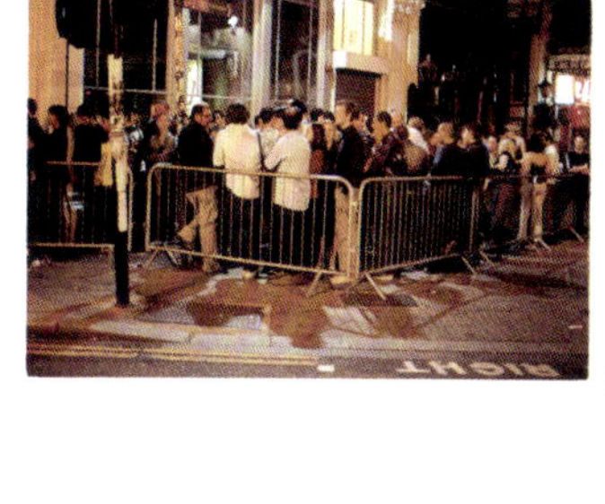

195—8

195—9

195—10

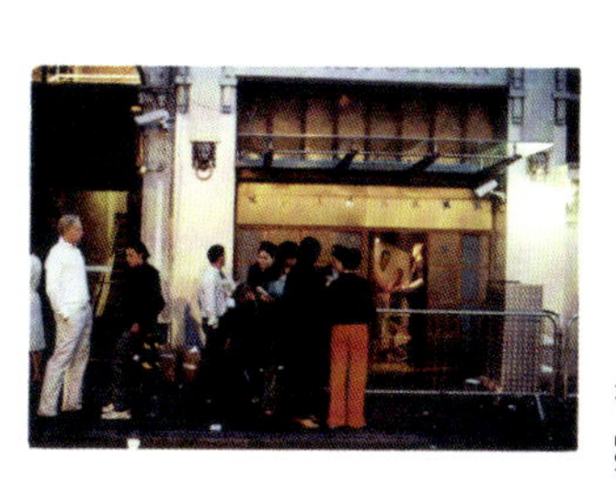

195—11

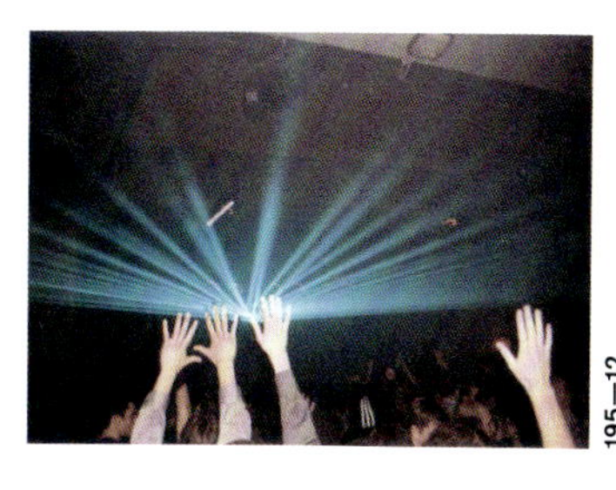

195—12

195—13

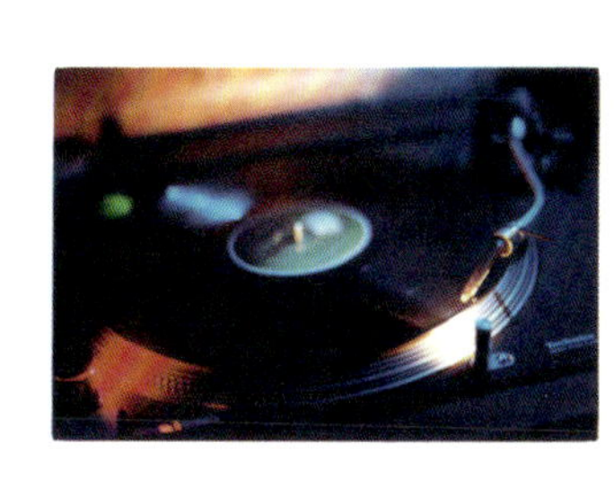

195—14

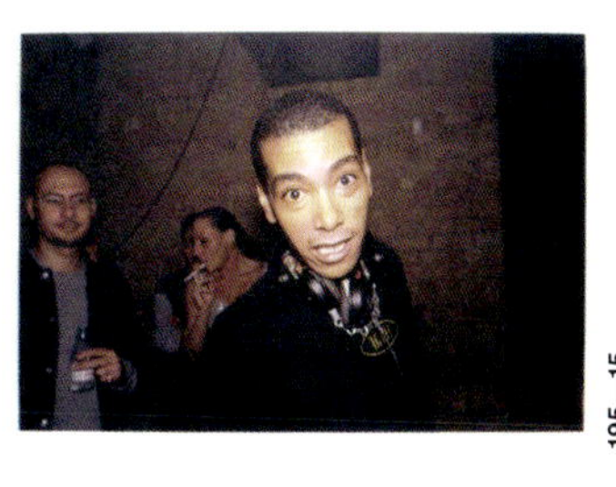

195—15

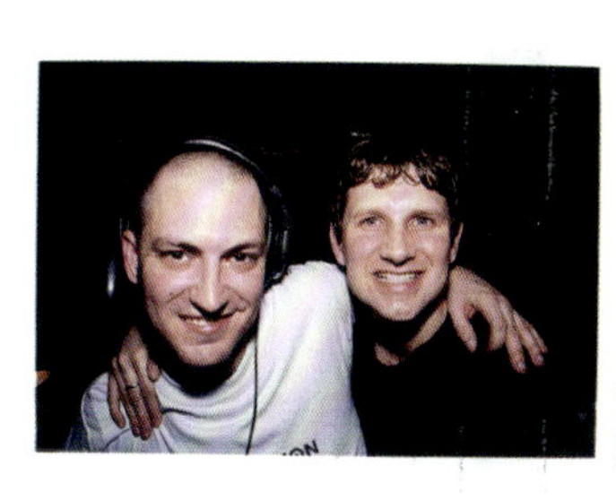

195—16

195—17

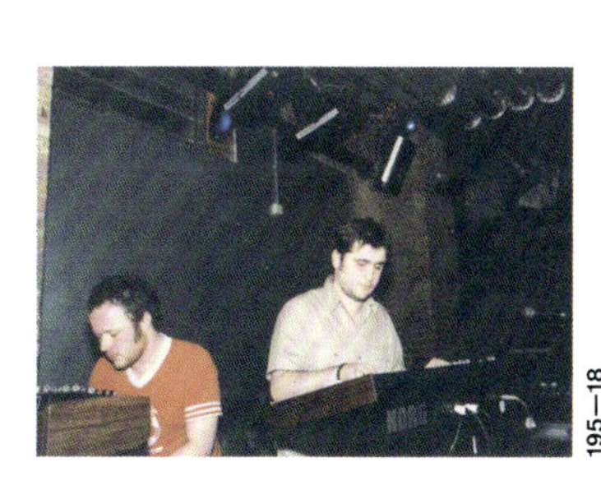

195—18

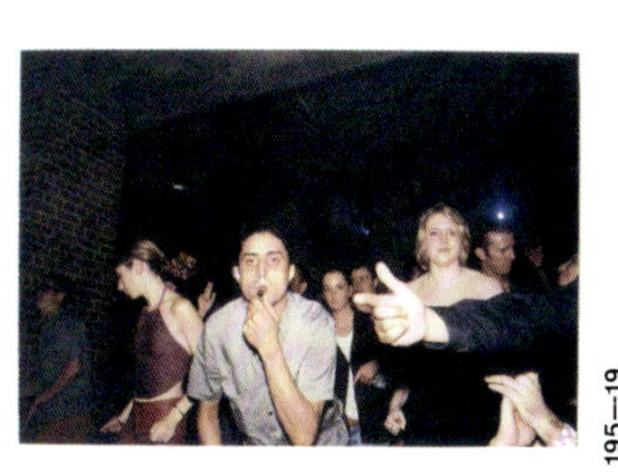

195—19

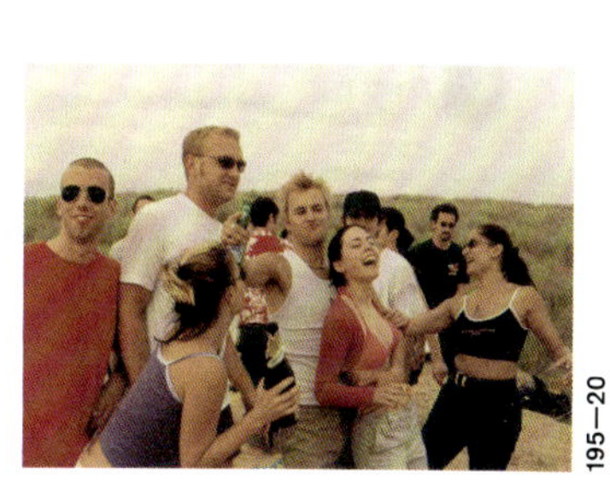

195—20

195—21

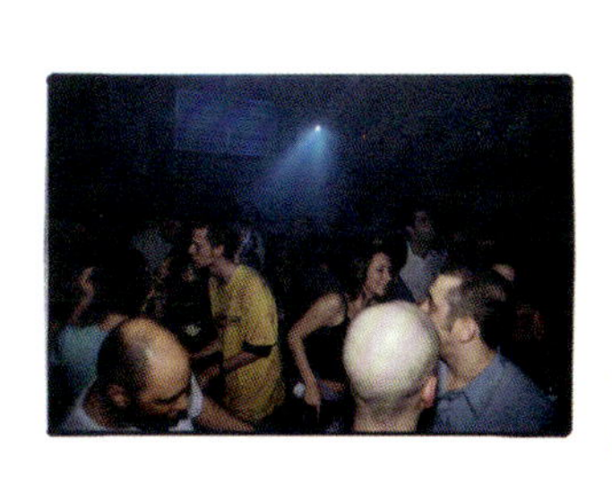

195—22

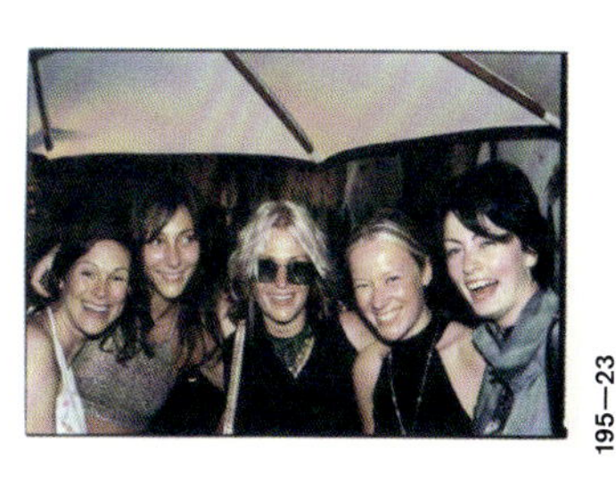

195—23

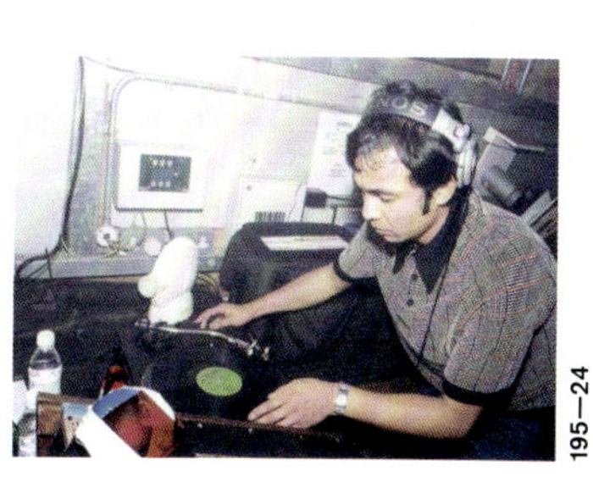

195—24

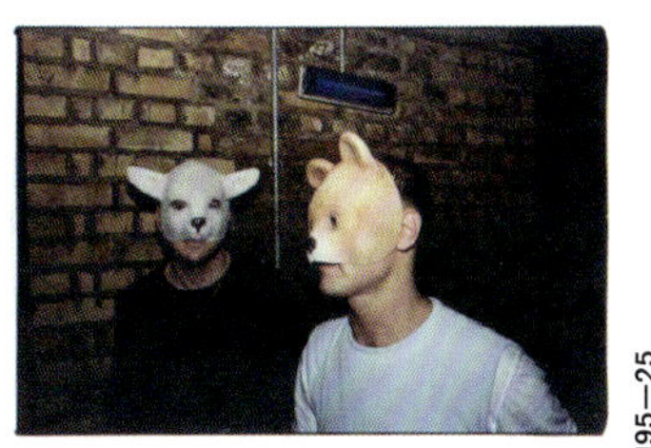

195—25

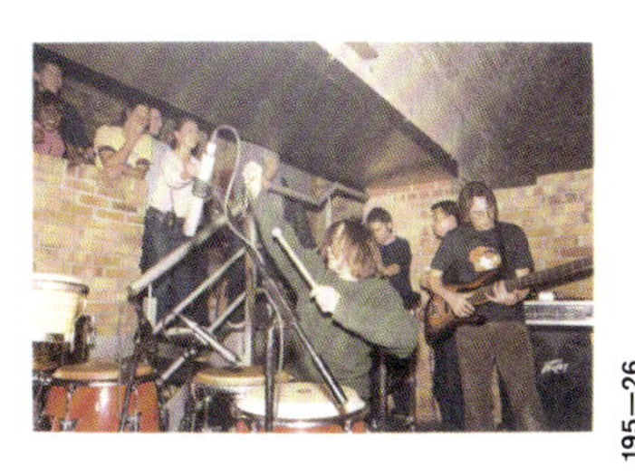

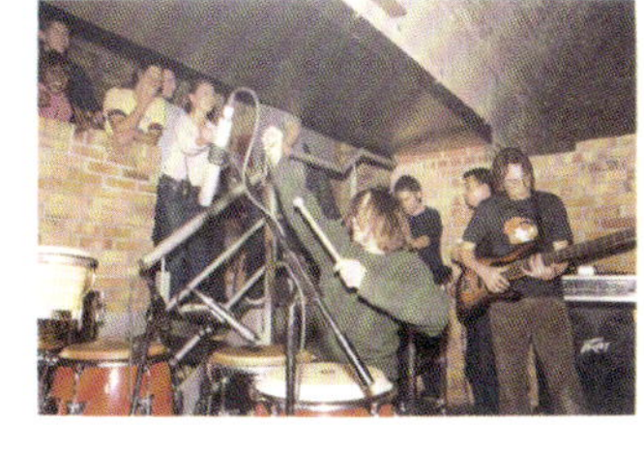

195—26

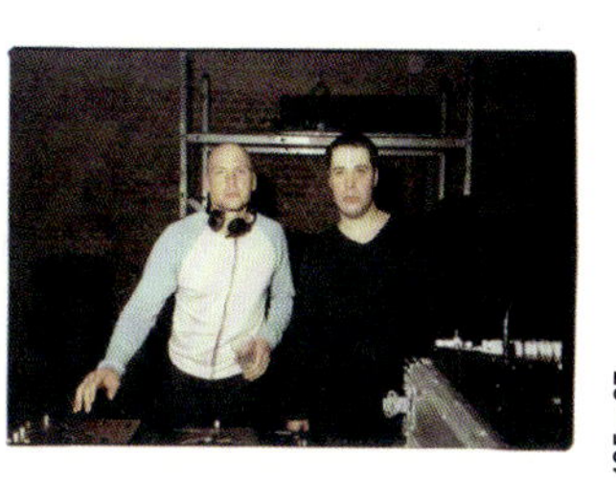

195—27

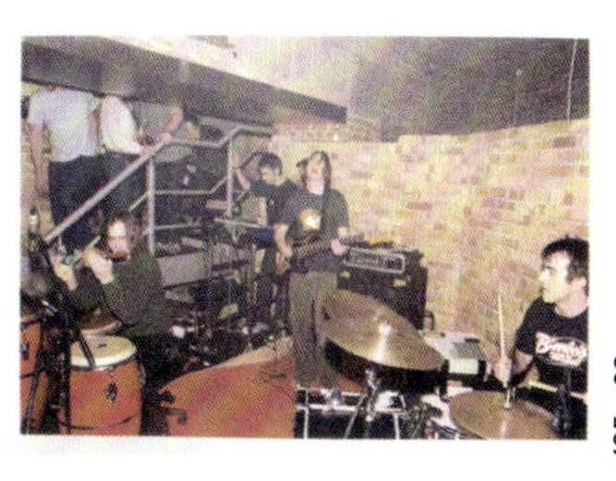

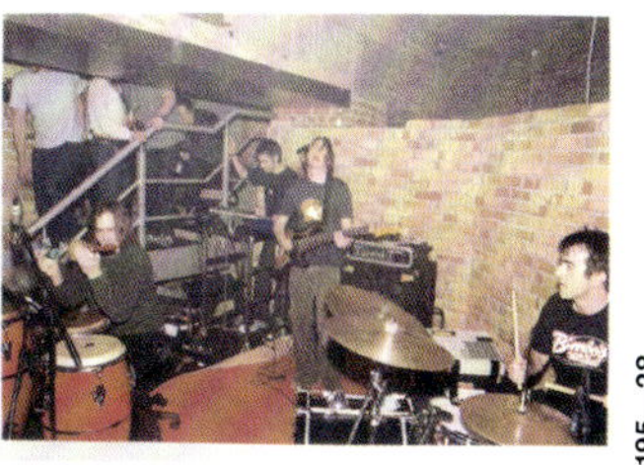

195—28

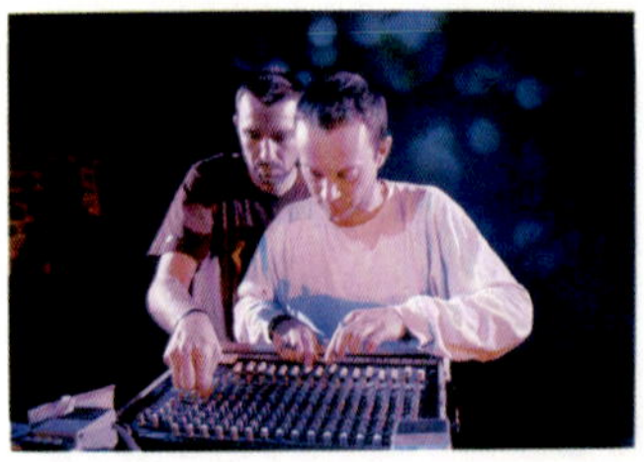

196–1

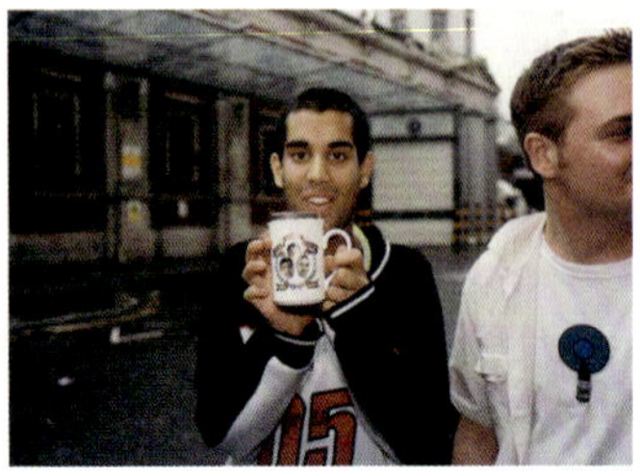

196–2

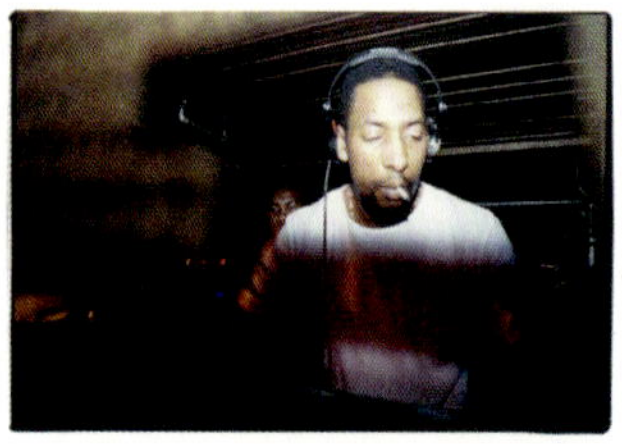

196–3

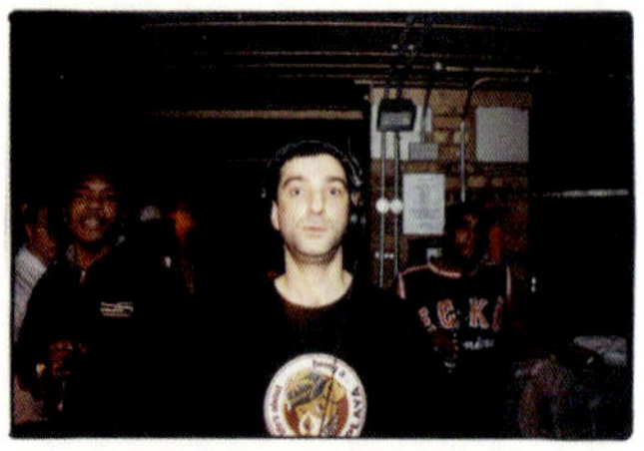

196–4

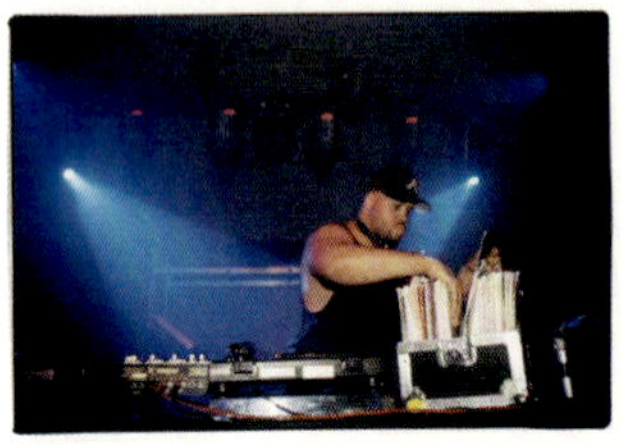

196–5

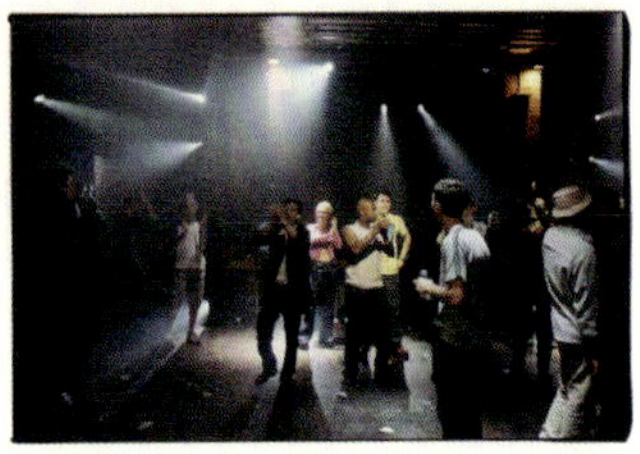

196–6

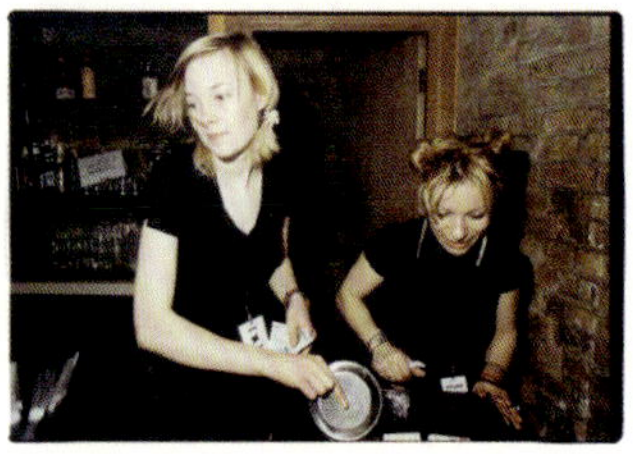

196–7

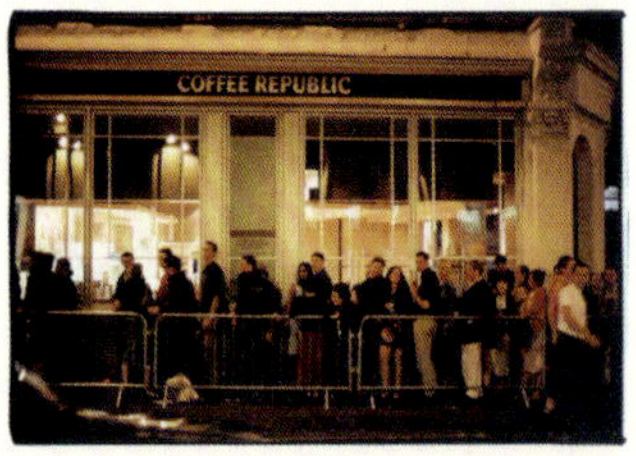

196–8

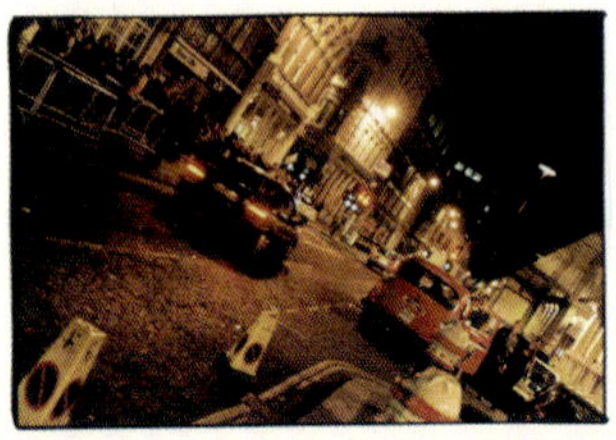

196–9

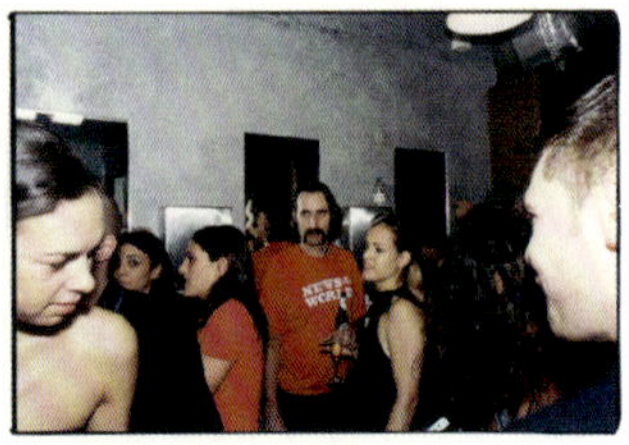

196–10

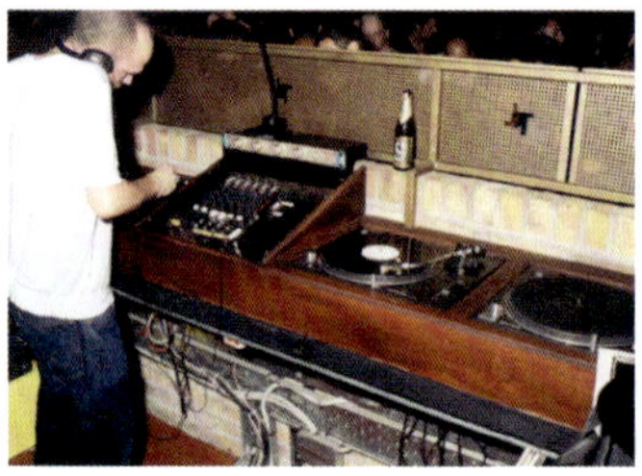

196–11

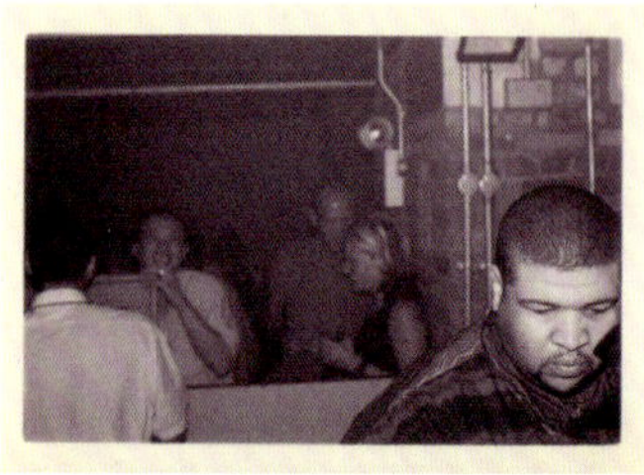

196–12

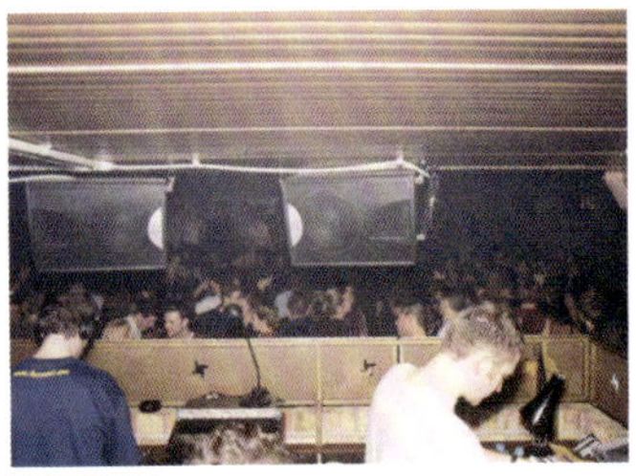

196–13

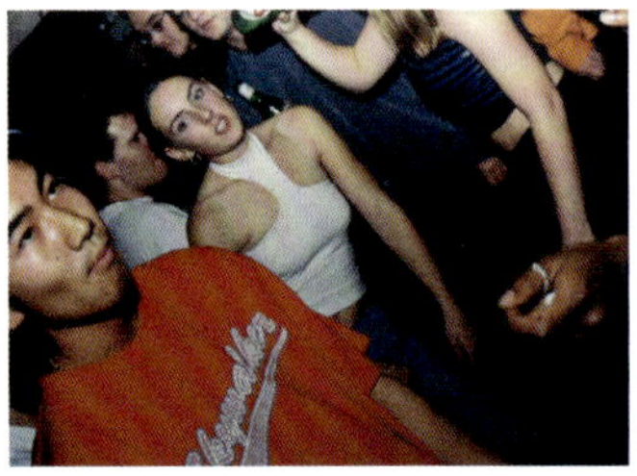

196–14

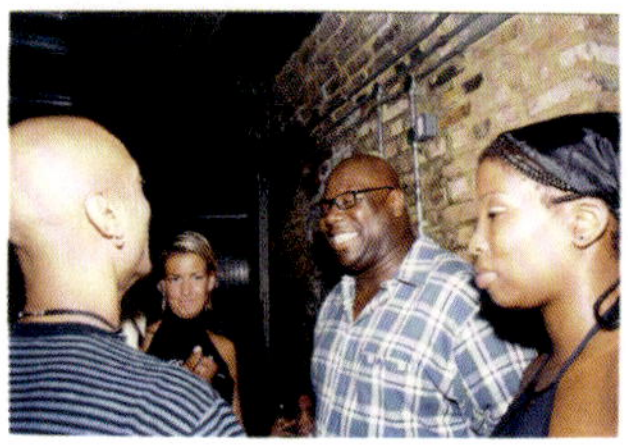

196–15

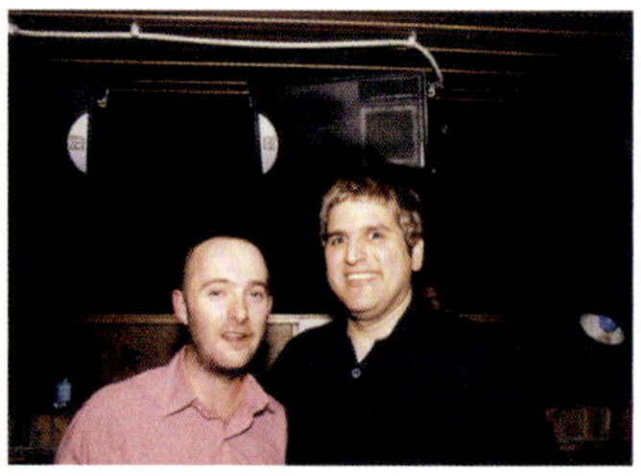

196–16

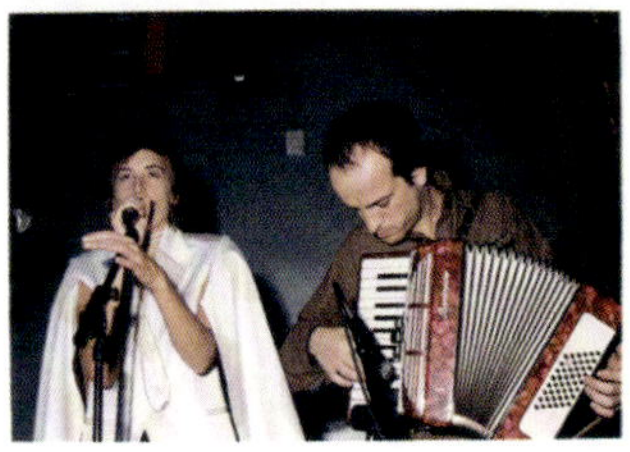

196–17

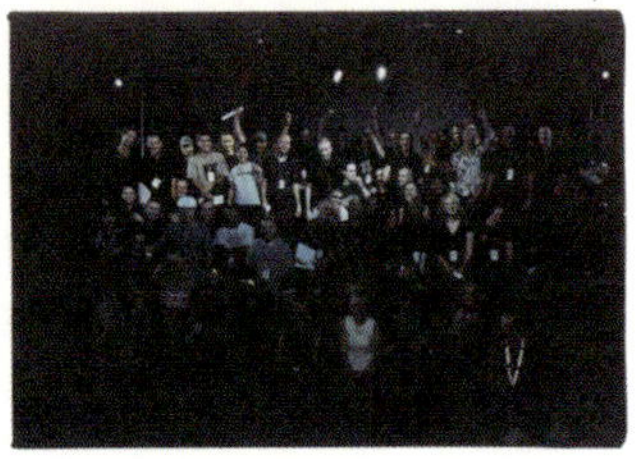

196–18

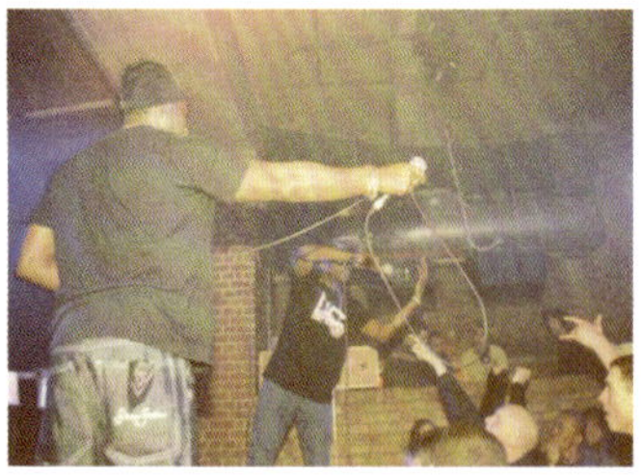

196–19

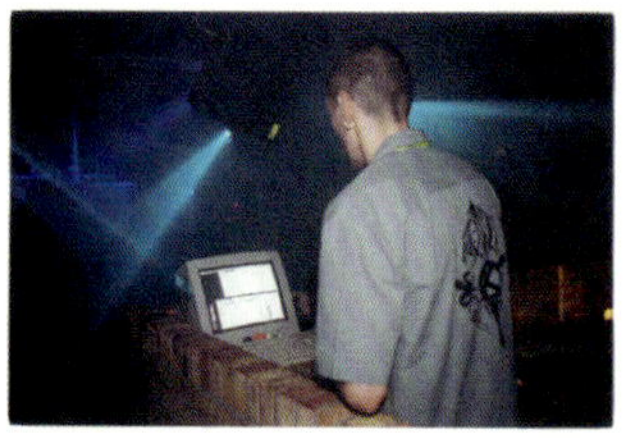

196–20

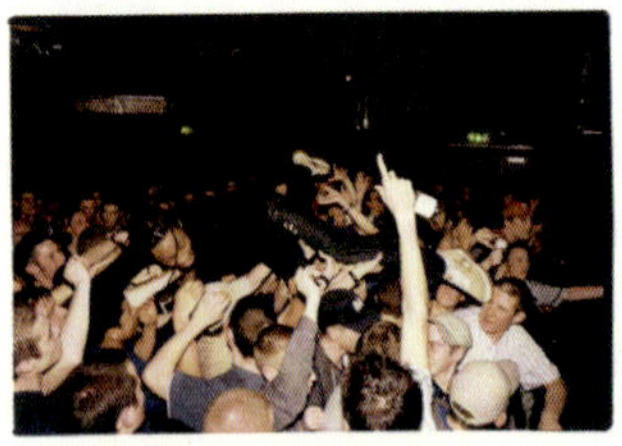

196–21

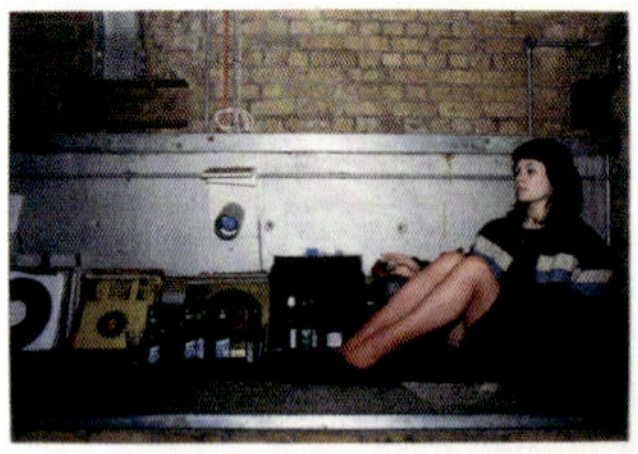

196–22

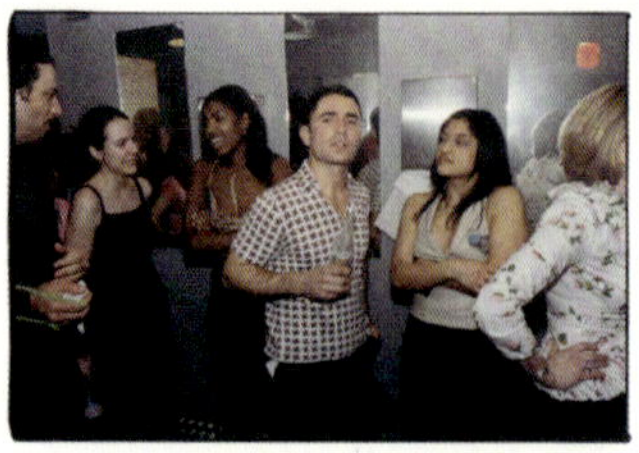

196–23

196–24

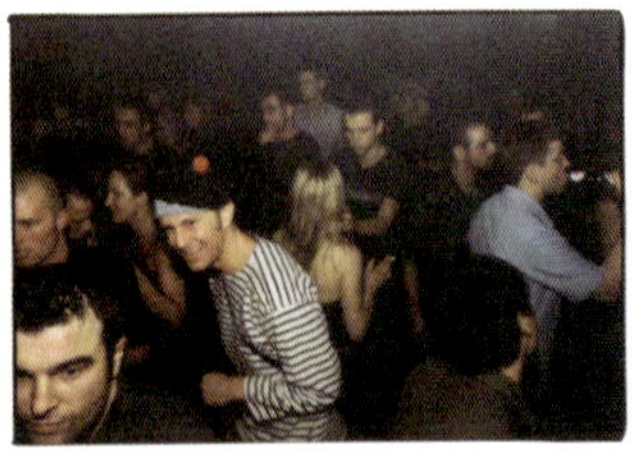

196–25

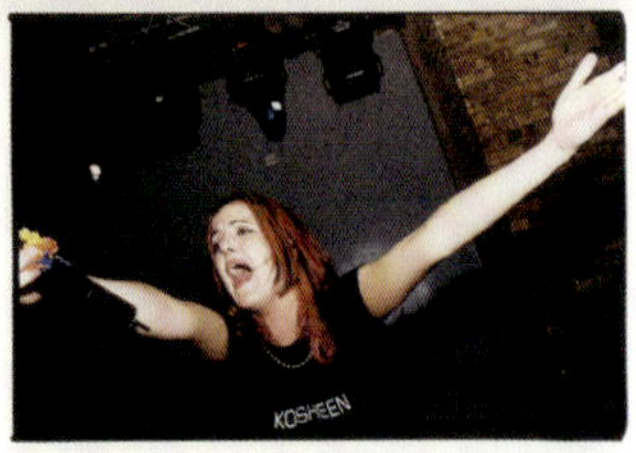

196–26

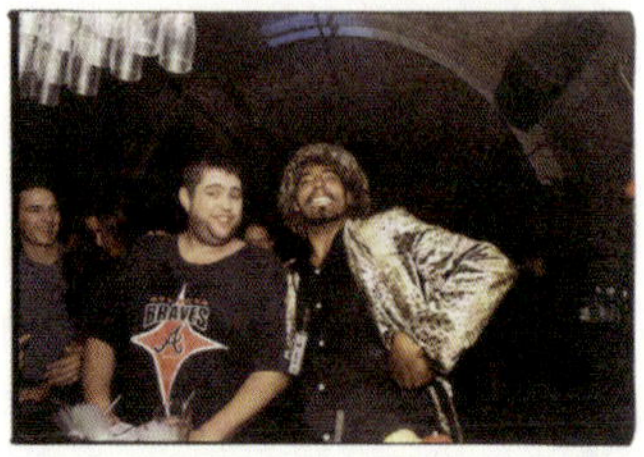

196–27

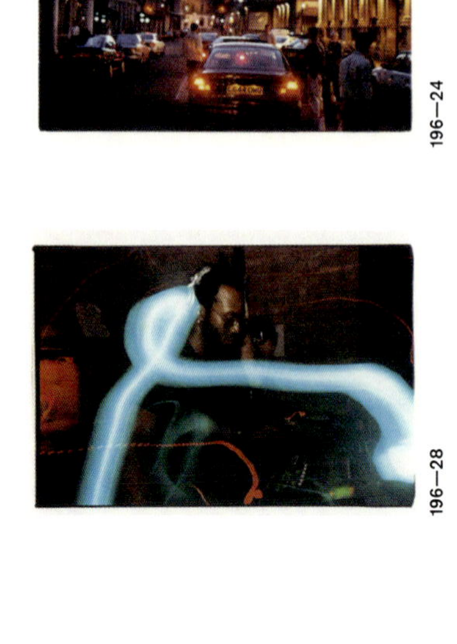

196–28

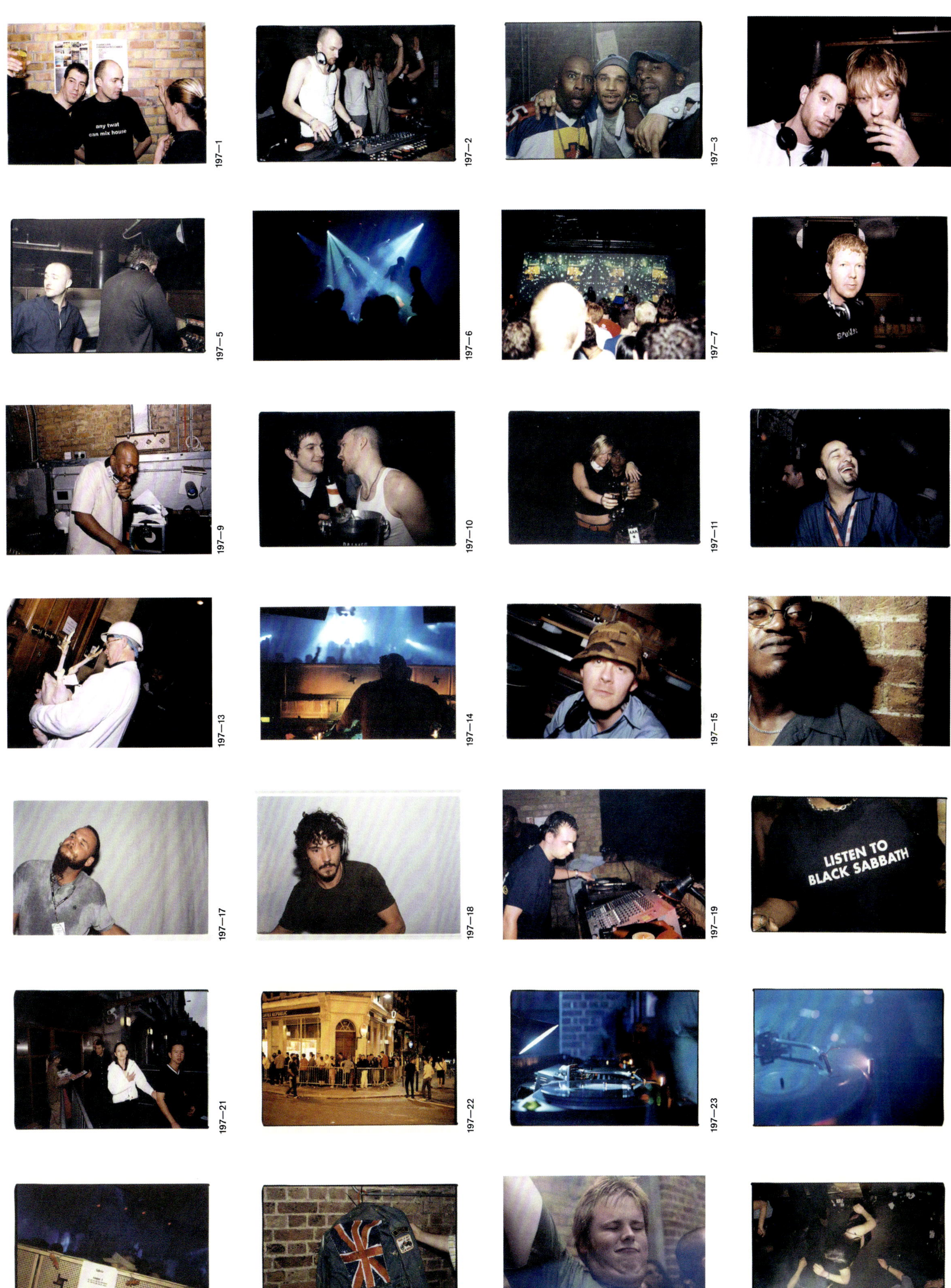

197—1 197—2 197—3 197—4
197—5 197—6 197—7 197—8
197—9 197—10 197—11 197—12
197—13 197—14 197—15 197—16
197—17 197—18 197—19 197—20
197—21 197—22 197—23 197—24
197—25 197—26 197—27 197—28

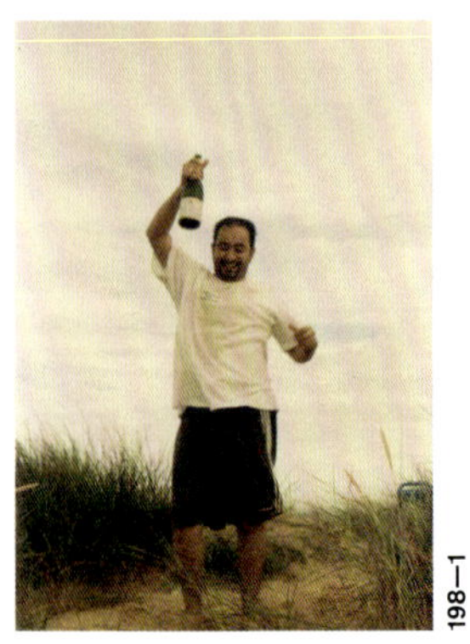
198—1

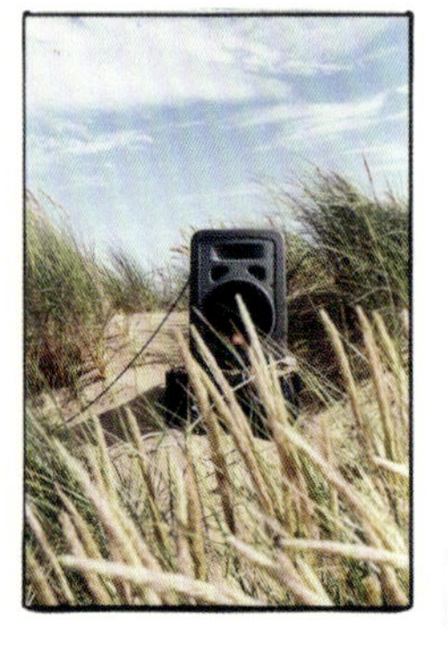
198—2

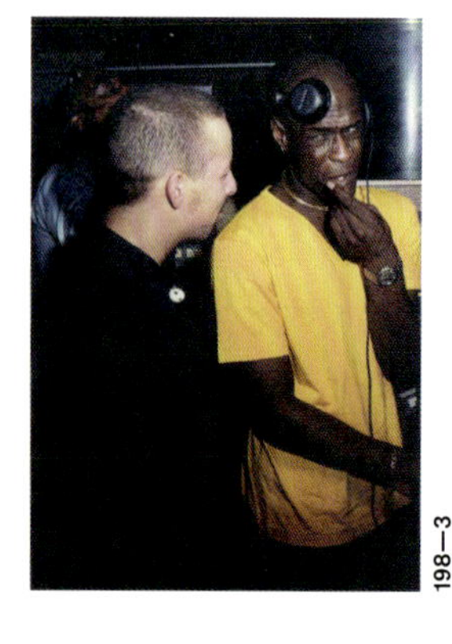
198—3

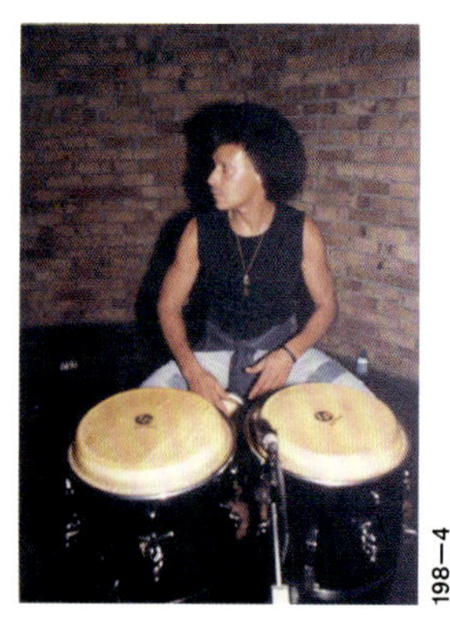
198—4

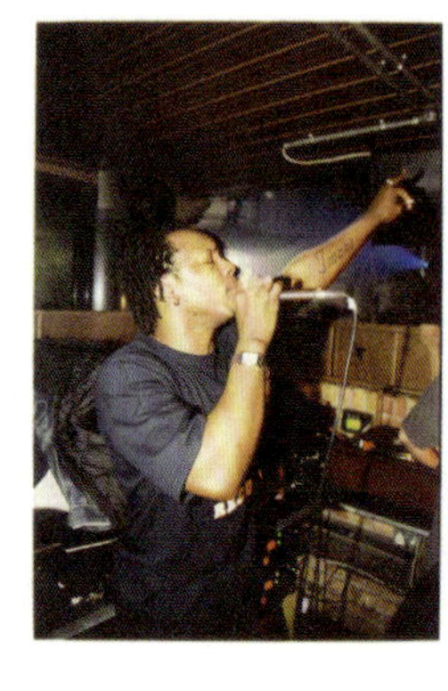
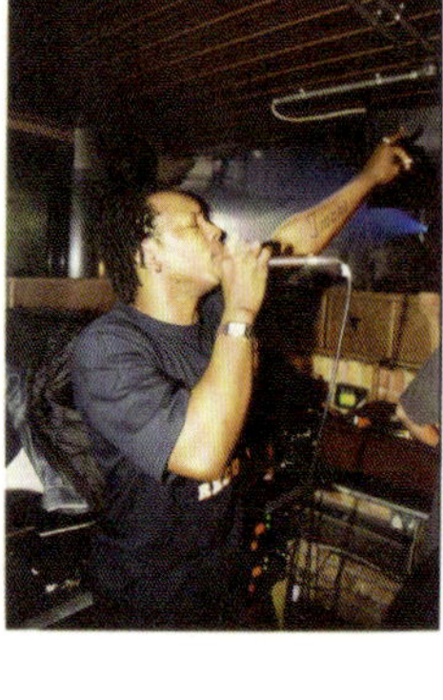
198—5

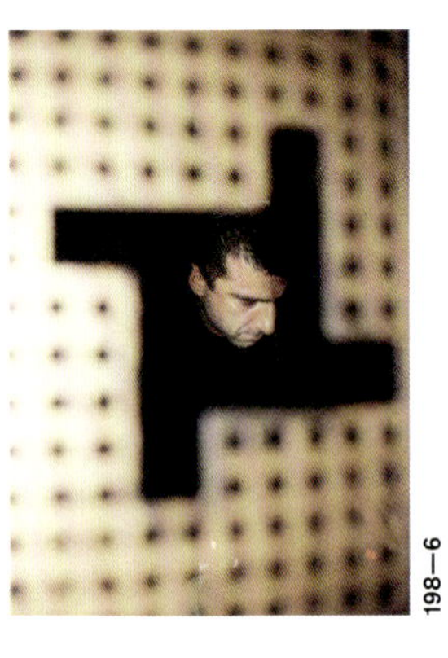
198—6

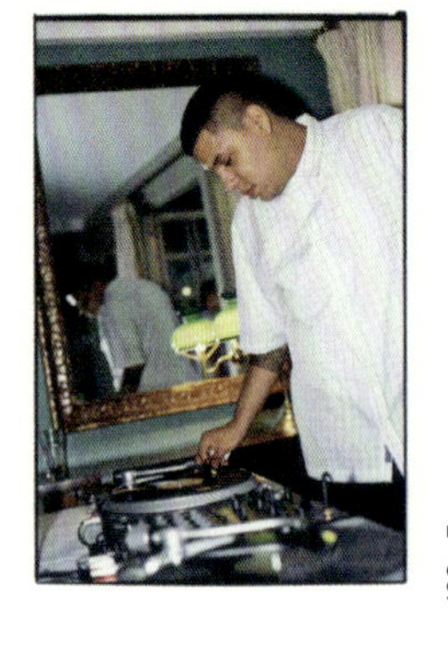
198—7

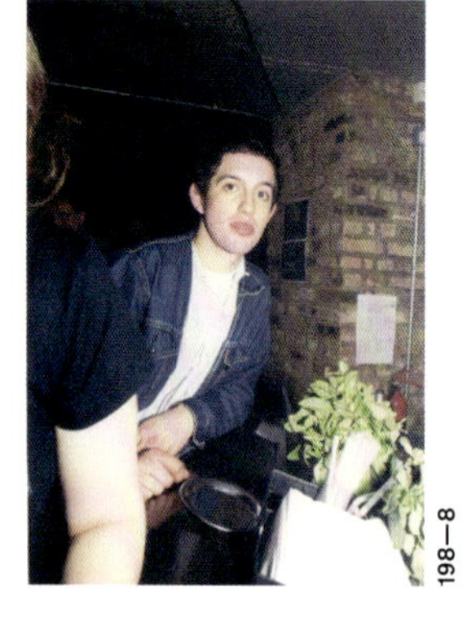
198—8

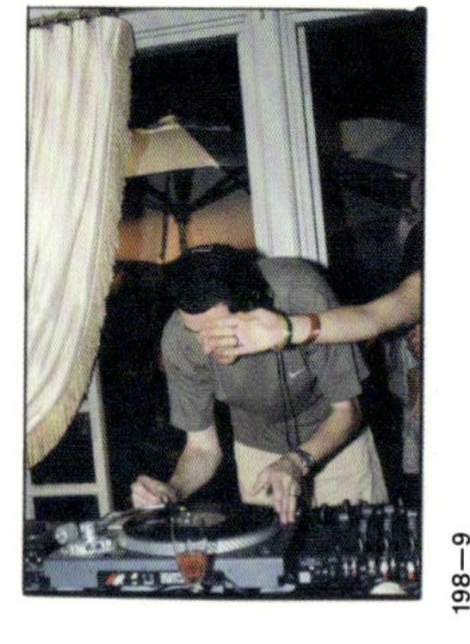
198—9

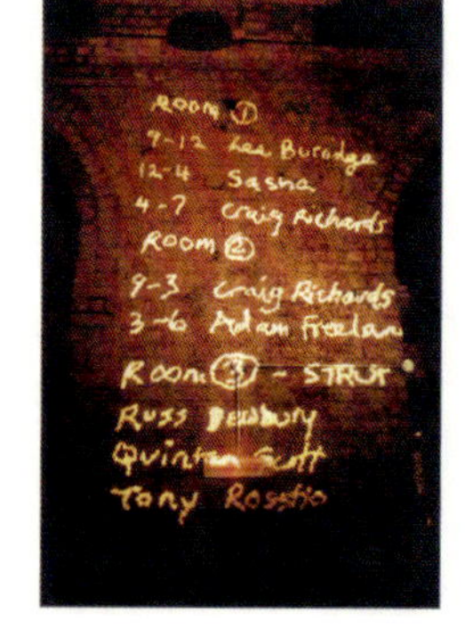
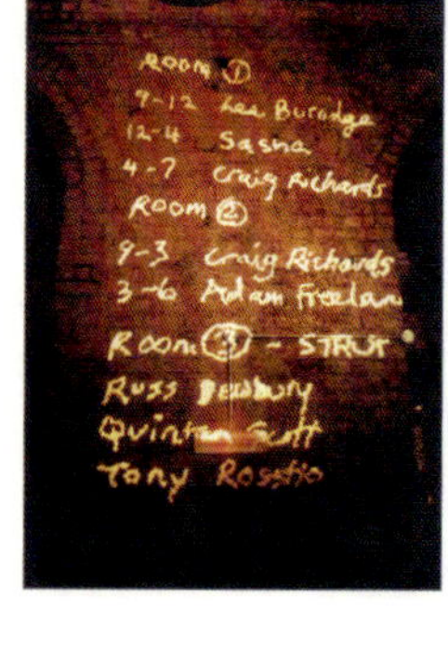

198—10

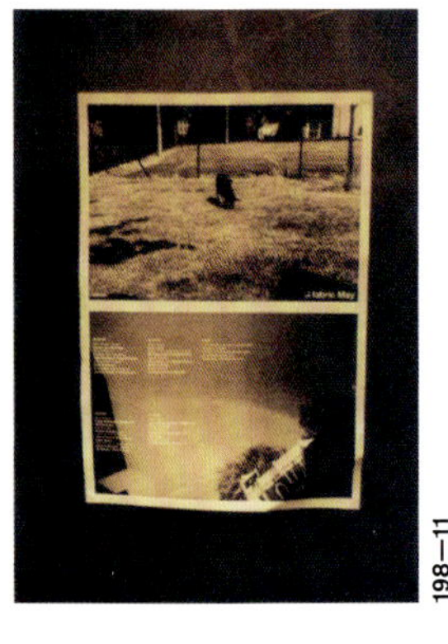
198—11

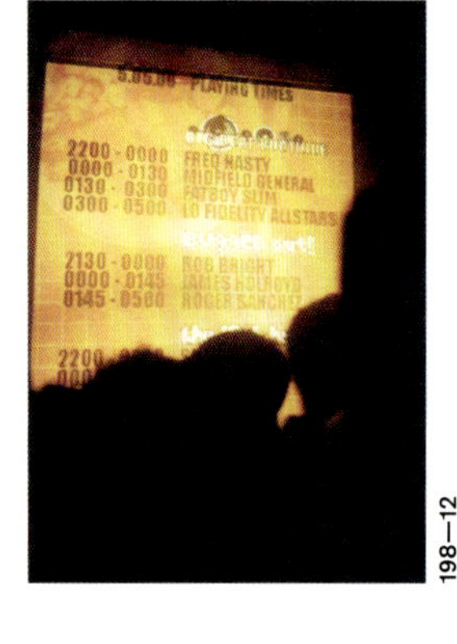

198—12

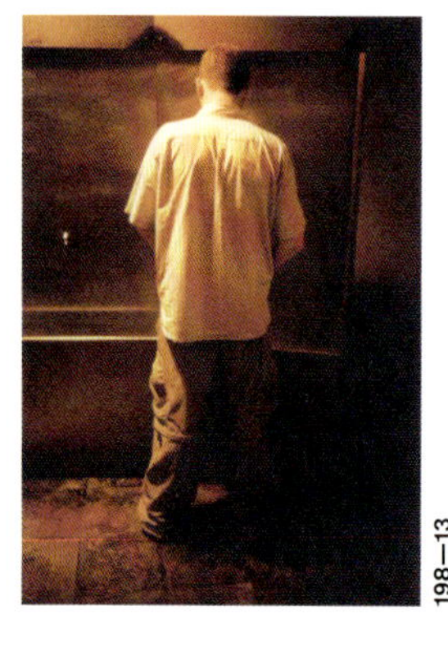
198—13

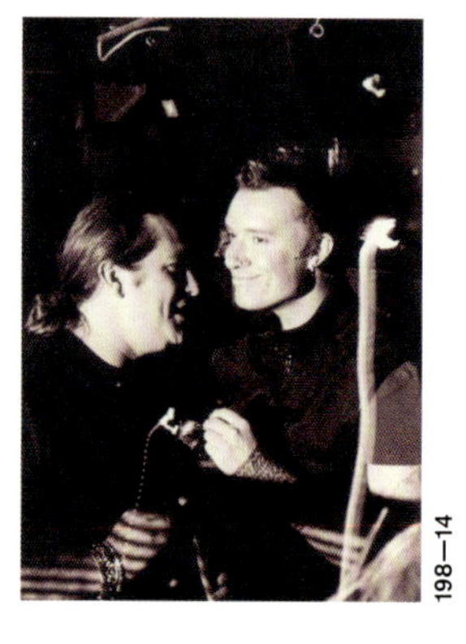
198—14

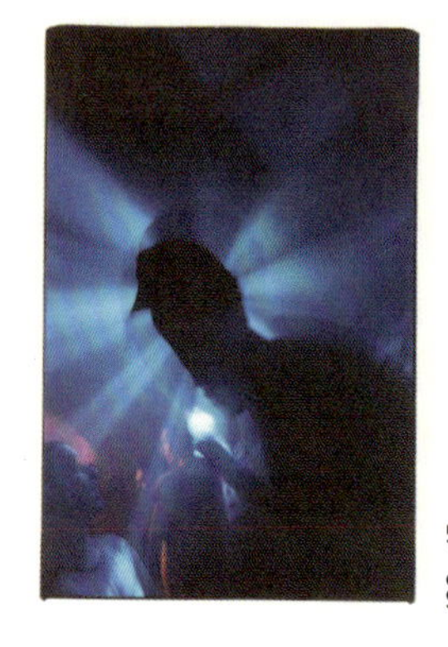
198—15

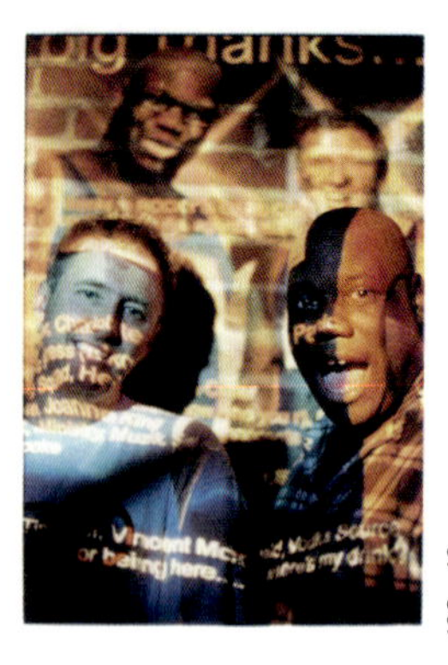
198—16

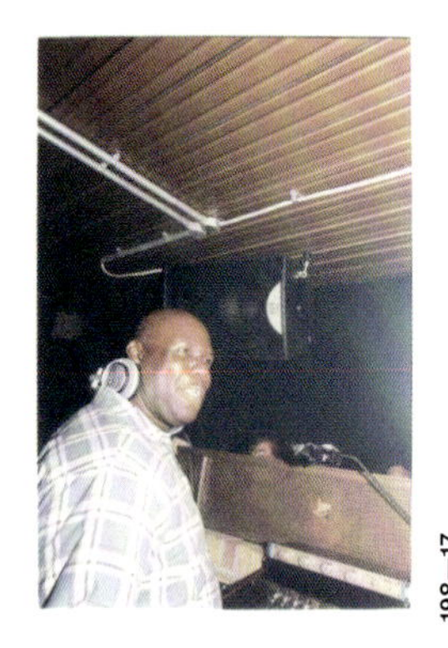
198—17

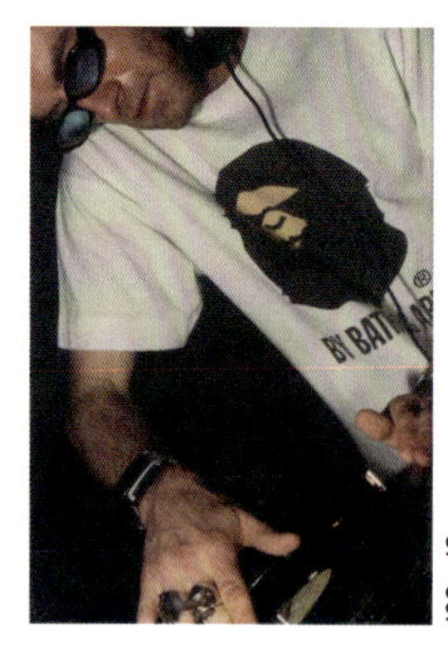
198—18

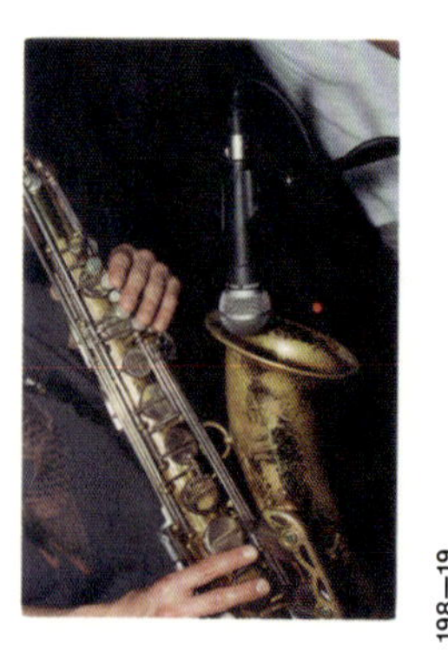
198—19

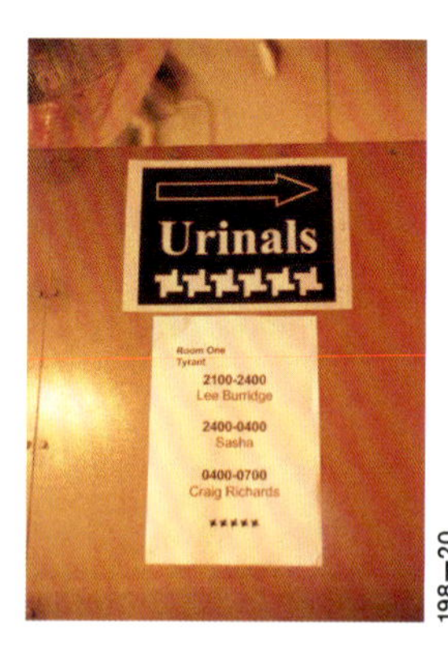

198—20

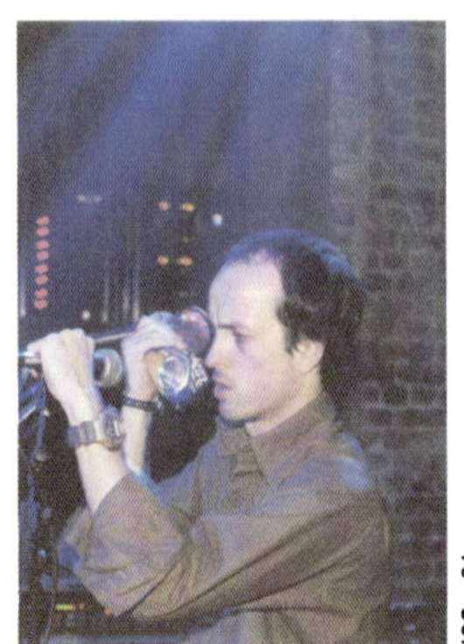
198—21

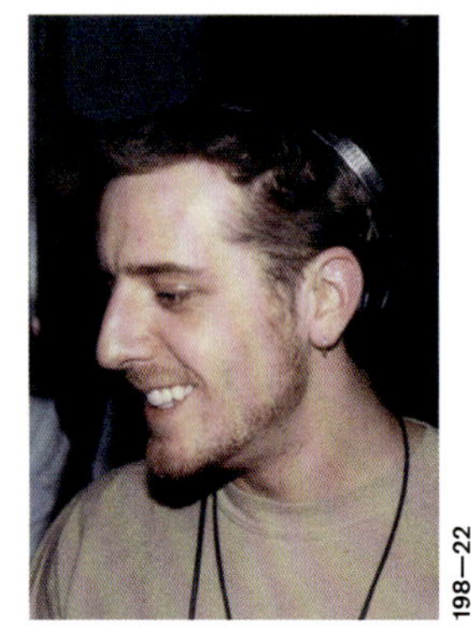
198—22

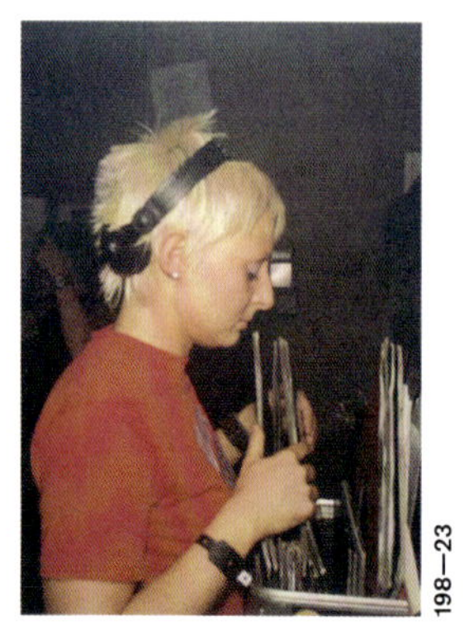
198—23

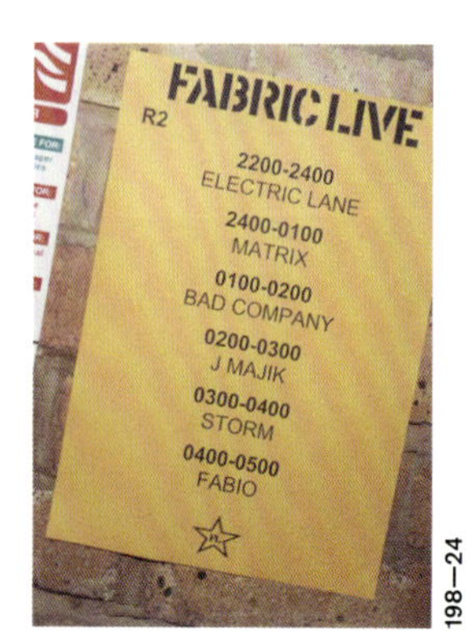

198—24

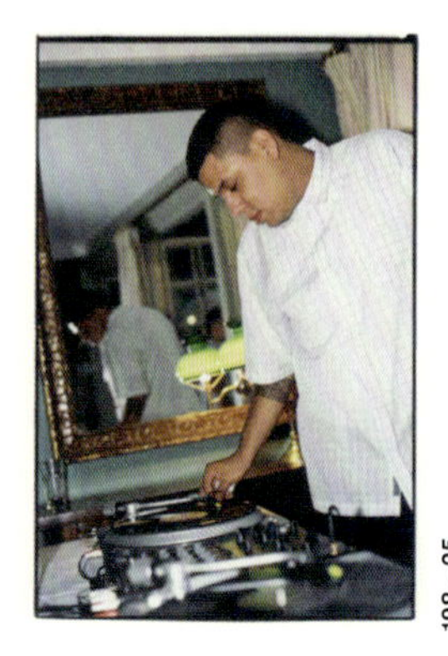
198—25

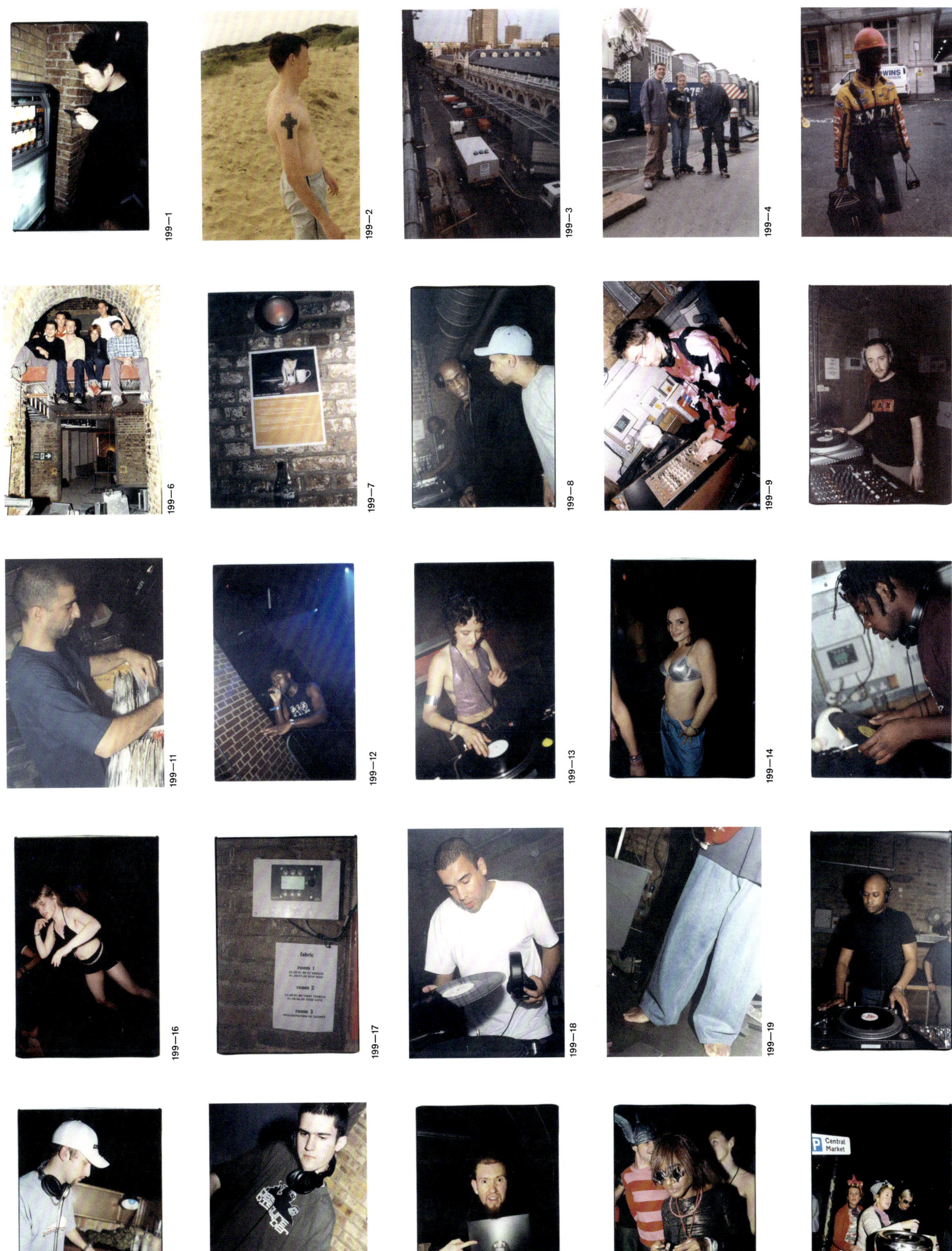

199—1 199—2 199—3 199—4 199—5

199—6 199—7 199—8 199—9 199—10

199—11 199—12 199—13 199—14 199—15

199—16 199—17 199—18 199—19 199—20

199—21 199—22 199—23 199—24 199—25

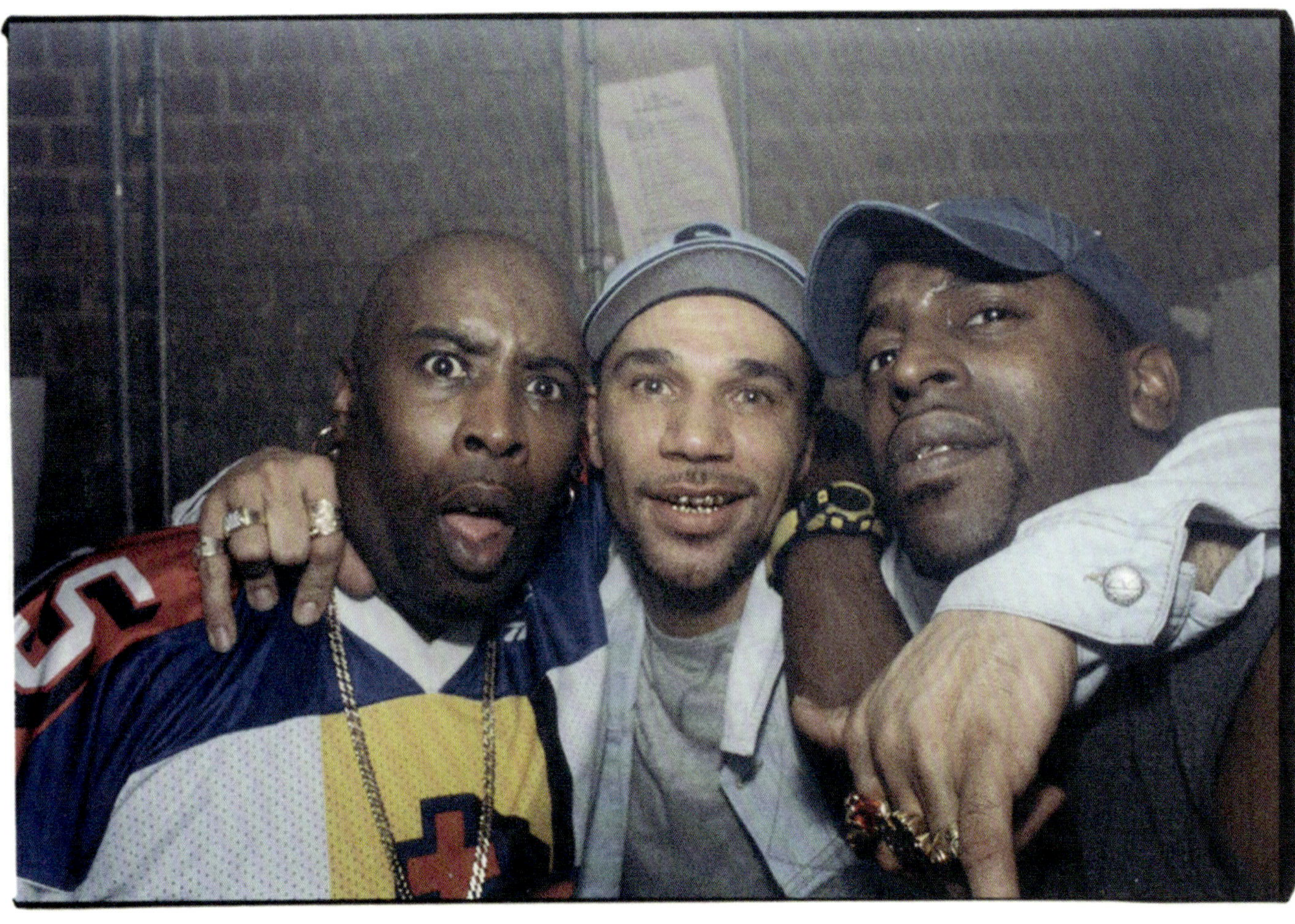

200—1

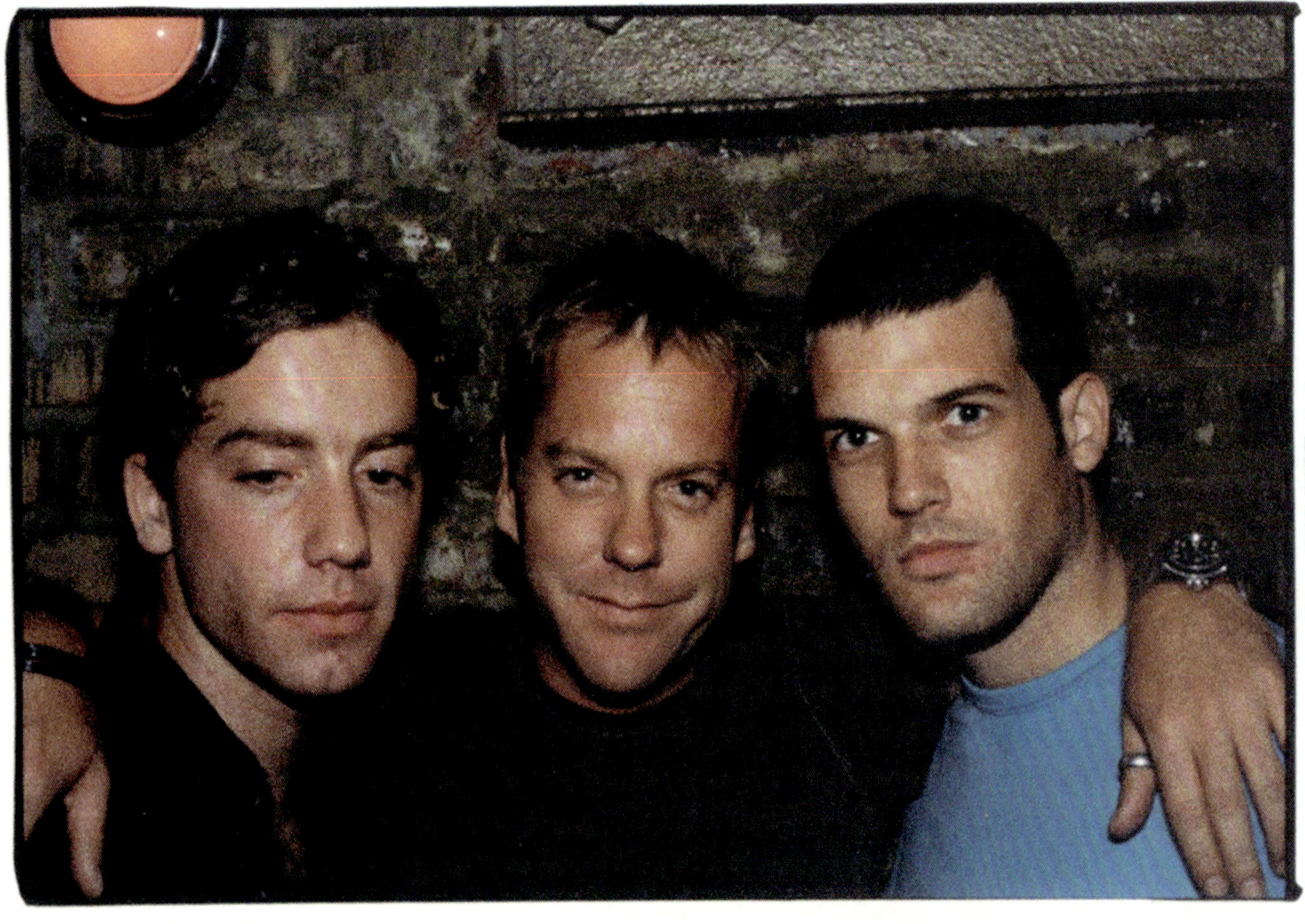

200—2

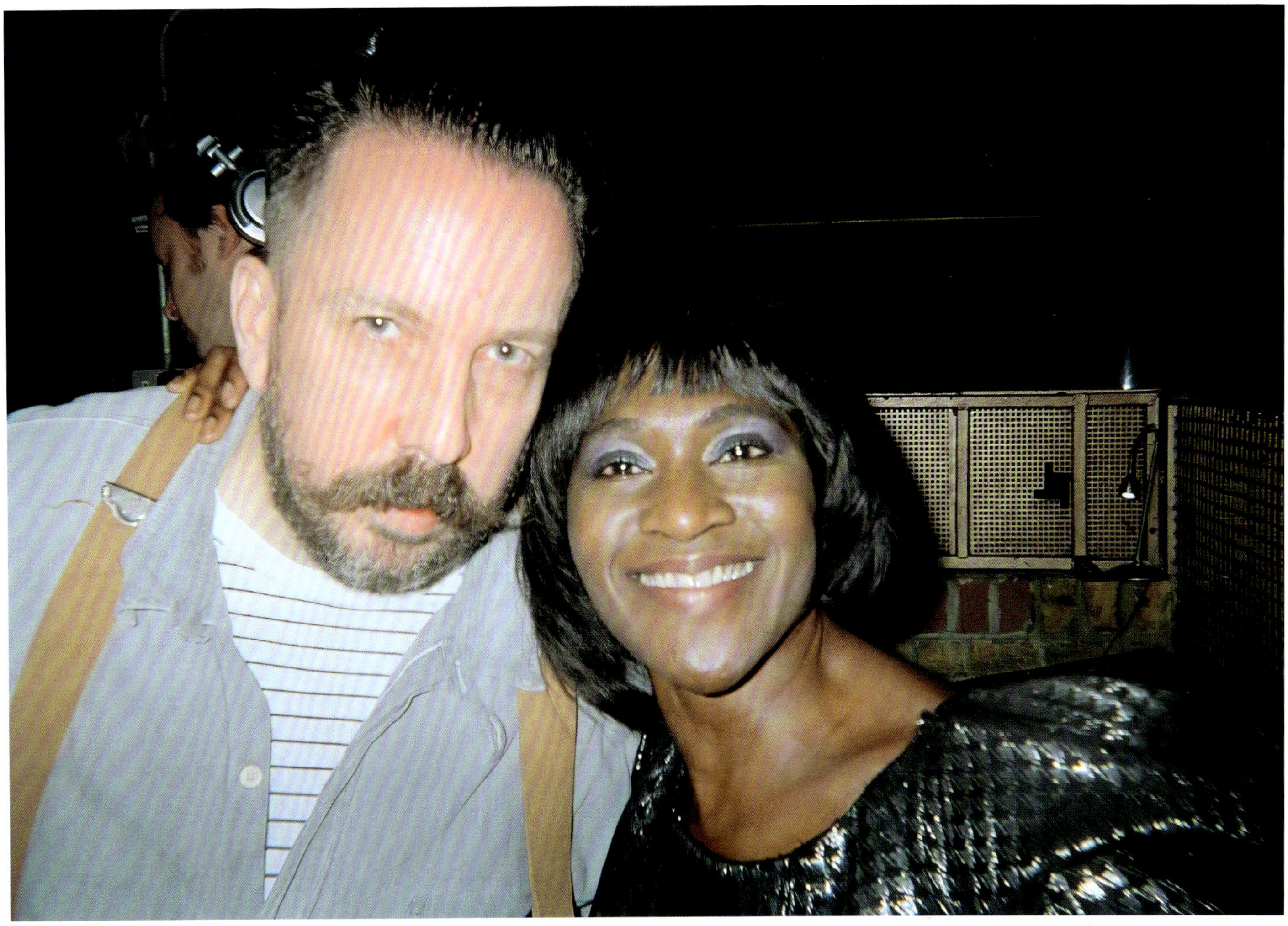

201—1

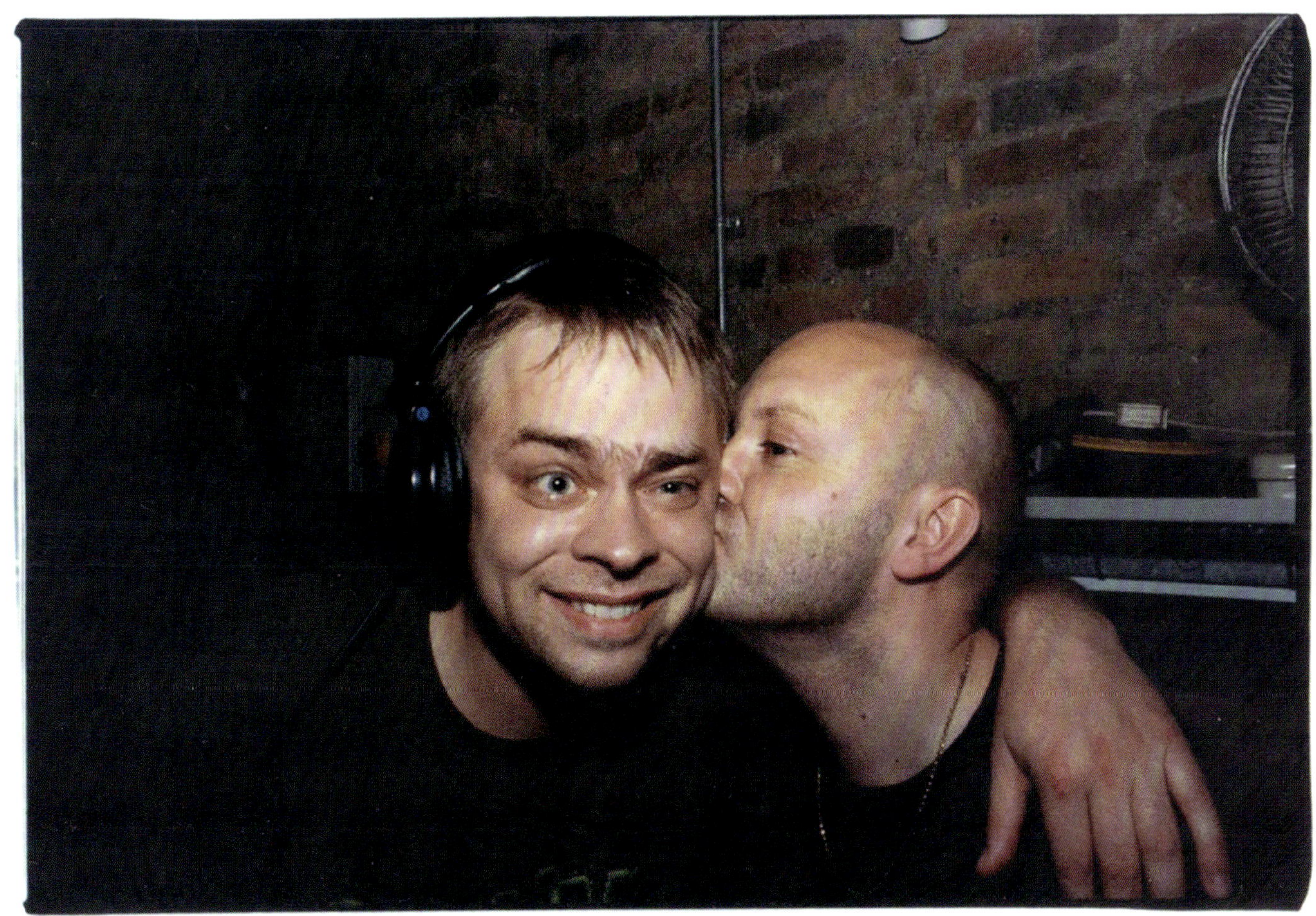

201—2

judy griffith

fabric is my life, my legacy, my london, my passion, my baby, my love – and the music programme is an extension of my soul. very nearly twenty-five years ago, i found my second family there, and i'm so grateful that i get to enjoy so many joyous moments with them all, and get spoilt hearing incredible music every single week.

most of my greatest times in life have been within those bricks. the special energy the space gives off – there's no other club where i get this feeling. you feel it walking down the stairs – still now – twenty-five years of good vibes, inspiring music, incredible sound, a beautiful community and the gift that is craig richards all soaked into the bricks.

the most joy, though, comes from the amazing (now global) community of like-minded people that we have built up over the years – it's such a rewarding family to be a part of. when we all come together, only magic happens. the dreams dreamt on that dancefloor, the people met and the creativity spawned from it in so many areas is inspiring and beautiful. even our new resident djs grew up on our dancefloor …

fabric has enabled us to give artists on the underground a bigger, safer platform to showcase their music, and always insisted that music was heard through the best sound system and on the best equipment. we have created an environment fuelled by love, passion and respect, and we are very grateful for the public's trust and belief in us over the years.

it's not been an easy ride, more an emotional rollercoaster. we've had so many outside obstacles that tried to take us down, but if fabric is anything, it is resilient and strong – and we've survived. we've all put blood, stress, tears, passion, fun and a lot of love into fabric – and may it continue … for ever.

craig richards

i knew keith from when he had his flyer company – he'd always be at gigs and outside flying afterwards, and i knew his brother billy from the cross – and we had a very thorough, slow-build friendship that coalesced through the scene. i was doing a night called freaky disco, which i did at the soundshaft at the back of heaven, which i then transferred to the cross. this was a night where we were muddling up the likes of swayzak, derrick carter, angel moraes – and terry francis and i were residents. it was the very beginning of what you could innocently call tech house – or 'housey techno', as we called it at the time. nobody talked about minimal at that time, but it was really stripped back and required a good sound system – vocals were out, and instead it was a bit trippier, tweakier, quirkier as a sound, but still had house roots, the bumping kind of feel of the us guys. we also loved warehouse party, one-off party culture, because it was no-frills, music first – but the catch-22 was that we wanted that, but also the luxury of a regular home with top-notch sound.

keith was into what we were doing – and he told us he'd found a possible new venue, and he'd like terry and i to be residents, not just as warm-up but with the night built around us, with us bookending the night and being representatives for the club's sound. we'd be involved with bookings, and using our record boxes to guide us would define the sound of fabric. it sounds terribly grand, but it's actually what happened. what a phenomenal opportunity it was. it was a more innocent time, a smaller scene, not as saturated. nowadays, there's so much choice, so much information, why would you have loyalty to just one club? but we had a solid group of people on that dancefloor week in, week out, and for a good ten years i was playing 4am to 7am week in, week out, and that allowed for a sense of nuance and experimentation that i could never have found in another situation.

one of the things i really shared with keith, and which helped cement our friendship and our ethos very early on, was that we would go record shopping together – so we experienced the music together, playing them on great speakers in our homes, comparing notes, putting them in context. he was, and is, an avid collector, a real music head. we both shared a particular love of all things simple and stripped back, music that does a lot with very little. music that was deep, soulful, atmospheric and without genre boundaries. we were very clear about what to represent at the club because we knew it intimately already, simply through research. we'd bought and talked about those records; we constantly went to gigs that had or hadn't worked and picked apart what was right or wrong about them, all that went into fabric and what it became. we had confidence from the start and knew what would work long term.

i remember repeatedly going down a ladder into that old meat fridge with keith, as we tried to envisage how it could function architecturally. we knew what we wanted, and in the end the space kind of defined itself because of its own depth and character. it always had enormous personality, under the road and up against the tube line. it had to be a multiroom venue, which would allow juxtaposition and allow different genres of music to flourish. that was always the point, rooms of different scale but with equal importance. this would allow us to present, say, fila brazillia with the same sense of pride and momentum as jeff mills or mark farina; basic channel with larry heard, tony humphries with steve bug. the list goes on … it was important that there was equality in the music, not just in the bookings but in ethos. all of that fitted itself into the space, and our imagination gradually inhabited that special part of east london. we were able to follow our musical instinct. for example, when andrew weatherall told me he'd seen this amazing guy called ricardo villalobos, that was enough for us to book him. ricardo came, was an immediate flood of inspiration, missed his flight home, stayed at my house and spent his whole fee on a cardigan. of course, i instantly fell in love with him and a great friendship began. he became a loyal and vital part of the club's message.

from those early days it just rolled out really. the competition with home – which was really a press confection – ended up doing us no end of favours because it drew attention to the fact that we were an underground music-focused space away from the lights of the west end. a crowd instantly formed, which led us as much as we led them: we stumbled forward into the dark together, following a torch light into uncharted territory, and through night after night after night, we discovered more and more of what we were about. keith and i had been clubbing since the very early eighties, since before acid house, so we had a sense of the long game – it was never about hype, and always about the dancefloor and the absolute magic that can be created with the right tunes, the right people and the right sound system in a darkened room. it was pre-social-media times, so we were in the moment, heads down and engaged with secrecy, not having to promote the product in the way one might have to now gave us breathing space and a chance to experiment. the audience was always behind us.

gradually, our message grew – the cds, the flyers, the back pages of muzik and jockey slut, magazines that don't even exist anymore – slowly what we were doing seeped into the public consciousness, by word of mouth more than anything. the experience of walking down those stairs into the club was intoxicating, and people came week after week to recount their experiences and establish friendships. in the present and the future, even in this instant-information era, fabric still stands or falls on that – on the experience people have if they come into the club on any weekend. fabric provides a bedrock for thousands of experiences that people had in the past that made them want to say, 'yeah, that's the place'. that loyalty got us out of tricky spots. the closure felt like we were under siege, and the people and the power of social media forced its reopening.

for me, personally, it's meant the world to me. i feel very, very lucky. to be that resident dj that honed his craft and learnt to take risks and put together line-ups that revolved around our tastes and passion was and is an unbelievable privilege. to have helped build something of importance in the city of london makes me very proud. half of my family are from poplar and bow, my grandfather worked in the docks. london is an incredible city for many reasons, but in terms of nightlife culture there is nowhere like it on the planet. fabric, with all its ups and downs and twists and turns, remains an institution and a reference point in the development of electronic music. what fabric did and continues to do is set a standard of quality and of exploration. my residency at this club made me the dj i am. despite the fact that i have played records all over the world, i never really enjoyed being on tour. being in the same place every week allowed me to grow up in my own city and to build a level of confidence that allowed me to play anything at any moment with courage and certainty.

instant impact has never been my thing. i prefer the coastal path rather than the motorway. projecting the message within the music is what djing is about. understanding how to challenge a crowd while still pleasing them is something i could never have grasped without weekly repetition in the same booth. learning bit by bit what works at the right time of the night allowed me to develop a very personal style of playing. i've had the time of my life in that brickwork labyrinth for a quarter of a century, and it shows no sign of stopping. i don't play every saturday anymore, but it remains my favourite place to play in the world. i curate and play at a few weekends each year and feel blessed that the train keeps moving. my career really feels as if it's just beginning, my festival shines after a turbulent start and thankfully i am still invited to play at wonderful parties. but always in the back of my mind is the sense of exploration and possibility which came from my beginnings at fabric.

terry francis

keith popped up behind me when i was djing in the soundshaft, going on about how he's got this amazing new place and did i want to be one of the residents and all this. in those days, you'd heard it all before already – but there was something about keith that i believed. he's a very convincing bloke, and my ears pricked up a bit. then i didn't hear anything for ages so i thought, oh well, that's that. but then i got a call from nikki smith, who used to work there. she invited me to go and have a look and meet keith properly, and that was that.

it was a fantastic gig from the start. play exactly what you want, good attitude from everyone there, treated you nicely, you got free drinks. so straight away i thought, ok, yeah, this is cool. i mean, it seems simple, but it's amazing how many people don't get it right. by this point i was playing quite a bit abroad, especially round europe – and it was much more normal there to get treated really nice, good hotel, picked up at the hotel, friendly people, nice dinner, not mucking around, being reliable, taxi ready afterwards, just treating the djs well. fabric did that too, and that made djs want to come back!

that meant everyone got on with each other too. all the regular djs knew each other, hung out, were friendly, and that was important too – again, it kept people coming back, and i think

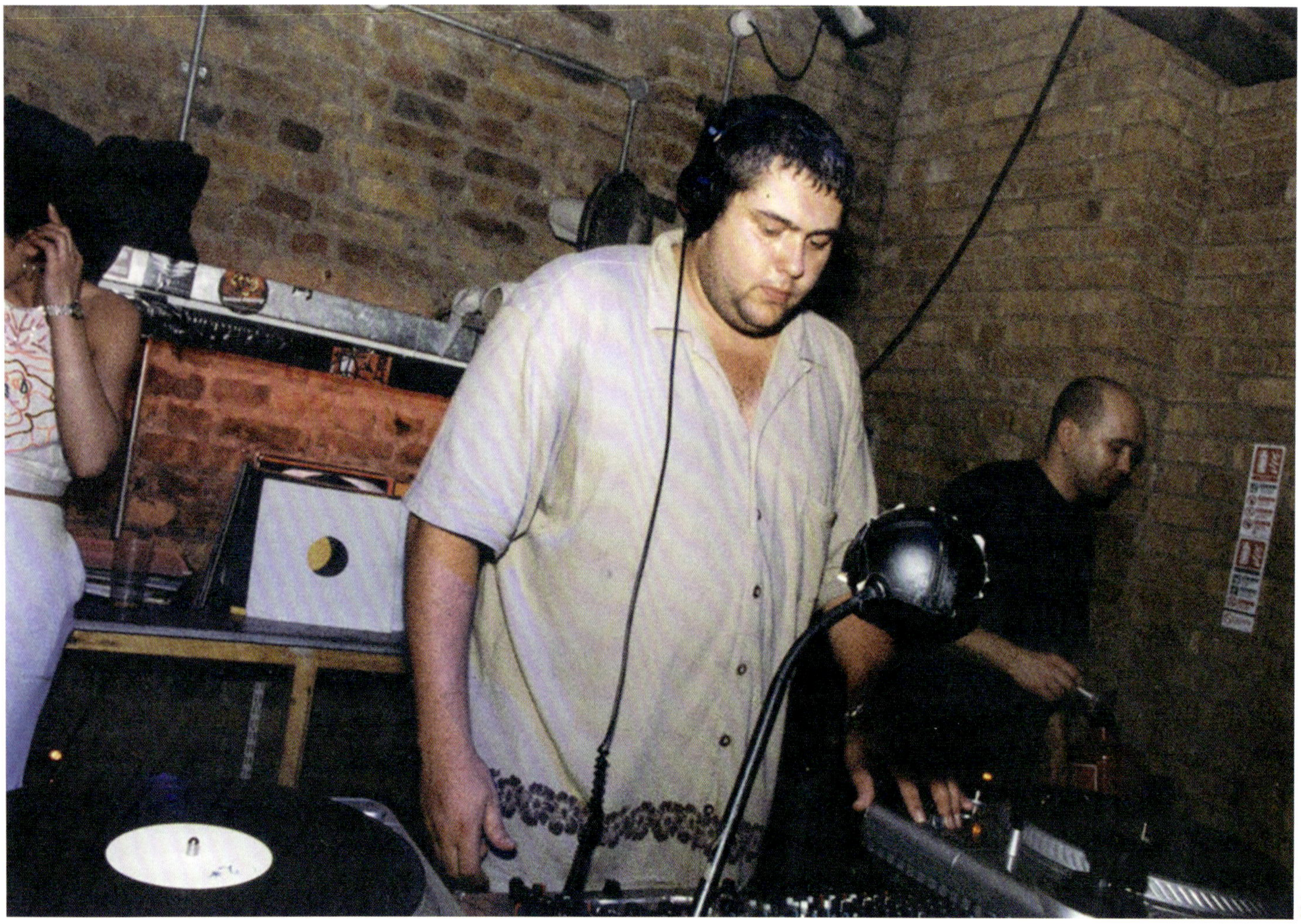

204–1

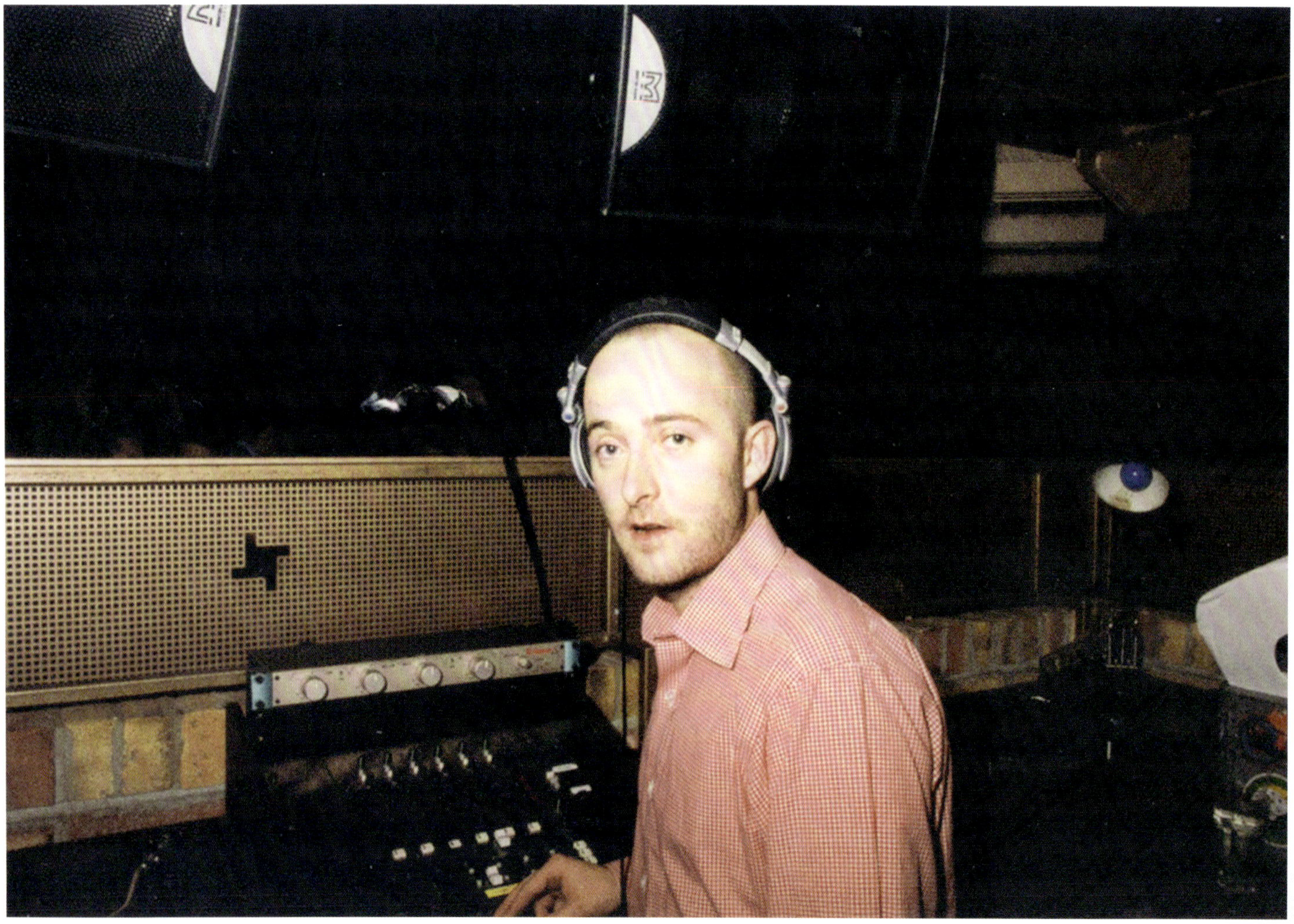

204–2

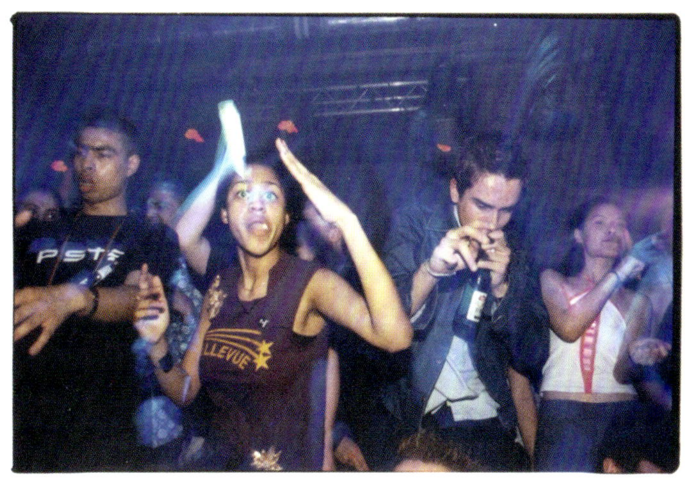

205—1

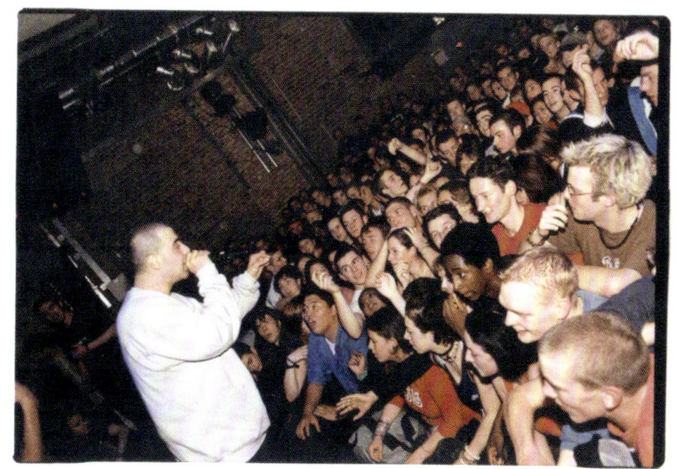

205—2

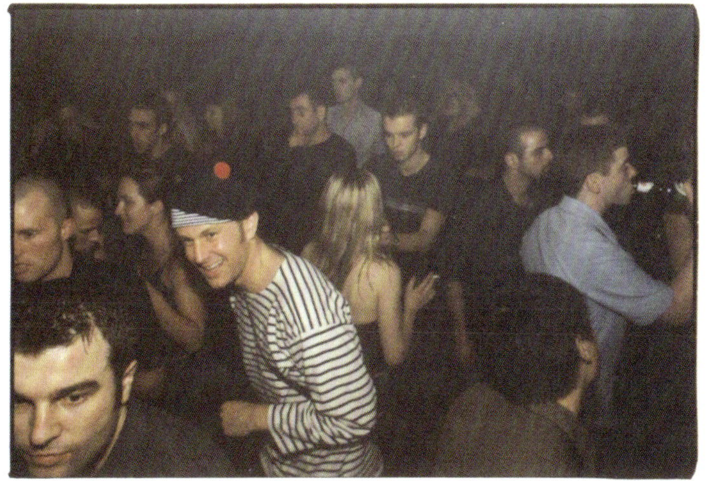

205—3

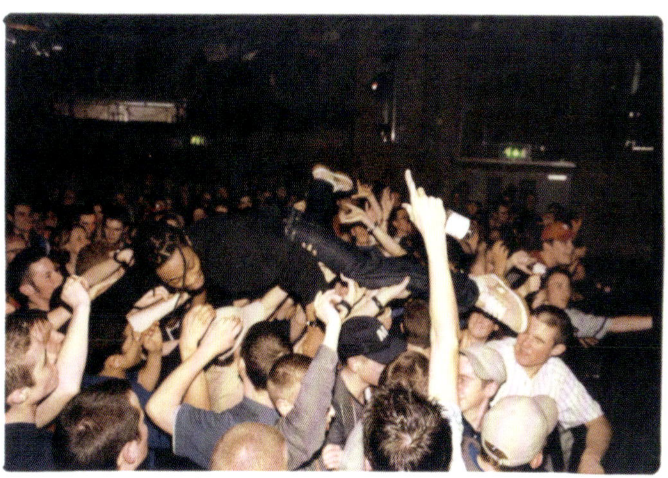

205—4

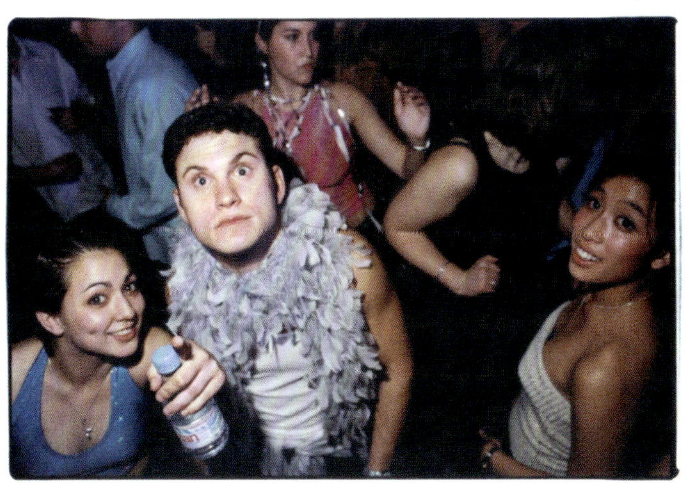

205—5

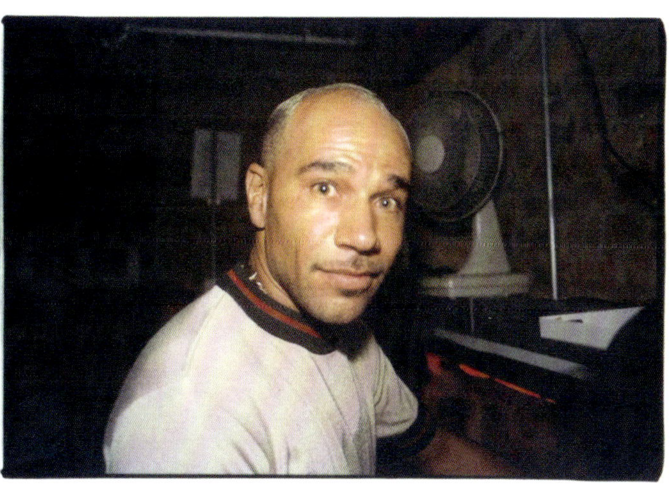

205—6

punters appreciated the vibe. fridays were pretty different to what we did, all that breakbeat stuff with james lavelle and howie b – bit more of a collegey, student crowd, where we were more hardcore-clubber based – but we got pretty matey. we'd always have a drink together.

i near enough lived there. i've eased off a bit, but i was in there every saturday night for twenty years – and i'd sometimes play a night midweek, or help out if someone dropped out on friday too. it was a lot of nights. and it always felt steady. i know there was ups and downs with the business, but inside the club it just kept on, you know? for me, it's four-four beats, how much can it really change? i play house, tech house; it might go through fads and changes, different influences coming in and out, but really it stays the same at the heart of it – and people love that now, same as they did back when we began.

ricardo villalobos

fabric means a lot. it's the one and only 'big underground club' in the world for me – meaning you have three floors with completely underground booking and not oriented to commercial, audience-catching mechanisms. it's totally about the content of the music, which is keeping the club alive and keeping the interest of the people who come from everywhere in the world for that experience, and it's like a melting point. it's the perfect size where people from different places and different cultures with different musical interests can flow together. i'm very happy to be part of this family and be accepted there – and, of course, i love playing there, because it's a club dedicated to music and to music sound quality and music culture.

they are just great people. it wasn't difficult to make friends with judy and craig and keith; from the very first time it was a welcoming family, very concentrated on the music – and on the vinyl culture too. every one of them believes in keeping subculture alive, and i think it's only possible in london to have something like this. in berlin you have it distributed over the whole city, not concentrated in one place – even berghain/panorama bar can't make any comparison to fabric. having this one special place is something very unique in the world, i think, and it's given so much to london. and the way people circulate around and it feels so away from the outside world makes magic; it's so concentrated energy, the energy can't leave anywhere so it stays in the space, like an experimentation glass for a scientist.

for me, being welcomed in with a residency – playing three, four, five times a year – meant a lot. the meaning of coming home to a place again and again allows you to create something special. it's a playground; with a sound system like this you can experiment and develop and start to produce tracks only for this sound system. the only other place i can do this is the robert johnson in offenbach am main – my only other residency and the only other club with a similar sound system. you can make music especially for this atmosphere, for this frequency range, for this room – it gives you a sense of special possibilities.

and, of course, that's helped me a lot in my career and my development in what i do. it's really a testing field; even for a year before alcachofa came out in 2003, i was playing those tracks and the fabric audience understood them. i could find out what was possible. it was basslines that were a bit deeper than the normal 808 or 909 kick, and really it was rare to find a sound system that could transmit these frequency ranges. and it's not just the frequency, but fabric is tuned to showing the sonic capabilities of vinyl, which is even more rare now. in the last twenty years it's got lost completely; in many places, if you play vinyl records, the equipment isn't tuned, it creates feedback.

i remember those early times at fabric, the sound engineer walking around with a computer, with a tablet, walking around the whole space, measuring the frequencies of the room at different times, which changed depending how many people were in there, then he'd come back and press one button and all feedback would disappear. it was amazing. that dedication to all the technical details, and to vinyl playing and how it should really sound – that is real care. it shows that they want it to be right, and it's really, really important.

i played saturdays, but i loved to go in on a friday too, because it was good to see how that sound system was good for dubstep and drum'n'bass and all that breaky music they played on fridays. it was a great proof of the system too! i think london understands that better than anywhere – except maybe miami bass people in florida! the vinyl mastering, the dubplates culture, london is a centre of bass transmission on vinyl, and it was very nice to see the heart of the club really concentrating on this. it had to be that way, because keith as the boss and initiator of all this was always a complete vinyl nerd – crazy about this – and it's necessary to have this, to have people who are completely freaky about these kind of things at the heart of subculture.

the magic of fabric is it's impossible to stop playing. they'd start with a three-hour set, but i had to get booked for longer and longer because it's impossible to stop. it was so funny, so much fun to play there, this little cage there with your limited amount of people and friends in with you, you feel safe, it's a very special and magical situation to be in. i always lose the sense of time completely – if someone comes in and said, 'you've had your three hours,' i couldn't even understand how this was possible. this would always happen to me in fabric, and, you know, it still does – no matter how long i play.

jaden thompson

to me, what makes fabric unique is its industrial rawness, with body shaking bass on the dance floor and an 'all about the music' policy.

i first visited fabric back in 2017, after i had just moved to london. it was the eighteenth anniversary of the club and ricardo was playing when i walked in at like 12 p.m.. that was one of my first experiences as a proper rave and i felt like it really inspired my later studio sessions.

playing at 8 a.m. on fabric's opening after lockdown a few years ago, after terry francis, is definitely one of my favourite memories at the club. i remember being quite nervous having terry behind listening to my set, but then assured when i turned round to see him enjoying the music.

in my eyes, fabric represents a melting pot of electronic music and culture. over the years, fabric has influenced our scene in so many ways by shining the light on upcoming talent and world-renowned names. it's one of those bucket list clubs that almost every dj wants to play at, and also a place that ravers travel across the world to visit.

anna wall

growing up in hackney, i was lucky to have such an abundance of nightlife on my doorstep. when i was too young to go to clubs i would listen to pirate radio all night until the early hours on my walkman, and that's where i discovered the rebellious sounds of jungle, d&b, uk garage and eventually house and techno. when i was old enough to be a rebel myself, i started exploring illegal raves. they'd often be shut down by the police, but i guess that was part of the thrill.

the first time i discovered fabric must have been around 2005. it was one of the first nightclubs i ever went to. i remember it blew my little mind, and opened my eyes to what a real clubbing experience could be. i was in awe when i stepped on the dancefloor in room 1; i was in heaven, and i never wanted to leave. although my memories are hazy from back in the day, i distinctly remember the wonder and excitement of it all. seeing craig richards for the first time, the booth in room 3 when it was tucked into the archway. sitting up there and talking to strangers, who quickly become your best friends.

at afterparties we'd be putting the first craig richards fabric mix cd on blast. it was a huge part of my music discovery – a lot of it stemmed from those early days. i was nineteen when i got a set of turntables, after finding a steal of a deal on gumtree from a guy selling two technics, a stanton mixer and pretty much his whole record collection, full of dubs and white labels. that was my starting point. i wanted to learn to play records at home to keep myself out of trouble, because i was going out way too much at the time. when i started djing it was in my bedroom, then at afterparties, but once i got the bug for it i couldn't stop.

i'll never forget the moment that i felt like things came full circle, when i got my first opportunity to play at fabric. it was in 2018, a three-hour set warming up for craig richards and seth troxler in room 1. it was a dream come true. i spent countless hours working on what i wanted to play, and they're records that i'll cherish to this day. hearing your records in that room is incredible; you hear so much depth and definition in tracks that you've never heard before on a system like that. it makes you listen to music in a different way. i'll never forget that night, and all the friends from near and far that came to support, even those who had long-since hung up their raving shoes. not long after the gig, in 2019 i became one the new residents. when i play at the club today i still get goosebumps, those butterflies in my stomach just like the first time.

harry mccanna

i used to come down from essex to fabric when i was in my teens with the group of older friends who had got me into djing. the first time i went with them we actually travelled in limos, because with a load of you it was cheaper than the train. that was a one-off, though, and i've spent many hazy mornings and afternoons on the train back since. a couple of years after that i was a resident for lost souls at public life in shoreditch, which is where i played back-to-back with peter from wetyourself! this then led to my first booking at fabric, on a new year's day with wys!, and then by the time i was twenty, i'd already managed to play in all three rooms – often playing room 3 on bank holidays when antony from lost souls had the room to programme, and then played room 2 on a random midweek student night when i was studying down in camberwell. i was and still am a huge fan of the club, visiting as much as i could – there was a point at the start of uni when me and my mate laurie had been seven weekends in a row.

my sound is strongly influenced by what i have experienced there. back in the uni days, we were going to see a lot of hessle audio, autonomic, addison groove, uk sound stuff – but then also seeing ricardo play, seeing cobblestone jazz live for the first time, seeing rpr every december when they played and always seeing craig whenever we went, so that naturally fed into what i do. now i will mainly play more minimal or tech house kind of rhythms, but there's always an element of uk bass to it, and that is definitely influenced by many hours spent in the club – especially the room 1 dancefloor, because you really can't beat the sound in there!

i gradually got to meet more people and build up a relationship with judy, who would come and watch me play at other gigs in london, and after a while i started to pick up a few saturday slots in fabric, then as we

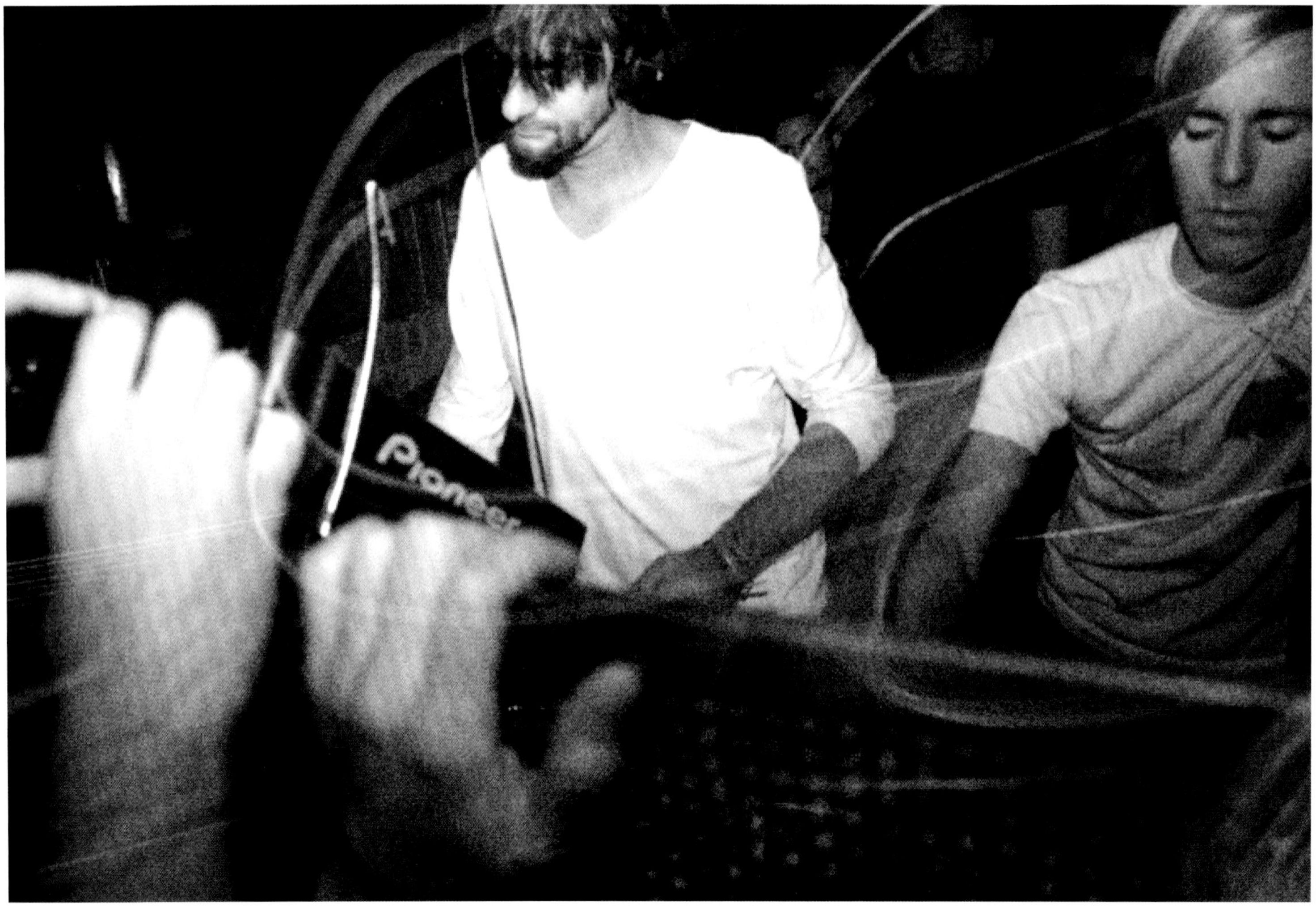

208—1

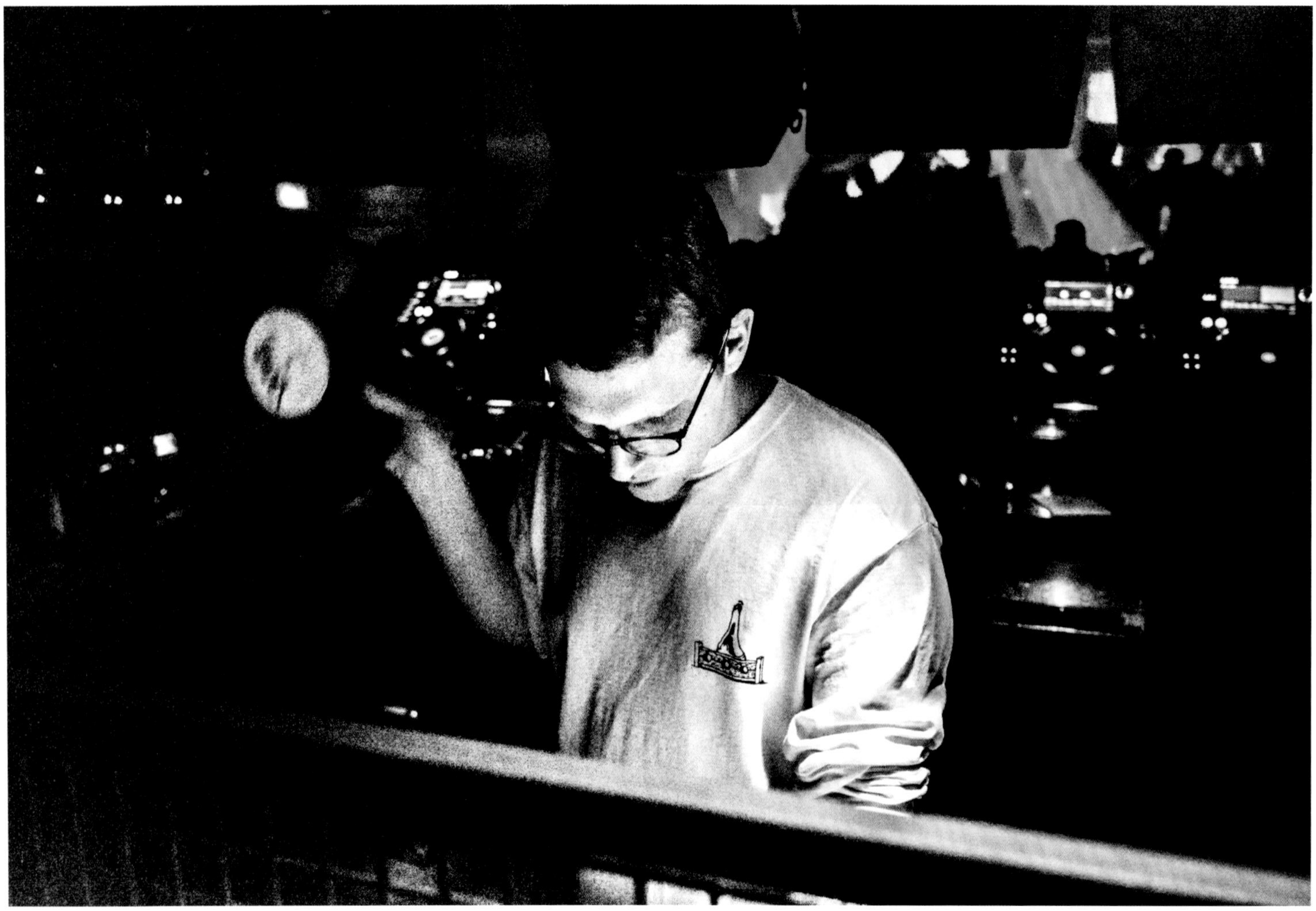

208—2

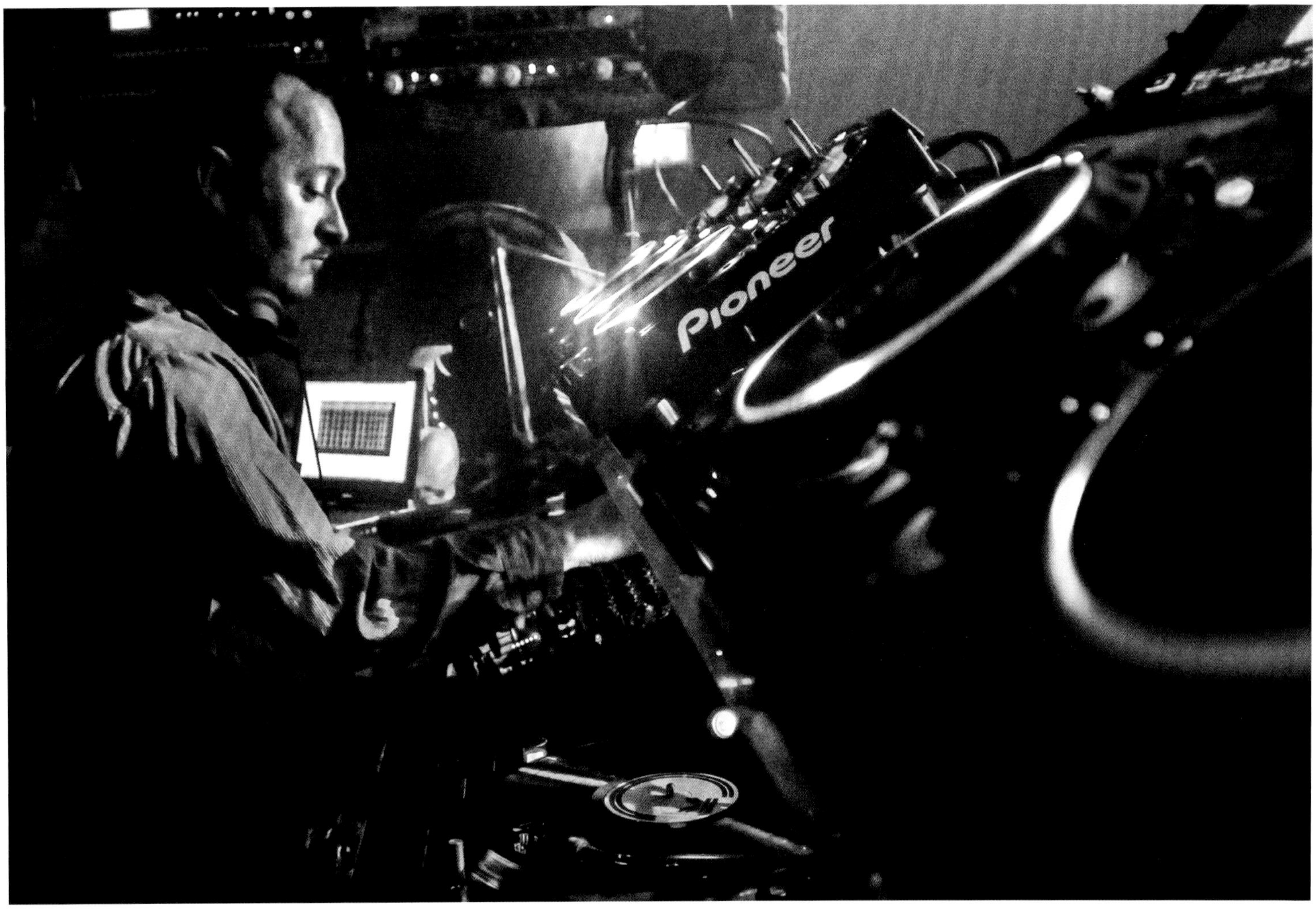

209—1

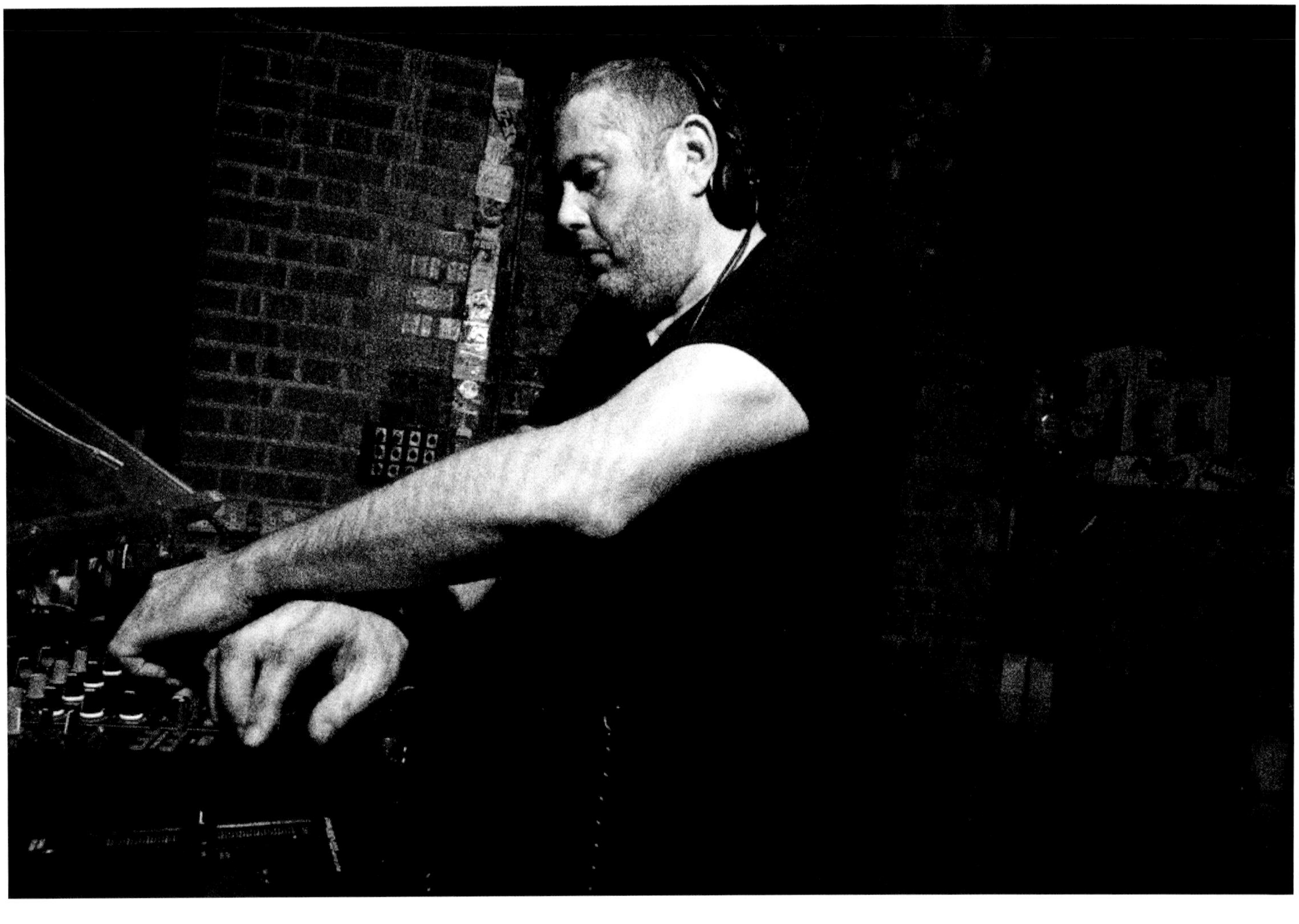

209—2

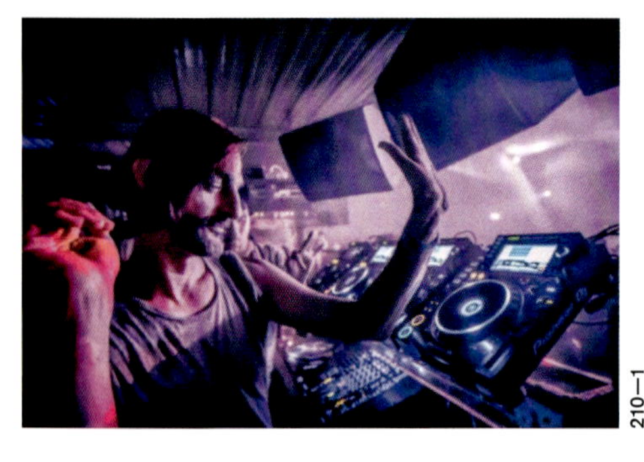
210—1

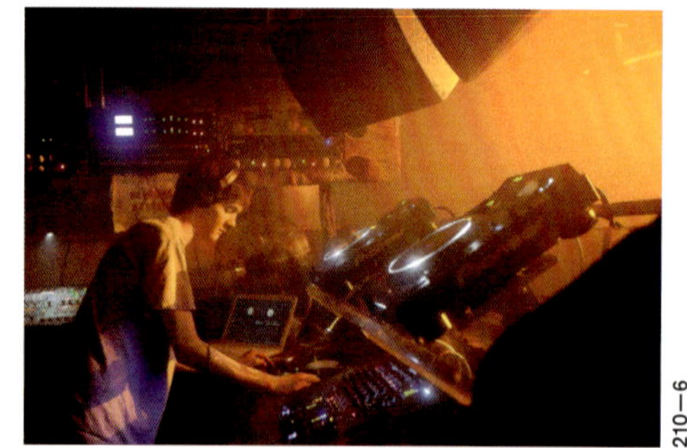
210—6

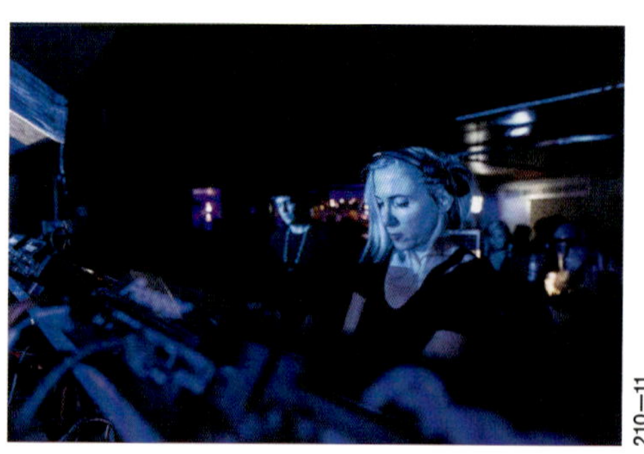
210—11

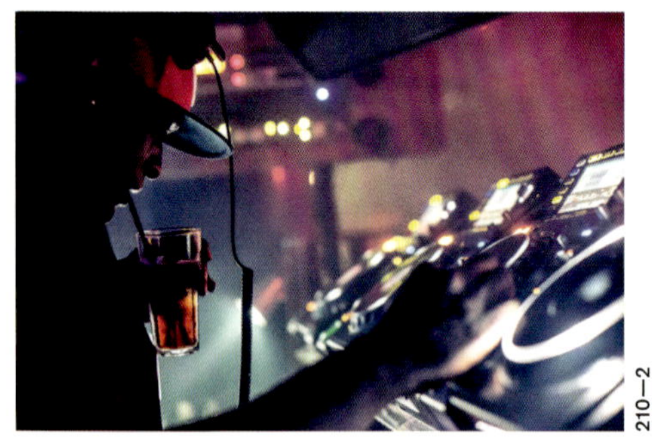
210—2

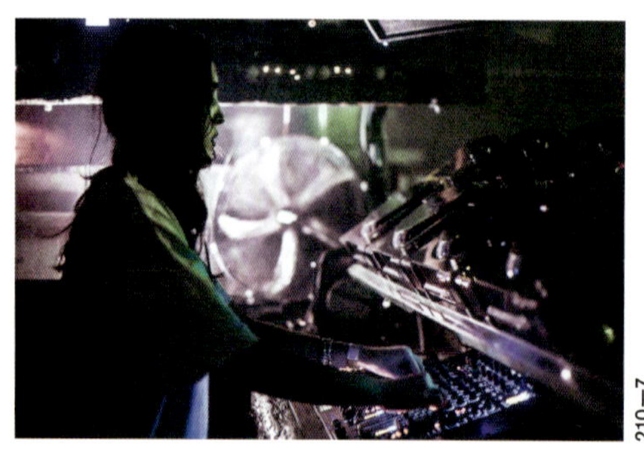
210—7

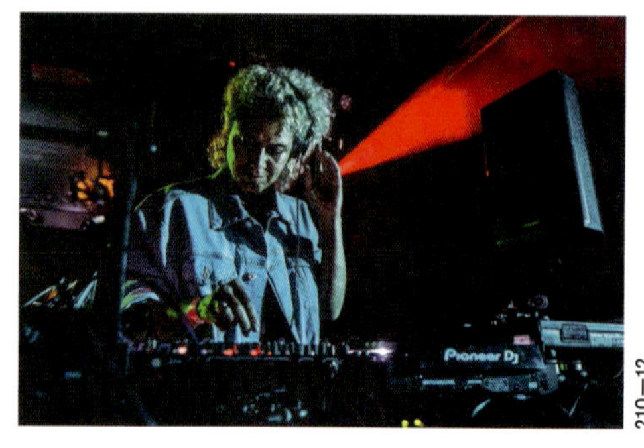

210—12

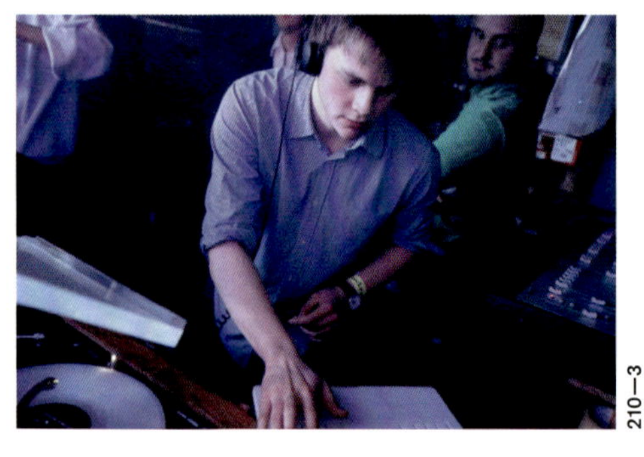
210—3

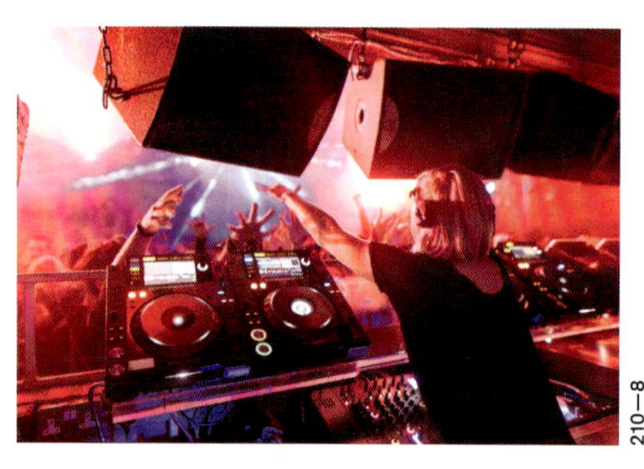
210—8

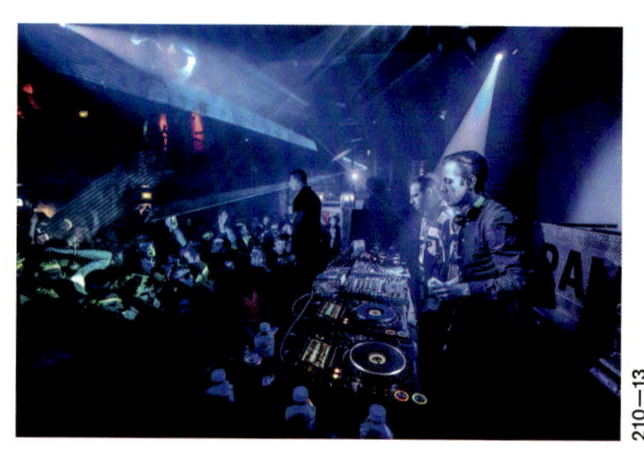
210—13

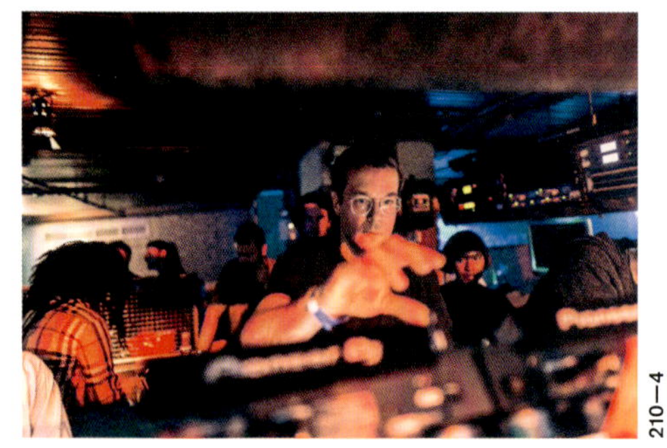
210—4

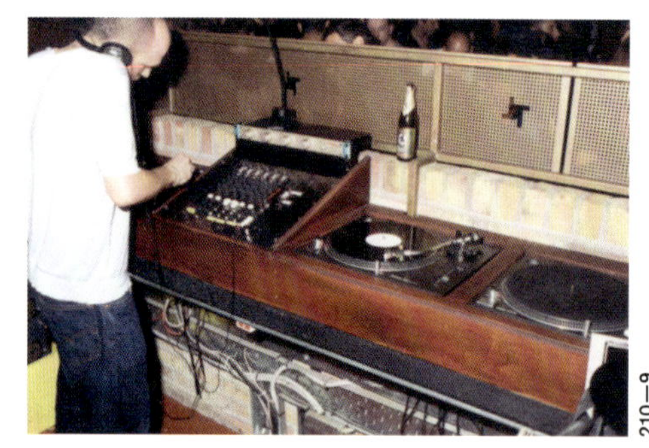
210—9

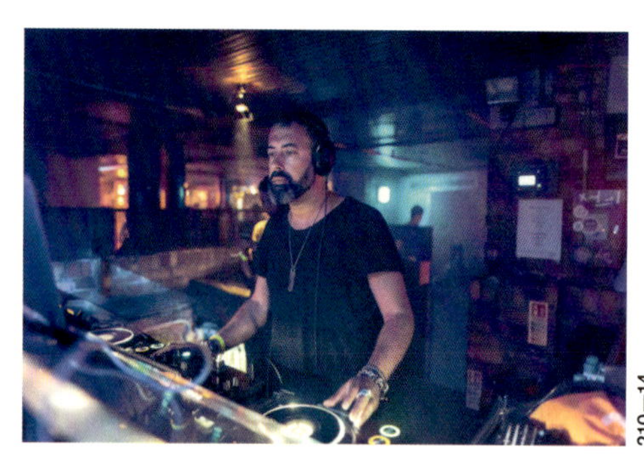
210—14

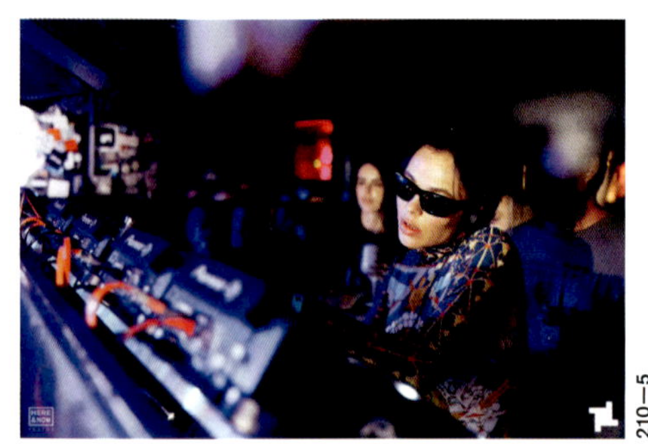
210—5

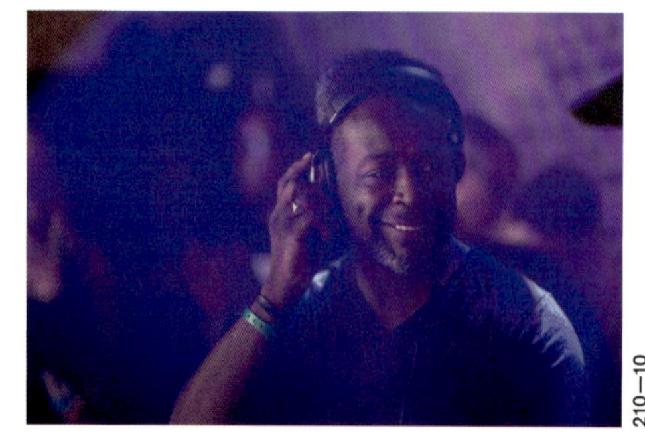
210—10

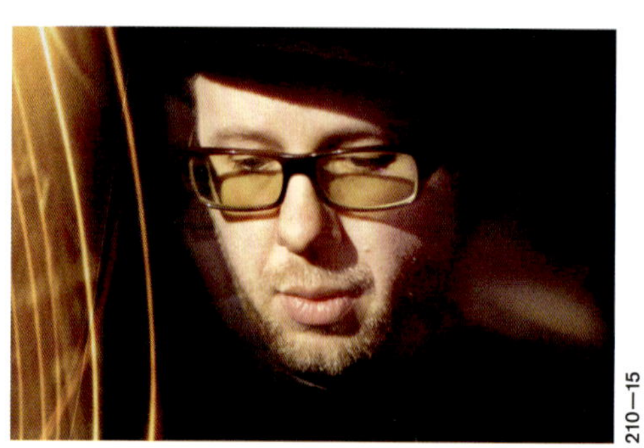
210—15

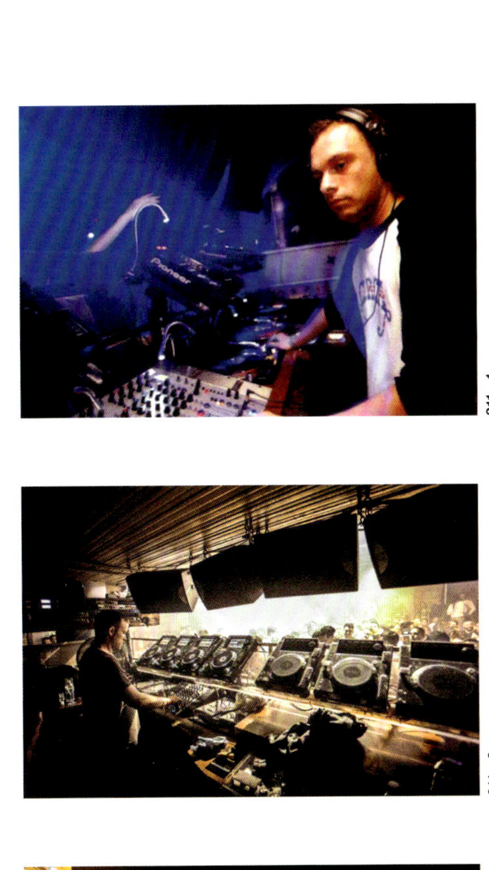
211—1

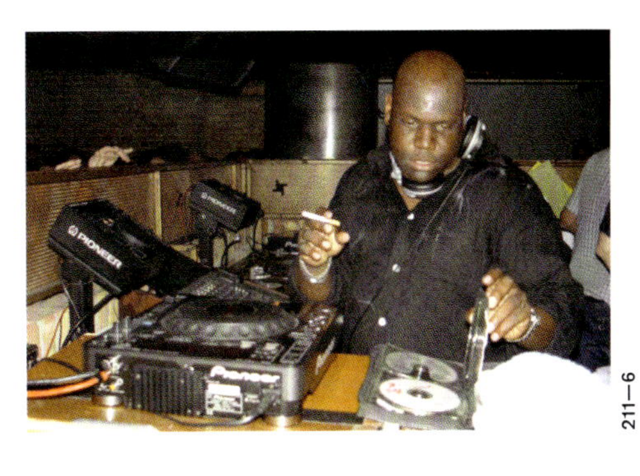

211—6

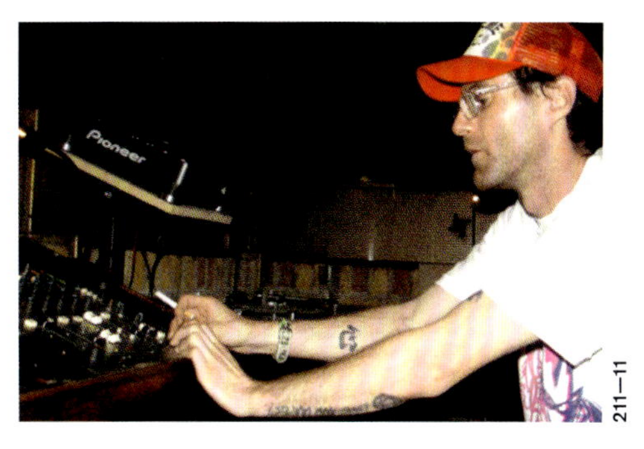

211—11

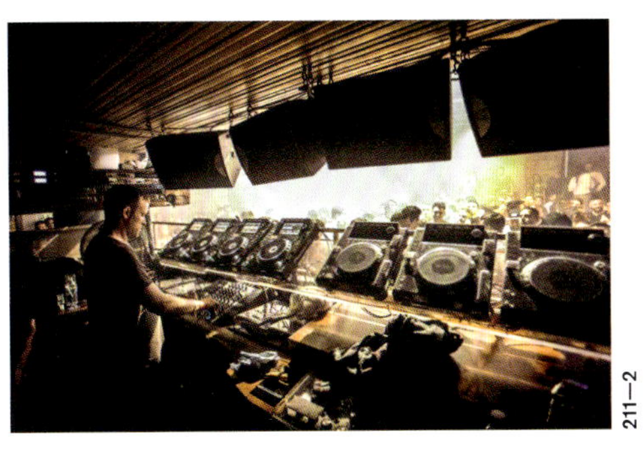
211—2

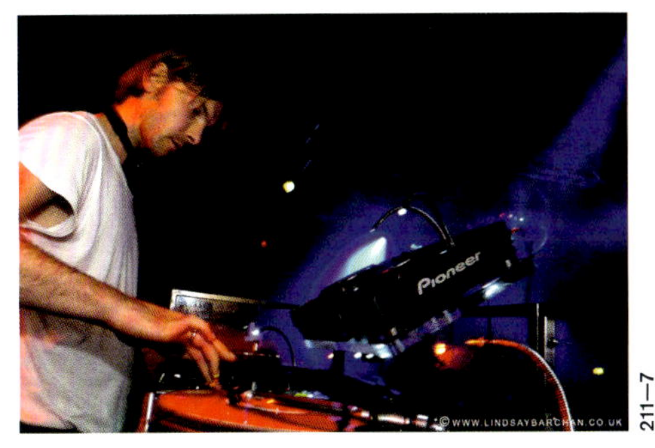

211—7

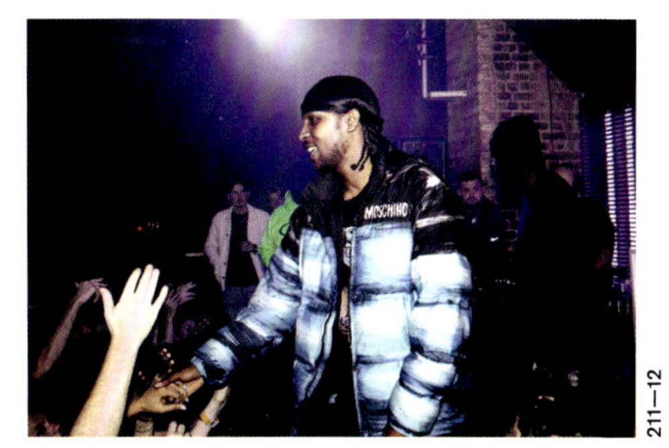

211—12

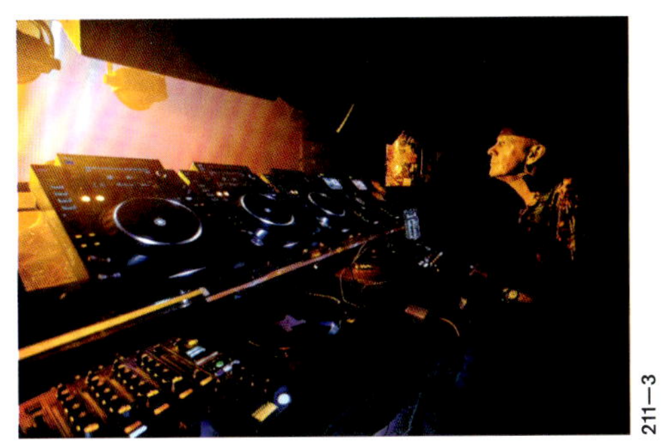
211—3

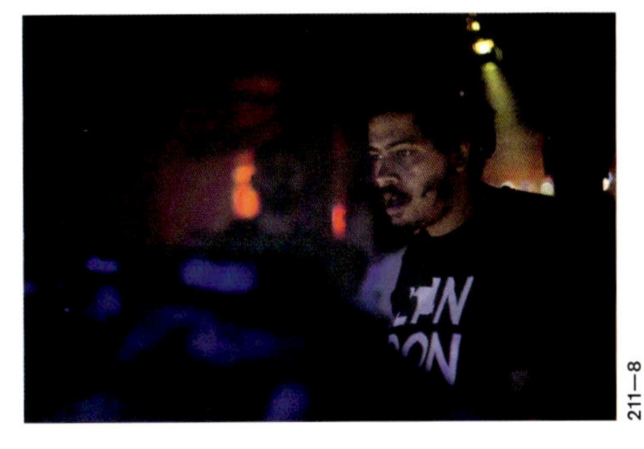
211—8

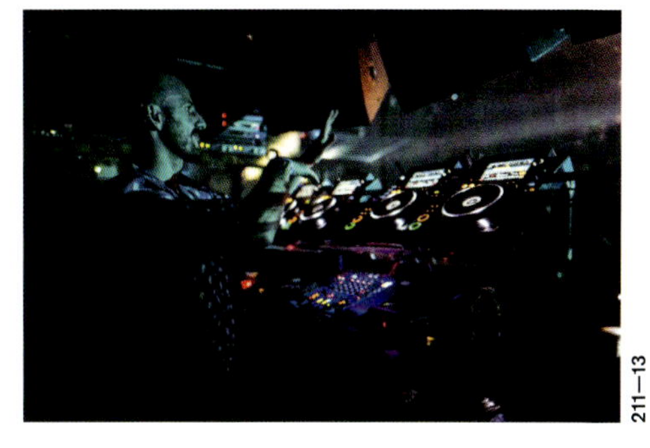
211—13

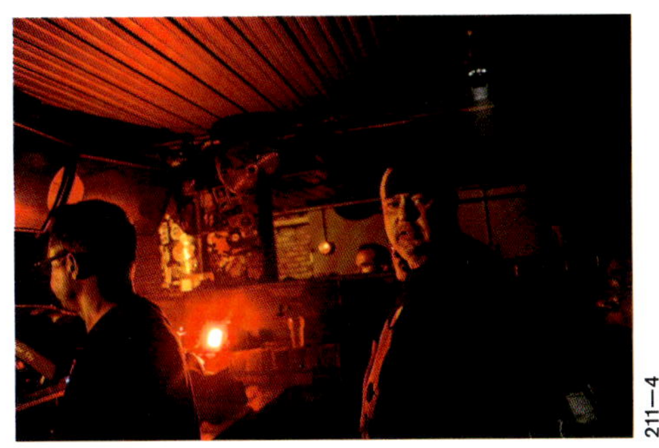
211—4

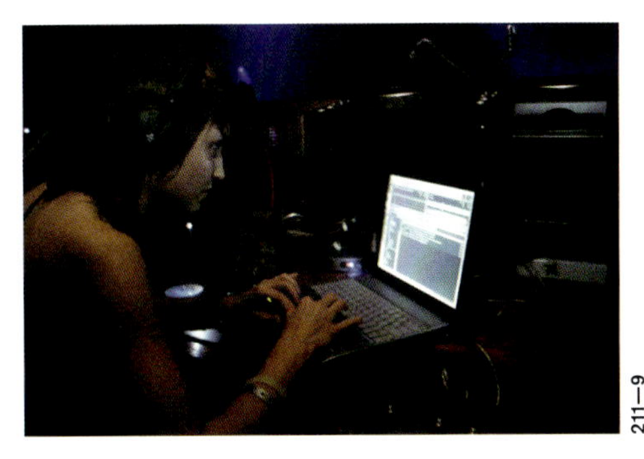
211—9

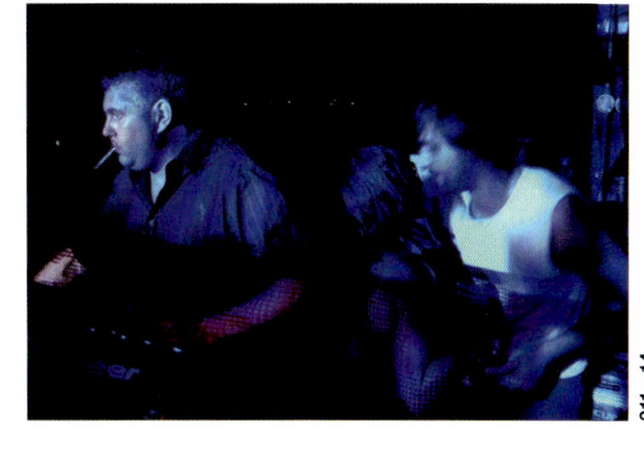
211—14

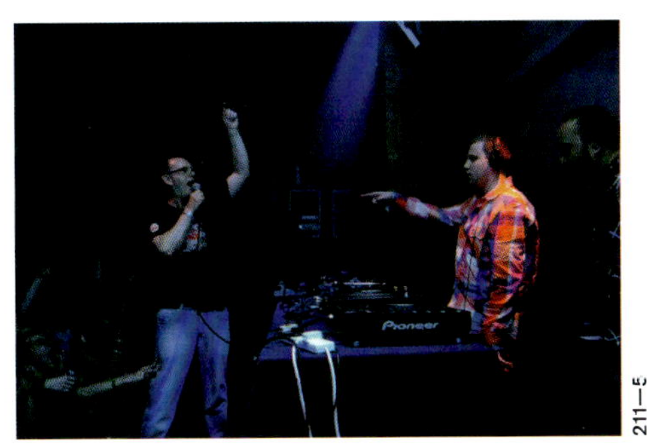

211—5

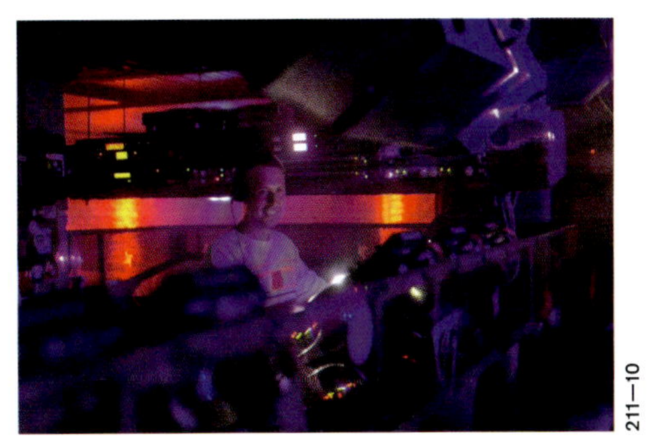
211—10

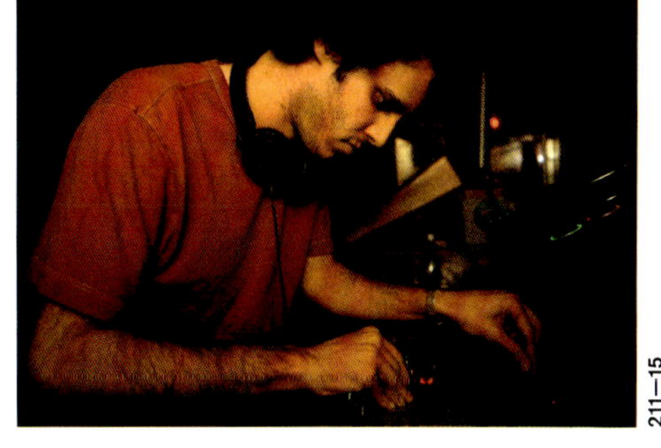
211—15

came out of lockdown i got offered the residency, and now here we are! i don't ever take it for granted. i'd been playing as a resident regularly for almost two years, but it was only at this twenty-fourth birthday that something clicked and i felt like i was truly part of the family. it's a real honour to be able to chat about music and the early days at the club to people like craig, who've built the sound of fabric, and now to be able to go forwards with my own sound.

josh caffé

i started going to fabric in the early 2000s, when they used to do dtpm on a sunday. this was a real melting pot for a lot of the queer community at the time, it was a really important club night for the time, and i went to it religiously for many years until it ended. then, after this, jacob started wetyourself! at fabric with cormac and peter pixzel, and this again was something that became a regular sunday party for me – the sunday 'naughty days' were definitely how my relationship built with fabric over the years.

through getting to know jacob and wetyourself! in general, in 2018 i got the opportunity to join up with him and start love child, which started monthly on a sunday, definitely as a nod to dtpm and wetyourself! and old-school london at the time, and at the same time i became a fabric resident. the very first party we did was a huge vogue ball, which was the first time that had happened in the venue – so that was an important and special moment for both fabric and the vogue/ballroom scene in london.

since then we've done various parties, always trying to bring back the queer presence to fabric. of course it was always there, but we just wanted to have something that was more standalone and stand-out. it was a real honour to be able to do this. having been part of the queer scene within fabric all the way back to the early days of dtpm, to come in as a resident, to create and curate a queer party in the space was something special. i think it's really important to carry on the legacy of fabric as a whole because there's so much that's important in its dna, but also it's about bringing in new blood – which in my case means bringing in young, queer artists from the uk and abroad and letting them be part of fabric's future dna.

tapefeed

fabric is a space with its own unique energy, like any iconic club should have. there's an intangible quality that you can only feel there, absorbing the energy from the great music played by djs over the last twenty-five years and all the people who have danced and lived life within its walls. what truly sets it apart is its inclusivity: it remains a club for everyone. fabric is accessible, welcoming and unpretentious, making it the club for every generation, from newcomers to seasoned veterans. this is really how a club should be, a place for everyone to be connected by music. it consistently promotes and prioritises quality, making it a standout institution in the world clubbing scene.

we've got quite a few memories, of course, but we'll pick three. firstly, our debut in room 1 was already set up to be an iconic moment, especially considering we were warming up for jeff mills – that's going to be a legendary night. it's an experience that we still find hard to believe was real. another memorable moment was during one of the first thirty-hour continuum events. due to a last-minute timetable change, we unexpectedly ended up playing on sunday morning at nine in room 1. we were initially concerned about the inconvenient timing for our friends to wake up early or stay out that late, but to our surprise, everyone showed up, and the energy was incredible! it turned out to be one of our favourite room 1 sets, creating a proper afterparty sexy vibe.

more recently, but equally significant, our hybrid live/dj set debut in room 2. we had been working and planning it for a long time, and performing for the first time at fabric was an incredible experience. the support we received made us feel truly at home, making it a very special occasion. and actually ... i know we said only three, but how could we forget about our all night long in room 3? that was also super iconic! we hope we can make another one soon.

being invited as residents during the pandemic was truly unexpected but immensely helpful in restarting positively. fabric's consistent support in shaping our profile, from curated line-ups to ep releases on houndstooth, has been gratifying and motivating. as residents, we embrace the responsibility of representing the club, understanding dancefloor dynamics in each gig, which simultaneously elevates our self-expression. it's such an incredible experience.

bobby connolly

i first went to fabric in 2006. before the boom of social media, before nightclubs and djs had followers, before every phone had a camera, my friends and i would make our weekly pilgrimage in the early hours of sunday morning. the full bodysonic vibrations of room 1 lured us back week after week. we went armed with trust, loyalty and commitment, often with no idea who would be playing, but safe in the knowledge it would be an exciting and inspiring experience.

i feel very fortunate to have experienced those original foundations, and it was just incredible for me that after almost thirteen years of dancing in those rooms, in january 2019 i was asked to be a new resident of the club. this was an opportunity i will be forever proud of and grateful for. with an understanding and respect of what came before, i approached the role with care and sensitivity.

having the good fortune to play in all three rooms, in very different situations, and alongside many of my favourite artists, has been the most wonderful and challenging process. from this i have learned more than i ever could have imagined about the true role of the dj. with the support of the ever-impeccable sound and artist teams, fabric is now my most comfortable place to perform in the world, and i feel confident representing the club's history and future every time i play. time passes and the world keeps moving, but legend lives on for ever.

hutch

i went to fabric for the first time on a sort of spur-of-the-moment night out after being sat in a pub. it was a playaz night in room 1, with bukem and friends in room 2. being a massive jungle and drum'n'bass fan i was desperate to go – and it straight up blew my mind, as i'm sure was the case for most people. the sound, the lights, the stairs, the toilets, the smoking area, losing my mates: everything about the club said to me, as a music fan, 'why have i never been here before?!' it became a place i would go to more often than any other club, and of course i instantly became a fabricfirst member and collector of the iconic FABRICLIVE cds.

i've been going to the club for years now and, just before covid, was approached by a member of the team then to talk about potentially being a resident of the club – then, of course, the world stopped and i was absolutely gutted, thinking it was never going to happen. but when fabric was reopening after covid, the bookings team approached me about the club reopening with some new residents and said that he wanted to put me forward. couldn't have been more excited. my first set was when the club reopened after covid, and i played in the newly refurbished room 2 straight after craig, who had just played a masterclass of a 140 electro set. to say i was shitting myself is somewhat of an understatement, but it was honestly the biggest honour, and i get goosebumps thinking back to that moment. now into my third year as resident, i'm still pinching myself that i get to play at that club on a regular basis.

what fabric has done over the years, as a venue purveying sounds from the farthest ends of the spectrum, is nothing short of astounding. it's given community to so many people, to so many sounds and so many cultures, and constantly delivers the underground club experience in its truest form. i've made lifelong friends there and i still have the utmost respect for every member of the fabric family – and, honestly, it really feels like a family – that put so much care into every detail of the club to make it what it is.

jossy mitsu

i moved to london for uni in 2014, and i remember just not wanting to go to any freshers' things – i just wanted to go raving and go to fabric! i went twice to weekend things picked at random, and it was pretty soon after that – in fact, i think it was the fabric birthday weekend in october – that i saw the advert saying 'come and work at fabric' and thought, wow, ok, i want to do that. the advert said to send a recent picture of yourself, and i specifically remember being in my uni halls and putting on loads of make-up to do the picture.

i worked there for about a year and a half, but i'd be in there on my nights off too. i was just there every weekend for a good two years – i met so many people who are still friends now, there'd always be someone to hang out with. one birthday i didn't even have plans for, just ended up going to fabric and hanging out with the staff – it was just the natural place to be. the very first shift i worked in the cloakroom, they let the new people finish work early – so i went downstairs, and bumped into elijah from butterz. i'd never met anyone who worked in the industry who i'd properly followed before. he was a bit 'i'll never get used to people recognising me', but actually he was really, really nice and encouraging, and we're still friends now close to ten years later.

i'd djed a bit in birmingham, nothing major, and i did a few student nights and stuff during the time i was working in fabric – but never got the chance to play there, so when it got shut down in 2016 i was gutted, i thought i'd missed my chance. but then, when it reopened, i finally got to do it. in fact, one of the earliest nights i did was opening room 1 for dj q's album launch with a load of butterz people playing. for a while i'd do a warm-up set every six months or so – then after covid, i did the residency for a year, and towards the end of that they let me curate two rooms of the club, which was just great.

because i'd been going regularly for the best part of a decade, i think i really learned a vibe or style of programming that i'd now try and keep to, or keep to the spirit of. it's never been about booking people because they'd get numbers in: fabric is about having good djs for the sake of good djs, and that's always something you need to be conscious of. the club has always been there, it's always been at the forefront of representing forward-thinking music – for me going there, it felt like a club you could trust, even without seeing a line-up, whether that's bass on a friday or techno on a saturday. still now, if i've got a night off, i'll end up there – and still, same as when i started, there'll be a community around whatever residents are there, the same feeling that i'll bump into old friends or people i haven't seen for ages. it's still fabric family.

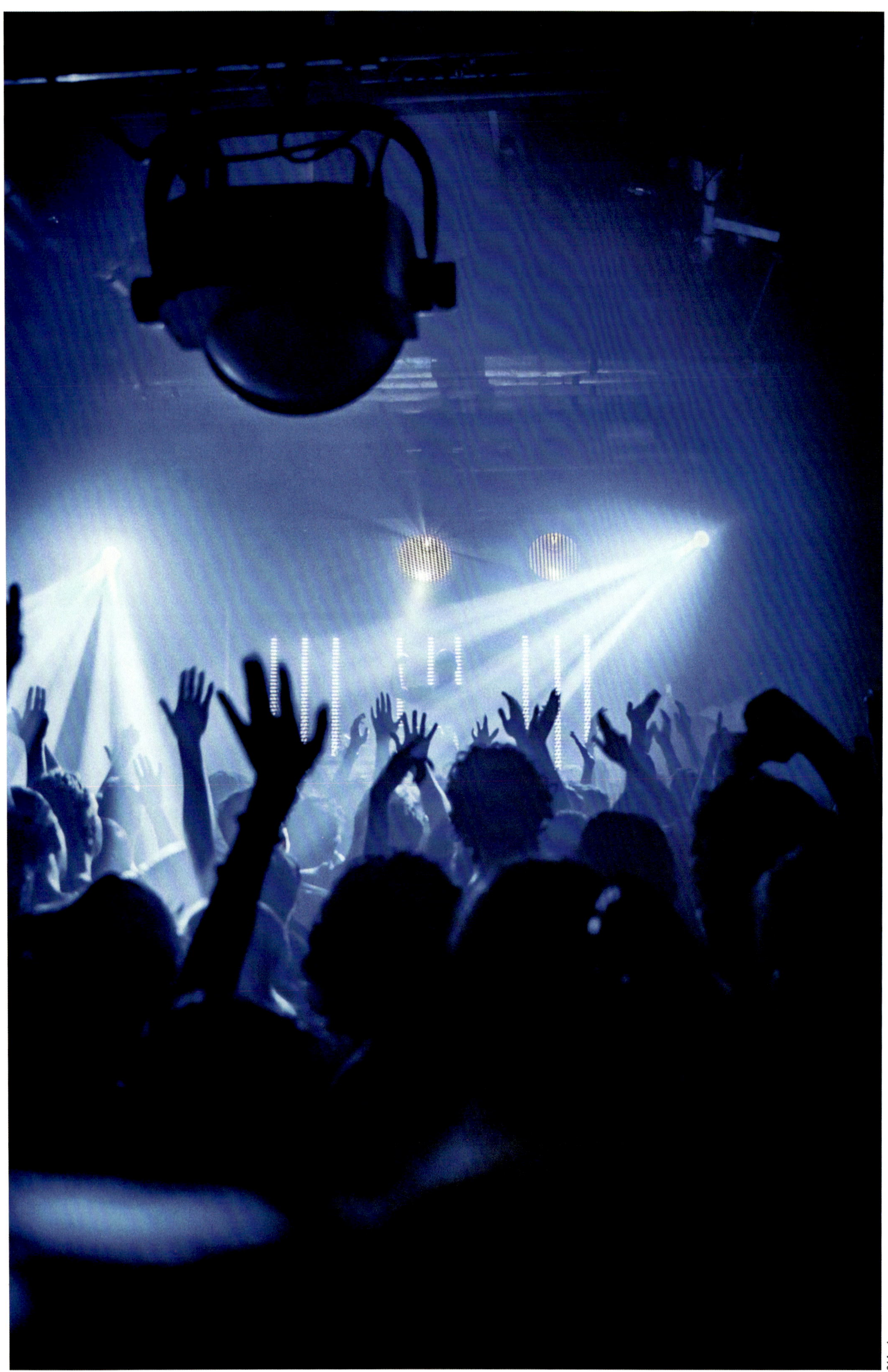

214—1

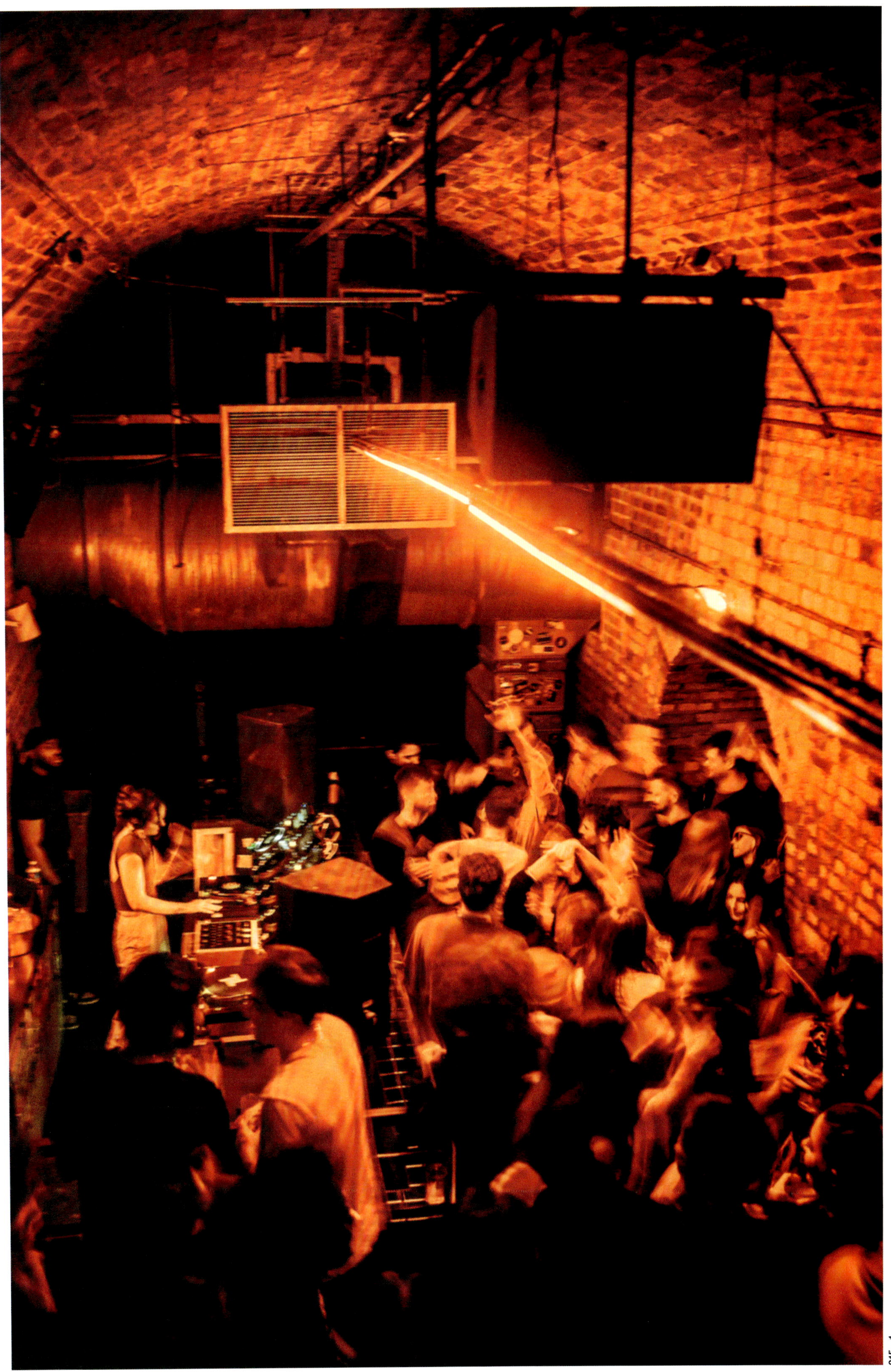

215—1

james lavelle

i first went for site visits to see it being built – i was meeting up with the original team, people like nikki smith, steve blonde, tubbs [tobias 'tubbs' west, guestlist picker and part of the founding team] and, of course, keith – and it was fucking mindblowing to see the ambition of what they were doing. it really felt like there was going to be a big change. of course, club culture in london was really rich and really happening at that point, but there hadn't been a purpose-built venue like that for our generation, i don't think. big events would be in these heritage places like heaven or the astoria, and there were smaller places and things like the blue note, where great things were happening, but nothing like this. with fabric there was this feeling that this whole big building was being built by clubbers, by people who were very invested in club culture – from taste to experience to sound to design, the whole aesthetic of everything, catering for every aspect of clubbing.

when it eventually opened i started djing, doing a mo' wax night once a month. the fridays kind of picked up where blue note had left off initially, with people like talvin singh, gilles peterson and us lot. over time i became very good friends with everybody there, and it was felt that it would be good to get more of a residency culture there – as they were already doing on the saturday with craig and terry, giving this idea of continuity in what they were doing. so FABRICLIVE grew out of that, with me as one of the residents regularly for about five years – and that was an interesting transition, coming out of mo' wax, my international gigs and the clubs i'd been doing like that's how it is at bar rumba and dusted at the blue note. already with that stuff i was maybe playing a little more electronic and contemporary than, say, gilles was – but fabric really made me lean more into that, and then what happened was a sound actually started coming out of the club. saturdays and fridays did keep their identities, but on saturday you had stuff like tyrant and sasha, and some of those hooj choons-related guys like hipp-e and halo, who were incorporating breakbeat into their uk house kind of sound – and it was a sound that was perfect for the club. and, in fact, that then came into the friday a bit, which became a lot more up-tempo breakbeat, just a lot more dancefloor orientated. when i first started there, there was still a lot more hip hop, but that world was changing: it was becoming a lot more backpacker-y, very male dominated – yet here we were with this amazing club, with amazing energy, and technology was changing, records were changing, there was a new crowd coming through … i was twenty-six, twenty-seven when i started playing there, and it was a hugely social thing, and really it changed my dj career. great records were coming through by people like layo and bushwacka! 'the healer' was a record i closed friday on religiously.

i think my FABRICLIVE mix, which launched the series, is a really interesting summation – because it's got one foot in where we were coming from and one foot in what it was changing to. the first half is definitely in that nineties kind of sound, but as it goes on, it gets more four-on-the-floor, which shows that dance energy we were bringing in. not that it ever became formulaic, mind you. there was usually drum'n'bass going on in the other room, then when i was playing we could bring in all sorts. i had south – a live band on mo' wax – play a few times, which was always mental. one of the busiest nights i ever did was me with liam howlett from the prodigy – the queues went right round the corner to turnmills! we put an anti-war benefit together with damon albarn and 3d – that had daft punk, massive attack and the first ever gorillaz show! some pretty mad nights …

i can see why it has lasted. at the time nobody could imagine on that timescale – club culture in the sense we understood it was still basically pretty new! but the thing is, fabric came from a very focused place; it's always maintained a very strong sense of its own identity, curation, of the actual character of the people involved – and it's done that because it's grown like a family business, rather a corporate business. there's a lot of people who've been there for a very long time, and that is absolutely key to any creative business's success, whether that's a record label, a club, a fashion label or whatever. of course it's changed and evolved over time, but just the fact that someone like craig richards is still there shows that the commitment to the club having a culture of its own has borne fruit and is why it has stood the test of time.

ellen allien

fabric for me was a very important club before i ever even played there – because looking from berlin i saw the line-ups and i was wishing and hoping to play there one day. it took many years until i did, but when i finally did – wow. it was amazing; it was such an interesting place, crazy crowd, very good sound system and so friendly and nice as an organisation, i just felt at home. i met cormac there and started playing for their parties on sundays, and, of course, i met judy – on my label bpitch control there's one track made by jay haze called 'lady judy', which is entirely to show her our love and our respect for everything she's done over the years. in fact, he uses it through his fabric.47 mix! and, of course, before that i made a mix cd too – fabric.34 – which i still love today, and this built my relationship even more. fabric was such an important club to me to understand the uk, to switch into the uk music world, and also seeing how the team work together was always an inspiration. most of all, it's about love, though; when i see judy to this day, it's so full of love to see her. i'm very thankful that i could be part of this journey with fabric, and really it is a very, very, very important club!

carl cox

i remember hearing about the concept of the club, it being somewhere you could hear music you wouldn't hear anywhere else, and straight away being interested. and, of course, it's about an experience too: from the moment you walk in, you're walking into a sonic experience – then you go right into the room 1 and get that full bodysonic immersion in the sound. that's something that's only there, the only place in the world you can go and see and hear and feel that is fabric.

so as a dj, when you play your music, you're hearing something new in your music too – and that inspires you to play outside of the box, to let the sound system sing for you. that's what i always associate with it, the sense i'll play 'a fabric set', not just a carl cox set that i'd play in a festival that'd have quite a few of the records you'd know me for. in fabric there's always a feeling of moving things much more forward than you'd play anywhere else – and it's not just me; just about any dj there will end up playing something extraordinary.

also, the people who go down there, they feel at home – everything is about what they want from the club, about what they experience for the whole night. there's none of this 'i'm going to see so-and-so dj, they're playing three till five so i'm getting there at two ready to see them' – you're there because it's fabric, and chances are you're there for the whole journey of the whole thing. it's why i like playing longer sets there – as far as i can remember it's the only place in london i've ever played an eight-hour set.

they weren't intentional eight-hour sets, mind. what happens is, you play up to a certain time and nobody's left – you'll look over to the fabric guys, they'll go, 'well, carry on if you like, they ain't done.' and at that point, where you go beyond the records you were expecting to play, that's where the real magic is. then it's, ok, we're all in this together, and i'm pulling out b-sides of records, tracks i'd wanted to play and couldn't fit in, but now had the space for. you start to feel really connected into it.

and they find people who can do that, consistently. it's fine if places want to book based on who's got a beatport top 10, or who's in the dj mag top 100 djs or whatever, but if you want to find someone who's going to create something really unique in the club, make it into an actual experience, then you've got to have the commitment that fabric have. every week of every year, you can walk through that door, down those stairs and instantly have that experience – whether it's drum'n'bass, whether it's trip hop, whether it's hard techno, whether it's funk and soul. the music prevails – and fabric is really the only club that's stood the test of time, even through all the pushbacks from local government, politicians, covid and everything else. it's never been easy for them, but here they still are – it's incredible!

ben ufo

i remember being in awe of fabric as a club space when i first attended as a visitor. it felt sprawling and labyrinthine, and having grown up going to smaller, single-room clubs, it took some time to adjust to the choose-your-own-adventure possibilities of multiple line-ups and rooms, dark corridors and staircases, and the chance of being separated from your friends; it was hugely exciting, though, and i enjoyed the sense of anonymity that comes with being surrounded by strangers, making new friends in the smoking area, and everyone in your group coming together at the end of the night having had slightly different musical experiences from one another. i realised later, of course, that the space isn't even that huge – but the sound, lighting and general vibe when it's busy all contribute to the feeling that you're entering this whole other dimension.

i think fabric was well positioned, with its three rooms of different sizes, to represent every different shade of london's dance music scene – the main-room acts would have to bring the necessary numbers in to fill the space, but they had two more rooms to experiment and get creative with. sometimes each of the three rooms would feel like a totally different club, and there wouldn't be much of a merging between them, but i think the club is at its strongest when they all feel integrated into a whole, and people are roaming freely between them. you could end up hearing loads of exciting new artists in room 3 having bought a ticket for a specific act in room 1, or vice versa.

hessle audio was one of many labels that shaun roberts and his co-promoter dave gamble saw potential in very early, and gave over responsibility for the third room. it was a big thing for us at the time, and they really left us to it and gave us creative freedom. we really loved it and learnt a lot, and by the end of our long residency, there we were, curating the line-ups across the entire space and headlining room 1 ourselves. the combination of the space having all these different possibilities and potential formats, and the trust and faith that everyone at the club had in their artists, meant that we could grow into it gradually, and i'm not sure there's another club in london where that would have been possible. this is the sort of dynamic that allows scenes to flourish in a longer-term way, and that's unusual in a world where things are generally more geared towards short-term impact.

i've got too many memories of playing the club to single out any in particular, but i'll always be proud to have played alongside such a wildly varied range of artists at our own residency parties and at the fabric birthdays. at fabric we were able to throw parties where kassem mosse would trip everyone out playing live and equinox would close us out with ninety minutes of tearing amens,

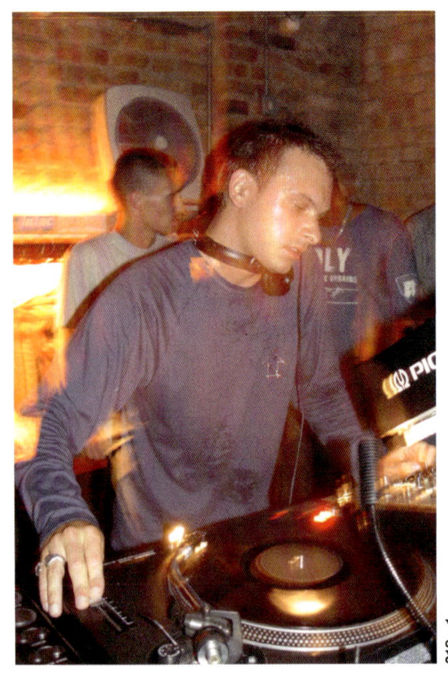
218—1

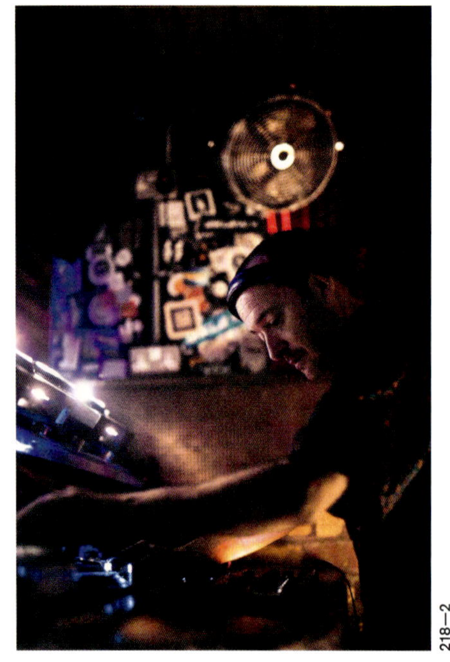
218—2

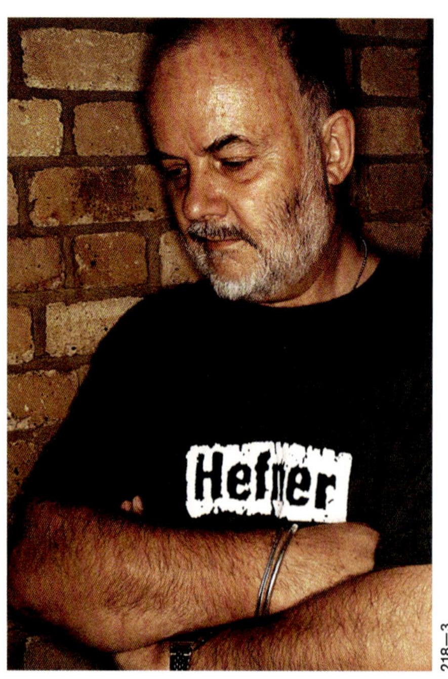

218—3

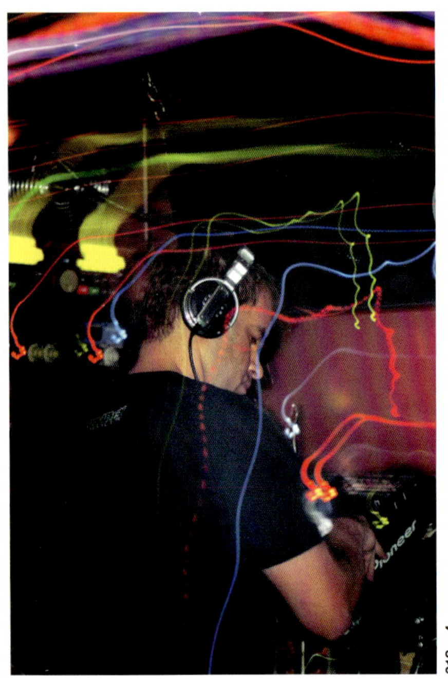
218—4

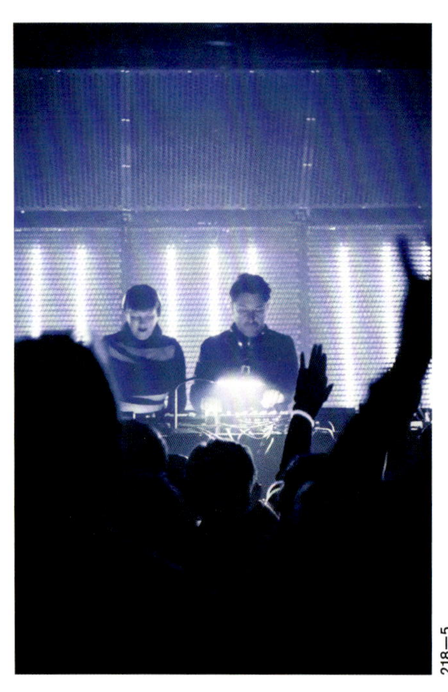
218—5

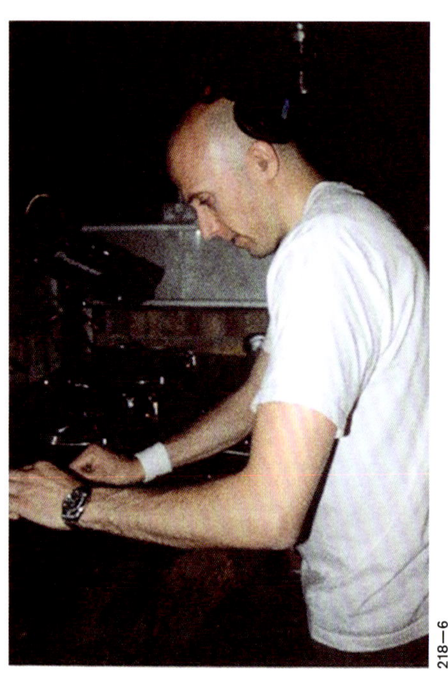
218—6

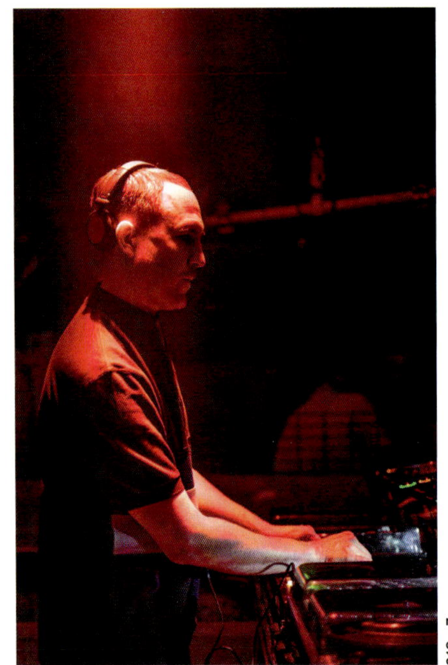
218—7

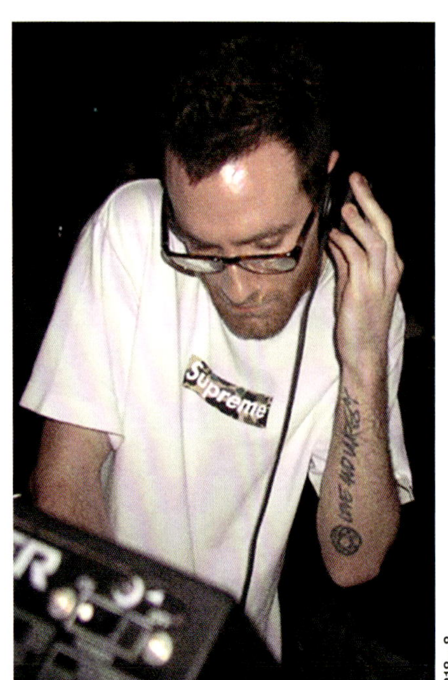

218—8

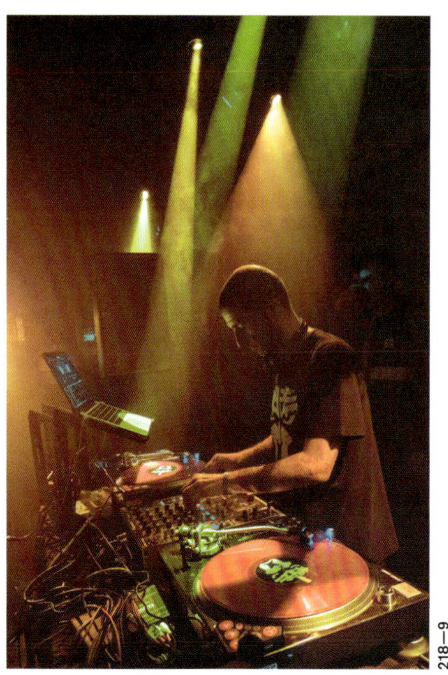
218—9

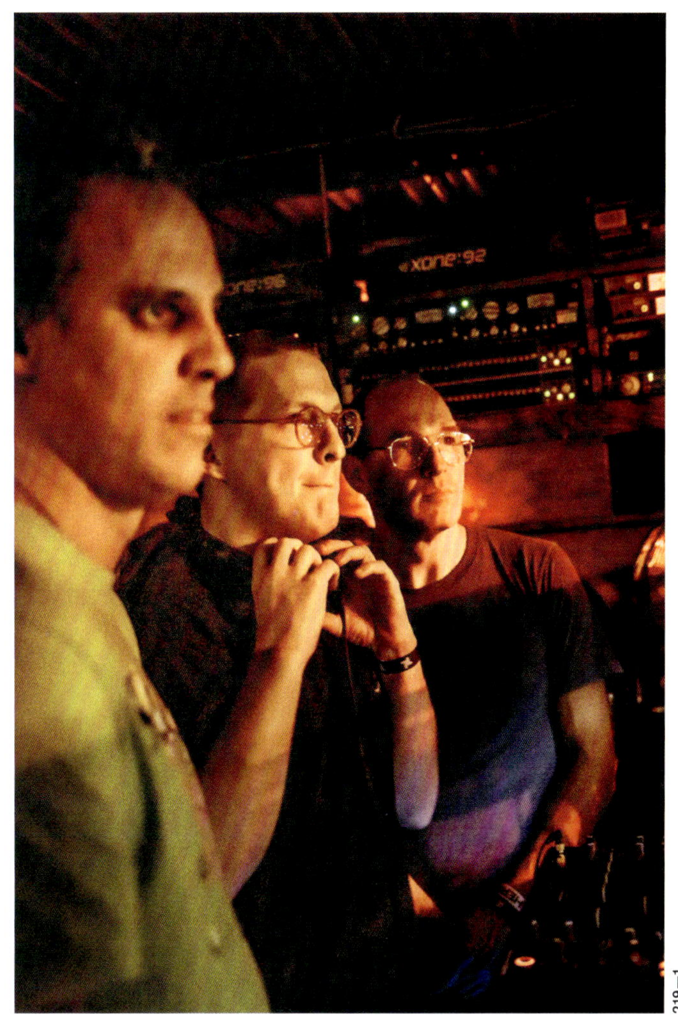

219—1

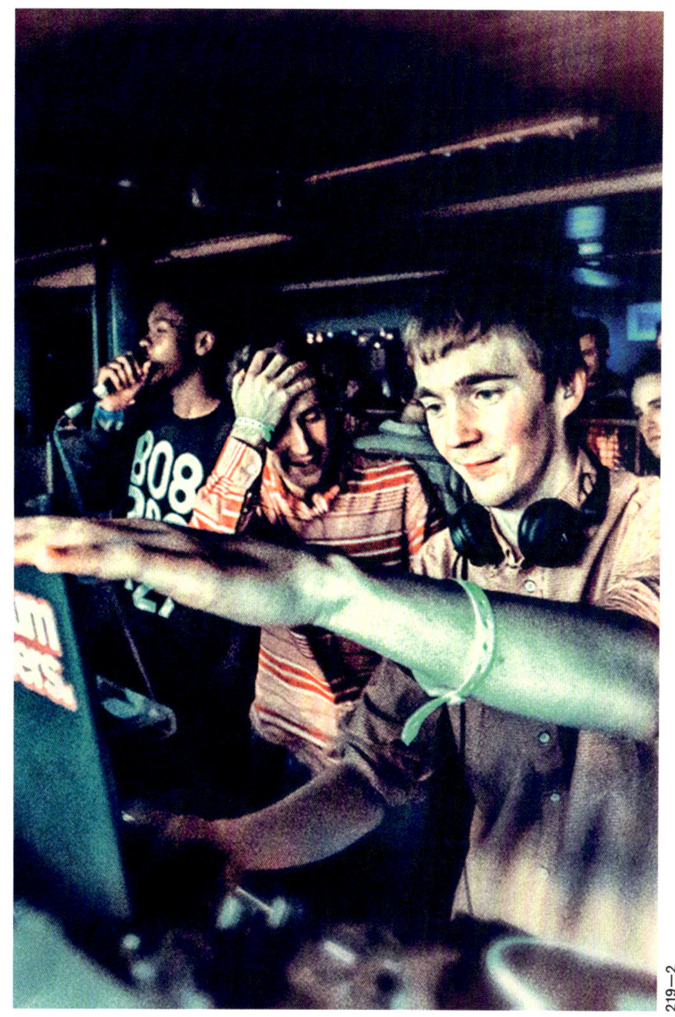

219—2

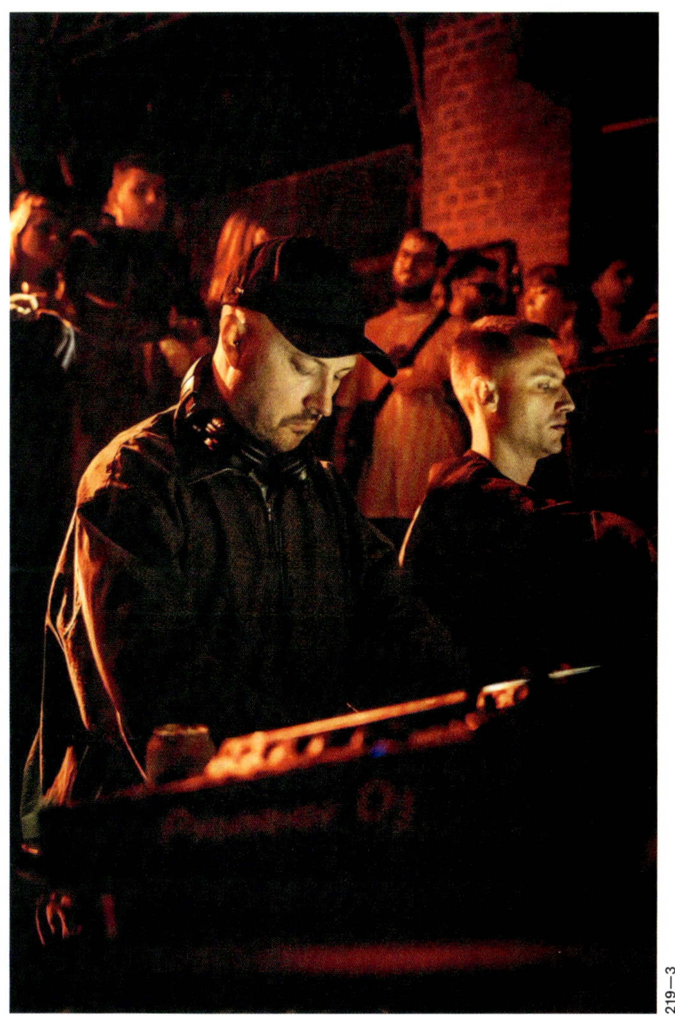

219—3

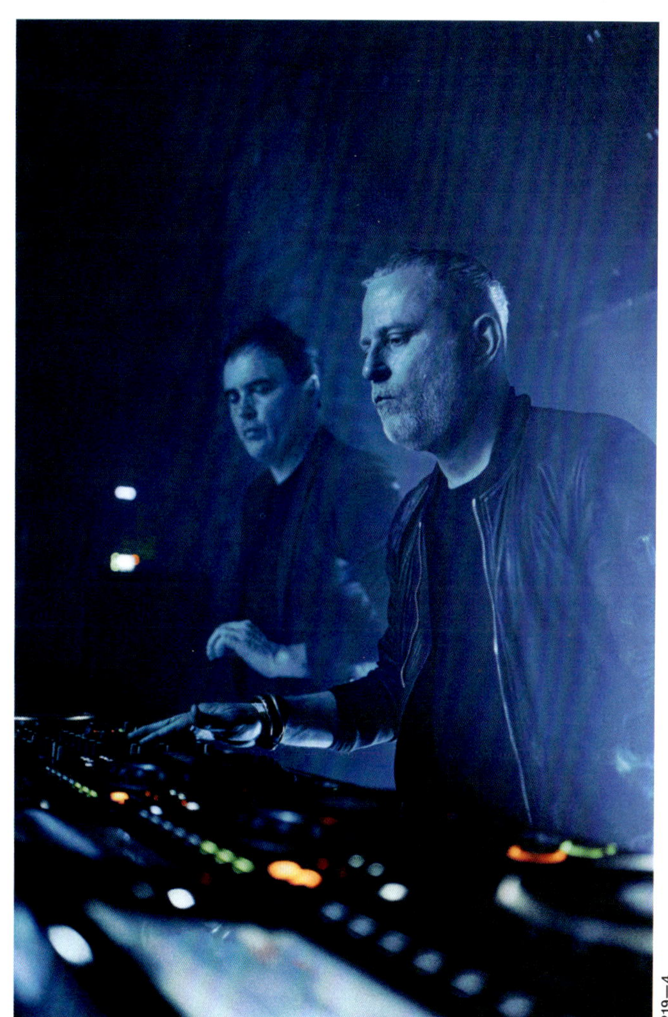

219—4

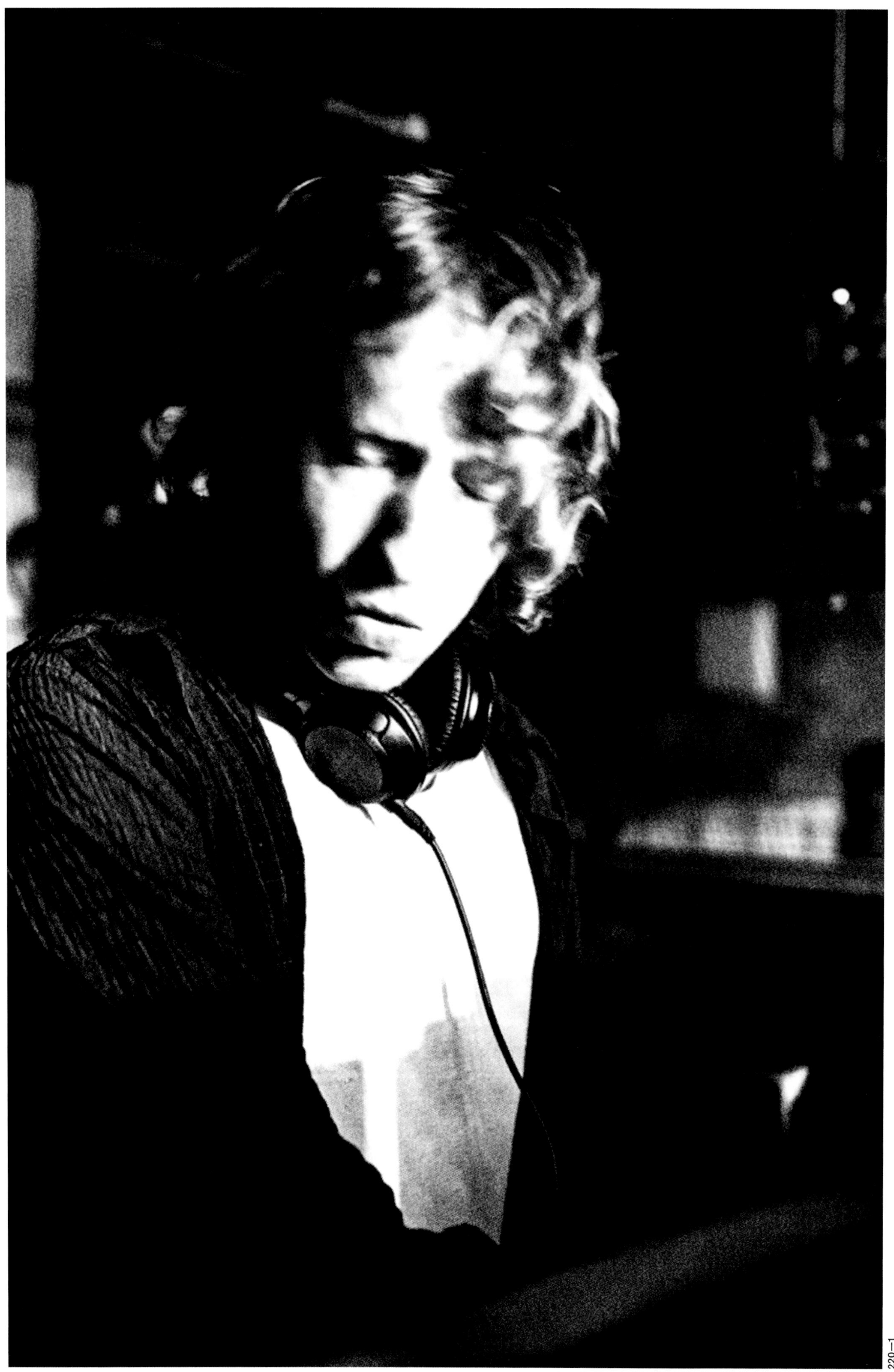

220—1

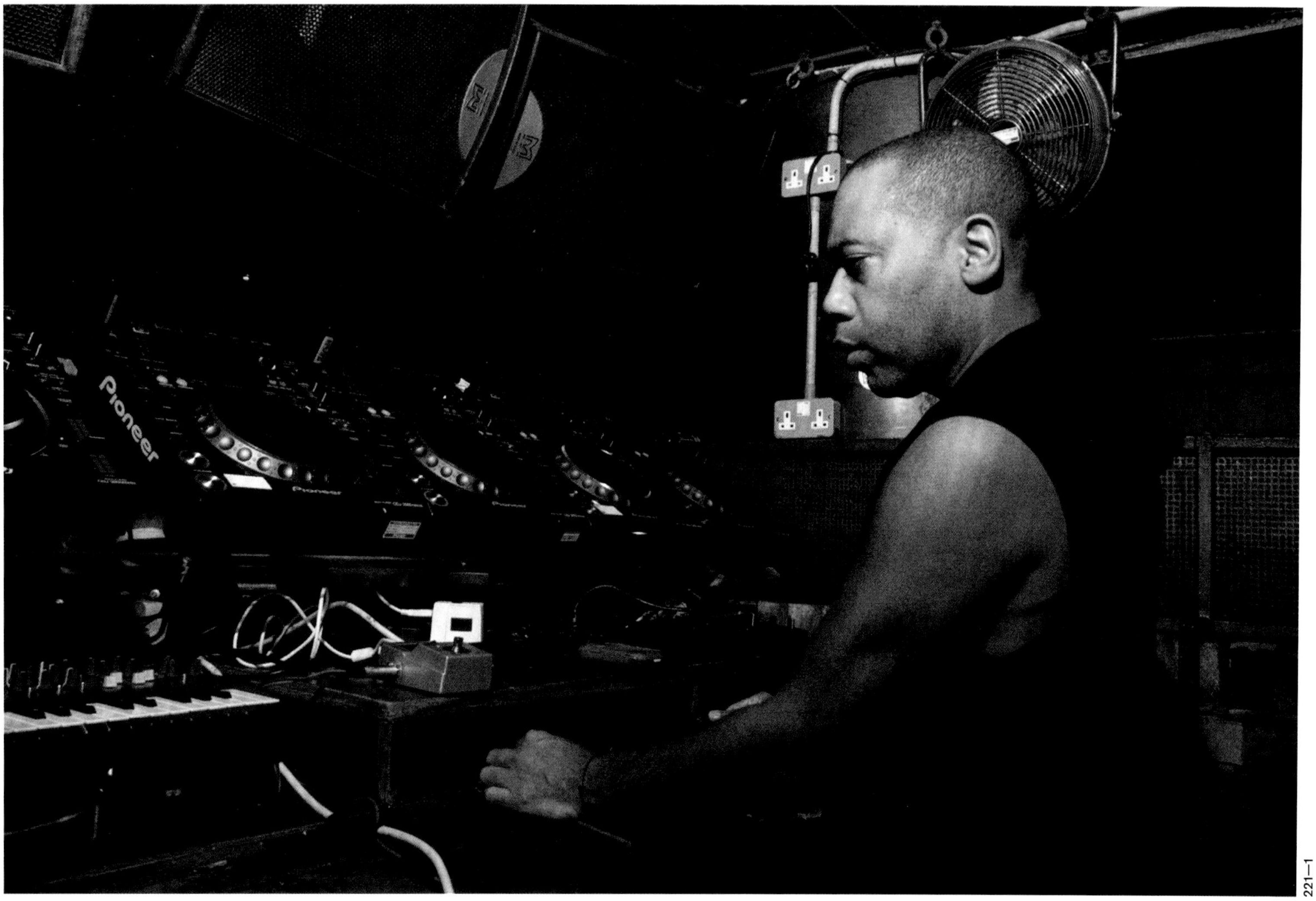

221—1

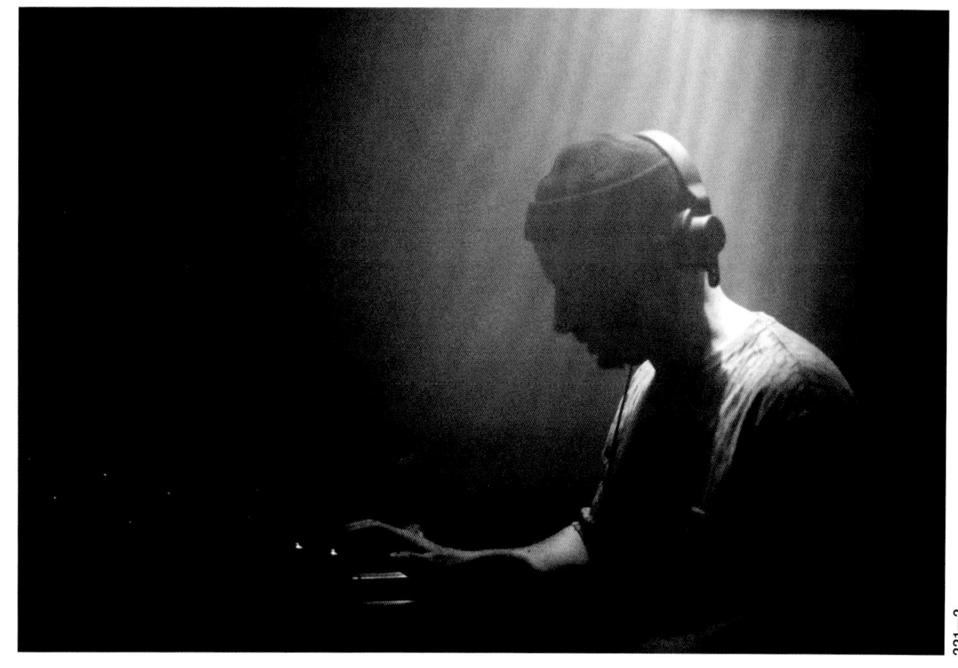

221—2

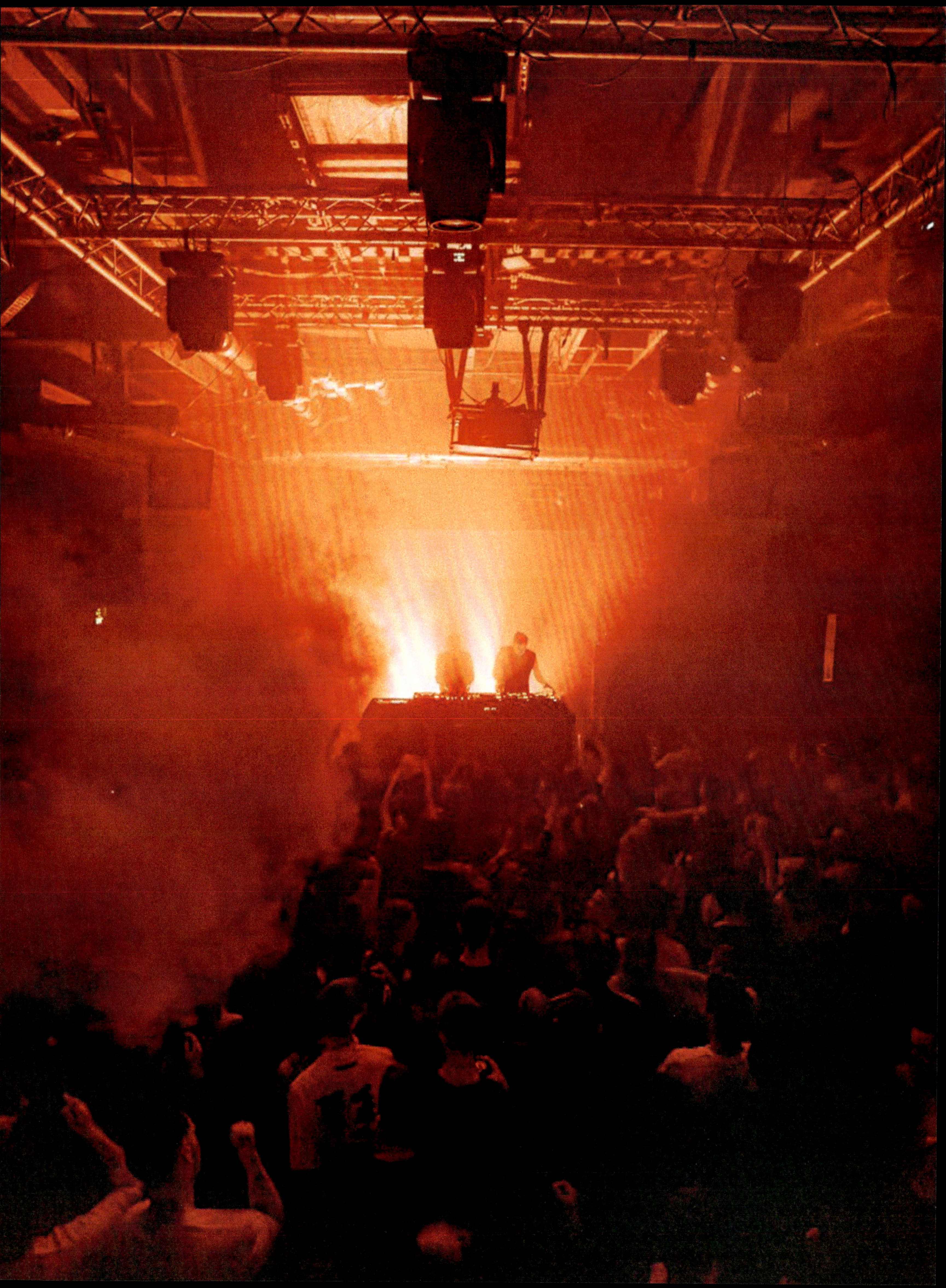

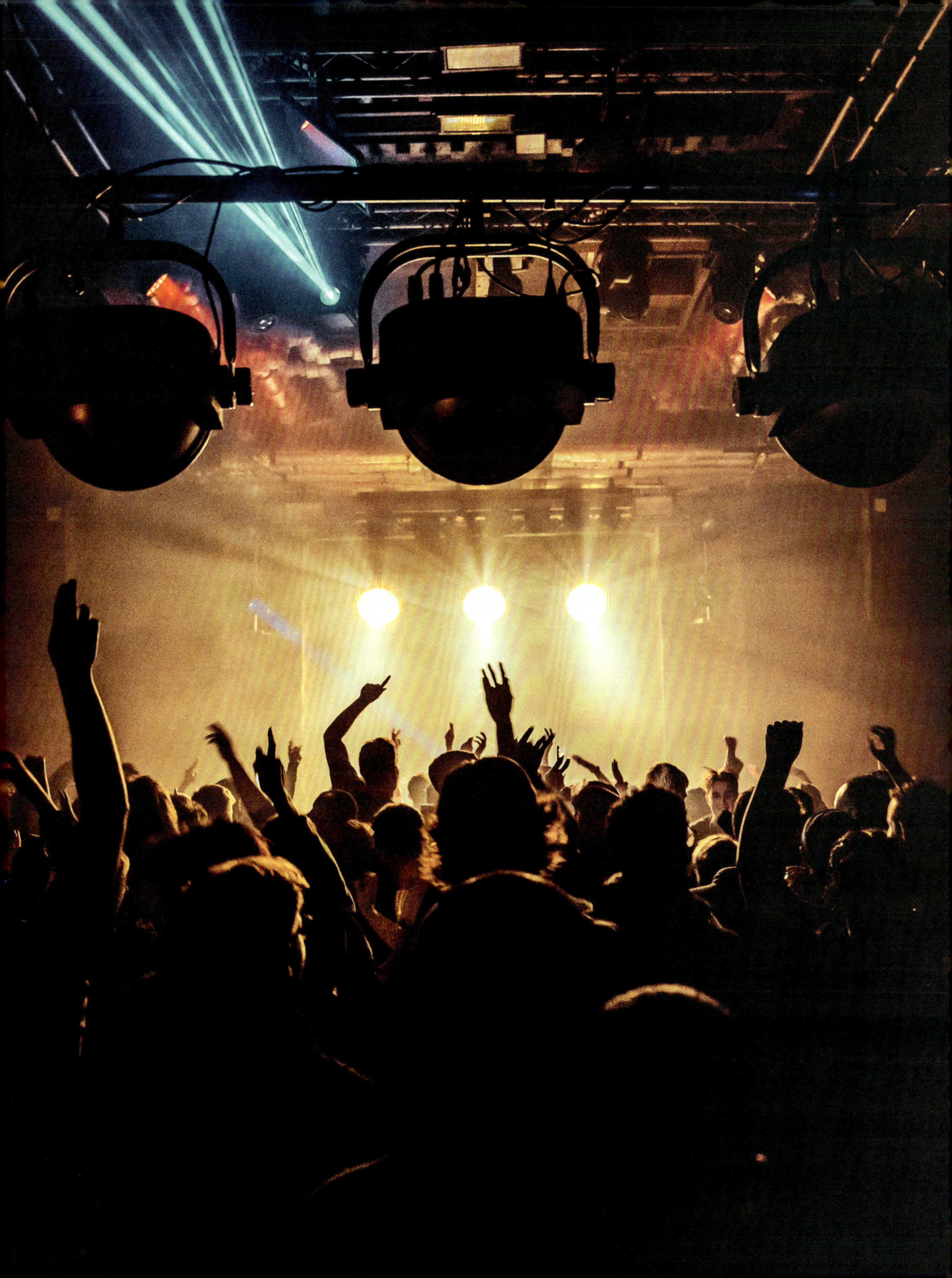

long before that sort of variation in a club night was considered normal. where else could you dj next to todd edwards and karizma one night, and villalobos & raresh the next? ⌖

tom rowlands (chemical brothers)

fabric has been hugely important to us, both for giving us amazing nights out and as a place to listen to new music we're making. hearing ideas you're developing on that incredible sound system is always a buzz. from the first time we played there, we immediately loved the venue. partly because of the spaces, but mainly because of the passion of all the amazing people who run it – music lovers and enthusiasts all, none more so than the much-missed, much-loved shaun roberts. so much attention to detail goes on behind the scenes at fabric. once the doors open, that attention translates into so much wild abandon that takes place on the dancefloor – every single time, without fail. ⌖

margaret dygas

shaun and i were flatmates for about two years. we became good friends, sister–brother kind of vibe; he was such an easy-going, lovely being who helped me so much. i really miss him and his cheerful spirit. i met everyone at fabric through shaun – he was doing friday's promotion and asked me to help at the door doing tickets. later, i was asked to help at the office now and again. it's how i met the fabric family and got to hang out with judy more and more – we had met a few months prior at another big club, home, where we both briefly worked. fabric was the hotspot when it first opened. everyone was curious about that state-of-the-art sound system with bass installed in the floor – this was really the talk of the town.

since i was mainly working for shaun on fridays, i was not very clued up with saturday line-ups. my clubbing background was influenced by the new york scene, which was very different from uk and europe, so saturdays were a bit of a riddle to me. fridays had hip hop, drum'n'bass, dubstep and so on, which is what i related to more at that time. but then i remember the first time hearing craig and lee [burridge] at their tyrant night – it was the usual lock-in, a big group of us on that dancefloor surrounded you, as if swimming in sound, a literally mind-altering experience. tyrant's no shoes, no cake is the album of that time, for me anyway, engraved in my soul for ever. i must have played it a million times.

as far as i'm aware, fabric was one of the first clubs to put so much emphasis on acoustics; sound engineers were doing rounds with portable tablets, continuously checking everywhere so that it sounded as best as possible – this made a big impression on me and gave me a passion for sound quality, which i value and am obsessed with to this day.

so now it has been a few months – well, it feels like it, time flies when having fun – since the opening, and there are so many memories, it's difficult to round them up in a short space. what matters most are the strong friendships we have built over this time.

judy and craig are two of the most inspiring people in my life. i cherish their honesty and share their passion for musical experience to give to everyone who is willing to join; they've inspired many on so many levels, including myself. the influence is beyond words.

music is frequency transmitted through air or aether, which has a great effect on our body, mind and spirit and on our wellbeing long term. sharing this natural phenomena should be with the best equipment possible, for the spirit and to show love by showing care for those who want to not only dance, but be able to feel music, maybe just listen in the corner somewhere and be able to hear every detail. it can be like a meditation session for some when sound is set up with care – with ears in mind. (if you have never seen how ears function, go take a look, because whoever designed them is an absolute genius!)

music is an international language, and fabric has been a great teacher for everyone who gave it their precious time to come in and experience something special. longevity and quality go hand in hand. to the entire fabric family: thank you for all those inspiring once-in-a-lifetime moments! love wins. ⌖

ben klock

honestly, when i think of the uk and london, i think of fabric. that's how much of an impact this place has. it's the first thing that comes to my mind. fabric also opened the doors to the uk for me a long time ago. i remember being really nervous the first years when i played at fabric, and even until this day i feel some of that, even though now i would call it more excitement than nervousness. it also feels a bit like a london home for me every time i come back. to have this strong support over the years in london always meant something unique and special to me.

sound-wise, room 1 was an interesting learning curve for me, since it's suited best for a crossover between house and techno, so there is a lot of room to experiment and find the groove in between the genres. i can't really name an individual special moment, but i can say that the most special memories i have are with extended sets where you really find the connection with the crowd and you feel the flow of energy between the dj booth and dancefloor. i also remember an endless back-to-back set with marcel [dettmann] in room 2 – i think it was a fabric birthday; that night was just pure magic. fabric is just such a longstanding name, an institution in the best sense of the word – after so many years a still amazingly well-curated club with devoted people behind it, always welcoming the artists in a way that make you feel special, and of course those fantastic sound systems. nothing is random. here electronic music means something. ⯮

nina kraviz

fabric has transcended its identity as just a club for me; it's been nothing short of an institution that has served as a gateway to the world of electronic music for many. it has introduced a wealth of great music to its audience. one of my very earliest experiences at fabric is etched in my memory like it happened yesterday. i performed in room 3, but before my set i went to listen to shackleton's performance. he has always been one of my favourite artists, and witnessing his live magic was a dream come true. his orchestration of every sound, weaving spells'n'drums into a voodooist symphony with that fabric sound system, was truly mesmerising. we also had an artist dinner before, and it was a one-of-a-kind experience to be in sam's presence.

when i recorded my fabric mix, i feel i was in my prime as an artist; i'd really found my own distinctive sound. it was a heady blend of acid techno that i still hold dear. around that time, i was just launching two labels, трип and galaxiid, and had a treasure trove of incredible music at my fingertips – old and new, released and unheard. i was so thrilled and excited to share my vision with people. some titles were rare, and there were concerns about licensing certain tracks. fortunately, everything fell into place seamlessly thanks to everyone at fabric's work. the cherry on top was the approval of a very special track by afx. experiencing that final nod of approval brought such a satisfying sense of completeness to the entire process. ⯮

jme

fabric holds all my early memories of raving. you can go to a club and you can party, you can go to a club for a showcase, you can go to a club for an event – but when i went to fabric in my early days there, i was raving. i'm there, and i'm spiritually connected to the music. all different music too – you go there for a certain tune from a certain dj in a certain room, but you end up wandering and experiencing new music and it's magical. really, it's a magical experience. it's weird, and it's magical. so fabric has been my barometer for all other venues. it's in the heart of london, you're mixing and mingling with anyone and everyone, you'll always bump into someone you hadn't seen for a time or you didn't know was going to be there or whatever. literally the whole thing is an experience, from the moment i pull up outside and park up, the fabric experience starts from outside. from that second, you're on london streets, those narrow little roads with double yellow lines, big skyscrapers on one side, barbican area, old london in the market buildings – but then you go from that into the most mind-opening musical surroundings. that's an experience that can't be replicated. and that's just going as a raver – but right to today, for me to be part of people's experiences too, i can't show nothing but gratitude for that. the fact people now have experiences like mine, but they're coming out to fabric and hearing my music and my vision and my creation – that's crazy. ⯮

jeff mills

london for dance music has always been one of those most special places. there are only so many on the planet like london, like new york, where as a professional dj and musician you really have to respect the understanding of the audiences. and the clubs in london that ran a regular programme – looking from the outside these clubs have always been very, very important for dance music. all of these clubs are an important barometer of what's going on in europe, and for fabric to do that so consistently over the years makes it special. playing there has always been something high-riding, very special, something you have to think about and prepare for before you stepped in the place. from when i first came to london, for places like club uk and lost, then the end, i knew these were audiences who connected deeply – they were places that i could test out new material, and fabric became one of those places.

the design and architecture of fabric was always exceptional. in terms of people really feeling the frequencies of the music, it makes the music more convincing – and then the visual aspect of it was vital too. you always felt that you were with the audience, not detached and away from it, looking at them like a one-dimensional picture. the architectural thinking of the place meant you were always inside the experience, and because of that – because of the level where you are – you could see the same amount of light they could see, you could feel the same amount of bass they could feel. and all of that affects the way you select and programme music; the reaction always influences what you can do next, and you're very close to that reaction. so i remember the nights reaching a very high point because of the response a dj could get in that set-up. not, of course, that other set-ups and other layouts can't work in their own way, but there's just something very, very special about being with the audience, being in the motion of them – and that comes, in my opinion, from a lot of knowledge from the people behind it and a lot of thought put into it. and it worked! ⯮

john digweed

every major city around the world has their legendary nightclubs, and for london it's fabric. i've been very lucky indeed to have played at the club pretty much every year since it opened. playing room 1 is a dj's dream, as you are in the thick of it on the dancefloor but just shielded enough to focus on your music. the dj booth is perfectly positioned and the monitors are crystal clear.

my bedrock showcases at the club, as well as my open-to-close sets, have so many amazing memories for me as a dj.

when fabric opened it went against the grain and did things on its own terms; especially, it had a reliably incredible music policy. that made it stand out from all the other clubs, and it became a weekly destination for clubbers around the world, as you could just know as a punter that all the djs who had been booked would deliver musically. the attention to detail in the actual experience of being in there has always been one of its strengths, too. i remember climbing down a ladder to look at the club when it was being built and being shown around this vast building site, trying to visualise how it would eventually look, but even after that, the finished project blew my mind, as it was so well thought-out.

i also love how it has always been maintained to keep it looking just like the first day it opened. it's so easy for clubs to let things slip, but fabric always took real care to make sure the customers got the best experience possible. to keep a club relevant for a few years is hard enough, but to stay at the top for twenty-five years is an incredible achievement – i think that's really worth paying attention to, because it just proves if you do things right consistently, then people will support you. it's evolved, of course, but in the way that you would expect fabric to do: with class and style. london's nightlife is such a different beast now, with six-thousand-people day parties and huge warehouse events on an almost weekly basis, but fabric has upped its game to meet that challenge and still just consistently delivers really strong and diverse line-ups that match anything else that's going on in london – and that's why, after twenty-five years, it really is still as relevant as it was when it first opened.

blackdown (keysound recordings)

the way i see clubland, fabric are the biggest good guys – and have sustained it impressively for years. at the base of the pyramid there's many small event communities putting on nights because they love the music. money would be a nice bonus, but let's be honest, the economics don't work. at the very peak are a small number of large events run by corporations, where the focus is on scale and profits – this drives commercial dj selections that rarely move musical scenes onwards. in this framing, fabric are the biggest of the grassroots good guys, as big as it gets while consistently making musical history. and that's why every dj always wants to play there.

skream

the first time i ever went to fabric was 2001, fwd>> was hosting room 3, hatcha was playing. i was fifteen and i hadn't been to a big club, ever, so i didn't understand ravewear. i got dressed up in a rollneck jumper, trousers, shoes and a trench coat – and, of course, turned up and everyone's in sweaty t-shirts and whatever. i remember it too because my brother said he had to go cos he had a headache, and i found out later he'd left with two birds … but really the reason i remember it is because it was one of the first times fwd>> had hosted a room in another space, and i'll never forget one of my tracks getting a reload and mc juiceman pointing at me through the crowd and saying, 'that kid's going to be the future!' in fact, i think it was the first time i even heard one of my productions in a club full stop. and literally the rest is history! my relationship with fabric over the years is well documented, and it holds a very, very special place in my heart. one birthday weekend i was dressed as a policeman-slash-clown – i think i got the bottom of the barrel of the fancy-dress box there – and that was the first time i ever played disco in fabric. judy said did i want to go and play? i was in no state, really, but i did it, and showed people i could … once again room 3 changing things for me! there's the iconic skream and benga shows, there's been so many, doing so many different things, it's just fully part of my life.

saoirse

i used to travel over from dublin to fabric, purely to go there as a punter. it was one of the absolute foremost reasons i decided to move to london and pursue a life in music, because of the experiences i had there. what makes fabric unique is the human side. i've never really worked at a club that has a group of people who are that committed to the space. there's people who've been there for so long that they're, excuse the pun, part of the fabric of the place. you really feel that when you go and experience a night there; you feel the dedication and family feel, it's part of everything, and it feels like people are there for the right reasons. i have too many favourite nights to even remember, but one that comes out on top is when i did my all night long in room 1 very recently, finished off with tiga & zyntherius 'sunglasses at night', and i put my sunglasses on, and as the vocals came in – 'i wear my sunglasses at night' – everyone on the dancefloor got their sunglasses out and put them on and sang along, and it was a very special end-of-the-night moment.

helena hauff

the night daniel avery invited me to play with dopplereffekt is the one that truly stuck in my memory. i'm pretty sure it was my first time playing at fabric. i played after dopplereffekt, and i was very, very nervous, with gerald donald being one of my idols. they played this amazing set and then just left the stage, but the music kept playing. it was just their machines left doing the job. i loved that image, and it was a perfect start for me – i had a great time djing after that. i've had so many great nights since then;

for me fabric is so unique because of the people that run it, and their incredible passion, enthusiasm and dedication. it's not just the club, but the label they run is fantastic. and it's honestly so easy to work with them. you can tell they are doing it for the love of the music and that shows; it's been a pleasure working with them every time. it's become such an institution to promote underground music i couldn't imagine london without it!

midfield general

from the off fabric felt different … there was a level of love and care that permeated everything they did. from the sound to the security and the bars to bathrooms.

it very quickly felt like home and, of course, shaun roberts played a big part in that. for the boutique it was really important that we had freedom not just to book a wide and varied range of guests, but to be able to find the perfect spot for them. and for me as a dj it was the perfect club; i genuinely didn't mind which room i found myself in at whichever time, as it satisfied all my different types of sets. warm up, back room or full-on tops off. it was an utter joy.

the amalgamation of soundz

at least two years before fabric opened, keith told us 'you guys are gonna be part of our residence set-up in my new club in east london.'

fast fwd a year or two, keith phones me at the shop (few mobiles and no internet to speak of at that time) and asks what we (mark and i) were doing the following evening. rendez-vous at charterhouse street: he wants to show us, along with his partner cameron, the site of his new big project. on go the hard hats, hi-vis jkts and down we go….

we climbed up a ladder in what is now known as room 3 to get a better vantage point and keith said 'this is your room when we open.' after that, i realised that this maverick, proud and sensitive london irishman is a man of his word and we never looked back…

in the eleven-plus years we were residents at fabric (btw, we played our first set the second saturday after opening), we must have played more than sixty times in and around those hallowed walls. and twenty-one years ago we released fabric cd12 to much aplomb including: time out compilation of 2003.

biiig papa love to nicky, judy, shaun (r.i.p), scotty and the lighting/sound teams who always went that extra mile for us. though we have not played there for a while, we feel great pride in having been involved (in some small way) in the development of one of the world's greatest underground clubs that NEVER pandered to the mainstream.

long may she reign xxxx

scratch perverts

we played the club for around fourteen years, once a month, starting on the second weekend of the club being open. we always felt incredibly blessed to have had fabric's support for so long. no more so than when curating our beatdown events. the club could have easily pulled the line-ups together themselves, but instead chose to curate the nights alongside us, insisting we shoot for the stars when picking the artists we wanted to play. so we did and from memory everyone said yes! it really spoke to the desire that artists across all genres had to play at fabric.

the ian brown stories have been told many times, but i remember a night where we shared the stage in room 1 with dj premier, an artist we had looked up to for so many years. we played after him and he stood behind us on stage as we started our set. i must have looked over my shoulder, nervously, at least a hundred times, hoping that we had the great man's approval. some whoops, cheers and back slaps from him said that we did. shaun told me that earlier in the evening, premier had respectfully declined a dinner invitation from the club, asking instead for a bucket of chicken. a real hero of ours and humble with it.

it's no secret that i, personally, spent a lot of time at the club. whenever you walked through the doors, the world outside ceased to exist and all that you needed was waiting for you inside. there's an art to making someone feel that welcome and no one possessed all of those qualities more than shaun. it was just who he was. i struggle to remember a time when i thought of shaun as someone i worked with. he was always just a friend and i miss him as such.

bradley zero

it's not just one thing that makes fabric unique – it's so many different elements coming together. the thing about it for me is that it's the gateway, it's like ground zero for people who come to the city and want to engage in this electronic music late-night culture. it was for me! when i first moved to london in 2006, it was on the top of my list of places to visit. but i think that, because it's so well known, people can become a bit complacent about its importance in the puzzle, and they shouldn't. there's always something newer or more underground – yet fabric has genuinely stood the test of time in the way that few other places have. so as much as it's the entry point for a lot of people, it's still pushing things forward, it's still putting on line-ups and bringing people through that are on the cutting edge, and it straddles so many echelons of our culture.

and the sound system in room 1, oh my god. i have to do a pilgrimage to fabric at least once a year to remind myself just how good that room sounds. there's really very few other places in the world i can think of that come near to it for the purist representation of music in

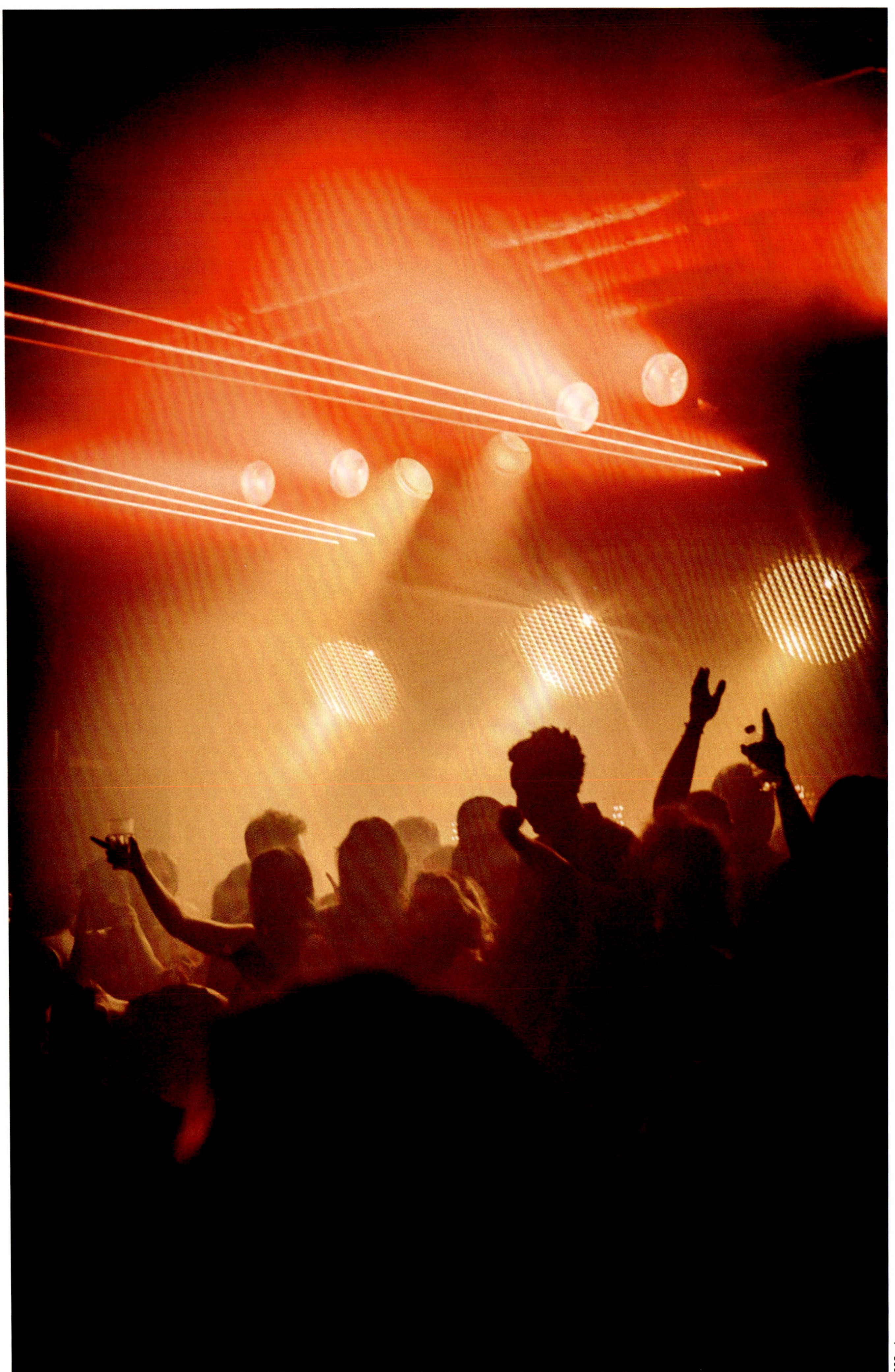

228—1

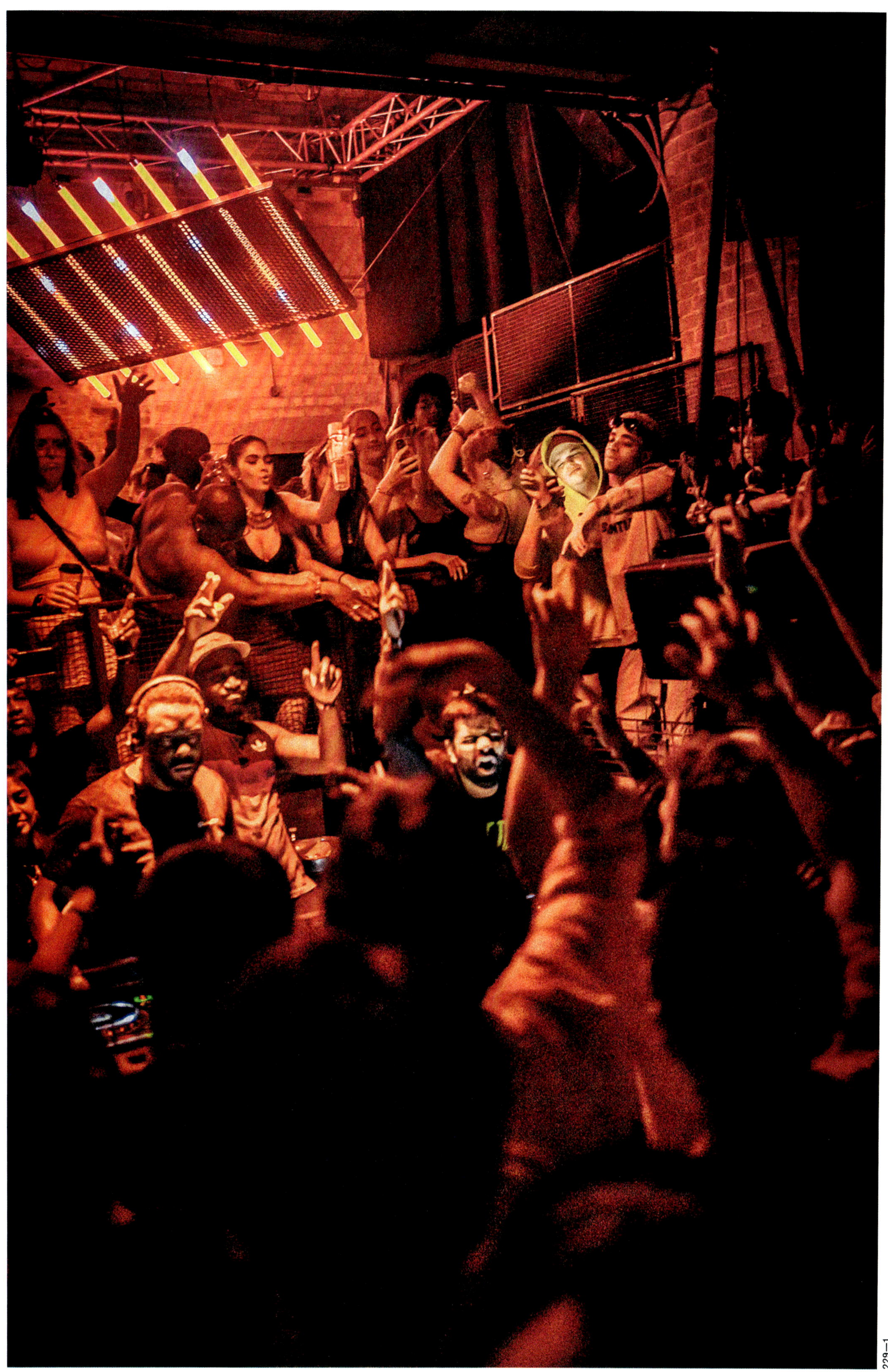

229—1

a club environment. it's nuts. most of my greatest memories have been of seeing ricardo on a sunday afternoon on the birthday weekend. i'll have breakfast, cycle up to farringdon at 8am to catch ricardo and just get taken to another plane. this is the peak for me. but there've been so many other great times too. we did rhythm section there very recently, and we brought in neue grafik and the orii crew to do a live jazz warm-up in room 1, really early, 8pm to 11, then we continued with the regular programming. and it was the most wholesome, community kind of vibe you could imagine, it was truly beautiful.

luke slater

i've seen clubs and venues come and go over my career – especially in london. yet fabric not only still exists, it's still rightly world famous and still pushes music forward. it's an absolute techno icon of london worldwide, and, of course, judy is the ultimate dancefloor queen. out of all the times i've played there, some unforgettable highlights were them hosting planetary assault systems live as a proper onstage band in room 2 in 2006, and when we used special 3d mesh screen visuals for my 'the messenger' live show. they were always among the very first to host those new shows. and to top it off, i met my wife at fabric!

damian lazarus

when i think of clubbing in london, playing behind the metal grill inside the main room dj booth is absolutely the first thought my memory opens up. not being able to see anyone's face in the darkness, but feeling the energy of that incredible, sprung dancefloor, technicians adjusting the sound using ipads, being squashed by friends and other djs packed into the space, judy dancing her ass off… it's a blissful thought, actually. the regular lock-ins when we'd close the club and keep playing to our closest mates, the tiny smoke-filled green room with people laying on top of each other, the early sets of tyrant, the launch party of my debut album, zoning out in the corner of room 2, ricardo playing thirty-minute tracks during our back-to-back session, the months i took to perfect my mix for fabric 54. the more i think about it, the more i realise it's incredible how much of my clubbing history is wrapped up inside this one building in farringdon, and more incredible still to think it feels just as fresh playing there today as it did over twenty years ago.

jumpin jack frost

the very opening weekend of fabric we had planet v in there, so i've got a very special connection to the place – it's almost spiritual – and i still feel that to this day. from that opening it was a state-of-the-art venue, cool layout, under-floor speakers and everything, but also the staff were second to none. even up to now, the staff are the best – they accommodate artists, they're very kind, very gracious, and just very professional. things like that make a big, big difference.

benga

fabric became the tastemaker club of clubs globally. it was a superclub in london, but it had everything to make it great for underground music. it just seemed to understand how to host parties – with people roaming from room to room and every one of them curated amazingly. fabric was special in build and sound, but it's definitely worth pointing out that the spirit of the fridays, which meant so much to us in dubstep as we broke out, owed a lot to shaun roberts, who placed the music and the people together beautifully.

kode9

it's good to have solid sound right across three rooms, but also important is that fabric is built like a tank. my greatest memory is definitely hyperdub's tenth birthday in 2014: being able to showcase the full spectrum of the label and have three distinct parties with separate vibes across the venue was great.

flowdan

fabric is one of the last of a dying breed. it's a venue that still encompasses the real raving values, and it's a place where, if you're a raver or mc or dj, you can still get into your vibe and stay in your vibe and not really be distracted by any of the other bullshit that really goes into what clubbing is about nowadays. undistracted, pure, unadulterated vibing. you can just vibe.

cooly g

about fabric … yeah, it's like a movie to me. it reminds me of some science fiction. when you get inside, you've got all these different ways to get somewhere. just the way it's laid out is all exciting, it's all dramatic. i think the first time i went, i came in through the front and it was, 'wowwww …' then the last couple of shows, i've got to go through the back, so each way is a new experience. but the sound is the best thing of all – every time i know i'm going to perform there i get so excited because of that sound. i know what i do is going to sound fine there. and yeah, i enjoy being in that movie. i don't know what the movie's called, but i love it!

dave clarke

the very fact that they have been around for a quarter of a century is in itself impressive, but to survive an ever-changing scene and still stand for quality, and not change that stance for twenty-five years truly is something to be applauded. so many events have become watered down over the years, scaled up and lost integrity along the way, but fabric is special in the fact it has been a caretaker of counterculture and i feel very privileged to have been a part of this journey since the very beginning. i think room 2 has always been my favourite bass cavern in the world.

the sound system has always been top notch and clubbers come there to dance – but what i like most of all is that it is not just the clubbers that dance; judy would also come down at the end of the evening and dance too most nights i played, and that is very special. singular favourite moments are hard to pick out, as the sheer consistency makes that quite a moot point!

andy c

back when it opened, the term being thrown around was 'superclub', but the first time i got down there i thought, well, this isn't what i consider an archetypal commercial club at all. this is an underground haven! it's a haven for our music. i've told this story a lot, but it bears repeating: i played room 2 at first, and i'd played a few times over about six months and didn't even realise there was a room 1. that maze-like set-up, so easy to get lost in and just hang out in the arches and walkways and stairs, meant i just didn't see it. then one night someone went, 'd'you want to go and check out room 1?' turned out there was someone massive in there, i think it was the chems – so i came through and, oh my god, there was this whole other world to it. a mind-blowing moment!

in those early days, though, i ended up there all the time, the fabric family, especially shaun of course, were genuine, proper champions of drum'n'bass, and it felt like i was doing literally every other friday night, sometimes more even. usually i'd be in the 5–6am slot to round things off, so i've got so many memories of rushing back through london from wherever else i'd been just to get to this incredible place – then even at 5am feel like i was getting home. it honestly did feel like a family, and people were there for the right reason – you'd go there to hear new beats and to get properly lost in the music and really in the zone, which you could really do in that space – and it was so important to drum'n'bass.

what it meant for us, for drum'n'bass, was not just a home, but a sense of possibility too. we'd been regulars in smaller clubs in london for years – then suddenly to have this major, major new spot championing us, not just hosting us but making friday nights synonymous with our sound, meant so much. it went on for years. i'd play room 2 when there was breaks stuff in the main room, i'd do true playaz in room 1 which was absolutely monumental, and then we moved ram there too after the end closed – which was so special with us all up on the stage in room 1. it was hilarious, not having even known there's a room 1, to graduate years later to having a whole record-label showcase in there. of course, we started doing ram nights at matter too, which was an incredible showcase.

it was always just so hospitable. the atmosphere wasn't just great on the dancefloor, but in the green room, in the dj booth, on the vip room above room 1. we had so many great nights there, mingling with the breaks or hip-hop guys like scratch perverts or whoever; there'd be shaun and josh robinson and everyone from fabric taking care of us, making sure everyone's got a drink – some really special, special times. but really that goes through the whole place. the sense of community on friday night – the same faces, you make friends for life, you've got the familiar crew to hang out with in the dj booth – it was fantastic.

i've seen so much progress for artists through that club. seeing chase & status play live for the first time, that was a really special one – they were signed to our label, and to have them perform their live show was a kind of proud parent moment. there've been so many major, major artists who are now proper festival headline acts, who've come through there because it was willing to fuel real underground music – in fact, throw fuel on the underground so it exploded and shone brighter than ever!

the same goes for me, personally. it was shaun that first suggested i do an all-nighter, i think. it went around the team and my agent, then suddenly it was actually happening: andy c all night at fabric. my first-ever six-hour-plus set in a club, and it's in room 1 at fabric! for my personal journey as a dj it was so important that the club supported me in doing that, in fact actively encouraged it, and that absolutely led to everything that's happening for me to this day.

âme – frank wiedemann & kristian beyer

frank: for me it starts with the experience going so deep into a basement, and being in a place where you never really have an overview of it all. that 'wait, where is room 2 again?' feeling. of course, now after so many years i know it well, but for a long time it confused me every time. the second thing is the sound. first time playing there, i remember sanj, the sound guy then, running around taking care of the sound the whole night – that was the first time i'd experienced someone taking such care during the night. and the third thing is being right in the heart of the room with all those people: it's such an intense, close experience.

kristian: the other thing, of course, is judy! the family feeling there is real. of course it is a big club, it's a machine, but i'm always having the feeling i'm coming to visit a family when i arrive. and musically, judy put so much trust in us from the beginning, and combined with that family feel, that's what made it special for me. and over all the years, it's so stable. of course there are new faces, some small changes, but the fact of the residents setting the pace and the people making the good atmosphere means it keeps its feeling through the years!

joy o

before i started doing the joy orbison project properly, i used to do a bit of djing for a friend's night. they used to

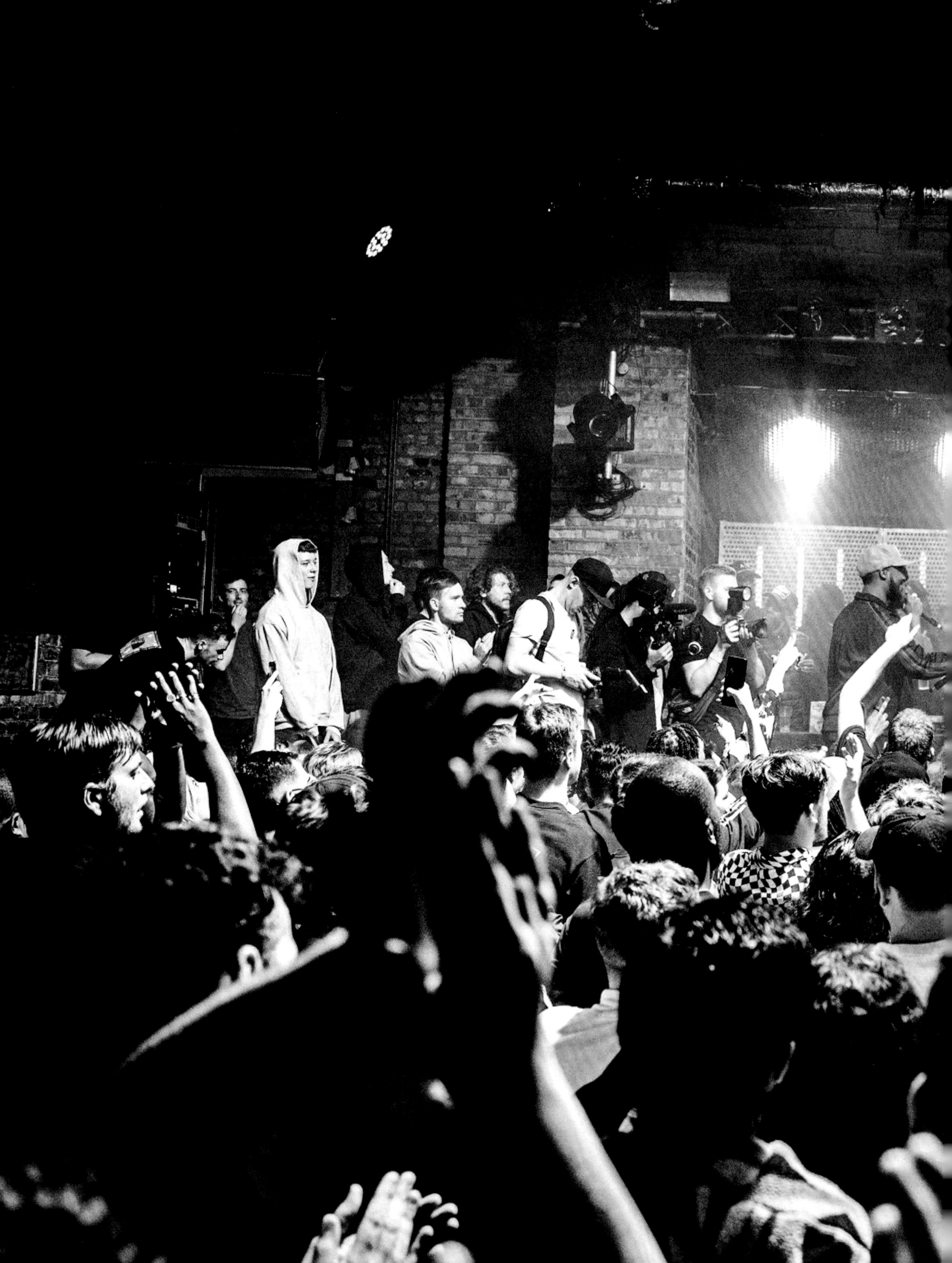

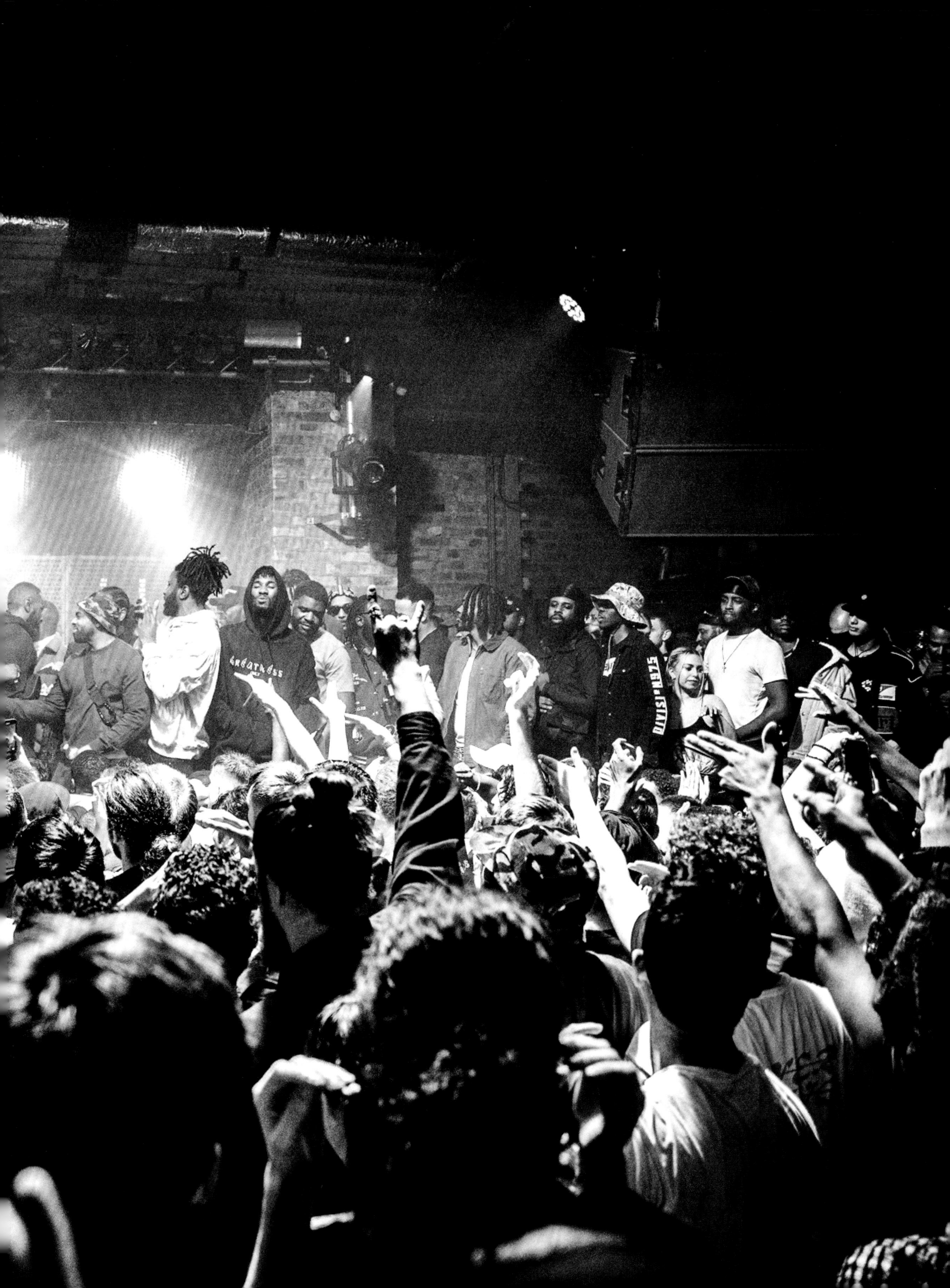

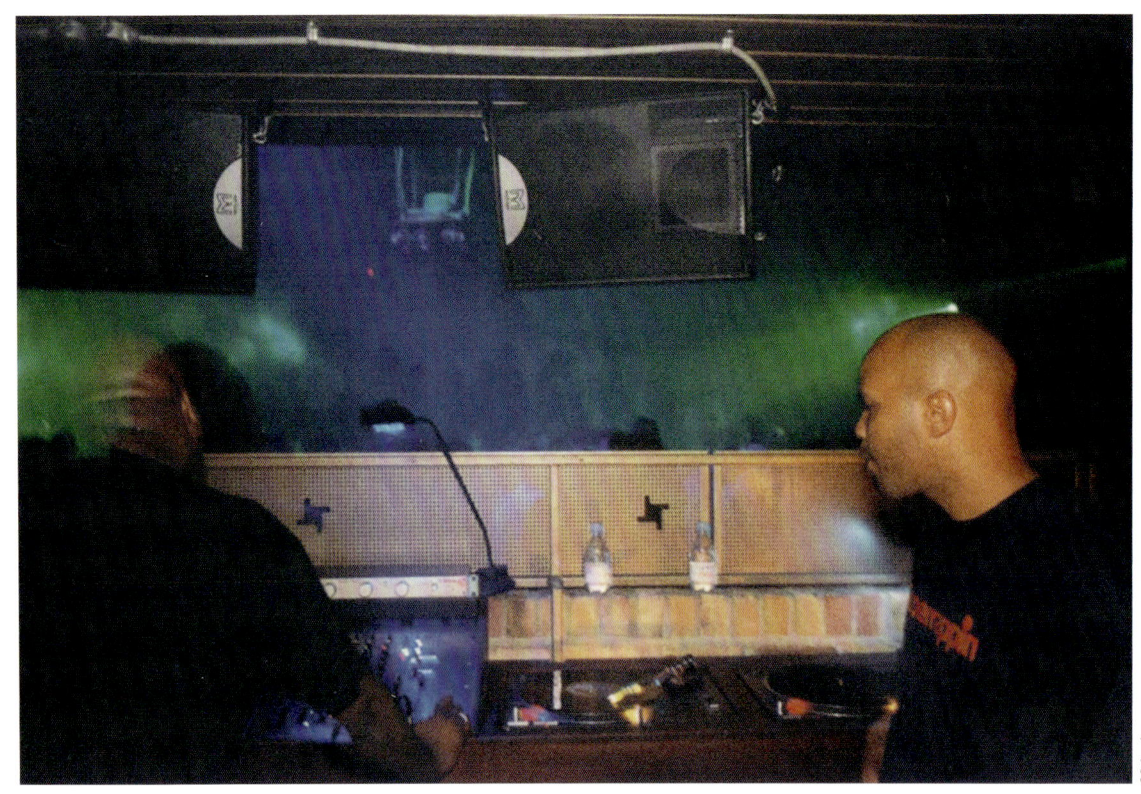
234—1

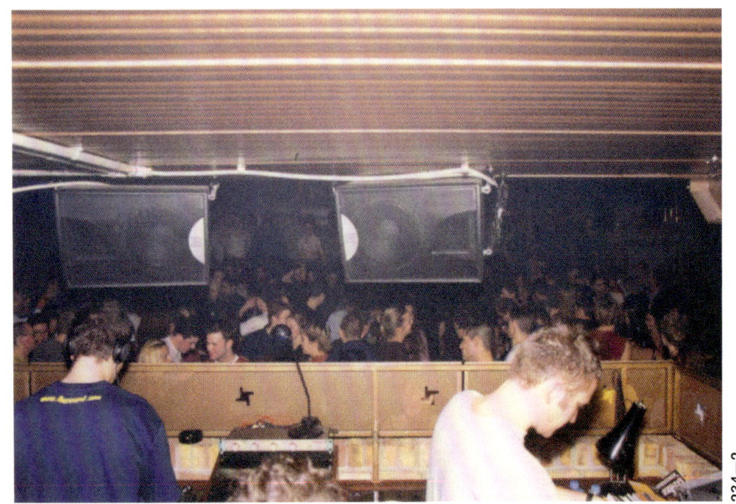
234—2

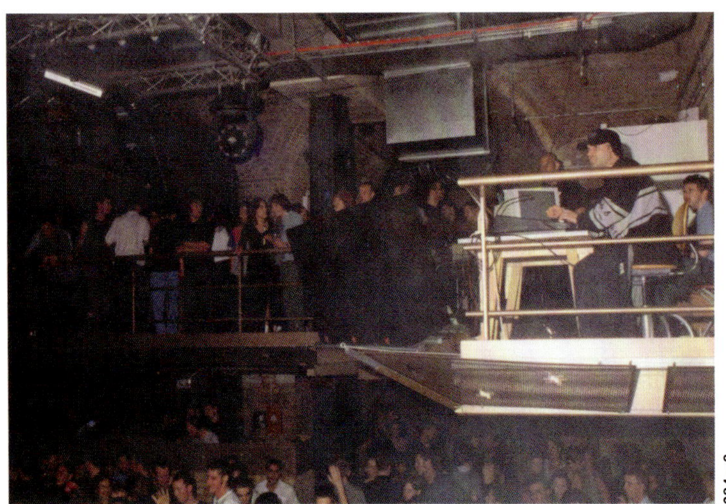
234—3

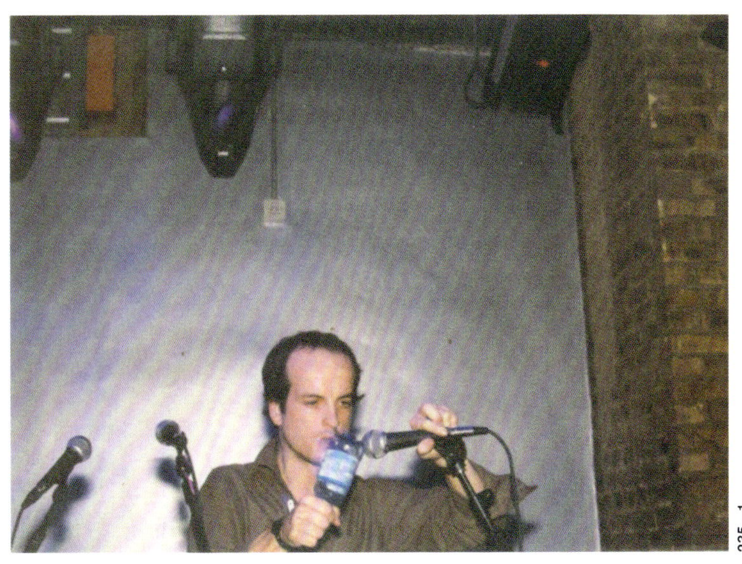

235—1

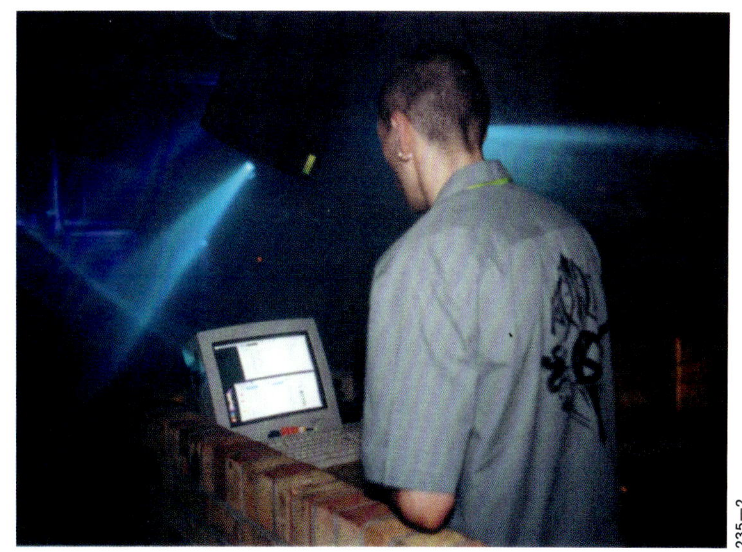

235—2

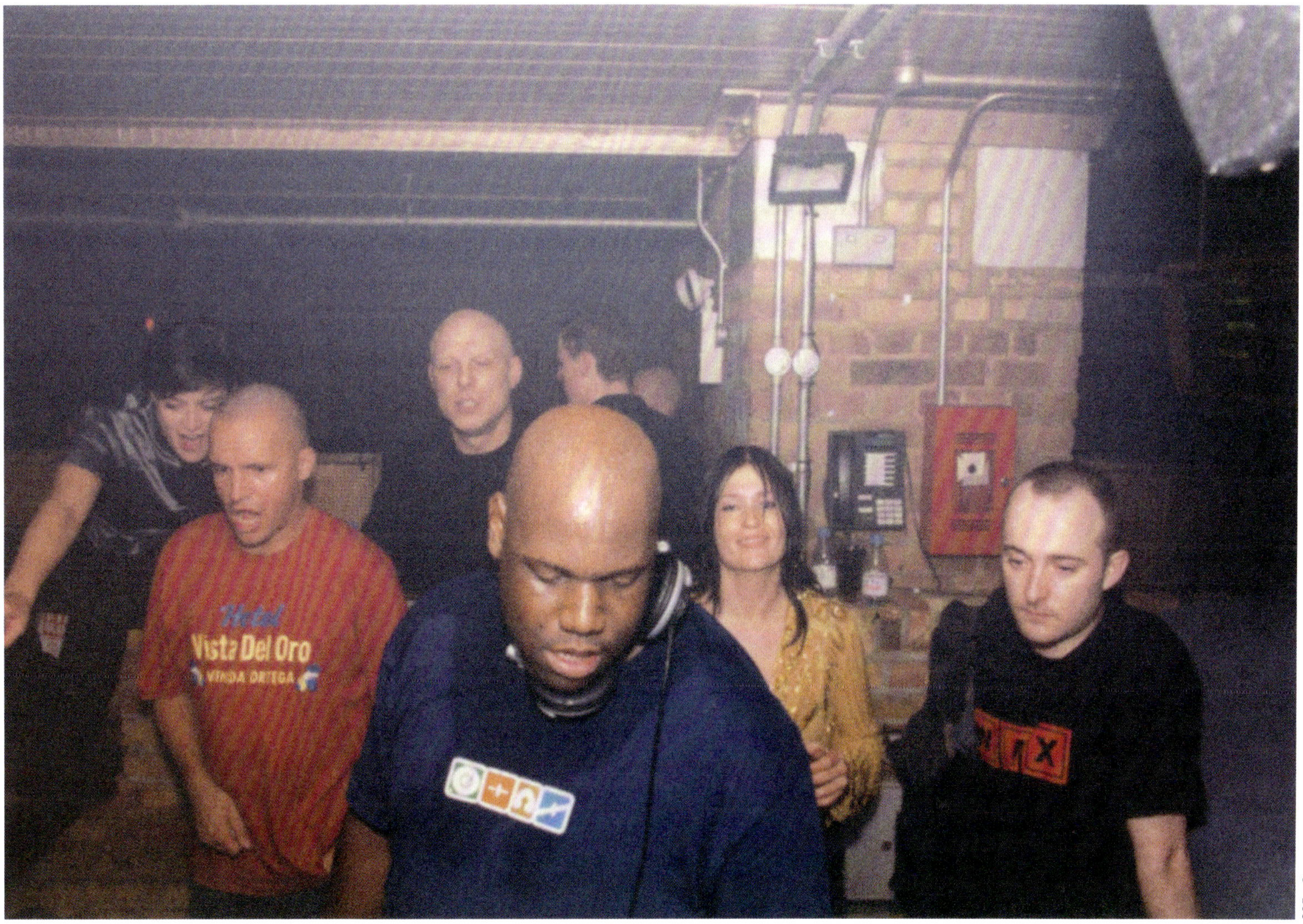

235—3

put on bands and djs, and i'd usually do a warm-up. one of them, they did a party in fabric, i was the warm-up and there was literally nobody in there, not one person. but i'd just that week made 'hyph mngo'; it was still only like a minute and twenty-five seconds – made for myspace!

so i played that at the end of my set. i went out the front to listen to it, a couple of mates with me, and we all went, 'hmm, yeah, doesn't sound too bad, does it?' i'd completely forgotten that for a long time, but it just came back to me recently – the first time i ever heard 'hyph' in a club was in fabric. so to think i've gone from that to now, running a residency in the club, in that exact room, is quite poignant for me.

but playing more major gigs in fabric did come fairly early on in my travels too, really – because shaun gave our sound a bit of a chance. he'd book whole three-room parties of essentially our new wave of stuff, and that was a lot in those days for our kind of thing. so that was important because it showed us that what we were doing could exist in those kind of bigger spaces. it gave us all the confidence to replicate it in bigger and bigger arenas.

roman flügel

i think for a club of this size, it's so well planned, not just the sound but the workspace for djs – there is just care taken to make it right. also, when you're in there, you can let yourself go and go with the flow around the three areas, three different types of music in the same night, and it's just great entertainment, the kind of place it's a pleasure to spend time in. i have some really profound memories from in there, but the biggest of them all would be playing live with alter ego back in the days when we had 'rocker' as a big hit in the uk. the place was absolutely rammed, everything was right, and people went completely ballistic when we played 'rocker', so much that we had to play it again! we were on stage, and judy and the whole crew were looking at us from the dj booth, and i will always remember the smiles and people freaking out to the track, then the encore of 'rocker' again going just as crazy. it's those people that make the place so unique, the team have so much power and creativity and they're just amazing people, which is why fabric was able to reinvent itself constantly. the constant choice of music – drum'n'bass, dubstep, house, electro, weird beats in room 3 sometimes – gives you so many different things going on inside that building, and that too makes it special.

howie b

i knew keith, not very well, but we'd crossed paths via the scene. then, late nineties, all of a sudden he started turning up at my gigs at places like 93 feet east – i'd see this face and go, hmm, him again? then eventually him and craig approached me about coming to play on a friday night, talked to me about the concept of the club and their intentions, and pretty much right there and then a great friendship started with both of them. it was extremely interesting they chose me, because i was a wild card at the time: i was concentrating more on putting records out rather than being a dj; my focus was on my pussyfoot label, stuff with mo' wax and also just being a producer with björk, u2, all of those kinds of things. djing was really just once, maybe twice a month, and mainly in europe.

but they asked me in, and i guess i fitted in quite well with the breakbeat, big-beat stuff that was around then. it was funny, because i'd dj at 128, 130, 133 bpm, but the music i was making was down in the 90s, so it was a bit schizophrenic for me – but i loved that, there was nothing that held me back. i was just walking into record shops all over london and europe, buying anything i loved and somehow fitting it in: trip hop sped up, jungle slowed down, slipping in some old james brown and r&b – anything that could fit into the breakbeat aesthetic. every time i played, i didn't know what was going to happen. i just went with whatever was going on, different every time, no rhyme or reason except for what record shops i'd been in that week – and that, i think, is what keith liked and what made the spirit of the club.

and the line-ups were crazy. i'd be playing with andrew weatherall one week, daft punk the next, drum'n'bass legends after that. and it was that good the whole weekend long. i'd play on a friday, come and see craig and terry and whoever they had on saturday, back on sunday – it was so easy to do that, it just felt like another home, honestly. if i wasn't in the club, we were all round each other's houses carrying on the party. people talk about getting lost in fabric, but it's the greatest thing – even if you know it like the back of your hand, it's just natural to wander around. you'll go there with a mate, suddenly they've gone off and you don't see them for two or three hours, then you turn round and there they are, next to you on the dancefloor, and you both go, 'waheyy!', and that's just part of the experience. it's fun. everyone working there loves and takes pride in what they put together. there's people coming in from tokyo, from berlin, from paris, all in the name of good music. it feels like such a meeting point, and it's bullshit-free. as a dj, if you dealt any bullshit, gave it the big i am, that would be the last time you'd play there. it was the opposite of superstar dj culture. it felt so great to have everyone on the same level, and i feel like they've maintained that to this day.

daniel avery

i can remember when i made a trip up to london as a teenager, just seeing the flyers everywhere, and not having a clue what it was but being really intrigued. but it was the FABRICLIVE cds, which trickled down to bournemouth where i grew up, that grabbed me most of all; i remember seeing them in shops and they seemed kind of alien in their metal boxes. at that age i had no idea who all these electronic artists were, so again it was intriguing, then when the john peel one came out in the middle of all that it was a proper startling and exciting moment.

i first went to fabric for a kill em all party run by filthy dukes – who i'd eventually go on to work with – as a student in about 2005. i was at university in southampton and working in a record shop at the weekends, and the shop crew all went up to london, got the first train home in the morning and worked all day on no sleep, but were just buzzing from the experience. i'd never been to any club on that scale, and it felt like a cavern, a maze. there's something kind of doctor who about it!

the first time i played was opening room 3, for a night called adventures in the beetroot field, which i think was actually on an easter thursday. more than anything else, seeing my name on one of those flyers was beyond anything i could have imagined before at that point. and it was around that time i met shaun roberts, too; i got on with him straight away, knew that he was a really funny guy, an interesting guy, and a genuinely charming person – which are not necessarily adjectives you'd usually jump to when describing a london club booker! he stood out instantly, but everyone on the team backed that up. i was absolutely a nobody at that time, yet everybody treated me like i was important that night, and that meant something. it really meant something.

of course, there are so many great memories subsequently, but a couple stand out. one was in 2012 when shaun called me up and asked to meet. he told me, 'the next FABRICLIVE artist has pulled out, and i want you to do it.' this is before my first album had come out, very few people knew who i was, but shaun and fabric as a whole took a chance on me, so i made FABRICLIVE.66 and it literally changed the course of my life. that obviously was just enormous for me.

the other one was when the club offered me in 2014 the chance to start curating a night, which i called divided love – where i was keen to show my love of live music as much as djs. the first line-up was helena hauff, myself, then dopplereffekt and factory floor, both live, and i was proud to bring that kind of stark, exciting sound to fabric with some of the best live acts around – some of my proudest moments in music right there.

but that's what fabric does. i've always looked to their line-ups for inspiration. beyond myself, they've taken chances on so many acts; they've always done so, they've always presented an underground vision in a way that feels elevated and on a grand scale. that's really difficult to do week in, week out, let alone for twenty-five years – but i still even now look at the fabric line-up purely as a fan, to see who they're interested in. it's important to me. there's never been a sense of dying passion with that club, or doing things half-heartedly; there's always been a new energy in who they're booking, and who they are. i'm their number one fan.

elijah

i went to the club pretty much as soon as i was eighteen, i think. would've gone before but it was strict with id. that was my starting point as a legit raver. i went to a run the road there, 2005, and i saw dizzee do a dirtee stank show too. i'd been to big concert-type venues, but i hadn't been to a purpose-built big club before. i'd been to bootleg-type places, theatres turned into clubs, pubs with a club room attached, but not a real, big sound-system vibe, and going into fabric was a definite, 'oh shit, this is different!'

it wasn't until much later that i even imagined i could do something there. maybe three, four years later i was on rinse – and suddenly fabric felt like an option. a lot of the labels that were on rinse were doing their own thing there – like hessle audio had a residency there, and they were the show before us, so i saw that, saw how they started in room 3 and worked their way up and thought, ok, cool, we could do something similar.

i might have a limited view of the club, because i don't think i've ever been on a saturday, but FABRICLIVE is a proper institution. i think it was an inspiration for a lot of people – or a lot of people just copied it – for a good while. it inspired clubs with that three-room thing to realise that you could mash a load of styles together. things are a lot more linear these days, but it definitely had that effect, and it's still doing that now.

i felt welcome in fabric, too. as a student i never felt like i was not going to get in. a lot of big clubs, i just never even tried – just assumed i wouldn't get in. and then shaun's support for us, for grime in general but particularly for butterz, that was the difference between having a night in london at a certain level and having nothing. all the bs that grime had to go through with form 696 and all the rest, a lot of clubs didn't want to host our music. so just being showed that our thing was legit showed other people, not just in london but uk-wide and internationally, that this was a serious operation.

we did actually have to prove ourselves. we did a couple of room 3s in 2011, asked to do room 2 and they said, 'no, you're not ready,' so we actually walked and did cable instead. they were mad about that, but when cable closed, they didn't hold it against us but said, 'ok you've shown you can do it on that scale, great,' and gave us room 2, then room 1. because with fabric it's not just about what's hot, what's popping that month – they commit to people, and that makes a big difference.

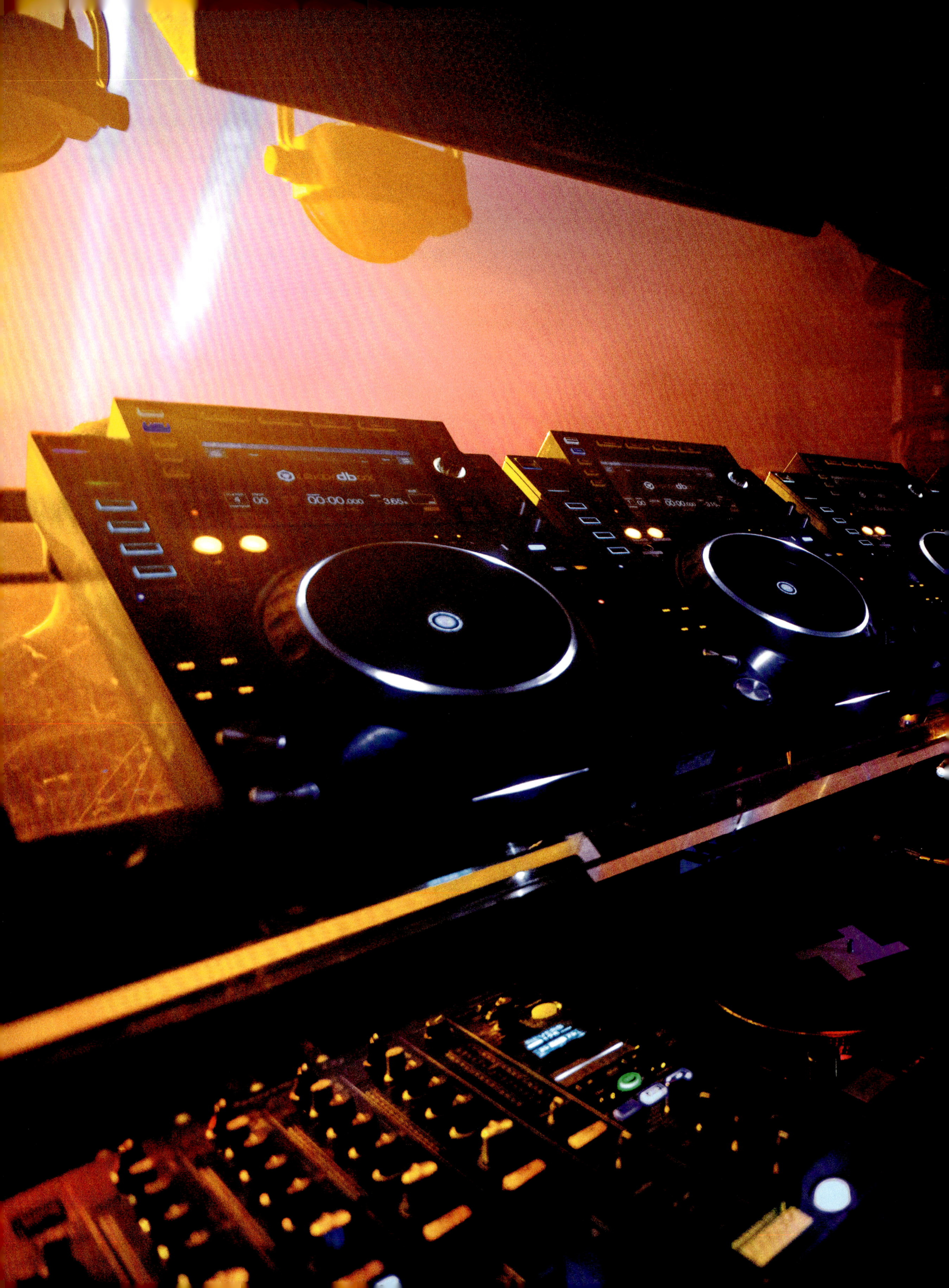

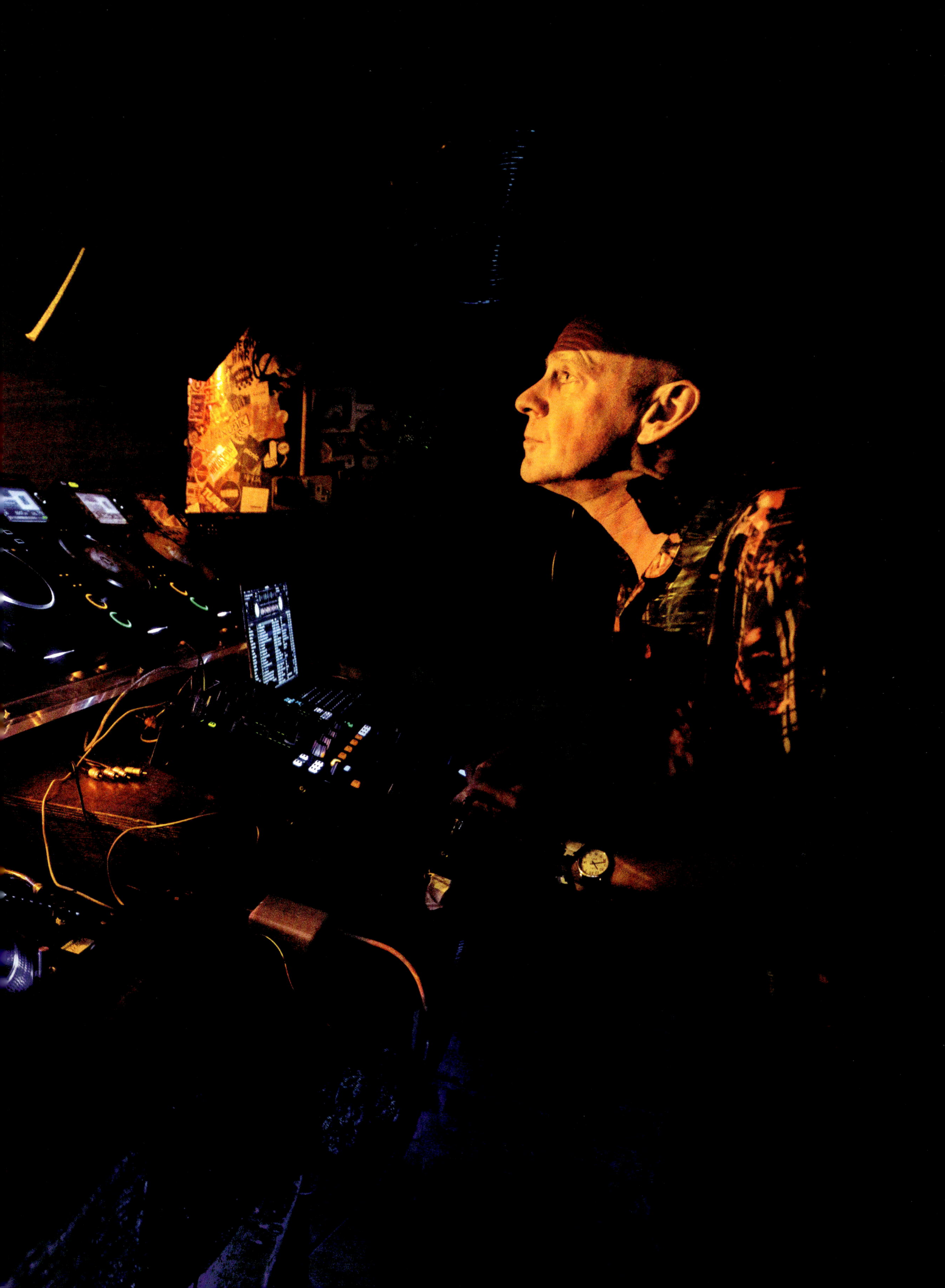

then, of course, we did the FABRICLIVE.75, which was another boost, this time to me and skilliam as djs. doing the launch for that was when skepta 'that's not me' was just coming out and was, i think, the first time he'd ever performed it in london. so imagine what that track became, and imagine seeing the first wave of that energy. it became like a trampoline for artists launching, do a fabric show then go on to bigger ones.

so fabric is a very special club for grime – it's not necessarily a club-based genre in the same way some other styles are, but it works in fabric, and fabric is probably the most important club for grime full stop. thinking from the perspective of the dancefloor, you get to see something in a big-enough room for it to feel epic, but not so big that it feels commercial.

that is a fine line, and that is why it works. if it was the size of room 1 and room 2 combined, it would be too big, but each one is just the right size to not feel overwhelming but still feel like a big room. it's not really that big, but it feels powerful; it's probably the exact threshold of what you can call a big room without losing the feeling. i don't think i've ever got lost there, mind – people say you get lost in fabric, but honestly it's just go from one room to another. catch a vibe, see a bit of this, ok, go to the next room, great.

sasha

from the beginning it was all about keith's absolute devotion to this purist idea of what a nightclub should be, how it should operate, the kind of people it should attract, the kind of people that should be working there, the kind of people who should be playing there, the sound … it was just such a clear conception in his head, and that spread to everyone else's. i think everyone else who got involved, the idea that he was cultivating and preaching converted a lot of followers to his thinking – and it became this unique beacon in this world of music that is so regularly corrupted by commercialism. they stayed true to their roots, even in the hardest times, when it would have been easy to just start throwing in some big commercial names just to make some money.

it couldn't be clearer now, looking back twenty-five years later, the contrast between home, which opened at the same time with these huge names on the bill right in the heart of the west end, and fabric, which was in a part of town that nobody really went to and focused entirely on music. but i went in with keith and craig before it opened – craig and i were practically neighbours at that point so i watched it all close up as it came together – and immediately when you walked into the space, i felt like it had a soul. the greatest nightclubs in the world, places that are truly close to my heart, are like that; there's something in the bricks and mortar you can feel. i felt that in the haçienda in manchester: you'd walk in and the building had a soul.

then they went on from that to install one of the greatest sound systems in the world. through my entire dj career i still hold fabric as the standard for what great sound is. i've played on some of the greatest systems in the world – twilo nyc, womb tokyo, some of the most expensive and perfectly assembled sound systems in the world, but fabric is still special. every time i come back, they've upgraded it, they've done a little something, they've bought a new gadget that's just tweaked that 0.03 per cent more. and so over twenty-five years, that consistent push for excellence, combined with the cultivation of the sound in terms of finding djs who are exploring and trying new things sonically, just keeps it ahead.

that attention to detail is representative of the personal approach to everything. it's the individual people that make up fabric as much as the building or the sound system. i can think of times i've got to the club and one of the regular people is off for a personal reason or whatever, and it's like there's a hole in the venue! obviously, some of the staff have been there for the longest time, some are newer, but it's always such an incredible welcome and they're there to the end. they care so much about what goes on in those rooms.

i've had gigs on the road where a promoter i've worked with for years will book me, but you'll get there and nobody is there in the organisation who actually cares about the gig itself; the promoter isn't there personally, and they're all just going through the motions. you can have a big crowd of people who've come to see you play, but when you know you're working with people who don't care, it can feel soul-destroying. what shines about fabric – and has done without a dip for the entirety of that twenty-five years – is the amount of passion and care for what goes on in that venue, for every single dancer's experience and for the dj's experience. you can't fake that.

musically, those early days, still playing vinyl in there, had a huge influence on me. we did the tyrant thing with me, craig and lee burridge from the very beginning of fabric. at the same time i was playing monthly with john digweed at twilo in new york, so i was between these two world-class venues and it was a really interesting pull in two directions. at twilo we were playing very stark, minimal, progressive house meets techno at 128 bpm, which really fit that room perfectly – while craig and lee were pulling me into this funkier, breakbeat, tech-house thing that fabric was really forging at the time.

i remember craig really schooling me in how not every record needs to get people's arms in the air – he wanted to focus on shaking their butts, and that pulled me and lee in that direction, i think. i could do whatever i wanted at twilo and festivals and so on, but that one gig a month with lee and craig, i used to prep for more than any other gig of the month – digging through my collection, doing special edits and cutting to acetates just to play at fabric. it felt very special to do every time. and i've done so many gigs there since then on my own, and it always still retains a bit of that.

paul woolford

fabric is an establishment built on pleasure, but also on everything being done in a very particular way. at the time in which it was first happening, the superclub era was coming to a close, and the fact fabric was built as an outpost for something more substantial meant it just thrived. it was reacting against the flashiness, but crucially it was about offering so much more.

it's just an amazing place, physically. for us, for artists, it's a fucking amazing place to play because those rooms are constructed from the ground up purely for us to get into the zone and continue in that zone for as long as possible. there's no greater fun than being in the environment where everything is in the right place and you're left alone to do exactly what you do. the team that run it, the team that built it, the team that continue to look after it – they're all completely about it. first, they know what they're doing, and second they're immersed in the culture of it all as well. they're not just people doing a job, performing a function; they're people with a passion, and the passion is what drives the whole enterprise.

i first played with craig, i think, in 2003. i'd been obsessing about it since it opened, then judy and craig gave me a spot – i opened, did a four-hour set, then craig played, then d'julz played, so i wasn't going anywhere. and just to get hold of that system for four hours at that stage, i couldn't believe it. i'd actually had a ridiculous session the night before, probably had an hour's sleep, turned up thinking, oh god, what have you done, you fucking idiot?, but ended up playing really well, again because that space is just made to bring the best out of you. i remember me and howie b doing an all-night back-to-back on a saturday in room 3 too. that was one of the greatest times – six or seven hours, just total freedom, playing dub, soul, all sorts of stuff, no house at all. the fact that fridays under shaun's tenure built such an incredible identity too is important – just having true playaz as such a stalwart for so long alone was an inspiration and another sense of the commitment that fabric had to maintaining things in the long term.

when rob booth came to the label, i'd already been keeping track of what he'd been doing with his amazing podcast – and he was a kindred spirit, another true enthusiast, and we immediately bonded. we had an absolutely amazing run with my special request things for houndstooth. i think i pushed them to the limit with the trying to do four albums in a year thing, and other mad ideas like a huge box set based on homer's odyssey that was going to be boxed up with a penguin classics book, but we're still mates now and that run really was something else. and to have the machinery of fabric in the background added confidence. at that point i'd been quite disillusioned with what was happening elsewhere in the music industry, but they just showed how capable and focused and ambitious it was possible for people to be, and how it was still totally legitimate to treat and package this music like beautiful works of art.

erol alkan

one of my best mates, john, did the electrics for fabric, so i was quite excited to find out about it. at the time it opened, me and my mates really went to indie/alternative nights, and just the occasional club thing like wall of sound at the end, but fabric just sounded exciting. we went to the opening and it was a bit, 'blimey, there's lots of celebrities here!' because it was the opening, but then when bugged out!/big beat boutique started, that's what really got me. at that time i was djing just about every night of the week on the alternative scene, but i'd take the night off from wherever i was djing on those fridays, and go to fabric. that was our big night out, we'd be one of the first in the door and the last out at the end. because i knew john, and i knew steve blonde who was booking then, i would often end up on the vip balcony above room 1 – not that i was bothered about the vip thing, but it was just really intoxicating because it was such a good vantage point to take in how majestic it was when it was packed, the incredible sound was in full flow, the lighting was so great and all of that. it was so different to anywhere else i'd been at that point.

it was one of the only places that truly felt eclectic, too, especially on those nights, and especially because of room 3. you could walk in and hear just about anything, which at that time, '99, 2000, was truly refreshing, because electronic music was taking on a new life, post this huge explosion it had already had. the appetite for the new was huge, and to have fabric popping up at that time, at that size, was just perfect. i felt such a sense of belonging when i went into room 3 and heard people playing records i recognised but that weren't from the big electronic scenes of that day – they weren't breaks, or techno, or whatever was big at the time, though obviously those styles were a big part of what was happening too. breaks was so big, i remember freq nasty would always play 'raize it up' by the freestylers – still a pretty mental track now, but then it was one of those tunes that would just blow room 1 apart. we knew he'd play it, we knew the effect it'd have, but it was always amazing every time.

at that time, trash was really starting to pick up, and jockey slut were always big supporters of ours; obviously johnno from jockey slut also ran bugged out! i got to know him and felt a really big sense of kinship with him – i could chat to him about the alternative scene, about electronic music, and i'd end up at afterparties at his house and playing on his decks, and he could see that i was actually doing something different in combining them. that led to him asking me to fill in for david holmes in room 3 at the last minute when he couldn't make it. i would have been at the night anyway, because i was still going to all the bugged out!/big beat boutique nights whenever i could, so i jumped at it!

i remember starting off in room 3, just moderately filled, and within three records it was packed, and it just went on from there – really fun, really natural, the perfect place because room 3 wasn't afraid of eclecticism. then halfway through, johnno came in, saw the vibe was right and asked if i wanted a residency for them! the next day it was, 'who's your agent?' 'oh, i don't have an agent', and within a week i'd been introduced to martje at decked out/primary, who has been my agent ever since. so it really was that one session that started so much that i couldn't ever have envisaged. i never had any ambition to be a dance dj, i just got invited to play a party, then another one and on it went …

i've got a poster in my office, the first time my name ever appeared on a poster. i think it's the last bugged out!/big beat boutique at fabric, so i'd played a couple for them, then this one i'm actually listed, so it's chemical brothers, felix da housecat, midfield general, rob bright, james holroyd, freq nasty, the unabombers, then right at the bottom 'erol alkan'. it's the first time i was called that; up till then i'd just been dj erol. my full name is erol alkan mustapha – alkan is my dad's name – but they asked how i wanted to be billed, i just decided to use that name and again, that was it! everything came together around fabric for me – literally everything.

there was a night in, i think 2005, where we had a benefit for a guy called manolis, who had a cafe on the road i used to live on. just this greek guy who had this amazing cafe, really quiet, super cheap, but i'd take people in there for meetings, i'd take djs in there if they were over from abroad and staying with me. business wasn't great, he was faced with closure, so we wanted to publicise it. so we went to shaun and asked if he'd be up for it, a party in room 3 to let people know about this cafe – and he instantly went, 'sure, of course.' i invited everyone who'd stayed with me and been to the cafe, so it was justice, pedro winter, paul epworth, feadz, mehdi … and they all came. basically, my house used to be the london ed banger hq, and manolis's cafe was where we ate. room 3 that night, you couldn't even breathe out it was that packed, hot, insane. that's one of my fondest-ever memories of fabric – just having an idea, doing it, so ridiculous and magical.

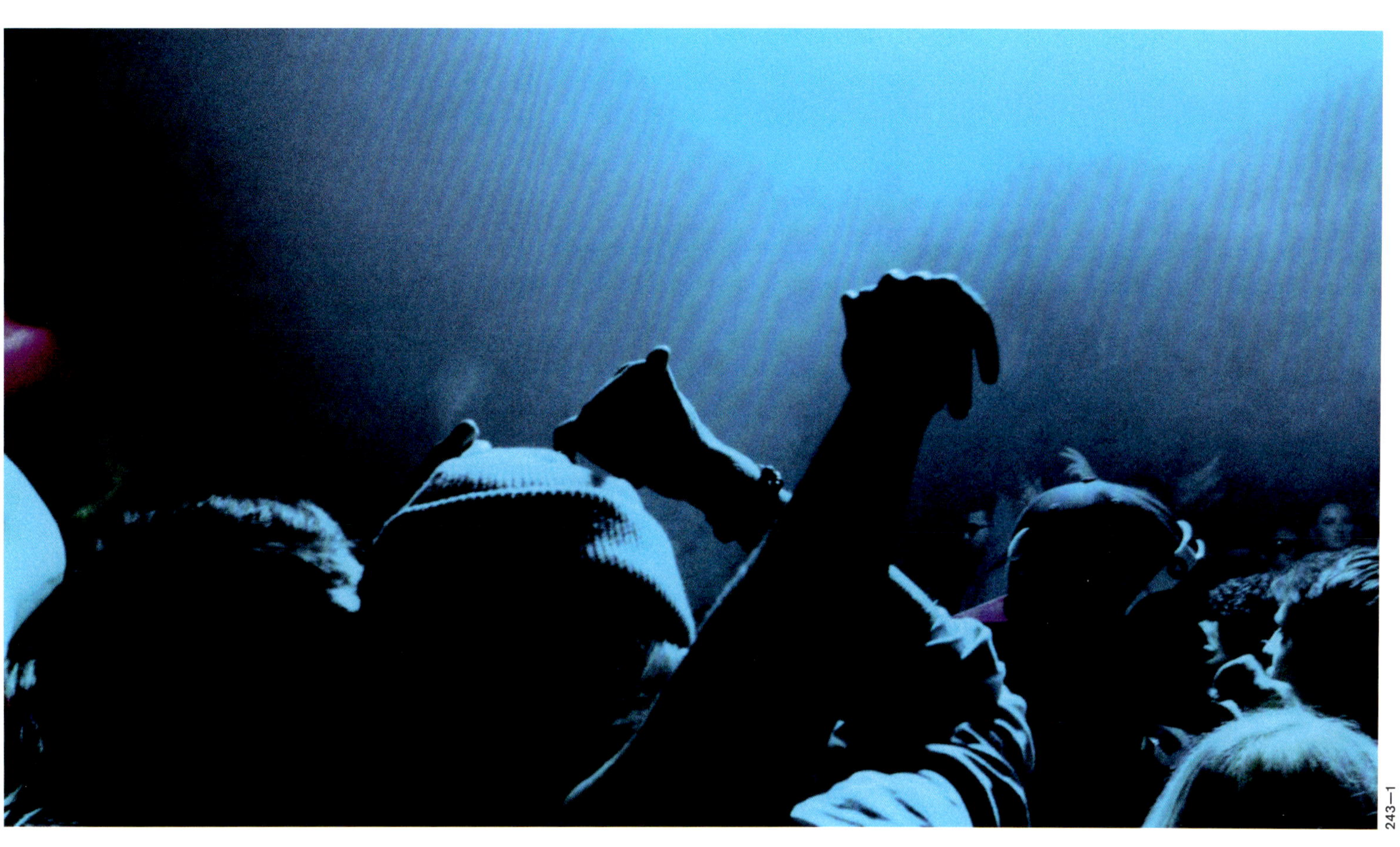
243—1

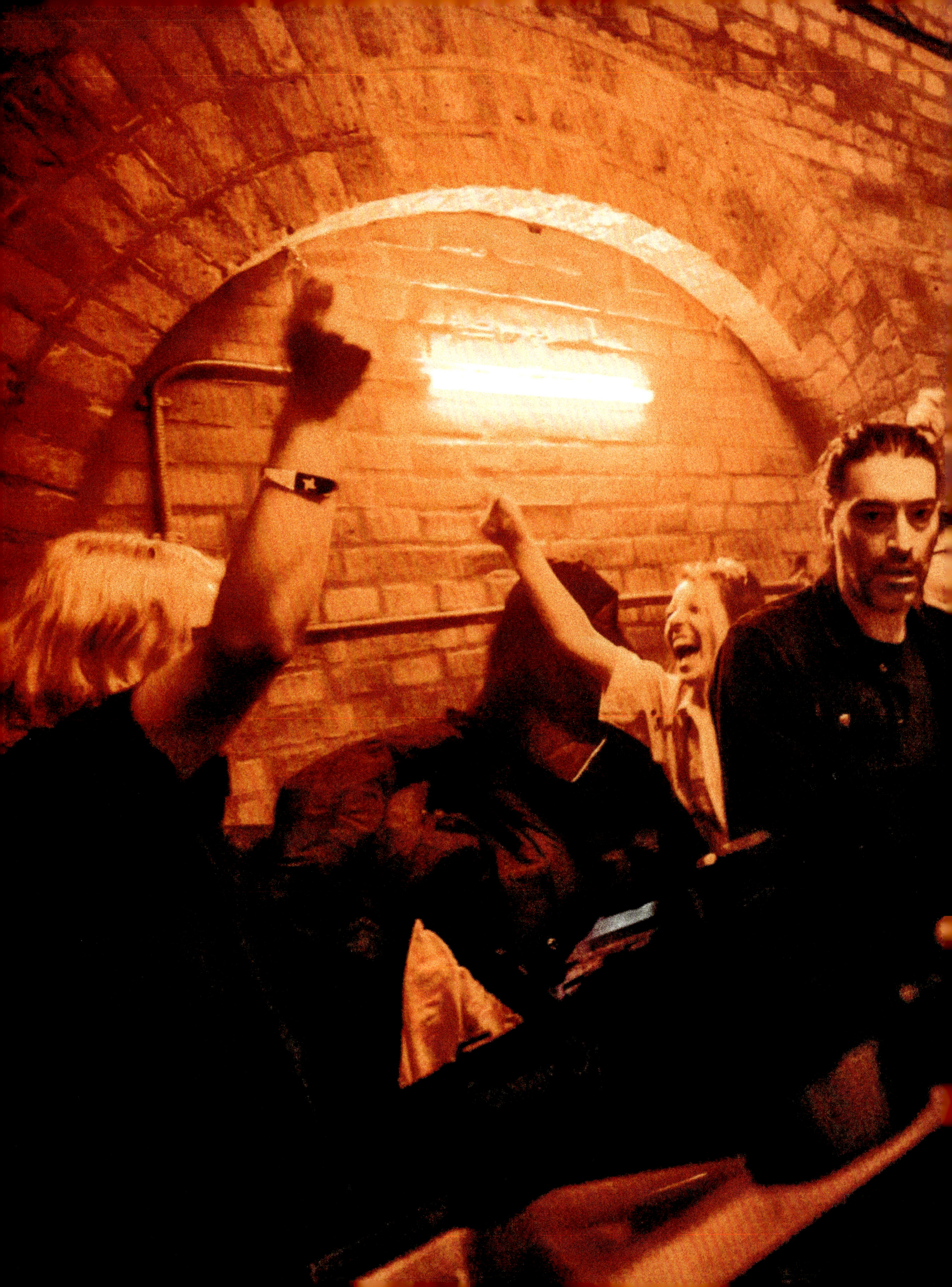

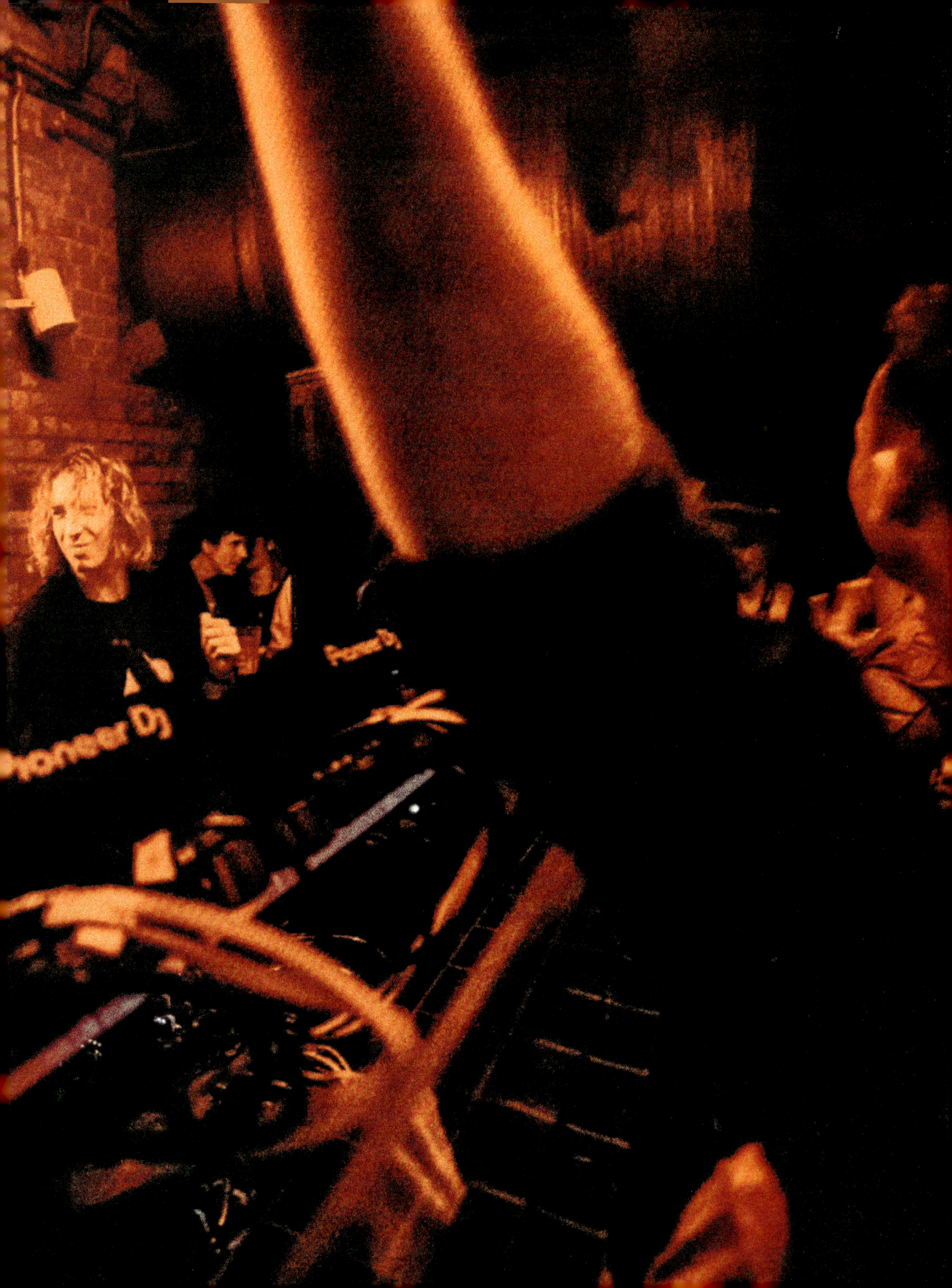

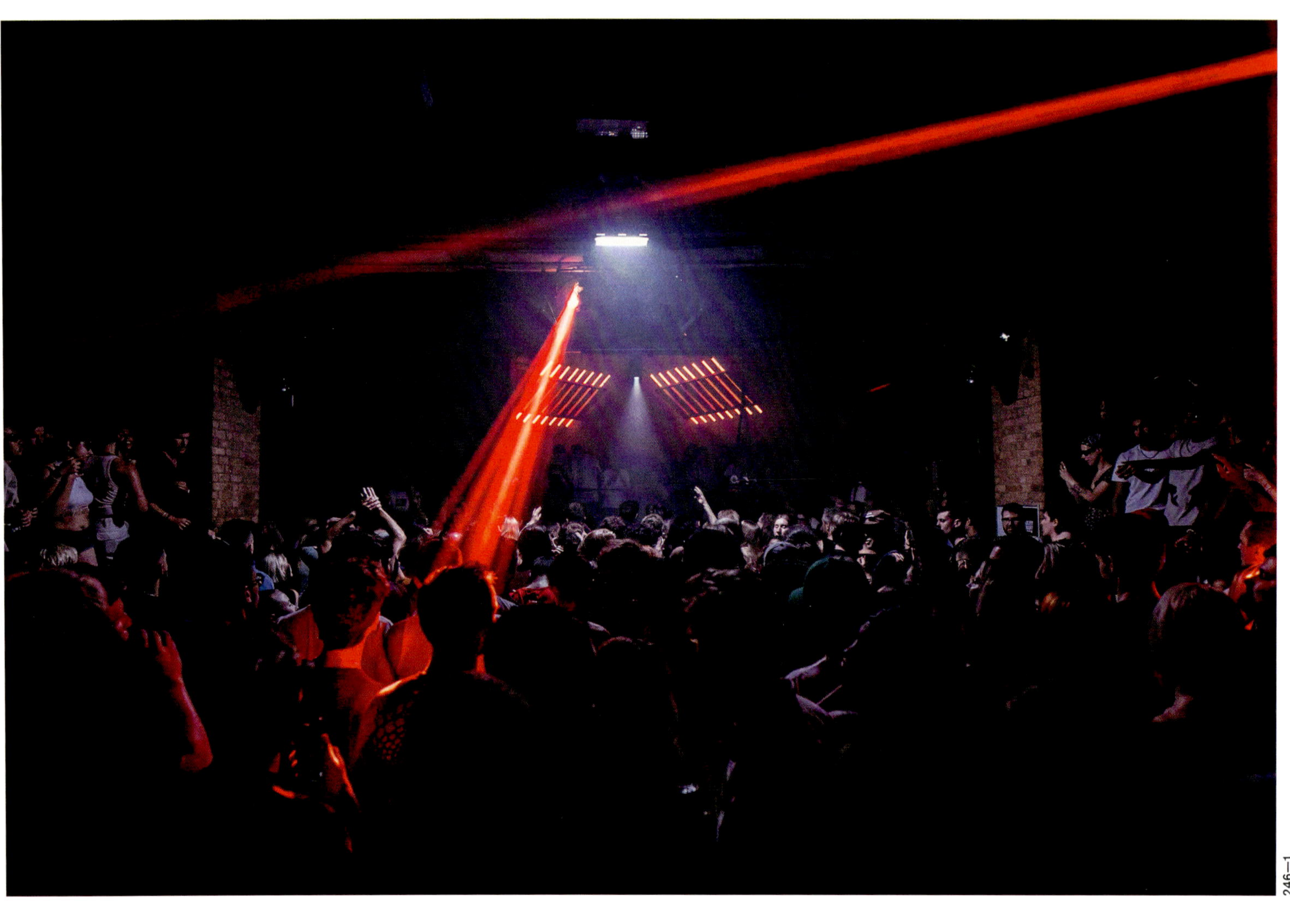

246—1

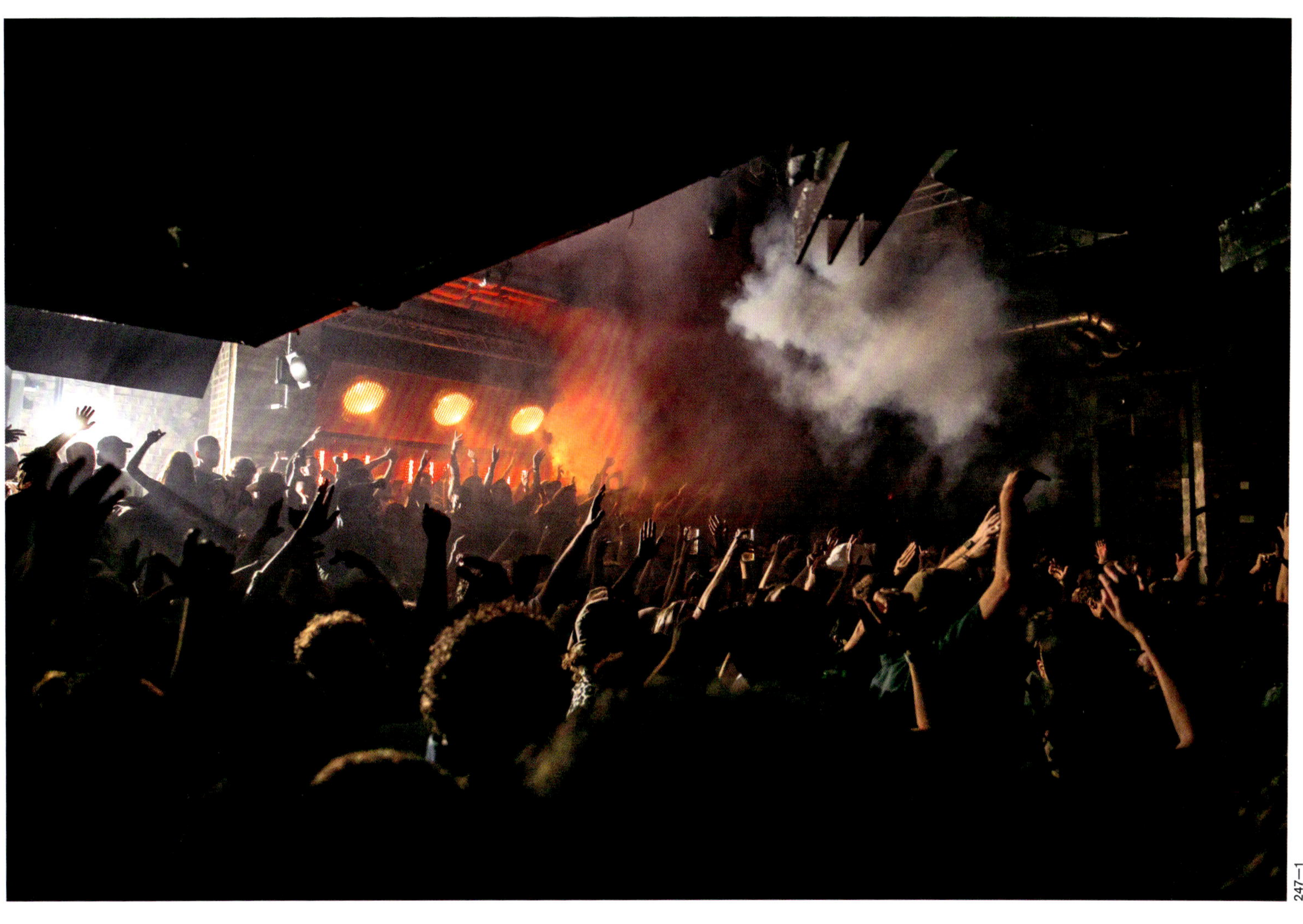
247—1

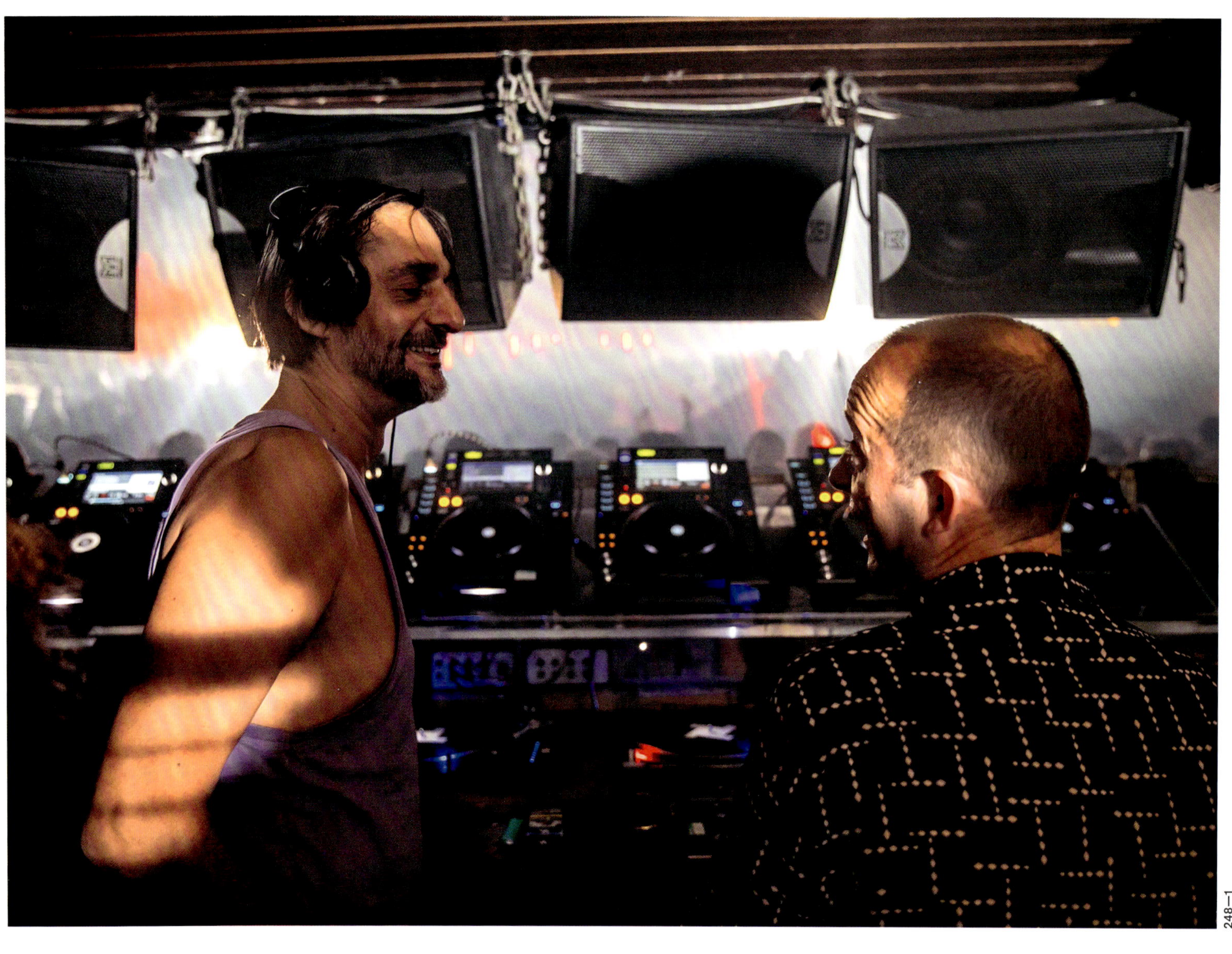

248—1

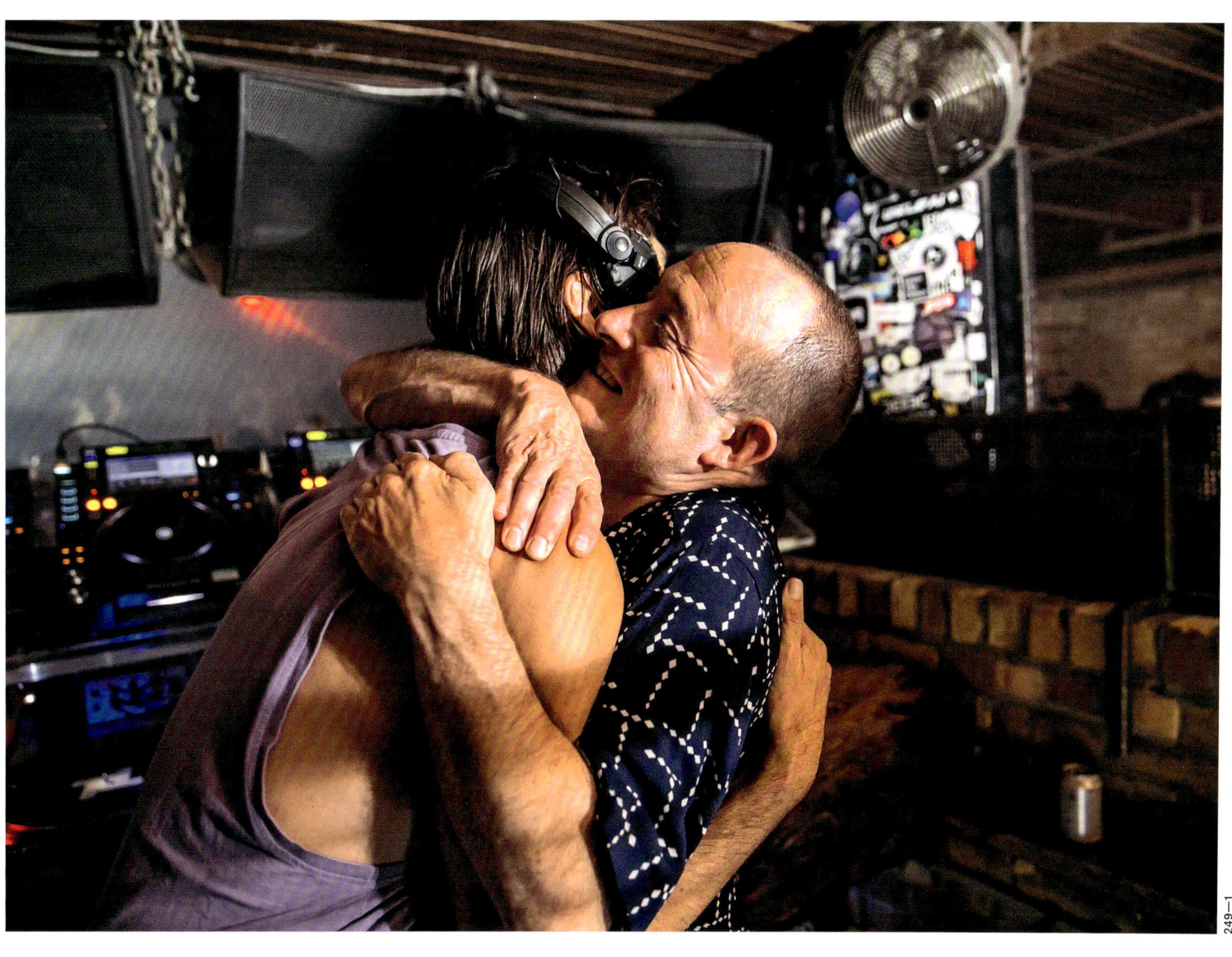

249—1

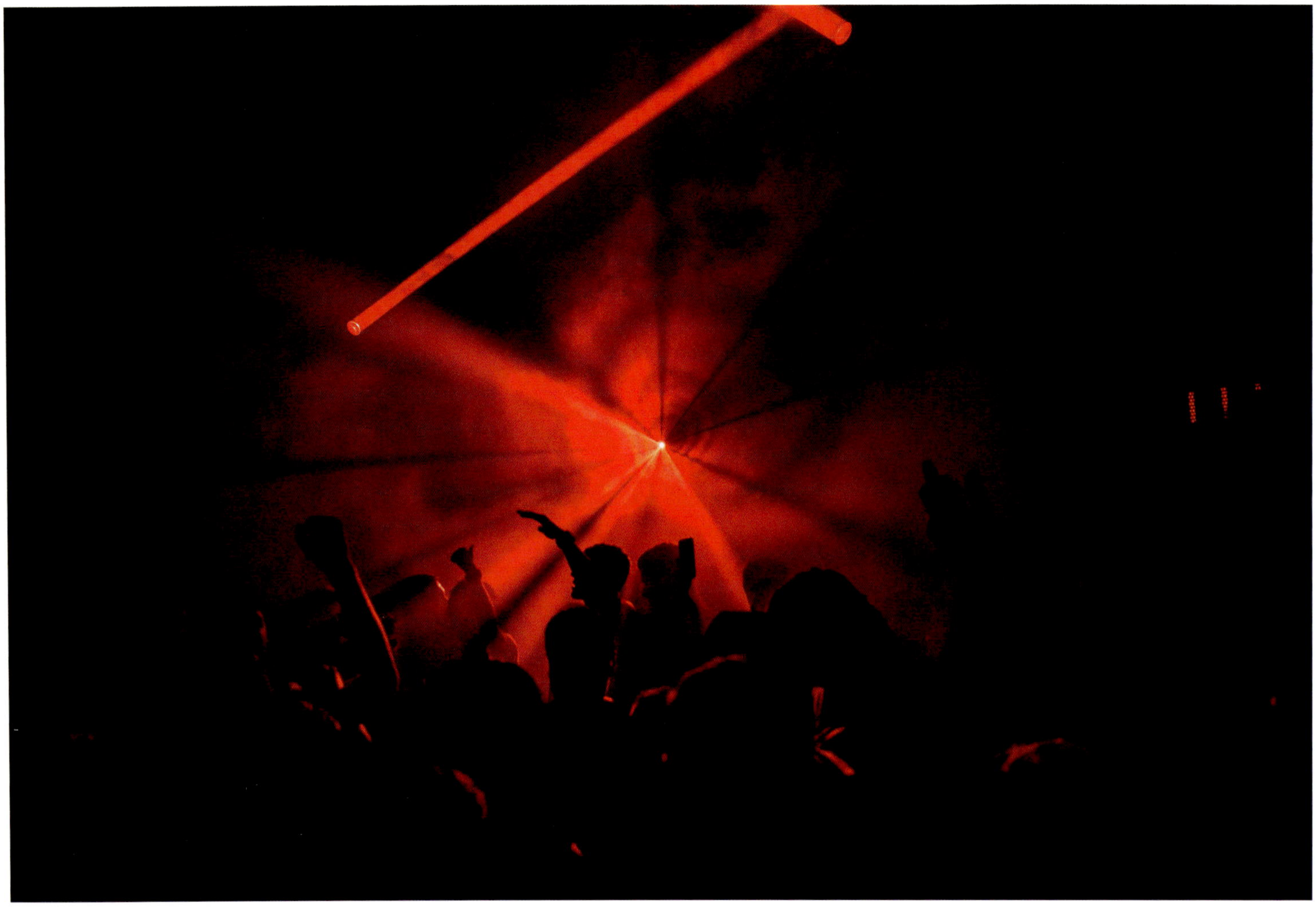

250—1

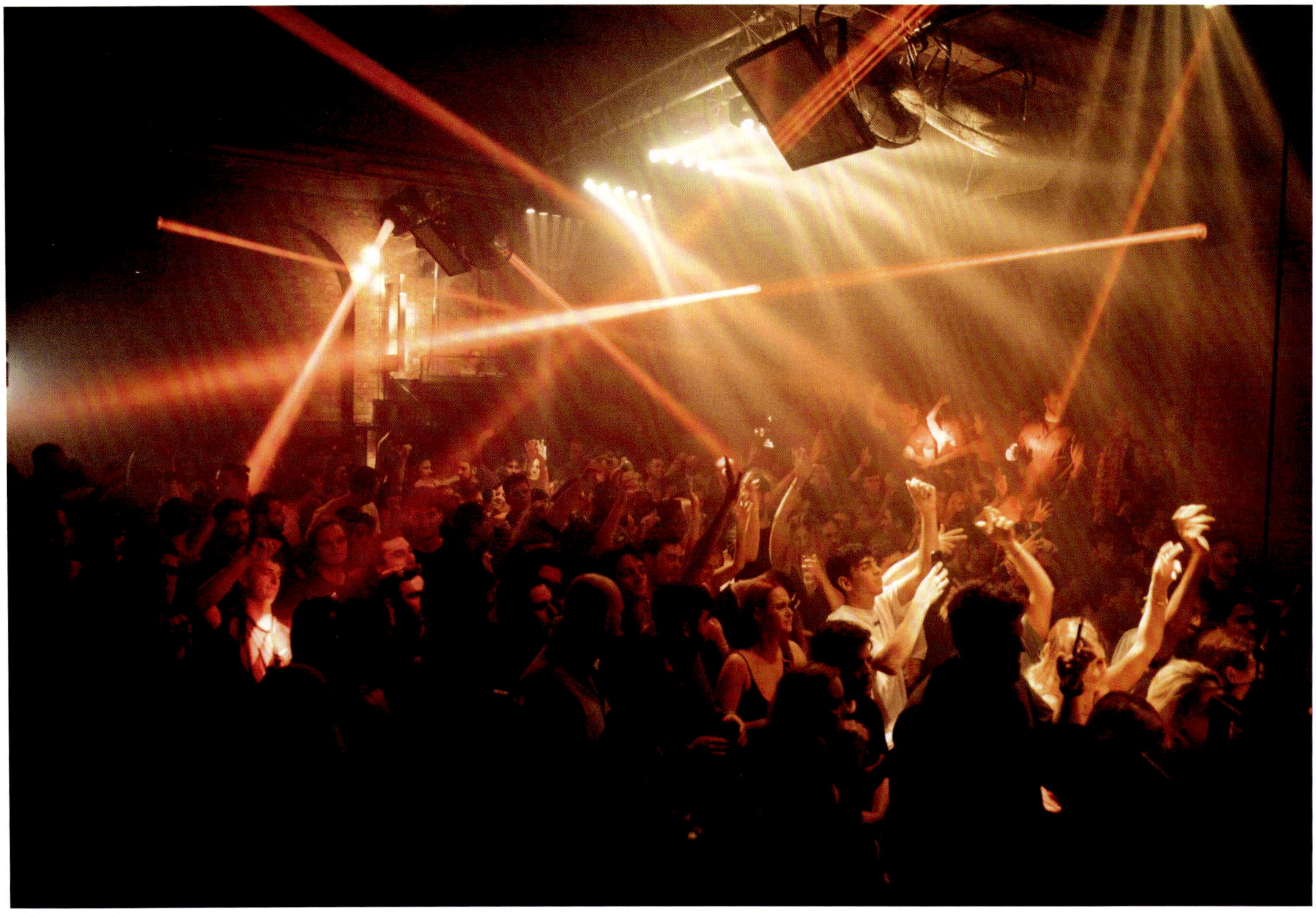

250—2

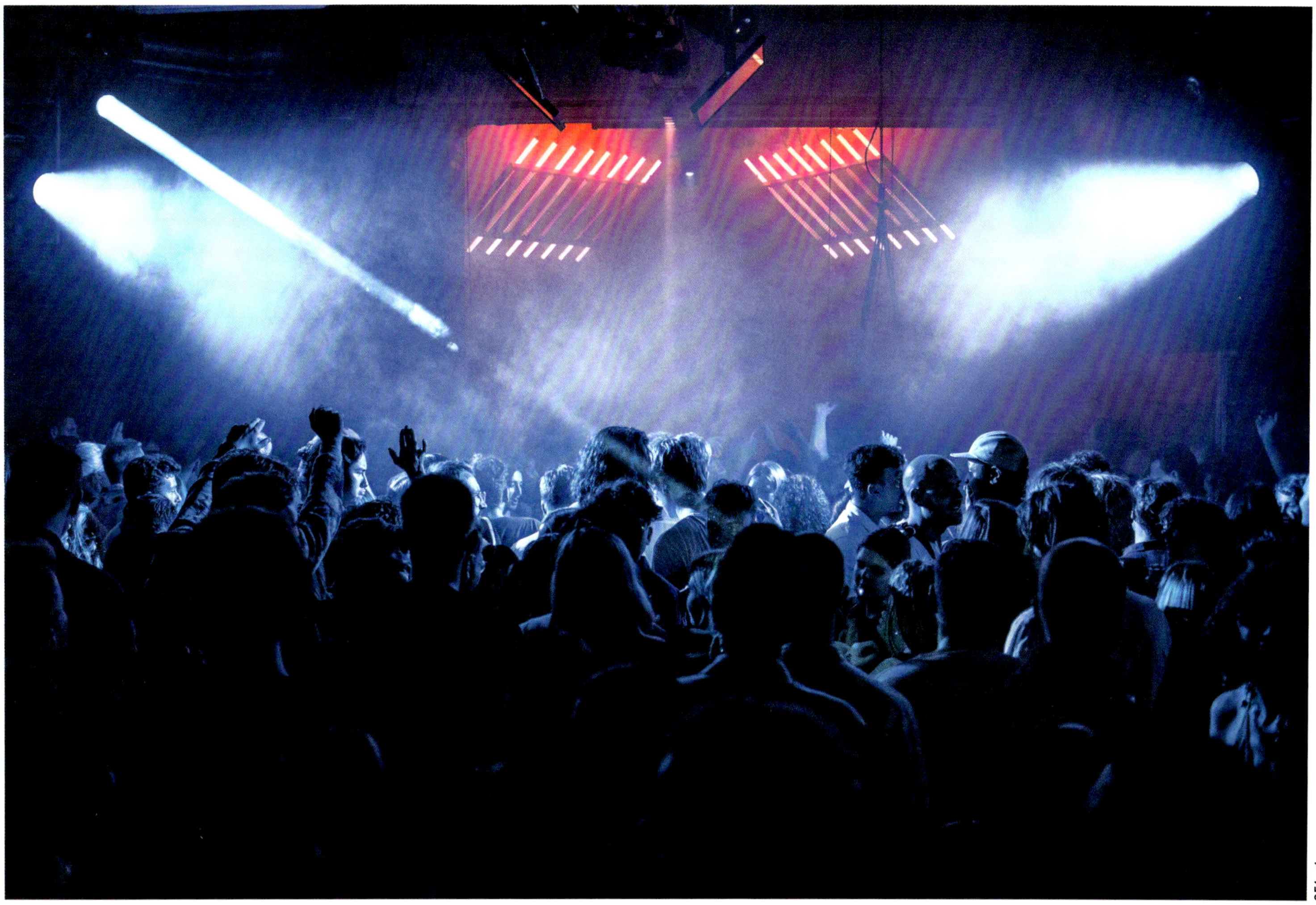

251—1

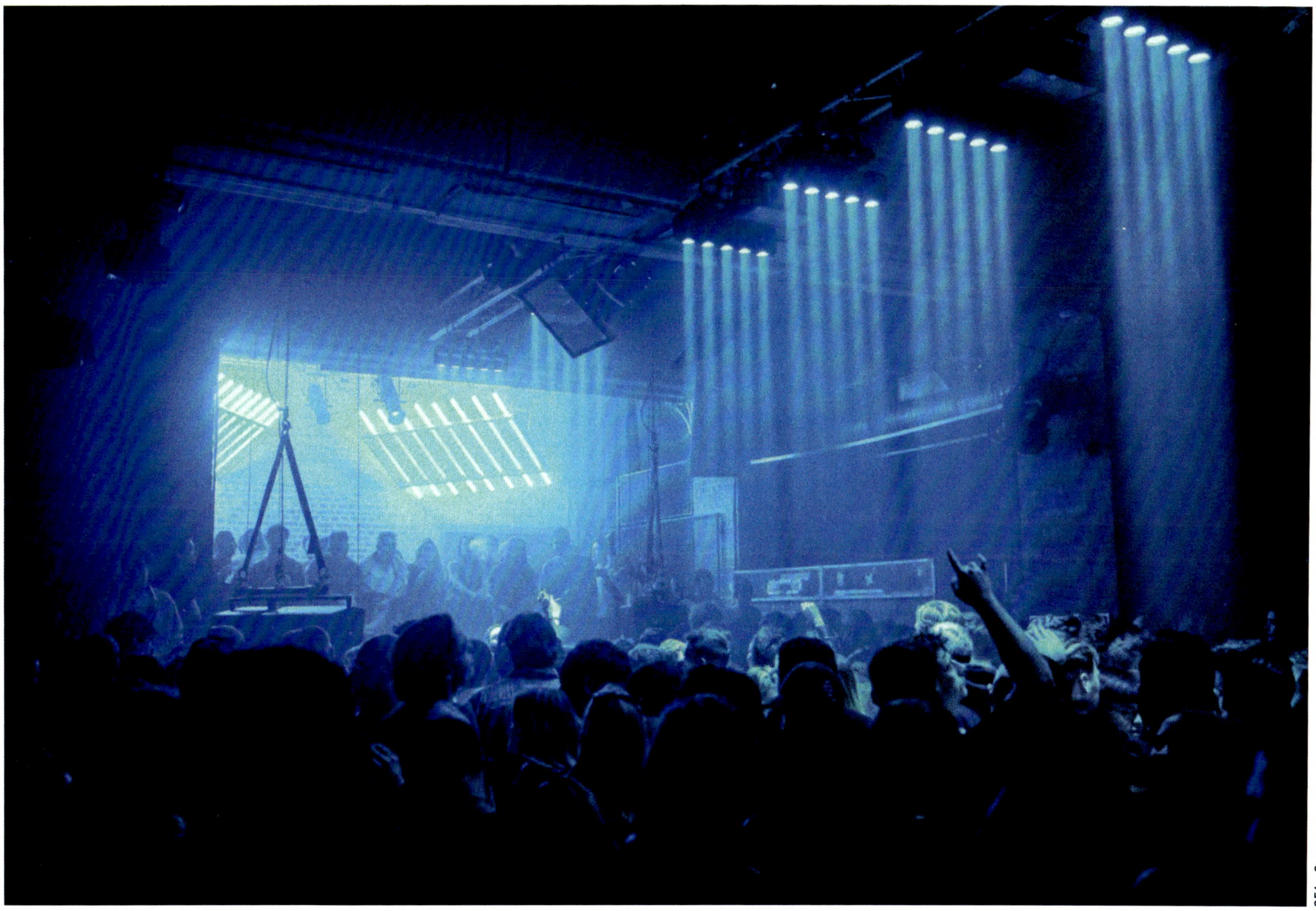

251—2

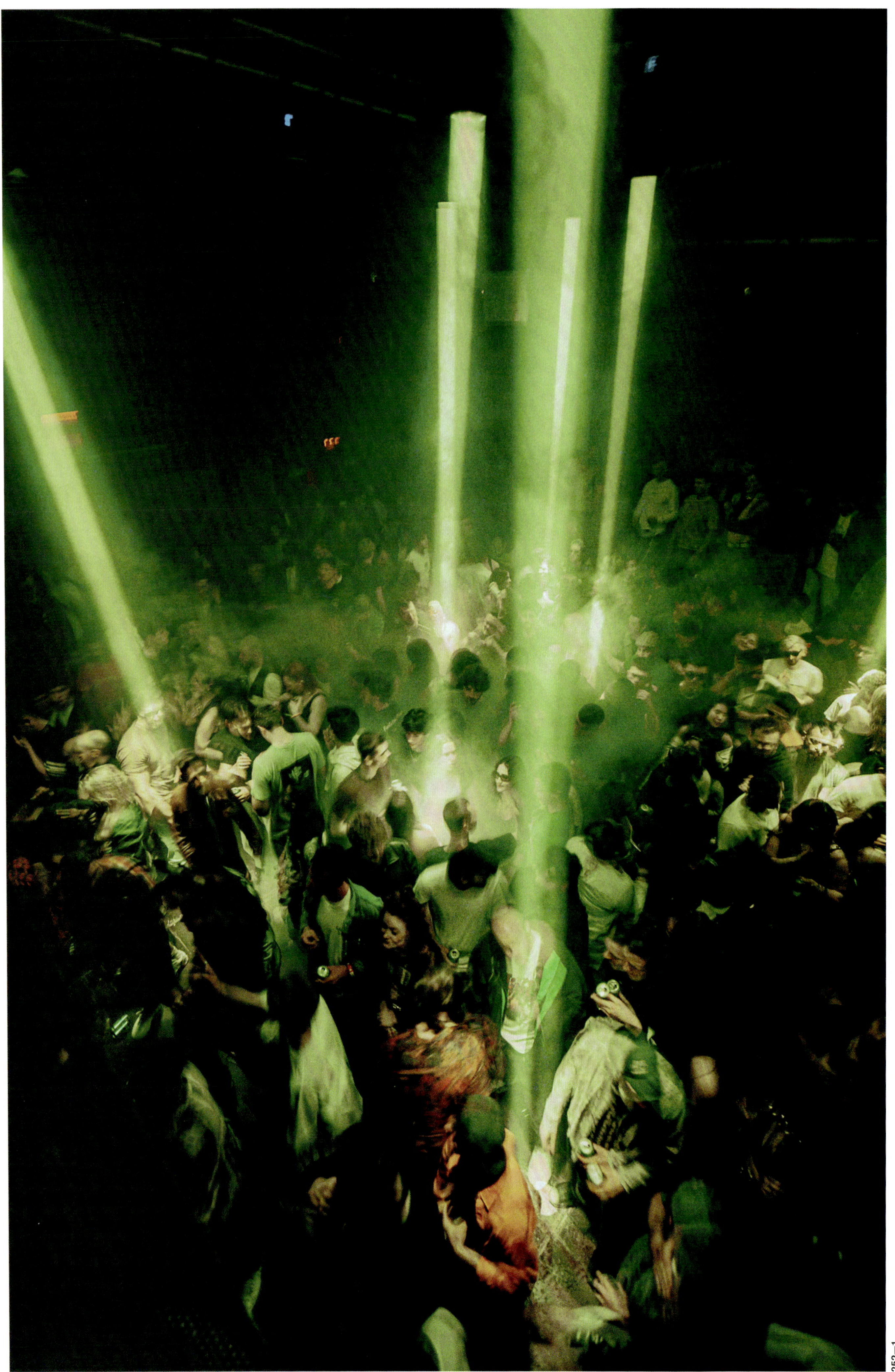

252—1

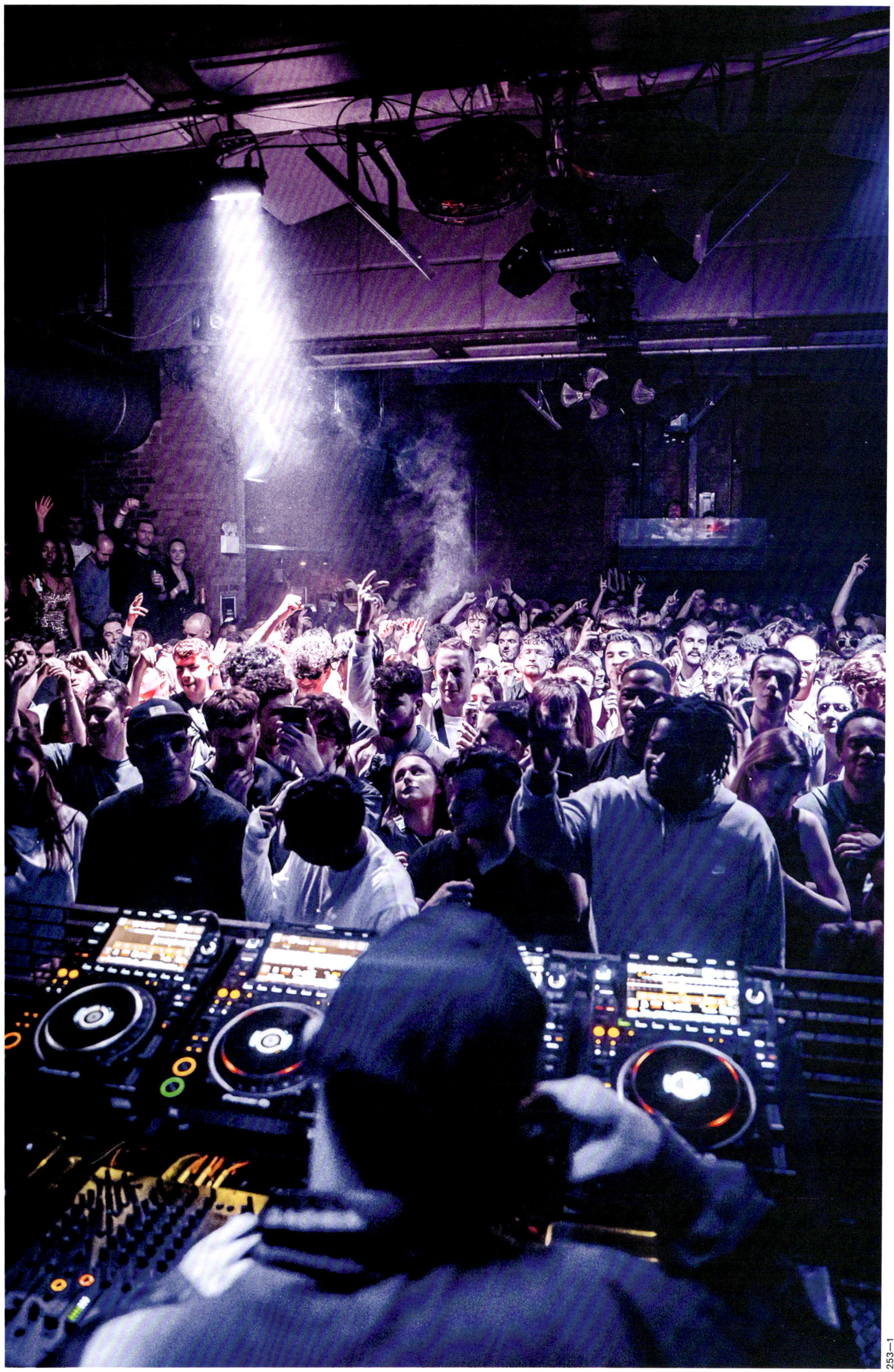

253—1

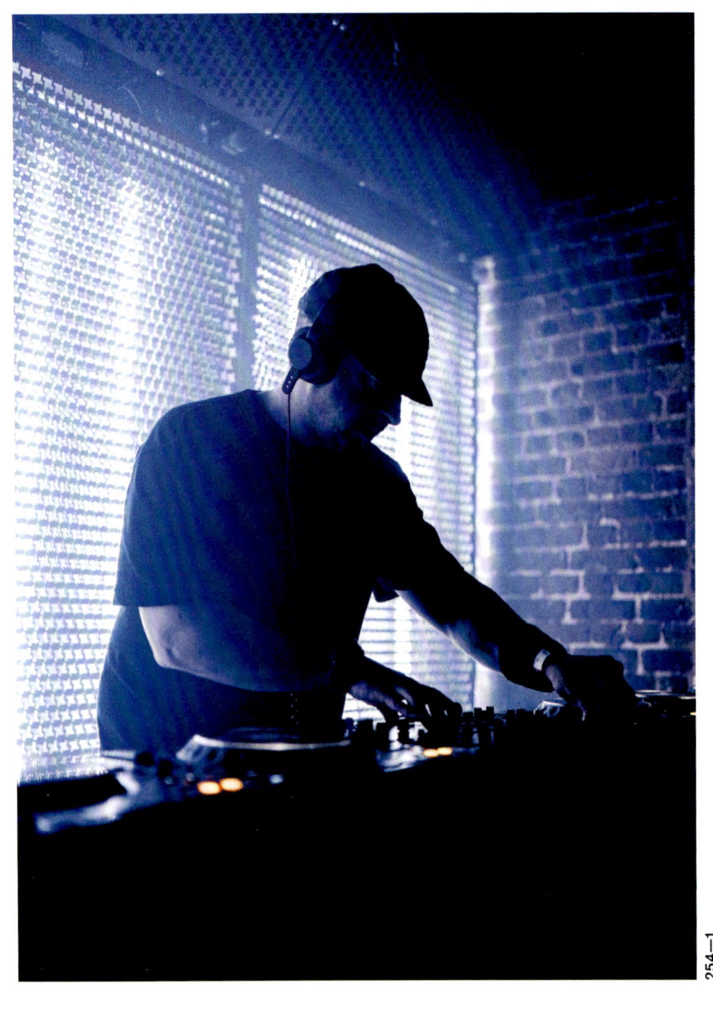

254—1

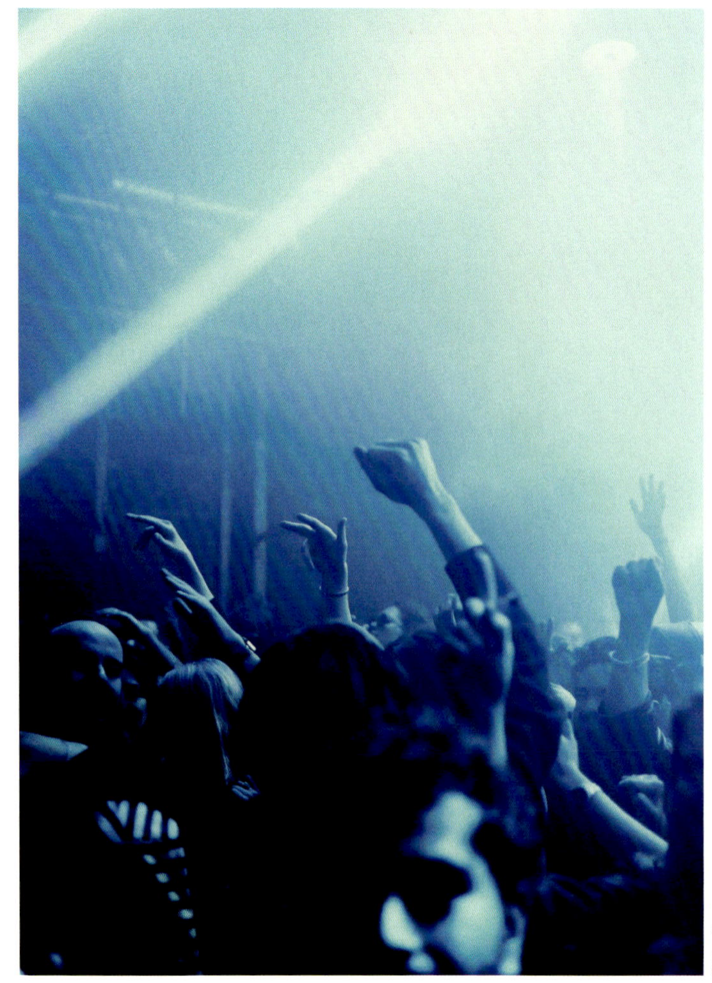

254—2

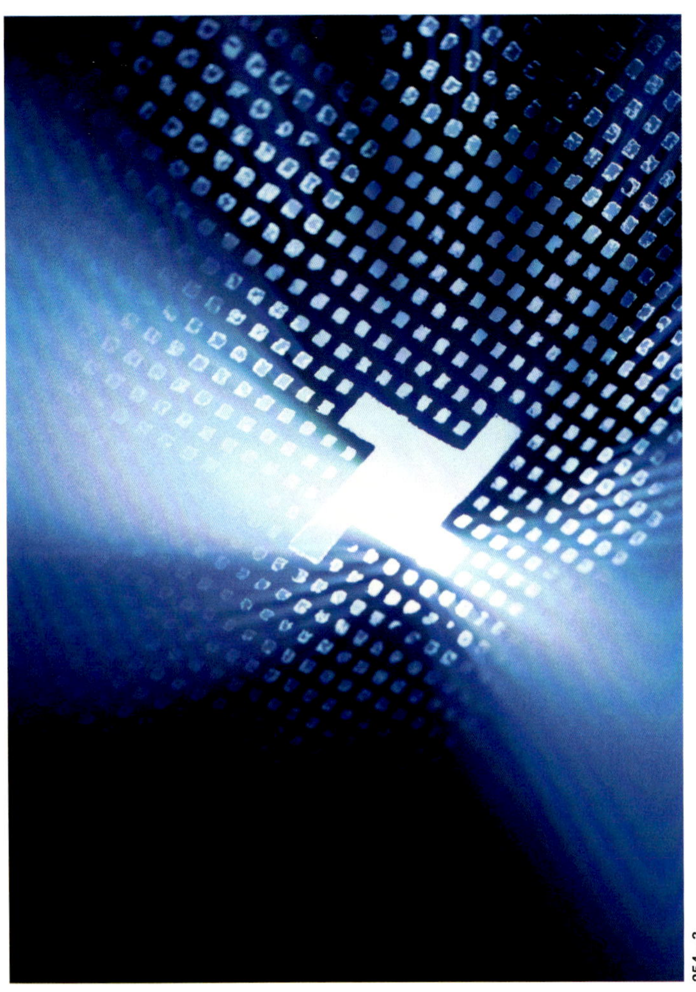

254—3

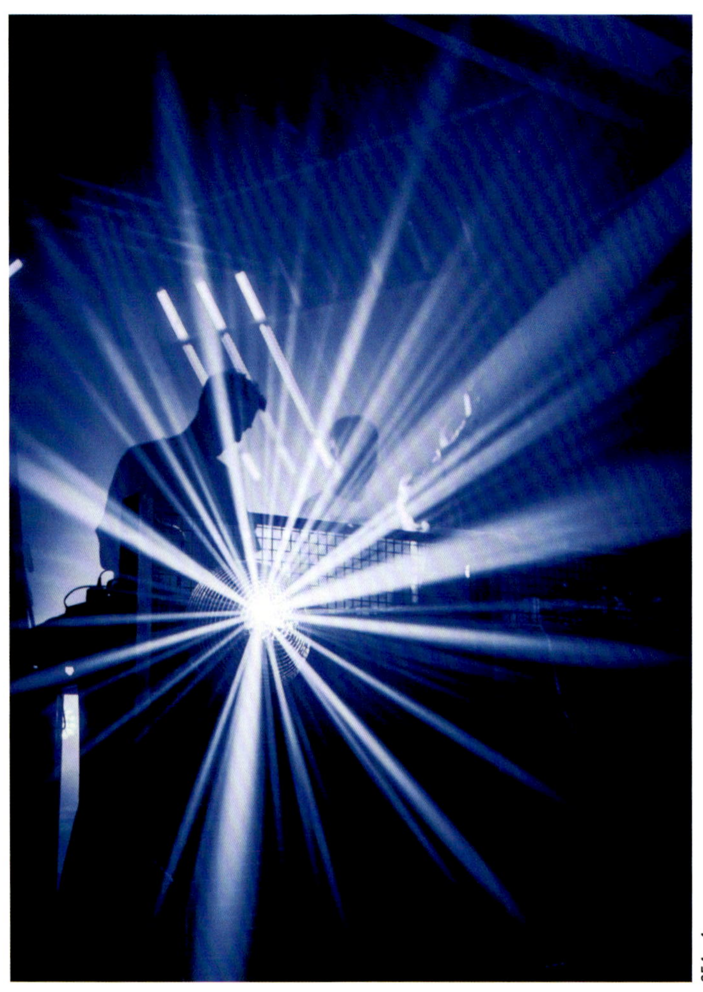

254—4

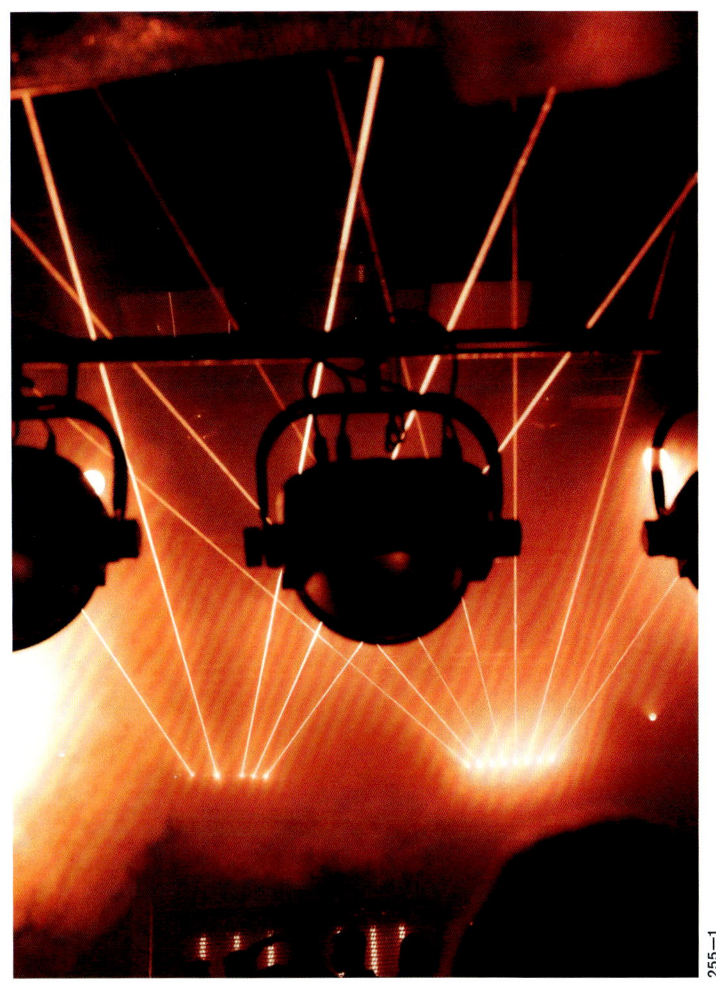
255—1

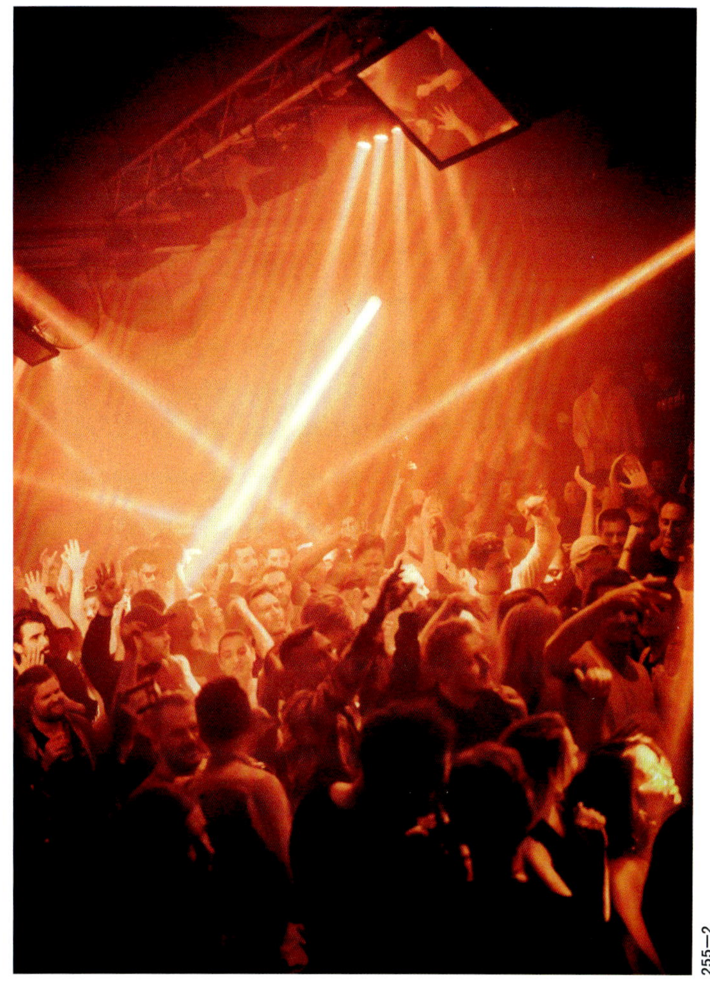
255—2

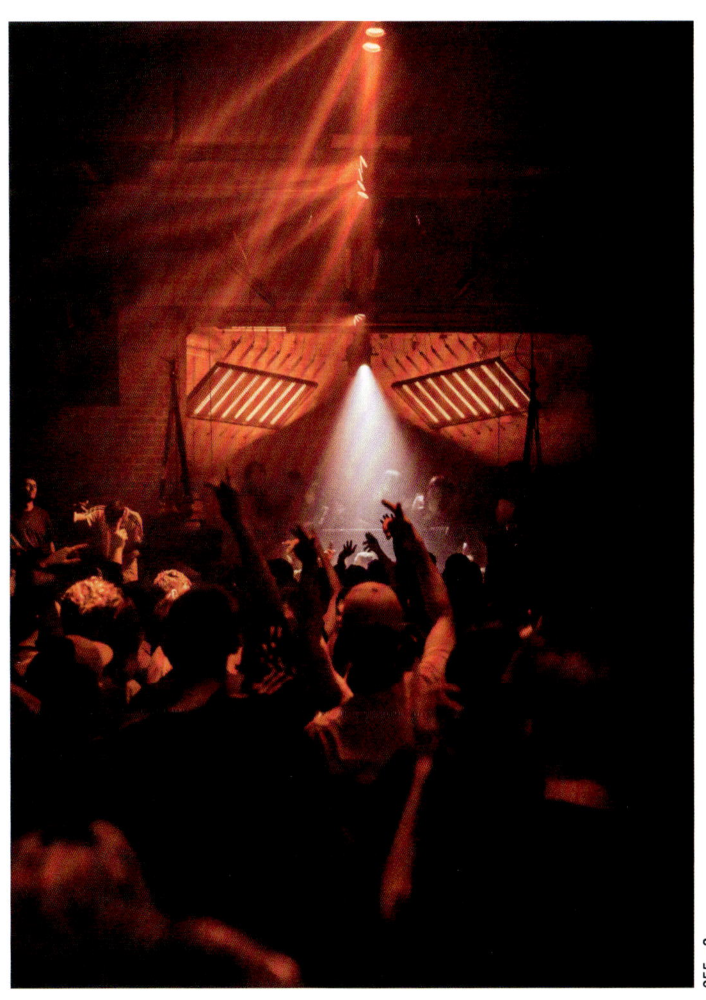
255—3

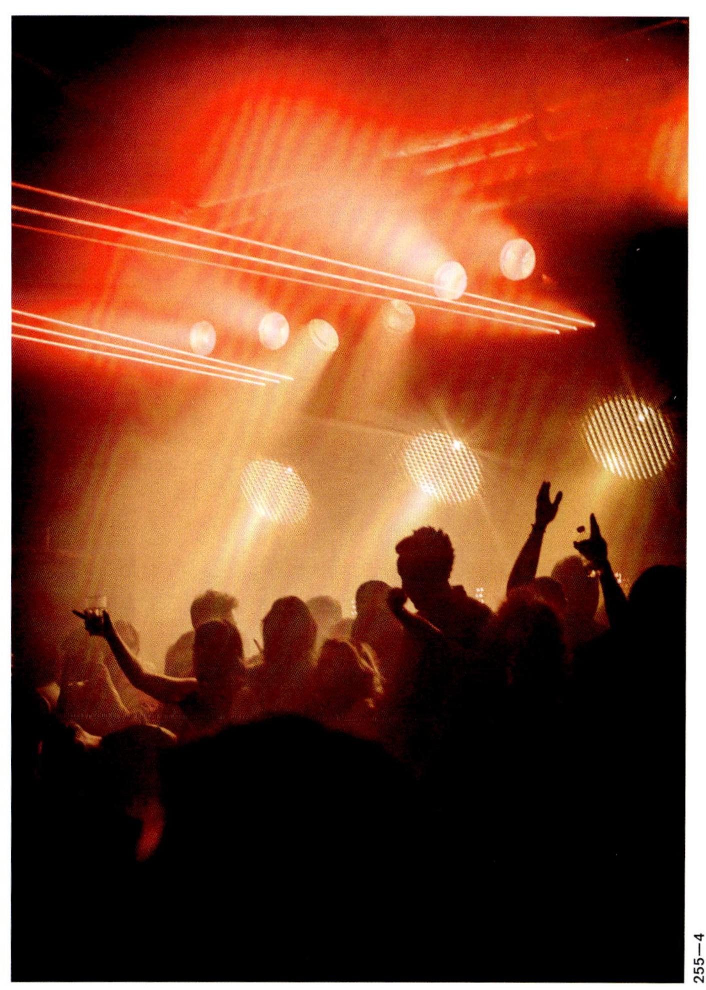
255—4

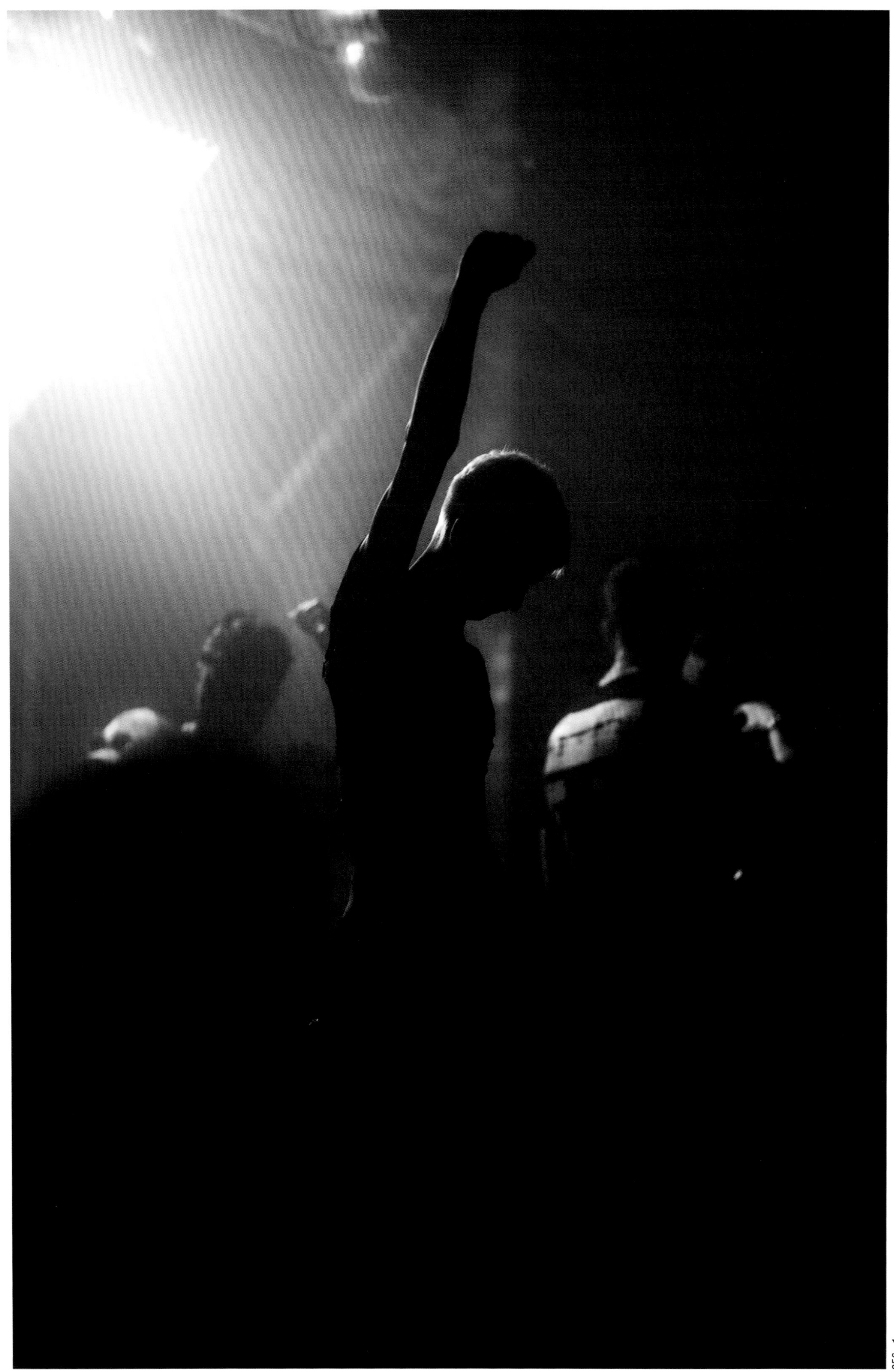

256—1

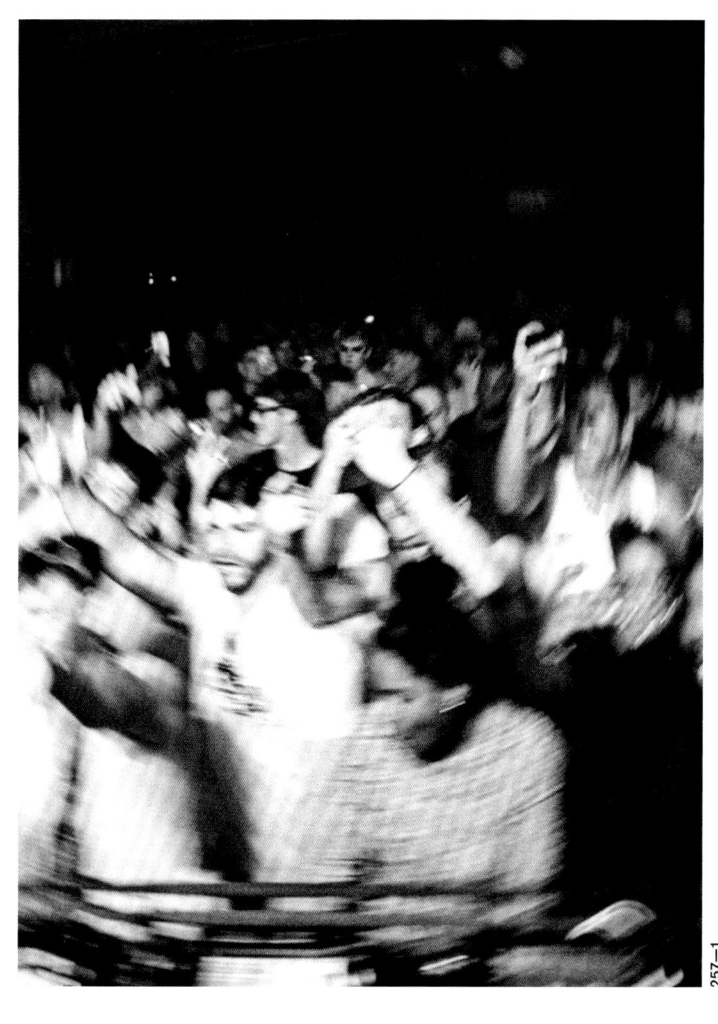
257—1

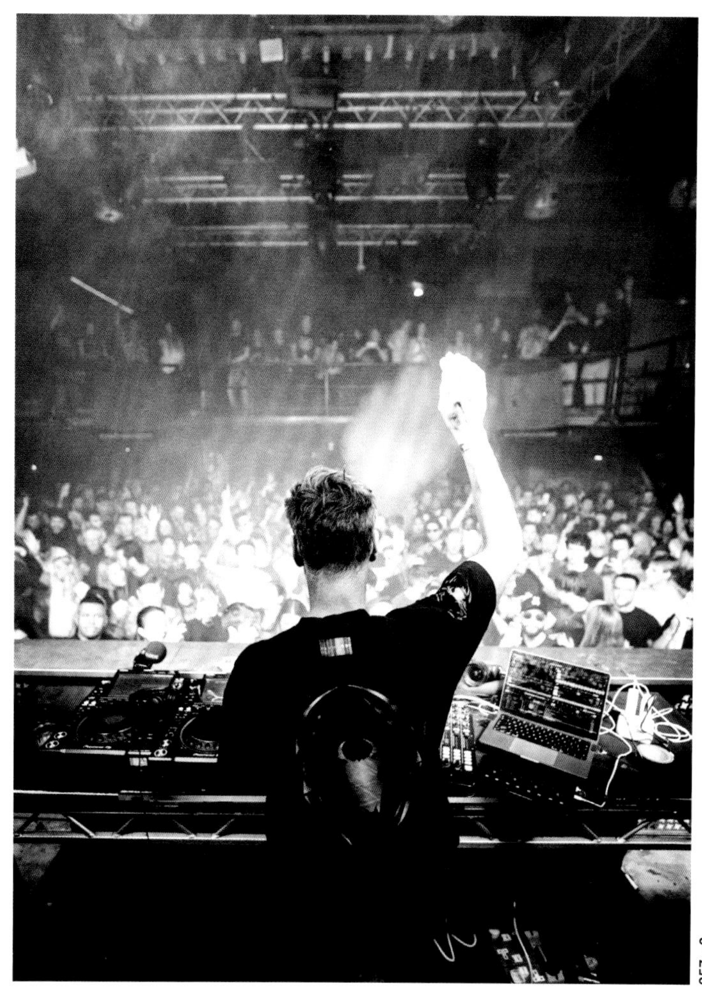
257—2

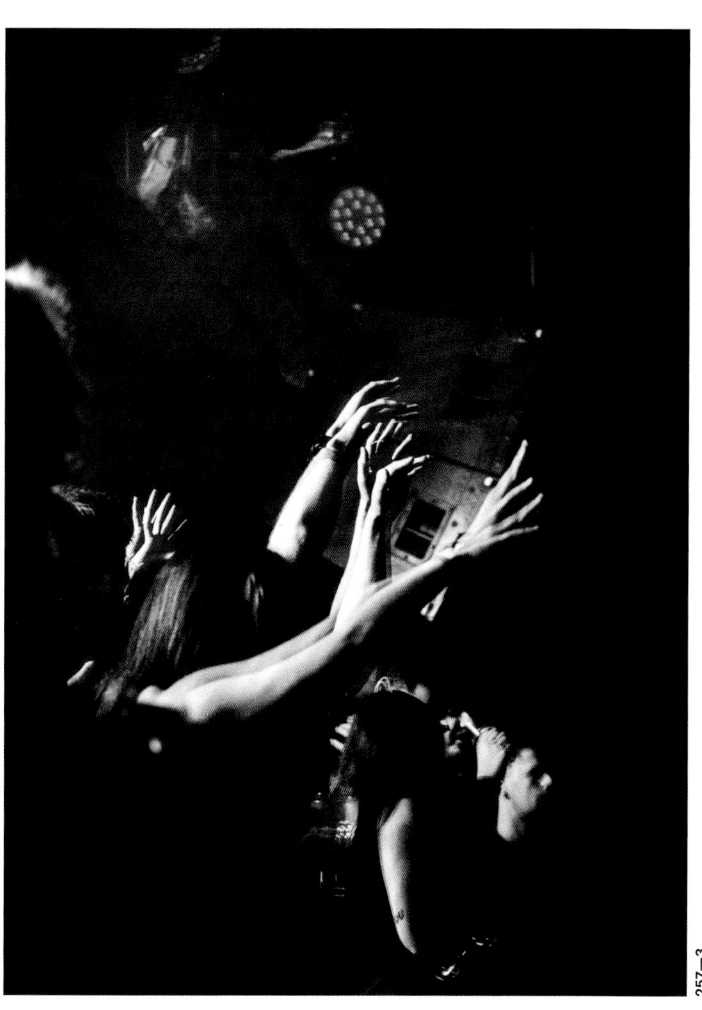
257—3

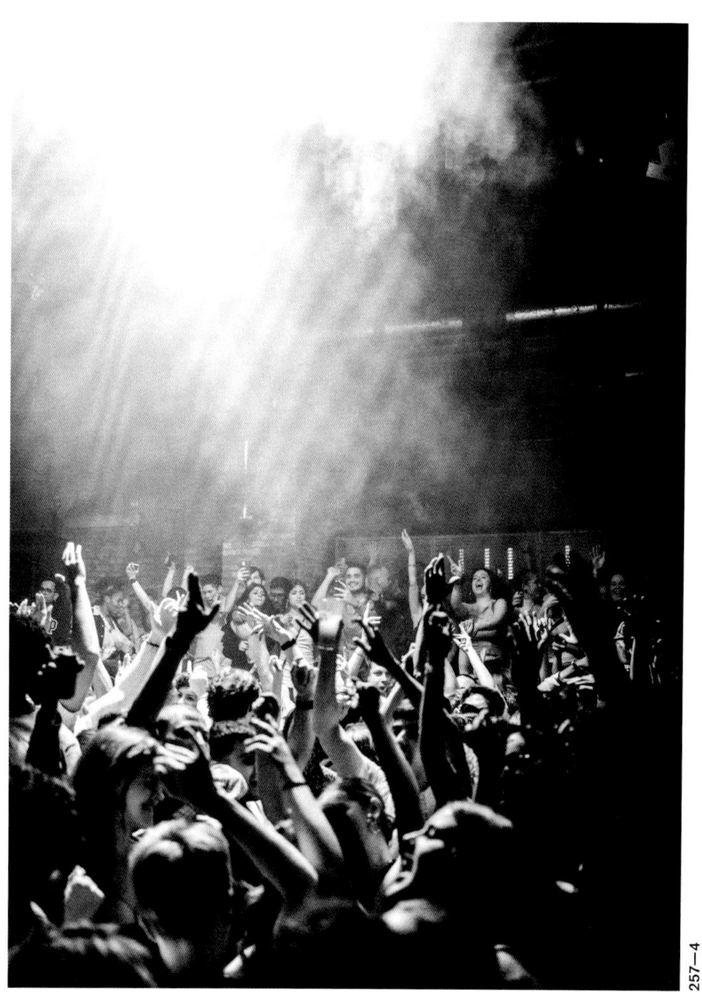
257—4

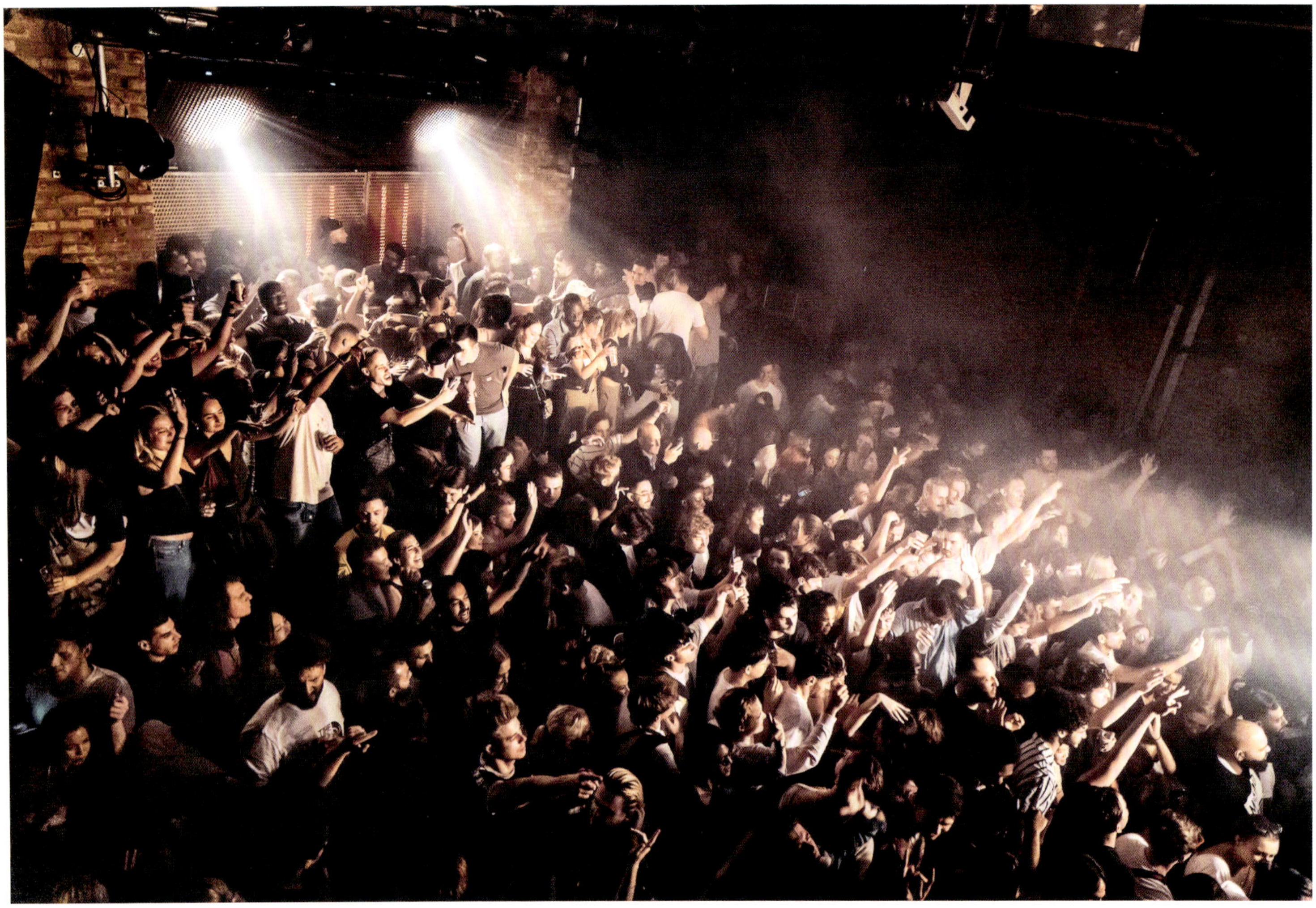

258—1

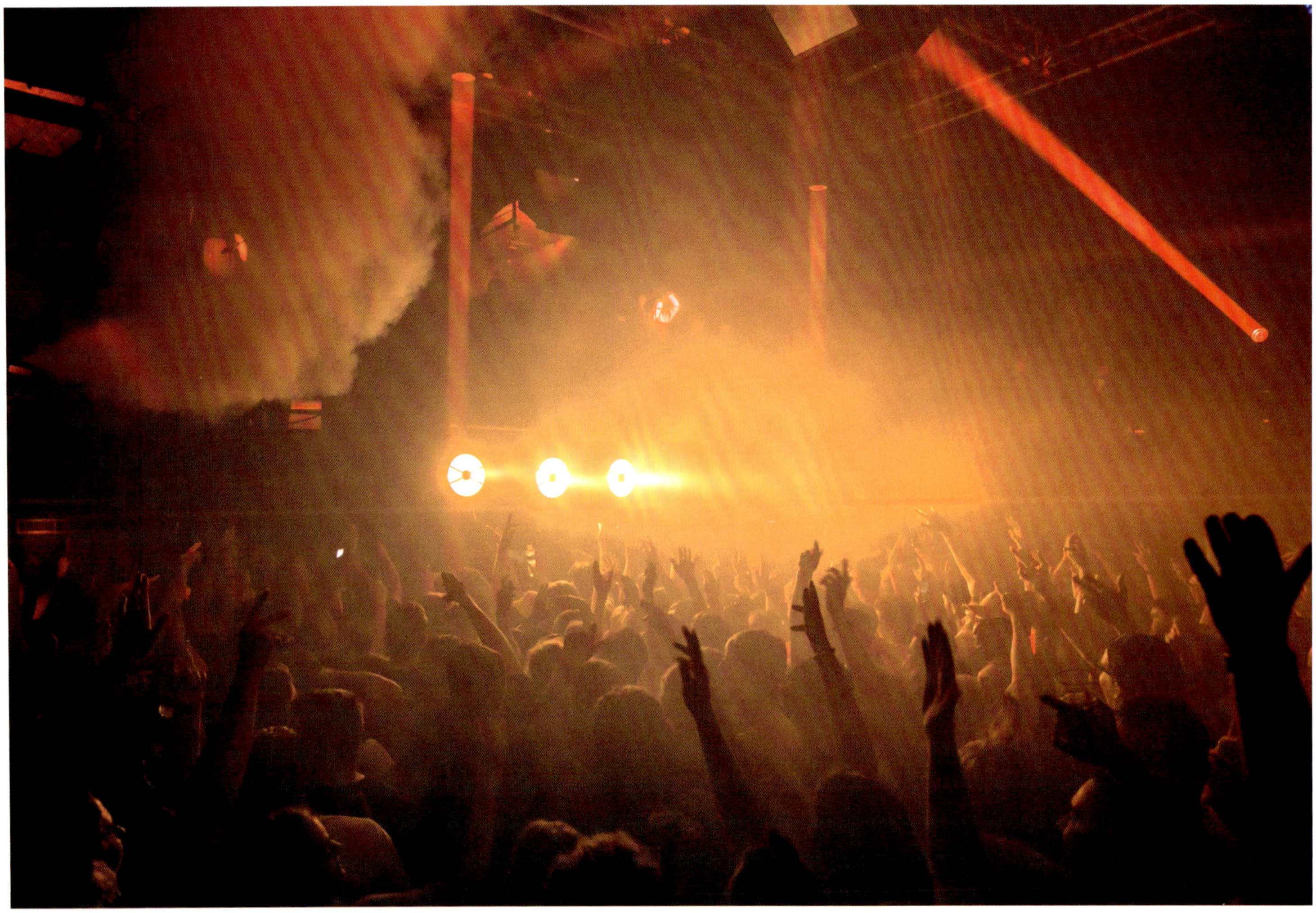

258—2

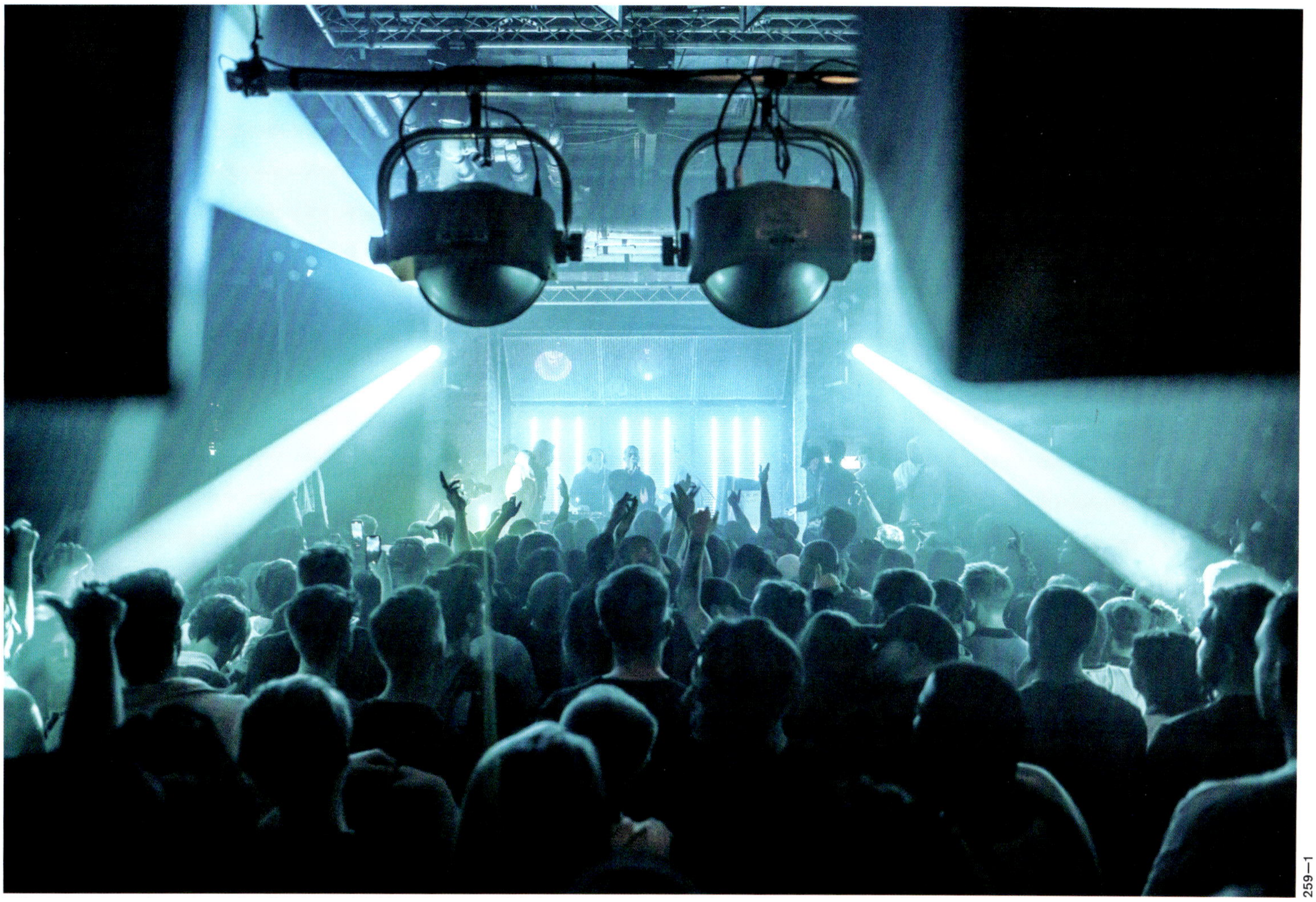

259—1

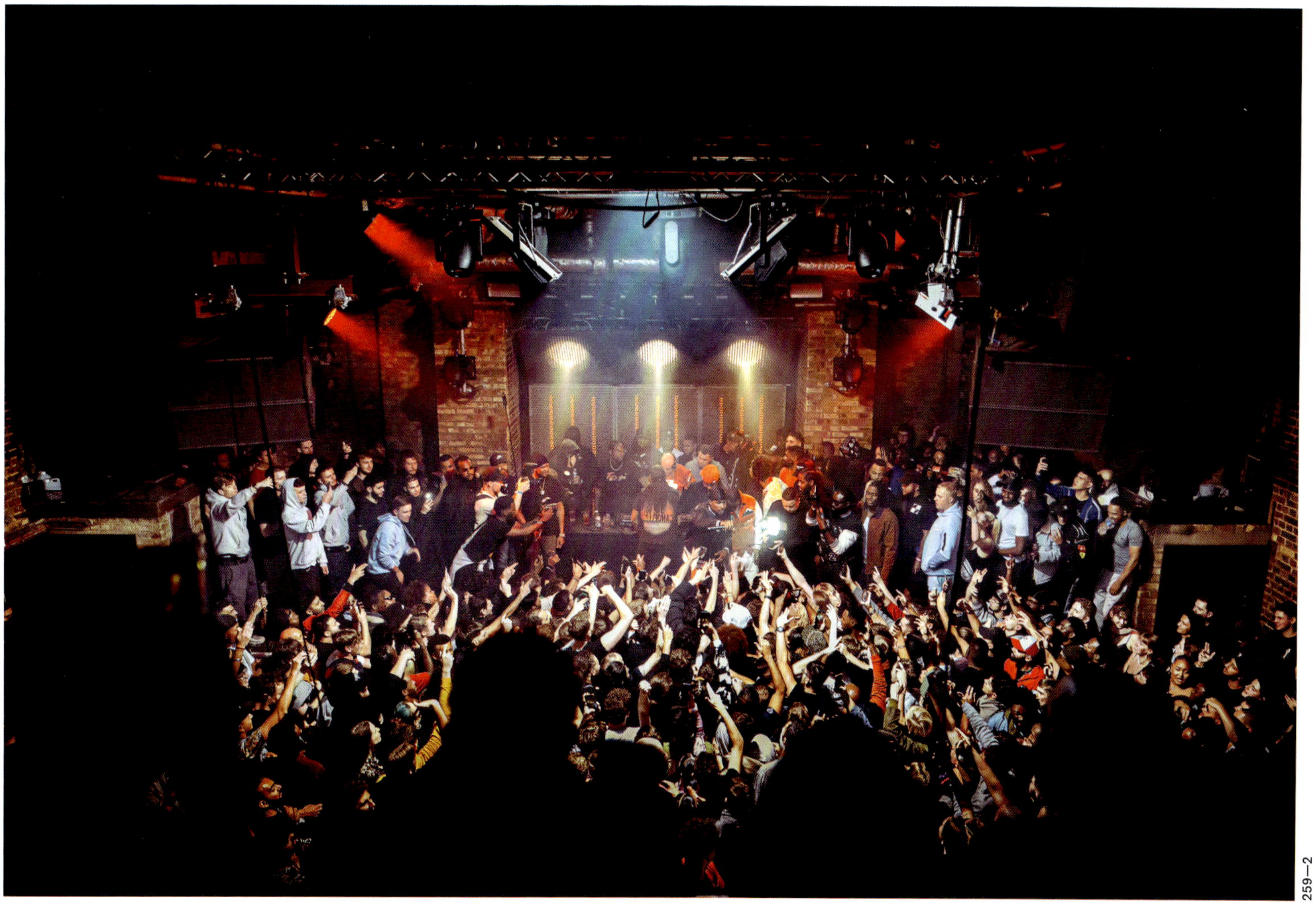

259—2

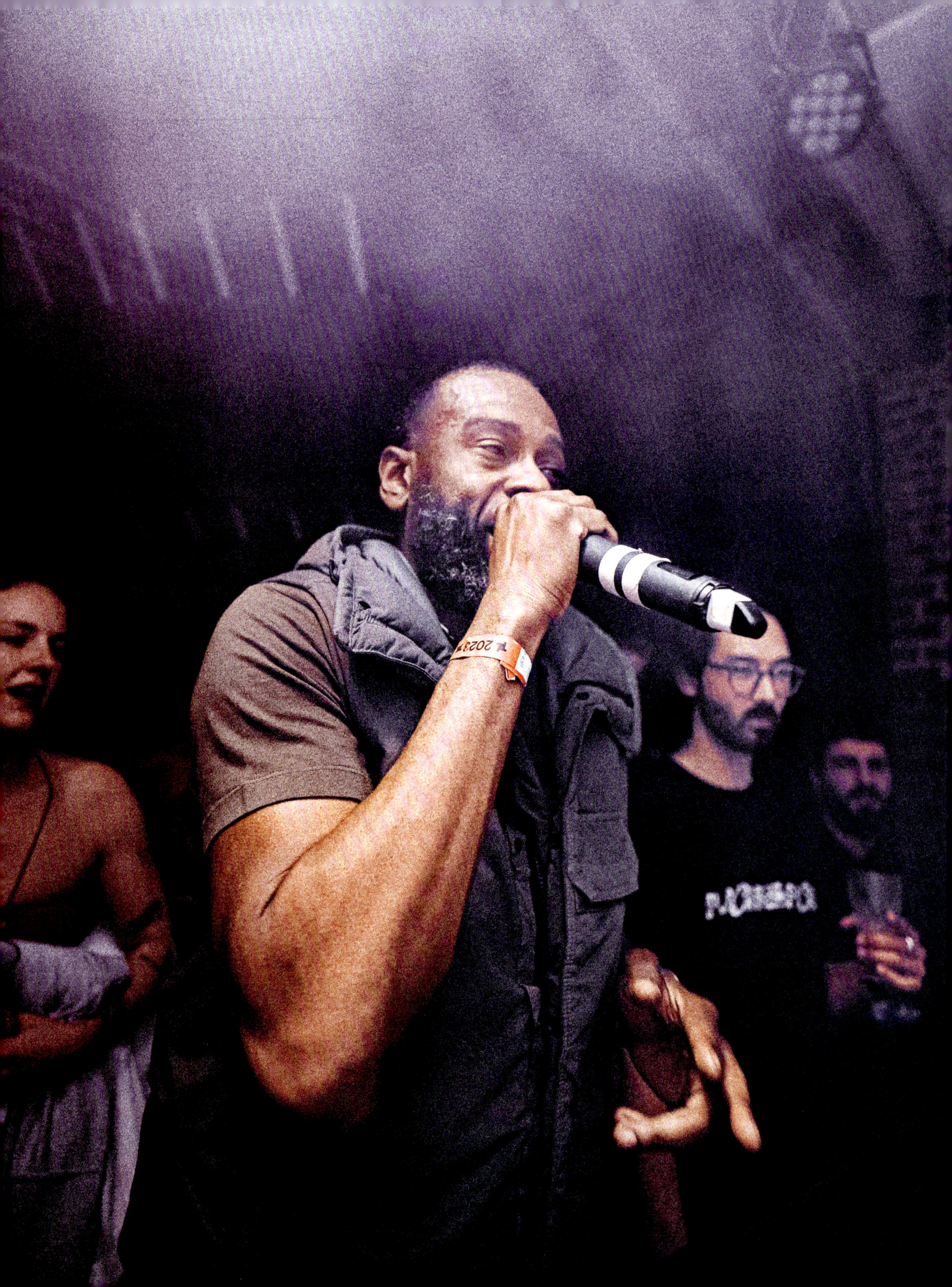

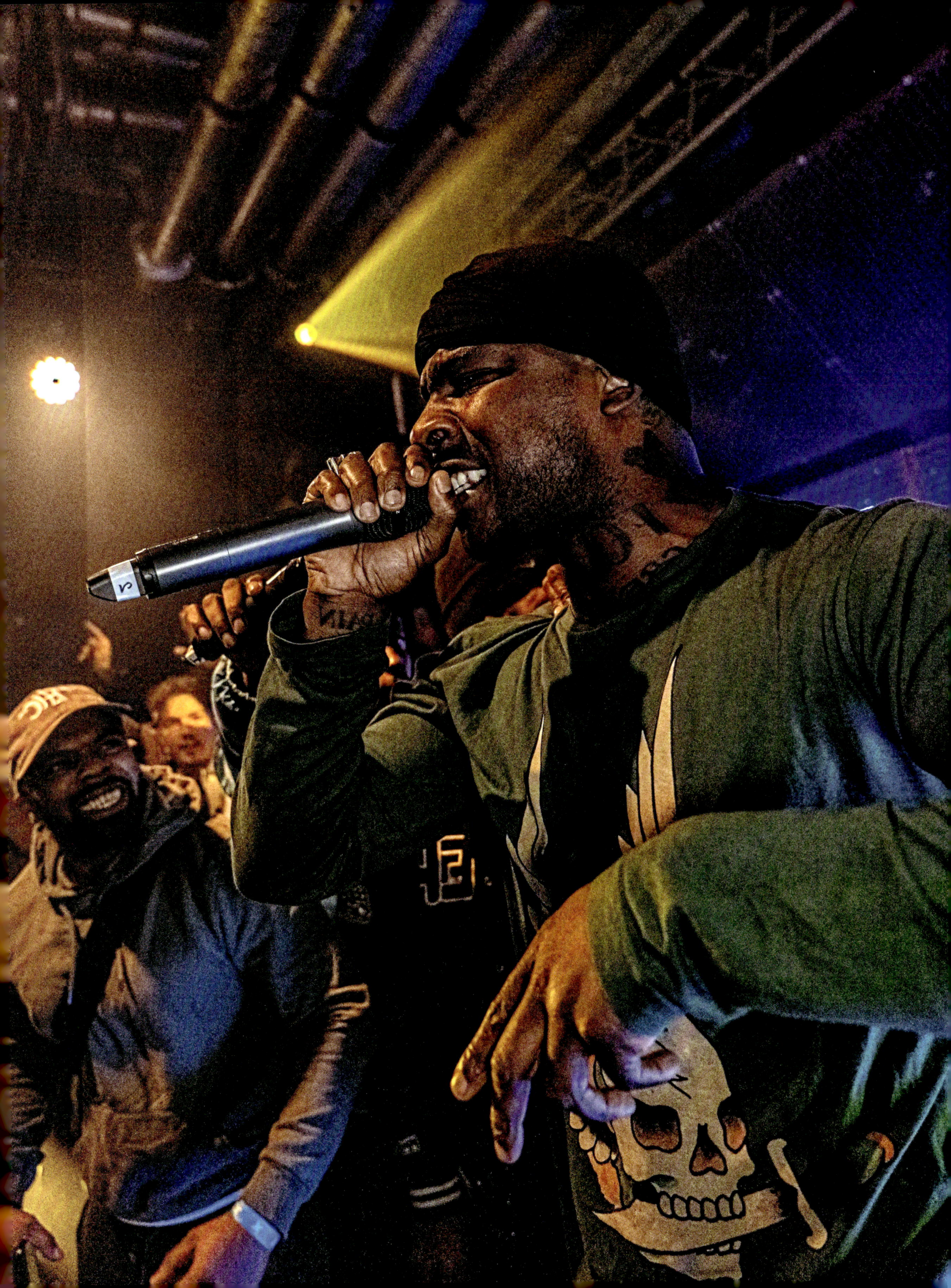

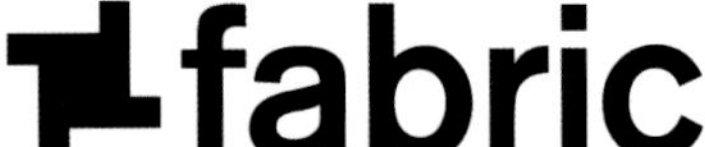

Fabric
77a Charterhouse Street
London EC1M 3HN
T+44 (0)20 7336 8898
F+44 (0)20 7253 3932
www.fabriclondon.com

June 2007

FAO – Danny Newman

Ref: Dizzee Rascal / Get Loaded 2007

Dear Danny,

As discussed on the phone I can confirm that the above named act – Dizzee Rascal has performed at fabric on a number of occasions. Each time has proved to be a successful trouble free event and a good showcase for his talents. We have never experienced any negative incidents linked to Dizzee and would and probably will happily have him perform at the club in the future.

Dizzee himself is a dedicated musician and can often get stereotypically pigeon-holed with certain groups of people who follow certain types of music. With any club night security and proactive measures are of paramount importance and with any music or any night there is always an element of risk associated – hence the need for a good solid operating and security plan.

I have not experienced at fabric any instances that would discourage us from having Dizzee back in the future. I would suggest however that any big event such as Get Loaded that thorough intelligence and due diligence be part of the build up and that would include research on any acts that are booked to play. I am sure that you will be on top of that with your lengthy experience.

I wish you all the best luck for the event and am fully contactable should you need to speak with me further.

Best regards,

Dan Coshan
General Manager
+44(0)207 549 4162 (direct)

262–1

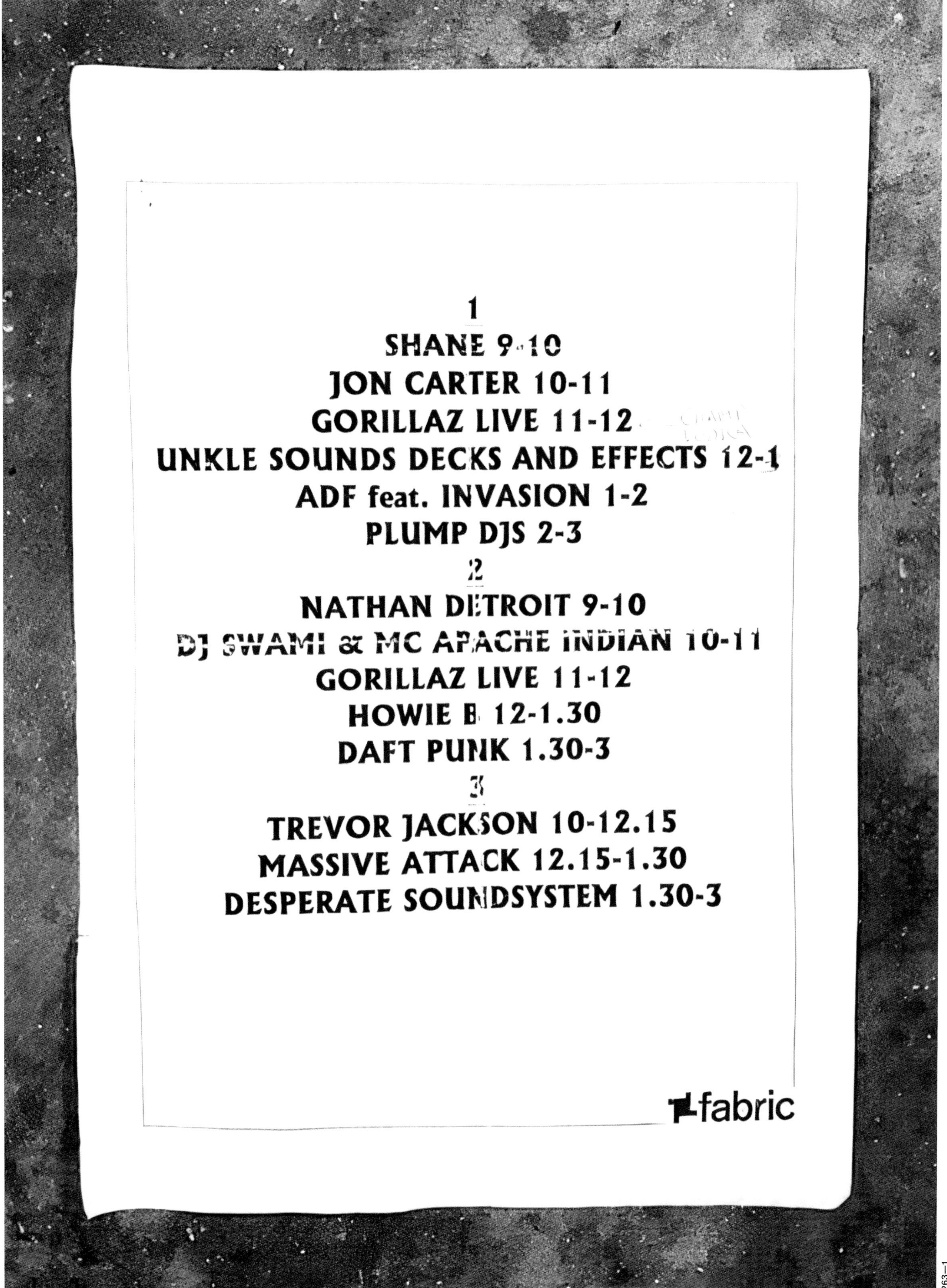
1
SHANE 9-10
JON CARTER 10-11
GORILLAZ LIVE 11-12
UNKLE SOUNDS DECKS AND EFFECTS 12-1
ADF feat. INVASION 1-2
PLUMP DJS 2-3
2
NATHAN DETROIT 9-10
DJ SWAMI & MC APACHE INDIAN 10-11
GORILLAZ LIVE 11-12
HOWIE B 12-1.30
DAFT PUNK 1.30-3
3
TREVOR JACKSON 10-12.15
MASSIVE ATTACK 12.15-1.30
DESPERATE SOUNDSYSTEM 1.30-3
fabric
263—1

#savefabric

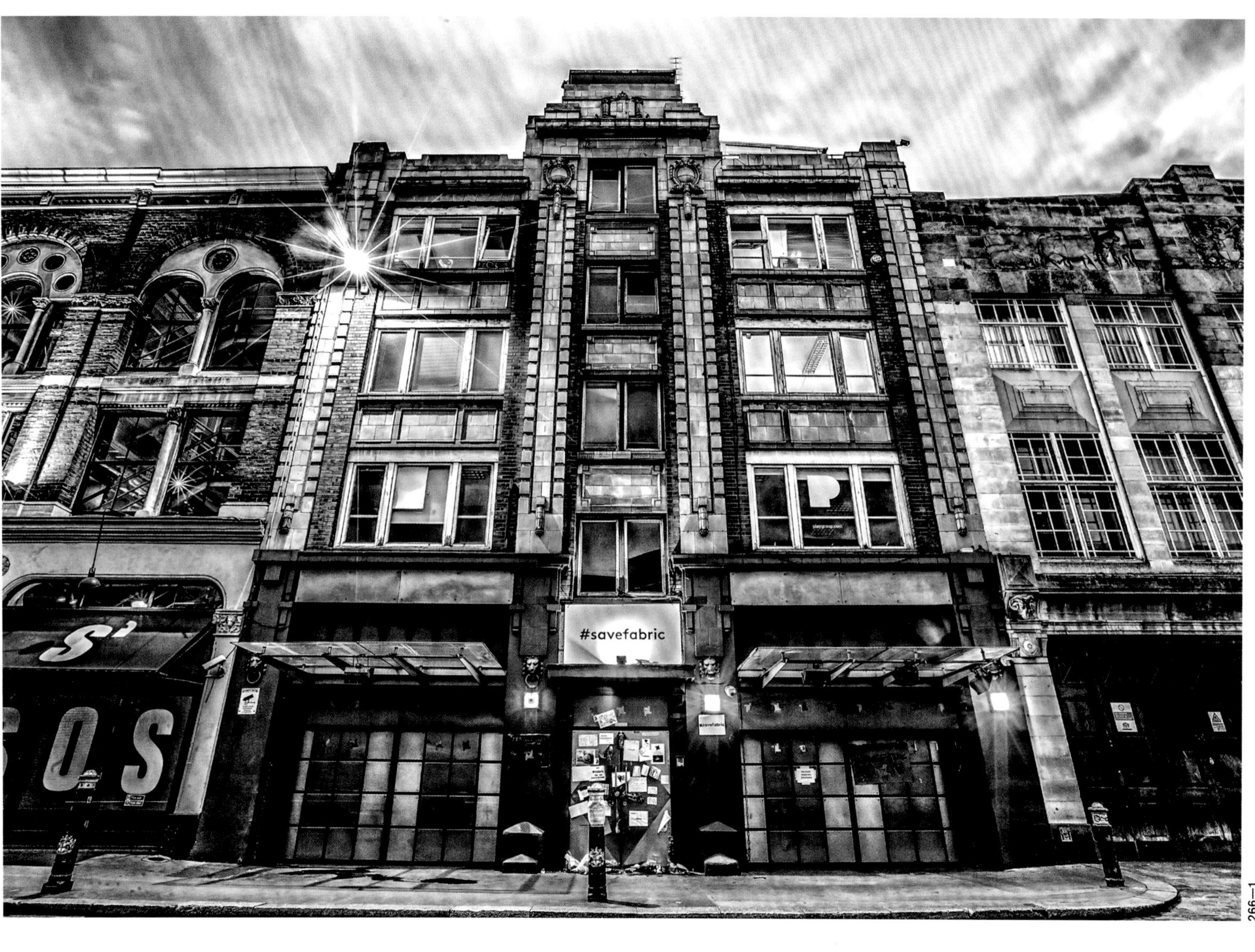

266—1

Almost as soon as fabric picked itself back up after the matter collapse, it was cooking with gas. The biggest nights from matter were folded into the fabric regular programming, so creatively and in terms of audience appeal they were, in fact, stronger than ever; 2011 to 2014 were halcyon years, with dubstep at its high-energy commercial peak, grime resurgent, and the audience for fabric's house and techno ever more global as the scene expanded beyond its European and North American centres. But although the business was back on track and the punters were extremely happy with what fabric provided, the authorities were increasingly not so into it.

In 2015 the Metropolitan Police asked them to join what was framed as a consultation, providing them with a hypothetical list of new measures to see what they would and would not consider signing up to. It seemed uncontroversial for the most part; in fact, the vast majority of things suggested, fabric already had in place. A couple they thought seemed a bit off but could maybe work, but there were a small number that rang loud alarm bells. Worst of all was a suggestion that the club should take sniffer dogs up and down the queue, and if the dog identified a customer as having been in contact with a narcotic, they'd not only be refused entry, but put on a national database and barred from licensed premises nationwide.

It all too quickly became clear that this wasn't just a suggestion, but was going to be imposed on them as a condition on their licence. Keith was shocked. 'We had a great relationship with Islington Council,' he says. 'We were their golden boys. If anyone was opening up a venue, they'd use us as an example. They'd say, "Read the fabric manual – this is the way to do it"!' It felt like they were being shaken down – and they couldn't just refuse; they had to go to court to prove it was unreasonable. 'Sniffer dogs are only 23 per cent accurate,' fumes Keith, 'so that's 77 per cent of people with their lives blighted for no good reason. What's more, even in that 23 per cent you could easily have just trodden on someone's discarded joint or whatever and then your life's fucked. But aside from all that, it's illegal! A dog search has to be done in private, and anyone we'd done it to in public would be within their rights to sue us.'

The judge not only ruled against the police and council in the most scathing terms, but without prompting reminded them that fabric had long been a beacon of good practice. Not only did fabric have superior facilities and training, she pointed out, but the club's medical staff had, over its fifteen years of life up till that point, saved the life of over thirty people who had not even been to the club, but had been found nearby and brought in for treatment. It was also noted in court that trials of sniffer dogs around clubs had been directly responsible for ten deaths, as it had caused young people to panic and swallow their entire stashes of drugs. It became clear that the idea had just been cooked up by the police in the cafe, with no evidence base or precedent, but had somehow got adopted as a flagship policy and foisted on the council.

'This particular unit of the police,' says Cameron, 'were particularly dogmatic, and did not appreciate being shown up like that. It's a shame, as they were actually trying to modernise licensing, but they were just doing it with a sledgehammer!' Keith is emphatic, too, that their attitude was never anti-police or antagonistic. 'We all need the police,' he says; 'we need order in society, we need to feel safe. But the way they're structured means they can never admit they're wrong, as we've seen so many times, from Hillsborough on down. So they couldn't forgive us for winning like that.' It was, in fact, made absolutely explicit that fabric's cards were now marked; one officer looked Keith in the eye as they were leaving the hearing and said, 'Don't think this is over!'

'We didn't know what would happen, of course,' says Cameron, 'but the time bomb was ticking from that point.'

What eventually happened was tragic. In the summer of 2016, in the space of under a month, two teenagers died after taking MDMA in fabric. There was an epidemic of overdoses at the time; the ability to buy drugs on the dark web in particular had led to a vast increase in availability of very strong and pure substances, and nationally and internationally deaths were on the increase. Indeed, as Keith points out, another nearby club of similar size had five fatalities that same year – but it was fabric where the hammer came down from the authorities. Their licence was suspended, the club closed, and a council licensing-review hearing was scheduled to see whether they could ever get it back.

The fabric team took the situation very seriously. As well as being nightmarish for the two boys who'd died and their families, of course, it had been traumatising for the staff and medics who'd dealt with the situations. This wasn't something they could be blasé about or pretend wasn't a problem – but at the same time they knew they'd been unfairly targeted, and they were determined to fight their corner. 'We thought we might get the licence back,' says Cameron. 'I guess we thought it was 50/50, and if we did get it back, it would be with complex conditions.' But nothing they did was ever going to be enough.

The night before their licence hearing, a broadly sympathetic councillor was replaced on the hearing panel by another – a former Pentonville prison governor who during his election had suggested policies including that council tenants convicted of cannabis possession should be evicted from their homes – and they knew they were done for. Keith is still incandescent about the situation: 'I wanted to shout at him, "How's it going, keeping drugs out of prisons? We have three thousand people through the door in a night, while a prison will have fifty visitors a day, with intimate searches, and they still can't stop drugs getting in. What hope have we got?' But, of course, I couldn't.' Theatrics and high emotion weren't going to help them; at this point, they had to scrupulously play everything by the book.

As they guessed, given this last-minute personnel switch, the licence was revoked, and fabric was closed – ostensibly permanently. They had to dismantle the company, giving notice to all the staff and leaving only a skeleton team of three to fight to overturn the decision and reinstate the licence, with some three months to wait before they could get an appeal court hearing. It felt bleak at first, but the sense of family once again made itself felt. Shaun Roberts, who'd moved on to pastures new in 2015, came back to help, while Sunday promoter Jacob Husley was a powerhouse, coordinating the #savefabric petition and corresponding with London mayor Sadiq Khan – and Houndstooth's Rob Booth threw everything into gathering exclusive tracks for what would become a 111-track monster compilation representing the entire underground. All this was done unpaid, for the love of the club. And support came from outside just as much. As Keith says: 'It turned pretty quickly in our favour, because in no time it became fabric and the world against the police and Islington Council!'

'The council were NOT prepared for what happened,' says Cameron, 'because they were just inundated by a tidal wave of support.'

It took no time for #savefabric to go supernova. From media editorials to celebrity endorsements – Goldie threatening to melt down his MBE was a particularly attention-grabbing one – and from banners on football terraces to individuals spreading the hashtag, it was everywhere. Feargal Sharkey, then CEO of industry body UK Music, spoke eloquently in their support, and Boiler Room ran live discussion panels about the situation. And as it all snowballed, two things became apparent. First up, it was truly global – messages were flooding in from South America, from Indonesia, from everywhere, not just from people who'd been, but from people who knew of fabric, who'd heard the mix CDs and dreamed of coming one day. Second, support was coming from other venues and rival promoters, who were even putting their money where their mouths were and contributing thousands to the fighting fund. Steadily, #savefabric became something bigger: it became #saveourculture.

One unforgettable boost to the campaign came from the re-emergence of a viral story from earlier that year. In May, fabric had had an unexpected visit on a Sunday night from a Polish couple in their seventies. Staff thought they must be lost or mistaken about the nature of the venue at first, but no, they enjoyed clubbing at home, had heard of fabric, and while they were visiting their daughter in Watford, they came along to dance all night. The story had exploded worldwide at the time – and when fabric's closure came, the couple, who'd stayed in touch with Jacob Husley after their visit, sent in messages of support. 'It was crazy,' says Jacob. 'Their story had been so popular that their message of support got shared almost more than the rest of the campaign put together!' It was cute, it was funny – but it was also a profound expression of fabric's way of turning small, individual dancefloor experiences into something bigger, and of the way the wider world grasped that.

It was a depressing year out in the wider world: 2016 was the year of Trump's victory, of the Brexit vote, of selfishness and division triumphing. Yet here was a global wave of community, solidarity, love. This one discotheque in an old meat-storage cellar had touched this many hearts, inspired this many people, been symbolic of so much that was important for those people; that it couldn't be brushed under the carpet by the powers that be like some passing annoyance. Cameron notes ruefully that the closure came in the same week that Berghain in Berlin was awarded high-culture status – placing it in a category with concert halls and museums. 'Yet here,' he says, 'we had a music institution in London getting shut because of social problems that existed outside the club, not because it was negligent in dealing with them. And even people who'd never been to the club could see that this wasn't right.'

Somehow, out of tragedy came something constructive. The whole world got to see what – ironically – only Islington Council had really known before: that for all its dedication to fun, fabric was a very, very serious operation, more scrupulous and painstaking in its commitment to safety and security than many more supposedly respectable nightlife spaces. 'I think,' says Cameron, 'the weight of that whole situation led to a whole different spotlight on the importance of venues. It was not long after that London got its night czar, new mediation groups were set up, and the police couldn't just railroad things into happening.'

All of this came, too, as the acid-house generation were maturing, reaching positions of power and responsibility, and club culture could be looked at in the round. It was no longer just 'a nineties thing', and no longer possible to write off as a set of disparate fads or mindlessly hedonistic – and it WAS possible to talk in the mainstream about club history as social history, and about clubs as key parts of the wider culture. 'It was the first time I really witnessed the power of social media,' says Craig Richards. 'The closure was horrible, but the fact people came together in recognising the importance of what we do was one of the greatest things in … well, in London's cultural history, really!'

This attention meant that fabric was taken that bit more seriously as well, by press, the general public and official bodies. The publicity showed the whole entity to the world: the nightclub itself, of course, with its passionate following, but also the close-knit family of big characters that made it run, and the prodigious musical output that it facilitated. Having heavyweights like Mary Anne Hobbs, Dave Clarke and Heidi showcasing chunks of the #savefabric compilation on the radio brought home to many people how much more it was than just a venue.

And that lasted. In November, before it could reach the High Court, an agreement was made with the police and council that fabric could reopen with stricter licensing conditions, including extra CCTV, ID scanners, lifetime bans for anyone caught trying to buy drugs, and pushing the lower age limit to nineteen. This was tough in a purely practical sense, let alone with the world's eyes on the club. 'In fact it was hell,' says operations director Luke Laws. 'We were essentially restarting from scratch as a new business with someone looking over our shoulder at every turn.' Nonetheless, from here the team began rebuilding fabric, and also their relationships with Islington Council and the local police – who, says Keith, 'I think were actually impressed by the showing we'd put up, and definitely by the amount of love that had been shown for the place.' Bruised but unbowed, fabric reopened with a new sense of maturity: confident in itself, and seen more by the outside world as a cultural institution, as well as simply a place to dance and socialise. And most of all, fabric had shown it was in it for the long haul.

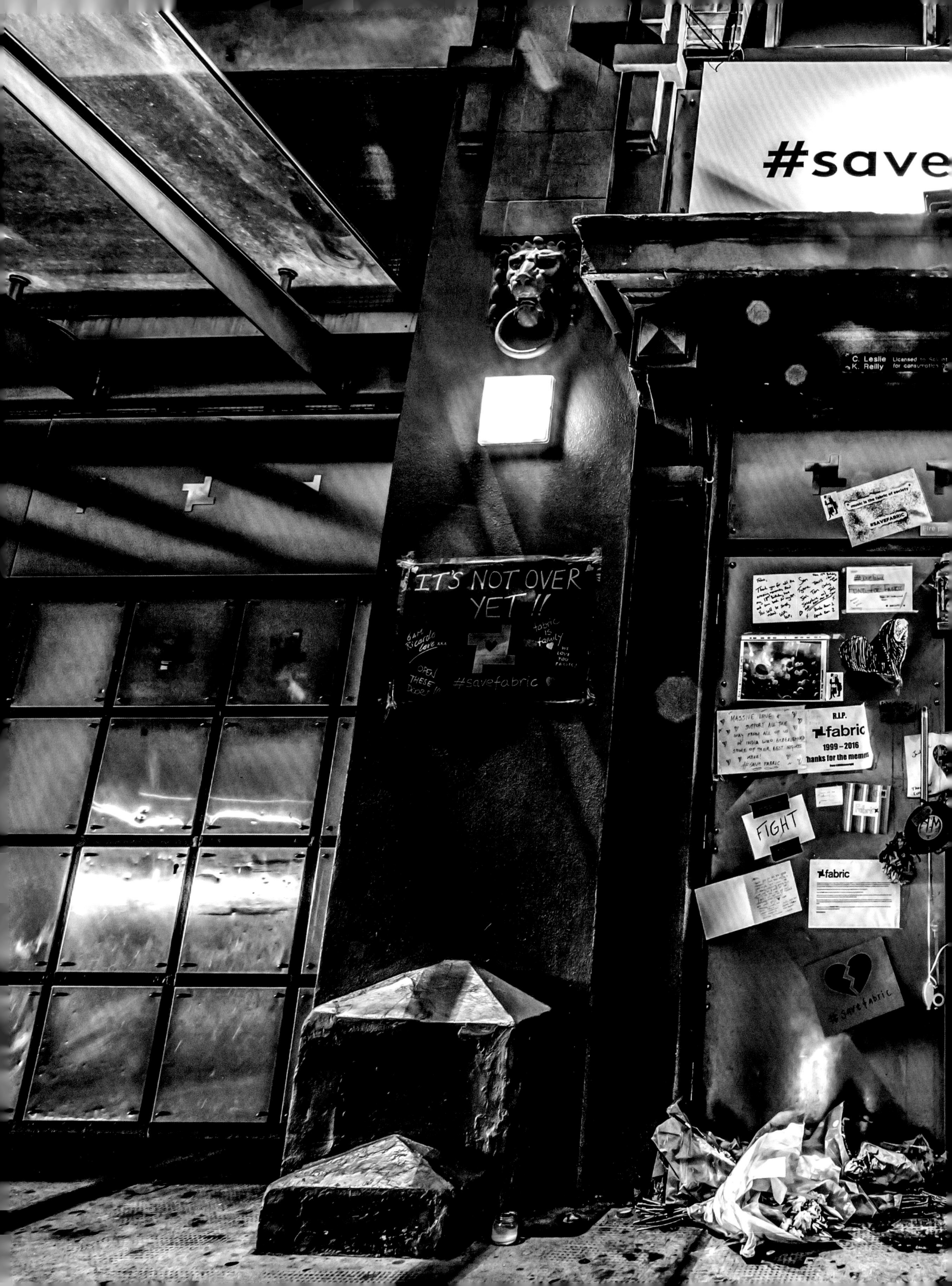
#save
C. Leslie
K. Reilly
IT'S NOT OVER YET !!
fabric is family
OPEN THESE Doors !!
#savefabric
MASSIVE LOVE & SUPPORT ALL THE WAY FROM ALL OF US IN INDIA WHO EXPERIENCED SOME OF THEIR BEST NIGHTS HERE!
#SAVE FABRIC
R.I.P.
fabric
1999 – 2016
FIGHT
fabric
#savefabric

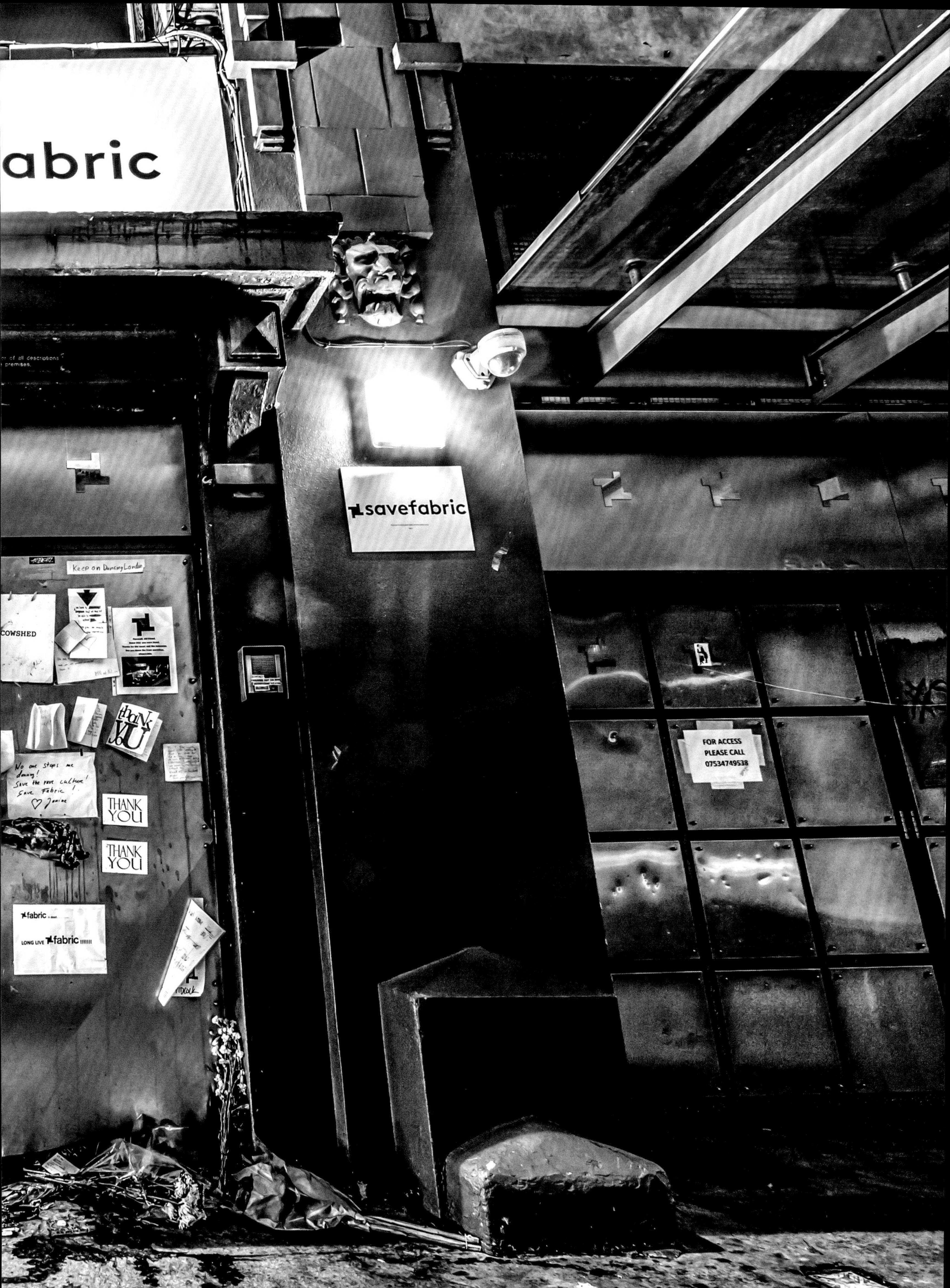
abric
savefabric
Keep on Dancing London
COWSHED
thank YoU
No one stops me dancing! Save the rave culture! Save Fabric! ♡ Janine
THANK YOU
THANK YOU
fabric
LONG LIVE fabric
FOR ACCESS PLEASE CALL 07534749538

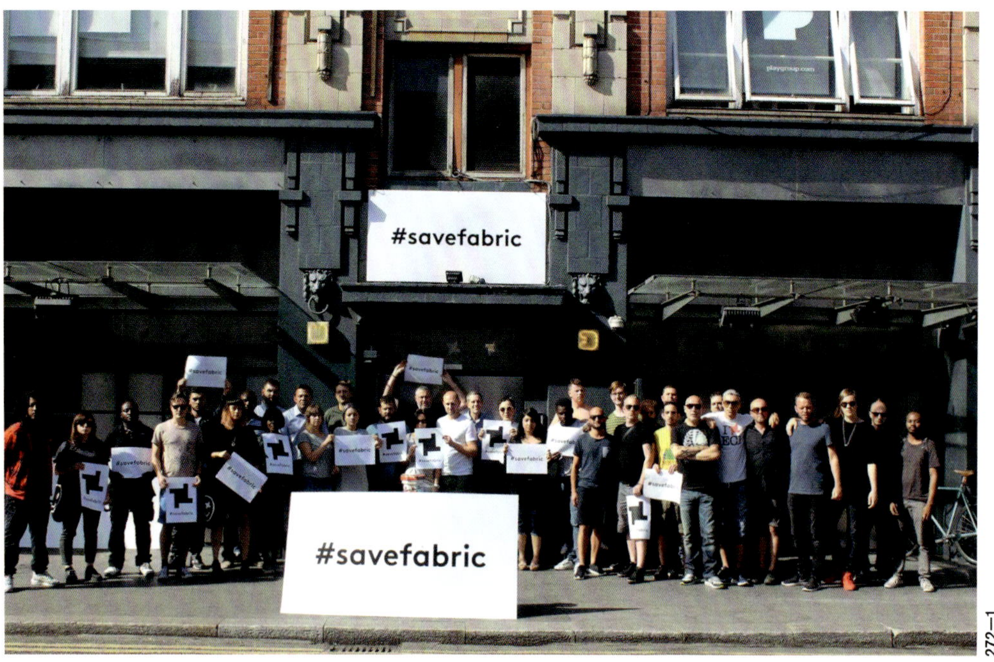

272—1

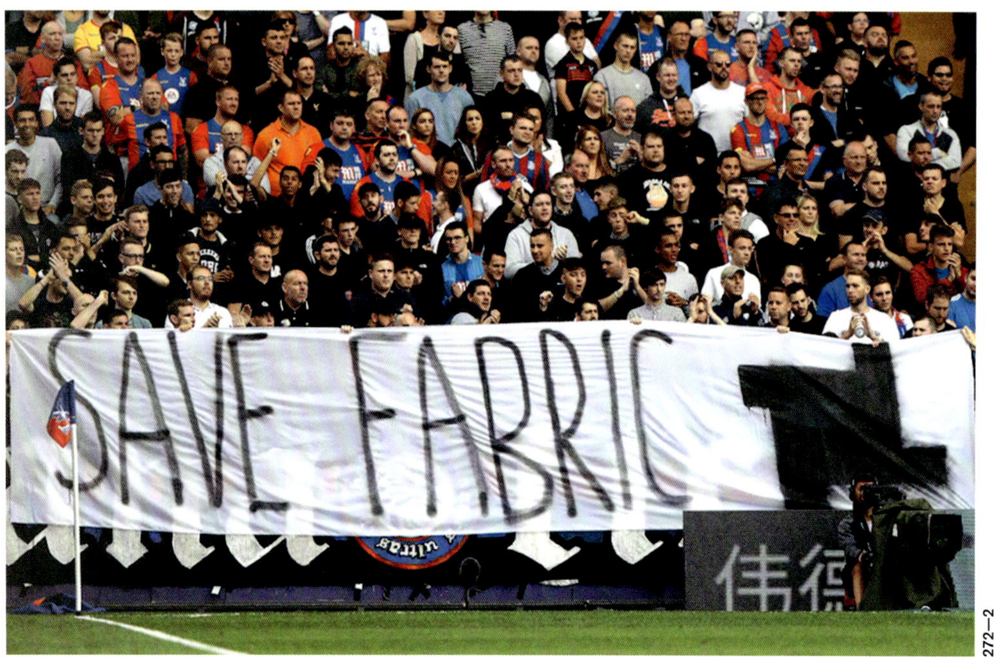

272—2

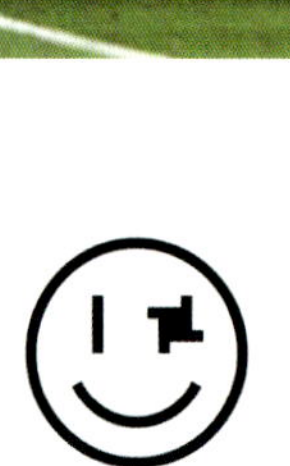

272—3

272—4

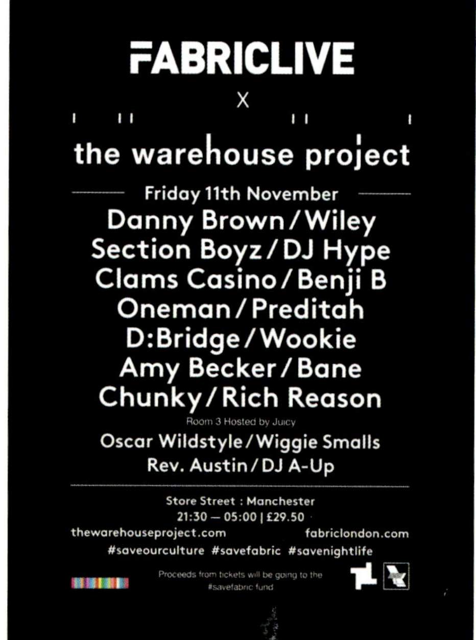

272—5

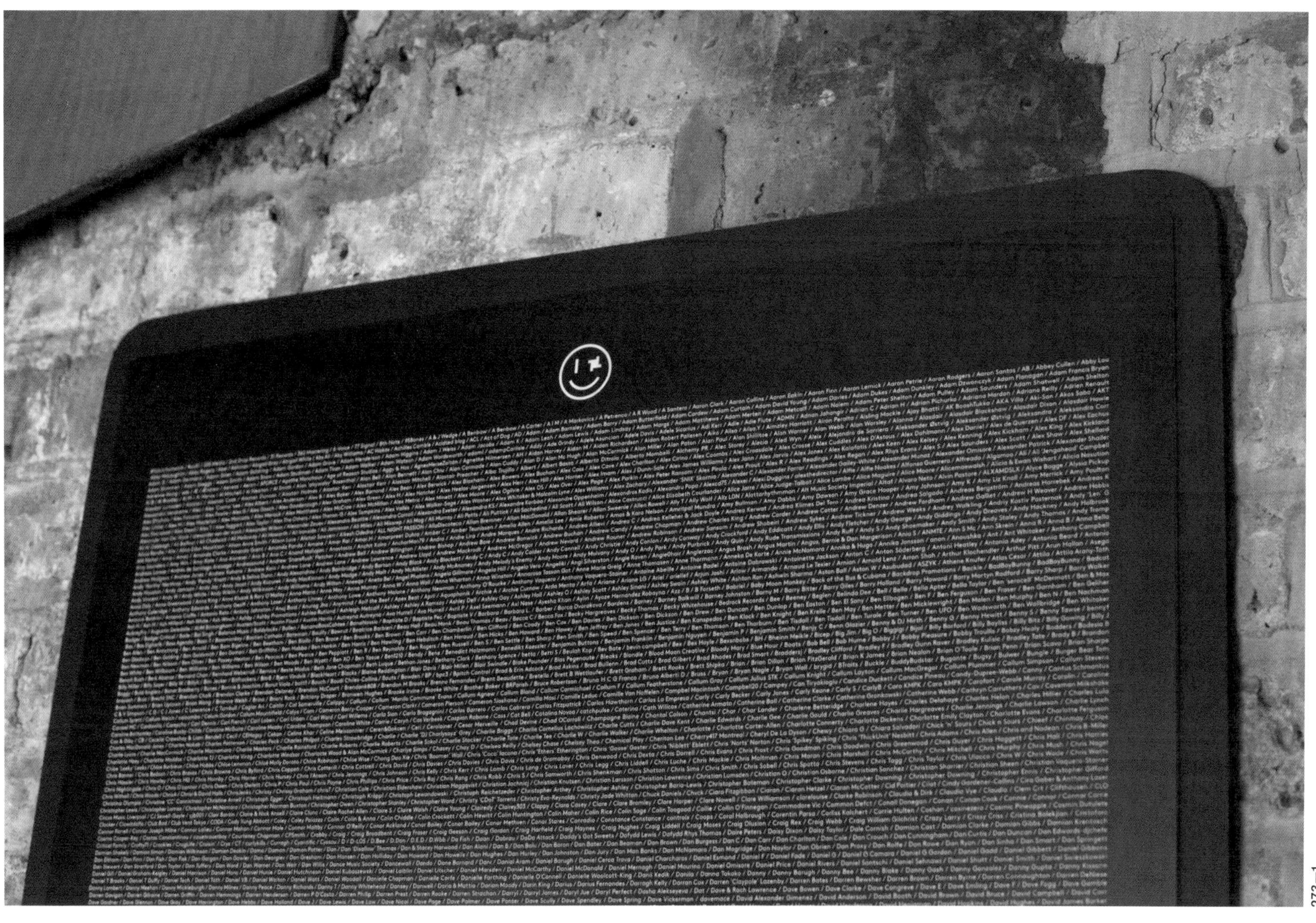

273—1

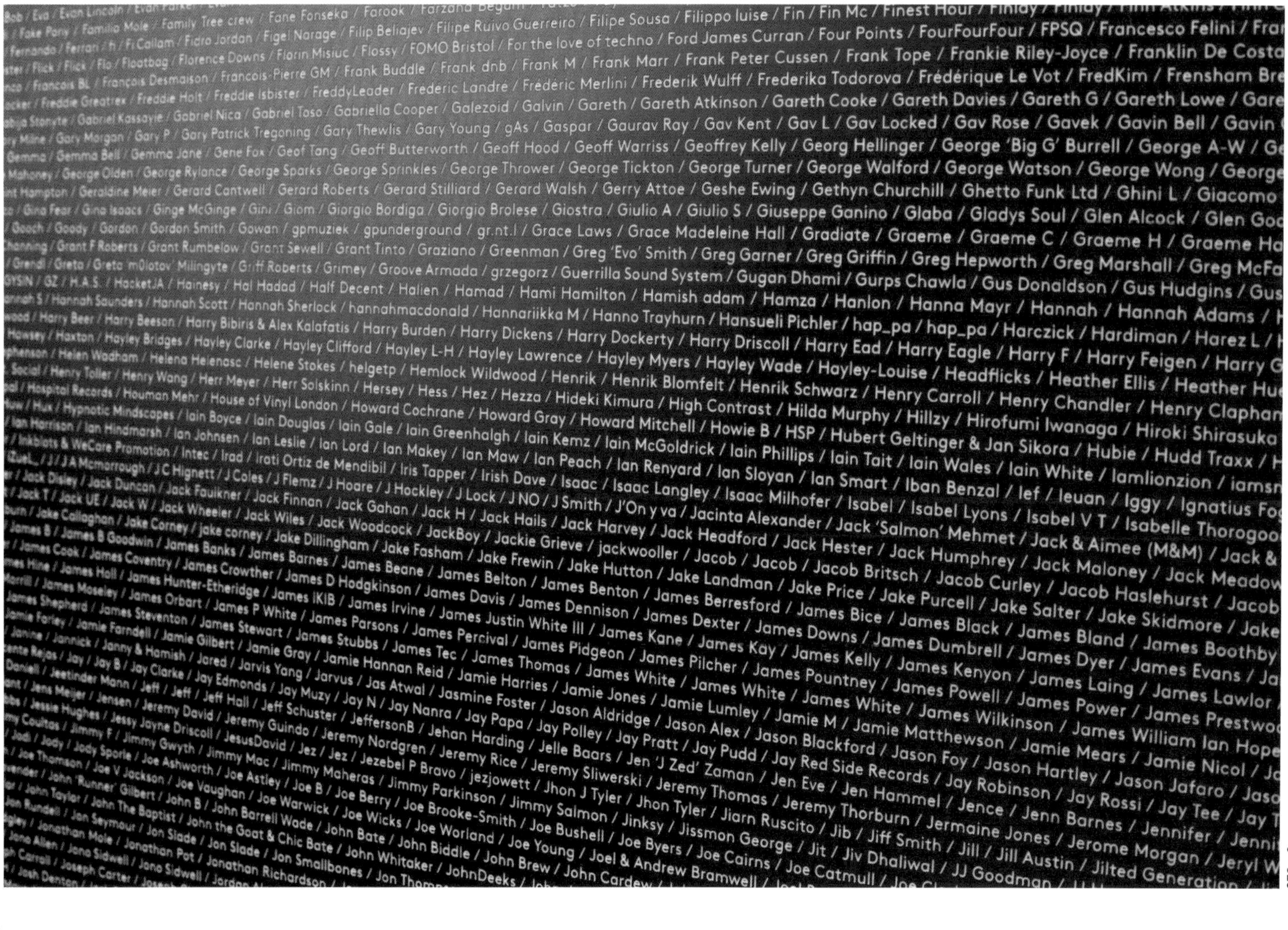

273—2

the meaning of fabric

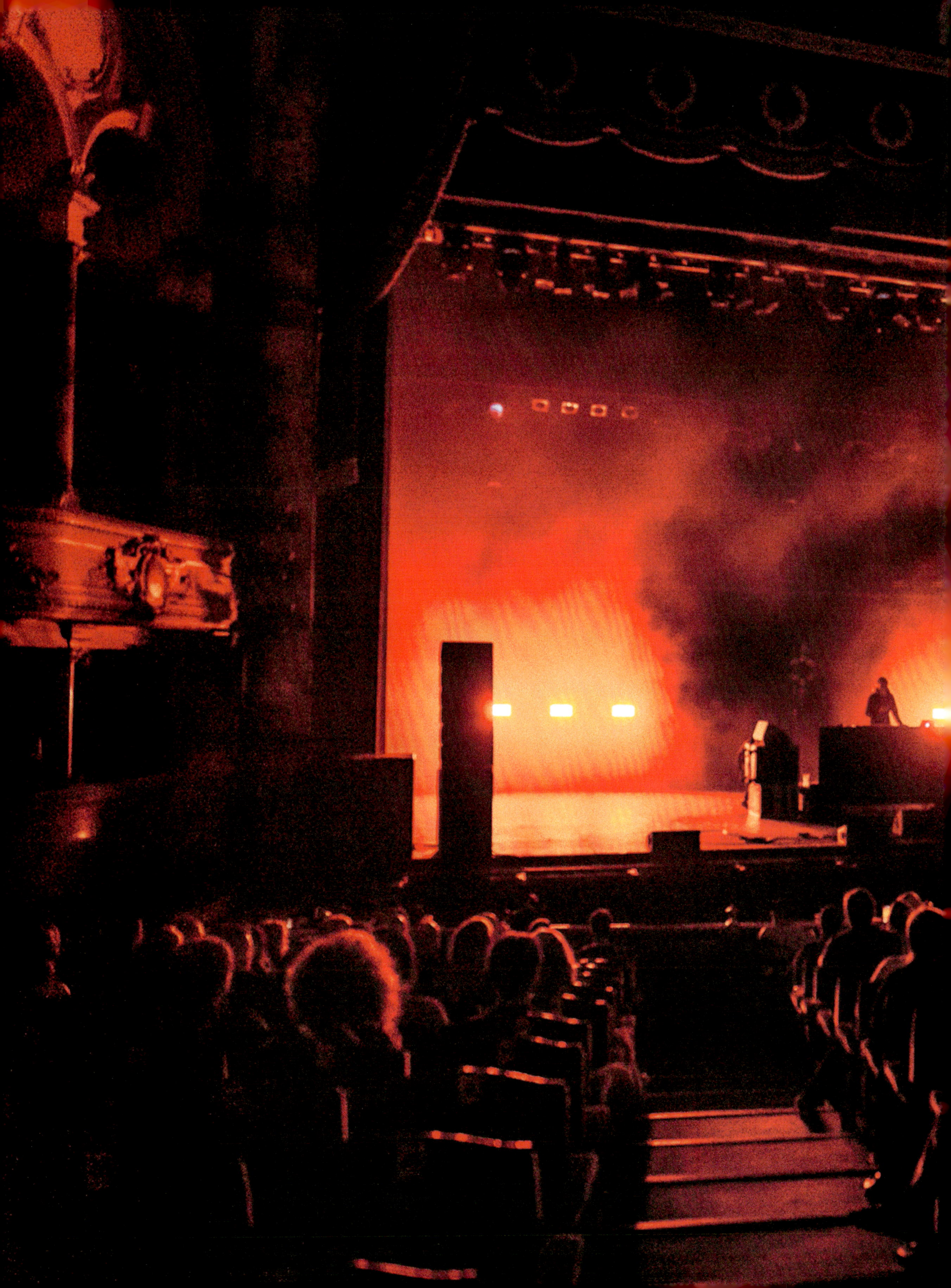

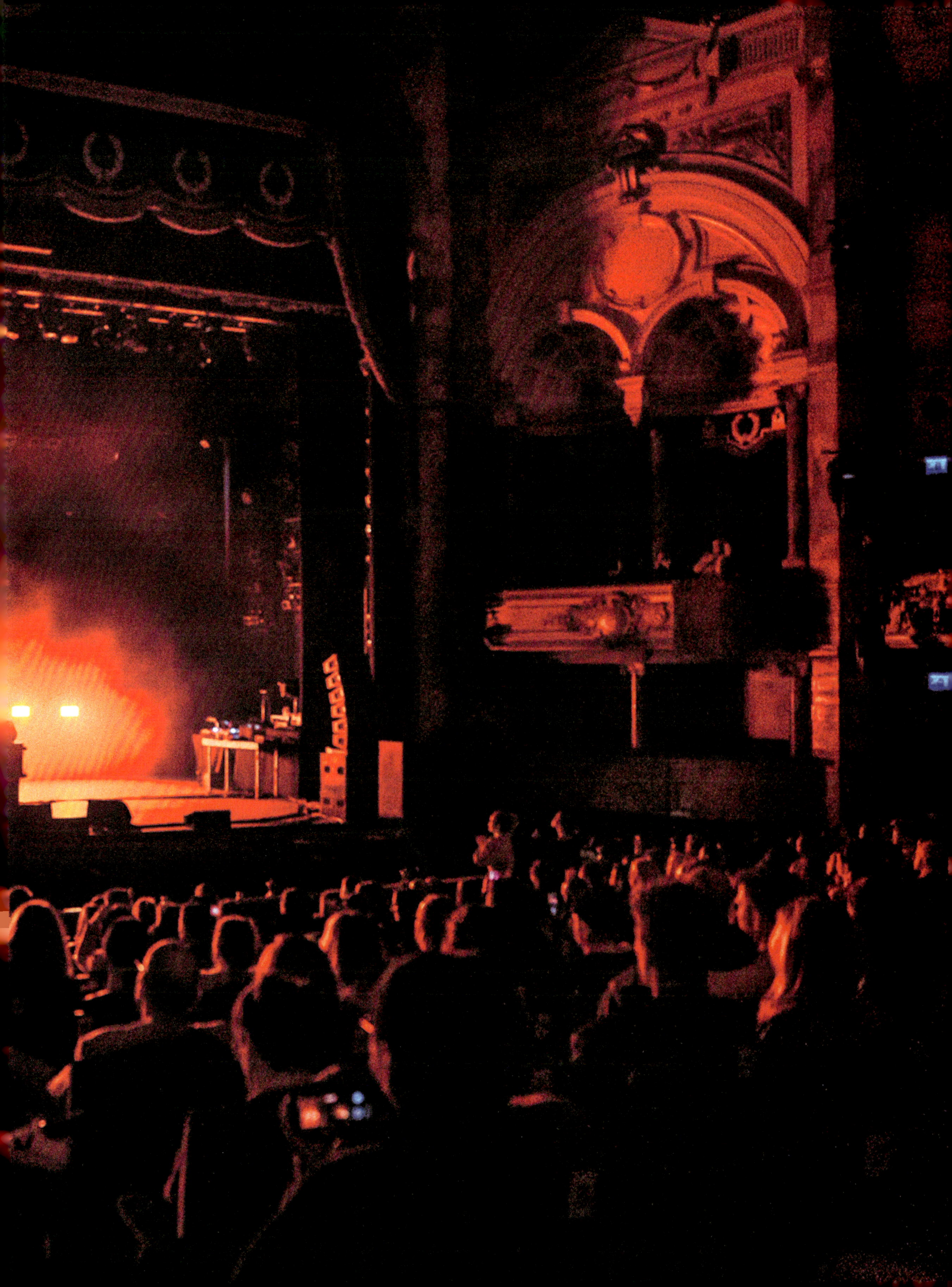

It feels a little unseemly – especially given the damage caused across the rest of clubland – to say that fabric had a good pandemic, but it is unavoidably the case. The thing is, the club and everyone involved in it desperately needed the breathing space. For almost exactly twenty years, through highs and lows, the club had been in a state of tumultuous movement: every weekend a near-constant party, every week spent preparing for the next weekend. In the period it was closed in 2016, uncertainty and frantic work to rescue the club precluded any hope of serious stock-taking – and even after the wave of love from the #savefabric campaign and subsequent reopening, things were, if anything, more hectic than ever. The club may have earned new respect from the authorities for its cultural importance and the seriousness of its operation, but it wasn't off the hook and was under constant intense scrutiny. 'We had to bring on a new security team, new measures, and still try and give people an experience they could actually enjoy,' says operations director Luke Laws. 'It was so much more work.'

So when lockdown hit in March 2020, even though there was yet more uncertainty, to say the very least, there was also a moment of calm. Unlike previous crises, there was no campaign to organise, no court case to fight, no global spotlight falling on fabric. The whole world had come to a stop, and there was time – nothing but time – to think about what would be best for the future. As for everyone in the wider world it was a traumatic and fearful time, but in this period of eerie calm it was possible to see glimmers of hope. Of course, pre-vaccine, there was no guarantee that clubs would ever open again, but – maybe because fabric had faced and escaped existential threats before, and maybe because bloody-minded pursuit of the best possible experience was baked into the company from the very beginning – it was decided that the only thing for it was to plan for better days anyway, and use the opportunity of this closure to refresh the club and company, materially and culturally.

The fundamentals were sound, mind. The layout of the club, the music that came through it, the late-night surrealism of its artistic vision – all of that made sense, as it did in 1999. Indeed, these things were precisely the reasons it had made it this far. What was needed was to boost and reassert all of that. So the whole sound system was rebuilt, architect and longtime friend of the club Giorgio Badalacchi was brought in to tidy up the look of the place, and Jorge Nieto was brought in as creative director.

The project was essentially to work out how fabric could be 'more fabric'. In Giorgio's case this meant, as he puts it, 'honouring the building's layers of history both as a former cold-meat storage for Smithfield Market; and second, as an iconic space which has redefined contemporary clubbing culture'. He revived original features, and added a mischievous nod to abattoirs with concrete, steel and PVC curtains. He also put the new concrete DJ booth in Room 2 right in the centre, 'allowing the public to be around the performer, and also behind at a higher level – so fabric's dancefloor has become a more inclusive, democratic space'. In other words, the refurbishment was about amplifying the fundamental functionality that had proved so resilient through the decades. With this done inside, Jorge's mission then became to take the spirit of fabric, which the fabric regulars and extended family understood implicitly, out into the world.

Jorge's involvement was an embodiment of fabric's international reach. He had grown up in Colombia throwing illegal drum'n'bass raves with his friends, and fabric had been a literally mythical presence to them – particularly via the FABRICLIVE mixes accessed online, but also through stories of their DJ heroes' residencies there. When he came to London to study, he quickly found work in clubland with venues like Village Underground, but it was always fabric he looked to for inspiration. So when the chance came to not just work there, but help expand what fabric actually was, it was a dream come true. Covid lockdown might have closed down clubs, but it also opened possibilities to reach captive audiences trapped at home and looking for stimulation online. With fabric's DJ connections, Jorge's wider arts world contacts and support from the Arts Council England, they set about placing dance music in some unlikely and magical locations.

DJs live-streaming wasn't new, nor was putting DJs in unusual places – but the London Unlocked series in 2021 achieved something magical. It took DJs throughout fabric's history, from those there at the very start to the newest rising stars, into spaces that were emblematic of London, both rarely seen (inside Tower Bridge) and very familiar indeed but made strange by their emptiness (the Royal Albert Hall, the V&A Museum, the

English National Opera at the Coliseum, the old Smithfield Market on fabric's doorstep), and filmed and framed them beautifully. Somehow it consolidated the sense of solidarity between the venue and the city that had birthed it, which had bubbled up during the #savefabric campaign five years before. And it asserted fabric's presence in the heart of the city – this was it reaching outside the walls of the old meat cellars, outside the sweaty dancefloors, and into London's most esteemed spaces and institutions, all with the world watching. It was a demonstration that fabric was more than just fabric.

When the club reopened, it was in one sense straight back to business as usual. Because that's what fabric does: it puts on fantastic dances with as little fuss as possible. But in another sense it was a rebirth. It wasn't only the crisp new sound system and zhuzhed-up interior that made fabric feel refreshed, but a renewed confidence, a shaking off of the pervading sense hanging over it since 2016 that it had to prove its right to exist every weekend – and a vast new sense of possibility outside its walls. And, funnily enough, though it hadn't been the conscious intention in reaching out to other cultural institutions for new partnerships, there was a plugging back in to some of Keith Reilly's more grandiose ambitions, which had been part of the fabric story going right back before its opening, before its mid-nineties conception, and all the way to those first warehouse parties he'd put on in 1979.

Back then it was the lowest of low-tech, ad-hoc attempts to create an interesting party environment with art made by whoever was in his orbit – a few banners here, some 'weird films' projected there. But in that, there was the innate understanding that the nascent dance culture held almost infinite possibility. It was always about pleasure and dancing, of course, but it was also about a space where unlikely people and unlikely ideas could meet and mingle and create something that had never existed before – that could never exist without that feverish, fertile atmosphere. And that fed into everything that came after: into the layout, sound, lights and booking policies of fabric; into the endless stream of surrealism that Jon Cooke and Roberto Rosolin's designs sent out into the world; into the brief explosion of deranged ambition that was matter; into hundreds of record releases; into literally millions of musical experiences and strange late-night conversations; and now, into the new sense of fabric as a respected cultural institution that could look venerable art galleries, churches and opera houses in the eye and collaborate as equals, speaking to the entire world.

fabric's existence has, by its very nature, involved flying by the seat of its pants. It has had to prove itself, again and again and again. Every night it's opened has involved bottling lightning, balancing chaos and control just so, maintaining the underground spirit of old but allowing new innovations in, and keeping up with the never-ending task of making sure there are clean glasses, toilet roll in the cubicles, fuses in the plugs and the right tickets on the right coats in the cloakroom. It's faced down gangsters, fraudsters, bankruptcy, the full might of the law and a global pandemic – but each time, it's come back stronger. Its quarter-century approaches, and people are dancing there now who weren't born when it opened, yet Cameron Leslie is still steering the ship in the office, Judy Griffith still greeting the DJs with a drink and a grin on a Saturday night, Craig and Terry still rolling out the eternal groove, and the excitement of walking down those stairs to the subsonic throb of Fridays is still as potent as it was in 1999. And somehow, not despite but because of all the crises and threats it's dealt with, there is still as much sense of possibility as there was in 1999, too. Twenty-five years of existence might seem like an excuse for nostalgia, but for everyone working in fabric, there's not much time for that because – as ever – it's not about past glories. It's about the next party.

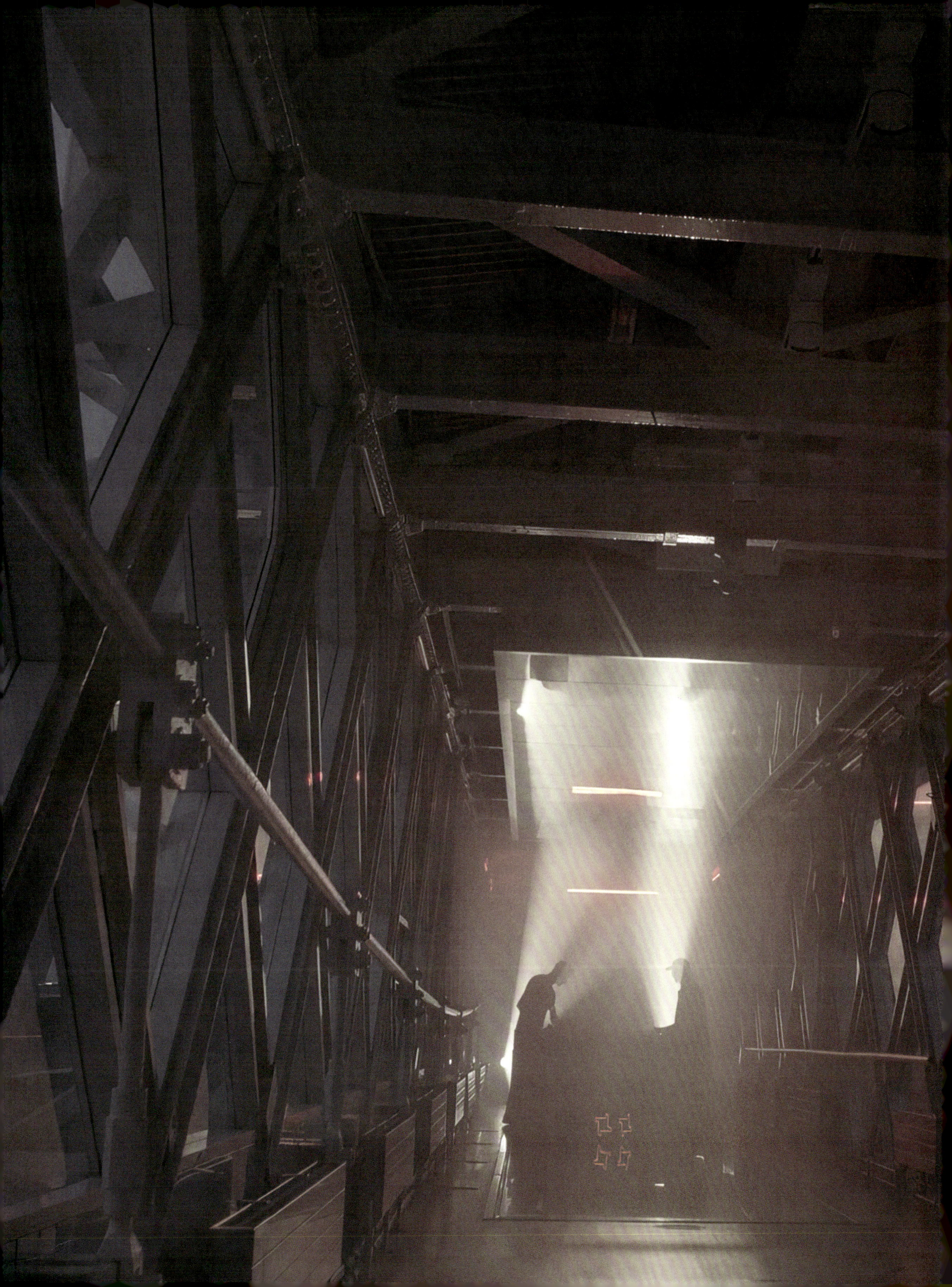

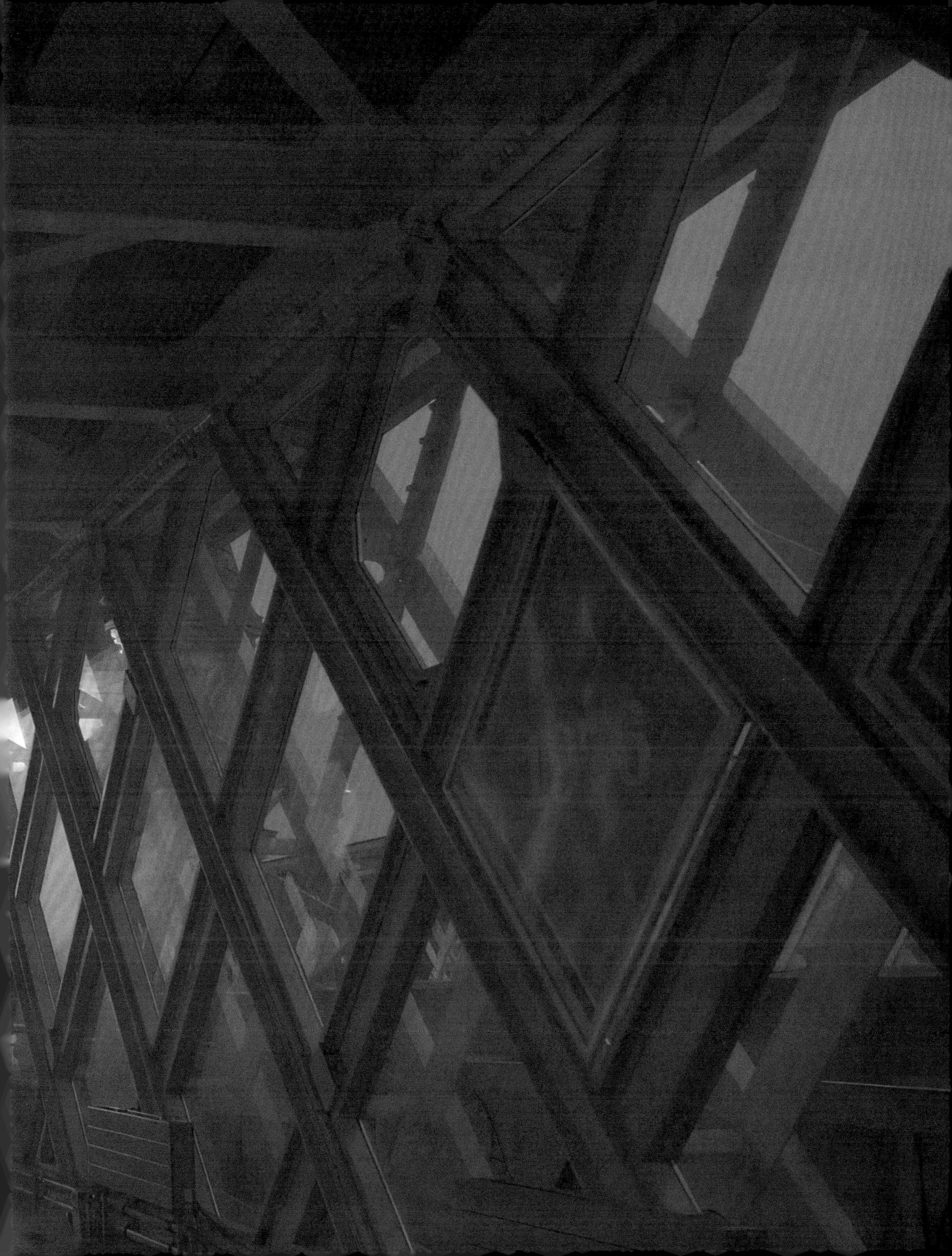

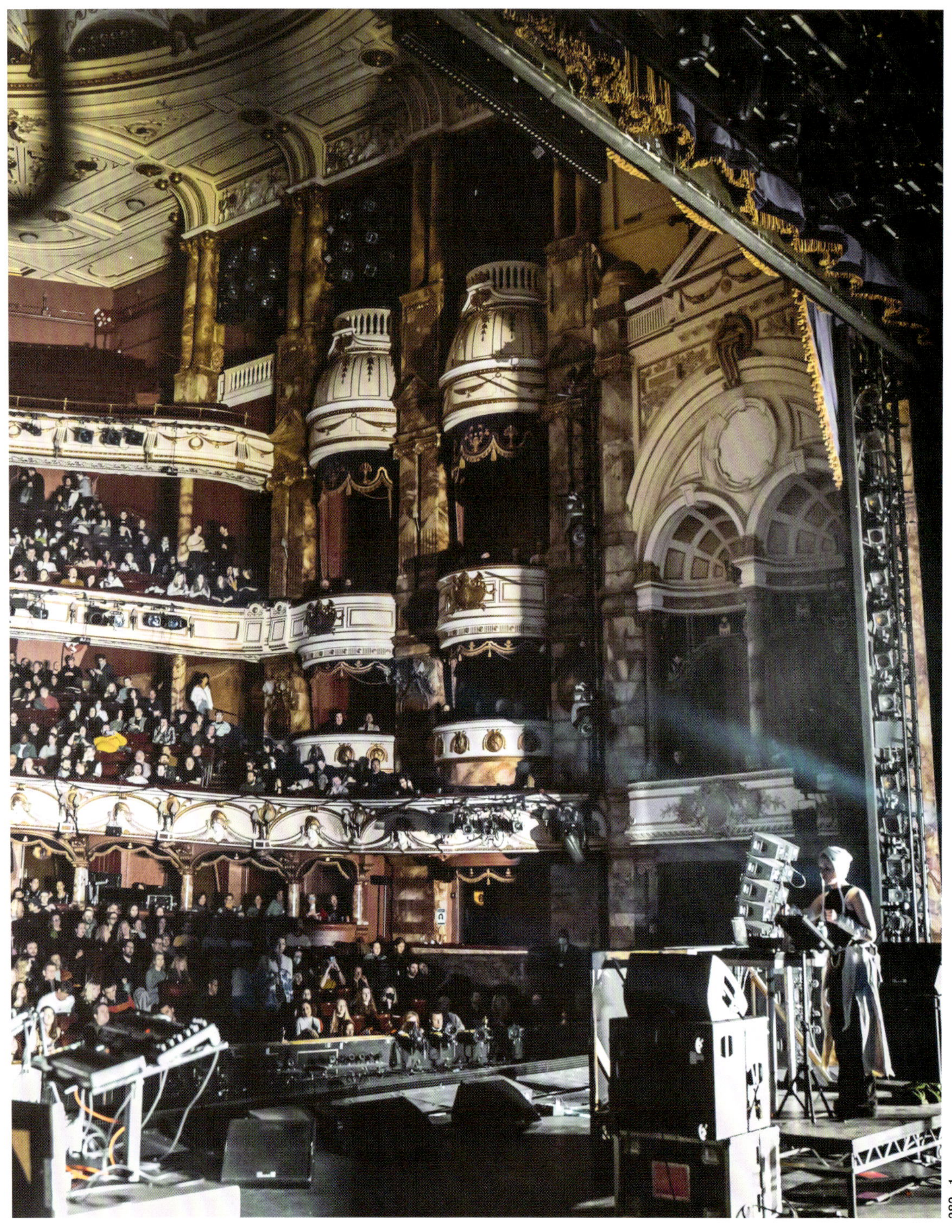

282—1

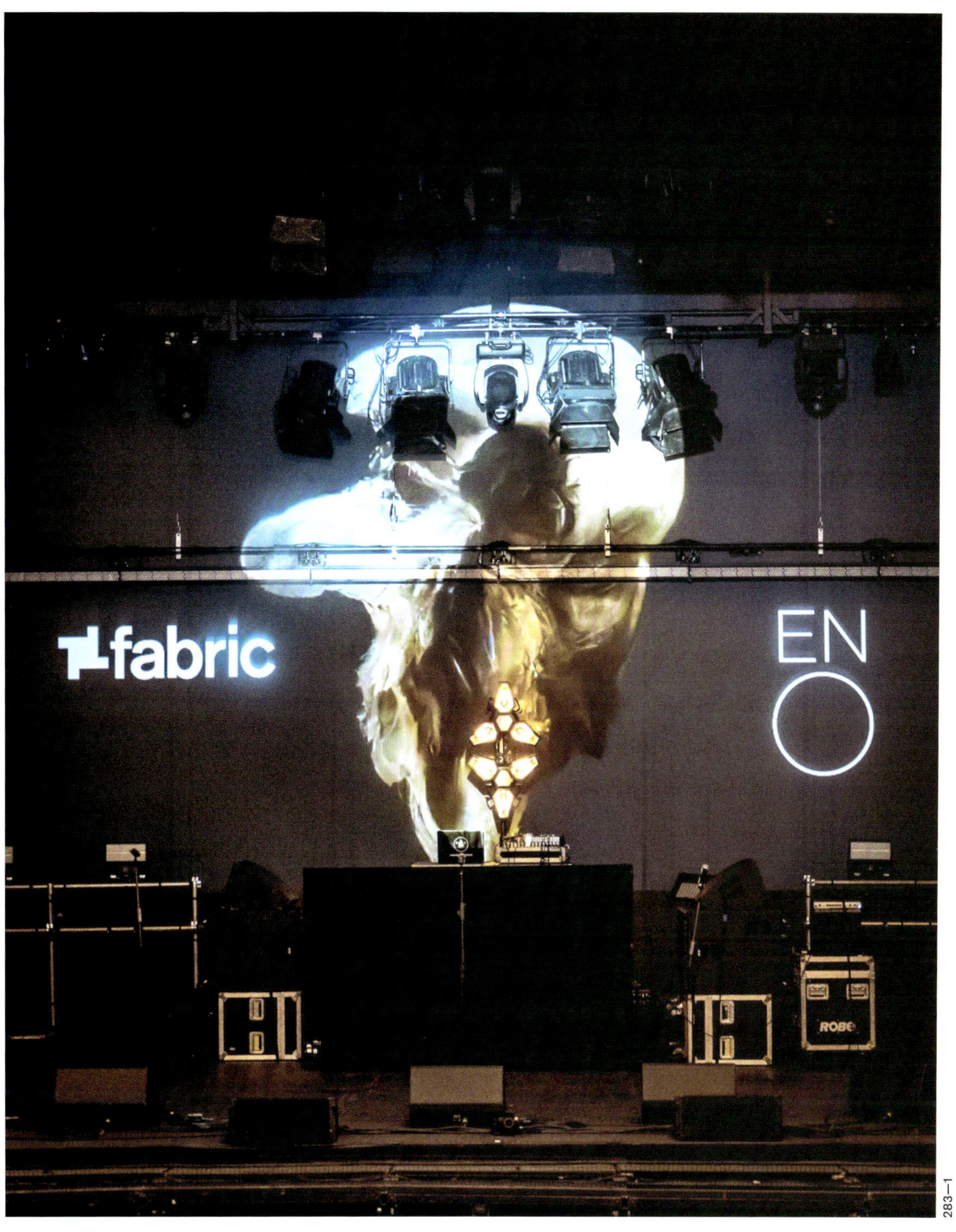

283—1

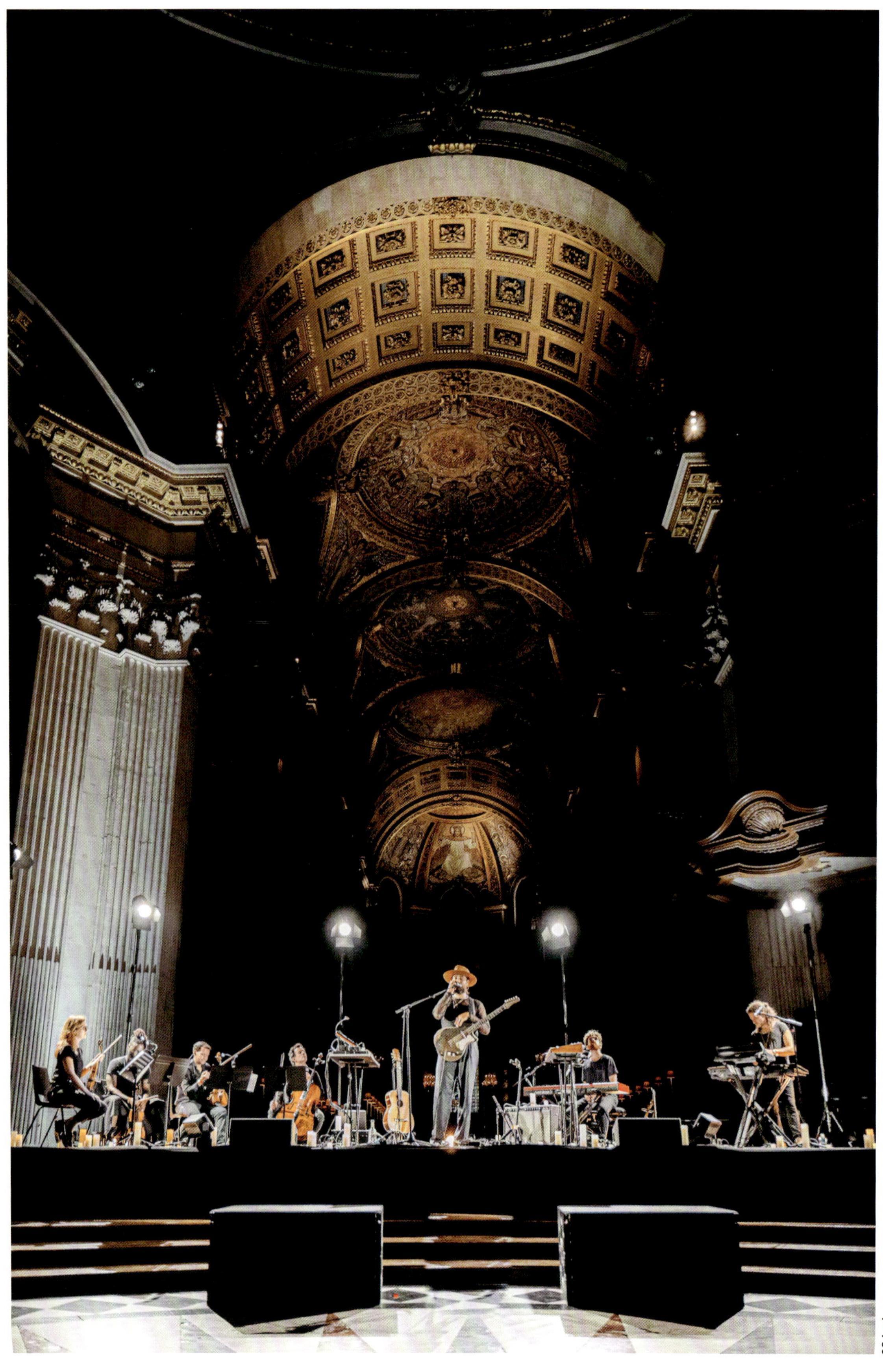

284—1

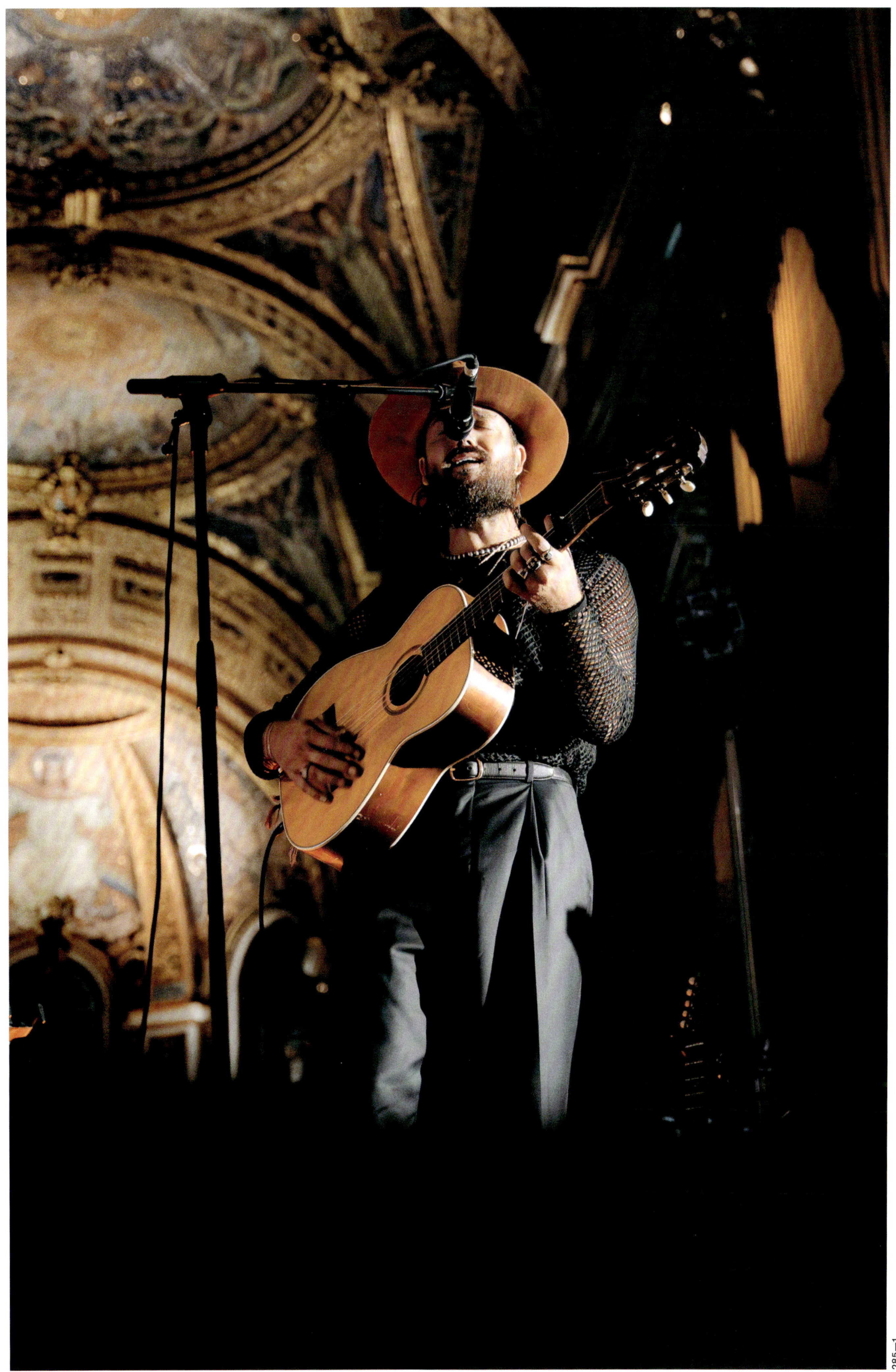

285—1

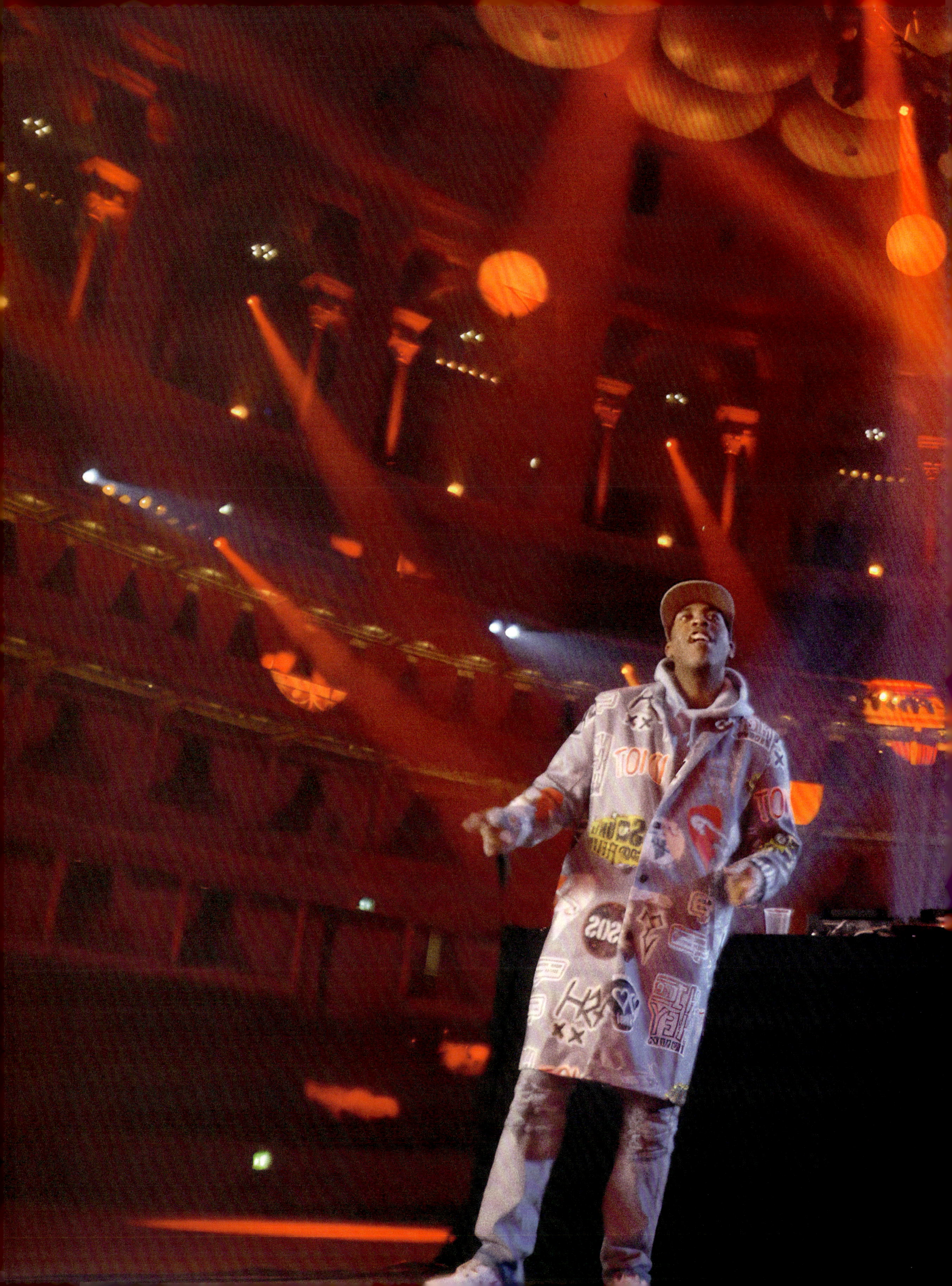

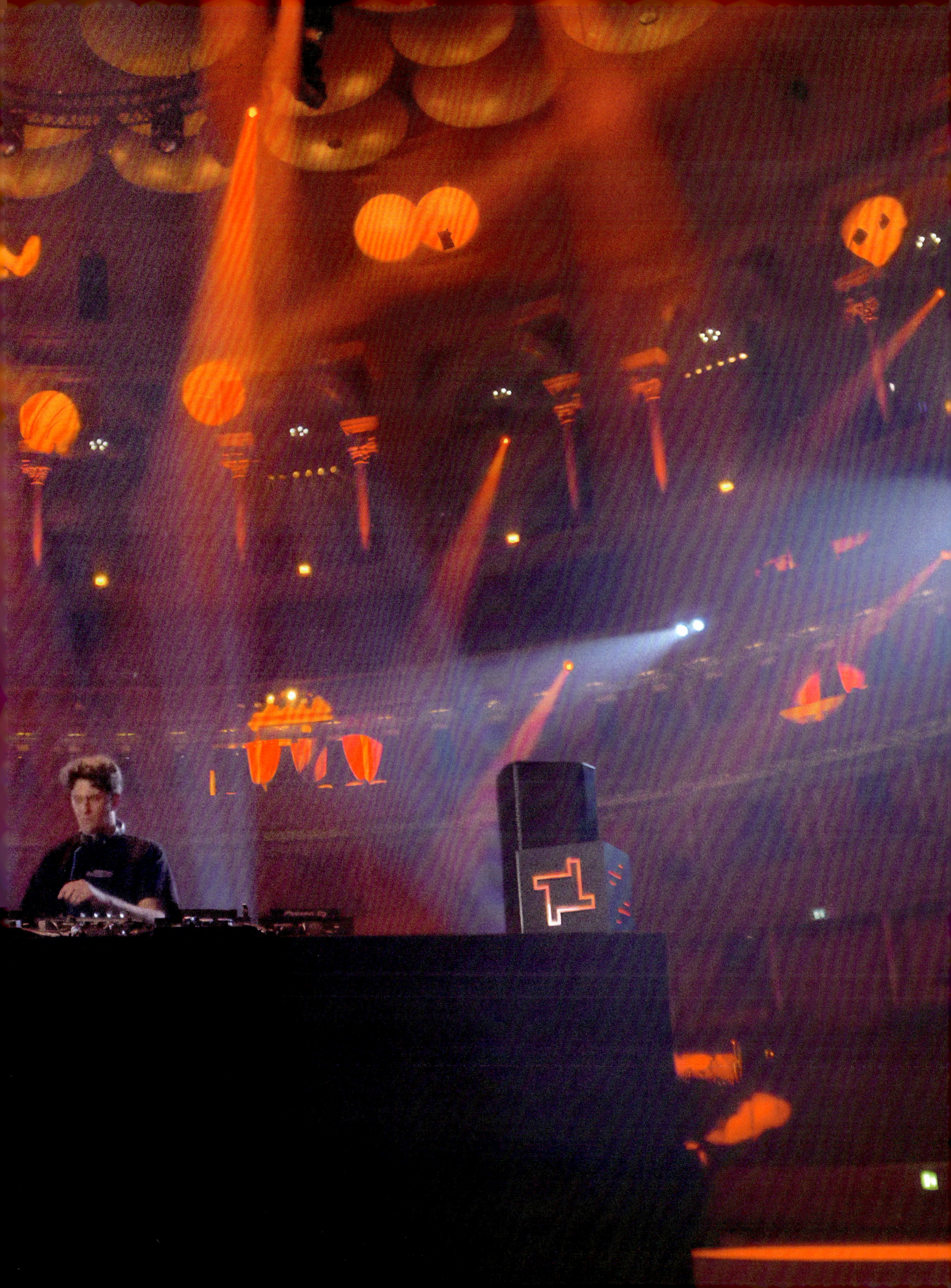

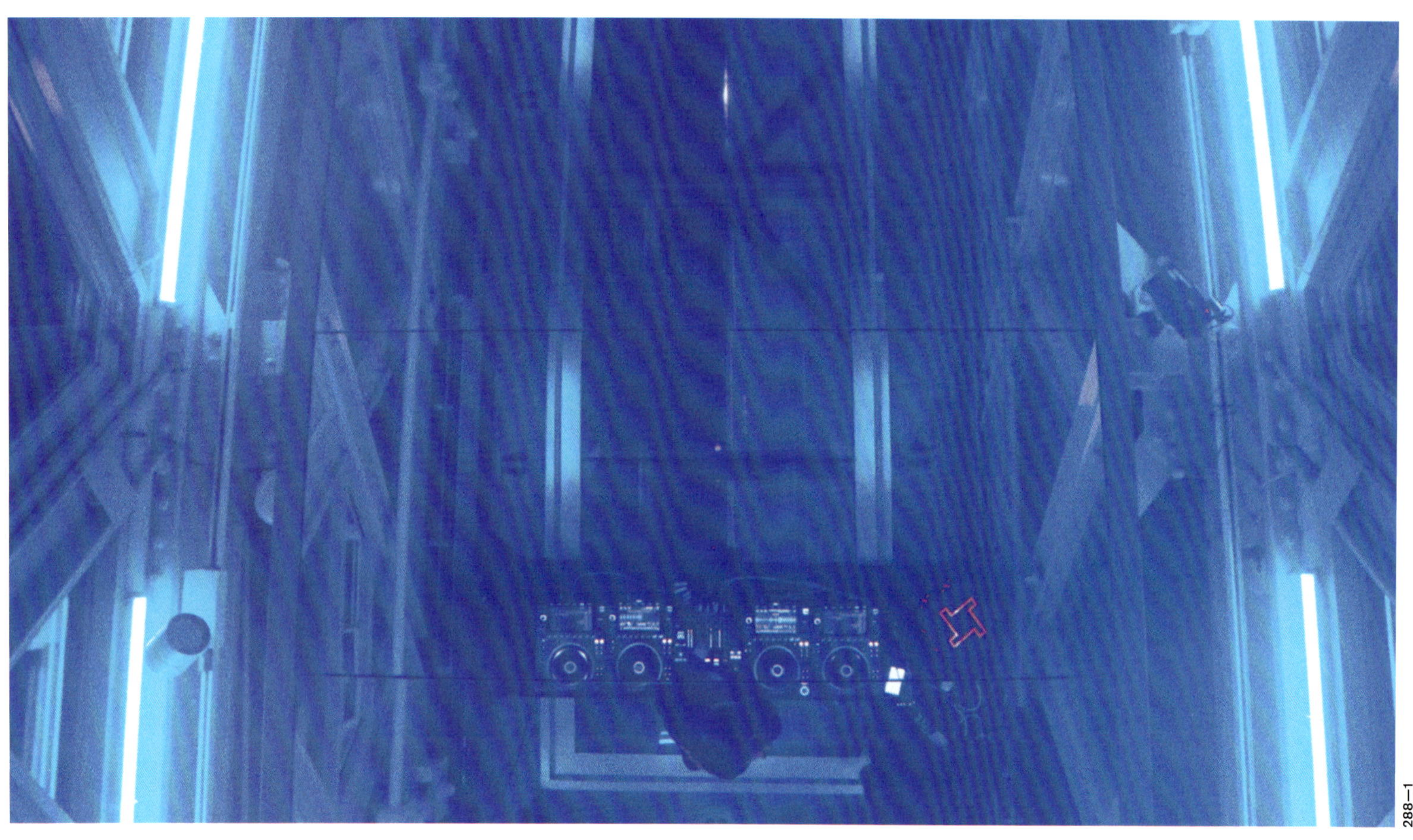
288—1

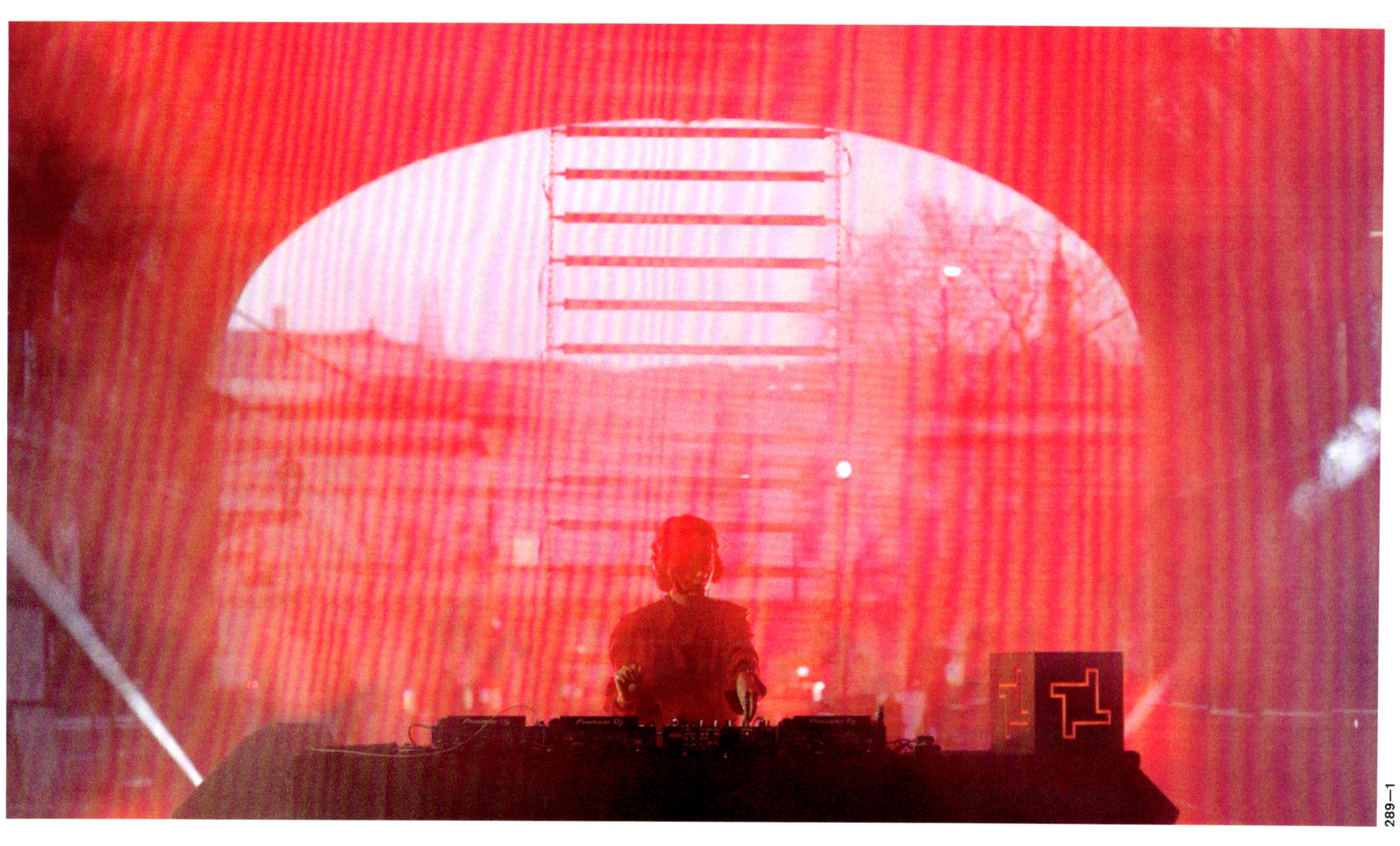

289—1

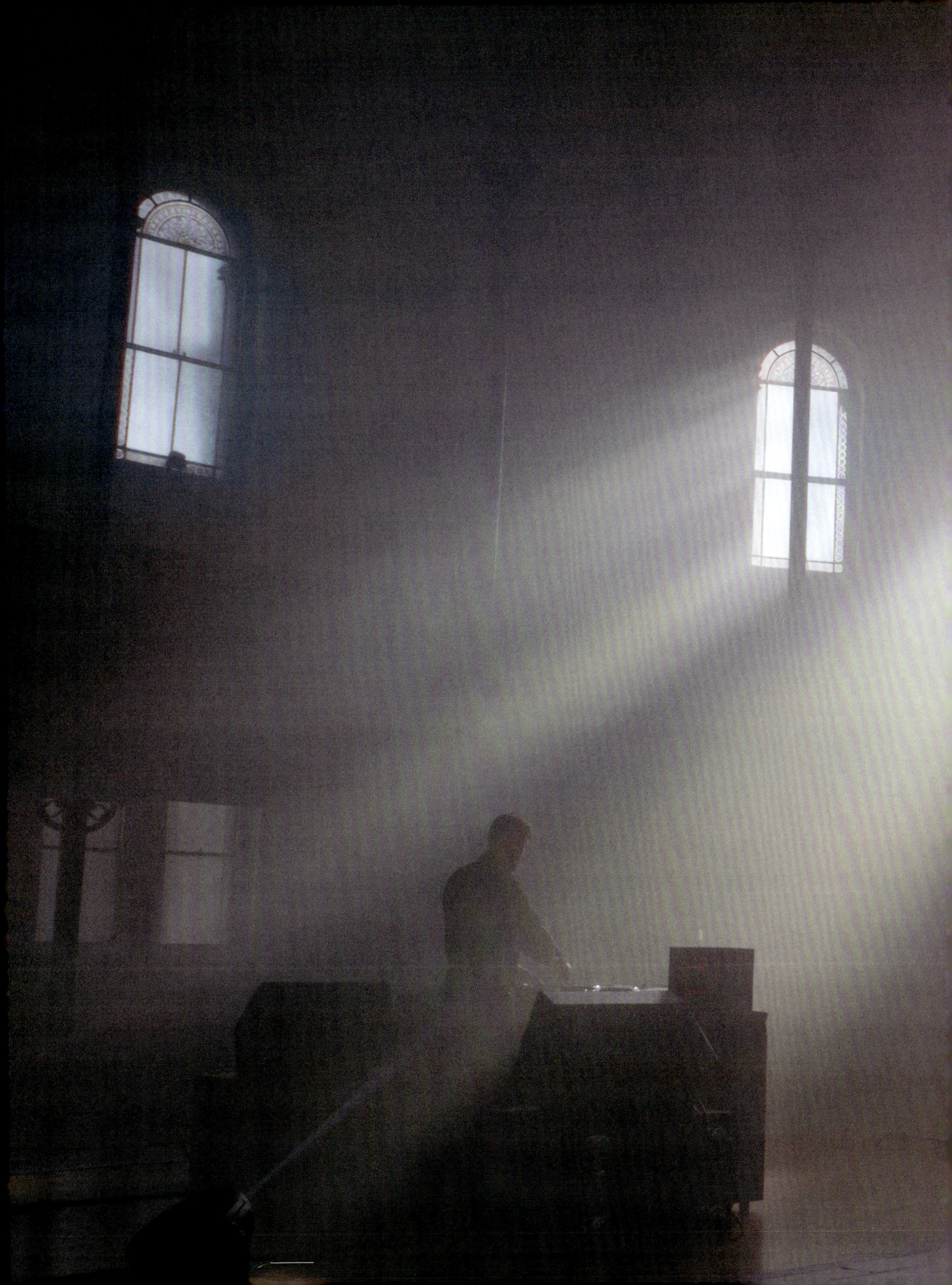

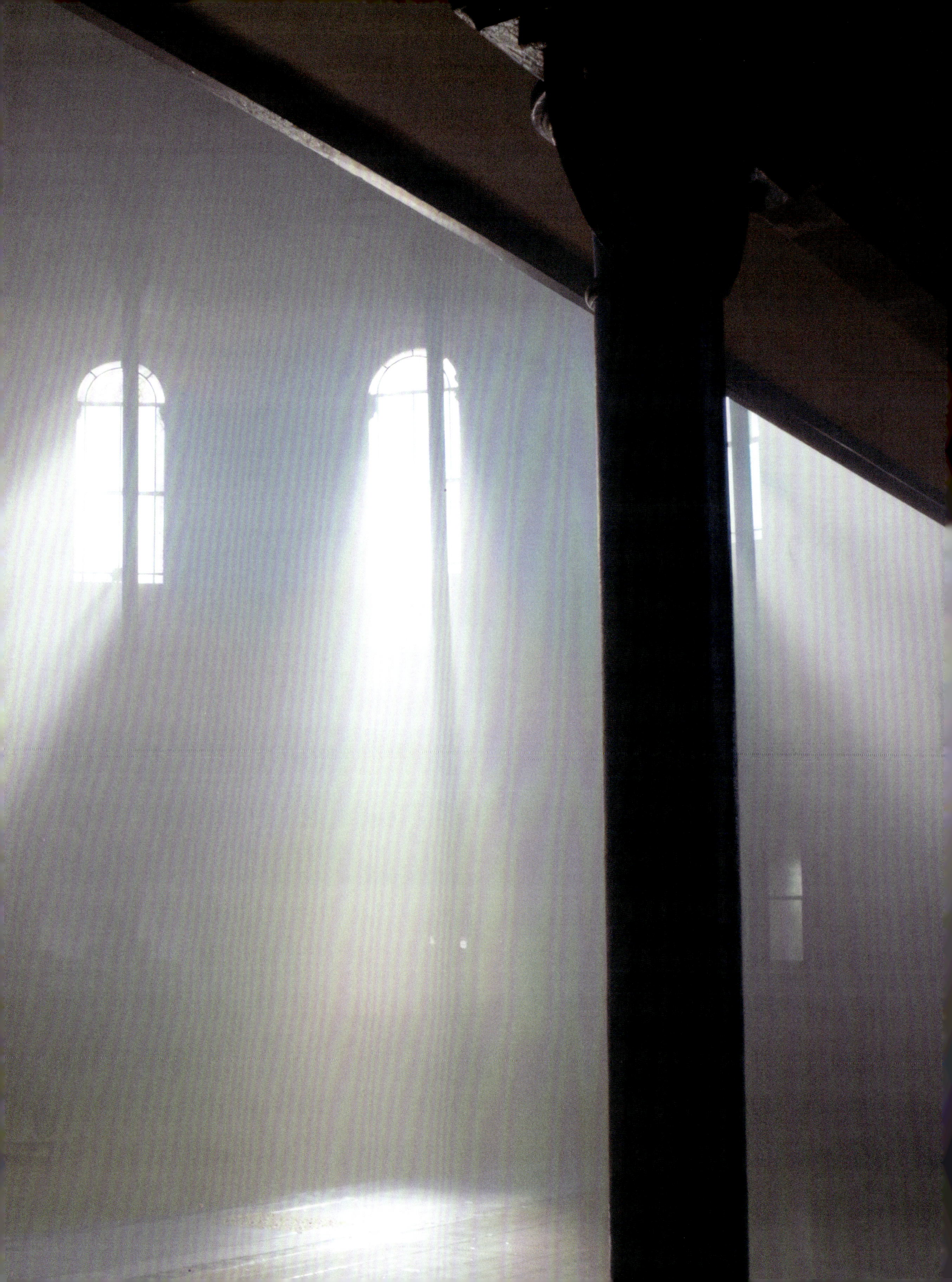

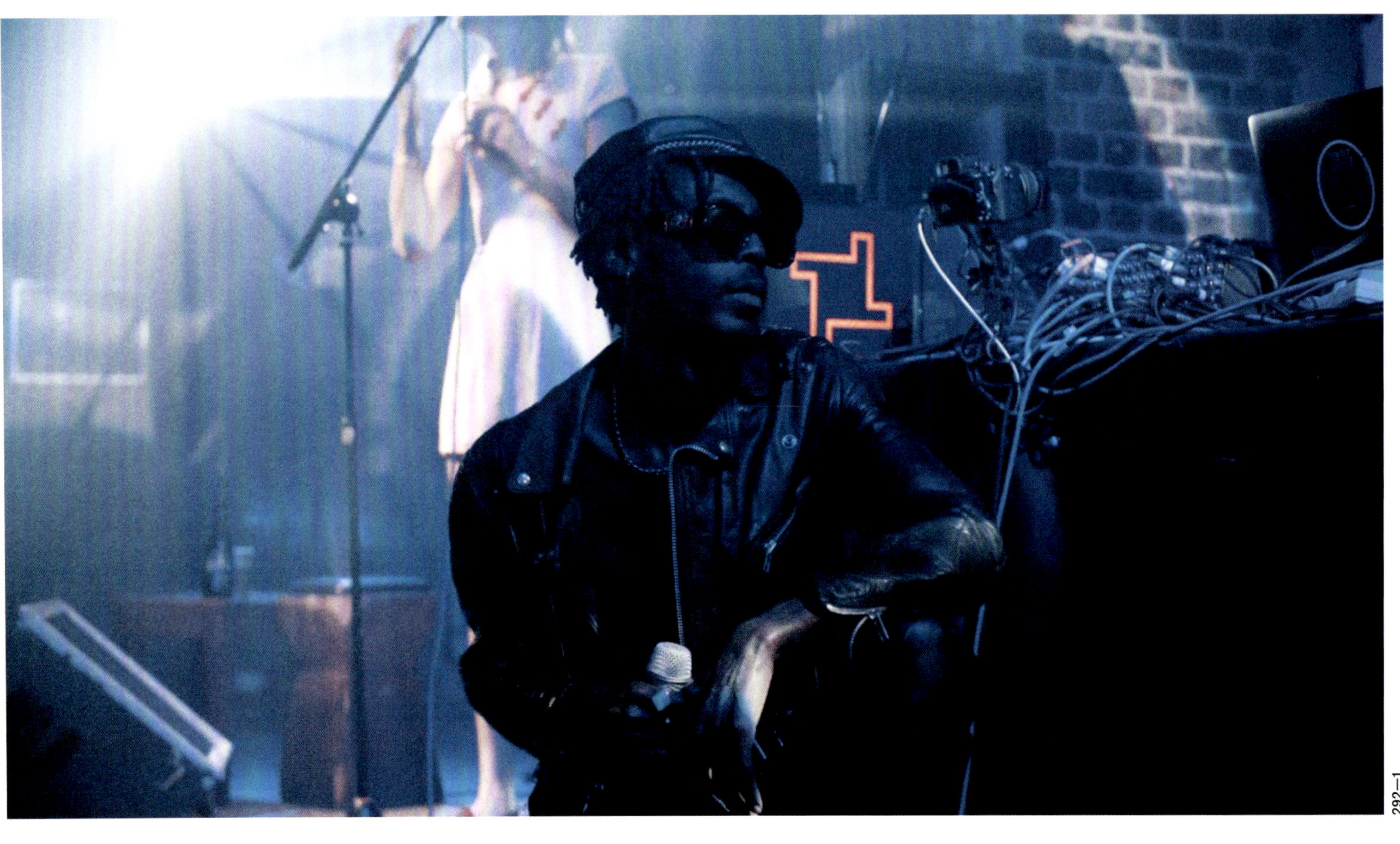

292—1

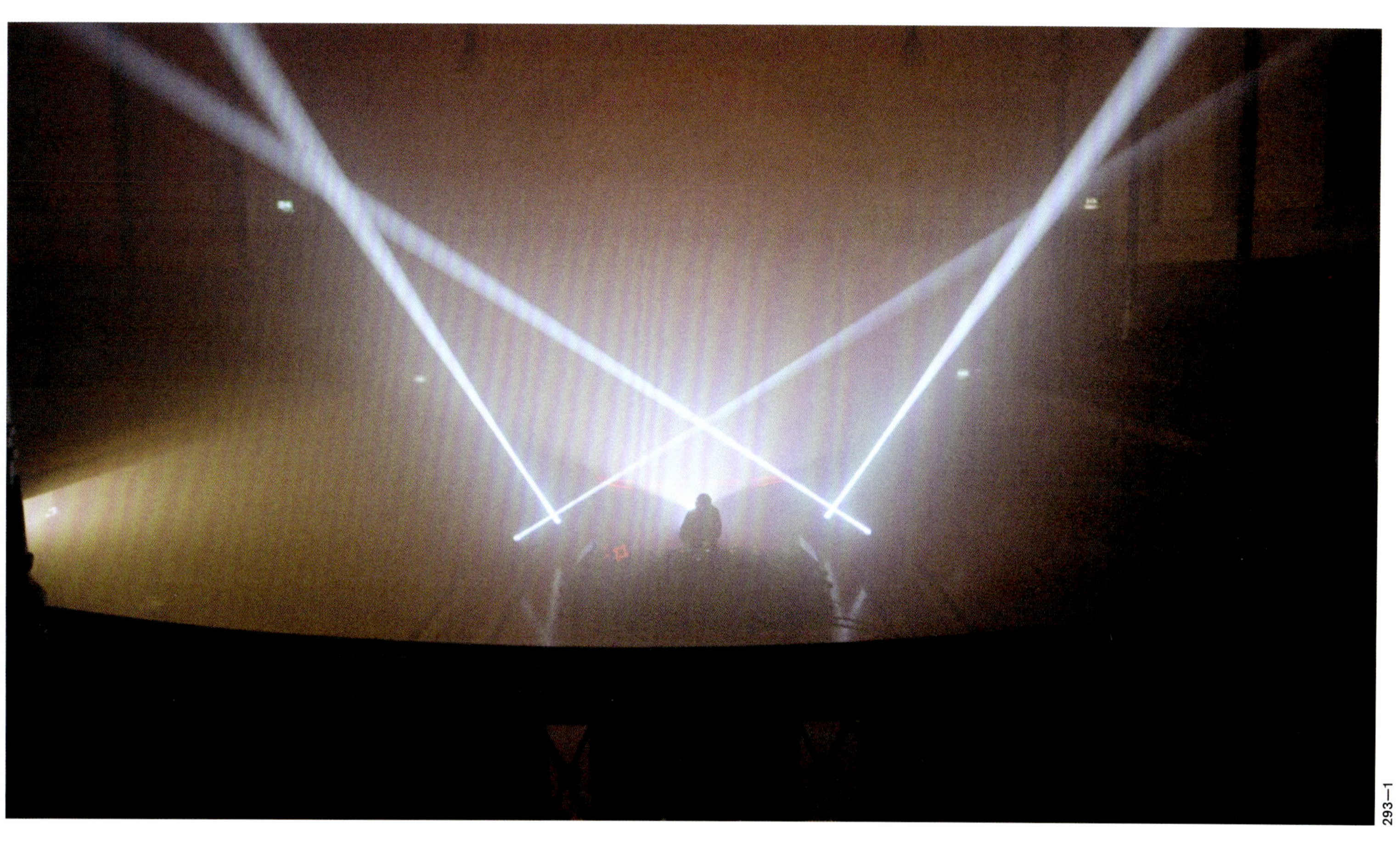

293—1

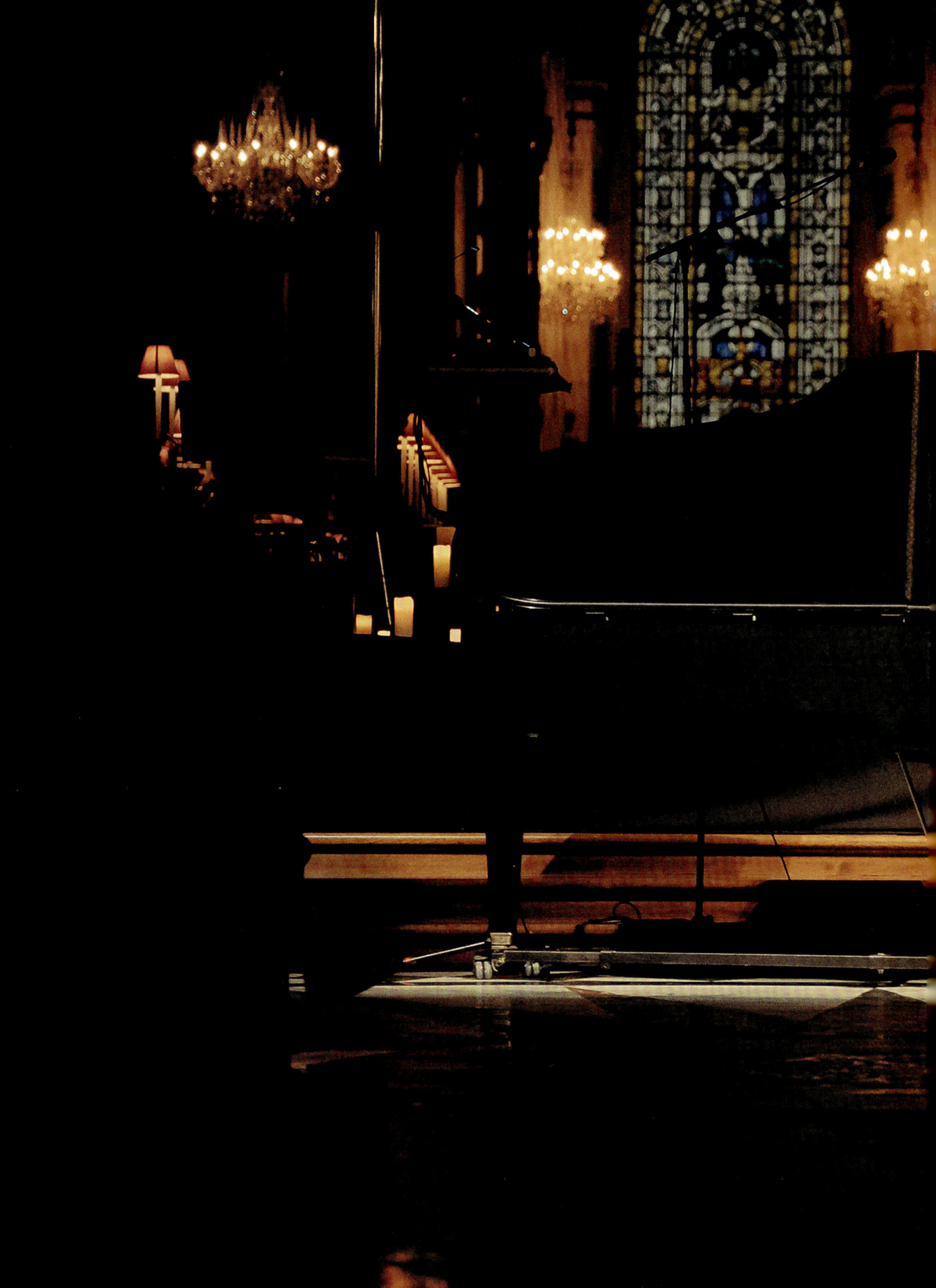

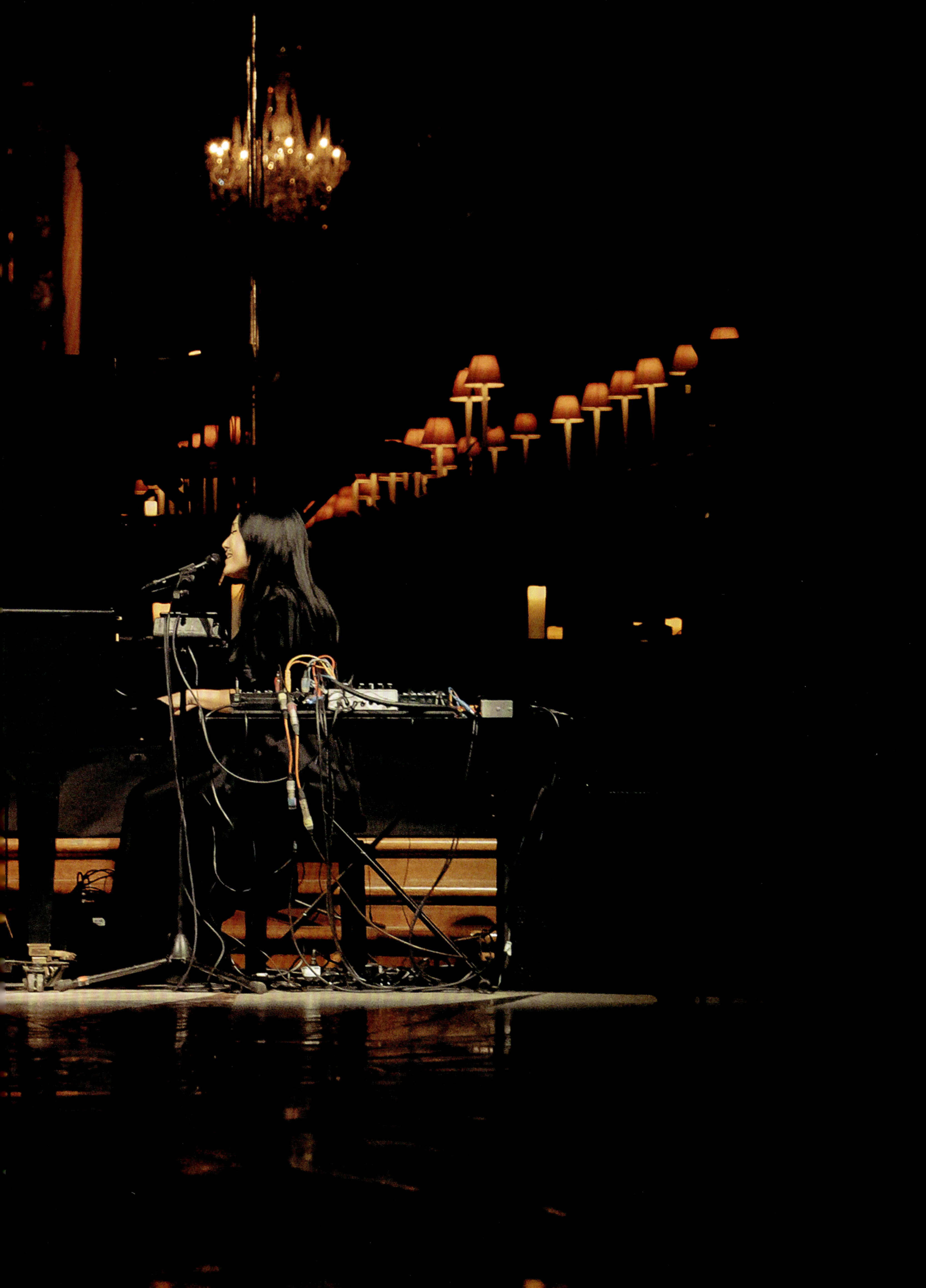

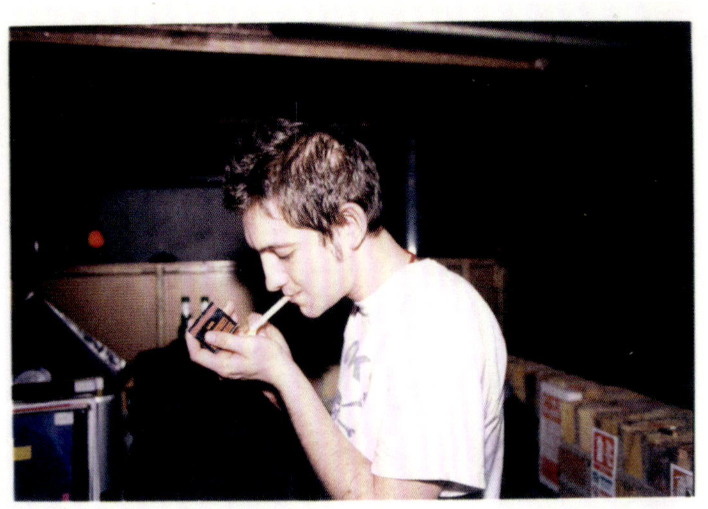

296—1

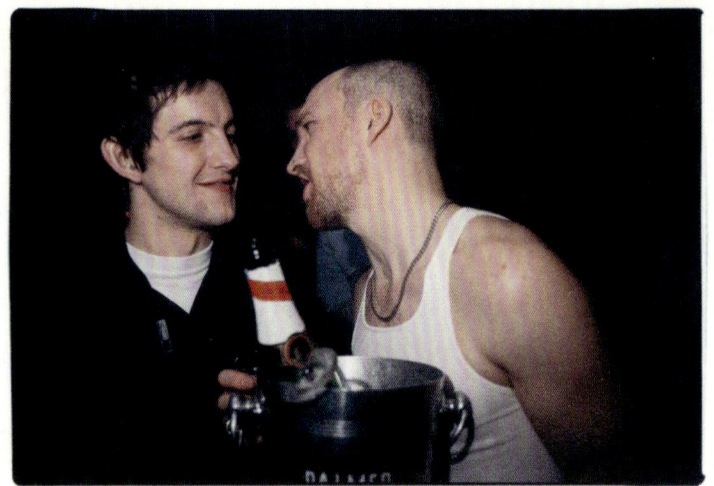

296—2

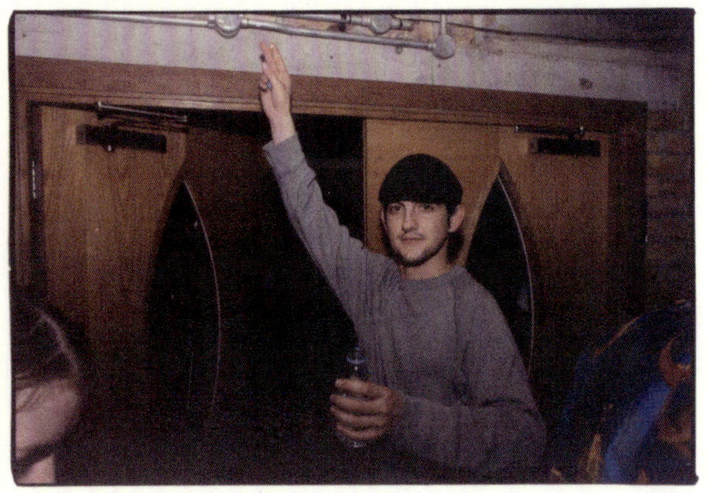

296—3

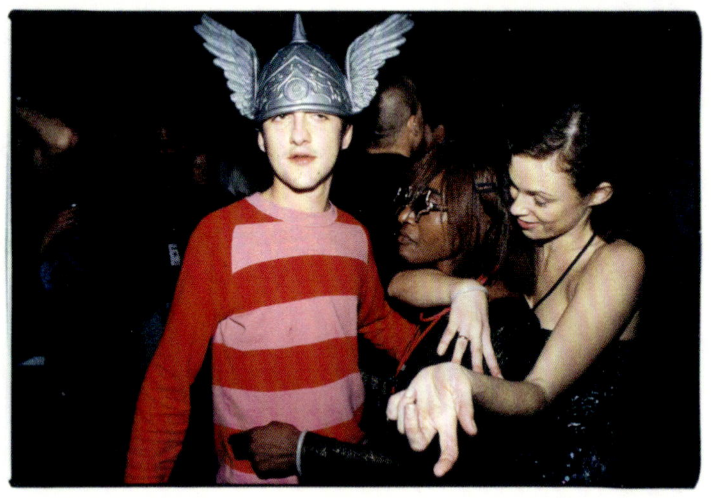

296—4

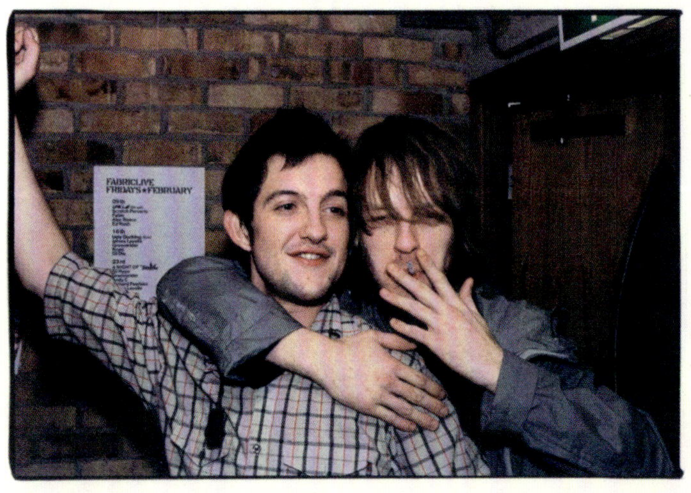

296—5

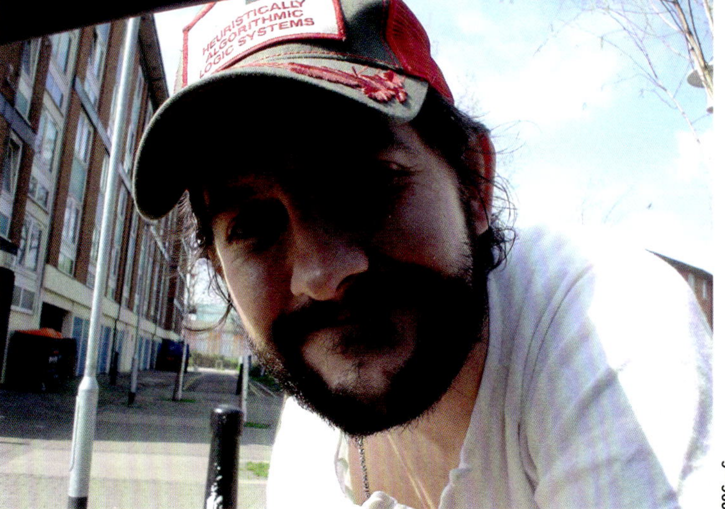

296—6

Shaun came into the company in the summer of 1999 – just a few months before we opened – as a flyer-boy, and that never left him.

It was in his DNA: a deep-rooted understanding of what made a good night, reading and understanding the crowd, knowing the essential building blocks of how and what to put on.

In those early days of FABRICLIVE he worked as a promotions assistant under Steve Blonde. Then when Steve left in 2006, Keith and I knew it was Shaun's time to shine. He just devoured that lead role and made it his own.

But in doing so he didn't change. He never got above his station or thought of himself as the kingmaker or lynchpin of the night; he'd be the one checking the posters were straight or making sure the set times and line-ups were correct. He didn't think for one second 'that's for the assistants'. He was and always would be a flyer-boy at heart.

Shaun was just a thoroughly good and decent person. When you have that as your basic modus operandi and you treat people the right way, no matter who they are – well, you can see the universal outpouring of love from across the industry and his countless friends at the news of his leaving us.

When it came to the fundraiser we hosted at fabric on Thursday, 18 November 2021, the good, the great and the even greater descended on the club to raise some much-needed funds for Shaun's late-stage cancer treatment. Annie Mac, Erol Alkan and The Chemical Brothers all performed. It was all so wonderful and simultaneously so damn sad, as all the money in the world wasn't able to save Shaun from that awful cancer in the end. But for that one night, the UK electronic music scene came together beautifully for one of their own: Jay Carder opened up in the main room, then a barefoot Fatboy Slim stepped up to the mixer before those Chemical Brothers, Tom and Ed, worked it out until the lights went up. Shaun was there too, still beavering away in the background and, in time-honoured tradition, not wanting a big fuss about his particular health predicament. When Shaun passed peacefully at 2 p.m. on Christmas Eve 2022, he was surrounded by some of his closest friends and family. Dan Avery and HAAi's elegiac 'Wall of Sleep' was playing at the close of day.

It's still hard to believe that Shaun Roberts is now gone. He was such a positive energy and a pure spirit with how he went about things. Shaun was the absolute consummate professional; he was dedicated to what he did, he was great at what he did and he absolutely loved our club. He bled fabric.

We all miss him terribly and life will never be the same without Shaun in it, but one thing is for sure: his spirit carries on in all of us and he'll forever be on the dancefloor.

Cameron x

djs

67. 747. 1991. 2562. 12592. 999999999. 'does it offend you,yeah?'. [0] phase. &me. $pyda. 10sui. 12th planet. 16bit. 1991 (uk). 2 bad mice. 2 shy. 20:20 soundsystem. 20:20 vision. 2000 and one. 28 costumes. 2many djs. 2shy. 2suckadjs. 3 channels. 3 reign. dj 3000. . 4 hero. 4am kru. 50 weapons…. 57th dynasty. 6th borough project. 92 points. a certain ratio. a for alpha. a guy called gerald. a human. a little sound. a made up sound. a man called adam. a plus. a skillz. a-bril. a-future. a-sides. a-trak. a.d.. a.g.. a.i. a.m. project. a.m.c. a.s.h. a1 bassline. aaa. aæe. aalson. aaron lacrate. aaron ross. aaronjay. aarron o'conner. ab. abdulla rashim. abe duque. able. abra cadabra. absolute.. ac mc. ac slater. ac13. accidental heroes. acemoma. acetate. acid arab. acid girls. acid mondays. acid pauli. acid ted. acoustic ladyland. acre. actress. ad. ada. ada regan. adam beyer. adam curtain. adam f. adam freeland. adam goldstone. adam marshall. adam mcgrath. adam port. adam shelton. adam x. adana twins. adapt. addiction. addison groove. adele moss. adesse versions. adiel. admnti. adnan. ado. adrian sherwood. adriana lopez. adriatique. adryiano. adsorb. adultnapper. advent. aeph. aera. aerofunk. aeroplane. aethority. affie yusuf. afrika bambaataa. afrika hi tek. afrodeutsche. afronaught. agent sumo. agents of time. aghnes. ago. agoria. agressor bunx. agy3na. ahadadream. ahmed salti. ai. ai people. aidan doherty. aidan orange. aim. air. air london. airod. airrica. airshots. aisha mirza. aj christou. aj tracey. ajax. ak sports. akala. akasha. aki. akiko kiyama. akira. akira kiteshi. akira the don. akito. akkord. akufen. akwaaba. al bradley. al doyle. al haca. al tourettes. al wootton. alan braxe. alan fitzpatrick. alan sims. alan vega. alb. alba heidari. albion forever. aldanya. alden tyrell. alec falconer. alecia hanna. alejandro fernandez. alejandro mosso. alejandro paz. alejo galvez. aleqs notal. aletha. alex. alex arnout. alex attias. alex bradley. alex celler. alex chase. alex cortez. alex coulton. alex downey. alex egan. alex gopher. alex jones. alex metric. alex murak. alex niggemann. alex nude. alex patchwork. alex picone. alex reece. alex smoke. alex t. alex tepper. alex under. alex virgo. alexander kowalski. alexander nut. alexander robotnick. alexandra. alexi delano. alexia glensy. alexis cabrera. alexis meshida. alexis raphael. alfie. alfy. ali b. ali tillett. alibi. alicia. alienata. alinka. alisha. alison marks. alitrec. alix alvarez. alix perez. allan pardo. allecto. alley cat. allez allez djs. alloy mental. aloud. alpha sect. also. alter ego. altered natives. altern 8. altino fernandez. alton miller. alvin c. alxzndr. ama. amadeezy. amaliah. amanda blank. ambivalent. amc. âme. amelie lens. amelièe. amémé. amen ra. americhord. amine edge & dance. amir javasoul. amirali. amit. ammara. amontobin. amoss. amotik. amy alford. amy becker. amy cutter. amy dabbs. amyelle. an toi. anabel arroyo. analogue cops. anastasia kristensen. ancient methods. and. andee. anden. andhim. ando. andre bratten. andre buljat. andré galluzzi. andrea giudice. andrea lai. andrea oliva. andrea parker. andrea rossi. andreas saag. andres campo. andrew. andrew baker. andrew curley. andrew gustav. andrew hill. andrew kay. andrew lyster. andrew stott. andrew thomson. andrew weatherall. andy bailey. andy bell. andy blake. andy bone. andy butler. andy c. andy george. andy luff. andy newland. andy smith. andy stott. andy vaz. andy votel. andy ward. andz. anek. anelisa. anetha. anfisa letyago. angel d'lite. angela hunte. angus taylor. anii. anikonik. anile. animistic beliefs. animus. anja ngozi. anja schneider. anna. anna morgan. anna wall. annie & timo. annie errez. annie mac. annie nightingale. annix. annix konichi & decimal bass. anonym. anotr. ansome. anstascia. answer code request. ansza. ant tc1. antal. antares. anthea. anthony 'shake' shakir. anthony collins. anthony naples. anthony parasole. anthony rother. anthony teasdale. antoine quesnel. antonio de angelis. antony diffrancesco. antony difrancesco. anz. aparde. apashe. apendics shuffle. apes & androids. apey. aphletik & dj morphingaz. aphotik. aphrodite. apollo 84. apollonia. apparat. appleblim. applebottom. apres:midi feat: aimee. aquasky. araabmuzik. archie hamilton. architect. architectual. archive. argia. argy. arian leviste. arielle free. aries. aril brikha. ark. arkaik. arkist. arkitech. armând. armanni. arnaud le texier. arne weinberg. arno. aroop roy. arp. arp 101. arpxp. arry h. art alfie. art brut. art department. art e fect. artche. arthi. arthrob. arthur baker. artifact. artificial intelligence. arto mwambe. artwork. asa tate. asad. asad rizvi. asadinho. asbo. asc. asch pintura. ash. ash a tak. ash lauryn. ash med school. ashatak. ashley arrez. ashley beadle. ashley slater. ashley wild. ashraf. ashworth. asian dub foundation. asok. aspects. asquith. asusu. aswefall. ata. athena. atipic. atjazz. atlants. atomic hooligan. atrip. attaboy. attaque. attention deficit disorder. attica blues. audio. audio bullys. audio werner. audiofly. audiojack. audion. audionite. august jakobsen. aum. auntie flo. aurbs. auric. aurora halal. austen/scott. autarkic. author. autobots. autocratz. aux 88. avatism. averse. avon blume. awanto 3. axel boman. aya. ayah marah. ayarcana. aychibs. ayme. ayn. azaad. azonica. azu tiwaline. azza. b live. b spoke. b traits. b-complex. b:thorough. b.love. b.o.t. b.traits. b12. baba stiltz. baby blu & mc peaches. baby ford. baby g. baby mammoth. baby t. babyhead. bachelors of science. bad anju. bad boy brown. bad company. bad cop/bad cop. bad habitz. badin brothers. badmarsh & shri. badness. badsista. bae blade. bahramji. bailey. bailey ibbs. bake. bakey. baltra. balzar. bambii. bambook. bambooman. bambounou. bamz. bandulu. bangkok impact. banksie. bannerworx. baobinga. bar 9. barac. barbie. bare up. barefoot doctor & carlos fandango. barely legal. barely royal & bunnie. barem. bareskin. barker. barker & baumecker. barlz & syntho. barnt. baron. barry ashworth. barry can't swim. bart b more. bart skils. bas ibellini. basement freaks. basement jaxx. basher. bashkka. basic soul unit. basim. basmati. bass clef. bass junkie. bass kleph. bassbin twins. bassboy. basshead. bassi. basslayerz. bassline. bassline smith. bassman. bassnectar. basteroid. battant. batu. bawrut. bb brown. bbymutha. bcee. bcuk. bdl. be svendsen. beaner. beanfield. beardyman. bearweasel. beat assassins. beat pharmacy. beat torrent. beatmania. beatnik. beatschubiger. beau. beautiful swimmers. beauty blender. beber. bec. becka diamond. becker. becky stroke. bedouin. beezy. bella mouki. bellaire. belle rouche. belly squad. bellyman. bempah. ben & pete. ben annand. ben clifford. ben cook. ben dillon. ben hauke. ben klock. ben martin. ben martin high sheen. ben murphy. ben pearce. ben pistor. ben rymer. ben sims. ben snow. ben sterling. ben ufo. ben verse. ben westbeech. beneath. benedikt frey. benga. beni g. benjamin berg. benjamin damage. benjamin fröhlich. benji b. benno blome. benny ill. benny l. benny page. benny v. benoit & sergio. bent. benteki. bentley rhythm ace. benton. beppe loda. bert bevens. bethbethbeth. bethegun. bex. beyond the wizard's sleeve. bianca oblivion. bicep. biesmans. big daddy kane. big hair. big miz. big narstie. big p. big tobz. big zuu. bigga. bigga world. biggie. biggoss. bigted. biig piig. bill brewster. bill patrick. bill shakes. billon. billy allen. billy bizznizz. billy blanks. billy daniel bunter. billy kenny. billy nasty. billy turner. binh. biome. bird peterson. birdsmakingmachine. birdy nam nam. bisoux bisoux. bizmarc. bjarki. bjorn torske. bklava. black affair. black asteroid. black barrel. black coffee. black devil disco club. black dog. black jazz consortium. black josh. black loops. black lotus. black milk. black sun empire. black wire. blacka. blackeye. blackhall & bookless. blackley. blacklist. blackout. blacks. blackstrobe. blade. bladerunner. blaise bellville. blak twang. blake baxter. blakey. blakkat. blame. blasha & allatt. blawan. blazey. blazey bodynod. blckshdw. bleak. blesid. blim. blind mic. blind minded. blk jks. blk.. blm. blm & jay massive. bloc2bloc. blocks. blokhe4d. blond:ish. blondes. bloodline. bloody mary. bloom. blotter trax. blowfelt featuring slarta john. blu bomma. blu mar ten. blue bear. blue daisy. blue hour. blue note set. bluejay. bluetoof. blunt instruments. bmb spacekid. bmotion. bnjmn. boaoabinga. boardroom. bob jones. bob moses. bobby & nihal. bobby & steve. bobby friction. bobby m. bobby o donnell. bobby pleasure. bobby.. bobmo. boca 45. boddika. body & soul. body by kenn. bodycode. bodyjack. boggy. bok bok. bok bok & manara. bolz bolz. bombay bicycle club. bonar bradberry. bonde do role. bone slim. bones & ramsey. bonkaz. bonobo. bontan. bonzai bonner. boo & ministre x. boo williams. boofy. booka shade. booker t. boomtac. bordello. boris werner. born n bread. born ruffians. borrowed identity. bot southern fried. botnek. bou. bougaïeff & yasuda. bowes. bowski. box clever. box mouse. boxcutter. boxia. boxwork. boy 8-bit. boy better know. boy-c. boycott. boys noize. brackles. brad laner. bradii. bradley zero. brady. bradzo. braiden. braindead. brakeman. brakes. brame & hamo. brandt brauer frick. branko buraka som sistema. brassica. braund reynolds. brawther. braxton. breach. break. break dj leacy. breaka. breakage. breakbot. breaker 1 2. breakestra. bredren. brenda russell. brendon moeller. brenmar. brennan green. brett johnson. brey. brian not brian. bricolage. brina knauss. brinsley. brinsley kazak. brisk. british murder boys. britta arnold. brix. brixx. brockie. brockie & det. brodanse. brodinkski. brodinski. brohn. broke 'n' english. broken english club. bromley. brookes brothers. brooks. brother brown. brothers black. brothers bud. brothers of set. brothers' vibe. brtsh knights. bru c. bruce. bruce wayne. bruk. brunelle. bruno pronsato. bruno schmidt. brunto balanta. bruza. bryan g. bryan gee. bryan zentz. bryte. btk. btraits. bu$hi. budino. bugz in the attic. bugzy malone. buki cole & free radical. bullion. bullitnuts. bungle. bunks. buraka som sistema. burnski. bushbaby. bushkin. bushwacka. busta. busy p. butane. butane & someone else. butch. butterz. buunshin. bwana. bxks. byetone. byron the aquarius. c1. c2c. c4. c90s. cab drivers. cabanne. cadans. cadence weapon. cadenza. caged baby. cajuan. cajun dance party. caleb calloway. caleesi. calibre. call super. callide. callum hammett. calvin clarke. calvin harris. calyx. calyx & teebee. camea. camelphat. cameo. cameron jack. camille leon. camo. camo & krooked. campagvelocet. campbell. campbell irvine. canblaster. capo lee. capsa. captain comatose. captain crunch. carasel. carbon. cardinal sound. cari lekebusch. caribou. carista. carl cox. carl craig. carl loben. carlita. carlito & addiction. carlo lio. carlos ryan. carlos valdes. carlota marques. carly foxx. carly wilford. carreno is lb. carsten jost. carsten klemann. carte blanche. cartier. cartoon. cartridge. casey spillman. cash money. casino times. casisdead. caski. casnova. caspa. casper c. cass & tom mangan. cassius. cassy. catching cairo. catchment. catz n dogz. causa. cause & affect. cause 4 concern. cc:disco!. cecilio. cedric benoit & matsa. cedric maison. cem. ceri. cern. cesar merveille. cesare vs disorder. cezar. chad andrew. chad dubz. chaim. chambray. champion. champion & serious. channel tres. chano. chaos in the cbd. charelle smith. charisse c. charla green. charles drakeford. charles siegling. charles webster. charli brix. charlie bones. charlie dark. charlie p. charlie pushamann. charlie rope. charlie tee. charlo. charlotte de witte. chase & status. chasing shadows. chateau flight. chavinski. chef. chef dee. chemical brothers. cherry. cherrywine aka butterfly. chew lips. chez damier. chic miniature. chickaboo. chicken lips. chief rockas. chimpo. chimpo & trigga. chinese daughter. chippy nonstop. chklte. chloe. chloe caillet. chloé robinson. chopstick dubplate. chords. chris carrier. chris carter. chris coco. chris duckenfield. chris farrell. chris finke. chris inperspective. chris interface. chris jay. chris liebing. chris lorenzo. chris maran. chris p cuts. chris parkin. chris read. chris rhythm doctor. chris sabian. chris schwarzwälder. chris stanford. chris stussy. chris su. chris wood. chrissy t. christian ab. christian bonanata. christian burkhardt. christian löffler. christian nielsen. christian prommer. christian smith. christine indigo. christophe. christopher just. christopher rau. chroma. chromatics. chrome hoof. chronik. chuckie. chuckster. chucky. chuckz. chunky. chunky bizzle. chunky fox. cicely. cici. ciel. cimm. cincity. cinnaman. cinthie. circlesquare. circuits. circulation. circulus. citizen. citizenn. city rockers. civil djs. cj beatz. cj c1. cj cam. cj jeff. cj yaxley. ckp. claire ripley. claptone. clara cuvé. clara moto. clarian. clarity. clarkee. clarky. claro intelecto. claude vonstroke. claude young. claus voigtmann. clbrks. cleido. clement meyer. cleric. cleveland watkiss. clickbox. client_03. clipz. clive henry. clive ingredients. clive morley. clock opera. clockwork. cloonee. clor. close a/v. clouds. clouwds. club autonomic. club fitness. cluekid. cmpnd. cmx. cobblestone jazz. coco. coco bryce. coco dubz. coco em. cocoon. codebreaker. coki. cold fusion. coldcut. colder. colette. colin boardway. colin chiddle. colin dale. collette warren. combine. command strange. commix. commix & lowqui. commodo. compa. complex. conair. concord dawn. conduct. conducta. conforce. congo dubs. congo dubz. congo natty. congorock. coni. connan mocaksin. connec. conrad. consequence. consouls. container. convextion. cookie monsta. cool kids. cooly g. coops. copacabannark. coppa. copy paste soul. cora novoa. corbi. cormac. correspondant music. corrie. cosmic kids. cosmicat. cosmin trg. cosmo. cosmo sofi. cosmos. cotesy. cottam. cotti. courtesy. crackhaus. crackin' skullz. craig bartlett. craig duranti. craig o'connell. craig richards. craig torrance. craig walsh. crash tracy. craze. crazy cousins. crazy d. crazy girl. crazy p. crazy penis. crazy titch. creatures. creed. cressida. crime rave. crispin dior. crissy criss. cristi cons. cristian vogel. cristoph. critical d. critical impact. critical sound. crmv nonsinthetik. crookers. croon inc. cropper. crossbreed. crossover. crosstown rebels. crowdpleaser & stplomb crymein. crystal castles. crystal clear. crystal fighters. crystallmess. crystl. ctrl. ctrls. cuartero. cuban bros. culoe de song. culprate. culprate & maksim. cult of the damned. culture shock. cupp cave. cuppa sounds. curses. curses!. cut chemist. cut copy. cutline. cutmaster swift. cw. cw/a. cyantific. cybin. cyrk. cyrus. czech. d bridge. d double e. d minds. d product & surge. d-bridge. d-lish. d. tiffany. d.dan. d.i.e.. d.i.m.. d'jules. d'lex (dollop). d'marc cantu. d'explicit. d'julz. d*minds. d/r/u/g/s. d1. da sunlounge. dabbla. dabs. dachshund. daddy earl. daddy freddy. daddy nature. daf. daffy. daggastar. daisy moon. daisybelle. dajusch. dakota sixx. dale mussington. dalunartikz. dam swindle. damian isaacs. damian lazarus. damian schwartz. damon martin. damu. dan & jon kahuna. dan andrei. dan beaumont. dan berkson. dan curtin. dan dnr. dan ghenacia. dan greenpeace. dan grindy. dan j spinney. dan shake. dan stacey & chantelle fiddy. dan the automator. dan wild. dana d. dana ruh. dance spirit. dandim. dandy jack. dangerous. daniel. daniel 2000. daniel avery. daniel bell. daniel curpen. daniel donnachie. daniel miller. daniel taylor. daniel wang. daniel wilde. danielle. danilo plessow. danja mc. danmass sound system. danny benedettini. danny byrd. danny c. danny cobbler. danny daze. danny drive thru. danny kaos. danny krivit. danny langan. danny m. danny macmillan. danny rankin. danny raper. danny snowden. danny spencer. danny t. danny t & tradesman. danny vito. danny wheeler. dano. dans le sac vs scroobius pip. dantiez saunderson. danton eeprom. danuel tate. dapayk daredevil & tigerstyle. daphni. dappa. dappz. dapz on the map. dar disku. darbak. daria kolosova. darius syrossian. dark circles. dark globe. dark sky. dark tantrums. dark0. darkhouse fam. darkid. darko. darkside. darkzy. darley. darq e freaker. darqwan. darren jay. darren roach. darrison. darshan jesrani. dart. darwin. das glow. das pop. daschund. dasha rush. data. data 3. data memory access. datkid. datsik. daughters of frank. dave. dave aju. dave angel. dave anthony. dave clarke. dave congreve. dave gamble. dave harrington. dave harvey. dave hill. dave jarvis. dave jones. dave martin. dave mothersole. dave owen. dave tarrida. davey boy smith. david alvarado. david duriez. david gtronic. david holmes. david kochs. david labeij. david rodigan mbe. david scuba. david sugar. david triana. davide decay. davide squillace. dax j. daxta. daz-i-kue. daze maxim. dazee. dazman. dbaudio. dbr uk. dbridge. dbx. dc breaks. de la swing. de-tü. dea dvornik. dead kids. deadbeat. deadboy. deadline. deadly avenger. deadset. deaf stereo. deamonds. dean marc. deanoloco. death invegas. death on the balcony. debbiesthuglife. deboa. debonair samir. deborah de luca. debukas. decal. decibel. decibella. decimal. deckwrecka. deefa. deego fresh. deeizm. deekline & wizard. deemas j. deep dish. deep teknologi. deepa dee. deepchord. deeper connections. deer jade. deetron. deft. dego. dego ranking. degs. dekker. del-30. delano smith. delicat. dellux. delphic. delsin records. delta funktionen. delta heavy. demarkus lewis. demarzo. demdike stare. demi riquísimo. demo. demolition man. demon. demuja. den haan. denaas. denham audio. denis horvat. denis sulta. deniz kurtel. denney. dennis cruz. dennis ferrer. dennis quin. denny. dense & pika. deploy. depthcharge. derek plaslaiko. derren smart. derren's disco. derrick carter. derrick may. desert sound colony. desiree. desperate soundsystem. dessert sound colony. desto. destruction. det. detboi. detlef. detoy selectah. detroit grand pubahs. detroit in effect. detroit love. detroit swindle. detropix. dev. devilman. devious d. devlin. devolution. devon miles. dewalta. dexcell. dexorcist. dexta. dexter. dexter kane. dextone. dhol foundation live drummers. diagonal. diane charlemagne. die. diefenbach. diego krause. diemantle. dieselboy. different drummer sound system. dig this. digable planets. digby. digital. digital farm animals. digital mystikz. digital niyabinghi. digitaline. digitalism. digs and woosh. dilate. dilemma. dilinja. dillinja. dillon francis. dimension. dimitry. dinky. dino lenny. diplo. dirtklod. dirty dike. dirty doe. dirty dog. dirtyphonics. disastronaut. discarda. disco 3000. disco bloodbath djs. disco bloodbath…. disco freaks. discodeine. diskjokke. diskokaine. dismantle. disprove. disrupta. distal. distance. distinction. distinkt. distorted minds. district. distro. diverge. dixon. diz. dizzee rascal. dizzle kid. dizzy doubledown. dj 279. dj 3000. dj adhd. dj alex. dj amaning. dj andy. dj apollo. dj argue. dj assault. dj babu. dj barely legal. dj believe. dj big ted. dj bizznizz. dj blakey. dj blitz. dj bone. dj boring. dj bpm. dj brockie. dj bryan gee. dj buck. dj bugzee. dj cable. dj calculon. dj cameo. dj cartier. dj cash money. dj champion. dj cloakroom. dj craze. dj dan. dj dar. dj deeon. dj deep. dj devil. dj dexter. dj dick & tweed. dj die. dj dominator. dj dough. dj drama. dj dsl. dj dub. dj dynamic. dj e. dj earl. dj edu. dj ej. dj emm. dj eva. dj ez. dj fiend. dj flight. dj food. dj format. dj fresh. dj fuckoff. dj funk. dj garth. dj gemini. dj go. dj gone. dj greenpeace. dj groove. dj guv. dj haus. dj hazard. dj heartstring. dj heather. dj hell. dj holographic. dj hype. dj hyper. dj hysteria. dj ink. dj iq. dj iron. dj jazz t. dj js-1. dj kane. dj kaos. dj kg. dj khalil. dj klever. dj kontrol. dj koze. dj krust. dj krystal. dj lee. dj lioness. dj listener. dj lok. dj love. dj luck & mc neat. dj lycox. dj madd. dj majestik. dj majesty. dj majic. dj marky. dj masda. dj maximum. dj mehdi. dj mell g. dj melon. dj mk. dj narrows. dj nate. dj naughty. dj no way. dj nobo. dj nobu. dj nodi. dj noize. dj nookie. dj ollie. dj one man party. dj orange. dj patife. dj paulette. dj paypal. dj phantasy. dj phantasy ft sas. dj philly. dj pierre. dj plead. dj pogo. dj polo. dj poolboi. dj pope. dj premier. dj presha. dj python. dj q. dj qdex. dj qu. dj randall. dj rap. dj rashad. dj red. dj redhot. dj riot. dj ritu. dj rocha. dj ron. dj rupert. dj s. dj s.e.f. dj s2. dj sammy b-side. dj say less. dj scratch. dj shadow. dj silversurfer. dj sizzla. dj skirt. dj skull. dj skully. dj slip. dj slow. dj sly. dj smj. dj sneak. dj sotofett. dj spen. dj spinbad. dj spinn. dj spinna. dj spit. dj spooky. dj sprinkles. dj ss. dj steaw. dj sticks. dj stingray. dj stingray 313. dj stix. dj stolen. dj storm. dj strangefruit. dj suki. dj suv. dj swagger. dj swamp. dj swingz. dj t. dj target. dj teenwolf. dj tennis. dj thiago. dj thinking. dj

thor. dj three. dj tlr. dj tool. dj tubby. dj twiz. dj unique. dj uniques. dj vibes. dj w!ld. dj w.m.d. dj warden. dj werner. dj whut. dj woody. dj yoda. dj zinc. django django. djebali. djedjotronic. djeff. djg. djinn. djoko. djq. djrum. djss. djt. djulz. djvadim. dk krush. dk7. dlr. dm & jemini. dmx krew. dna. do or die. do servini. dobbs. doc daneeka. doc martin. doc scott. dochi. doctor. doctor p. document one. dodge & fuski. dodha. dog. dogger. dogtanian. doktor. dolby anol. dolenz. dolle jolle. dolly daggers. dollz at play. dom & roland. dom 877. dom chung. dom donnelly. dom hz. dom sum. domenic. domenic capello. dominator. doms & deykers. domu. don diablo. don letts. don rimini. donae'o. donato dozzy. donch. doneao. donna edwards. donna leake. donna williams. donnacha costello. donovan 'badboy' smith. donovan kingjay. donsurf. doorly. dop. dopplereffekt. dorian paic. dorsia. dose. dosem. dossa. dot allison. dot major. double g. double helix. double o. double u. doudou md. downhill djs. downshifter. dozia. dr banana. dr bob jones. dr dubplate. dr eps. dr maz. dr s gachet. dr. gonzo. dr. lektroluv. dr. rubinstein. dr. s. gachet. dr.d lorean. dr.shingo. drama. drama society. dramatic. drea. dread. dread mc. dreadnought. dreadzone. dream. dreamrdreamr. dreps. driia. droog. drop the lime. drs. drs in session. drstab. drum monkeys. drumattic twins. drumcell. drums of death. drumsound. drumsound & bassline smith. drumtalk. drumterror. dsb soundsystem. dt. dub cartel. dub head. dub healy. dub marines. dub phizix. dub phizix & strategy. dub pistols. dub syndicate. dub terror. dub woofa. dub-4. dubfire. dubkasm. dubphizix. dubphizix & strategy. dubplate mex. dubrunner. dubtil. dubwise. dudley perkins. dudley scavenger. duels. duke dumont. dullah beatz. dullahbeatz. duncan forbes. dungeon meat. duowe. duplex. duppy. durrty goodz. dusk & blackdown. duskee. dusky. dustin swint. dusty kid. dutch. dutchie. dutchie & joe morgan. dutta. dvs1. dvsmc. dvwlx. dwarde. dwayne sodaberk. dyed sounderom. dyed soundorom. dylan. dylan rhymes. dylantheinfamous. dylhen. dynamic. dynamite. dynamite mc. dynarec. dyzen. e-ll. e.m.m.a.. eagles & butterflies. earful of wax. earl gateshead. earlybird. east end dubs. eastman. eastwood. easy rider. eat the beat. eat work play. eats everything. ebk. ebony bones. echocord. echonomist. echospace. eclair fifi. éclair fifi. eclecticist. ed case. ed darling. ed davenport. ed dimmock. ed dmx. ed funk. ed pitt. ed rush. ed scissor. ed sheeran. ed solo. ed:it. edan. eddie. eddie 'flashin' fowlkes. eddie leader. eddie ricards. eddie richards. eddy seven. eddy temple-morris. edit. edit select. edott. edson amw. edu imbernon. eduardo de la calle. eduardo de le calle. edward. edward oberon. edwin oosterwal. efdemin. effy. eg. eglo. ego trippin. ego troopers. egoless. egyptian hip hop. egyptian lover. egyptrixx. ehst. ehua. eich. einzelkind. ejeca. ekko. ekkohaus. eksman. el jharno. el-b. el-p. ela minus. electric lane. electro elvis. electrocute. elektro guzzi. elektrons. eleonora cutaia. eleven8. elf kid. elgato. eli & fur. eli brown. eli verveine. elif. elijah. eliphino. elise massoni. elite force. eliza rose. elkka. ell murphy. ella. ella sop. ellen allien. elli acula. ellie cocks. ellie prohan. ellie stokes. elliot adamson. elliot eastwick. elliot schooling. ellis dee. elmono. elodie. eloi. elvin zed. ema. emalkay. eman. emanuel satie. emcee recordings party. emerald. emerson todd. emily crooked. emma b. emma g. emma lou. emma-jean thackray. emmma. emperor. emperor machine. emz. enada. enamour. enchante. endo. enei. enemie. english teacher. enrica falqui. enrico sangiuliano. envelopes. envoy. enzo siragusa. eon. eprom. eps & phantom. equiknoxx. equinox. eren. eric borgo. eric rug. eric volta. erick navas. erlend ove & the full effect. ernesto ferreyra. erol alkan. errol. error djs. esa. esa williams. escape. escher. eskman. esmeralda. esser. esteban adame. estella boersma. estelle. etapp kyle. etch. ethel. etherwood. ethyl. etienne de crecy. euphonique. eva lazarus. eva808. evan baggs. evenson allen. eveson. evil b. evil dust. evil nine. evm128. evoke. evonii. ewan mcvicar. ewan pearson. ewen pearson. excalibah. excel & moodie. exercise one. exile. exit99. exodus. exos. extended players. extrano. ez. ez rollers. ezlv. f. fabe. fabio. fabio florido. fabrice lig. fabricio maurizi. fabrizio mauriza. fabrizio maurizi. fabz. facs. factory floor. fade black. faded. faff. faith sfx. fake blood. falko brocksieper. fall forward. fallacy & fusion. falle nioke. falty dl. fantastic twins. farrago. fat camp. fat freddys drop. fatboy slim. fatima. fatima al qadiri. fatima yamaha. fatman d. fats. fauna. faux naif. fauzia. fava. faze. faze action. faze miyake. fb julian. fbr. fc kahuna. fd. feadz. fear of flying. fear of music djs. fearful. fearless. fearless dread. fedele. federico molinari. feed me. fekky. felipe venegas. felix da housecat. felix dickenson. felix dickinson. felix. cw. felon. felon 5. felon5. female allstars. femi b. fen. fenin. fer ber. ferenc. ferreck dawn. ferro. feux. fideles. fiedel. fierce. fila brazillia. filip motovunksi. filthy dukes. filthy gears. filthy luka. fineart. fink. finn. finn lewis. finn mccorry. finnebassen. finwa. fiona kraft. fiona maguire. firas. first rate. fish. five 0. five alive. fix. fixate. fiyahdred. fjaak. fka.m4a. flabbergast. flash. flat-t. flatline. flaty dl. flava d. flavio falco. fleur shore. flex. flight. flint. flipz. flirt. flirta d. fliss mayo. flix. flo dan. floating points. flohio. floorplan. florentia. flori. flosstrodamus. flowdan. flowrian. floyd lavine. flux. flux pavillion. fluxion. foals. foamo. fokus. folamour. fold. fonti. fool's gold. foostie. footprintz. footsie. ford. foreign beggars. foreign concept. foreigner. forest. forest drive west. forester. format b. fort knox five. fort romaeu. fort romeau. fossil archive. foundation. four tet. fourward. fox. fox n wolf. foxy. fra soler. fracture. frak. fran hartnett. france copland. francesca lombardo. francesco del garda. francesco maddalena. francesco tristano. francis. francis harris. francisco (pigna). francisco allendes. franck roger. françois k. françois x. frank & tony. frank de wolf. frank kusserow. frank martiniq. frank tope. frankee. frankee d. frankey & sandrino. frankie chan. frankie staywoke. frankievalentine. frankievalley. franklin de costa. franky greiner (alter mahnn). franky nuts. franky rizardo. franky wah. franz costa. fraser cook. frazi.err. fre4knc. freakenstein. fred asquith. fred everything. fred p. fred paka black jazz consortium. fred v & grafix. freddie foxx. freddie foxxx. freddy fresh. freddy k. frederic robinson. fredventura. free zing. freeform five. freek & kit. freestyle. freestyle man. freestylers. french fries. frenchy. frenzic. freq nasty. frequency. frequency 7. fresh. fresh randall. freshta. friction. friend within. friendly fires. friends of the bride. frisco. frivolous. frosty. frozemode. fryars. fuckpony. fudge fingas. fujiya & miyagi. full nelson. fumez the engineer. fumiya tanaka. fun. function. funk butcher. funk d void. funki porcini. funkin pussy sound squad. funkineven. funkstepz. funktion. funktional. funky dee. funky flirt. funkystepz. funsta. funsta mc. funster. funtcase. fur coat. furney. fused. fusion. future boogie. future cut. future funk squad. future prophecies. futureboogie. futurebound. futurecast. fuzion. fuzz against junk. fuzzbox. g -double- e. g dub. g-ha. g-pal. g'mac. g33. gabbs. gabriel ananda. gabriel torres. gabrielle kwarteng. gadi mizrahi. gaiser. gallivanter. gamal kabar. gamma. ganja white night. gantz. gap shakk. gardens of god. gareth hansome. gareth wild. garth (grayhound). gary beck. gary k. gary strife. gaskin. gasslyte. gatekeeper. gatto fritto. gavin fraser. gavin herlihy. gavsborg. ge-ology. geddes. geeneus. geiom. gemi. gemini. gemmy. gene on earth. general degree. general levi. general levy. general ludd. general midi. genetika. genius of time. gentle friendly. gentleman's dub club. gentlemen's club. geoff barrow. geoffroy (mugwump). george fitzgerald. george pringle. george smeddles. georgia. georgia girl. georgie bee. georgie marshall. georgie riot. georgio oniani. gerardo niva. gerd. gerd janson. gerra & stone. gerrardo. gerry read. gerry rooney. ges-e. gesaffelstein. get fucked. ghetto. ghost culture. ghostland observatory. ghostphone. ghoulish. giammarco orsini. gianluca de tiberis. gianni callipari. giant swan. gid & karen normal. giddy. gideon. gideön. giganti. gigi fm. gil (the youngsters). giles smith. gilles peterson. gin. gina breeze. gingy. gino. gino ginelli. giom. giorgia angiuli. girl unit. girls don't sync. girls of the internet. giulia tess. giuliano lomonte. giuseppe cennamo. giz. gizla. glacci. glade marie. glenn underground. glimpse. glitch city. global communication. glowal. glume. glxy. godderz. gold chains. gold panda. golden bug. golden lady. goldie. golesworthy. gomes. good shoes. goodhand. goods. goon club allstars. goose. gordon ritchie. gorgon city. gorgon sound. gorje hewek. goth-trad. gotsome. goya music. gq. grace sands. grafix. grafta. grainger. gramme. grandmixxer. grant nelson. grass roots. greco-roman soundsystem. green velvet. greena. greenlaw. greenmoney. greenmoney djs. greenskeepers. greg dredzone. greg packer. greg pidcock. greg venezia. greg wilson. gregor tresher. grey code. greymatter. gridlok. griff. grim sickers. grima. grimm. groove armada. grooverider. groovy d. grum. gta. guad. gucci soundsystem. gui boratto. guido. guido schneider. guilhem monin. guillaume. guillaume & the coutu dumonts. guilty beatz. guilty simpson. guinee conakry. gully b. gunnar haslam. guns n bombs. gus da hoodrat. gus gus. gusto. guti. guv. guy gerber. guy j. gw harrison. gwenan. gydra. h-productions. h foundation. haai. hacke. hackman. hadouken. hagan. hainesy. hakan lidbo. half hawaii. half queen. halo. halo varga. halogenix. hamid. hamilton. hamish & toby. hammer. handsome rob. hanfry martinez. hank limit. hannah. hannah holland. hannah wants. happa. hard house banton. hardhouse banton. hardt antoine. haribo. haris. harmonic 313. harri. harriet jaxxon. harrimannn. harrison bdp. harrison f. harry james. harry love. harry ludermann. harry mccanna. harry shotta. harry wills. harvard bass. harvey. harvey mckay. hashman deejay. hatch. hatcha. haus. haydn. haywire sessions. hazard. hazard,. haze. hazel marimba. head high. headhunter. headless horseman. headman. heartbreak. hearthug. heartless crew. heartthrob. hecha. hector. héctor oaks. heels & souls. hefner. heidi. heiko laux. heiko m/s/o. heiko mso. heimlich knüller. heist. helena hauff. heléna star. hemera. henning baer. henri bergmann. henrik schwarz. henry dell. henry krinkle. henry saiz. henry st social. heny g. herbert. herbzie. herck. hercules. heron flow. herve. hervé. hesseltime. hey today!. hi5ghost. hidden agenda. high contrast. high maintenance. high rankin. hijack. hijak. hipp-e. hird. hiroko yamamura. hito. hizzle guy. hobo. hodge. holger zilske. holic:. holloway. holy ghost!. holy goof. honcho. honestjons. hoomance. horror inc.. horse meat disco. horsepower. horsepower productions. hosh. hostage. hosted by. hostox. hot chip. hot city. hot cross fun. hot natured. hot since 82. hotflush records. house of black lanterns. house of house. housekeeping. housemeister. howie b. hrdvsion. hucci. hudson mohawke. huerco s. huerta. huggy. hugh hardie. hugo. hugo massien. hunee. hunter/game. hutch. huw lloyd. huxley. hvob. hybrid. hybrid minds. hybrid theory. hybris. hydra x blueprint. hydro. hyenah. hyetal. hyjack. hypah. hyper. hyperactive mc. hyperaktivist. hypercolour. hyrogifics. hyroglifics. hysterics. i g culture. i hate models. i-f. i:cube. i.d.. iain taylor. ian brown. ian dpm. ian o'brien. ian pooley. ic3. icarus. icey. icicle. icicle entropy. icon. id. idjutboys. ifan dafydd. ifeoluwa. iffy. ig culture. ignacio morales. ika. ikay. ikonika. ila brugal. ilija rudman. ill blu. ill truth. illaman. illario allicante. illmatika. illum sphere. illyus & barrientos. ils. imanu. imogen. impact & kuedon. impact mc. impey. in aeternam vale. in flagranti. in:most. indian ropeman. indidjinous. indigo. indiji. indira paganotto. infamous. infamousizak. infinity ink. influx uk. inforce. infusion. initial research. inja. injekta. ink. inka. inkke. inland. inland knights. inna. innellea. inner zone. innervisions. insideinfo. insomniax. instinct. instra:mental. intec. intense. inter. interference. intergalactic gary. international chrome. interplanetary criminal. interstellar-funk. introspekt. invaderz. invadhertz. invoker. invt. inxec. ion ludwig. ipman. ipso facto. irah. iration steppas. iris menza. iron curtis. irondread. irrelevant. isa. isa gt. isabella. ishan sound. isolee. ital. ital tek. italoboyz. itoa. ivan kutz. ivan smagghe. ivory. ivy. ivy lab. iwizz. iz & diz. izco. izzie gibbs. j casa. j da flex. j distant. j kenzo. j majik. j oh zee. j phlip. j rocc. j spaceman & john coxon. j sweet. j tijn. j walk. j wilz. j wow. j-double. j-zef. j:kenzo. j:s. j. phlip. j.b.. j.g.. j.jeff & l.e. bass. j.o.s.h.u.a. j.sparrow. j'rome. j33. jac the disco. jack. jack beats. jack dat. jack de marseille. jack dee. jack junior. jack ling. jack master. jack mirror. jack sparrow. jack srow. jack swift. jack wickham. jackbeats. jackdat. jackdate. jackmaster. jackson & his computer band. jacky (uk). jacky murda. jacob husley. jacopo latini. jacques greene. jacques lu cont. jacques renault. jade. jade seatle. jaded. jadell. jaden thompson. jael. jafar. jagga. jaguar. jaguar skills. jagz kooner. jahcoozi. jai baisden. jaime doom. jake beautyman. jake fairly. jake holloway. jake manders jakes. jakes. jakwob. jam city. jam d bongo. jamakabi. jamback. james dean brown. james dexter. james friedman. james grant. james hillard. james holden. james lavelle. james marvel. james massiah. james mcardle. james mollison. james mowbray. james murphy. james o'connell. james pants. james prentice. james priestley. james puentes. james ruskin. james tec. james teej. james welsh. james what. james yuill. james zabelia. james zabiela. jameson. jamie 3:26. jamie aramayo. jamie duggan. jamie george. jamie jones. jamie o'dell. jamie russell. jamie thinnes. jamie vex'd. jamie xx. jamiu. jammer. jammz. jamz supernova. jan blomqvist. jan krueger. jan kruger. jane fitz. janette slack. jansons. janus rasmussen. japanese popstars. jape. jappa. jared wilson. jargon. jarvis cocker. jason kaakoush. jason kaye. jasper james. jasper thevinyl junkie. jasper tygner. jasss. javeon mccarthy. javi redondo. javier carballo. jawside. jay. jay 5ive. jay carder. jay clarke. jay cunning. jay daniel. jay duncan. jay haze. jay jay revlon. jay karim. jay massive. jay shepheard. jay swift. jay tripwire. jayar. jaycee. jayda g. jaydaa. jaydan. jaydes. jaye ward. jaymo. jaz. jazzanova. jazzcool. jazzie b obe. jazzy jeff. jc. jd. reid. jdh & dave p. jds. jean nipon. jeannie hopper. jeep girlz. jef k. jeff bennett. jeff metal. jeff milligan. jeff mills. jeff samuel. jehst. jelani blackman. jen. jenia tarsol. jenifa mayanja. jenna g. jennifer cardini. jenny cheng. jeno & garth. jens bond. jens zimmerman. jensen interceptor. jeremy newall. jeremy olander. jeremy p. caulfield. jeremy underground. jeroen search. jerome hill. jerome six. jerome sydenham. jerry dammers. jerry lionz. jerry rooney. jeru the damaja. jesper dahlback. jesse callosso. jesse calosso. jesse maas. jesse rose. jessie jo. jetsss. jey mellen. jezar. jezta. jim stanton. jim-e stack. jimi jules. jimmy edgar. jimmy franks. jimmy k tel. jimpster. jj. jjess. jk flesh. jkarri. jman. jme. jnr tubby. jnr windross. joakim. joaquin 'joe' claussell. job jobse. jody wisternoff. joe. joe & will ask. joe 2 grand. joe armon-jones. joe claussell. joe corti. joe davis. joe ellis. joe ford. joe goddard. joe hart. joe hot chip. joe nbo. joe peng. joe ransom. joe raygun. joe syntax. joefarr. joel compass. joel deep. joel martin. joel mull. joey anderson. joey beltram. joey jackson. joey jay. joey negro. johannes heil. john b. john barera. john beech. john daly. john digweed. john dimas. john heckle. john keys. john monkman. john peel. john roberts. john talabot. john tejada. johnny b. johnny dub. johnny hiller. johnny hunter. johnnyd. joi. jojo de freq. joker. joker & buggsy. joker & footsie. joker d. joker of the scene. jokers of the scene. jolliffe. jolyon green. jon carter. jon convex. jon hester. jon hopkins. jon k. jon kennedy sound system. jon marsh. jon pleased. jon rundell. jon rust. jonah sharp. jonas kopp. jonas rathsman. jonathan kaspar. jonathon cooke. jonathon more. jones kopp and pfirter. jonny banger. jonny dub. jonny rock. jonny slut. jonny trunk. jook. jools butterfield. jordan nocturne. jordan peak. jordan vickors. jordanv. jordss. jordy g. jorge martins. jorge nieto. jori hulkkonen. joris voorn. jos. joseph capriati. josey rebelle. josh baker. josh butler. josh caffe. josh caffé. josh constanzo. josh gigante. josh gregg. josh idehan. josh t. josh wink. joshua (iz). joshua idehen. joshua iz. jossy mitsu. journeyman v barrcode. jovonn. joy orbison. joy orbison,. joyhauser. jozif. jp enfant. jrocc. jrumhand. jscience. jt donaldson. jt the goon. jtc. juan atkins. juan basshead. juan forte. juan maclean. juana. juba. jubei. judda. juergen junker. juiceman. juicy djs. juicy romance. juju & jordash. julenn. julia govor. julian alexander. julian anthony. julian fijma. julian jeweil. julianna. julien chaptal. juliet. juliet fox. julietta. julio bashmore. juls. juma. juma phist. jump up cave djs. jumpin jack frost. june miller. jungle jam djs. jungle jam residents. jungle warriors. junior dangerous. junior red. junior sanchez. junior tubby. juniper. junki inoue. jupiter black. jus ed. jus now. jus-ed. just be. just blaze. just jam. just lauren. just william. just.kelly. justcye. justice. justin drake. justin harris. justin lee. justin long. justin martin. justin miller. justin robertson. justus kohncke. justyce. justyce lowqui. jwarn. jxn coco. jyclrk. jyoty. jyrrel. k eye. k means. k motionz. k swing. k-eye. k-lone. k-motionz. k-rock. k[9]*. k15. k2k. k4ptur3. kabinett. kade. kadosh. kahn. kai alcé. kai campos. kai king. kaida. kaiju. kal-i. kalli. kalyde. kamerol. kamixlo. kane solo. kangding ray. kango's stein massiv. kanijira. kanine. kanji kinetic. kanjira. kano. kareful. karen lopez. karen nyame kg. karenn. karizma. karl o'connor. karma. karma kid. karotte. karyendasoul. kasha. kasien. kasper. kasra. kassem mosse. kassian. kate rathod. kate simko. katewax. kathy brown. katie barber. katja. katya. katy b. kavinski. kay. kaya fyah. kays. kaz. kda. kearun. keaton. keb darge. keeno. kego. keith lawrence. keith reilly. keith tenniswood. keith tucker. keith worthy. kele le roc. kellie allen. kelly lee owens. kelvin andrews. kelvin krash. kelz. kemarr. kemo. ken ishii. ken mac. kendo. kenneth christiansen. kennith. kenny glasgow. kenny hawkes. kenny ken. kenny knots. kenny larkin. kentaro. kerala dust. kerb staller. kerenn. kerizma. kerri chandler. kerrie. kerry wallace. kessler. kevin de vries. kevin g. kevin gorman. kevin griffiths. kevin knapp. kevin mcphee. kevin saunderson. kevlar. key clef. keyrah. kezman. kgb. kgw. khan. ki creighton. kiara scuro. kiasmos. kicks like a mule. kid 606. kid acne. kid batchelor. kid blue. kid carpet. kid drama. kid flamingo. kid fonque. kid k. kid kenobi. kid sister. kid twist. kidkanevil. kidloco. kidnap. kidnap kid. kie. kikelomo. kiki. kikiorix. kiko. kiko bun. kilig.. kilimanjaro. kill em all. killa kela kindness. killa p. killa's army. killawatt. killjoy. killsonik. kim ann foxman. kim turnbull. kimii. kimyan law. kincaid. kindness. kinetic. king britt. king cannibal. king grubb. king hydra. king kashmere. king original. kingdom. kings of the rollers. kink. kinnerman. kirbstomp. kirby t. kirilik. kirk degiorgio. kirk paten. kirsti. kirsty hawkshaw. kismet. kissy sell out. kitbuilders. kitcha. kito. kittin. kitty amor. kiwi. klangkarussell. klartraum. klashnekoff. klaus 'heavyweight' hill. klax. klaxons. klen. kleu. klever. kling klang djs. klinical. klip & outlaw. klose one. kloser deal. kloudmen. klute. koan sound. koast. kobe 1. kobosil. kodah. kode 9. kode9. kodh & netic. koek sista. kofi & fallacy. kofi b. kojak. kojay. koko (it). kollektiv turmstrasse. kölsch. kolter. koma & bones. kombo. komonazmuk. kompis. kon. kone r. konetix. konkord. konrad black. konstantin sibold. kontrol. konx om pax. kookie scientist. kool keith. kornél kovács. korolova. korrode. kosheen. kotekan. kove. koven. kowton. kozo. kozzie. krafty kuts. krafty mc. krakota. krankbrother. krash slaughta. krause duo no.2. kreon. krept & konan. kreutziger. krif. kris menace. kris wadsworth. kristoffer. kristy harper. krl. kronikz. krooked. kruse & nuernberg. krust. kruz leone & renz. kruz leone. kryptic minds. krysko. krystal klear. krywald & farrer. kt. kuedo. kuhn. kurtis mantronik. kurupt fm. kush jones. kusp. kutmah. kutz. kxvu. ky. kyle hall. kylin tyce. kyri. kyrist. kyza. l 33. l double. l f o. l major. l plus. l u c y. l-side. l-vis 1990. l.e.bass. l.e.x. la fleur. la gosse. la la. laani. lady chann. lady lena. lady lykez. lady shocker. lady sovereign. lady starlight. lady v dubz. lady waks. ladyhawke. ladytron. laelo black. laffnar. lagoon femshayma. laidlaw. lais pattak. lakeway. lakuti. lamache. lamola. lancey foux. lando kal. landslide.

lapalux. lara. larrikin love. larry cadge. larry heard. lasermagnetic. last japan. late of the pier. latmun. latte. lauer. lauhaus. laura harvey. laura jones. laurel halo. lauren duffus. lauren faith. lauren lane. lauren lo sung. laurence. laurence guy. laurent garnier. laurine. lava la rue. lawrence. lawson. layer 3. layo & bushwacka!. lazare hoche. lazer sword. lazersonic. lazy days. lazyeye. lb aka labat. lcd soundsystem. lcy. ld. ld50. le carousel. le hammond inferno. le loup. le lutin /tko. le motel. leadbelly. leaf. leaf dog & bva. leala-rain. leandro gamez. leaving laurel. lebreton. leda stray. lee burridge. lee burton. lee coombs. lee curtiss. lee douglas. lee foss. lee gamble. lee hume. lee jones. lee pennington. lee rands. lee scott. lee scratch perry soundsystem. left/right. leftfield dj. leftlow. leftwing & kody. legion. legowelt. legroom. lehar. leif. leisure life. lemon d. lemon jelly. lemonade. lemos. lemzly dale. len faki. lengoland. lenka toma. lenny fontana. lens. lenzman. leo belchetz. leo elstob. leo greenslade. leo pol. leon. leon switch. leon vynehall. leonardo. lerosa. leroy roberts. les gammas. les petits pilous. leslie lawrence. lester. lethal b. letherette. lets go outside. lev. levela. levelz. levon vincent. lewis boardman. lewis fautzi. lewis g.burton. lewis james. lewis ryder. lex amor. lf system. lfm & mali. lhf. liam bailey. liam howlett. liam palmer. light surgeons. lil c. lil louis. lil silva. lil tony. lil' louis. lili chan. lilith marlene. lilly palmer. limited. lindsey matthews. lindstrom. lindstrom & christabelle. linguistics. linkwood. linquistics mc. linus. linus loves. lioness. lipton. liquid earth. lis sarroca. lisa maffia. literon. little chris. livio & roby. livity sound. livsey. liz edwards. liz-e. lj high. lo shea. lo-fi-fink. lo-fidelity allstars. lo*kee. lo5ive. loa szala. load b. loadstar. loadstar & mc texas. lobster boy. local group. locked groove. locklead. locky. loco dice. locuzzed. loefah. lofty. logan. logan d. logan sama. logistics. logos. lois & pearl. lokane. loko. loksin. lola haro. lombardo. london elektricity. london modular. lone. lookleft & bearight. lopaski. lopazz. loran bruno fornaro. lorca. lord apex. lord gosh soundsystem. lord of the isles. loren. loren heer. lorenzorsv. lory d. los hermanos. los updates. losoul. lost. lost & dismantle. lost & found djs. lost desert. lottie. lottie croucher. lou & nova. louche. loud mouth. loud-e. louie austen. louie dunmore. louie vega. louis guilhem. louis jay. louis slippaz. louisahhh. louise chen. love affair. love child. lovebirds. lovefingers. low b. low jack. low steppa. lowqui. loxy. loz. loz contreras. lp giobbi. lsb. lsg. ltj bukem. lu.ree. lubdub. luca andreozzi. luca c. luca lozano. luca saporito. lucia blayke. luciano. luciano esse. lucy. lucy randall. ludo m. luigi madonna. lukas wigflex. luke benjamin. luke black. luke carr. luke envoy. luke handsfree. luke hazell. luke hess. luke howard. luke slater. luke solomon. luke una. luke unabomber. luke vb. luke vibert. luke wynter. luke.envoy. lukevibert. lukid. lula circus. lulah francs. lumiere. lumieux. lump. luna city express. luna semara. lunar c. lung. lunice. luomo. lurch. lusine. luther vine. luttrell. luud. luuk van dijk. luv*jam. luxe. lv. lx one. lxury. lynx. lyza jane. m a n i k. m-a-x. m-high. m.a.n.d.y.. m.a.x. m.i.a. m.o.p. ma1. maayan nidam. mac wetha. maceo plex. mach 4. machine. machine drum. machine woman. machinedrum. mackaveli. macky gee. macphearson. macpherson. mad mel. mad miran. mad professor. mad rush. mad.again. mada. madam x. madato. madcap. made by pete. madlib. madman. madox. madteo. maduk. madvilla. madz. maelstrom. maetrik. mafia boyz v nan kole. mafia kiss. maga. maga bo. magda. magdalena. magic jase. magic mountain high. magika. magistrates. magit cacoon. magnetic man. magnus (c-soul) & simon atkinson. magnuss. maher daniel. main phase. mains ignition. maison sky. majestic. majistrate. major ace. majora. mak. makam. makaton. make a dance. mako. makoto. maksim. mala. malady. malaika. malaky. malandra jr. malarkey. mall grab. malux. mama (pa). mama shamone. mama stylist. mampi swift. man power. manami. manara. manare. mandar. mandidextrous. mandrake. manfredas. manga. manga saint hilare. manik mc. manlyk redz. manni dee. mano le tough. manoo. mant. mantmast. mantra. manu. manu gonzalez. manuel de lorenzi. manuel tur. manuk. manuka honey. mara le fay. marathon men. maratrax. marc almond. marc ashken. marc faenger. marc houle. marc hughes. marc lessner. marc mac. marc roberts. marc romboy. marc schneider. marcel dettmann. marcel fengler. marcelina wick. marcello miele. marcellus pittman. marcin czubala. marco bailey. marco bernardi. marco carola. marco del horno. marco faraone. marco passarani. marco shuttle. marco strous. marcos cabral. marcus fix. marcus intalex. marcus nasty. marcus visionary. marcus worgull. marga. margaret dygas. maribou state. marie montexier. mariiin. marijan felver. marina trench. marino canal. mario bianco. mario d'ambrosio. mark ambrose. mark archer. mark b. mark broom. mark chambers. mark collings. mark dinimal. mark du mosch. mark e. mark ernestus. mark farina. mark gwinnett. mark healy. mark henning. mark james. mark jenkyns. mark jones. mark more. mark pavitt. mark pritchard. mark radford. mark rae. mark robertson. mark ronson. mark shadow. mark system. mark turner. mark xtc. markantonio. markee ledge. markle & jbliss. marky. marley marl. marlie. marly. marquis hawkes. marrøn. marsh. martelo. marten hørger. martin brew. martin buttrich. martin heywood. martin kemp. martin landsky. martin larner. martin liberty larner. martin marner. martinez. martsman. martyn. martyné. marvin & guy. mary anne hobbs. mary lake. marysia osu. masaya & gildas. masomenos. mason. mason collective. mason maynard. massaï. massano. massimiliano pagliara. master h. master x. mastomic. mat carter. mat the alien. mat zo. mat.joe. matador. mateo murphy. math head. mathame. mathew burton. mathew jonson. mathias kaden. mathias schaffhauser. matias aguayo. matrix. matrixxman. matt brown. matt cantor. matt cc. matt dicks. matt frost. matt jam lamont. matt jn. matt kenny. matt masters. matt neale. matt playford. matt simmons. matt smooth. matt the alien. matt tolfrey. matt walsh. matteo manzini. matthew burgess. matthew burton. matthew dear. matthew harrington. matthew herbert. matthew simmons. matthew styles. matthias heilbronn. matthias tanzmann. mattia trani. mattias mimoun. mattjohn. matty g. matty j. maurice fulton. mavs. max chapman. max cooper. max dean. max mohr. max sedgley. max sinàl. max the tribrid. max vaahs. max.. maxi jazz. maxime cescau. maximono. maximous. maximum. maximum (bbk). maximus. maxwell d & doller. maxwell owin. maxwelld. maxxi soundsystem. maya jane coles. maya q. mayaan nidam. maze & masters. mazi. maztek. mc 2shy. mc a.d.. mc ad. mc asbo. mc bellyman. mc biggie. mc bluejay. mc boxer. mc bunzi d. mc carlton 'kilowattvalley. mc cd. mc chickaboo. mc conrad. mc crazy d. mc creed. mc dappa. mc det. mc drs. mc dt. mc face-t. mc fava. mc felon. mc flux. mc flyte. mc fokus. mc gq. mc gusto. mc hotch. mc id. mc jakes. mc jc. mc kaos. mc kie. mc koast. mc kofi b. mc linguistics. mc mg. mc moose. mc onoe caponoe. mc pean. mc phantom. mc pranksta. mc prankster. mc rage. mc ranking. mc rhymes. mc rymetyme. mc script. mc serious. mc serocee. mc shantie. mc starky. mc system. mc texas. mc tonn piper. mc vapour. mc versatile. mc viper. mc whizzkid. mc wrec. mc youngman. mcde. mcleod. mcs det. mcs toddlah. mcs: dynamite. mcs: gq. mcs: moose. mdr. meat. meat katie. mechanism. medic. medicine. medis. medusa odyssey. meduza. mef jus. mefjus. meg paine. megan leo. mehlor. mekar. mekon. mel. melanie kyrklund. melchior productions ltd.. melé. mella dee. melo. melody. melody kane. melon. melysma. memtrix. menendez brothers. mensah. mental overdrive. mentat, sireman & shameless. mentsh. meph 13. meraki. merky ace. mervella. messy. messy mc. meth. metope. metrik. metrist. metrix. metro area. metrodome. metronomy. mez. mez & duppy. mez & spitz. mgun. mi-el. mia. mia aurora. mia dora. mia koden. mic man frost. mic newman. mica. mica coca. micachu & the shapes. micah earnshaw. michael. michael bibi. michael black. michael c. michael fentum. michael james. michael koppleman. michael mayer. michael morley. michael reinboth. michal ho. michel cleis. michelle. michelle manetti. mickey finn. mickey moonlight. mickey pearce. micky finn. micofcourse. micronauts. mid vortex. midfield general. midland. midnight juggernauts. midnight operator. midnight snacks. midz. mighty moe. miguel campbell. miguel e. migz. mihai popoviciu. mihigh. miim. miina. mijk van dijk. mikael stavostrand. mikal. mike 'ruffcut' lloyd. mike 'agent x' clark. mike dehnert. mike delinquent. mike drop. mike dunn. mike healey. mike huckaby. mike monday. mike morrisey. mike parker. mike ruffcut lloyd. mike servito. mike shannon. mike simonetti. mike skinner. mike slocombe. mikee mikel metal feat paul st.hilaire. mikhail & clement meyer. mikix the cat. mikki most. milan s. miles hollway. miley serious. milhouse. milky. millbrook. miller. millz. milo spykers. milton bradley. mimi love. mina. mina rose. mincy. mind against. mind vortex. mindscape. mindstate. mineo. minilogue. ministre x. mint. mint royale. minuit. mira. misanthrop. misc.. misfya. miss bliss. miss ill. miss kittin. miss melody. miss modular & sudanim. miss red. miss trouble. missingno. missrepresent. mistajam. mistakay. mista me. mit. mitch tilson. mitchell brothers. mitsabishi. miura. mixhell. mixmaster mike. mixologists. mixtress. miz. mizz beats. mj cole. mjk. mlr. mm/km. mmm. mo fingaz & bobafatt. mob tactics. mochakk. mocky. model 500. modelizer. modeselektor. modula. mofaux. mogwai. moleskin. mollie collins. molø. molotov. moma ready. momma's boy. momma's boy. monchhichi boy. monchhichi boys. mongrel. monika kruse. monika ross. monk audio showcase. monkey maffia. monkey safari. monkey wrench. monki. monoblock. monolake. monoloc. monty. monty luke. mood hut. mood ii swing. moodtrap. moody boys. moody boyz. moody manc. moodymanc. moodymann. moon boots. moon unit. mooqee. moose. mor elian. more fire crew. moreofus. morgan elder. morgan geist. morgan zarate. moritz. moritz von oswald. moritz von oswald trio. morphosis. mosai. mosaic. mosca. mosus. mota. mota mc. mother earth. motion. motions. motive. motor. motor city drum ensemble. motorcitysoul. mount kimbie. mountain people. move d. moveya!. moving fusion. mowgli. moxie. mozey. mpho skeef. mr beatnick. mr c. mr g. mr hudson. mr jones. mr joseph. mr keas. mr lif. mr maqs. mr mentsh. mr mitch. mr oizo. mr pauli. mr scruff. mr shiver. mr thing. mr tophat. mr velcro fastener. mr virgo. mr wong. mr wood. mr. c. mr. g. mr. jones. mr. redley. mr. scruff. mr. top hat. mr.c. mrd (no). mri. mrk1. mrsa. mrti2bs. ms bratt. ms. dynamite. mssingno. mtox. mu. mu-ziq. muffler. mullett. multi function collective. mumdance. mumu. mungo's hi fi. mungo's hi-fi. mungolian jet set. mura masa. murat. murder he wrote. murdock. murkage present tonga. murlo. murmur. murray. mushkilla. mustapha 3000. musumeci. mutants. mutated forms. my favorite robot. my friend. my my. my nu leng. my robot friend. myd. mydas. myles mears. mylo. myriam. mystery. mystery jets. mystic state. mystro. mystry. mz bratt. n-type. n-gynn. n-type. na'sayah. nacho bolognani. nacho marco. nadastrom. nadia ksabia. nadia rose. nadia struiwigh. nadine noor. nadja lind. nah eeto. naibu. nail. naina. nakamo. nala brown. namedrop. names (a-z):. nanci ninjah. nancy. nancy noise. nandu. nanny banton. naomi //. naone. napt. nass aka geiger. nasser baker. nastee boi. nastia. nasty jack. nat home. nat jenkins & the delmars. nat self. natalie williams. natanya popoola. natasha. natasha diggs. nathan barato. nathan coles. nathan colinet. nathan detroit. nathan fake. nathan gregory wilkins. nathan haines & vaceo. nathan scott. nathan x. natty lou. navigator. nd_baumecker. neana. necessary mayhem. nedd. need for mirrors. neek. neffa-t. negativ. neidex. neil & johnny. neil landstrumm. neil mac. neil parkes. neil quigley. neil thornton. nekes. nelson. nene h. neon chambers. neon heights. neon neon. neonlight. neoteric. nepo. neptizzle. neptune. nerm. nero. netik. netsky. neverdogs. neville watson. new build. new flesh. new york transit authority. newham generals. newworldaquarium. nguzunguzu. nia archives. niamh. nic + kaleb. nic fancuilli. nic tasker. nicholas. nick agha. nick craddock. nick curly. nick dare. nick doherty. nick höppner. nick monaco. nick name. nick rapaccioli. nick simoncino. nick sinna. nick thayey. nick williams. nickname. nicky blackmarket. nicky elisabeth. nicky macha. nicky siano. nicky soft touch. nico purman. nicola cruz. nicolas jaar. nicolas lutz. nicolau. nicole moudaber. nige. night moves. night shift. nightbreed. nightmares on wax. nightmoves. nihal. niki sadeki. nikk. nikki lucas. nikki nair. nikniknik. nils hess. nima gorji. nina kraviz. ninetoes. ninjasonik. nirvan. nisekay. nite fleit. nitetrax. nitework. nitin. nitin sawhney. niv ast. nkc. no artificial colours. no concept. no fakin' djs. no lay. no pain in pop djs. no regular play. nocturnal. noel jackson. noisey djs. noisia. nolay. nonames. nonplus. noob. nookie. norm de plume. norm talley. norman jay. norman nodge. norris da boss windross. north base. north lake. nosa. nosaj thing. notion. novelist. noyeahno. noze feat. dani siciliano. nsdos. nto. nu balance. nu elementz. nu:logic. nu:tone. nubreed. nuclear digital transistor. nuklear. nv. nvrsoft. ny ny. nymfo. nyra. nyta. ø [phase]. o the ghost. o.bee. o.children. o'flynn. o/v/r. ob-server. object blue. objectiv. objekt. oblig. obscure shape. obskür. oc & verde. oceanic. ocelot. octa push. octane. octave one. october. oden & fatzo. of norway. offkey & nv. ogz. oh91. ohmydais. oil gang. oiram gar. ok williams. okain. okmalumkoolkat. oko. okouru. okular. okzharp. ol drift. olanskii. oli furness. oli marlow. oli silva. olive f. oliver. oliver $. oliver dollar. oliver hafenbauer. oliver ho. oliver huntemann aka h-man. oliver koletzki. oliver moon. oliver schories. oliver way. oliverse. ollie drummond. ollie seaman. ollie teeba. olly g. olly groves. olof enar. olympe. om unit. omar. omar (uy). omar-s. omri smadar. on-off. onallee. one records. one87. oneman. ones. onetrueparker. onirik. onlymatt. onno. onoe caponoe. onset. onur özer. onyvaa. operahouse. oppidan. optical. optimo. optimo espacio. optiv. opus. or:la. orange hill. orange hill soundsystem. orchestral world groove. ordio kid. orgasmic. orgue electronique. orien. orifice vulgatron. original. original sin. orinwalters. oris jay. orlando voorn. orphan101. orson. os:man. oscar mulero. oscar wildstyle. oshana. oskar offerman. oslo records. osmani soundz. ossie. ost & kjek. osunlade. other echoes. otik. oto. ourman. outboxx. overmono. owen howells. ownglow. oxia. oxide & neutrino. p money. p-jam. p-rallel. p0gman. p5nt0. pablo (butch cassidy soundsystem). pablo cahn speyer. pablo modrono. pach. paco modinos. paco osuna. pacodilliocircus. padded cell. paige eliza. paige tomlinson. pal 'strangefruit' nyhus. palace. paleblu. paleman. palm skin productions. palmistry. palms trax. palstician. pametex. pan-pot. pangaea. pangaea,. panico. panka. paolo francesco. paolo mojo. papa nugs. par grindvik. para one. paradox. paragon. parallelle. paramida. paranoid london. pariah. paris. parker. parly b. parris. parris mitchell. part chimp. partiboi69. particle. pascal. pascal hetzel. pase rock. pasteman. pastrymaker. pat hurley. pat mahoney. pat wilson. patchwork pirates. pathaan. patrice bäumel. patrice scott. patrick chardronnet. patrick dawes. patrick forge. patrick grooves. patrick topping. pattn. paul agripa. paul arnold. paul cawley. paul chambers. paul daley. paul devro. paul epworth. paul johnson. paul kalkbrenner. paul louth. paul mac. paul mcguire. paul mogg. paul murphy. paul neary. paul richards. paul ritch. paul sg. paul soul. paul stephan. paul stubbs. paul t. paul thomas. paul wain. paul woolford. paula tape. paula temple. paulo moreno. pawsa. pax. pbr streetgang. peach. peak & swift. peanut butter wolf. pear djs. pearson sound. peart. peder mannerfelt. pedestrian. pedro. peel seamus. peggy gou. pender street steppers. pendulum. penelope. penfold. pennygiles. people are germs. pep. pepe bradock. pepe deluxe. perc. perch. percy x. perel. perempay. performance. perlon. peshay. pete cannon. pete dafeet. pete graham. pete heller. pete herbert. pete moss. pete simpson. pete tong. pete z. pete zorba. peter goodwin. peter hook. peter kruder. peter pixzel. peter van hoesen. petre inspirescu. petter nordkvist. peverelist. pezzner. pfel. pfn. ph project. phace. phaction. phaeleh. phantasy. phantom. pharoahe monch. phase. phase fatale. phat phil cooper. phat plastic. phatplayerz. phatworld. phi life cypher. phil asher. phil cooper. phil hartnoll. phil jones. phil k. phil kieran. phil klein. phil mison. phil moffa. phil tangent. phil towers. phil weeks. phil:osophy. philgood & ram. philip k. philip stirzaker. philipp ort. philth. phon.o. phone traxxx. phonique. phoreski. phossa. photek. photes. phuture. picture house. pied piper. pier bucci. pierre lx. pig & dan. pillowtalk. pilooski. pinch. pinch guido. pinty. pioneer. pior. pipes. pipes present tonic. pirate copy. pitch. pitch 92. pk. plaid. plain suede. plan b. planet mu dj's. planetary assault systems. planningto rock. plastic little. plastician. platt. playdead. plaza de funk. pleasure. pleasure club. pleasurekraft. plex. ploy. plugs. plump djs. plus one. plussounds. pmt. point g. point nemo. point.blank. poirier. poirier & mc zulu. poison anna. pokes. pola & bryson. polder. pole. polyrhythmic. pony pony. popof. populette. portable. portara0000. posij. post scriptum. posthuman. potential badboy. poussez. powell. prankster. praslea. praslesh. precision cuts. predita. preditah. premiesku. presence. presha. preshus. president t. pressure drop. prfct mandem. priku. prime cuts. prince fatty. prince language. prince paul. princess nokia. princess superstar. prins thomas. probe. problem central. problem child. proc fiskal. profile. project pablo. project89. prolix. promo zo. propz. prospa. prosumer. proteus. protone. proxima. proxy. prozak. prunk. psg. psycatron. psychemagik. psyk. public lover. punctual. punks jump up. puppetz. pure science. purg. purge. purple. pursuit grooves. pushamann. putsch 79. pvblic xcess. pvc. pyramid. pyrelli. pyrrah girls. pythius. q & rossano strut. q burns. q project. q-bert. quantic soul orchestra. queenie. quelza. quest. quinton scott. qzb. r.e.d. r.o.t.f. r.o.y. r1 ryders. ra+re. rabit. rachel barton. rachel k. collier. rachel wallace. rack n ruin. radio 4. radio slave. radioactive man. radioclit. radioslave. rae & christian. raf daddy. raf daddy (the 2 bears). raf rundell. raffertie. rafik. rage. ragga twins. rahaan. rahzel. raiders of the lost arp. raiser. rakim under. ralph lawson. ralston. ramadanman. ramin rezaie. ramon judah. ramoss. rampa. rampage. ramses. ramson badbonez. ramzee. rancido. randall m. random factor. random movement. random noise generation. randomer. rankin. ranking. rap saunders. rapha. raphael pellizzaro. rapture 4d. rareman. raresh. ras kwame. rasco. ratpack. rattus rattus. raudive. raul midon. raw silk. raw t. rawtekk. ray keith. ray mono. ray okpara. ray rampage. ray stanley. rayfield. raymundo rodriguez. raz ohara. razor. razor rector. razor rekta. rbc. re-up. re:ni. re.you. read the news. readymade. real artillery. real gang soundsystem. reamz. rebekah. rebekah aff. rebel clash. rebolledo. reboot. recloose. recondite. red axes. red eye hifi. red greg. red one. red rack'em. redders. redhot. redinho. redlight. redpill. reds. redshape. reebz. reece spooner. reecha. reecha & magic. reek0. reelow. rees. reeshy. reggae roast. regis. reidy. reinhard voigt. reiss. remain & mlle caro. remarc. remedy. remi mazet. remidy. remotif. renaissance man. renato cohen. rene lavice. rene wise. renegade soundwave. renelle 893. rengade. rennie pilgrem. reseo. reset robot. resin dogs. reso. resom. resound. response. retroactif. rev. milo speedwagon. reverend & the makers. reverso 68. rework. rex the dog. reynold. rezident. rhadoo. rhymestar. rhythm + sound feat. tikiman. rhythm doctor. rhythm plate. rhythmic theory. ribbz. ricardo villalobos. riccardo piazza. rich beats. rich nxt. rich reason. richard bartz. richard davis. richard dorfmeister. richard fearless. richard grey. richard rowell. richard seeley. richard sen. richard thair. richard x. richie dan. richie hawtin. richie weaver. richy ahmed. richy pitch. rick hopkins. rick wade. rick wilhite. rickinzi. ricky ranking. rico tubbs. rider shafique. ridikule. rido.

rie kiriiaka. rikki rokkit. rikky rock. riko. riko dan. rinocerose. rio jay. rio tashan. riotous. riotous rockers. ripraw. risky. ritchie rundle. ritmo ldn. riton. riva. riva starr. rival. riya. riz la teef. riz mc. rizzle. rjd2. rob amboule. rob burden. rob cockerton. rob da bank. rob data. rob mac. rob mello. rob paine. rob pursey. rob smith. rob summerhayes. rob swift. rob wood. robag wruhme. robbie doherty. robbo ranx. robert bratu. robert dietz. robert hood. robert james. robert owens. roberto. roberto mello. robin. robin ordell. rocc. rocco harris. rocha. rockers. rocketnumbernine. rocks foe. rockwell. rod azlan. rødhåd. rodneyp. rodriguez jr.. roger gerressen. roger23. rogue element. rogue star. roi perez. roland appel. rolando. roll deep. roller express. rolling like kingz. rolls n do. romain bno. roman flügel. roman lindau. romana imi. romans. romare. romeo. ron bacardi. ron morelli. ron obvious. roni size. ronnie loko. ronnie spiteri. rontrent. roosevelt. roots manuva. rootsteady. rory phillips. ros. rosa. rosa pistola. rosa red. roska. ross allen. ross caiden. ross clarke. ross from friends. ross mccormack. rossi. rossi b & luca. rossi.. rossko. rough tempo djs. route 94. rowl. rowney. rowpieces. roxanne shante. roxy. roy davis jr. roy green. royal t w.. royal-t. royksopp. rpr soundsystem. rrose. rroxymore. rsd. rtkal & roxxxan. rub n tug. rub'n'tug. rubi dan. ruby savage. rude kid. rudimental. rudolf. ruede hagelstein. ruff sqwad. ruff stuff. ruffhouse. rui da silva. rumme. run hide survive. runaway. rune lindbaek. rush hour. rushy. rusko. russ cuban. russ dewbury. russ gabriel. russ yallop. russell. russko. russo. rustie. ruthless. ruthless mc. ruze. rv. rvs music. ryan crosson. ryan elliot. ryan elliott. ryan o gorman. ryan shaw. ryme tyme. s 1 futures. s_m music. s-candalo. s-venus. s.a.m.. s.c.d.d. hazmat team. s.moreira. s.p.y. s9. saachi. sable sheep. sabre. sabrina. sacha yonan. sadidas. sahar. sahau. sai. saichotic. saint ludo. sainte vie. sakro. salo. salò. sâlo. salome. sam bangura. sam binga. sam blenk. sam gellaitry. sam interface. sam luke. sam paganini. sam russo. sam shure. sam sparro. sam supplier. sam tiba. sam wolf. sama' abdulhadi. samba. samim live & miguel toro. sammy dee. sampha. samrai. samsön. samtheman. samtotolee. samu.l. samuel andre madsen. samuel bellis. samuel deep. samuel kerridge. samuel l session. samuel sessions. san proper. sancho panza. sandman. sandra. sandrien. sandwell district. sansibar. santé. santogold. santos. santos resiak. sany pitbull. saoirse. sappo. sara siu. sarah kreis. sarah love. sarah rodin. sarah story. sarah sweeney. sas. sasasas. sascha braemer. sascha dive. sascha funke. saschienne. sasha. sasha crnobrnia. sasha go hard. sasse. satl. satori. satoshi tomiie. savas pascalidis. savio testa. saxon soundsystem. saxxon. saytek. sbtrkt. scally. scan x. scan7. scandalous unltd. scanone. scape one. scar. scar duggy. scarlett o'malley. schatrax. schlachtofbronx. scissor sisters. scissors for lefty. scntst. scott fraser. scott garcia. scott grant. scott grooves. scott hendy. scott nixon. scott rozario. scottie b. scratch perverts. scratcha dva. scratchclart. script. script mc. scrufizzer. scsi-9. scuba. scuba v scb. sean brosnan. sean canty. sean doron. sean johnston. sean rowley. seanie b. search & destroy. seb chew. seb zito. seba. sebastian. sebastian ledher. sebastian mullaert. sebastien san. sebastien voigt. sebo k. sebra cruz. second storey. secondcity. secret machines. sedef adasi. sef kombo. sei a. seiji. seiul. semifinalists. semtex. sender berlin. sendex. sense. sense mc. sensei lo. sensible sundays djs. sensor. sentre. sepalcure. seph. sepia. seren seo. serene. serge. serge devant. serge santiago. serial killaz. serious. serocee. serum. session victim. setaoc mass. seth troxler. setoac mass. sety. seuil. sev raven. seven davis jr.. severino. sevie. sg lewis. sgt pokes. sh?m. shabba. shabba d. shackleton. shadow child. shadow dancer. shadow demon coalition. shady novelle. shaf huse. shaka. shake. shakedown. shakes. shall ocin. shameless. shampain. shanique marie. shannen sp. shannon. shanti celeste. shantie. shapes. shapeshifter. sharda. sharky major. sharnie. shaun reeves. shaun roberts. shaun soomro. shaun.p. shauwdii. shawny elstar. shay malt. shaydee. shdw. sheba q. shed. shelley parker. shenin amara. shenoda. shepdog. sherelle. sherry s. shifted. shimon. shimz343. shinedoe. shinichi osawa. shit disco. shit robot. shitfted. shockin mc. shonky. shortee blitz. shortstuff. shorty. shox. shu. shubostar. shur-i-kan. shut up and dance. shxcxchcxsh. shy fx. shy one. shychild. shystie. shyun. si baker. si begg. sian anderson. sian evans. sicaria sound. sick rick. sicknote. sid le rock. sideshow. sidetrack. sidewinder. sidney charles. sieg uber die sonne. siege mc. sierra sam. siggy smalls. sigha. sigma. signal. silas. silencer. silent dust. silent servant. silent witness. silicon. silicone soul. silk road assassins. silkie. silva snipa. silver city & dubble d. silver columns. silver storic. silver team. silverlining. silversurfer. silvie loto. simbad. simian mobile disco. simo cell. simon atkinson. simon baker. simon bassline smith. simon dk. simon doty. simon haggis. simon kurrage. simon morell. simon rigg. simon scott. simon shreeve. simon smugg. simon young. simone de kunovich. simone ellis. sims. simula. sinál. sinàl. sinden. sinéad. sinjin hawke. siobhan bell. siopis. siopsis. sir corey. sir dj corey. sir spiro. sir spyro. sireman. sis. sisterhood. sisters of transistors. sit. sivey. six blade. six sunsets. sixblade. sk vibemaker. skankandbass. skantia. skayy. skee mask. skelecta. skeme. skepsis. skepta. skeptical. skibade. skibadee. skilliam. skimming. skinny macho. skinnyman. skism. skit. skittles. skitz & rodney p. skizzo. skool of thought. skream. skudge. skull juice. skunkrock. skynet. sl8r. slackk. slagsmals-klubben. slam. slang banger. slartajohn. slaughta mob. slay. slb & j swif. sleeparchive. sleeper. slim soledad. slimzee. slipmatt. slipz. slow hands. slt mob. slumvillage. sly moon. sly one. slyde. smak pony. small saul. smalltown djs. smash hits. smash tv. smasher. smith-n-hack. smoggy. smooth. smurph. smuskind & saunders. smutlee. snare surgeon. sneak. sneaky. sniff. snoops. snowboarding. so large. social logic. soft rocks. softchaos. softi. sohmi. soho. sol ortega. solah. solardo. solid blake. solid doctor. solo. solomun. someone else. something something & eidna. somne. son of philip. sonic router. sonik gurus. sonja moonear. sons of slough. sonz of count ossie. sophie. soraya. sosa. sosa uk. soul capsule. soul clap. soul designer. soul intent. soul mekanik. soul of man. soul structure. soulchild. souljazz soundsystem. soulphiction. soulvent residents. soulwax. soulz. sound pellegrino thermal team. sound proof. soundproof. soundstream. source direct. south. south central. south london ordnance. south rakkas crew. sp: mc. sp:mc. space dimension controller. spaceape. spacek. spacemaster. spaceship god. spacetravel. spade. spam chop. spank rock. sparkz. speaker junk. special request. specialist. specialist moss. spectral. spectrasoul. speeka. spektre. spektrum. spencer. spencer parker. spice. spin doctor. spin eb. spinline. spinn. spirit. spirit catcher. splitloop. splurgeboys. splurgeboys x pap. spoils. spook. spooky. spor. spyda. spyro. spyro w. footsie. squarehead. squarewave. squeak e clean. ss. st files. st germain. st john da ziva. stacey pullen. staffan linzatti. stagga. stalawa. stamina. stamina mc. stan. stanton warriors. stanza. stapleton. star eyes. star.one. stark. starkey. starski & tonic. starsmith. start the vibe. state of mind. statik. stavroz. stay-c. ste robert. ste roberts. stealth. steel banglez. steelzawheelz v western allstars. stefan goldmann. stefano nicolaou. steffan deux. steffi. steinski. stella marbles. stellar om source. stenchman. stenny. steo. stephan bodzin. stephan greider. stephane ghenacia. stephanie sykes. stephen brown. steppa. sterac. stereo 8. stereo mcs. stereo underground. steve bicknell. steve bug. steve da conga. steve hanson. steve lawler. steve longwill. steve o sullivan. steve rachmad. steven dunn. stevie kotey. stevie wonderland. stewart walker. stian. sticky. stimming. stingray. stinkahbell. stinkin slumrok. stirlin. stix. stompmakingme. stoner. stones throw. stonez. stooki sound. stööki sound. stopmakingme. storm. storm mollison. stormzy. stranger. strategy. stray. stray beast. streetlife djs. stretch armstrong. strip steve. stripes showcase. stu clark. stuart patterson. stuart rowell. style of eye. stylo g. sub basics. sub focus. sub level feat lillia. sub zero. subb an. subb-an. subjective. subliminal. submerse. submorphics. subscape. subsonic. subsoul djs. substance. subtension. subterra. subtle element. subtle mind. suburban knight. subzee d. subzero. sucasa. sue veneers club. sugar free. sukh knight. sully. sumgii. sumo. sun of selah. sunil sharpe. supa d. supa nytro. super flu. super midz. super nashwan. superfreq. superpitcher. superthriller. supplier. surface noise sound system. surge. surgeon. surkin. survey. survival. survival & silent witness. suspect. sustance. suzana rozkosny. suzanne kraft. sven andersson. sven tasnadi. sven väth. sven weisemann. svengalisghost. swag. swan e. swarvo. sway. swayzak. sweat x. sweely. sweet irie. sweetlight. sweet n' candy. sweetpea. swift. swifta. swindle. swing ting. swingz. switch. switchbitch. swoop. swoose. swzk. sy sez. sybil. syd gris. syer b. sylphe. sylvie marks. sync 24. synkro. syreeta. system. system of survival. system sound. syv. szare. t dunn. t man. t q d. t raumschmiere. t williams. t-bone. t-man. t. williams. t.i. t++. t>i. taahliah. tacteel. tadeo. taelimb. tai lokun. taiki nulight. taiko. tailor jae. taimur agha. take. tal fussman. tale of us. tali. talik. talker. tallmen785. talos. talvin singh. tama sumo. tamra. tañ. tane. tangun. tania vulcano. tanner ross. tantrum desire. tanz. tape fear. tapefeed. tarek charbonnier. tarquin. tarzsa. tash lc. tasha. tasker. tasman-uk. taxman. tayir. tayla. taylah elaine. tayo. tayo iku. tayylor made. tc. tc1. tcts. tdj. tech itch. technasia. technimatic. techriders. tectonic plates. teddy killerz. teebee. teenage bad girl. tekel. teki latex. telekinesis. telekom. telepopmusik. tempa t. temper d. temple. tempza. tendai. tengu. tensnake. tepeli feat. elif. tephra & arkoze. terence fixmer. teresa. terminalhead. terr. terrence parker. terror. terror cell. terror danjah. terrorist. terry farley. terry francis. terry hall. terry hunter. terry lee brown junior. terry mitchell. terry-m. tes la rok. tesen. tessela. tessellate. tesslea. test icicles. tetris. tevo howard. texas. thadeus concept. thc. the 12 ball experience. the 2 bears. the advent. the aliens. the allies. the amalgamation of soundz. the bays. the beat junkies. the beat monkeys. the beatnuts. the beatseekers. the bees. the beta band. the black dog. the black ghosts. the blast djs. the bodysnatchers. the boogie knights. the bpm. the breakfastaz. the bug. the captain. the caracal project. the carps. the chap. the clones. the cocknbullkid. the count. the count and sinden. the coutu dumonts. the creators. the crystal method. the dexorcist. the diaz bros.. the earls. the element. the emperor machine. the exaltics. the extremists. the fear ratio. the fmg. the four owls. the freestylers. the gaslamp killer. the ghost. the glimmers. the golden boy. the guvnors. the hacker. the heartless crew. the heatwave. the herbaliser. the house that chicago built. the infadels. the insiders. the invaderz. the invisible. the jazzassins. the joy formidable. the juan maclean. the kelly twins. the last skeptik. the liars club. the light sound-system. the light surgeons. the little men. the lovely jonj. the lovely jonjo. the maccabees. the martinez brothers. the menendez brothers. the mole. the monchichi boys. the neon dreams. the nextmen. the nothing special. the other. the pachanga boys. the phenomenal handclap band. the presets. the producers. the propellerheads. the prototypes. the proxy. the psychonauts. the purist. the pushamann. the qemists. the ragga twins. the reagenz. the real escobar. the revenge. the rub. the rumblestrips. the runaways. the rurals. the sauce & mc fox. the secret agency. the separatists. the shout out loads. the soft pink truth. the soul providers. the square. the subliminal kid. the subs. the sunshine underground. the town karve & kazey. the upbeats. the vanguard project. the whip. thee mike b. thefft. thelem. thelena. thelma. themba. themroc. theo kottis. theo nasa. theo noble. theopilus london. theoretical girl. these new puritans. theteenagers. thetouch. thevangelis. thevisitor. the young knives. theyoungsters. thievery corporation. think tonk. third face. third side. this & that. tho. thoma bulwer. thomas brinkmann. thomas dolby. thomas hessler. thomas melchior. thomas muller. thomas roland. thomas tantrum. thomas urv. three. thris tian. thristian br. throwing snow. thugfucker. thunderball. thys. tia cousins. tia talks. tibi dabo. tibor. tidal. tiefschwarz. tiffany calver. tiga. tiger & woods. tigerskin. tigerskin aka dub taylor. tigerstyles. tiggs da author. tijana t. tikiman. tim engelhardt. tim exile. tim green. tim holmes. tim love lee. tim paris. tim parker. tim red. tim sheridan. tim sweeney. tim wester. tim westwood. tim wright. timewriter. timmy regisford. timo maas. timothy j. fairplay. timoti. tinchy stryder. tini. tinman. tino. tiny k. tippa. tipper. titia. tittsworth. tj. tk. tko. tlr. tna. tnt. to my boy. toast. tobi neumann. tobias. tobias thomas. toby tobias. tocadisco. todd bodine. todd edwards. todd hart. todd sines. todd terje. toddla t. tolfrey. tolga fidan. tom baker. tom cottrell. tom demac. tom dinsdale. tom furse. tom gillieron. tom kerridge. tom mangan. tom middleton. tom rio. tom roberts. tom shorterz. tom staar. tom szirtes. tom trago. toman. tomas andersson. tomas barfod. tomas more. tomas station. tomb crew. tomboy. tommie sunshine & science. tommy b. tommy evans. tommy four seven. tommy gold. tommy sparks. tommy vercetti. tomoki tamura. tomoya. tomoya mizuno. tomson. tomvek. tone of arc. tonga. toni d. toni rossano. tonika. tonn piper. tony allen. tony hewitt. tony humphries. tony s & ali mac. tony vegas. tony y not. toob. tooshy. top cat. top cat and don caesar. topcat. tori beaumont. tortured soul. toru. tosh ohta. toshiki ohta. total fitness. total recall. total science. totally enormous extinct dinosaurs. totherockrecords. toto chiavetta. touché. tourist. township rebellion. toyc. trace. traces. trade. tradesman. tramp! djs. trancemicsoul. transient. transit mafia. transparent sound. traumatik. traumatize. traumer. travis. traxman. trc. treatment. trevino. trevor jackson. trevor loveys. trevor rockliffe. trex. trg. triangle orchestra. tribal brothers. trickski. trigga. trikk. trilla. trim. trimer. trip. trish & kash. tristan. tristan da cunha. trixie. trojan soundsystem. trolley snatcha. tronik youth. trouble soup. troy gunner. troy pierce. tru fonix. truant. truant (uk). truce susan. true tiger. true tiger collective. truemendous. truly madly. truncate. trus'me. truss. truthos mufasa. ts2w. tsasha. tsha. tsuba. tsuki. tsvi. tuccillo. tucker. tuff culture. tuggzy. tunik. tunnidge. tunnindge. turbowolf. turner. turno. turzi. tweed'. twista. twisted individual. two & eight. two inch punch. two lone swordsmen. two shell. ty. tygapaw. tyger dhula. tyke. tyler t bone stadius. tyrant. tyree cooper. tyreece. tyrone. tyrone 'mixologist' francis. uberzone. uffie. ufo. ugandan methods. ugly duckling. uk apache. ulterior motive. ultrasone. umek. umfang. umwelt. unabombers. uncle dugs. underground paris. unders. unglued. uniiqu3. unit 4. united vibez. unitz. unkle. unknown error. unknown t. unsung heroes. untitled musical project. untold. up bustle & out. upbeats. upgrade. urban dawn. urban nerds. urbandawn. ursula 1000. used. usherenko. ussy. utah jazz. uz. v.i.v.e.k.. vadim svoboda. vakula. vale budino. valentino. van she tech. vandal. vandera. vanessa maria. vanille. vapour. varg^{2}™. variations. various production. varoslav. vatican shadow. vector lovers. vectorvision. velcro fastener. velocity boy. ventress. vera. verb t. verbz. verdine logie. verna francis. veronica vasicka. veronika fleyta. verraco. versa. verse. vertical drop. vessel. vex'd. vhs or beta. via seri. vian. vibezin. vicarious bliss. vicious. vicious circle. vicky kroon. victor rosado. victor ruiz. victorville. videeo. video wall of visuals. vigro deep. viken arman. vikter duplaix. vil (pt). villa. villem. villem & mcleod. villem, mako & fields. vince watson. vincent lemieux. vintage culture. vinyl dialect. violet. violet (pt). viper. viper mc. virgil abloh. virginia. virgo four. virus syndicate. visages. visionist. visionobi. visionquest. vista. vital techniques. vitalic. vitaminka. vitess. vithz. vivek. vlad caia. vlada. vodex. voices from the lake. voigtmann. voiski. volatile cycle. voltage. volte-face. volte-face bleed. volvox. von d. von sudenfed. voodeux. votuma. vowel. voyage. voyeur. vril. vrilski. vtss. vuur. vxrgo. vyvyan. waajeed. waff. wager. wagon cookin'. wah wah 45s soundsystem. waifs & strays. walk:r. walker & royce. walker hintenaus. wallwork. wally callerio. walsh. walshy. walter meego. walterego. walton. wamdue kids. wandy. war. wareika. warlock. warm. warren g. warren mooney. warrior one. warrior queen. was a be. watch the ride. wavey garms. wax. wax magic. wax on mare st.. wax wings. wayfarer. wayne holland. waze & odyssey. wbeeza. we are scientists. we have band. wedge. weeji. weiss. wen. wendy. werkha. werner niedermeier. wes baggaley. west london deep. west norwood cassette library. western allstars. westman. wheats. whiney. white rose movement. whitey. whomadewho. why. whyt noyz. wickaman. widow. wiggie smalls. wiggie smalls juicy dj's. wighnomy brothers. wild geese. wildchild. wilde renate. wildkats. wiley. wilfred giroux. wilkinson. will bankhead. will martin. will saul. will taylor. will. b. willer. william djoko. william kouam djoko. william noble. willie burns. willikens & ivkovic. willow. wincent kunth. winston hazel. wisdom teeth. woesum. wolf & lamb. woo york. wookie. wooly. worakls. wordz. workforce. works of intent. workshop 10. worries outernational. wouter de moor. woz. wraetlic. wrec. writz. wrongtom. x-coast. xample & lomax. xenia beliayevas. xenogears. xerox teens. xi. xing xing. xo chic. xosar. xosé. xpansul. xpress 2. xrabit & dmgs. xrs. xtrah. xxteens. xxxchange. xxxy. y-zer. ya hu. ya z an. yacine dessouki. yakine. yam who?. yamen & eda. yapacc. yasmin. yaw evans. yazzus. yemz. ygg. yizzy. ynez. yo majesty. yo speed. yoofee. yosh. yossi amoyal. yotam avini. yotto. you say party! we say die!. youan. youandewan. young & lost djs. young marco. young turks. young'un. youngman. youngman mc. youngsta. youngsters. yours collective. yousef. youthmovies. yoyo. yuis. yulia niko. yunè pinku. yung singh. yungun. yusek. yushh. z lovecraft. z.i.p.p.o. z@p. zach murray. zach nohame. zak frost. zandervt. zane lowe. zed bias. zeitgeist. zen. zenker brothers. zero 7. zero g. zero t. zerofg. zha. ziggy kinder. zilla. zinc. zip. zøe. zombie disco squad. zombie nation. zombies in miami. zongamin. zulu. трип.

photographs

2-3, 247—1, 250—1, 258—2 room 1, fabric reopening after covid, 2021. 8-9 danny the minicab controller, charterhouse street, 1999. 12—1 queue on charterhouse street, 2000. 18—1 front of the club as a building site, 1998. 23—1 charterhouse street, 1950. 28—1, 36—1, 38—1, 39—1, 42—1, 43—1 to 43—9 interior of the space during construction. 31—1 hythe, kent, circa 1972. 40—1, 40—2, 41—1 fabric promotions team (james mac, nikki smith, richard welch, tubbs, steve blonde, keith reilly). 44—1 room 1 booth, 2015. 44—2 room 3, 2015. 45—1 mezz bar, 2015. 45—2 room 2, 2015. 46-47 room 1, 2015. 48—1, =49—1 staircase 1, 2015. 50—1, 51—1, 52—1, 52—2, 53—1 to 53—3 room 2, 2021. 56—1, 60—1, 61—1, 61—2, 62—1, 63—1, 63—2 matter, 2008. 61—3 toilets at matter, 2009. 66—2 main room at matter, 2009. 64-65 main room at matter, 2010. 66—1 main room at matter, 2009. 66—3 ram at matter, 2010. 66—4 skybridge at matter, 2009. 66—5 laurent garnier at matter, 2010. 66—6 unkle at matter, 2010. 67—1 main room at matter, 2009. 67—2 main room at matter, 2009. 67—3 main room at matter, 2009. 67—4 nick fanciulli, 2009. 67—5 main room at matter, 2009. 67—6 room 2 at matter, 2009. 96—1 terry francis. 98—1 shaun roberts, 2004. 98—2 farsin, seth troxler, anna zuchara & dave poll, 2013. 98—3 rami & griff, 2014. 99—1 tayo. 99—2 saul press & scott paterson, 2009. 99—3 steve blonde, 2003. 99—4 seth troxler, 2013. 99—5 seth & charlie soul clap, 2013. 99—6 scott paterson, 2013. 99—7 hannah reilly, 2009. 99—8 conrad black, natalia & derren smart. 99—9 natalia & derren smart. 100—1 10th birthday line up, 2009. 102—1 richie hawtin, 2014. 102—2 zip, 2014. 102—3 marisa & ignacio garrido, 2009. 102—4 craig richards & felix dickinson, 2015. 102—5 jamie jones & craig richards, 2015. 103—1 crowd, 2009. 103—2 carl craig & cassie, 2009. 103—3 peter pixel, jacob husley & cormac, 2015. 103—4 henrik schwarz, 2009. 103—5 phuture dj pierre & spanky, 2014. 103—6 fabriclive 2shy, 2014. 103—7 appolonia & jovonn, 2014. 103—8 ms. dynamite, 2016. 104—1 ricardo villalobos, 2009. 105—1 dancer, 2012. 106—1 ricardo villalobos. 106—2, 199—25 tea ladies at fabric's 1st birthday, 2000. 106—3 dan coshan & jj, 2009. 106—4 —dj three & judy griffith, 2014. 106—5 peter pixel & cormac, 2010. 106—6 saul press, 2013. 107—1 johnnie wilkes, optimo. 107—2 kevin saunderson, 2015. 107—3, 193—13 crowd, 2002. 107—4 craig richards. 107—5 matthew jonson, 2014. 107—6 kimi, leo, natalie & kate, 2014. 108—1 seth troxler, ricardo villalobos, craig richards, 2014. 108—2 martinez brothers, 2015. 108—3 raresh, 2016. 108—4 mike shannon & dewalta, 2016. 108—5 fabriclive, 2016. 108—6 carl cox, 2015. 108—7 surgeon, 2016. 108—8 dave clarke, 2016. 108—9 fabriclive, 2015. 108—10 maya jane coles, 2015. 108—11 ricardo villalobos, 2014. 108—12 crowd, 2016. 109—1 front of the club, 2013. 119—1 artwork outside the main toilets, 2002. 164—3, 164—4, 164—13, 164—14 fabric x stussy t-shirt, 2003. 164—6. 164—7 fabric x 55dsl shirt, 1999. 164—10, 164—11, 164—12 fabric x stussy t-shirt, 2000. 164—15, 165—1, 165—12, 165—13 fabric x duffer st george, 2000. 175—1 fabric tote bag in room 2 booth, 2022. 176—1, 176—2, 176—3, 176—4, 176—6 fabric afterparty flyers, image by david shrigley. 177—1 to 177—4 front of the club for the 20th year launch, 2019. 180—1 skream & benga, 2023. 182—1 room 2, 2024. 188—1, 188—2, 195—20, 195—21, 198—1, 198—2, 199—2 staff party at camber sands, 2000. 188—2 staff party at camber sands, 2008. 188—3 staff party at camber sands, 2009. 188—4 staff paintballing, 2001. 188—5 team in front of the club, 2009. 185—1 keith reilly, 2023. 185—2 cameron leslie, 2023. 189—1 fabric management, promo, ops, marketing, finance & record label teams, 2023. 190—1 queue on cowcross street, 2000. 190—2, 205—1 queue from charterhouse street round on to cowcross street, 2000. 191—1, 191—2 queue on charterhouse street, 2000. 192—1 carl cox & craig richards, 2000. 192—2 shelley preston & jon cooke, 2000. 192—3 deep c, 2000. 192—4 fabio, 2000. 192—5, 193—17, 197—2 touche, 2000. 192—6, 193—3, 193—4, 194—16, 194—17, 194—21, 197—9, 197—16, 198—24, 199—22, 205—2, 205—4 fabriclive, 2000. 192—7 judy griffith & nikki smith, 2000. 192—8. 192—9 mampi swift & mc gq. 192—10 james lavelle, 2000. 192—11 lemonjelly, 2000. 192—12 john tejada, 2000. 192—13 room 3. 192—14. 192—15 back of house. 192—16 afrika bambaataa. 192—17 the rookery party, 2000. 192—18 richard file, 2001. 192—19, 197—14 room 1 booth. 192—20, 192—23, 192—24, 193—11, 193—25 to 193—27, 196—3, 196—5, 196—19, 196—21, 198—4, 198—5, 198—23, 199—12 fabriclive, 2001. 192—21 x-press2, 2000. 192—22 room 3, 2001. 192—25 craig richards & lee burridge, tyrant, 2000. 192—26 dubfire. 192—27 tayo & craig richards, 2000. 192—28 ed rush & optical, 2001. 193—1 metalheadz, 2001. 193—2 goldie & sanj, room 2, 2001. 193—5, 197—19 andy c, 2000. 193—6 richard file & james lavelle, room 1, 2001. 193—7 doc martin, hipp-e & halo, 2000. 193—8 moby, duane shepherd, sasha, 2000. 193—9, 193—10 live art in fabric, 2000. 193—12, 198—18, 211—11, 218—8 james lavelle, 2001. 193—14. 193—15, 194—2 to 194—5, 194—10, 194—25, 195—19, 196—14, 196—18, 196—22, 196—23, 197—6, 197—7, 197—28, 198—14, 198—15, 199—1, 199—16, 205—5 crowd, 2001. 193—16, 194—6, 195—11 front of the club, 1999. 193—18 ruth enfield, daniella, nikki smith, shelley preston, christina, 2000. 193—19. 193—20 nikki smith & rob da bank, 2001. 193—21. 193—22 pedro, tim payne & friends, 2001. 193—23. 193—24 john digweed & moby, 2000. 193—28 lee burridge, 2000. 194—1 lee burridge & rosanna maldonado, 2000. 194—7 foyer, 2000. 194—8 rosanna maldonado, lewis pennington, tubbs, nikki smith, lee burridge, 2000. 194—9, 194—11, 195—3, 195—12, 195—13, 195—22, 197—21, 199—14 crowd, 2000. 194—12 slam featuring envoi (hope), 2000. 194—13 howie b, 2001. 194—14 craig richards & terry francis, 2001. 194—15 dom butler, stanton warriors, 2001. 194—18 tyler stadius, 2000. 194—19, 194—20 aril brikha, 2001. 194—22 front of club for everyman cancer event, 2000. 194—23. 194—24. 194—26 udoh, nikki smith, craig richards, 2000. 194—27, 205—3 cameron leslie, 2001. 194—28 mezz toilets, 2001. 195—1 aril brikha, 2000. 195—2 get fucked, 2000. 195—4, 195—5. 195—6. 195—7 nils hess, 2000. 195—8 crowd on corner of charterhouse st & cowcross st, 2000. 195—9 craig richards & james lavelle, 2001. 195—10. 195—14. 195—15 dave angel, 2001. 195—16 fred everything & ralph lawson, 2001. 195—17 nathan coles & dave fly, 2001. 195—18 cameron leslie, 2000. 195—23 dave gamble, shaun roberts, judy griffith, scott paterson in room 1, 2021. 195—24. 195—25. 195—26 room 3, 2000. 195—27 circulation, 2000. 195—28. 196—1 swayzak, 2000. 196—2 crowd with birthday mug, 2000. 196—4 dj hype, 2001. 196—6 crowd, 2002. 196—7 bar 2, 2001. 196—8 queue on charterhouse street, 2000. 196—9, 197—22 charterhouse street, 2000. 196—10. 196—11 craig richards, 2002. 196—12 boo williams, 2000. shaun roberts & keith reilly, 2012. 196—15 apu, helen coates, carl cox, glow rockliffe, 2000. 196—16 craig richards & doc martin, 2000. 196—17 herbert (live), 2000. 196—20 chris binks, 2002. 196—24 charterhouse street, 1999. 196—25 matteo manzini, 2018. 196—26 kosheen, 2001. 196—27 terry francis & chico, 2001. 196—28 stacey pullen, 2001. 197—1 hallo, inland knights, nikki smith, 2000. 197—3 stamina, goldie & fats, 2001. 197—4 james lavelle & richard file, 2001. 197—5 craig richards & terry francis, 2000. 197—8 john digweed, 2000. 197—10 shaun roberts & touche, 2001. 197—11 nikki smith & judy griffith, 2000. 197—12 sanj, 2001. 197—13 smithfield market worker, 2000. 197—15 tony vegas, 2001. 197—17. 197—18. 197—20. 197—23 room 2, 2000. 197—24. 197—25 room 1 booth, 2000. 197—26. 197—27. 198—3 fabio & friend, 2000. 198—6, 199—11 dj hype, 2000. 198—7 andrew weatherall, 2002. 198—8 shaun roberts, 2001. 198—9 keith reilly at the rookery party, 2000. 198—10, 198—20 tyrant, 2000. 198—11, 198—12, 199—7 line-up, 2000. 198—13 urinals, 2000. 198—16 rocky & carl cox, 2000. 198—17 carl cox, 2000. 198—19. 198—21, 235—1 matthew herbert, 2000. 198—22 ali b, 2000. 198—25 hipp-e, 2000. 199—3 ac chiller arrives, 1999. 199—4 keith reilly, nikki smith, tubbs, 1999. 199—5 kid batchelor, 2000. 199—6 tubbs, richard welch, steve blonde, nikki smith, james mac, keith reilly, 1999. 199—8 goldie & fabio, 2000. 199—9 michael morley, 2001. 199—10 craig richards, 2000. 199—13 electric lane, 2000. 199—15 tayo, 2000. 199—17 line-up, 2001. 199—18 clive henry, 2000. 199—19. 199—20 grooverider, 2000. 199—21 joel clements, scratch perverts, 2000. 199—22 tom middleton, 2001. 199—24 judy griffith, 2000. 200—1 stamina, goldie & fats, 2001. 200—2 kiefer sutherland & friends, 2001. 201—1 andrew weatherall & judy griffith, 2001. 201—2 nathan coles & jon cooke, 2000. 204—1 terry francis, 2001. 204—2 craig richards, 2001. 205—6 goldie, 2002. 208—1 ricardo villalobos & richie hawtin, 2005. 208—2 floating points. 209—1 craig richards, 2014. 209—2 terry francis, 2014. 210—1 ricardo villalobos, 2017. 210—2 fabio, 2014. 210—3 pearson sound, 2009. 210—4 roman fluegal. 210—5 nina kraviz. 210—6 ben ufo, 2009. 210—7 helena hauff. 210—8, 210—11 ellen alien. 210—9 craig richards, 2023. 210—10 a guy called gerald, 2017. 210—12 cassy. 210—13 chase & status, 2010. 210—14 dave clarke. 210—15 chemical brothers, 2007. 211—2 ben klock. 211—3, 238-239 fatboy slim, 2021. 211—4 nathan coles & terry francis, 2016. 211—5 david rodigan. 211—6 carl cox, 2001. 211—7 marcel dettmann. 211—8 seth troxler, 2018. 211—9 magda, 2011. 211—10 joy orbison, 2017. 211—1 andy c. 211—12 jme presents grime mc fm, 2021. 211—13 midland. 211—14 terry francis, judy griffith, ricardo villalobos. 211—15 fourtet, 2012. 214—1, 255—4 room 1, 2022. 215—1 room 3, 2023. 218—1 andy c, 2001. 218—2 craig richards. 218—3 john peel, 2002. 218—4 stanton warriors, 2006. 218—5 miss kittin & the hacker, 2022. 218—6 lee burridge, tyrant, 2001. 218—7 âme. 218—9 dj hype, 2002. 219—1 four tet, daphni, floating points, room 1, nyd 2023. 219—2 ben ufo, 2011. 219—3 overmono, room 2, nyd 2023. 219—4 sandwell district, room 1, 2024. 220—1 daniel avery, room 1, 2024. 221—1 carl craig, 2009. 221—2 kode 9, 2021. 222—1 sandwell district, room 1, 2024. 223—1 frisco presents the den, room 1, 2022. 228—1 room 1, 2022. 229—1 ahadadream b2b champion, room 2, 2022. 231-232 frisco presents the den, room 1, 2022. 234—1 udoh & deep c, 2000. 234—2 room 1, 2000. 234—3 phydeaux mcavoy on lights, 2000. 235—2 chris binks on lights, 2001. 235—3 darren hughes, carl cox, nikki smith, craig richards & friends, 2000. 243—1 crowd in room 1, 2024. 244-245 haai, erol alkan, daniel avery, 2021. 246—1, 250—2 room 2, fabric reopening after covid, 2021. 248—1, 249—1 ricardo villalobos & craig richards, 2021. 251—1 room 2, 2021. 252—1, 255—1 room 1, 2023. 251—2 room 2, 2022. 253—1 overmono, room 2, nyd 2023. 254—1 kode 9, room 1, 2023. 254—2 crowd, room 1, 2024. 254—3 club detail, 2023. 254—4 phone traxxx, room 2, 2022. 255—2, 255—3 room 2, 2022. 256—1 dancer in room 1, 2024. 257—1 room 2, 2023. 257—2 joris voorn, room 1, 2023. 257—3 room 1, 2024. 257—4 fabriclive birthday, room 1, 2022. 258—1, 304—1 room 1. 259—1 jme presents grime mc fm, room 1, 2021. 259—2 frisco presents the den, room 1, 2022. 260—1 flowdan, room 2, 2023. 261—1 skepta, room 1, 2021. 262—1 —letter from dan coshan to danny newman supporting dizzee rascal, 2007. 266—1, 270—271 front of fabric while closed, 2016. 272—1 team in front of the club for #savefabric, 2016. 272—2 holmesdale fanatics, crystal palace #savefabric, 2016. 273—1, 273—2 supporters who helped save fabric, 2017. 276-277 rival consoles, fabric at the opera, 2022. 280-281 giant swan, fabric presents london unlocked at tower bridge, 2021. 282—1 lcy, fabric at the opera, 2022. 283—1 fabric at the opera, 2022. 284—1, 285—1 ry x live at st paul's cathedral, 2023. 286-287 skream & crazy d, fabric presents london unlocked at royal albert hall, 2021. 288—1 lcy, fabric presents london unlocked at tower bridge, 2021. 289—1 object blue – fabric presents london unlocked at smithfield market, 2021. 290-291 archie hamilton, fabric presents london unlocked at round chapel, 2021. 292—1 josh cafe, fabric presents london unlocked at fabric, 2021. 294-295 hinako omori live at st paul's cathedral, 2023. 293—1 kode 9, fabric presents london unlocked at round chapel, 2021. 296—1 shaun roberts, 2000. 296—2 shaun roberts & friend, 2001. 296—3 shaun roberts, 2004. 296—4 shaun roberts, judy griffith, ruth enfield, 2000. 296—5 shaun roberts & richard file, 2002. 296—6 shaun roberts, 2020.

promotional materials

70—1 art direction: roberto rosolin. illustration: yin zhen chu, 2019. 73—1, 78—70 to 78—72, 87—2, 87—4, 87—6, 149—1 art direction: roberto rosolin. photography: mads perch, 2013. 78—1, 79—1, 80—1, 84—1, 84—2 to 84—6, 85—1, 138—4, 138—9, 138—19 art direction: jonathon cooke. design: juan cortes, 2001. 78—2 to 78—7, 79—2 to 79—7, 80—2 to 80—6, 81—1, 88—1, 138—1 to 138—3, 138—5 to 138—8, 138—12, 138—17 art direction: jonathon cooke. design: juan cortes, 2002. 78—8 to 78—13, 79—8 to 79—13, 81—2 to 81—6, 85—2 to 85—6, 138—10, 138—11, 138—13 to 138—16, 138—18, 140—1 art direction: jonathon cooke. design: juan cortes, 2003. 78—14, 78—16 to 78—19, 79—14 to 79—19, 90—1, 138—20 to 138—24, 141—1 art direction: jonathon cooke. design: juan cortes, 2004. 78—15 art direction & design: craig richards, 2004. 78—20 to 78—25, 79—20 to 79—25, 138—25 to 138—30, 138—33, 138—35, 138—36, 142—1 art direction: jonathon cooke. design: juan cortes, 2005. 78—26 to 78—31, 79—26, 79—31, 138—37, 138—38, 139—2, 143—1 art direction: jonathon cooke. design: juan cortes, 2006. 78—32 to 78—36, 79—32, 79—33, 89—1, 139—7 to 139—10 art direction: jonathon cooke. design: juan cortes, 2007. 78—37 to 78—39, 82—1, 138—39, 139—6, 144—1 art direction: jonathon cooke. design: tom darracott, 2007. 78—40 to 78—42 art direction: jonathon cooke. design: juan cortes, 2008. 78—43, 145—1 art direction: jonathon cooke. design: village green studio, 2008. 78—44 to 78—47 art direction: jonathon cooke. design: village green studio, 2009. 78—48, 79—49, 139—18, 139—19, 146—1 art direction: jonathon cooke. design: peter richardson, 2009. 78—49, 79—46 to 79—48 art direction: jonathon cooke. design: ryan belmont, 2009. 78—50, 79—50, 79—51, 147—1 art direction: jonathon cooke. design: peter richardson, 2010. 78—51 to 78—53, 82—2, 82—4, 82—6 art direction: jonathon cooke. design: tom darracott, 2010. 78—54, 78—55, 139—22, 139—23, 139—25 to 139—27, 139—29 to 139—31 art direction: roberto rosolin. photography: thomas de hoghton, 2010. 78—56, 78—57, 78—59 to 78—61, 83—1 to 83—3, 139—34, 139—35 art direction: roberto rosolin. photography: thomas de hoghton, 2011. 78—58 art direction & design: roberto rosolin, 2011. 78—62 to 78—66, 79—62 to 79—64, 83—5, 83—6 art direction: roberto rosolin. photography: thomas de hoghton, 2012. 78—67, 78—68, 79—65 to 79—67, 139—36, 139—37, 148—1 art direction: roberto rosolin. illustration: luca zamoc, 2012. 78—69 art direction: roberto rosolin. illustration: luca zamoc, 2013. 78—73 art direction & design: roberto rosolin, 2013. 78—74, 78—75 art direction & design: roberto rosolin, 2014. 78—76 to 78—79, 110—1, 111—1 art direction: roberto rosolin. photography: mads perch, 2014. 78—80, 78—81, 78—85, 79—80 to 79—82, 154—1 art direction: roberto rosolin. photography: mads perch, 2015. 78—82 to 78—84 art direction & design: roberto rosolin, 2015. 78—86 to 78—90 art direction: roberto rosolin. photography: mads perch, 2016. 78—91, 79—86 to 79—91 art direction: roberto rosolin. photography: enrico policardo, 2016. 78—92 to 78—96, 79—92 to 79—94 art direction: roberto rosolin. photography: enrico policardo, 2017. 78—97 to 78—99 art direction: roberto rosolin. photography: enrico policardo, 2018. 78—100, 79—97 art direction: roberto rosolin. photography: mads perch, 2018. 79—27 to 79—30, 138—41, 138—42 art direction: jonathon cooke. design: ryan belmont, 2006. 79—34 to 79—36, 139—3 to 139—5 art direction: jonathon cooke. design: ryan belmont, 2007. 79—37, 138—32, 139—11, 139—12 art direction: jonathon cooke. design: tom fearn, 2007. 79—38 to 79—43, 86—1, 86—3, 86—5, 139—13 art direction: jonathon cooke. design: tom fearn, 2008. 79—44, 79—45 art direction: jonathon cooke. design: tom fearn, 2009. 79—52 art direction: village green. design: tom fearn, 2010. 79—53 to 79—55 art direction & design: roberto rosolin, 2010. 79—56 to 79—61 art direction: roberto rosolin. photography: enrico policardo, 2011. 79—68 art direction & design: roberto rosolin, 2012. 79—69 to 79—73 art direction & design: roberto rosolin, 2013. 79—74 to 79—76 art direction & design: roberto rosolin, 2014. 79—77 to 79—79, 151—1 art direction: roberto rosolin. photography: enrico policardo, 2014. 79—83 to 79—85 art direction & design: roberto rosolin, 2015. 79—95, 79—96 art direction: roberto rosolin. photography: mads perch, 2017. 79—98, 79—99 art direction: roberto rosolin. illustration: luca zamoc, 2018. 79—100 art direction: roberto rosolin. illustration: yin zhen chu, 2018. 82—3, 82—5 art direction: jonathon cooke. design: tom darracott, 2008. 83—4, 139—24, 139—38, 139—39 art direction & photography: roberto rosolin, 2011. 86—2, 86—4, 86—6, 91—1 art direction: roberto rosolin. photography: roberto kusterle, 2012. 87—1, 87—3, 87—5 art direction & photography: roberto rosolin, 2014. 92—1 art direction: roberto rosolin. photography: enrico policardo, 2023. 92—2, 92—3 art direction & design: roberto rosolin, 2022. 92—4 art direction: roberto rosolin. photography: mads perch, 2021. 92—5, 92—6, 93—1 to 93—3, 112—1, 113—1 art direction & design: roberto rosolin, 2023. 101—1 art direction & design: village green studio, 2009. 116—1 pre-opening promo sticker, 1999. 121—1 fabric christmas card, 2000. 122—1 launch month with scheduled events, 1999. these never happened due to fabric's delayed opening. 123—1 an event that took place just after the revised opening, 30 october 1999. 124—1 fabric saturdays, november 1999. 125—1 millennium night, 31 december 1999. 126—1 fabric saturdays, december 1999. 127—1 events brochure, 2004. 128—1, 129—1 pre-opening press pack, 1999. 130—1, 130—2 original launch date that got delayed, 1999. 131—1, 131—3 complimentary ticket for launch saturday 2nd oct that got delayed, 1999. 131—2, 131—4 complimentary ticket for launch friday 1st oct that got delayed, 1999. 132—1, 133—1 flyer for the launch weekend that got delayed, 1999. 134—1, 135—1 pre-opening teaser promo flyers, 1999. 136—1, 137—1 art direction: jonathon cooke. design: juan cortes, 2000. 138—31, 138—40, 139—40, 139—41 art direction: jonathon cooke. design: ryan belmont, 2005. 138—34, 139—20 art direction: jonathon cooke. design: juan cortes, 2009. 139—1 art direction: jonathon cooke. design: tom darracott, 2006. 139—14, 139—15 art direction: jonathon cooke. design: ryan belmont, 2008. 139—16, 139—17 art direction: jonathon cooke. design: peter richardson, 2008. 139—21 art direction: jonathon cooke. design: tom darracott, 2009. 139—28 art direction: roberto rosolin. photography: enrico policardo, 2010. 139—32, 139—33 art direction: roberto rosolin. photography: roberto kusterle, 2011. 139—42 art direction: jonathan cooke. design: village green studio, 2018. 150—1 art direction: roberto rosolin. photography: enrico policardo, 2013. 152—1, 153—1, 155—1 art direction: roberto rosolin. photography: enrico policardo, 2015. 156—1, 157—1 art direction & photography: roberto rosolin, 2015. 158—1 art direction & photography: roberto rosolin, 2019. 159—1 art direction & photography: roberto rosolin, 2020. 160—1, 161—1, 161—2, 162—1, 162—2 art direction & photography: roberto rosolin, 2013. 163—1, 163—2 art direction & photography: roberto rosolin, 2012. 164—1, 164—2, 165—4, 165—5, 165—9 fabric t-shirt, 2009. 164—5, 164—8, 164—9, 165—2, 165—3 fabric t-shirt, 2019. 165—6 #savefabric t-shirt, 2016. 165—7, 165—8 fabriclive x rolling rock, 2000. 165—10 fabric t-shirt, 1999. 165—11 ac fabric staff football team, 2004. 165—14, 165—15 fabric t-shirt, 2022. 166—1 fabric t-shirt, 2001. 167—1 fabric t-shirt, 2000. 168—1 socks birthday gift, 2022. 168—2, 169—8 aaa wristband, 2001. 168—3 hot99 fabric pre-opening pendant, 1999. 168—4 keyring, 2005. 169—1 flyer holder, 2004. 169—2 ice tray birthday gift, 2007. 169—3 oven gloves birthday gift, 2001. 169—4 mug birthday gift, 2000. 169—5 fridge magnet birthday gift, 2008. 169—6 friend of fabric silver card, 2000. 169—7 laces birthday gift, 2023. 170—1 teddy bear birthday gift, 2004. 171—1 tea towel birthday gift, 2002. 172—1 art direction & design: roberto rosolin, 2010. 173—1 photography: roberto rosolin, 2010. 174—1 logo design by roberto rosolin, 2016. 176—5 image credit: isis salvaterra, 2012. 263—1 afghanistan benefit concert line-up, 2001. 272—3, 272—4 #saveourculture event at great suffolk street, 2016, 272—5 fabriclive x whp, 2016

image credits

55dsl 164—6, 164—7 asia ella 221—2 banksy 119—1 ben mcquaide 211—12, 251—2 benedict priddy 175—1, 180—1, 182—1, 214—1, 215—1, 218—5, 219—1, 219—3, 219—4, 220—1, 222—1, 223—1, 228—1, 229—1, 231-232, 252—1, 253—1, 254—1, 254—2, 254—3, 254—4, 255—1 to 255—4, 256—1, 257—1 to 257—4, 259—2, 260—1, 276-277, 282—1, 283—1, 284—1, 285—1, 294-295 chris davison 218—3 david lothian 28—1, 36—1, 38—1, 39—1, 40—1, 40—2, 41—1, 42—1, 43—1 to 43—9 david shrigley/fabric 176—1 to 176—4, 176—6 dosed 280-281, 286-287, 288—1, 289—1, 290-291, 292—1, 293—1 duffer st george 164—15, 165—1, 165—12, 165—13 evie williams 209—1 fabric in-house photographer 8-9, 12—1, 18—1, 96—1, 98—1, 99—1 to 99—5, 99—7 to 99—9, 100—1, 106—2 to 106—4,107—1, 107—3, 107—4, 190—1, 190—2, 191—1, 191—2, 192—1 to 192—28, 193—1 to 193—28, 194—1 to 194—6, 194—8 to 194—28, 195—1 to 195—19, 195—22 to 195—28, 196—1 to 196—28, 197—1 to 197—28, 198—1 to 198—25, 199—1 to 199—25, 200—1, 200—2, 201—1, 201—2, 204—1, 204—2, 205—1 to 205—6, 208—1, 208—2, 210—4, 210—5, 210—7 to 210—9, 210—11, 210—12, 210—14, 211—1, 211—2, 211—5, to 211—7, 211—11, 211—13, 218—1, 218—2, 218—6 to 218—9, 234—1 to 234—3, 235—1 to 235—3, 258—1, 272—1, 296—1 to 296—6, 304—1 ian walton/getty images 272—2 jake davis 2-3, 246—1, 247—1, 248—1, 249—1, 250—1, 250—2, 258—2 jamie dixon 261—1 keith reilly 31—1 larry jordan 251—1 london metropolitan archives 22-23 louis nesbitt 259—1 luke kirwan 50—1, 51—1, 52—1, 52—2, 53—1 to 53—3 matter in-house photographer 66—1, 66—3, 67—1, 67—2, 67—4, 67—5 max von mensenkampff 177—1 to 177—4 nick ensing 98—2, 98—3, 102—1 to 102—5, 103—1 to 103—8, 104—1, 105—1, 106—5, 107—2, 107—5, 108—1 to 108—12, 109—1, 209—2, 210—10, 211—4, 211—8 to 211—10, 211—14, 211—15, 221—1 nick torrens 99—6,106—6 pentagram 56—1, 60—1, 61—1, 61—2, 62—1, 63—1, 63—2 sarah ginn 44—1, 44—2, 45—1, 45—2, 46-47, 48—1, 49—1, 61—3, 64-65, 66—4 to 66—6, 106—1,107—6, 185—1, 185—2, 189—1, 210—1 to 210—3, 210—6, 210—13, 210—15, 211—3, 218—4, 219—2, 238-239, 244-245, 266—1, 270—271 stussy 164—3, 164—4, 164—10 to 164—14, tamsin isaacs 66—2, 67—6 tom mcewan 168—3 vanessa galvin 188—5 vickie parker 67—3 zak watson 243—1. photos on 186-87 are the contributors' own. all other images © fabric.

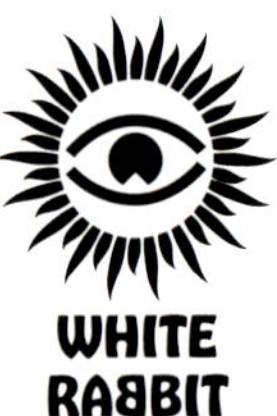

First published in Great Britain in 2024 by White Rabbit,
an imprint of The Orion Publishing Group Ltd
Carmelite House, 50 Victoria Embankment
London EC4Y 0DZ

An Hachette UK Company

A CIP catalogue record for this book is available from the British Library.

ISBN (Hardback) 9781399620987
ISBN (Hardback special edition) 9781399622417
ISBN (Hardback deluxe edition) 9781399622424
ISBN (eBook) 9781399627641

Editor: Lee Brackstone
Art Direction: Liam Relph
Design: Daniel Streat, Visual Fields
Project Editor: Sarah Fortune
Production: Sarah Cook

Origination by f1 Colour
Printed in China by C&C Offset Printing Co., Ltd

www.whiterabbitbooks.co.uk
www.orionbooks.co.uk

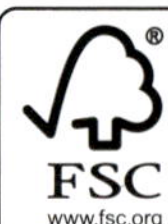

MIX
Paper | Supporting responsible forestry
FSC® C104740

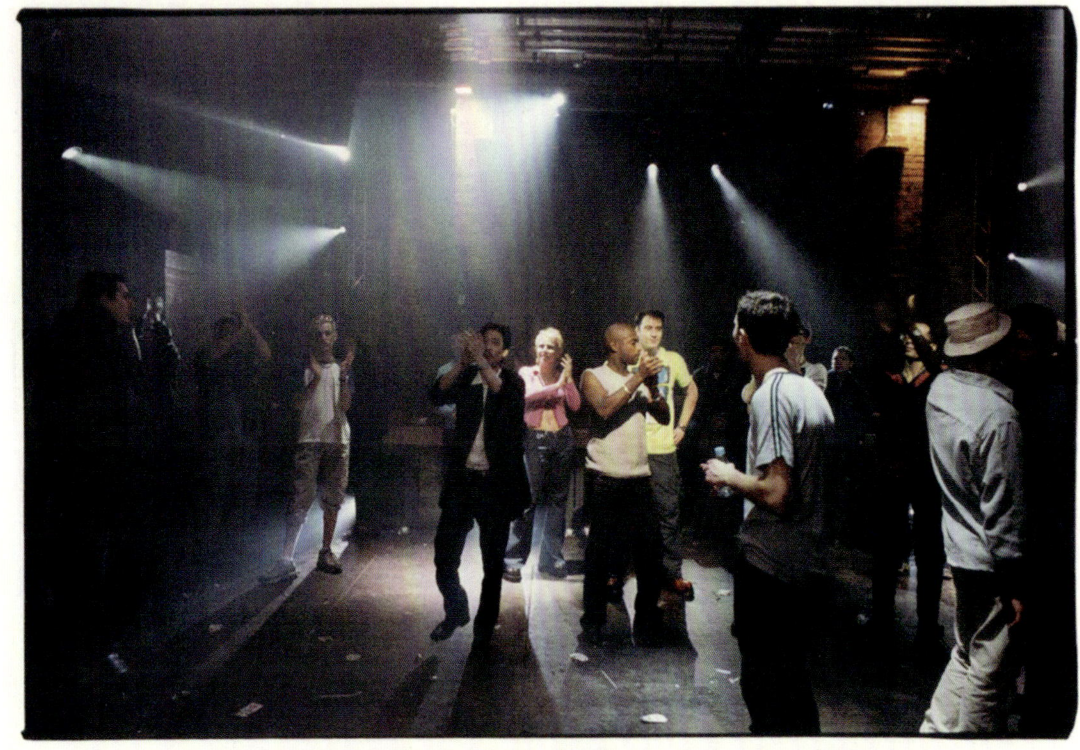

304—1